THE CHURCH IN CHINA
ONE LORD TWO SYSTEMS

Eph 3:20-21

THE CHURCH IN CHINA
ONE LORD TWO SYSTEMS

Michael D Suman

2006

The Church in China: One Lord Two Systems
by
Michael D Suman

Published by Michael D Suman
Email: mdensuman@yahoo.com

ISBN 81-7525-693-1

Concept, design and layout by SAIACS Press.

Printed by SAIACS Press,
SAIACS, PO Box 7747
Kothanur, Bangalore-560077, India
saiacspress@saiacs.org
http://www.saiacs.org

DEDICATION

This dissertation is dedicated
to

my faithful wife
Ella Nora Suman – Pearson

and in memory of my father
Otho Ulysses Suman
1915-1998

and my mother
Clara Mae, Sally, Suman – Diehl
1919-1969

INSPIRATION

On this rock I will build my church,

and the gates of Hades will not prevail against it.

ACKNOWLEDGEMENTS

Initial thanks go to Dr. Graham Houghton for affording the opportunity to be a part of South Asia Institute of Advanced Christian Studies, SAIACS, and being my sustaining advisor. It is with gratitude that I mention Dr. David Benedict who helped in an advisory capacity in the USA where a major part of research was accomplished and for his encouragement to search in places I would have only dreamed of going in research. Their help was assisted by the editing skills and comradeship of Dr. Richard Wing who trimmed the text and kept me on track to the finish. I am grateful to Dr. Idicheria Ninan who read my dissertation and gave constructive comments on how to sharpen its focus.

It is with utmost thanksgiving to OMS International as my mission board to extend the opportunity, and through my faithful constituency to sponsor the endeavor to pursue this terminal degree.

Gratitude to He Yanli who accompanied me on two trips into China and lectured on its history, customs, traditions and politics while we traveled. He made arrangements both in China and in the Chinese communities of Spain for interviews. He and his wife Chu Lijung helped translate when needed. Authors Gail Coulson, Dr. Jonathan Chao, Britt Towery, Drew Liu, Samuel Wang and Kathy Call not only helped with information in their writings but introduced me to other contacts for materials or valuable interviews.

I am sincerely grateful for Steven Liu, Shen Chengen, and Bao Jiayuan who invited me to meet them in China and arranged introductions to religious leaders in the Three-Self Patriotic Movement offices and East China Theological Seminary in Shanghai, China Christian Council and Nanjing Theological Seminary in Nanjing, and independent Christian communities in Beijing for interviews on behalf of my research.

A heartfelt thanks is due for the help of these individuals:

Dr. Douglas and Minnie Atwood who arranged for my research at Harvard University where I roomed with Charles and Mary Glenn. Dr. Raymond Lum facilitated finding data from the Harvard Yenching Library and procured the assistance of the staff of the Harvard Divinity School Library, Widener Library, Emerson Library, the Harvard Law School Langdell Library and the Harvard China Research Center. I appreciate the help and hospitality of Li Yading at Yale University where Martha Smalley and library staff graciously contributed with assisting in archives, documents and references at the Yale School of Divinity Library. Dr. Brent Fulton, managing director of the Institute of Chinese Studies at Wheaton College, provided assistance with Chinese political data. I am obliged to Clive and Angela Harffey of the United Kingdom for their gift of documentaries on China. The faithful services of L.Johnson Jagannadham and staff at SAIACS Library, librarian and staff at Union Theological College Library at Bangalore, India; George Bennett and staff of the Houghton College Willard J. Houghton Memorial Library; and the late Linda Doezema's assistance for interlibrary loans were much appreciated.

A special note of gratitude is due to Allen Shea for setting up my computer system, Glen Avery for his expertise, Cindy Lastoria and staff at the Houghton College Help Desk for their assistance with computer technology, and especially Seth Taylor for aggressively pursuing computer problems encountered. Finally, to my wife, Nora, who read the complete work for legibility and sons, Matthew and Andrew, for their patience and readiness to assist in spelling and defining words throughout this time of research and writing. To God be all honor and glory.

TABLE OF CONTENTS

LIST OF ABBREVIATIONS

AD	*Anno Domini,* Year of our Lord
AM	*Ante Meridiem,* Before Noon
ANS	Amity News Service
BC	Before Christ
CCC	China Christian Council
CCP	Chinese Communist Party
CCRP	China Committee on Religion and Peace
CMI	China Ministries International
CPPCC	Chinese People Political Consultative Conference
IMB	International Mission Board
KCR	Kowloon Canto Rail
MTR	Mass Transit Rail
NCC	National Christian Council
NPC	National People's Congress
PLA	People's Liberation Army
PM	*Post Meridiem,* After Noon
PRC	People's Republic of China
PSB	Public Security Bureau
RAB	Religious Affairs Bureau
TSPM	Three-Self Patriotic Movement
TULIP	Total depravity, Unconditional election, Limited atonement, Irresistible grace, Perseverance of the saints
UFWD	United Front Work Department
UNESCO	United Nations Educational, Scientific, and Cultural Organization
U.S.	United States, usually related to currency
USA	United States of America
WCC	World Council of Churches
YMCA	Young Men's Christian Association
YWCA	Young Women's Christian Association

TABLE 1*

THE CHINESE DYNASTIES

Five Emperors (Mythical)
    Xia (Mythical)   ca. 1994 B.C. – ca. 1523 B.C.
    Shang (or Yin)   ca. 1523 B.C. – ca. 1028 B.C.
    Zhou   ca. 1027 B.C. – 256 B.C.
    Qin   221 B.C. – 207 B.C.
Western (Earlier) **Han**   202 B.C. – 9 A.D.
Xin   9 – 23
Eastern (Later) **Han**   25 – 220
The Three Kingdoms
    Shu,   221 – 263 A.D.
    Wei,   220 – 265 A.D.
    Wu,   222 – 280 A.D.
Western Jin   265 – 317 A.D.
Eastern Jin   317 – 420 A.D.
Former (Liu) Song   420 – 479 A.D.
Southern Qi   479 – 502 A.D.
Liang   502 – 557 A.D.
Chen   557 – 589 A.D.
Northern Wei   386 – 535 A.D.
Eastern Wei   534 – 550 A.D.
Western Wei   535 – 556 A.D.
Northern Qi   550 – 577 A.D.
Northern Zhou   557 – 581 A.D.
Sui   590 – 618 A.D.
Tang   618 – 907 A.D.
Five Dynasties + Ten Kingdoms
    Later Liang,   907 – 923 A.D.
    Later Tang,   923 – 936 A.D.
    Later Jin,   936 – 947 A.D.
    Later Han,   947 – 950 A.D.

Later Zhou,	951 – 960 A.D.
Liao	907 – 1125 A.D.
Northern Song	960 – 1126 A.D.
Xixia	990 – 1227 A.D.
Southern Song	1127 – 1279 A.D.
Jin	1115 – 1234 A.D.
Yuan	1260 – 1368 A.D.
Ming	1368 – 1644 A.D.
Qing	1644 – 1911 A.D.

* June Teufel Dreyer, *China's Political System* (Boston: Allyn & Bacon, 1996), p. 27.

ABSTRACT

The Church in China:
One Lord Two Systems

by
Michael Dee Suman
Doctor of Philosophy in Missiology
South Asia Institute of Advanced Christian Studies, 2000
Dr. Graham Houghton, Chairman

This dissertation addresses the emergence and development of the Chinese Church as the Body of Christ in China through the historical and sociopolitical context of that nation. The focus on the last half of the 20th century is supported by a concise overview of the political history of China from its dynastic era and international influence on its Church history.

A special study is made of the sociopolitical and religious facets of China's history to provide an understanding of the Chinese context into which the Church was introduced. The manner in which the Church found its way into China also affected its reception.

This research shows that missionaries came into China in the wake of international domination that caused resentment from the Chinese ruling class. The Chinese Christian believers formed a dependency on foreign mission boards and missionaries' patronage for financial and legal advantages.

The fact that the Chinese Communist Party came into power for the final half of the 20th century was given significant consideration. The chairmanship of Mao Zedong was of particular consequence since he actually led China into the era of Communism and set the pattern of how the Communist Party functioned in China for over a quarter century. The formation of his thought and its impact on his leadership and state policy served as the basis for the government's treatment of the Church in China.

Another aspect of this study considered the Chinese Church's response to the control of a totalitarian government. The Three-Self Patriotic Movement made it possible for the Chinese Protestant Church to exist and function legally. The political events that occurred during the era of Communist rule affected the patriotic organizations and how they managed religious activities.

The entity of the Church that refrained from legally joining the patriotic organizations because of their association with an atheistic government was considered, especially since this group makes up the majority of the Christian Church in China. The political dynamic that this faction created formed a dimension that contrasted with the totalitarian governing principle of the Communist Party.

Another group taken into account for this study operated outside the boundaries of any established defined organization. The intellectuals considered Christianity from beyond Protestant or Catholic roles and examined Western Christian literature for study and translation. They were not comfortable with the legal Church for its restrictive measures, nor did they associate with the autonomous Christian communities because of their lack of tolerance and intellectual stimulation.

The results show that the indigenization of the Chinese Church was in its adaptation to its context. In highly politically controlled areas of China, the Church continues to grow, even under oppressive circumstances, for it is more than an organization that can be manipulated. It is an organism of belief that has penetrated Chinese society.

1
INTRODUCTION

DESCRIPTION OF THE STUDY

This study defines the Church in China as it emerged from the context of China's sociopolitical history of the last 4,000 years, and reports how it adapted to a culture formed by the accumulation of unique and varied facets of historical events. Initially, the Church's introduction into China at various stages of history through Catholic missions failed, as their missionaries were expelled repeatedly. Finally, after the imperialistic thrust of Western nations subdued the governing dynasty, the Church became established in the land of China if not in the hearts of the Chinese. Within the last half of the 20th century, the Chinese Communist government in the People's Republic of China provided another distinctive element to the context within which the Church adjusted and survived. Foreign aspects were eliminated, and the Church sought to become self-governing, self-supporting, and self-propagating. Within this framework constitutional documents and regulating organizations were formed for the legalization of religious belief. At this point the Church took on different facets of identity: the Three-Self Patriotic Movement, or TSPM, as the legalized Chinese Protestant Church; the autonomous Christian communities that declined relations with the TSPM; their Catholic counterparts; and the intellectuals referred to as Culture Christians.

In this study, the researcher analyzes the historical events and how they formed the contextual environment into which the Chinese Christian Church expressed itself in an indigenous form, and he explores the factors that caused it to perpetuate and grow through suppression. The focus of the research is on what the Chinese Christian Church has become in the final half of the 20th century.

A Synopsis Of The History Of The Church In China

To set the Chinese Protestant Church in its proper context, the backdrop of political history was examined from the beginning of ruling dynasties. This was provided to demonstrate the construction of the mindset of the Chinese as ethnic people and the political setting in which the Chinese Church emerged.

Coupled with the political history, the history of the Chinese Church was investigated from the era of Nestorianism, beginning in 635AD. Throughout the history of the Chinese Church the political environment of China shaped the Church into what it had become by the end of the 20th century.

To properly analyze the Church in China, five strata that affected its developmental process must be examined. The political regulations that outline the legality of religious activity may be defined as one layer through which the Church must be viewed. Another was the TSPM as the legal patriotic Protestant organization approved by the Chinese Communist Party, CCP, in which the Protestant Church must legally operate. Third, the autonomous Christian communities, identified as the house church movement in some references, originally formed during the time of Church persecution in China and traditionally meeting in private homes. Fourth, the Catholics within the legal Chinese Catholic Church and its patriotic association not affiliated with the Pope and the Roman Catholics that claim loyalty to the Vatican. This fourth strata was placed outside the focus of this study and is only dealt with briefly. The final layer was a Christian phenomenon among the intelligentsia, the Culture Christians. It was through the interaction of these influences on the Church that the indigenous Chinese Church had emerged.

Significance Of The Study

An attempt is made to write from the viewpoint of the Chinese and their perceptions; therefore reasoning their actions and reactions. The concept of the Church utilized in this study is that

18

of Christians whose faith rests in the Lordship of Jesus Christ, which is inclusive of the Catholic Christians as well as Protestants, the registered and official churches, and unregistered independent meeting points. This is not an endeavor to promote a universalistic, unificatory, or ecumenical Church, but an attempt to define the Body of Christ in China. Neither is it an effort to discredit any missionary, scholar, or author in his or her particular viewpoint, for each has a reasonable argument as to specific cases. The question is in the emphatic generalizations that tend to become harsh and unjust to the other perspectives.

The controversy regarding the legal aspects of the Church in China left it in a quandary of definition. This dilemma forged two camps of support: those who recognized only the legal entity of the Church within the framework regulated through the patriotic organizations and the CCP, and the portion that remained independent from registration with the Religious Affairs Bureau, RAB, as part of the Communist Party.

The Constitution of China guaranteed freedom of religious belief, and the TSPM, under the biblical concept that God placed a Communist government into power in China, strove to strengthen the growth of the Church in China. However, another segment, the house church movement, cited persecution they had suffered for their belief at the hands of the TSPM, and affirmed that in cooperation with the government, the TSPM infringed on their independence, dictated doctrines, and stipulated venue boundaries of worship. Therefore, they concluded that the TSPM should not have their cooperation as it was unequally yoked to an atheistic government according to the Christian Bible, in II Corinthians 6:14.

Any reference to the Church in China favors either its legal or the unregistered entity to identify it. Britt Towery, Philip Wickeri, and Han Wenzao are among the authors and religious leaders who favor the legalized method of registration through the RAB for the Church to follow. They maintain the view that those who operate outside this realm of legality do so at the risk of criminal charges. Jonathan Chao, David Adeney, and Tony Lambert are examples of those authors and leaders who support the independent church groups even as far as helping to supply the needed training and literature in clandestine manners. These maintain the view that those who cooperate with the atheistic government are compromising the Christian message. Bishop

19

Ting, in whom the autonomous Christian groups do not express confidence, was the only Christian leader who made strides to become inclusive in reference to the Church and suggested an integration of effort.

The hypothesis of this dissertation is that neither portion of the Chinese Church, the segment registered with the government through the Religious Affairs Bureau, RAB, and joined to the Three-Self Patriotic Movement, TSPM, nor the unregistered autonomous Christian communities can claim to be the only true Church in China. In private most Chinese Christians from each persuasion seem ready to recognize and accept all who claim Jesus Christ as Lord to be a part of the Chinese Church. Moreover, this also includes those believers of the Catholic faith. The great differences have arisen over the way Chinese Christians have adapted to the political context with a Communistic government.

In defining the Church in China with its complex context, the author's initial investigation purported that research leading to a major sociopolitical historical study of China and its Church would contribute to the understanding of the context to which the Chinese Church adapted and established its own identity.

In the discussion of indigenization of the Church, Bruce Nicholls has aptly described the Church in an article 'The Gospel in Indian Culture' as the "extension of his (God's) incarnation in the world."[1] He cites the Lausanne Covenant stating that dependence on the Holy Spirit is inevitable for the transformation of cultural forms, because all elements of each culture contains perversions of sin. He then defined indigenization as "relating the Gospel to the traditional cultures of the people."[2] However, in his book Contextualization: A Theology of Gospel and Culture, Nicholls endorsed the goal of indigenization first introduced by Henry Venn, Rowland Allen and Melvin Hodges as " a church that is self-governing, self-supporting and self-propagating."[3] David Bosch added in his book, Transforming Mission, that "there is the 'indigenizing' principle which affirms that the gospel is

---

[1] Bruce J. Nicholls, 'The Gospel in Indian Culture,' M. Ezra Sargunam (ed.), Mission Mandate, Kilpauk, (Madras: Mission India 2000, 1992), pp. 379. (God's) added by author.
[2] Ibid., p. 386.
[3] Bruce J. Nicholls, Contextualization: A Theology of Gospel and Culture (Exeter: The Paternoster Press, 1979, p. 20.

Introduction

at home in every culture and every culture is at home with the
gospel."[4] He, along with Charles Brock and Keith Minus, agreed
with the definition of indigenization provided by Nicholls as the
"three-selves."[5]

The articles written by Bong Rin Ro, Lorenzo Bautista, Hidalgo
Garcia, and Sze-Kar Wan in The Bible & Theology In Asian Contexts
agree with Paul Hiebert in his book Anthropological Insights
for Missionaries that indigenization is used in response and
understanding of the gospel in terms of the culture of a people.[6]
Tissa Weerasingha, looking at the Buddhist perspective, said that
indigenization has to do with "local forms of communication,
methods of transmission, and personnel."[7] Wing-hung Lam
supported Ch'eng Ching-yi's view of indigenization for China
as to "render Christianity suitable to the needs of the Chinese
and to accommodate it to the customs, environment, history, and
thinking of the Chinese culture."[8]

For this study, indigenization of the Chinese Church is defined
as the Church governed, supported, propagated, controlled, and
structured within China by Chinese Christians. The operation
and adaptation within the unique sociopolitical context of China
was the distinctive of the Chinese Church's situation.

RATIONALE OF INTEREST

The exposure of having lived in Asia for over two years and then
having worked with those in the Chinese community in Madrid,
Spain, for a total of thirteen years since 1986 inspired an interest in

---

[4] David J. Bosch, Transforming Mission (Maryknoll, NY: Orbis Books, 1991),
p. 450.
[5] Ibid.; Charles Brock, Indigenous Church Planting, (Nashville: Broadman
Press, 1981), p. 12; Keith Minus, 'Missions and Indigenization,' A Compendium
of the Asia Missions Congress '90, World Missions: The Asian Challenge, 1992,
p. 260.
[6] Bong Rin Ro, 'Contextualization: Asian Theology, Bong Rin Ro and Ruth
Eshenaur (ed.), The Bible & Theology In Asian Contexts, (Taichung: Tai Shin
Color Printing, 1984), p. 64; Lorenzo Bautista, Hidalgo B. Garcia, and Sze-Kar
Wan, 'The Asian Way of Thinking in Theology,' Ibid., p. 177; Paul C. Heibert,
Anthropological Insights for Missionaries, (Grand Rapids: Baker Book House,
1985), pp. 189-190.
[7] Tissa Weerasingha, 'A Critique of Theology from Buddhist Cultures,' Bong
Rin Ro and Ruth Eshenaur
(ed.), In Asian Contexts, (Taichung: Tai Shin Color Printing, 1984), p. 305.
[8] Wing-hung Lam, 'Patterns of Chinese Theology,' Ibid., p. 331.

21

the Chinese peoples. In Madrid, the author helped to establish the Chinese Evangelical Church in the Chinese community of Madrid, and he anticipates returning to the orient in a teaching capacity. It has been reasonable to form an interest in the development of the indigenous Chinese Christian Church and important to understand the dynamics of the Chinese sociopolitical system in regards to religion as well as the cultural-ethnic aspects of Chinese Christian worship. Also, this study will help those contemplating Christian service in China.

DECLARATION AND CLARIFICATION

The author declares that this dissertation is an original work from his research that was documented to indicate credit to authors and sources of reference. Any direct quotes were set off by quotation marks or indented for that significance. All interviews were recorded on cassette tape or in the form of written notes that have been preserved for verification.

When the word Church is addressed by using a capital C, it is in reference to the universal Church as the Body of Christ, or as a particular proper name of a church, the Protestant Church, or Catholic Church. In contrast, church written with the lower case c refers to a location or building used for Christian worship.

Any italicized words refer to book titles, foreign words – other than foreign names—or words that the author wished to emphasize for clarification of the text.

RESEARCH SCOPE AND METHODS

The primary sources of evidence for this study were materials collected during visits to China. During a tour of observation to visit family members of those who were a part of the Chinese Evangelical Church of Madrid, the author entered many cities and villages, some where a foreigner had never been before. The experience of staying with these Chinese in their natural context, hearing their testimonies of faith and experiences of China's political events such as the Cultural Revolution from 1966 to 1976 and the Tiananman Square incident of June 4, 1989, and attending worship services with them provided insights into the Chinese Church situation. Fifteen churches ranging from the great city churches, with 1200 in each of the five services held on a Sunday, to the churches of towns that had over 1000 members and numerous training sessions on a weekly basis, and to the many rural churches that had lay leadership and 5 trained pastors who serviced 125 churches in a district were visited. Traveling with and in the mode of the Chinese and interacting with them brought perspective of how wide spread Christianity really was in China. It also provided a view of reality between generations of Christians, with the older Christians who sustained their faith from before the Communist Revolution in 1949 being reluctant to pass on their belief for fear of political consequences. Travel also provided opportunity for the escort, a Chinese man, to lecture on the culture and politics of China. Different sites of cultural and political significance were visited that verified observations, writings and verbal communications.

Another trip for primary sources was with the purpose of formal interviews. Working with authors Britt Towery, Gail Coulson, and Jonathan Chao, introductions were made with officials of the TSPM and professors of the Far East Theological Seminary in Shanghai, officials of the China Christian Council, CCC, and professors of the Nanjing Union Theological Seminary in Nanjing, and pastors and elders of autonomous Christian communities who were interviewed. Other Chinese professors, students, sociologists, and those in the discipline of Chinese studies were also interviewed.

Interviews with Chinese residing in Spain gave a realistic perspective to life in China and the condition, ministry, extent and pressures on the different facets of the Church from outside the context of China. In this setting, even though most names were withheld to protect family members still residing in China, there was an openness to reveal politically sensitive information.

Collections of documents, articles and resources were found in Harvard's libraries. Harvard's Yenching Library offered material on the TSPM and its function as the patriotic organization for the Protestant Church in China. Harvard's Divinity School Library provided materials relating to the ministry of the TSPM. Widener Library was a source for testimonials of religious persecution within China. Harvard Law School's Langdell Library included materials of legal significance toward Chinese constitutional religious rights. The Emerson Library at Harvard was a source for documents of Christian congresses. Access to the Harvard China Resource Center provided translated materials of cultural and political significance. Assistant librarian of Harvard-Yenching

Library, Dr. Raymond Lum, afforded access to Harvard's extensive computer resources through Ovid Citations.

Supporting materials were found in the Yale Divinity School Library, including microfilms of translated archives of articles and documents pertaining to Christian history of China. The opportunity to room with a Chinese student at Yale University, under the official auspices of the Church in China, provided an interview and a sense of reality in regard to religion and politics within China from outside that setting.

The Church of the Nazarene headquarters at Kansas City, Missouri availed its archives to the researcher for materials of reports on statistics regarding different mission stations throughout China. Letters between the missionaries and mission headquarters' personnel, documents of mission polity on how to treat political issues as a mission organization, on relations between the missionaries and national church leaders, on experiences of property confiscation, on donations given to the national churches, and on the sale of certain items provided historical information on the function of a mission during the missionary era of China.

Other collections with Chinese Christian religious material included those at South Asia Institute of Advanced Christian Study Library and Union Theological College at Bangalore, India. Historical materials during the missionary era were made available toward this research including information on the Opium Wars and the Boxer Rebellion.

Resources were sought at the Willard J. Houghton Memorial Library at Houghton College for historical materials regarding the Chinese Church both for modern and pre-Communist eras and for sociopolitical changes in China. A number of articles, national policy documents, speeches by political and religious leaders, and literature were borrowed through interlibrary loan from libraries throughout the United States. The Institute of Chinese Studies at Wheaton College provided resources on Chinese political issues with the Church in China.

The methods used by the researcher involved an initial review of materials relating to the political history of China from the prehistory legendary era throughout the dynasty periods. It also involved an initial review of the historical literature for Chinese Christian Church history from the Nestorians of 635 AD

Introduction

through the missionary era. It was from these readings that the formulation of an outline of study with the research questions presented was established.

The next stage consisted of the research of sources to establish the historical and political context of the Church in China and to find the philosophical mindset of the people and the social customs that influenced the receptivity to Christianity. Another aspect derived from the international contact that not only confirmed the reputation of the foreigners but also the Christianity they represented. The TSPM organization that represented the Protestant Church after the Communist Revolution and establishment of the People's Republic of China was researched for its historical foundation, connection to the government in relation to the United Front Work Department – UFWD – and the Religious Affairs Bureau – RAB, extent of its cooperation with the government, and its administrative objectives of establishing a socialist Communist society and ministry. The impact of Mao Zedong's leadership was explored for the significance of the precedence he set as the first chairman of the Chinese Communist Party.

The major dimension of the research was through materials found at Harvard's libraries and research center, Yale Divinity School Library, and interviews to establish the ministry and significance the TSPM and CCC had on the development of the Chinese Church after the Cultural Revolution. Reports from the autonomous Christian communities and their interaction with the TSPM were also of significance to understand the pressures projected by and characteristics of the TSPM since its revision in 1979.

Significant research through interviews and current articles identified sects and cults that were prevalent in China. Some of these attempted to gain credibility by identifying with one of the five religions authorized by the Chinese government. The significance of the study of these sects and cults was their identification as criminal and counter-revolutionary by the government, and the unregistered Christian groups being identified as one of these covert groups. Thus, the scope of persecution was brought into perspective and the dimension of the Church in China defined.

25

RESEARCH QUESTIONS

To answer the inclusive question, "What is the Church in China?" the principal questions focused on by the researcher were the following:

1. What constituted the indigenous aspects of the Chinese Christian Church? Were there particular elements that made it unique? Did indigenous indicate isolation? Could the indigenous Church of China be identified as one entity?
2. What formed the context into which the Chinese Church emerged? What historical events of China shaped the development of the Church? What political contributions affected the character of the Church?
3. How did the Chinese Church express itself within its context? Was the Church effective in the same manner throughout all of the Chinese provinces? Had power shifts and policy change affected religious activities of the Church in China?

In addition, these supplementary questions were considered:

1. What caused the changes in philosophy of the TSPM after the Cultural Revolution? Did these changes affect the direction or ministry of the Church in China? Why were these changes introduced?
2. Had the growth of the Church affected governmental policy change?
3. How could those who viewed China from abroad better understand and best encourage Chinese Christians?

DISSERTATION CHAPTER ORGANIZATION

This study is presented in a chronological topical arrangement. Chapter 2 presents the political history of China, describing its developments, cultural lifestyle and philosophies from the earliest dynasties. The events that led to China's exposure to the Western world and Opium Wars in the first decades of the 19th century are discussed. The framework of the time of the treaties following the first Opium war of 1842 to the time of the overthrow of the dynastic rule in 1919 leads into an analysis of the formation of Mao Zedong's character and origin of the Chinese Communist Party in 1921. The Chinese Communist Revolution of 1949 is cited with the policies and their consequences on Chinese society during the period when Mao was chairman and following his death in 1976.

The focus of chapter 3 is that of Chinese Church history from before the Nestorian period beginning in 635 AD through the missionary era from the early 1800s until the expulsion of foreign missions that commenced in 1949 and was completed in 1952. The period of national perpetuation of Christianity then extended from soon after the conception of the People's Republic of China in 1949 to the limit of this study in 2000.

Chapter 4 offers specific historical data on the Three-Self principle, promoted by the government agencies, for the authorized religions and specifically the Chinese Protestant Church. Its philosophy and the extent and intent of its policies were explored as to the political discipline of operation to specified socialist objectives as well as the motive of ministry in fulfillment of spiritual needs of the people of China. This study then considered the results of the TSPM and its administration as to the enforcement of the intent of policy in comparison to the benefits or adverse effects on the Church.

Chapter 5 covers the time after the Cultural Revolution and events leading to the 1979 revision of the philosophy and practices of the TSPM. This includes the political structure and policy changes and the effects of these changes on the Chinese Christian believer.

In chapter 6 the discussion focuses on the realities of political pressure applied by the government through the TSPM on the churches to comply in conformity to socialist ends. Both the liberties for conformation and consequences of deviation from policy are discussed.

Chapter 7 shows the relation of the autonomous Christian communities to the TSPM and compares the orthodoxy of belief and the extent of the TSPM's guardianship of the orthodoxy of doctrine. Indigenization of the Church in China is defined through its manifestation in governing, supporting, propagating, controlling, and structuring itself as the Body of Christ, adjusted to Chinese society in its sociopolitical context. Some future expectations and projections are presented to indicate the direction in which Chinese society will continue to affect the Church as it adjusts to these changes.

The conclusion in chapter 8 provides a summary of the study

and states the deductions found by the author in defining the Church in China as the body of believers who place their faith in the person of Jesus Christ and his teachings as expressed in its different forms.

In addition, a chart of the Chinese dynasties, a table of abbreviations, and an administrative map of China are provided for the convenience of the reader to more fully grasp an understanding of the sociopolitical context of the Church of China.

2
POLITICAL HISTORY:
CHINA IN CONTEXT

Each civilization has shaped the culture and mindset of its people through the context of its history. The longer a history of a civilization, the more deeply ingrained the patterns of thought are etched into the heart of the people, and customs are formed around these events to become a culture. China was the cultural center of East Asia for well over four thousand years as the oldest continuous civilization; therefore, the accumulation of history has formed her people into what China has become.

China was called *Zhongguo*, literally as the central nation or the Middle Kingdom. The Chinese were *nei*, of the inside, while all others were *wai*, of the outside. China's emperor was a divinity figure of everlasting stature called Son of Heaven and Lord of Ten Thousand Years. For the Chinese, he had power to rule the world, ideally, by the principles of wise, philosophical teachings and exemplary lives of the past sages. The emperor was to exemplify the highest virtue of moral behavior and inspire his subjects to achieve a high moral standard. Thus, as all of society followed his pattern, everyone lived in harmony. The ultimate standard of exemplary moral behavior was always in reference to those sages of the past. Therefore, China was a civilization that reflected much on her history.

The history of China was lived out by dynasties in a cyclical pattern rather than marking linear time, as in the West, through centuries. Each dynasty prospered, grew, declined through disaster, and was succeeded through internal struggle for power, but without outside intervention. According to the Chinese, the cyclical pattern of time began before the first recorded dynasty when China developed the calendar. While the West used the birth of Christ as the focal point in dating, the Chinese used the invention of the calendar attributed to the legendary Emperor Huangdi in 2637 BC. The Chinese dating system began at 2637 BC and designated years in cycles of 12 with an animal as the symbol of each year of that cycle. Then five of the twelve-year cycles made up a sixty-year cycle. The year 2000 AD, on the Western calendar, therefore, was the 17th year of the 78th sixty-year cycle on the Chinese calendar. China also used the lunar month with the 15th on the day of the full moon. At times, between the Western and Chinese calendar systems, it was difficult to accurately define a particular date. The successions of dynasties were not rigidly defined, as one dynasty may overlap another because of factors regarding area boundaries under the influence and rule of each dynasty.

Each succeeding dynasty had contributed to the context of Chinese history, and in each instance had made a contribution to the world. Even before the recorded dynasties, China had developed agriculture, herbal medicines, and acupuncture. The Xia, Shang and Zhou dynasties had their centers of power in three different locations and their co-existence seems to be evident. The Xia Dynasty, 1494-1523 BC, was defined as a late stage of Neolithic Longshan culture. In both the Xia and the Shang, 1523-1028 BC, dynasties, the emperor had rituals of shamanism in communication with ancestors for the confirmation of ruling power. Royal burials were often accompanied by human sacrifices. The utensils used in these rituals as well as in their weapons of warfare and chariots were made of bronze. The Shang developed a written language and they lived in an elaborate society, dressed in silk and furs, produced many works of art, and resided in ornamental buildings.

The Zhou rulers, originally subservient to the Shang, overpowered them in 1040 BC. The Zhou Dynasty, 1040-256 BC, claimed an impersonal deity who sanctioned the rule of the family morally worthy of the responsibility. Through this doctrine the ruler maintained accountability to a supreme moral force that guided humanity. During the Zhou Dynasty a national university was founded, and history was recorded with a developed written language of over two thousand characters.[1] The king of Zhou was dethroned by the king of Qin in 256 BC.

The Qin Dynasty, 221-207 BC, was very short. Though established to last ten thousand generations, it was terminated within fourteen years. This dynasty gave China its name. Emperor Qin Shi Huangdi or the First Emperor, the title he had created for himself upon defeating the other states, divided his new empire into 36 *jun*, or commandery states, subdivided into *xian*, as counties. Therefore, *junxian* signifies centralized bureaucratic rule of unification as opposed to *fengjian*, the decentralization of feudalism.[2]

Qin encouraged the mass production of farm tools and axles for carts all the same width in conjunction with a network of roadways that were constructed from the capital of Xi'an or Sian. A system was established that allowed the peasants to have the land which removed the nobles from the line of taxation. Work on the Great Wall began in 214 BC as a noted historical monument to this era. Laws were unified with severe penalties by strangulation, castration, decapitation, branding, cutting off hands and feet and mutilation as introduced by Lord Shang and the Legalists. The Legalists advocated state-enforced rule of law, regardless of who may commit a crime. These laws were to be posted outside the city gates.[3] Qin Shi Huangdi had secured immortality through monumental strides in society and government. In 1974 there were 7,500 life-sized ceramic soldiers found in his tomb near Xian, the area was still under excavation in the year 2000. He died at the age of 49 in 201 BC, after which the Qin Dynasty quickly disintegrated.

The successors of Qin continued the methods of his bureaucratic control as emperors of the Han Dynasties.[4] Liu Bang, a rebel general, who conquered the Wei Valley in 207 BC, destroyed Xiang Yu, a descendent of the Chu generals who had led rebellions throughout the empire. Liu established himself as emperor in 202 and took the name of a major tributary of the Yangtze River, Han, as his dynastic name. His descendents reigned until 8 AD. The Han dynasty recognized the ruling power of the emperor's widow after his death.

---

[1] John King Fairbank, *China* (Cambridge MA· The Belknap Press, 1992), p. 35-42.
[2] Ibid, p. 56.
[3] June Teufel Dreyer, *China's Political System* (Boston: Allyn and Bacon, 1996), p. 28
[4] Fairbank, *China*, p. 57.

It was the Western Han Dynasty, 202 BC-9 AD, that started making paper during the first century before Christ, which led to revolutionary progress in recording written material. This dynasty was expansionist, adding new territories into the south and southwest China including North Vietnam, parts of central Asia and North Korea.[5] It was also the Han that brought China out of feudalism with land placed on the market rather than granted as fiefs to the Nobles who were paid for there services in rice.[6]

The resurrection of the Han dynasty took place after a brief usurpation as the Eastern Han Dynasty, 25 AD-220AD. The Western and Eastern Han corresponded in time, prestige, and historical magnitude as that of the Roman Empire of the Western world. The Chinese, as a people, were continually referred to as the Han through the 20st century, and even writing in Chinese was denoted as Han characters.

Li Shihmin, of Chinese and Manchurian mixed ancestry from Shanxi Province, captured the capital city of Chang-an in 617 AD, and placed his father on the throne in 618 AD. In 626 AD he had his father abdicated, his brothers eliminated, and he ruled until 649 AD, an era of consequence for the Tang dynasty. The Tang Dynasty 618-906 AD took the position along with the Han dynasty as the golden age of the Chinese Empire. The expanse of territory under the Tang extended from Siberia to Southeast Asia and as far toward the west as the Caspian Sea.

The third Tang emperor, Kao Zung, was weak and dominated by his Empress Wu, who ruled after his death through young successors. In 690 Empress Wu assumed the title and as the only woman ruler of China changed the dynastic name to Chou. She was a superior politician but maintained control by murderous means.[7] Empress Wu was dethroned by coup in 705, and Xuanzong assumed rule in 712 after some years of disorder. His forty-four year reign was the most prosperous point of the Tang dynasty.[8]

During the Tang dynasty the civil service examination was introduced as a selective process for Chinese officials. Great care

[5] Alasdair Clayre, *The Heart of the Dragon* (Boston: Houghton Mifflin Company, 1984), p. xi.
[6] Dreyer, *China's Political System*, p. 38.
[7] Fairbank, *China*, pp. 81-82.
[8] John K. Fairbank, Edwin O. Reischauer and Albert M. Craig, *East Asia* (Boston: Houghton Mifflin, 1998), pp. 98-99.

was taken for fairness; the examiner could not be prejudiced and the students could not collaborate on the writing of an eight-part essay over the Confucian classics. Less than one percent passed the examination and gained the prestige of position. This system produced intelligent officials, established an orthodox belief system, and it rewarded merit, which provided social mobility.[9]

The first six dynasties plus the early Tang ended the period of ancient Chinese history. The history of the later Tang and Song dynasties formed what had been considered typical Chinese during the past millennium.[10] The key to advancement of the Northern Song Dynasty, 960-1126, was the application of the Chinese invention of printing, by the first century BC, in the development of the technology of the printed book.[11] It was also during the Song dynasty that a neo-Confucianism formed with elements of Buddhism, Taoism and the incorporation of the *feng shui*, the spirits of wind and water, and calmness signified harmony.[12]

The Juchen or Tungusic tribes of Manchuria appropriated the Song territory north of the Yangtze River. Emperor Kaozong restored Song rule in the south to make up the Southern Song Dynasty, 1127-1279, with the capital at Hangzhou in Zheijiang Province. Although Southern Song was a remnant state, it occupied the economic heartland of all China, and it procured economic growth even in its situation between war and peace.[13] The cost of defense from the required build up of bureaucracy became a weakness of the Song, which the Mongols conquered in 1279.[14]

As a peasant, Chu Yungchang formed a rebel band that seized Nanjing in 1356 and conquered the Yangtze Valley in 1367. He asserted himself as the first emperor of the Ming, or Brilliant, Dynasty, 1368-1644, and chose Hangwu as his reign title, which signified vast military power. He made Nanjing the imperial capital and built a sixty-foot high, twenty-mile wall around the city as the longest city wall in the world. The fourth son of Hungwu, Yunglo, moved the capital to Beijing in 1421.[15]

The Ming dynasty was known for superior shipbuilding and

[9] Dreyer, *China's Political System*, pp. 32-33.
[10] Fairbank and others, *East Asia*, p. 116.
[11] Fairbank, *China*, p. 93.
[12] Dreyer, *China's Political System*, p. 29.
[13] Fairbank and others, *East Asia*, p. 151.
[14] Fairbank, *China*, pp. 108, 121-122.
[15] Fairbank and others, *East Asia*, pp. 179-180.

long sea voyages.[16] It also maintained the reputation as one of the eras of orderly government and social stability throughout history with relative peace for 276 years. In 1628, Li Zucheng as a Shanxi postal employee lost his job because of famine and joined his uncle in banditry, and by 1643 held much of Shanxi, Henan and Hebei provinces. Early 1644 he raided Beijing and the Ming emperor committed suicide by hanging himself on Prospect Hill that overlooked the Forbidden City. Therefore, it was Chinese rebels who had destroyed the Ming dynasty before the Manchurians took rule and retained the major governmental institutions that the Ming had established.[17]

There were five dynasties before Christ on the Western calendar with thirty-one more dynasties and kingdoms following of which the Han, Tang, Song and Ming were most influential. The genius exhibited during these dynasties of China contributed many inventions and discoveries: gunpowder, suspension bridge, watertight compartments on ships, sternpost rudder, the abacus, movable type, examination system, seismograph, and vaccine for smallpox. The Chinese had technological developments beyond the level that Western scholars had presumed possible, in mathematics, medicine, chemistry, and astronomy. This misconception was rectified when Joseph Needham, of both the Fellow Royal Society and Fellow British Academy, Master of Gonville and Caius College and Cambridge foreign member of Academia Sinica, authored a encyclopedic research, *Science and Civilization in China* in five volumes. The table that Needham compiled included the lunar theory for tides, equatorial astronomy, clocks, the evaluation of *pi* along with other advanced theories.[18] These discoveries reflect the early advancement of Chinese thought.

Throughout her history, the principle philosophy of China was that of Master Kong Fuze, known to the West as Confucius, who became the authority for a well- ordered society during the Zhou Dynasty. Confucius developed a system of hierarchical relationships for the child to be subordinate to the parents, wife to husband, younger brother to older brother, younger friend to older friend, subject to ruler, and the emperor as father to his people.[19] A major

---

[16] Dreyer, *China's Political System*, pp. 40-41.
[17] Fairbank and others, *East Asia*, pp. 177, 209-210.
[18] Jean Chesneaux, Marianne Bastid and Marie-Claire Bergere, *China, from the Opium Wars to the 1911 Revolution* (New York: Pantheon Books, 1976), p. 41.
[19] Dreyer, *China's Political System*, p. 26.

Confucian principle was that man was perfectible through proper schooling and conditioning.

Another philosophical school that had an influence on the Chinese society was a School of Names, referred to as the Logicians. The Logicians under the leadership of Gongsun Long sought a system of logic through debate in defining absolute from relative terms. They believed that a system of laws and government could be established only through properly defined names.

The cosmology of China rested on the concept of the *yin-yang* a contribution of the Naturalists. The *yin-yang* represented the two natural or social complimentary aspects of opposites that gave the world its movement in alternate and reciprocal action: female and male, darkness and light, winter and summer, moon and sun, passive and active, cold and heat, wet and dry, soft and hard. These independent and complementing aspects gave balance and rhythm to life as one compensated for the other in its cycle. The Naturalists conceived of the combination of fire, water and earth, wood and metal that comprised the pseudoscience of all nature.[20] The Chinese respect for harmony of the human cohabiting with nature is signified in the *feng-shui*. When the winds and water, *feng-shui*, are placid there is peace and harmony or when troubled with breaks of waves there will be disaster. A phenomenon of relationship also existed between the *wen* and *wu*. *Wen* is the written word that spreads morality and culture while the *wu* signifies military order through violence.[21]

A set of norms and values was noted through the hierarchy of four levels of Chinese society. The highest level was the scholar, *shi*, then the peasant working class, *nong*, after which was the artisans, *gong*, then lastly the merchants, *shang*. Outside these four levels were the non-productive soldiers, prostitutes, servants, vagrants, and others who were considered parasites on society. The military was of the lowest realm of society, and to avoid concentrations of military power to organize an overthrow of a dynasty, the Chinese troops were scattered in small units throughout the country. If it became necessary to suppress a peasant rebellion the units could be called together.[22]

Those known by the Chinese as officials and scholars, *shenshih*, or

---

[20] Fairbank, and others, *East Asia*, p. 50.
[21] Fairbank, *China*, p. 69.
[22] Chesneaux and others, *China-1911*, p. 19.

the gentry class, as termed by the English, were individual degree holders and their families as land holders. To make up this class the degree-holders and landlords overlapped to a considerable extent but somewhat indiscriminately. This class was an asset to the Confucian government for they raised funds for public works, took responsibility for public morals, supported the academia as well as orphanages and care for the aged, compiled the local history, provided relief during disasters and organized militia without remuneration when defense was required.[23]

More than a decade before the Manchurians took the rule from the Ming Dynasty; they imitated the administration of Beijing in Mukden. The Manchu conquest of 1644 proved that it was easier to take China as an outside force rather than an inside revolt. From outside, the Manchus learned the ways of the Chinese. The Manchu rule became the Qing Dynasty, which subjected the Chinese[24] and made all Chinese men wear the long braid, a *queue*, as a token of dependence. A barber could report anyone without a *queue* to authorities, and that person would be in danger of being beheaded.[25] Manchu troops were placed in fortresses in all major cities throughout China. Every Manchu regardless of status was allotted a quota of rice without charge. Anti-Manchu feelings were prevalent even though they shared the official power, for there was a repugnance of humiliation sensed with their rule.[26]

Within 120 years, the Qing Dynasty under the Emperor Kangxi had extended the Chinese Empire to its greatest extent through economic growth and social change. China was not interested in any foreign relations and to avoid difficulties would give gifts with pretense of sincerity. Peoples from outside China were referred to as barbarians who were merely seeking to find what China could contribute to their knowledge and wealth. Chinese leaders believed that China could not benefit in any manner from collaborating with or seeking any developments of another nation. Everyone who came to establish relations with China was expected to *kowtow*, to kneel three times and prostrate nine times in submission, to recognize the emperor's sovereign rule. Gifts from foreign powers were delivered as tribute, starting in the late thirteenth century

---

[23] Fairbank and others, *East Asia*, p.193.
[24] Fairbank, *China*, p. 143.
[25] Chang Tieh-Cung, *China in Revolution* Part I (Documentary Video, an AMBRICA production, 1989).
[26] Chesneaux and others, *China-1911*, pp. 19-20.

with Mongol expeditions. About a hundred years later the Ming Dynasty's first Emperor Hungwu sent envoys to Japan, Korea, Vietnam, Champa, Tibet and others. Later the rulers of these countries started sending tributary missions to China. In the early 1400s Cheng Ho, a eunuch, with an expedition of ships up to four hundred feet in length with a dozen watertight compartments and navigational instrumentation, sailed along South East Asia, Ceylon, India, the Middle East and East Africa. He visited about fifty new countries and those rulers became tributaries.[27] Any relationship extended to a foreign country was for the purpose of benefiting China not to befriend the foreigner.[28] It was in this context that China faced the nineteenth century and the intrusion of the West with its technology, military power, opium and religion.

EVENTS LEADING TO OPIUM WARS: 1800-1839

Throughout recorded history the Chinese had maintained a superior civilization of self-sufficiency. Only once in their history had they borrowed anything on a large scale from another nation, and that was their adaptation of Buddhism from India in about 100 AD. This was a result of the loss of the dominating influence of Confucian scholars and individualism introduced through Taoism, or Daoism which stressed the supremacy of personal choice. Since that time, the sole modification even noticed by the majority of Chinese within the past millennium had been the hair style, the *queue*, a single braid as a sign of submission imposed by the Manchu Emperor Kangxi in1662. As they entered the modern age after limited contact with the outside world, the popular opinion in China was still that foreigners should copy the clearly superior civilization of China.[29]

By the time that the Manchurians had conquered China, Westerners had reached the Central Kingdom during the Ming Dynasty, 1368-1644. The Portuguese not only arrived, but by mid-sixteenth century had established a colony on the island of Macao, which they finally held through 1999. The Russians began to encroach upon the areas in the north, while the Spanish and the Dutch had been building settlements along the seacoast.[30] These

---

[27] Fairbank and others, *East Asia*, pp. 49, 195,198.
[28] Fairbank, *China*, p. 161.
[29] Edwin E. Moise, *Modern China*, 2nd edn. (London: Longman, 1944), p. 35.
[30] Lucian W. Pye, *China An Introduction*, 4th edn. (New York: Harper Collins Publishers, Inc., 1991), p. 107.

contacts were a threat China's passivity under the ruling gentry, who maintained the Confucian teachings of living in the harmony of a frugal agrarian life style rather than being urban and expansive. Merchants had been discredited as parasitic and manipulative; to work contently in one's own fields without concern for even the next village was held as the ideal.[31] This Confucian goal of living in harmony and tranquility had been interrupted with revolution and rebellion against the old authority with civil and international wars.[32] The beginning came through a Buddhist religious sect, the secret White Lotus society, that led a rebellion during the years 1796 to 1804, which appealed to peasants in their state of poverty through promises to restore the Ming Dynasty. They professed that Maitreya Buddha, who would descend to remove suffering, disease and disaster in this life, would accomplish this relief and secure happiness in the following life.[33]

POWER STRUGGLE WITH WESTERN COUNTRIES

Conflict on an international level, however, began with contact from the Western nations on a commercial basis. Because of their nation's great size and a sense of self-sufficiency and disinterest in foreign diplomatic relations, the Chinese were slow to respond to the economic value of trade. The demand for imported goods was very limited and the extent of exports was tea and silk, products that did not stimulate modernization.[34] The heart of Britain's interest in China was tea, which England alone consumed 20 million pounds a year and by the late 1820s escalated to about 30 million pounds, or approximately two pounds of tea for every man, woman and child each year.[35]

The first attempt to establish diplomatic relations with the Imperial Court of China was by the British representative Lord Macartney in 1793 who had determined to secure mutual respect. The conflict came over the controversy of the humiliating *kowtow*, rendered in submission by bearers of tribute to recognize the

---

[31] John K. Fairbank, Edwin O. Reischauer and Albert M. Craig, *East Asia*, Rev. edn. (Boston: Houghton Mifflin Company, 1989), p. 436.

[32] Pye, *Introduction*, p. 123.

[33] John King Fairbank, *China A New History* (Cambridge, MA: The Belknap Press of Harvard University Press, 1992), p 189.

[34] Fairbank and others, *East Asia*, pp. 437,439.

[35] Peter Ward Fay, *The Opium War: 1840-1842* (Chapel Hill, NC: The University of North Carolina Press, 1975), p. 17.

sovereignty of the emperor. Again the British tried to establish an international relationship with China through Lord Jeffery Amherst in 1816, which again was curtailed over the issue of delivering the *kowtow*. A haughty mandate was delivered by Jia Qing, the new emperor, in retaliation for refusal to comply with this courtesy.[36] Maintaining the proper relationship with the barbarians in a state of submission to the emperor was more important than prospering in commercial trade.

Western countries, motivated by desire for raw materials, aggressively sought commercial influence. As rapid modifications came through industrialization, the societies of the Western world had been revolutionized socially, economically, morally, intellectually and politically, and they had the military power to become masters of the world. The British, according to international law, which they claimed to follow, had to relinquish treaty rights in recognition of the sovereignty of each nation by accepting their refusal and withdraw or negotiate a satisfactory modification. However, in the nineteenth century that was not the attitude of Britain toward non-Europeans.[37]

Corresponding to China's fast population growth was expansion in production and trade plus the establishments that sustained them. As late as 1800, but before the expansion of science and industry, China considered herself relatively self-sufficient while still functioning with a manpower economy. Irrigation, transportation, handicrafts and the rice culture had a high degree of efficiency even though production was just keeping abreast of population growth. After 1820, the contact with Western countries became too complicated to control, and a noted decline in Qing Dynasty rule became evident.[38]

The legal system set up during the Qing was elaborate and well organized to function through five punishments. Depending on the severity of the offence, beatings with light or heavy bamboo, servitude, exile or the death penalty was administered. The major aim was to preserve the social order of relational hierarchy.[39] Each level had the responsibility to set an example and give praise or place blame on all events under its jurisdiction The local level was

[36] Pye, *Introduction*, pp. 112-114.
[37] Kenneth Scott Latourette, *The Chinese, Their History and Culture*, 3rd edn. Rev. (New York: The MacMillan Company, 1959), pp342, 344.
[38] Fairbank, *China*, p. 163.
[39] Ibid, p. 184.

that of magistrate who sought every means to avoid trouble, to the extent of enlisting bandits as part of the local police force rather than providing justice. Magistrates with their public office responsibilities, confused the use of private and public funds by exacting money, or a squeeze, to supplement their own income received as a farmer. This type of corruption exhausted the financial resources of the dynasty.[40] In 1829, this corruption affected the official exchange rate causing it to change from 4,000 copper coins for one tael of silver, to 1,000 per tael. However, an edict recorded rates as high as 4,600 still being charged peasants who were paying their taxes in copper, as well as suffering a shortage of revenue.[41] Therefore, foreign currency, namely the Spanish sliver dollar was preferred in trade and was being hoarded. Problems increased when the copper coin that had a hole in the center to enable stringing them together in bundles was reduced in size by one-third. The smaller size increased the amount of cash to be minted and encouraged counterfeiting of an even cheaper coin.[42]

In foreign trade, the British sought to equate the rate of their exports to China to their imports from China of tea and silk. They were paying in silver for the variance between the little they exported and the great amount imported. Therefore, the British began the export of opium through their East India Company to make up the difference.

OPIUM INTRODUCED INTO CHINA

Opium, made by multiple incisions in about eighteen thousand poppy capsules per acre to allow the opium to ooze out, yielded about twenty pounds of processed opium. By 1838 India's Ghazipur factory was processing over 400,000 acres of poppies, or 4,000 tons. At 170 pounds per chest, over 47,000 chests of opium were destined for China per year.

The Chinese ate and drank opium, as the Indians did for years, until they started mixing it with tobacco or betel into what was called *madak*. Many turned to smoking it in a pipe for relaxation to the extent that there was a temptation to associate opium pipe smoking with the Mongoloid features of the Chinese.[43] Smoking

---

[40] Fairbank and others, *EastAsia*, pp. 441-442.
[41] Jean Cheneaux, Marianne Bastid and Marie-Claire Bergere, *China, from the Opium Wars to the 1911 Revolution* (New York: Pantheon Books, 1976), p. 43.
[42] Fairbank and others, *East Asia*, p. 455.
[43] Fay, *Opium Wars*, pp. 4-5,7.

of opium by actually inhaling it in water vapor only started in the 17th century after tobacco smoking was introduced to China from America by way of Manila, the capital city of the Philippines.[44] For processing *chandu*, the smokable extract of opium, it was necessary to ship it in a partially moist form, which the Bengal agencies had solved, by shipping it in cakes. The Ghazipur factory turned out 6,000 to 7,000 cakes a day with 100 or so cake-makers each forming about a dozen cakes an hour, working from May to early September. With the mark of East India Company, the buyers were assured of receiving the pure and full weight of the best Patna and Benares types of processed opium. These shipments were rarely confiscated even though the trade was illegal, and it was delivered in a way that the risk was totally absorbed by the Chinese.

From Calcutta the opium was taken by the fast clipper ships, of which the most famous was the "Red Rover," not directly to the docks at Canton but was relayed to merchantmen as floating depots of receiving ships, such as the well known Lintin ship.[45] Therefore, the opium was sold while it was still afloat, to stay within the written law that smuggling was the actual delivery of the illegal goods to the shore. The Chinese then carried out the smuggling, although the East India Company supplied their means of smuggling. These receiving floating warehouses were heavily armed and organized as broker houses while the smuggling boats, fast crabs or scrambling dragons that took the drug to the shore, were also armed and manned by sixty or seventy oarsmen. Both the British of the East India Company and the Chinese merchants propagated the opium trade.[46] The emperor discovered that even those of his palace guard were using the drug.

China started to administer regulations for incoming foreign commercial vessels with a duty tax, customs, pilotage and other fees. Each ship had to secure an exiting permit before it could leave for Macao, and the passengers could not go into the countryside, into the city suburbs, or wander along the city wall. Not all of the regulations were enforced, but the foreigners were fairly well controlled.

---

[44] Fairbank and others, *East Asia*, p. 450.
[45] Fay, *Opium Wars*, pp. 12-13, 49
[46] Fairbank, *East Asia*, pp. 451-452.

CHINA'S FIGHT AGAINST THE OPIUM TRADE

The first edict from Beijing was issued in 1729 against opium. As the use of the drug spread from the coastal provinces of the south and the grade of opium of low morphia enriched to the *chandu* form, the official decrees against it multiplied. In the early nineteenth century the declarations of prohibition of opium from the governor-general of Guangzhou or Beijing were ordered about once a year.[47] This was such a regular activity that an actual ritual at Namoa was devised as described by William Hunter of Russell and Company who resided in China for several years:

The new arrival dropping anchor close by a little piece of land called Brig Island; a suitable wait; then comes a Mandarin seated on an armchair in a sort of open scow; he climbs gravely aboard, walks to a clear space on deck, draws from his boot an edict ordering the barbarian vessel away, reads it, and steps into the cabin for a glass of wine and a cheroot; after which merchant junks stand out from the mainland to receive the new arrival's chests. This was the way the coast opium business went.[48]

The British encouraged the production of opium in Bengal and Madras through the East India Company during the early nineteenth century. By 1830 China was undergoing a major outflow of silver just to pay for the amount of opium being imported over the products of export. This expenditure had a major effect on their currency and economy.[49] At the 1837 rate of consumption, 57 percent of Chinese imports were designated to opium. In 1839 Lin Zexu, the Chinese official who later took a leading role in the events that ultimately led to the opium war, had calculated that each year 100 million taels of silver was spent by addicts on opium. The Chinese government's entire annual revenue was a mere 40 million taels.[50] Just before the opium war, the value of a tael of silver had increased from 800 copper coins to around 1,600. The Manchu government only accepted silver for taxes, but the peasants sold their produce for copper coins. Therefore, they were paying in taxes double the amount previously required.[51]

---

[47] Fay, *Opium Wars*, pp. 34-35, 42-43.
[48] Ibid, p. 122-123.
[49] Pye, *Introduction*, p. 109.
[50] Cheneaux and others, *China-1911*, pp. 54-55.
[51] Tung Chi-Ming, *An Outline History of China* (Hong Kong: Joint Publishing Company, 1982), p. 210.

The West maintained the attitude that smoking opium was contemptuous and all the Chinese had to do to stop the opium trade was to stop being addicts. They also held in contempt the corrupted officials that they bribed to keep the trade open, because they were corruptible. On the other hand, the British adopted all they saw could be used to their advantage from the Chinese such as their civil service system and the practice of competitive examinations, which they first implemented in their Indian ports. Later the Parliament established these Chinese procedures into the British system.[52]

Genuine free trade with competition was realized in 1833 when London officials terminated the monopoly of the East Indian Company. A British superintendent of trade was sent to China to oversee the trade interests of Britain. He ridiculed the tribute system supported by the Qing court and refused to deal with the Chinese merchant Hong, the anglicized word for *hang,* licensed brokers responsible to conduct trade. He insisted on negotiating only on a diplomatic-equality basis with Qing officials, but to accept this level of equality would destroy the superiority of the emperor and demean his position in China.

The newly-manufactured steam gunboats of the British discouraged any hope for the Qing administration to ever destroy the opium smuggling operation or undertake trying to enforce an embargo of trade with Britain. As early as 1836 there were advocates encouraging legalization of the opium trade, since its prohibition could not be enforced.[53] Nevertheless, in 1838 Lin Zexu, as imperial commissioner, was appointed to eliminate the drug traffic. He virtually placed the entire foreign community of Gunagzhou under house arrest and demanded that all of the opium under their possession be relinquished. Then he required that all merchants render a formal agreement not to be involved in its transport into China.[54] Lin referred to the British as rebels, for they had brought disorder to the harmony of the Chinese society. Along with the authorities, he agreed that the harmony could only be restored through the refusal of diplomatic negotiations.[55] The emperor,

---

[52] Steven W. Mosher, *China Misperceived* (Montclair: A New Republic Book, 1990), p. 37.
[53] Fairbank, *China*, p. 199.
[54] Latourette, *The Chinese*, p. 345.
[55] Cheneaux and others, *China-1911*, pp. 61-62.

by the end of 1838, decided to enforce an anti-opium campaign by imposing the death penalty against all those that cultivated, distributed and used opium. Opium dens were destroyed, dealers were executed, and by the winter of 1838-1839 trade had practically been eliminated. This statute included all foreign importers, and he refused to communicate with the superintendent of British trade without the Chinese characters for *qing yuan*, meaning petition, to head his letters, which implicated that it was sent from an inferior to a superior.[56] These events, leading to further complications and strained international relations and rebuttals, built up to explosive proportions.

OPIUM WAR LEADING TO THE TREATY OF NANJING: 1839 – 1842

The struggle for a new order and the opium trade were the themes of concern in China coming into the mid-nineteenth century. Britain dominated the opium trade through their colony of India. Both Indian and British traders, those of private trade as well as those licensed by the East Indian Company, sold opium at auction and then had it shipped. The opium bought by the Chinese traders in Guangzhou paid for the tea consumed in England. This arrangement made a prosperous India-Chinese-England trade circuit. The outlay of silver as a drain on China and her people caused apprehension on the part of the governing administration of the Qing Dynasty, who had appointed Lin Zexu as the official to eradicate the importation of opium.[57] In England, opium was not illegal and many well-known statesmen like Samuel Taylor Coleridge regularly used it. Opium was regarded as less harmful than alcohol; therefore, the new laws published by Lin went unheeded.[58] Lin's efforts to end the opium trade escalated to the confiscation of all the opium in Guangzhou, which eventually led to events of the Opium War from November 1839 to August 1842 with few casualties but many consequences.[59]

---

[56] Fairbank and others, *East Asia*, p. 456.
[57] John King Fairbank, *China, A New History* (Cambridge, MA: The Belknap Press of Harvard University Press, 1992), p. 198.
[58] Jonathan D. Spence, *The Search for Modern China* (New York: W. W. Norton, 1990), p. 151.
[59] Lucian W. Pye, *China: An Introduction*, 4th edn. (New York: Harper Collins Publishers, Inc., 1991), p. 115.

Political History: China in Context

Events that Activated the Opium Wars

Lin Zexu was quite ingenious in his methods of executing his duty to terminate opium traffic. He used the traditional Confucius examination system as a tool by requesting a special assembly of over 600 students. Along with answering the conventional examination questions, the students were asked to name anonymously and voluntarily any opium merchants. Then these students were requested to propose a suggestion on how to deal with the vendors to stop this commerce.[60] By March of 1839 he had approximately 350 foreign distributors of opium confined to their living quarters in Guangzhou. Although their servants were ordered to leave the foreign compound, the foreigners were not physically harmed or prohibited from securing food. However, they were restricted from leaving until all opium supplies were relinquished for destruction. With these restrictions, the trade was practically obliterated and the dealers were left with an overabundant supply of unsold opium. Captain Charles Elliot, the British representative, collected and yielded over to Lin approximately 1,000 tons of accumulated opium from these merchants.[61] A letter written from the frigate *Conway* by Captain Bethune to Sir Frederick Maitland on May 28, 1839, argued that the Chinese were more concerned about losing silver than the issue of immorality of opium use.[62]

Many Chinese were also arrested in connection with the opium trade and indulgence. Opium dens were raided and destroyed, cakes of opium were confiscated and burned, and all smugglers were tried and sentenced.[63] The Qing administration tried to curtail the trade with a crusade that proved too late to coincide with the interests that were generated in Guangzhou.[64] In July of 1839, a thirty-nine-article statute was submitted to enforce the death penalty on all varieties of opium offences. Opium smokers were given eighteen months to become rehabilitated with the help of the sanitarium Lin opened just outside Guangzhou.[65] The Chinese imperial government appealed to the West, but these foreign powers presented the fact that opium

---

[60] Spence, *The Search*, p. 150.
[61] Edwin E. Moise, *Modern China*, 2nd edn. (London: Longman, 1994), p. 31.
[62] Peter Ward Fay, *The Opium War 1840-1842* (Chapel Hill, NC: The University of North Carolina Press, 1975), p. 185.
[63] Ibid, p. 119.
[64] John K. Fairbank, Edwin O. Reischauer and Albert M. Craig, *East Asia*, Rev. edn. (Boston: Houghton Mifflin Company, 1989), p. 455.
[65] Fay, *Opium War*, p. 172.

45

was raised in China, and if the demand were not supplied through importation, it would be produced domestically.[66]

Further damaging Sino-British relations, a drunken English soldier killed a Chinese villager, leading to the first naval battle of the first Opium War in November 1839. However, the Guangzhou tea trade continued under the American flag by Russell and Company, who worked with a hong distributor contact, Houga, in the interest of the British.[67]

The Chinese courts decided to act through the imperial commissioner to apprehend over three million pounds of British raw opium.[68] Five or six miles above Chuenpi, where the creek and river met, the high commissioner had two basins constructed with wooden sides and a flat stone floor. Fresh water from the river filled these basins, then coolies shoved twenty thousand cases of cakes and crushed balls of opium into the water and covered it all with lime and salt. More coolies used hoes and shovels to make a putrid mixture, which flushed into the creek, and the watery mess was washed into the sea.[69] This action stimulated the West into taking military action.

THE FIRST OPIUM WAR INSUED

On the dawn of Wednesday, May 26, 1841, a letter from Captain Elliot rationalized that the move on Guangzhou was to demonstrate to the Chinese that Britain could not be intimidated. However, the British were not to enter the city for fear of injury to innocent citizens that would harm their cause.[70] Another motive for this action was the British abhorrence of the Chinese judicial system's arbitrary arrest and torture of people merely accused of an offence. In 1784, the British had refused to submit to the Chinese courts' jurisdiction, and the United States of America, USA, joined this stand in 1821. The foreign powers promoted an extraterritoriality policy in China that put each foreign nation in jurisdiction over their own citizens, but the Chinese had not agreed to this arrangement.[71]

With the motives defined, the British decided to strike swiftly

---

[66] June Teufiel Dreyrer, *China's Political System* (Boston: Allyn and Bacon, 1996), p. 46.
[67] Fairbank and others, *East Asia*, p.457.
[68] Dreyer, *Political System*, p. 46.
[69] Fay, *Opium War*, p. 160.
[70] Ibid, p. 294.
[71] Fairbank and others, *East Asia*, p. 453.

and intensely without prior written warning. They believed that the Chinese should not only pay for the costs of the war but also recompense the value of the confiscated opium and suffer any expense incurred in the course of collection.[72] Britain demanded these terms, which were to be negotiated by Captain Elliot as their representative and chief superintendent.

Although there was little problem with translation through Robert Morrison, the first Protestant missionary in China, the discussion to reconcile the differences between the two countries lasted six hours between Elliot and Kishen, the Chinese governor-general. Kishen tried to subordinate Britian by referring to the differences in status of rank between himself and the British official. He also referred to the two incidents when "little England" sent Lord Macartney in 1793 and Lord Jeffery Amherst again in 1816 as tribute embassies to the "Celestial Empire" in Beijing. Elliot remarked that the Chinese were determined to smoke opium and only the influence of proper instruction could gradually wean them from their cravings, but violence could not stop them. Therefore, an impasse left the two negotiators in an irreconcilable situation.[73]

Plenty of public criticism arose from both Britain and America on the basis of forcing opium trade on China, but little dispute was voiced against the rights of Western powers to demand the stipulations for what was considered legitimate trade.[74] However, because the British cargo of opium had been destroyed, Britain made a decisive reaction. British forces set up a blockade at selected points along the Gulf of Guangzhou, the major port of Amoy, and at the mouths of the Yangtze and Yellow Rivers.[75]

Since the Chinese officials perceived that Lin Ze'xu was responsible for the retaliation of the British, which he was unable to control, in September 1840 he was disgracefully recalled and sent to the Northwest into exile.[76] However, he had already earned the title of *The Author of the China War* with the distinction of having destroyed British property worth over 2.5 million British pounds. He was called from exile in 1845, but in transit to his new assignment

---

[72] Fay, *Opium War*, pp. 192-194.
[73] Ibid, p. 233.
[74] Kenneth Scott Latourette, *The Chinese, Their History and Culture*, 3rd edn., Rev. (New York: The MacMillan Company, 1959), p. 345.
[75] Fay, *Opium War*, p. 242.
[76] Jean Cheneaux, Marianne Bastid and Marie-Claire Bergere, *China, from the Opium Wars to the 1911 Revolution* (New York: Panthcon Books, 1976), p. 63.

Lin died near Guangzhou the autumn of 1850.[77]

On May 30, 1841, British brigands came to Sanyuanli near Guangzhou and were very surprised when tens of thousands of peasants from 103 neighboring villages rushed to surround them at the predetermined sound of a gong. While they fought, armed with hoes, shovels, axes and other tools, the Chinese peasant women and children supplied the men with food and water. These peasants killed or wounded more than two hundred of the British,[78]the only real Chinese military victory in the first Opium War. The British continued to pursue their goal of China's submission. If the British would conquer Beijing, the Chinese knew that the shame would destroy the dynasty, for it was the primary duty of each Manchu to preserve the dynasty.[79]

THE TREATY OF NANJING

The capture of Chinkiang, in July of 1842, cut off all communication between Beijing and the South at the point where the Grand Canal crossed the Yangtze River. The order to invade Nanjing had been given, which forced the Qing Dynasty to come to terms with the Treaty of Nanjing in August of that year.[80] The Manchu plenipotentiaries, Qishan along with his successor Qiying, negotiated the conditions of the treaty, which was signed by Qiying and the British representative, Pottinger, on August 29, 1842.[81]

The treaty provisions included (1) extraterritoriality (foreign consular jurisdiction over foreign nationals), an upgrading of an old Chinese practice, (2) an indemnity, (3) a moderate tariff and direct foreign contact with the customs collectors, (4) most-favored-nation treatment (an expression of China's "impartial benevolence" to all outsiders), (5) freedom to trade with all comers, no monopoly (long custom at Kashgar).[82]

The Qing gave the island of Hong Kong in perpetuity to Britain and opened five ports for trade including smuggling of opium. Hong Kong at that time was a barren island of a few fishing villages. Its location just forty miles from Macao and a bit more than forty

---

[77] Fay, *Opium War,* p. 369.
[78] Tung Chiming, *An Outline History of China* (Hong Kong: Joint Publishing Co., 1982), p. 214.
[79] Fay, *Opium War,* p. 357.
[80] Latourette, *The Chinese,* p. 346.
[81] Cheneaux, and others, *Opium Wars to 1911,* p. 63.
[82] Fairbank, *China,* p. 200.

to Bogue was very suitable for opium transactions.[83] Beyond the ceding of Hong Kong, an indemnity of 21 million Mexican dollars was required to cover debts of the hong merchants and pay for the confiscated British opium cargo along with reimbursement to the British-Indian government for the cost of the war.[84] There was no agreement to terminate opium traffic into China; rather, further inroads for trade were opened in the five ports of Guangzhou, Amoy, Fuzhou, Ningbo and Shanghai. Foreigners were allowed to reside in these port cites, and consulates were to be permitted. Perfect equality of relations between Britain and China was established with the Cohong to be abolished and a reasonable tariff of custom duties determined.[85] The Treaty of Nanjing with its obvious one-sided stipulations was the first of a series of unequal treaties with which China yielded to comply.[86]

No other time in history had there been such blatant imperialistic aggression on any nation similar to this Anglo-Chinese war of 1839-1842 with its successive treaties. Moreover, it was a war initiated by the Chinese government's effort to terminate the insidious contraband smuggling of opium.[87] Now that foreigners infested their land by traveling, trading, and forming their own communities along with propagating new ideas through merchants and missionaries, the Chinese began to adopt traits of the alien culture.[88] The events of the Opium War had contributed to many changes in China both positive and negative, which prepared her entrance into the modern world.

FROM THE 1842 TREATY TO 1920

The sense of decline was more acute for the Middle Kingdom, because they had never confronted a technologically superior power.[89] This encounter with Britain forced China to engage in the trade of opium, which was a detriment to the social-economic order of the Confucian society. The resistance offered by the residents of

---

[83] Fay, *Opium War,* p. 170.
[84] Fairbank and others, *East Asia,* p. 460.
[85] Fay, *Opium War,* p361-362.
[86] Raymond Whitehead and Rhea M., *China: Search for Community* (New York: Friendship Press, 1878), p.13.
[87] Fairbank and others, *East Asia,* p. 454.
[88] Latourette, *The Chinese,* p. 342.
[89] Raymand L. and Rhea M. Whitehead, *China: Search for Community* (New York: Friendship Press, 1978), p. 13

Guangzhou was evidence that the Qing rulers had submitted to the demands of Britain rather than the Chinese people. The political awareness displayed in their resolve to deter the enemy caused apprehension in the assailants as well as their rulers. The Qing Dynasty, ruled by Manchu usurpers, was always on guard against the capability of the Chinese people to displace the dynasty.[90] Through the resolution of the Opium war, concluded by the Nanjing Treaty, the country became a semi-feudal system under the suppression of foreign powers and the ruling Manchu Qing Dynasty.[91]

FURTHER WESTERN INTRUSION

There was a time after the war that it seemed as if the British aggressors were leaving China. For many of the Chinese this blessing was perceived as if China had won the war, and indeed there was a time during which the results of the war and treaty had left the fundamentals of daily life unaltered.[92] However, the official political ramifications from the denial of their right to international isolation had closed doors to trade in China except those approved on a State by State basis.[93]

In time it was quite obvious that the Westerners had not returned home, as they turned their attention to the Northern ports in persuasion that they would offer an even more lucrative, yet illegal, opium trade than the five ports opened by treaty. The Western powers' approach to China was different from the way they had divided Africa into separate colonial claims, or from the appropriation tactic the British had imposed upon India as the Russians did in Central Asia. These Western nations literally perforated China with total subordination, for they lived, traveled, worked, propagated teachings, built ships and factories, founded hospitals, schools and universities, published newspapers, established legal and postal systems and managed banks at will. In spreading the message of Christianity, they not only preached and persuaded the Chinese to become believing converts but became involved in the social services

---

[90] John Gittings, *A Chinese View of China* (New York: Pantheon Books, 1973), pp. 51-53.
[91] Tung Chiming, *An Outline History of China* (Hong Kong: Joint Publishing Company, 1982), pp. 217, 219.
[92] Peter Ward Fay, *the Opium War 1840-1842* (Chapel Hill, NC: The University of North Carolina Press, 1975), p. 363.
[93] Victor Purcell, *The Boxer Uprising* (Cambridge: The University Press, 1963), p. 269.

of education, hospitalization and technical training.[94]

These imposed services displaced the gentry's function within the Chinese society. The upper gentry class obtained academic degrees through excelling in examinations, but the lower gentry, principally landlords, received their degrees by recommendation or purchase.[95] The lower gentry class by 1850 made up three-tenths of the ruling class of about 1,100,000 men throughout China.[96] The willful independent attitude of the foreigners toward this ruling class generated an atmosphere of insubordination.

The foreigners of the West filled China with all varieties of imported goods. The cheap and often better commodities from abroad saturated a market where handicrafts once were a source of extra income on the local community level. Peasants became dependent upon the world and national markets along with the merchandise of local commerce.[97] On October 8, 1843, Britain established trade in the form of most-favored nation clauses, which persuaded other nations to follow their lead to urge China to extend compatible agreements for their particular desired treaties. The American president, John Tyler, dispatched Caleb Cushing to negotiate with Chiying for extraterritoriality rights that would allow Americans to be governed by their own laws in China. Thereby, the USA obtained the Wanghai Treaty on July 3, 1844; the French also secured a treaty on October 24, 1844, to protect missionaries. Belgium in 1845, Norway and Sweden in 1847, and Russia in 1851 each established a treaty encompassing the most favored nation clause.[98] Spain, Portugal, Italy, Austria, Germany and Japan all managed to establish ratified relations with the Qing government.[99] These treaties exposed China to Western commerce and culture against her will. July 1854 marked the development of British, American and French international settlements and concessions of self-government with their own local taxation, roadway service,

---

[94] Fay, *Opium War*, pp. 364-365.

[95] John King Fairbank, *China, A New History* (Cambridge, MA: The Belnap Press of Harvard University Press, 1992), pp. 102-103.

[96] John K. Fairbank, Edwin O. Reischauer and Albert M Craig, *East Asia*, rev. edn. (Boston: Houghton Mifflin Company, 1989), p. 570.

[97] Cheneaux, Jean, Marianne Bastid and Marie-Claire Bergere, *China, from the Opium Wars to the 1911 Revolution* (New York: Pantheon Books, 1976), p. 218.

[98] Lucian W Pye, *China An Introduction*, 4th edn. (New York: Harper Collins Publishers, Inc., 1991) p. 116, and Fairbank and others, *East Asia*, p. 460.

[99] Cheneaux and others, *China-1911*, p. 250.

and police enforcement.[100]

The most favored nation status was used to expand the opium market, along with another social evil that developed in China late in the 1840s. Male laborers were shipped under contract, mainly from the ports of Xiamen and Macao as well as other harbors, as cheap labor for sugar plantations of Cuba, Peru, Hawaii, Sumatra and Malaya in what was termed as coolie trade.[101] Often this form of contract work was but a little better than slave labor, for the workers were completely dependent on those for whom they worked for proper food, clothing, shelter and care along with any hope of ever returning to China.

THE SECOND OPIUM WAR

The treaty imposed on China after the Second Opium War in 1860 reserved the right for all Chinese to be at liberty to become a part of the labor force in any British colony and other places abroad. This was only to legalize coolie trade for the rubber and tin plantations in Java and the Straits Settlements and workers in the gold mines and railroads of California.[102] By 1880 a unilateral action agreement confirmed cooperation between the Western powers and China to prohibit the abuses that had corrupted the understood stipulations of the treaty.[103]

Under the strain of apprehension that the treaty system would deteriorate without an updated extension, the British drew a pretext for war in an incident at sea in October of 1856. The Chinese owned lorcha *Arrow*, with a Western hull and Chinese rig, had been registered in Hong Kong to a British captain accompanied by a Chinese crew and was flying the British flag. While docked in Guangzhou at Pearl River, Chinese officers boarded the *Arrow* and arrested most of the crew for a recent act of piracy, then lowered the British flag. The British claimed that their sovereignty had been violated and the British flag disgraced, but the Chinese offered no satisfactory recompense. With the execution of a French missionary for subversion in Kwangsi, an area of rebellion, the French cooperated with the British by joining fleets, captured

---

[100] John K. Fairbank, and others, *East Asia*, Rev. edn., p. 476.

[101] Ibid, p. 466.

[102] Gittings, *Chinese View*, pp. 59-60.

[103] Kenneth Scott Latourette, *The Chinese, Their History and Culture*, 3rd edn, Rev. (New York: The MacMillan Company, 1959), p. 368.

Guangzhou in December 1857 and took the obstinate Viceroy, Yeh Mingchen, as prisoner to Calcutta.

Along with Britain and France, the USA and Russia joined to assert conditions on Beijing. Under duress the emperor conceded to negotiate and his brother, Prince Kung, signed the Treaties of Tientsin in June 1858. These treaties increased indemnities to Britain and France by two million teals of silver each, plus two million more teals for compensation to Britain for losses suffered by their merchants.[104] The British secured Kowloon Peninsula and the French, through deceit, procured the right for the Catholic Church to hold properties in the interior of China. In the attempt to ratify the treaties in June 1859 at Beijing, the British and French were repelled. Then, in October 1860, Britain and France returned in force, entered and captured Tientsin and Beijing while the emperor fled to Jehol. They burned the Yuang Ming Yuang, a summer palace built from the plans of Jesuit architects for Emperor Qianlong's pleasure.[105] The Treaty of Beijing was assessed as follows:

The Treaties of Tientsin (1858) and Peking (1860):

(1) New ports were opened.... (2) The merchantmen of the powers were given permission to use the Yangtze River. (3) Peking, although not technically made an open port, was to have the hated alien living within its walls... They were, moreover, to be received as representatives of independent nations on a footing of equality with China. (4) Foreigners, when armed with proper passports, were to be permitted to travel anywhere in the interior. (5) To Christians, both aliens and Chinese was given the privilege of propagating Christianity... (6) The French convention of 1860 gave further sanction to the promise made in imperial edict of 1846 that the Chinese Government would restore to Roman Catholics the religious and benevolent establishments confiscated during the persecutions of the preceding century and a half.... (7) An elaboration of the regulations for extraterritoriality, (8) the cession to Great Britain of a bit of mainland opposite Hong Kong, (9) the payment of indemnities, and (10) in a new tariff drawn up in 1858 in pursuance of the treaties of Tientsin, the legalization of the opium traffic by placing of a duty on the drug.[106]

---

[104] Tung, *History of China*, pp. 226-227.
[105] Fairbank and others, *East Asia*, p. 477-478.
[106] Latourette, *The Chinese*, p. 351.

These agreements represented an even more humiliating defeat to China than did those of the Nanjing Treaties. Eleven more ports were opened including in Northern Manchuria; Taiwan and as far up the Yangtze River as Hankow, or Wuhan.[107] Further concessions within different cities were granted to both Britain and France. Shanghai rapidly became a center of foreign trade. In 1863 Britain, France and the USA established international settlements almost completely independent of Chinese rule.[108] More disturbing than the steamships that permeated China's waterways were the railroads that disrupted the *feng-shui*, or the pseudoscience applied to the lay of the land, crossing canals and farm-land as well as intruding upon burial grounds. The sentimental value of land made it an extravagant investment.

To add to the insult, opium was legalized with imports peaking in 1879 to 87,000 chests but subsequently declining as Chinese-grown opium supplied the continued growing demand. Tea exports to Britain rose to 150 million pounds through the 1880s, then declined because tea had been transplanted from China to colonized India. Likewise, Chinese silk exports declined from the superior European and Japanese market organization and technology of disease prevention while China failed to adequately modernize;[109]although their private workshops began to switch to machine production. In 1861 Fuzhou merchants started using automation in making tea-bricks; in 1863 the Hung Sheng Rice Dealers were mechanically husking rice, and by 1880 the silk merchants of Nanhai, Kwangtung, had set up mechanized silk filature.[110]

After the wars and treaties, China entered the Tongzhi, the Emperor's reign title signifying unified government, reformation period in which Prince Gong, the important Manchu reformer reasoned that the destruction of the palace indicated that the foreigners apparently did not desire to conquer the land or people of China. Therefore, the Qing government could still control them while pursuing recovery. Zeng Guofan, the Hunanese scholar-general and important representative for restoration, promoted the reinstitution of the traditional Confucian curriculum in schools, with restoration of harmony dependent upon hierarchical organization

---

[107] Fairbank and others, *East Asia*, pp. 482-483.
[108] Latourette, *The Chinese*, p. 348.
[109] Fairbank and others, *East Asia*, pp. 575, 582-583, 590.
[110] Tung, *History of China*, pp. 239-240.

in proper roles with norms of conduct by *li,* or principles of social usage. The superior man would gain moral authority through his virtuous example while legal punishment would serve as only a governmental supplement.[111] Mathematics and science could be part of the curriculum with a foreign language program included. Many changes took place in China for advancement as the Grand Canal was reopened, a new tax system installed, and a coal mine opened. The military was modernized with regionally-based armies and navies, and Chinese army officers were sent to Germany to study military technology. Further international contribution was encouraged through instituting foreign offices, and some students had been sent to the United States to study at Yale University.[112] However, the only thing to be adopted from foreign powers would be the manufacture of solid ships and effective weaponry.[113] This led Chang Chihtung, a powerful regional reformer for self-strengthening, to challenge the academy training of officers for strengthening the military defense. According to Chang, this was an erosion of the Confucian principles of *wen* over *wu,* or civil over military.[114]

CHINESE REBELLIONS AGAINST THE QING RULERS

As the Qing government worked to avoid compliance with the treaty agreements and for reformation, there were over a hundred peasant insurrections. The major concern after 1851 was from the impact of a domestic revolt, the Taiping Rebellion.[115] This uprising was initiated by some misinterpreted teachings of missionaries from the West. Hong Xiuguan, the leader of the rebellion, had attempted to become a Confucian scholar-official but failed the provincial examinations three times. He lived with Reverend Issachas J. Roberts, an American missionary who held fundamentalist Christian doctrines. These teachings led Hong to destroy the idols in Buddhist temples, though he rationalized that only he and his close associates could have harems while

---

[111] Fairbank and others, *East Asia,* p. 568.
[112] June Teufel Dreyer, *China's Political System* (Boston: Allyn and Bacon, 1996), p. 47.
[113] Jonathan D. Spence, *The Search for Modern China,* (New York: W. W. Norton, 1990), pp. 195-197, 200 as found in Teng Ssuyu and John K. Fairbank, *China's Response to the West* (Cambridge, MA: Harvard University Press, 1954), pp. 47-48, 53-54.
[114] Fairbank and others, *East Asia,* p.622.
[115] Dreyer, *Political System,* p. 46.

others abstained.[116] He reasoned that the Qing rulers were devils in conflict with God as Confucianism diverted the Chinese from righteousness.

On January 11, 1851, Hong declared himself the *Taiping Tianguo*, or the Heavenly King.[117] His revolutionary plan was primarily altruistic for serving the peasant population of China. He promoted the redistribution of land from the feudal landlords to encourage an agrarian system, which ensured every man and woman an entitlement of land. Even those under sixteen years of age were to acquire a half of an adult share. Women's equality was established on a political and economic level with the arranged marriage system abolished.[118] The opium trade and use was forbidden along with gambling, slavery, adultery, witchcraft, and use of alcohol and tobacco.

The God Worshippers Society, as Hong's followers were called, staged their first armed opposition against the imperial soldiers in Kwangsi at a village near the West River in July 1850. By September 1851 their flag of dynastic sedition was raised over the departmental city of Yungan.[119] These forces captured about 600 walled cities from 16 of the 18 provinces. However, they were not able to govern the areas they had subjugated because they focused on the next area and neglected those already conquered. They took, by conservative estimate, 20 million lives and left the country ravaged.[120]

Hong Xiuguan was obsessed with the idea that he was the younger brother of Jesus Christ, and he extended his influence and control over a large section of China with a capital established in Nanjing.[121] He indulged in luxuries, concubines and debauchery with little consciousness of what was taking place in other parts of his realm.[122] Finally, the decline of the Taipings was inevitable from jealousy over the unscrupulous Yang Hsiuching's claim to receive power through trances and experience visitations from God. Yang then challenged Hong's superiority, and in 1856 Hong

---

[116] Pye, *Introduction*, pp. 127-128.
[117] Jonathan D. Spence, *The Search for Modern China* (New York: W. W. Norton, 1990),p. 172.
[118] Tung, *History of China*, pp. 222-223.
[119] Fairbank and others, *East Asia*, pp. 469-470.
[120] Pye, *Introduction*, p. 128.
[121] David H. Aleney, *China: The Church's Long March* (Ventura, CA: Regal Books, 1985), p. 40.
[122] Purcell, *Boxer*, p. 171.

arranged for Wei Changhui, the Northern King to assassinate Yang.[123] In the end there was such an acute shortage of food that Hong committed suicide. In July 1864, with only a few thousand men of the Taiping able to defend Nanjing, they fought the Hunan soldiers to the last man.

The foreign powers declared themselves neutral in the first phase of the Taiping Rebellion but secretly had sold arms to the Qing government. Later, after the West had forged the Qing regime into their docile instruments as result of the Second Opium War treaty, the Western powers then sided with the Qing rulers to defeat the Taiping.[124] Zeng Guofan, a scholar-statesman from Hunan Province and commander, was instrumental in suppressing the Taiping Rebellion and initiating steps to regain Confucian order through moral revival.[125]

The Nien, or Torch-Bearer, Movement began in Kiangsu, Anhwei, Shantung and Honan during the early phase of the Taiping Rebellion. At one point it became an ally with the Taiping in the North, whom they imitated by wearing long hair, and after the defeat of Nanjing a division of the Taiping joined them.[126] The first Nien were bandits who claimed no unified leadership, ambitious goals, religious or political agenda. They predominated north of the Huai River in southwest Shandong, northwest Jiangsu, east central Henan and northern Anhui.[127] Organized as an alliance of five bands, each with a banner of a different color: red, blue, white, yellow and black. They formed a secret society with elaborate rituals, secret symbols and blood oaths.

In 1855, the Nien harassed the police, pillaged the *yamen* or government offices, attacked prisons, ambushed official convoys, and held landlords and merchants for ransom. They were finally defeated on August 27, 1868, in Shandong, and all survivors were executed.[128] The Qing court offered sacrifices as thanks for victory in the temples of their ancestors and of the god of war. Li Hongzhang, who financed the Qing soldiers was given the honorable title of the Grand Guardian of the Heir Apparent.[129]

---

[123] Fairbank and others, *East Asia*, p. 472.
[124] Tung, *History of China*, pp. 230-231.
[125] Fairbank, *China*, p. 212.
[126] Tung, *History of China*, p. 233.
[127] Spence, *The Search*, p. 184.
[128] Cheneaux, *China-1911*, pp. 108,139.
[129] Spence, *The Search*, p. 188.

Another noted suppression of rebellion was that of the Triad, of which the first were known as the Dagger or Small Knife Rebellions at Xiamen and Shanghai in 1853 to 1855. Dissention among the Triad leaders caused the downfall of these rebellions. The imperial soldiers defeated and took all captives and anyone associated with them to Guangzhou where they were executed by beheading at the rate of about 800 a day until nearly 100,000 were slain. Estimations were that in Kwangtung Province alone a million people were executed during the Triad suppression.[130]

The Taiping movement had extended influence to other rebel groups. The Miao, a minority oppressed by the Qing Manchus, revolted in 1854. The Hui was another minority group settled in Yunnan and the Northwest China. It had prospered in agriculture, mining and trade with Burma, but had risen in insurrection because the Qing officials levied heavy taxation and frequently confiscated their land.[131] In the area of Yunnan a conflict between the Moslem and non-Moslem tin miners led to rebellion in 1853. The Qing used this contention as a motive to act in opposing the Moslems, against whom they had discriminated for some time, in the form of a brutal massacre in May 1856. The differences between the Moslems and non-Moslems soon turned anti-dynastic.[132] The Moslem, or Panthy, Rebellion headed by Tu Wenhsiu was based in Talifu and continued until 1873 when the Chinese scholar-officials, who were loyal to the Confucian order rather than the Qing government, overthrew the revolt.[133] The Chinese suppressed most of the rebellions and only used Western arms for their purposes without soliciting their direct involvement. These rebellions followed the traditional pattern of movements for change with the peasant-oriented revolts suppressed by action of restoration. It is estimated that China's population in 1850 was 410 million and by 1873 had been reduced to 350 million.[134]

Within China, the rebellions were initiated by internal strife against the Qing Dynasty and foreign influences, which by 1869 were compounded by the opening of the Suez Canal that allowed a more direct trade route from Europe and further commercial

---

[130] Purcell, *Boxer,* p. 167.
[131] Tung, *History of China,* p. 235.
[132] Cheneaux, *China-1911,* p. 113.
[133] Latourette, *The Chinese,* p. 363.
[134] Fairbank, *China,* p. 216.

pressure on China. China was drawn further into the world economy when telegraph cables were laid connected Vladivostok, Nagasaki, Shanghai, Hong Kong and Singapore with those from London to San Francisco.[135] Also, the death of the Xianfeng Emperor on August 22, 1861, left the throne to his five-year-old son, Tongzhi, in whose name the Tongzhi Reformation had been undertaken. The empress consort Cian and Cixi, as the mother of the new emperor, became Empress Dowagers. Shortly after taking up official power at the age of eighteen, Emperor Tongzhi died on January 12, 1875, of exhaustion from overindulgence in the pleasure quarters at Beijing, but his death was officially recorded as smallpox.[136] The weakened dynasty was caught between internal rebellion and foreign aggression.

WEAKENING OF THE QING DYNASTY

The dynasty was also weakened through further agreements and natural disasters. A British expedition from Burma to Yunnan in 1875 to develop a new overland trade route ended when an armed Chinese killed a British interpreter. The British demanded apology, indemnity and further regulations on trade and international relations in the 1876 Chefoo Agreement.[137]

A flood in five southern provinces in 1876 was followed in 1877 and 1878 by drought in the North.[138] In the resulting famine people pulled down their houses to sell the wood to buy grain, and during the winter dug deep pits where 30-40 people would huddle to keep warm. Millions died and their bodies were left along the roads, to be eaten by dogs and birds. Women were loaded in carts to be sold as prostitutes and slaves.[139] These tragedies demanded relief funds to further deplete the national treasury.

The Sino-French war in 1884-1885 was the result of French aggression in taking over Vietnam, from part of Yunnan and Kwangsi provinces.[140] The Tientsin Treaty of 1885 secured Vietnam for France along with open trade in Southwest China.[141] Britain annexed Burma in 1886, and Portugal finally confirmed her claim to Macao in 1887. The concessions gained by the West threatened

---

[135] Fairbank and others, *East Asia*, p. 581.
[136] Sponce, *The Search*, pp. 216-217.
[137] Fairbank and others, *East Asia*, p. 601.
[138] Latouritte, *The Chinese*, p. 363.
[139] Whitehead, *China Community*, p. 14.
[140] Tung, *History of China*, p. 244.
[141] Cheneaux, *China-1911*, p. 195.

the Confucian order in the East. Japan, Korea, Burma, Vietnam and Thailand, neighbors which historically gave tribute to China, perceived China's weakness and not only insisted on autonomy, but also acquired courage to become as intimidating as the West.[142]

China and Japan came to a confrontation over Korea, and China declared war on August 1, 1894. China had been modernizing her military, but Japan, with support from the USA, had been more successful, and even with the difference in size defeated China in 1895.[143] Through the Treaty of Shimonoseki Japan took Taiwan as a colony, and led Western powers in exploiting of China's resources and low cost labor force to initiate industry in the treaty ports. During this period there was a surge of railway investments.[144]

Then ensued a clamor for concessions, as Britain obtained a 99-year lease on Kowloon in 1898 while France secured a 99-year lease on the bay of Kwangzhou in Southwestern Kwangtung.[145] Russia, in a Russo-Chinese treaty of alliance, finally acquired her coveted warm-water port with a 25-year lease of Liaotung Peninsula, the size of France, on the southern tip of Manchuria. Japan, with Britain, France, Germany, Russia and the USA, began to establish banks with capital exported to China.[146]

Imperialist powers exploited China more during the three years from 1895 to 1898 than the previous fifty-five years. They had granted China loans that amounted to 370 million teals, while the central treasury annual income totaled only 80 million teals.[147] Finally, China was bankrupted with a foreign debt of 200 million teals. Mining, shipping and railway concessions were made as security for these debts; and as a guarantee these foreigners were allowed to superintend the Qing government revenue.[148]

During the late 1890s more floods hit in Kiangsu and southwestern Shantung, which forced the victims to survive by eating tree bark and grass roots. An estimated 170,000 lost their lives.[149] Many sold their children, and farms were abandoned after the houses were washed away and land inundated. Many became vagabonds.

---

[142] Pye, *Introduction*, p. 120.
[143] Cheneaux, *China-1911*, p. 285.
[144] Tung, *History of China*, p. 254.
[145] Latourette, *The Chinese*, p. 382.
[146] Fairbank and others, *East Asia*, p. 625.
[147] Cheneaux, *China-1911*, pp. 300-301.
[148] Purcell, *Boxer*, p. 173.
[149] Tung, *History of China*, p. 267.

25

Local officials refused them entry when they attempted to enter southern provinces across the Yangtze River from Kuazhou; thus they formed mobs and attacked the *yamens,* or government offices. By the spring of 1898, 100,000 hungry people were wandering from place to place begging for food.[150] The external and internal strains on the Chinese society were extraordinary, and China was left struggling for identity and dignity.

The USA proposed the open-door policy in 1899 to demonstrate an apparent sympathetic concern for preventing the division of China into colonies. This policy was an agreement among all countries for access into each country's sphere of influence throughout China and that each realm would not cease to be a part of China.[151] However, the outcome of the open-door policy created an atmosphere of hostile nationalism that Empress Dowager Cixi nurtured. She remained in power after her emperor son, Tongzhi, died in 1875 by a maneuver that illegally placed her three-year-old nephew on the throne, after the death of Tongzhi's pregnant wife. Her nephew reigned under the name of Guangux, or Glorious Succession. The successor, by law of dynastic succession, was to be of a generation younger than was his predecessor, and the regent was to be the widow of the previous emperor not the mother. However, with the death of the widow, Cixi seized the power of the throne for her own interests.

Except for a few months in 1898 when reformers convinced him to transform the Empire into a constitutional monarchy, Emperor Guangxu remained under the rule of his aunt, Cixi[152]. During these months he called for four major changes in the Qing government: a reform of the examination system, opening of vocational institutes, reforms in commerce, and strengthening of the armed forces.[153] Cixi sensed a threat to her power and had the Emperor imprisoned, then sent Jung Lu, one of her devoted supporters, to Tientsin as Viceroy of Chihli to control the army.[154] Cixi sanctioned units of the militia, the Righteous Harmony Fists, or *Ye Ho Tuan,* who the Westerners termed Boxers from the gymnastic exercises they practiced. She endorsed the outbreak of the Boxer Rebellion as a means to eliminate foreign influence from the Empire.[155]

---

[150] Purcell, *Boxer,* p. 177.
[151] Edwin E. Moise, *Modern China,* 2nd edn. (London: Longman, 1994), p 40.
[152] Cheneaux, *China-1911,* p. 259.
[153] Spence, *The Search,* p. 229.
[154] Tung, *History of China,* pp. 263-264.
[155] Latourette, *The Chinese,* pp. 389-390.

BOXER REBELLION AGAINST FOREIGNERS

The Boxers, generally very young agricultural peasant laborers, were involved with Daoist sorcery rituals that included a recitation of an incantation, breathed through clenched teeth. They foamed at the mouth and believed they were possessed by spirits who made them impervious to bullets,[156] although according to Hykes' record of eyewitness accounts, during the Boxer suppression many of the Boxers were seen dead of rifle shots in the street.[157] Women were organized into Red lantern girls, Blue Lantern middle age wives, Black Lantern older wives and Green Lantern widows.[158] By 1899 the Boxers began to openly disturb Westerners, and by June of 1900 Christians were massacred in Chihli and all foreigners were in danger.[159]

The Boxer Rebellion was intended to drive out the alien intruders and their political, social and religious traditions. This effort resulted in the death of over 1,900 Chinese Protestant Christians and some 30,000 Catholics. There were 188 Protestant missionaries and dependents along with 47 Roman Catholic priests and nuns killed during the rebellion.[160] From June 29 to August 14 in the Beijing legislation quarter alone, the Boxers slaughtered about 3,000 Chinese Christians, 475 foreign civilians, and 450 troops of eight nations. They had also killed about 150 racing ponies for food.[161]

Finally on August 14 some 16,000 foreign troops from Japan, Russia, Britain, the USA, Germany, France, Austria, Italy, Belgium, Spain, Hungary, Portugal and Sweden entered Beijing. Upon news of their approach, Empress Cixi, at the age of 65, and her trusted followers, disguised as peasants, fled to Xian in carts where they stayed for over a year. These foreign troops systematically plundered the city and slaughtered Boxers more extensively than the Boxers had annihilated others.[162] August 17th marked the end of the Boxer Repression with a triumphal march through the Forbidden City, after which officers returned to inspect and do some looting of the Palace.[163]

Li Hungchang, the emissary of the Manchu government, signed

---

[156] Fairbank and others, *East Asia*, p. 634.
[157] Hykes, *The Boxer Rising* (New York: Paragon Book Reprint Corp., 1967), p. 50.
[158] Cheneaux, *China-1911*, p. 330.
[159] Latourette, *The Chinese*, p. 390.
[160] Adeney, *Church's March*, p. 41.
[161] Fairbank, *China*, p. 231.
[162] Cheneaux, *China-1911*, p. 334.
[163] Hykes, *Boxer*, p. 108.

the Protocol of 1901 agreement for indemnity payment of 450 million teals of silver, or 333 million U.S. dollars, on September 7, 1901. With the 4 percent interest spread over 39 years until December 31, 1940, the total summed to precisely 982,238,150 teals.[164] Under the Protocol, examinations were to be suspended in 45 cities as punishment to the gentry class, plus formal apologies, execution of high officials, expansion of the Legation Quarter, access to Beijing by railroad, and a 5 percent increase on the import tax.[165]   Later the USA set its portion of the indemnity aside for scholarships for Chinese students to attend American universities.[166]   Therefore, along with the remission of Britain, defeat of Tsarist Russia and Germany the actual indemnity payment was reduced to less than a third of the original Protocol requisition.[167]   Nevertheless, for the next twenty years foreigners who lived arrogantly in a known conquered nation manipulated and exploited the dynasty while the Chinese reserved any demonstration of resentment.[168]

Japan initiated her penetration into Northeast China with an agreement in 1905 for a portion of land held by Russia.[169] During these first years of the new century Empress Dowager Cixi continued to hold the dynastic power. In 1905 she sent a delegation of five princes and officials to the USA, Britain, France, Germany, Russia and Italy to study their governments for the institution of constitutional reform.[170] In August of 1908 the constitution was written to reflect a limited democracy based on that of Japan.

Emperor Guangxu, at 37 and in apparent good health, died from poison in 1908 and was succeeded by another minor, Puyi, the great nephew designated by Cixi.[171] Puyi reigned under the name of Xuantong from 1909 to 1912 with his father, Prince Chun, as regent.[172] However, Empress Dowager Cixi, respectfully called the Old Buddha, survived her nephew, Emperor Guangxu, by only a few hours and died on November 15, 1908.[173]

[164] Spence, *The Search*, p. 235.
[165] Fairbank and others, *East Asia*, p. 640.
[166] Steven W. Mosher, *China Misperceived* (Montclair: A New Republic Book, 1990), p. 44.
[167] Fairbank and others, *East Asia*, p 641.
[168] Latourette, *The Chinese*, p. 394.
[169] Tung, *History of China*, p. 280
[170] Spence, *The Search*, p. 246.
[171] Dreyer, *Political System*, p. 53.
[172] Cheneaux, *China-1911*, p. 351.
[173] Latourette, *The Chinese*, p. 360-361.

THE FALL OF THE QING DYNASTY

Throughout China there was unrest and dissatisfaction with a governing dynasty, which though weak, was nevertheless continually suppressive. Sun Yatsen, an American- educated Chinese and founder of the Nationalist movement, formed a revolutionary society, the *Hsing Chung Hui*, or Revive China Society, in Honolulu, Hawaii, in 1894.[174] He organized a rebellion on October 26, 1895, with the help of some secret societies of the Guangzhou region. The motive spearheaded by the unrest of discontentment sought the deposition of the Qing Dynasty in favor of the formation of a republic. Yet, some local reformers were executed when Sun's plan was discovered, and he sought refuge in Japan.[175] From there Sun went to San Francisco and London to study Western political and economic theory. An attempt to kidnap him to return to China for trial and execution was unsuccessful.[176] Many young Chinese patriots were attracted to Sun Yatsen's intent for a Republican form of government. He had stated his three principles of government in the first issue of the *Min Pao*, or the People's Newspaper: *Min Chu*, the patriotic nationalism, *Min Chuan*, democracy as governed by the people, and *Min Sheng*, people's livelihood with a means of subsistence.[177]

Sun studied continuously to polish his political ideas while he raised funds. He founded a new organization in 1905, the *Tongmeng Hui*, or Alliance society, which later became the Kuomingtang or Nationalist Party. Four maxims stated the purpose: terminate Manchu rule, restore China to the Chinese, institute a republic, and equalize land ownership.[178] The three stages of revolution to realize the type of government Sun had anticipated were first to be ruled as a military state; second, become a political protectorate; and finally to be governed through the regulations of a written constitution.[179]

Along with the formation of the new Nationalist Party determined to displace the dynasty that was just recovering from its weakened

---

[174] Anne Fremantle (ed.), *Mao Tse-tung An Anthology of His Writings* (New York: New American Library, 1972, pp. xiv-xv.
[175] Cheneaux, *China-1911*, p. 307.
[176] Spence, *the Search*, p. 228.
[177] Tung, *History of China*, p. 283.
[178] Dreyer, *Political System*, p. 54.
[179] Fremantle, *Mao Writings*, p. xx.

state, China suffered more floods and droughts throughout Hunan Province in 1909. Landlords and merchants hoarded rice while the peasants ate only tree bark and grass roots. Finally in revolt, the enraged masses raided over one hundred rice shops, set fire to the governor's yamen, the police bureau, the Ta Ching Bank, churches, foreign businesses and the Japanese consulate.[180]

For years a new army had formed an anti-Manchu opposition and finally organized a revolt in Wuchang the capital city of Hupeh Province on October 10, or double ten, which is considered the beginning of the 1911 Revolution. Teachers and students from all parts of China distributed leaflets urging the masses to declare independence from the Qing government.[181] The Revolutionary League, as professional reformers, established the Republic of China and placed Sun Yatsen, who had just arrived from Europe for the convention, as Provisional President on January 1, 1912, at Nanjing.[182] His inauguration was marked by the change from the lunar calendar of the dynastic dating; on the Western calendar, 1912 became the first year of the Chinese Republic. The Revolution of 1911 was considered by the Chinese historian Tung Chiming to be a bourgeois-democratic revolt that displaced a feudal monarchy and prepared a means for the development of national capitalism and inspiration of a democratic republic.[183]

FORMATION OF THE NATIONALIST GOVERNMENT

Yuan Shikai, the Chinese commander of the Beiyang army who came from a line of officers and had never taken the examinations but had purchased a minor degree in 1880, tried to balance his support and loyalty between the revolutionaries and the Qing Dynasty. He blatantly asked for offers from each side, and upon the proposal to become President of the new republic, withdrew his allegiance from the dynasty. At the end of January 1912 the finality of the Qing was determined by a telegram sent from 44 senior commanders to the Qing Court urging the formation of the republic in China. Yuan and the Senate of the provisional government guaranteed that the young Emperor Puyi and his family could continue to reside in the Forbidden City with possession of the imperial treasures along with

[180] Tung, *History of China*, p. 289.
[181] Fremantle, *Mao Writings*, p. xv.
[182] Fairbank, *China*, p. 250.
[183] Tung, *History of China*, pp. 294-295.

a annuity of 4 million U.S. dollars and protection of all Manchu ancestral temples. On February 12, 1912, the Qing Court announced the abdication of the emperor, who continued to live in the Forbidden City until 1924 when it was turned into a historical museum. He then went to live in the Japanese concession of Tianjin.[184]

Britain and the USA had supplied loans to Yuan as the head of the northern warlords in Beijing in favor of establishing parlimentarianism, which failed. These Western nations had withheld their support from Sun Yatsen, even though he was educated in the West.[185] However, with Sun's assistance, on February 14, 1912, the Nanjing council unanimously elected Yuan Shikai as Provisional President of China. Yuan's government survived on foreign loans since there was no base of financial support from the mass population.

Sun Yatsen went to Japan in 1914 to reorganize the Kuomintang after Yuan's troops suppressed his attempted revolt of 1913. Sun's insurgency opposed the direction Yuan had advocated in Kiangsi, Anhwei and Kwangtung provinces. In July 1914 at Tokyo, the Chinese Revolutionary Party was instituted, and Sun published the first manifesto that September. This new party organized a coup in Shanghai that same year.

On January 18, 1915, Japan presented the infamous Twenty-one Demands that were designed to reduce China to a Japanese colony and pressured Yuan to accept them in return for promised aid in attaining the throne, for Yuan had declared his intent to be enthroned on January 1, 1916. These demands would allocate more rights to Japanese subjects in Manchuria and Inner Mongolia and secure joint administration of the Han Ye Ping iron and coal foundry in central China. They would create access to all ports or islands to foreign powers, give placement to Japanese police and economic advisors in Northern China and acquire expanded commercial rights in Fujian Province. These demands resulted in anti-Japanese rallies throughout China.[186]

Still, Yuan ratified four of the five sections of Japan's stipulations, and rebellion against his rule broadened.[187] He was forced to abandon the throne that he held as emperor for eighty-three days.[188] Yuan

[184] Spence, *The Search*, pp. 266-267, 288.
[185] Fremantle, *Mao Writings*, pp. xx-xxi.
[186] Spence, *The Search*, pp. 278, 284-286, 294.
[187] Fremantle, *Mao Writings*, p. xxi.
[188] Gettings, *Chinese View*, p.86.

Shikai's death on June 6, 1916, from uremia-compound at the age of fifty-six left his Vice President,[189] Li Yuanhang, who never assented to the restoration of the monarchy, to be elected as President of Yuan's opposition government established in Guangzhou.[190]

The central government was reduced to warlord rule by various generals while the Republic of China remained in place at Beijing to handle foreign relations.[191] Sun Yatsen still could not secure support from the West, and Russia had intruded upon Mongolia while Britain invaded Tibet. Therefore, during World War I, Sun Yatsen opposed any union of China with the Allied Nations.[192]

FORMATION OF THE CHINESE COMMUNIST PARTY

Under the political condition of warlordism in which China was placed, Duan Qirui, a warlord general and political leader of the Beiyang group, gained the premiership of China in 1916. Duan was receptive to the compensation offer from the Japanese for recognizing their position in north China at Germany's expense. Japan's loan of 5 million yen of gold in January 1917 helped to bring pressure for Duan's compliance. Over the next year, Duan procured another loan from Japan for an additional 140 million yen, or 70 million U.S. dollars at the exchange rate of the time. Duan Qirui had utilized the loans to build up his military power, but lost the territory of Shandong controlled by Germany, which China expected to recover when the Treaty of Versailles was finalized. He then resigned in October 1918, but continued to build his relation with Japan with a network of secret financial arrangements.

China fully anticipated receiving the Shandong territory for it naval assistance in World War I, with the loss of 543 at sea and some 2,000 Chinese workers who died in France and Flanders.[193] After Britain, France and Italy had signed a secret treaty with Japan for the rights to Shandong, China was shocked to have been humiliated again by the West. The news was received with bitterness on May 3, 1919, which led to the May Fourth Movement. This movement nurtured young radical students like Mao Zedong and Zhou Enlai who became leaders in the revolution that dealt

---

[189] Spence, *The Search*, p. 287.
[190] Latourette, *The Chinese*, p. 403.
[191] Moise, *Modern China*, p. 46.
[192] Fremantle, *Mao Writings*, p. xxi.
[193] Spence, *The Search*, pp. 288-290, 292-293.

with these issues.[194]

On the morning of May 4, 1919, about 3,000 students from thirteen different academic institutions gathered on Tienanmen Square and drew up five resolutions:

One protested the Shandong settlement reached at Versailles conference; a second sought to awaken "the masses all over the country" to an awareness of China's plight; a third proposed holding a mass meeting of the people of Peking; a forth urged the formation of a Peking student union; and a fifth called for a demonstration that afternoon in protest of the Versailles treaty terms.[195]

Merchants closed their shops in protest and organized labor-union strikes spread throughout all major cities. There was a boycott of all Japanese goods and Japanese residents were molested, and for over a year students promoted the eradication of Japanese markets in China.[196] It finally led to the dismissal of three pro-Japanese officials, the resignation of the cabinet and China's refusal to sign the Virsailles Treaty.[197]

The May Fourth Movement that formed was the transformation from the old type to the new democratic revolution. Marxism was guiding China to become part of the world proletarian-socialist culture,[198] although anarchists were the main socialists on the Chinese political arena.[199] However, warlords remained in control of the central government and Sun Yatsen had established a supportive southern-based government. For nearly a decade after 1917 there were two governing bodies in China pursuing international recognition.[200] The intellectual activity of this time period did not lead to any social action, but it became a New Culture Movement with a re-evaluation of values and an interest in Western literature.

FORMATION OF MAO ZEDONG THOUGHT: 1893 - 1920

There are many sources of input into what made up the character of Mao Zedong, a peasant from rural Central China of Hunan

---

[194] Whitehead, *China Community*, p. 17.
[195] Spence, *The Search*, pp. 310-311.
[196] Fairbank, *China*, p. 267.
[197] Fairbank and others, *East Asia*, p. 770.
[198] Tung, *History of China*, pp. 316-317.
[199] Fairbank, *China*, p. 275.
[200] Pye, *Introduced*, p. 136.

Province, Siangtan County in Shaoshan village.[201] He grew up with the knowledge of the traditions, myths and folklore through the Confucian education he received. He was, however, a part of the first generation that had the opportunity to explore Western knowledge. Even though he came from rural China, seemingly isolated from the impact of what was taking place in urban China and in the port areas, he sought to become knowledgeable of the world of politics, and different experiences formed his sense of justice that gave incentive to revolutionary ambition. Eventually with experience as a soldier, ideologist, planner and leader of the guerrilla struggle for Chinese Communism, Mao focused beyond the duties of administration to that of engineering mankind and society into a new form through active government.[202]

The emotional world of Mao, clearly an intricate part of the making of his leadership, must be explored in the realm of political psychology. He is not to be analyzed solely on the basis of his intellect or ability as a strategist, for that would limit understanding of his ultimate role in history. Rather, with Mao there was a craving for power and dependence on the worship of his followers. He had certain anxieties about being ignored. [203] Mao had an intense focus, revealed in his expression of controlled emotion. While attending normal school, he passed through a time of seeking personal identity, when he was referred to as an "unkempt person." He allowed his hair to grow longer than was fashionable and in general dressed in an unconcerned manner. Along with the change in his appearance, he had become unconcerned about personal possessions and the quality of his clothing, in contrast to his time in primary school.[204] Mao was observed as aloof and by willpower able to dominate his emotions. Often he gave the impression of being emotionally detached from the present situation.[205]

PRIMARY INFLUENCES ON MAO

On December 26, 1893, Mao Zedong was born into a family that was progressing economically through the efforts of his

---

[201] Anne Fremantle (ed,) *Mao Tse-tung, An Anthology of His Writings* (New York: New American Library, 1972, p. vii.
[202] Lucian W. Pye, *Mao Tse-tung* (New York: Basic Books, Inc. Publishers, 1976), p. 5.
[203] Ibid, pp. 7, 12-13.
[204] Ibid, p. 20.
[205] Ibid, pp. 27-28.

father, Mao Jensheng. Mao's grandfather, a poor farmer of little success, had built the original house where the family dwelt. It is significant that Mao's parents neither gave proper reverence to the grandfather nor taught their children to do so. The family did not observe this fundamental Confucian tradition that governed this basic Chinese value.

However, Mao's father had earned the family a position of leadership within the Mao clan. Mao Jensheng, as a young man, was compelled to sell his small farm of fifteen *mu* or about two and a half acres of land, for payment of debts accrued through poor management by Mao's grandfather. Even though the military was considered as a low position in society, Mao Jensheng joined the army for several years because of his financial situation.[206] After returning to the village, through hard work and shrewd business dealings, he was able to recuperate his land and buy more. He then advanced from being a "poor" peasant to becoming a "middle" peasant. By being frugal in selling his surplus rice, the elder Mao finally became a "rich" peasant[207]. Because his father was prosperous and was treated with respect by others of the extended family, Mao Zedong had sense of confidence and security. However, when he left the village and the reinforcement of confident respect it provided, Mao was not recognized, and he developed a resentment which was manifested through withdrawal and shyness.[208]

Mao resembled his mother, Wen Chimei, in physical characteristics. Although she was illiterate, her generosity and gentleness were easily noted in her care of others in need. She was a devout Buddhist with a faith wrapped up in the local superstitions. Though his father was not a believer, Mao was attracted to his mother's interest in the spiritual realm. She gave her children instruction in religious matters, and this is where Mao gained his understanding of an order beyond observed events or his control. This religious training also helped to form his concepts and perspective of historical context, for he had developed an appreciation for the value of gratification delay.[209]

In this setting, Mao cultivated his first sense of equity by sharing his lunch empathetically with a poor boy at school, who had no

---

[206] Ibid, pp. 112-113.
[207] Fremantle, *Mao Writings*, p. viii.
[208] Pye, *Mao Tse-tung*, p. 73.
[209] Ibid, pp. 75, 77-78.

lunch. He observed the compassion of his mother who, after this incident, sent him to school with two lunches.[210] His mother contributed to his self-assurance by her responsiveness to his every wish, which made him feel very special and gave him the confidence to defy his father, who was severe in his dealings with Mao. It also made him feel that in his defiance against his father, he was in turn protecting his mother.[211] The bond that he experienced with his mother was fractured with the birth of his other two brothers and the adoption of a sister. Even though his confidence had been established through her undivided attention feeding his sense of worth, he felt as if his mother had neglected him by shifting her affections towards the other children.[212]

News arrived at the village of Shaoshan only by word of mouth. Since there were no newspapers, all information or new government policy was read aloud to the 2,000 village inhabitants at the village meeting and a copy displayed on the school building. The village was a setting in a world of its own, insulated from society. Even though Mao Zedong grew up in this village community of daily routine and seasonal cycles, there were stories of some villagers who had left the Hunan region to become generals and great statesmen of high status. Zeng Kuofan and Zo Zungtang were heroes of the century who had helped suppress rebellion and crime which were plentiful in that region.[213] These stories drew Mao's attention from his work for his father, with dreams of adventure.

Mao Jensheng was very demanding of his son, Mao Zedong, forcing him to be the bookkeeper for the family business at a very young age and always badgering him to improve his manners. Even though it was highly resisted by Mao, this was the characteristic traditional Chinese method by which a father showed his concern and trained his son to take responsibility and attain the character of success.[214] Mao learned the value of hard, physical, productive labor from his father.[215] However, to deal with Mao's character of defiance, his father decided on a traditional method that was typical in Chinese culture to curb a son's behavior by forcing him to marry

---

[210] Ross Terrill, *Mao* (New York: Harper & Row Publishers, 1980), pp. 6, 9.
[211] Pye, *Mao Tse-tung*, p 80.
[212] Ibid, p. 82.
[213] Ibid, pp. 69-70.
[214] Ibid, pp. 119-120.
[215] Steven Uhalley, *Mao Tse-tung, A Critical Biography* (New York: New Viewpoints, 1975), p. 2.

as a 14-year old. Though the girl was six years older than Mao was, he went through with the ceremony and even behaved according to the accepted traditional behavior for a new groom. Then he refused to live with her and according to his account never even touched her.[216] This formed in his mind the concept of injustice about marriage arrangements that he later addressed in writing.

One incident of injustice, witnessed by Mao in the village that influenced his sensitivity towards peasant suppression, concerned the peasant-founded Elder Brother Club. This group had a dispute with a landlord of the Shaoshan region over rent payments. The landlord brought a lawsuit against them and bribed the magistrate to win. Pang, a blacksmith and a member of the club, led the Elder Brothers in a riot that ended in his beheading. Pang became Mao's first hero for the cause of the peasants. Another time there was a food shortage because the rice harvested for the winter was eaten before the new rice could be harvested. Mao's father was one of the "Big House" landlords, and the hungry peasants confiscated one of his shipments of rice to be sold at the capital city of Changsha. Even though Mao did not agree with the tactics of the peasants, he did not sympathize with his father, but according to Ross Terrill, he stated that "...the first capitalist I struggled with was my father."[217]

MAO'S REACTION TO AUTHORITY

Mao linked his father's authority to the source of injustice and discovered an effective manner in counteracting these injustices by referring to a higher authority. He used this tactic against his father when they had an argument: he would quote the Confucian classics, using a Western manner of putting one authority up against the other. However, he never completely submitted to any authority, even to that of Marxism. His ultimate sense of justice remained within his own will.[218] This was evident in 1909, when Mao was sixteen years old, six years older than the majority of those in his class and a poorly-dressed peasant.[219] He was refused admission into the Tungshan primary school on the grounds, according to the headmaster, that he was unqualified. He insisted until one of the teachers came to his aid with a proposal that he be admitted on

[216] Terrill, *Mao*, p. 12.
[217] Ibid, p. 13-14, 16.
[218] Pye, *Mao Tse-tung*, p. 139.
[219] Uhalley, *Mao Biography*, p.4-5.

a five-month trial basis. Of course this arrangement did not gain acceptance with the other boys, who teased him because of his size and poor clothing. Mao displayed a very sensitive attitude, not accustomed to being teased, and he responded by becoming a bully. His focus then was to establish acceptance and gain attention from his teachers.[220]

Mao developed an admiration for some of his teachers who made an impression on him. He told Edgar Snow:

Another influence on me at this time was the presence in a local primary school of a 'radical' teacher. He was 'radical' because he was opposed to Buddhism and wanted to get rid of the gods. He urged people to convert their temples into schools. He was widely discussed personally. I admired him and agreed with his views.[221]

When Mao had a disagreement with a teacher, he sought the support of fellow students to stand with him. He would show anger and incite incidents, even resort to physical violence, endangering personal relationships.[222] In one incident he refused to stand to recite, which infuriated the teacher who forcibly tried to make him stand. Mao freed himself and wandered around in close proximity of home for three days, and after returning he related that "My father was more considerate and the teacher more inclined to moderation." It impressed him how successfully this incident indorsed the concept of a "strike."[223] After this incident, Mao was instrumental in organizing students of other schools he attended against teachers whom he felt were unjust.[224]

MAO'S FOCUS ON PROBLEMS OF CHINA

As was usual for Mao, he extended beyond the range of the given curriculum of school to read two publications that his cousin, Wen, had given him. These were some "issues of the *Journal of the New People*, edited by Liang Qiqiao, the leading writer of political issues of that time, and *Reform Movement of 1898*, a manifesto of reform by Kang Youwei."[225] It was these books that formed his first political

---

[220] Pye,*Mao Tse-tung*, pp. 149-151.
[221] Edgar Snow, *Red Star over China* (New York: Grove Press, Inc., 1973 edn.), p.136.
[222] Pye, *Mao Tse-tung*, pp. 153-154.
[223] Terril, *Mao*, pp. 9-10.
[224] Uhalley, *Mao Biography*, p. 3.
[225] Terrill, *Mao*, p. 20.

concepts, for he learned of the humiliation that China had suffered from foreign governments and the progress of Japan.[226]   At the middle school in Xiang Xiang, where he attended only four weeks, Mao read *Three Kingdoms*. He had thought that the novel was an actual account of the Warring States era. The headmaster burst his disillusion, and Mao's naivety was revealed. He submitted a petition for the replacement of the headmaster to the Mayor of Xiang Xiang and forced classmates to sign it. Mao's intellectual style, from that point, was the "oblique approach" of "scorn" for those who differed with him.[227]

It was during the spring and summer of 1911 that Mao saw his first newspaper and learned that there were living heroes and martyrs, not just those in the books of history.[228]   The newspaper *Strength of the People* featured an article on an unsuccessful revolt led by Huang Xing in Guangzhou. With his acquired defiance of authority and development of an independent character, Mao had lost his respect for the monarch as a ruler who he saw as an oppressing authority. In September, at the age of seventeen, Mao wrote his first political article suggesting rather innocently Sun Yatsen as President, Kang Youwei for Premier and Liang Qiqiao as foreign minister of a new government. He was the first of the students to cut off his pigtail, or *queue*, the mark of loyalty to the Qing dynasty. He and another student forcibly cut off the pigtails of ten of their classmates for the anti-Manchu cause. In October of 1911, in the city of Wuhan, the revolutionaries rebelled against the Manchus and within a month ended the dynasty that had ruled China for 267 years.[229]

In 1911 at the fall of the Manchu Empire, when he was 18 years old, Mao Zedong, with the enthusiasm of his revolutionary spirit, joined a Republican revolutionary army regiment.[230] His enthusiasm was not the result of his father being a former soldier. If anything, that would have had a negative influence on him. Only his passion for the liberation of China through revolution persuaded him to enlist. Mao enlisted into the army for six months, and during that

[226] Uhalley, *Mao Biography*, p 5.
[227] Terrill, *Mao*, pp. 21-22.
[228] Pye, *Mao Tse-tung*, p.159.
[229] Terrill, *Mao*, pp. 22-23.
[230] Alian Bouc, trans. Paul Auster and Lydia Davis, *Mao Tse-tung: A Guide to His Thought* (New York: St. Martin's Press, 1977), p. 5.

time he spent more time reading newspapers than receiving his military training.[231] He learned the power of the printed page, and this medium established a lasting influence on him as the future leader of China.[232]

After the six months, Mao left the army to return to the more suitable role of a student, doing some reading in the Hunan Provincial Library. Another student, Tan, whose father was an official, made the statement that the end of the monarchy and the beginning of a republic signified "We could all be President." After he gained Mao's interest, Tan went on to explain that the "will to struggle" was of more importance in making a political leader than was learning from books. This began a new political worldview for Mao.[233] Self-assured, he internalized these statements of radical political significance.

Mao became very fascinated with newspaper advertisements and was easily convinced to try the suggestions. In this manner he was persuaded to inquire about enrollment into different schools. First it was a police school to improve law and order, then a soap-making school to promote hygiene, later a law school for political contacts. Finally he pleased his father by enrolling in a commercial school. His self-centered, proud personality was exemplified in his experience of entering the commercial school for one month, after which he quit because the instruction was mostly in English. He spoke of his lack of English as a matter of an unchangeable absolute rather than something that could be gained with effort on his part. Therefore, he dismissed the importance or essentiality of learning another language. His skill in the Chinese language would enable him to modify China, and he did not care to adapt to Western culture by learning English or humiliate himself as a "beginner" in the view of others.[234]

From the time Mao resigned from the army to when he enrolled into the First Normal School of Hunan that offered free tuition,[235] there was a time of aimlessness in his life. With the opportunity of unstructured time outside of a classroom, he spent every minute he could in the library discovering developments in

[231] Jaques Gillermaz, Wilson (ed.), 'The Soldier,' *Mao Tse-tung in the Scales of History* (Cambridge: Cambridge University Press, 1977), pp. 118-119.
[232] Pye, *Mao Tse-tung*, pp. 161, 164.
[233] Terrill, *Mao*, p. 26.
[234] Pye, *Mao Tse-tung*, p. 165-167.
[235] Fremantle, *Mao Writings*, p. xvii.

Germany and England through translations of works available by the authors Darwin, Kant, Feverbach, Hegel, Paulsen, Mill, and Adam Smith.[236] His search for knowledge was a compulsive drive for personal development that gave him the sense of still being a student by forming his own academic curriculum, but without the challenge of competition from others or written exams.[237] Upon reading *Great Heroes of the World*, Mao marked the paragraphs on Napoleon, Lincoln, Peter the Great, Catherine the Great, Washington, Montesquieu, Gladstone and Rousseau and remarked that China needed great people like these. He then quoted the scholar Gu Yenwu, 1613-1682: "Every common man has a hand in determining the fate of his nation."[238] The news from Europe was an opportunity for Mao to find its parallel in the history of China as a comparison in "living history," the descriptive term he coined for his value of newspapers that later would enable him to establish a strategy for the revolution of China.[239]

Newspapers had an interesting effect on Mao, for he was attracted to the influence of advertisements. His character of rebellion, linked with a search for friendship, led him to advertise in the Changsha newspaper for "young men interested in patriotic work," hoping to attract to himself, as leader, those of his own interests. With this group he formed the formal society, *Hsin Min Hsueh Hui* or the New Peoples' Study Association, which became a student political group of Hunan and earned a national reputation.[240]

In 1917 there was much disorder with the Hunan armies fighting the armies of the northern warlords. The different armies were occupying the schools of Changsha, and the Northern Warlord Army wanted to occupy the First Normal School. Mao was instrumental in organizing the athletes into a union to barricade the doors and arm themselves with rifles left by a band of soldiers that had been there before. The soldiers turned away leaving the buildings intact. This was the first military victory for Mao.[241] Later, Mao led this union in protest against Japan with their "Twenty-one Demands" and other humiliating acts against China. Through this band of men he saw the value of people with different abilities and declared

[236] Bouc, trans. Auster & Davis, *Mao: Thaought*, p. 5.
[237] Pye, *Mao Tse-tung*, p. 169.
[238] Terrill, *Mao*, p. 21.
[239] Ibid, p. 30.
[240] Pye, *Mao Tse-tung*, pp. 173-174.
[241] Fremantle, *Mao Writings*, p. xxi-xxii.

PhysicalDiscipline## Political History: China in Context

that everyone has strong points, most at individual pursuits and others at organization.[242]

PHYSICAL DISCIPLINE

With confidence, discipline and single-mindedness in 1917, at the age of 23, Mao published his first essay on physical exercise. It was not a highly brilliant work of academic insight, but it addressed the literate on a subject of the virtues more common to the illiterate. He described a series of exercises that he taught himself and proudly displayed as a quality of discipline by a self-taught man. It was this quality that he demonstrated throughout his life.[243] Mao was inspired by the ascetic practices of a teacher he had chosen as his ethical model in 1915 at the Changsha First Teacher's Training School. Yang Changji was Western-educated and had a rare skill of making disciples, but he was a gentleman with a streak for subversion, in the flow of reforming China.[244] Mao entered an era of building up the body through exposing the body to physical adversity. He even engaged in shouting into the wind to develop the voice and more importantly to be exhilarated by putting the will up against resistance.[245] In building up the body Mao engaged in the exposure of hiking, camping, taking sun baths, wind baths, rain baths, stripping and running naked in the open air and seeking danger,[246]and he developed a denial of all romance and sex. This carried over into his exertion with the wits and wisdom of man to build a will for social struggle.[247] Moreover, as a means of self-discipline to test his power of concentration, Mao studied at noisy South Gate.

MAO'S INTRODUCTION TO COMMUNIST PRINCIPLES

At the First Teacher's Training School at Changsha, Yang had ranked Mao as third best among his thousands of students. However, the students chose Mao as the "school's model for ethical quality, courage and eloquence in speaking and writing." Some described him as "a wizard" or "the brain." One of Mao's important accomplishments in the years 1917-1918 was that he had written over a million words

---

242[242] Terrill, *Mao*, p. 32 33
[243] Wang Gungwu, Wilson (ed.), 'The Chinese,' *Mao Tse-tung in the Scales of History* (Cambridge: Cambridge University Press, 1977), p. 275.
[244] Terrill, *Mao*, p. 29.
[245] Ibid., p.31.
[246] Fremantle, *Mao Writings*, p. xix.
[247] Pye, *Mao Tse-tung*, p. 177–178.

7777

of comment just in the margins of books.[248]   One example of his commentary that showed his strong convictions was in the book of the German neo-Kantian, Friedrich Paulsen, Mao wrote:
The goal of the human race lies in the realization of the self, and that is all. What I mean by realization of the self consists in developing our physical and mental capacities to the highest degree...Whenever there is repression of the individual,...there can be no greater crime. That is why our country's "three bonds" must go, and why they constitute, with religion, capitalists, and autocracy, the four evil demons of the realm...[249]

In 1918 at the age of twenty-five, although physical fitness and political revolution were his convictions and are factors of Marxism, Mao still had not learned of Marxist doctrines.[250]

At this opportune point in his life in 1918, when he was being recognized for his achievements and had just graduated from the First Normal School, Mao left for Beijing.[251] There, Yang Changji, his professor from Changsha, who had moved to Beijing, sponsored Mao for a job at the Peking University library and introduced him to different intellectuals. During this time Mao lived in Professor Yang's home, and met his daughter, Kaihui, whom he later married.[252]

Students from Hunan planed on going to France for a "work and study" program sponsored by the Franco-Chinese Educational Association, a program created to benefit France through the labor force that these Chinese youth provided during the First World War.[253] Mao had the opportunity to go to France, but besides not caring to study the French language and not having the money, his attention was concentrated on the humiliations of China.[254]

After World War I, The Versailles treaty revealed the secret agreements that premier Duan Qirui had made with the Japanese for loans in September 1918. He had used these loans to build up his own military power before he resigned that October. Then Japan required Great Britian, France, and Italy to sign a secret treaty for the disposal of Germany's rights in Shandong, China, for their

[248] Terrill,*Mao*, p.34-35.
[249] Stuart R. Schram, *Mao ZeDong* (Hong Kong: The Chinese University Press, 1982), p. 5.
[250] Terrill, *Mao*, p. 35.
[251] Bouc, trans. Aster & Davis, *Mao: Thought*, p. 7.
[252] Pye, *Mao Tse-tung*, p. 174.
[253] Fremantle, *Mao Writings*, p. xxii.
[254] Terrill,*Mao*, pp. 39-40.

naval assistance during the war in 1917, and for compensation of China's debt. Therefore, all Chinese who were expecting to recover the Shandong rights for China's contribution to the allies during the war were shocked to be humiliated again by the West in favor of Japan. The news arrived on May 3, 1919, and in Beijing on May 4, known as the beginning of the May Fourth Movement, three thousand students representing thirteen academic institutions demonstrated at the home of a pro-Japanese official.[255]

Mao basically ignored these protests until after he left Beijing to organize the Changsha wing of May Fourth. He organized girls to harass shop owners into destroying imports from Japan. There were no romances during this time as he remarked that there was no time then, and even made a pact among the "three heroes," Chi Hesen, a member of the Changsha chapter of the May Fourth, his sister, Chi Chang, and Mao, to never marry.[256]

Along with some of the Chinese intellectuals in France, Mao was under the persuasion of anarchism.[257] Mao compared the "extremely violent" Marxism to anarchism as the means "to resist powerful people who harm their fellow men."[258] However, when he returned to Beijing for three months, and under the influence of the librarian, Li Ta-chao, his mentor and employer, Mao read in translation the *Communist Manifesto*, Kautsky's *Karl Marx's Okonomische Lehren*, and a history of socialism by Kirkupp. Through the ideology expressed in the content of these books his concepts changed, and Mao finally considered himself a Marxist by the summer of 1920.[259]

After the first month that he was in Beijing, his mentor Yang died, but the loss also gave Mao an opportunity to become intimate with Yang's daughter, Kaihui. That which began as a "trial marriage" produced a child in less than a year after his spring trip to Beijing.[260] Mao had formulated his thought on marriage and new roles for women, contrary to tradition. When he returned to Changsha, a girl had been forced to marry and she ended her life by suicide. Mao Zedong wrote nine articles in less than two

---

[255] Uhalley, *Mao Biography*, pp. 18-19.
[256] Terrill,*Mao*, pp. 42-43.
[257] Benjamin I. Schwartz, *Chinese Communism and the Rise of Mao* (Cambridge MA: Harvard University Press, 1979), p. 26.
[258] Terrill,*Mao*, pp. 44-45.
[259] Pye, *Mao Tse-tung*, p. 195.
[260] Terrill, *Mao*, p. 48.

weeks for "the great wave of freedom to love" and reforms in marriage customs.[261]

FORMATION OF THE CHINESE COMMUNIST PARTY

In Changsha he started to organize various groups including the Russian Affairs Group for sending students to Russia and the "Marxist Study Group, which in time became the key Communist cell in Hunan and sent Mao to Shanghai for the founding of the Chinese Communist Party."[262]

After their father's death, as heir, Mao took his brothers and sister into his charge. He sent his younger brother, Zemin, to First Teacher's Training School. Zetan, the third boy, was sent to a good middle school, and his adopted sister, Zejian, was placed in a teacher's training school in the nearby village of Hengyang. Mao had ensured that his brothers and sister were in the preparation stage for being a part of his movement toward the Chinese Communist Party.[263]

In June 1921, Comintern agent Gregori Voitinsky traveled from Beijing to Shanghai to make arrangements for the First Congress of the Chinese Communist Party.[264] Sometime in July 1921 – sources do not agree on the exact date[265] - the First Congress of the Chinese Communist Party was held in Shanghai's French Concession at the Po-Ai girls' school that was closed for summer recess.[266] Thirteen delegates attended the congress, representing seven different communist groups formed in 1920 with fifty-seven members. After being interrupted by the Concession police, the congress members reconvened aboard a boat on Niehpu Lake in Chekiang. For Mao, as the Hunan delegate, the congress was quite anticlimactic, especially in that neither Professor Li Tao-chao nor Professor Chen Tuh-siu was in attendance. Mao expressed his opinions with authority, but

---

[261] Pye, *Mao Tse-tung*, p. 193.

[262] Ibid, p. 198.

[263] Terrill, *Mao*, p. 52.

[264] Fremantle, *Mao Writings*, p. xxv.

[265] Jean Chesneaux, Francoise Le Barbier and Marie-Claire Bergere, *China*, trans. Paul Auster and Lydia Davis, (New York: Pantheon Books, 1977), p. 89. Fremantle, the author of *Mao Writings* cites that there is some discrepancy in the accounts of the foundation of the Party. Chen Tanchiu, a participant, writing in *The Communist International*, said that the meeting took place "in the second half of July." Mao himself said it was in May… The author notes a possible discrepancy due to the lunar calendar.

[266] Uhalley, *Mao Biography*, pp. 23-24.

the other views expressed were not in line with the basics of his thinking.[267] This congress endorsed the Party statutes and laid the basis of cooperation under Sun Yat-sen between the new Communist Party and the Kuomintang. Chen Duxiu was chosen by the congress as the first head of the Chinese Communist Party.[268]

Mao's aspiration for the leadership of the Communist Party can be attributed to the formation of his thought and character during his early years. The attitude of scorn he adopted toward opposition and the self-assurance he displayed in superior organizational values invoked him to seek the position. The influence he observed in the printed page gave him the means of behavioral impact and control of governmental affairs. His initiative and self-discipline to be informed helped him succeed in leadership.

Communism as an ideology appealed to Mao from the ascetic practices he adopted from his teacher, Yang. This political view can also be attributed to the humiliations he had observed China to suffer for the decisions of the West stated in the Versailles Treaty. His initial attitude toward languages made him distant in his relations regarding the Western nations and thought. Communism satisfied the empathy Mao felt toward the peasants and their plight. The different works he read shaped his thought and self sufficient approach in philosophical belief. By rejecting the religious teachings of his mother, which he practiced until his adolescence,[269] he concluded that religion was a demon and a bond of China.

CHINA DURING THE DAYS OF MAO ZEDONG: 1920 - 1976

China, from World War I until the autumn of 1931, experienced a turning point from foreign control to regaining the advantages of autonomous sovereignty.[270] It was these first years after the war that brought economic growth through prominent foreign investment because of China's abundant human resource of inexpensive industrial labor and potential market for the products. For several years before 1923, the foreign share of investment in shipping

---

[267] Terrill, *Mao*, pp. 56-57.
[268] June Teufel Dreyer, *China's Political System*, (Boston: Allyn and Bacon, 1996), p 65.
[269] Schram, *Mao Zedong*, p. 16.
[270] Kenneth Scott Latourette, *The Chinese, Their History and Culture*, 3rd edn. Rev. (New York: The Macmillan Company, 1959), p. 419.

stabilized at about 77 percent and in cotton spindles at 45 percent.[271] However, the Chinese used their mass potential coupled with their sense of nationalism to their advantage against the alien intruder. Their power to boycott foreign commodities, even though Chinese merchants were not enthusiastic about their loss in this participation, proved an effective instrument of warfare. Boycott, agitation and force finally brought an extended international conference in Beijing from 1925 into 1926 to allow the Chinese to determine their own duties for merchandise being imported and exported.

In 1928 and early 1929, with the exception of Japan, the foreign powers conceded to the agreement of China's autonomy in tariffs.[272] It was also during these years just after World War I and the new independence from the Qing Dynasty that the Chinese made a mass migration into the Manchurian northern territory where in its isolation there was prosperity and order from famine and the civil war under the Republic. By 1930 it was considered the greatest movement of population on earth as people relocated into these three eastern provinces.[273]

MAO ZEDONG BECAME POLITICALLY ESTABLISHED

Mao Zedong was thoughtfully regarding the situation of China during the days of shame under the yoke of unequal treaties and exploitation by the Western nations and Japan. He had been involved with the struggle for liberation from the rule of the Manchurian Qing Dynasty. Because of China's situation, he became involved in the formation of the Communist Party. Mao was one of the thirteen charter representatives, from seven different Communist groups formed in 1920 with fifty-seven members, that organized the first congress in July 1921 that met in Shanghai and Chekiang. Although he was not chosen at that time as the leader of the Chinese Communist Party, nor was impressed with the proceedings – especially since his opinions, although expressed with authority, were not readily considered – he committed himself to its ideology. Mao did not attend the Second Party Congress held in a secret meeting place, for he had forgotten the address and could not manage to make contact. The Third Party Congress, in July 1923, built on the basis established in the First Congress for cooperation

---

[271] Jonathan D. Spence, *the Search for Modern China* (New York: W. W. Norton, 1990), p. 329.
[272] Latourette, *The Chinese*, pp. 420, 426-428.
[273] Ibid, p. 432.

under Sun Yatsen. Mao successfully called for a united front with the Kuomintang. He was elected to the Chinese Communist Party's central committee and soon after became head of the Party's Organization Department. At the date of this third congress the party numbered 342 members throughout all of China.[274]

While none of the imperialist countries wanted to help the Kuomintang in its effort to stabilize China as a governing body, Russia offered to assist the reorganization of the Kuomintang for China to become united.[275] Adolph Joffe, the Russian representative of the Communist International Comintern, contacted Sun and in January 1923 the Sun-Joffe Manifesto was signed. Sun recognized the advantage of a helpful friendship with Russia, although Joffe acknowledged that the connection with Russia was not necessary for China's adaptation to Communistic ideology. With the Chinese Communist Party joining the Kuomintang, the First United Front was formed.[276]

Mao Zedong admired Sun Yatsen and his Three Principles of the people's nationalism, people's democracy and the people's livelihood. For Sun, the last principle became increasingly socialistic; and although it proved to be an impossible task, Mao became an important catalyst between the Communist and Kuomintang parties.[277] In July 1925 Mao was appointed secretary of the Propaganda Department of the Kuomintang and later was the deputy head of the department. In connection with the new status of the Communist Party in a united front with the Kuomintang, Mao advanced his political influence while remaining dedicated to Marxist doctrine. In March of 1926 he returned to Shanghai to head the Peasant Department of the Chinese Communist Party. Then in August of that year, he returned to his home province of Hunan to just rove that familiar countryside and investigate the rural conditions. He published his findings in January 1927 as a peasant movement report.[278]

---

[274] Stephen Uhalley, Jr., *Mao Tse-tung A Critical Biography* (New York: New Viewpoints, 1975), pp. 25-26.
[275] Chen Lifu, Nationalist Officer, interview, Sue Williams, *China In Revolution, Battle for Survival 1911-1936* (Documentary: An AMBRICA Production, 1989)
[276] June Teufiel Dreyer, *China's Political System* (Boston: Allyn and Bacon, 1996), p. 58.
[277] Uhalley, *Mao Biography*, p. 27.
[278] Lucian W. Pye, *Mao Tse-tung* (New York: Basic Books, Inc. Publishers, 1976), p. 203.

As the leader of the Kuomintang Party, Sun Yatsen had been a very successful propagandist and idealist. He died on March 20, 1925, while in conference with warlords of the north, Feng Yu-hsiang, the Christian general, and Chang Tsolin, the marshal of Manchuria. Sun's last will was regularly read publicly, and his book *San Min Chu I*, or *Three People's Principles*, became the party manual. The Kuomintang developed popular slogans made of the three principles – government by the people and for the people, a sufficient livelihood for all and freedom from the control of foreign nations – into an effective and skilled use of propaganda. However, though an attempt was made to adapt Communism to China, Sun rejected the Marxist class war concept and stood in opposition to the Communism of Russia.

CHIANG KAISHEK SEVERED ALLIANCE WITH THE CHINESE COMMUNISTS

Chiang Kaishek, trained and mentored by Sun, became the leader of the Kuomintang or Nationalist Party after Sun's death. Chiang realized with alarm that the Communists leaned toward the destruction of religion and Confucius principles of the Chinese society.[279] The influence of the Communists in Guangzhou was stopped by Chiang's coup on March 20, 1926. Chiang then relieved Mao of his position as deputy head of the Propaganda Department in May of 1926.[280]

He continued to use the united front with the Communists to unite China and to take Shanghai in 1927. Nonetheless, in the Shanghai massacre of April 12, 1927, Chiang turned on the Communists and executed them.[281] Some men in plainclothes approached a Communist worker, and when guards asked them the password the men began to shoot at workers walking towards the machinegun emplacements on street corners.[282] More than 100 people died and many were injured on Baoshan Road, which the rain soon turned into a river of blood. The surviving workers were arrested but remained defiant.[283]

In February 1927, Chaing made his intentions clear to expel the

---

[279] Latourette, *The Chinese*, pp. 407-409.
[280] Uhalley, *Mao Biography*, p. 29, 32.
[281] Raymoand L. Whitehead and Rhea M., *China: Search for Community* (New York: Friendship Press, 1978), p. 17.
[282] Wu Fuhai, Communist worker, interviewed, Williams, *China Revolution*.
[283] Xu Deliang, Ibid.

Communists. As head of the Nationalist government in Nanjing, Chiang Kaishek reinforced his position in the party when he married Soong Meiling, the sister of Sun Yatsen's wife. Upon suppressing the opposition of Yen Hsishan and Feng Yuhsiang in the autumn of 1930, Chiang secured authority. He remained the most powerful man in China, although students demonstrated against him for not taking stronger action against Japan. He then resigned as head of the civil political system but remained the dominant government military leader.[284]

Incidents of foreign oppression continued to reinforce the Communist vision of a People's Republic. On May 15, 1925, in Shanghai, a Japanese textile mill foreman killed a Chinese worker, which resulted in Chinese student demonstrations at the international settlement on May 30. This demonstration resulted in twelve students being gunned down by British police. Later, on June 23 of that year, a demonstration of workers, students and military cadets in front of the Shameen Concession area at Guangzhou was ended as British soldiers fired upon them and killed fifty-six of the demonstrators. Through the impact of these occurrences, the Communist Party grew from 995 at the beginning of 1925 to 10,000 by November with another 9,000 in Youth Clubs.[285]

MAO LINKED THE CHINESE COMMUNIST REVOLUTION WITH THE PEASANTS

Although Communism appealed to the intellectuals, including Mao Zedong, as an immediate political solution to the situation in China, there was a realization that Marxism needed to be modified to the Chinese realities. As early as 1921 Li Dazhao, an author and professor at China's prestigious Beida University, understood that the peasants of China needed to be liberated from ignorance, sufferings, and defects before the nation could experience liberation. According to Li the people must be made aware of their situation for them to know that they should demand liberation.[286] To achieve this awareness, their sufferings must be brought to their attention with encouragement to discard their ignorance and be people who plan their own lives. Mao recognized that the participation of the peasants depended upon awakening them to their circumstance

---

[284] Latourette, *The Chinese*, pp. 409-411, 413.
[285] Uhalley, *Mao Biography*, pp. 27-28.
[286] Spence, *The Search*, p. 308.

and inciting their willingness to cooperate. Only education could instill the values and attitudes desirable for successful social transformation. To accomplish this, the educational system was restructured with local authority taking over from the centralized system with the introduction of half-time schools to amplify the opportunities.[287]

Marxist revolution became the solution in Mao's mind, for it opposed the imperialistic forces and economic oppression by the corrupt landlords as the source of Chinese misery.[288] Mao dedicated the years 1921 and 1922 to the organization of the labor movement in Hunan. In 1923 and 1924 he built up his political organizational influence as a member of the Chinese Communist Party's Central Committee, and he was a member of the Executive Bureau of the Kuomintang in both Guangzhou and Shanghai. He distinguished his leadership in 1925 to 1927 as he organized the peasant movement.

His writings during this six-year period linked the masses with his concept of nation. Mao identified the peasantry and the urban proletariat as the main force for revolution, while the feudal landlords were adversaries to revolt. He insisted that the main power of revolution against feudalism, warlords and imperialism resided in the peasants rather than the workers, students and merchants of the cities. By 1927 Mao started to mobilize the peasants as he realized their revolutionary potential and believed there should be support for them in the strategy as part of the United Front. His first inclination of breaking with Chiang Kaishek was the class distinction the Kuomintang made against the peasants.[289]

Mao had learned by November of 1928 that to maintain a political system among the workers and peasants, a solid mass base must be developed with Party organization supported by a strong Red Army and resources for sustenance. Mao had established the "Three Rules of Discipline for the Red Army": Prompt obedience to orders, no confiscation of peasant property and delivery to authorities any confiscated items. Also there were "Eight Points for Attention": Replace doors when leaving a house, roll up sleeping mats after use, be courteous and polite to the people and help them, return

---

[287] Uhalley, *Mao Biography*, p. 79.
[288] Whitehead, *China Community*, p. 19.
[289] Stuart R. Schram, *Mao ZeDong* (Hong Kong: The Chinese University Press. 1982) pp. 8-11.

borrowed articles, replace anything damaged, be honest in all transactions with payment for merchandize bought, and maintain good sanitation. The discipline of the army won their popularity among the people.

The key to Mao's success in developing party relations was his willingness to spend time with the workers in the Anyuan coal mines of southern Hunan. By being with these expendables of society he learned of their hardships and used the experience to build the base upon which to improve the condition of workers.[290] These laborers, even some as exploited children, worked 17 hours a day. With Communist indoctrination, a progressive worker would convince these miserable employees that people were not born to be poor. He would argue that poverty was the result of exploitation by the capitalists and labor contractors; while the people worked, these profiteers took the money. The care and concern of the Party certainly encouraged these workers to improve their condition and society.[291] The priority for Mao was to educate the peasants for revolution to be carried out by them and for them. Their asset was that the masses were poor, which gave incentive for change and a desire for revolution, and they were uninformed to be impressed and shaped by instruction.[292]

According to Marx, there are certain stages of human social development. The primitive stage is the communal system with everything being held in common. The system to own and work slaves derives from communities in conflict. Eventually, working for a noble lead to a feudal system, which then develops into the capitalist system. Humanity finally will evolve socially and politically into the socialist system that ultimately would develop into Communism. This ultimate utopia is without struggle as a classless society. Lenin developed this theory with the Communist Party as a priesthood of infallibility, unable to collectively make a mistake. For Lenin, revolutionary morality was what counted as real morality.[293]

Mao agreed with the ideology of Marxist theory, but he did not

---

[290] Uhalley, *Mao Biography*, pp. 24, 37-38.
[291] Qui Huiying, Communist wife, child labor, interviewed, Williams, *China Revolution.*
[292] David H. Adeney, *China: The Church's Long March* (Venura, CA: Regal Books, 1985), p. 98.
[293] David Aikman, 'Marxism & Christianity, David Aikman (ed.), *Love China Today* (Wheaton, IL: Tyndale House Publishers, Inc., 1977), pp. 106-110.

agree that the socialist revolution must originate with the industrial proletariat. He held to his hypothesis that, in China, revolution must arise from the peasants, which cost him good standing with the Party until 1931 when he was reinstated and ultimately became its head in China.[294]

Mao Zedong developed strong narcissistic feelings and focused energy toward his own ego, which allowed him to detach his emotions from external realities. He had confidence in his own creativity and ability to accept change if he sensed that he had initiated the change. His charismatic appeal was not dictated by the context, but he was able to remain calm when there was tension, or he could create tenseness when the situation was relaxed to maintain control. The masses perceived him to be distant and unemotional while his colleagues found his demeanor threatening, never knowing their status in relationship to him as a powerful superior.[295]

THE LONG MARCH

After the United Front against the Japanese disbanded from a confrontation between the Communists and the Nationalist armies, Mao led the Communists into turbulent revolution. The Red army was based in the Chingkang Mountains of south central China surrounded by Chiang Kaishek's forces. From that position Mao led his troops – an estimated 100,000 men and 35 women, one of them Mao's pregnant third wife – on the legendary Long March.[296] This march lasted 370 days from October 15, 1934, when they set out from Jiangsi, until October 20, 1935, ending at Shaanxi in the northwest of China.[297] They walked over 6,000 miles through ten provinces covering China's most rugged terrain of 18 snow-covered mountain ranges and 24 rivers[298] plus the dreaded marshlands. Nothing was in the marshlands; no trees or houses, just grass on soft sponge-like ground and very dangerous, for if someone sank up to his or her chest their life could not be saved.[299]

Fifteen of the days during the march they met the Nationalist

---

[294] Latourette, *China*, p. 3.
[295] Pye, *Mao Tse-tung*, pp. 262, 275-276.
[296] Dreyer, *Political System*, pp. 70-72.
[297] Uhalley, *Mao Biography*, p. 48.
[298] Arthur Wallis, *China Miracle* (Columbia, MO: Cityhill Publishing, 1986), p. 27.
[299] Wang Xinlan, Officer's wife on Long March, interviewed, Williams, *China Revolution.*

Armies in armed conflict. By the time they reached the Xiang River nearly half or at least 30 to 40,000 of the troops deserted rather early as they marched day and night. Many complained because they did not know where they were going. Even Mao was exhausted as he marched with the troops,[300] and he was reported to have given his rations of three little steamed buns to a weakened soldier. He was known to take very good care of those on the march.

It was during the Long March that Mao's position as leader of the Chinese Communists was established.[301] When they found out through a newspaper that there was a Communist base in the caves of Yenan in Shaanix province, they decided to go there to reorganize. Fewer than 7,000 of those 100,000 who left Jiangxi arrived in Shaanix, but Mao assured them that those who arrived were much stronger and like purified gold.[302] Here the values of frugality, simplicity, and dignity of physical labor were established among the Chinese Communist leadership, which has been a continuous characteristic of the Party.[303]

Mao Zedong assumed the leadership of the headquarters in Yenan, consolidated the structure of the Chinese Communist Party, and created an army among the peasants disciplined in Communist ideals. Lenin did not consider Mao's use of peasants, rather than industrial workers as the base of their revolutionary program, as true Communism. However, with these peasants the Chinese Communists led a double-faceted conflict not only with the civil strife against the Nationalists, but also with the Japanese. They carried on a guerrilla strategy against the attacking Japanese, but Chiang Kaishek's Nationalist troops took the main thrust of Japan's brutal invasion to occupy Manchuria.[304]

NATIONALIST'S DETERMINATION TO ELIMINATE COMMUNISM FROM CHINA

Chiang was not ready to fight against Japan, and the Nationalists resorted to persuasion to detour the Japanese aggression.[305] The Nationalist policy was internal pacification as stated by Chiang.

---

[300] Wang Ping, Communist on March, interviewed, ibid.
[301] Xu Deliang, on March, ibid.
[302] Wu Xiuquan, on March, ibid.
[303] Whitehead, *China Community*, p. 19.
[304] Latourette, *China*, p. 4.
[305] Chiang Weikuo, Chiang Kaishek's son, interviewed, Williams, *China Revolution*.

Chiang had determined to eliminate the Communists before resisting the Japanese.[306] He went to Xian in Shaanxi to convince Zhang Xueliang, the son of a warlord killed by the Japanese, to annihilate the Communists before initiating a confrontation with the Japanese. Zhang had been influenced by the Communists to make Japanese resistance a priority over Chinese fighting Chinese, and in what became known as the Xian incident, he had Chiang kidnapped.[307] The Nationalist Central Committee held meetings the day of his kidnapping for negotiations for saving him, and Madame Chiang was flown to Xian.[308] The nation as a whole considered this a mutinous act, disabling the only real sense of leadership it had. The Soviet Union intervened with a telegram to the Chinese Communists from Stalin demanding them to release Chiang or he would publicly "disavow them as Communists" and label them as common "bandits." Zhou Enlai, the political commissar, entered into the negotiation for Chiang's release.[309]

The Communists appealed to the country to unify against Japan, rallying support among Chinese everywhere. However, the Nationalist police repressed a unification student demonstration in Beijing on December 9, 1935.[310] Finally, peace between the Nationalists and the Communists was reestablished in 1936. After a long struggle, the nation had been weakened in its resistance against Japan. Chiang Kaishek was the most powerful leader of the Nationalists and was endeavoring to unify China. His most obdurate adversaries were still the Communists.[311]

During the ten years of the Nationalist regime, between the Communists and Japanese, the nation experienced constant conflict. Japan invaded Manchuria in 1931; in 1933 it occupied Jehol province, and Hebei and Chabar provinces in 1935. Later the Japanese instigated the war on July 7, 1937 that concluded in 1945.[312] On the evening of July 7, 1937, an encounter in an area outside treaty bounds at the extremity of Beijing, between Chinese and Japanese soldiers practicing military maneuvers, resulted in Japanese occupancy of Beijing within the month.[313] Chiang Kaishek made Nanjing the capital and had

[306] Wang Tiehhan, Nationalist officer, interview, ibid.
[307] Lucian W. Pye, *China Revolution*, 4th edn. (New York: Harper Collins Publishers, Inc., 1991), p. 148.
[308] Chin Lifu, Nationalist officer, interviewed, Williams, *China Revolution*.
[309] Pye, *Introduction*, p. 148.
[310] Uhalley, *Mao Biography*, p. 58.
[311] Latourette, *The Chinese*, p. 441.
[312] Pye, *Introduction*, p. 143.
[313] Latourette, *The Chinese*, p. 443.

the name of Beijing changed from *Peking*, or the northern capital, to *Peiping*, northern peace. Most residents of Beijing retained the original name until the Japanese in occupation replaced the original title of the capital. Then, to demonstrate their nationalist spirit, the Chinese people called the city *Peiping* in rebellion against the Japanese. This name remained until the Communist Liberation in 1949 declared the name to be *Peking*, or Beijing.[314]

Chinese in retreat from the advancing Japanese departed Shanghai in November 1937, and in early December, the Nationalist government evacuated Nanjing. Japanese troops proceeded on a slaughter and rape orgy for days and beat, stabbed and shot to death about three hundred thousand helpless prisoners, women and children. This outraged the civilized world.[315] Japan was in command of the railways, navigable rivers and ports. To demonstrate their cooperation with the Chinese, the Japanese put elderly anti-Nationalist Party Chinese in control of Beijing, professing to liberate China from the Communists and Chiang Kaishek's regime.[316] However, throughout China the Japanese were merciless as described in the account of a village where over a period of three days they killed 46 families and all the animals. When they entered a house and shot into the cellar, children cried to be let out. The father was stripped to the waist and tied up with ten other men, and the family finally found him in a pit with bullet holes in his chest.[317] Another man had been put into a pit full of people, and while he was there they pushed in about two hundred more, then commenced to shoot them. This man was shot in the hand and did not move, but escaped into the night. When he arrived home, fresh earth in the courtyard signified graves. He found his grandmother, mother and two sons buried, and his wife and three-year-old had been thrown into the well.[318]

Madame Chiang delivered speeches to the West on the calamities of the war in China, and an appeal to boycott Japanese merchandize.[319] Chiang Kaishek's decision to stop the progress of the Japanese

---

[314] Pye, *Introduction*, p. 149.
[315] Steven W. Mosher, *China Misperceived* (Montclair: A New Republic Book, 1990), pp. 46-47.
[316] Latourette, *The Chinese*, pp. 444-445.
[317] Liang Xihua, woman victim of Japanese, interviewed, Williams, *China Revolution, Fighting for the Future, 1936-1949* (documentary: An AMBRICA Production, 1989)
[318] Lu Chuancheng, man victim of Japanese, ibid.
[319] Madame Chiang Kaishek, speech, ibid.

armies by rupturing the dikes without warning the people caused the death of hundreds of thousands of Chinese and destruction to farm land that produced suffering for millions even years later.[320] Chiang then established his wartime capital in Chongqing of Sichuan province.[321]

Mao Won the Chinese to Communism but Lost His Family

The support for the Communists increased its membership from near 20,000 in 1936 to 1,200,000 by 1945 with its control over most of the north to include over 95 million people.[322] The Communist Party wanted to appeal to the rich farmers because the poor farmers could not afford to stop working and they were not as progressive.[323] In the poor peasant villages the women had no rights and no self-esteem.[324] The Communist cultivated the equality of women so they would be free to choose whom they would marry and unbind their feet. Mao promoted women's equality years earlier when he refused to live with the girl his father forced him to marry at the age of 14. He also had written articles on the subject before he became involved with the Communist Party.

However, the marriage relations that Mao practiced seemed only for his personal benefit, without a traditional sense of responsibility. His second wife was the daughter of his mentor professor, Yang Kaihui, who bore him three sons. Kaihui was captured and killed in 1930 by the Nationalist while Mao was in the Chingkang Mountains. Two of their sons were imprisoned then put on the streets to pick garbage for seven years. They were then sent to Russia for training and protection, and Mao had one sent to a peasant farm for work education and he was finally killed in Korea. The younger son was declared insane and never came back to Mao's household.

Two years before Kaihui was killed, Mao, at the age of 35, on the field had started sharing his bed with Ho Tzuchen, age 18, who became his third wife. Tzuchen had their fourth daughter on the Long March, who was given to peasants along the way as her three older sisters had been. After they arrived in Yenan, Tzuchen had

---

[320] Uhalley, *Mao Biography*, p. 63.
[321] Williams, documentary, *China Revolution*.
[322] Ibid, p. 57.
[323] Li Hengxin, rich farmer Communist Party member, interviewed, Williams, *China Revolution*.
[324] Wang Xinlan, Communist officer wife, interviewed, ibid.

their fifth daughter. Mao became interested in other women and had Tzuchen and their fifth daughter sent to Moscow to undergo treatments for a nervous disorder.

In 1937 Mao met and fell in love with an actress Lan Ping, who took the name Jiang Qing. His marriage to Tzuchen had complicated the romance so that marriage was dissolved in 1938, and Mao and Jiang Qing were married in April 1939. They had two daughters who lived at home and went to the University of Peking.

Mao utilized the parting with eight of his ten children as leverage, which provided him the right to demand fellow Party members to sacrifice their children for the revolution, rather than having recognized them as the tragedies they were.[325] Even with the death of his parents, which put his siblings in his care, Mao had placed his own brothers and adopted sister in schools for training to serve the purpose towards China's liberation.

JAPAN'S ATTACK ON PEARL HARBOR LINKED THE USA AND CHINA

In the autumn of 1938 students went to Yenan under sacrificial conditions to study at the Anti-Japanese University. There were classes in current affairs, philosophy and other courses along with drills for weapon use against the Japanese.[326] At the news of Japan's attack on the United State's Pearl Harbor there was celebration by both Communist and Nationalist, for it determined that the USA would declare war on their common enemy.[327] However, when the Americans helped relay the Nationalists to Beijing by air to combat the Communists, the Communists retaliated by not fulfilling their agreement to arrange for the National Assembly. Chiang Kaishek rallied the citizenry of China to defy and repress the revolt.[328]

The USA sent a delegation to Yunan to help reconciliation between the Nationalists and the Communists, but the lack of cultural sensitivity was evident when Major General Patrick Herley arrived with a Choctaw war whoop upon his descent from the airplane. He had difficulty remembering the Chinese names and showed his lack of preparation and respect for Chinese authority figures when

---

[325] Pye, *Mao Tse-tung*, pp. 205, 210, 214, 217-223. Parts confirmed and added by Dreyer, *Political System*, p. 104, and Uhalley, *Mao Biography*, p. 74.
[326] Guo Quimin, Communist woman in training, interview, Williams, *China Revolution*
[327] Dreyer, *Political System*, p. 79.
[328] George N. Patterson, *Christianity in Communist China* (Waco, TX: Word Books, 1969), p. 41.

he referred to Mao Zedong as "moose dung" and other nicknames in a blatant display of ignorance.

The Communists mistrusted General Herley; therefore, the Officer of Foreign Service, John Davis communicated to the Communists that they had the potential to win in China. He described them as a democratic force, which he recognized as a misnomer, in that they had potential and popular support.[329]

General Joseph Stillwell was sent from the USA to China to help in the resistance against Japan, but he found that Chiang Kaishek was unwilling to commit military personnel to encounter the Japanese. Chiang was reserving them to expel the Chinese Communists and had committed 500,000 troops to blockade the territory occupied by the Communists.[330]

Stillwell observed corruption within the ranks of the Nationalists starting with some of Chiang's family members who held office.[331] Reportedly the soldiers were bound in small groups of five or six to travel so they would not desert. The officers would replace the rice they stole with sand and left the soldiers with moldy rice and sand to eat. The soldiers were told that they had been recruited to fight Japan, but in reality were being used to roust the Communists. Nearly 1.5 million men starved to death and the rational for corruption was poverty, saying only food and clothes produce good ethics.[332]

Again Madame Chiang went with speeches to the USA to appeal with propaganda against Japan and the plight of China in request for money and supplies.[333] Stillwell aired the corruption he observed along with the arrogance of Chiang and wanted to place American officers in key positions, which was not acceptable to Chiang. Their greatest disagreement was over supplying the Communist armies with weaponry to unite against the Japanese.[334]

The Communists were working to unite the peasants through land reform. The campaign for cooperatives began on January 25, 1943. Mao was gambling; this adventure would interfere with accustomed farming practices, and it must produce positive results

---

[329] John Davis, Foreign Service officer, interviewed, Williams, *China Revolution.*
[330] Edward Rice, Foreign Service officer, interviewed, ibid.
[331] Williams, Documentary, ibid.
[332] Xie Shaohan, Nationalist soldier experience and Tsai, Wentchih, Nationalist general observed, interviewed, ibid.
[333] Madame Chiang Kaishek, speech, ibid.
[334] Soong Hsilien, Nationalist officer, interviewed, ibid.

to influence the peasants. The village was the logical natural unit to be used.[335]   Landlords were attacked and all they owned including their land was taken and redistributed among the peasants. These peasants also struggled against the landlords, in mob trials, trying to exact confessions of exploitation. Even parents of Communist Party members who were landowners were brought together to mass rallies of struggle.

These struggles often became unreasonably belligerent.[336] Often middle peasants were confused with rich peasants in struggle, and Mao tried to counter this tendency. He realized that the status of middle peasant was the desired standard, for they maintained the desire and were able to support the revolution. Mao deplored brutality and forbid killings without clear discrimination. Late in the spring of 1948, he attempted to curtail land reform unless the majority of the farm laborers, poor and middle peasants demanded it.[337]

The context of China can be described as turmoil, for there remained the Western foreign influence especially in the major port cities and the encroachment of the Japanese from the North. There were internal struggles between the Communists and the Nationalists who were polarized in their efforts. The Communists, allied with Russia, rallied the masses with land reforms and promised equality while the Nationalist, aligned with the USA, were attempting to boost modernization appealing to the cities with a capitalistic lifestyle. Both the Communists and the Nationalists were anxious about the Japanese but avoided confrontations with them. During this time the country suffered floods, some of which were induced, and famine that put it in a state of economic bankruptcy with starvation and corruption. The currency system was in chaos and changed many times. The *fabi* was changed to the new *fabi*, which changed to the gold *yuan*. Without enough gold *yuan* the *Yuan Shiki* silver dollar was introduced. Gold and even U.S. dollars were being used. When employees were paid in the morning they needed to rush to buy household goods before prices doubled by the afternoon.[338]

In this context, the USA continued to aid the government of

---

[335] Uhalley, *Mao Biography*, p. 76.
[336] Zhang Jingzhi, peasant woman and Li Hengxin, rich farmer Communist Party member, interviewed, ibid.
[337] Uhalley, *Mao Biography*, pp. 97-98.
[338] Rong Yiren, industrialist, interviewed, Williams, *China Revolution*.

Chiang Kaishek, because of the Chinese Communists alliance with the Russians in light of the cold war between Russia and the USA. It was concluded that military aid might contribute to the survival of the Nationalist government.[339]

CIVIL WAR BETWEEN THE NATIONALISTS AND THE COMMUNISTS

The Communists had established sixteen bases for revolution throughout China by the end of 1944. They controlled 635 counties and an army of nearly one million men. Mao Zedong had confirmed leadership in the Communist Party by the spring of 1945. When the Seventh Congress convened in Yenan from April 23 to June 11, 1945, with 544 delegates and 208 alternatives, there were 1,200,000 members of the Party. In his leadership position, Mao recalled the story of the foolish old man determined to remove two mountains. He started digging and when confronted with that impossibility replied that with his sons, their sons and so forth the mountains would finally be removed. Relating to the story, Mao declared that the two mountains that weigh on China are imperialism and feudalism, and as the Communist Party perseveres, it will touch God's heart. Furthermore, God was none other than the Chinese People, who would stand together with the Party to dig up these two mountains.[340]

The civil war was carried out in the three-stage strategy that Mao had envisioned. July 1946 to June 1947 was defined as the defensive stage as the Communists drew the Nationalist offensive deep into North China and Manchuria. In the summer of 1947, during the second stage of a limited counter offensive, the Communists extended their scope of engagements with mobile warfare. Then a strategic thrust of publicity on December 25, 1947, made the Nationalists insecure as Mao revealed his strategy.[341] As Chiang Kaishek had already overextended his military resources in North China, his soldiers were deserting to the Communists in battalions. The Communists, who had arrived in the northeast with 100,000 soldiers, soon were 500,000 strong. Much of the equipment used by the Communists had been captured from the Nationalist Army, supplied by the USA to Chiang Kaishek. They even made a joke that their best supplier of American weapons was Chiang, who

[339] Edward Rice, State Department, ibid.
[340] Uhalley, *Mao Biography,* pp. 62, 80, 86.
[341] Ibid, pp. 92-93.

should receive a metal for assisting them to win the war.[342]

The Nationalists failed, for they had lost the support of the people. During the Northern Expedition, the people showered them with flowers and food and in the conflict with Japan they provided intelligence, but once the Civil War with the Communists started the Chinese people would not even give the Nationalists road directions. As a saying in China portrays it: "the water that carries the boat can also overturn it."[343] Although missionaries from the West tended to support Chiang to the end, journalists and diplomats agreed that the best interests for China lay in the victory of Mao Zedong.[344]

The third stage of the Communist offensive was strategically conducted in four campaigns with the People's Liberation Army of over two million soldiers. The first, led by Chen Yi, on September 24, 1948, shocked the Nationalist Army with the capture of Jinan. Lin Piao conducted the second campaign in Northeast China with twice the manned army as the Nationalists. The third, known as the Huai-Hai Campaign, produced a clear passage to the Yangtze River. On the forth campaign, in the Beijing-Tientsin area, Tientsin was captured on January 15, 1949, and within a week Nationalist General Fu Tsoyi surrendered Beijing, then *Peiping*, to Lin Piao.[345]

Even after the overwhelming Communist victory and the prearranged retreat of Chiang Kaishek to the island of Taiwan along with many of China's art treasures and the Chinese Central bank reserves as well as aid and munitions already redirected there, the Nationalist stepped up an anti-Communist thrust in China.[346] They arrested Communists and had them executed, even though it was certain that the Communist Revolution would succeed.[347] Chiang Kaishek's first order of organization in Taiwan was to make an effort to examine mistakes on the domestic and international levels. Then he determined to recover Mainland China under the Nationalist government. His plan was not to take the mainland by force but help the people there overthrow the Communist regime.[348]

---

[342] Lu Zhengcao and Wu Xiuquan, Communist officers, interviewed, Williams, *China Revolution.*
[343] Shenzul, Nationalist security police, interviewed, ibid.
[344] Mosher, *Misperceived,* p. 48.
[345] Uhalley, *Mao Biography,* pp. 100-101.
[346] Williams, documentary, *China Revolution.*
[347] Qui Huiying, Communist wife, interviewed, ibid.
[348] Chiang Weikuo, Chiang Kaishek's son, interviewed, ibid.

Preparation for this strategy had been in place since their arrival in Taiwan under the reasoning of a Chinese proverb: "It is easy to seize power but difficult to maintain it."[349]

THE PEOPLE'S REPUBLIC OF CHINA ESTABLISHED

China had been forced open and remained open for nearly a century, but on April 20, 1949, Communist guns fired upon the English cruiser *Amethyst* as she navigated a stretch in the Yangtze River.[350] The British sustained more casualties in this incident than in the entire Opium War. At that moment, China closed again to foreigners.[351] The Communists on the mainland sent delegates from twenty-three democratic organizations to *Peiping* in July 1949 as a Preparatory Committee for the election of a Standing Committee to set regulations for the People's Political Consultative Conference. This conference then met in *Peiping* from September 21 to 30, when the name of the city was changed from *Peiping*, Northern Peace, to *Peking* or Beijing as the Northern Capital.[352]

The historical moment for the Chinese Communists' liberation of China was at Tienanmen Square, the Gate of Heavenly Peace, on October 1, 1949. After Mao Zedong rode through the streets of Beijing in a captured American jeep,[353] he proclaimed, "Countrymen! The People's Republic of China has been established. The Chinese people have stood up."[354] This day also saw the arrest of Huang Wei, a Nationalist general who was placed in a War Criminal's Prison for thought reform. He never changed his convictions and his loyalty to Chiang Kaishek and remained locked up for 27 years.[355]

Learning Socialism

Mao considered the most important business for the Chinese Communist Party was to establish friendly relations with the Soviet Union, even though the Soviets had disagreed with his use of peasants in the Chinese Communist revolution. On December

---

[349] Williams, documentary, ibid.
[350] Peter Ward Fay, *The Opium War 1840-1842* (Chapel Hill, NC: The University of North Carolina Press, 1975), p. 365.
[351] Pye, *Introduction,* p. 115.
[352] Uhalley, *Mao Biography,* p. 103.
[353] Whitehead, *China Community,* p. 20, combined with Dreyer, *Political System,* p. 80.
[354] Guo Quimin, in attendance, interviewed, Williams, *China Revolution.*
[355] Huang Wei, Nationalist general, interviewed, ibid.

16, 1949, six days before Stalin's birthday and just two and a half months after the establishment of the People's Republic of China, Mao arrived in Moscow. The years that followed were characterized by mobilization campaigns interspersed with intervals of ordinary life for Chinese society.[356] Chinese Communism definitely took on the personality of Mao Zedong as its helmsman with his determination to hold the power of the Party. His ideas for advancement for the country, along with Communistic progression in its socialistic order and personal position as Chairman, motivated his energies of leadership.

Before 1949, Mao Zedong theorized that the revolution could be achieved by atheists who had no concern for life after physical death or consequential judgment with a conscience that would preclude them from participating in violent acts against class enemies for liberation. The post-revolution demanded the type of individual who lived above corruption and committed to the construction of socialist society of highest spiritual endeavor.[357] He declared, "Ours is a just cause! A just cause is invincible!"

The people were ready to fight for the ideal of liberation toward the formation of China as a new socialist country. Eventually the people adjusted to the new concept of work unit assignments,[358] which meant responsibility and accountability as well as provision for the welfare and social order. This concept was carried out with children who were integrated into the Young Pioneers, and students, primarily in urban areas, were encouraged to join the Communist Youth League to shape their philosophy with strong atheistic teachings of Marx, Lenin and Mao Zedong.[359] The promise was that the people would be the masters of the country and their own lives. Even the custom of arranged marriages would be terminated with the new well-received policy that couples could marry those they loved.[360]

---

[356] Uhalley, *Mao Biography,* p. 106-107.
[357] Adeney, *Church's March,* p. 100.
[358] Wang Ruoshui, Communist Party member, interviewed, Williams, *China Revolution, The Mao Years – Catch the Stars and the Moon, 1949-1960* (documentary: An AMBRICA Production, 1989)
[359] Adeney, *Church's March,* p. 89.
[360] Yang Ge, woman Communist Party member, interviewed, Williams, *China Revolution.*

Liquidation of Dissidents

The first years after liberation were marked with change of regulations and education and a time of cleansing the society of the undesirables. Some would term 1950 to 1952 as the years of terror, when landlords, capitalists, counter-revolutionaries and those considered spies were brought before the people's court for condemnation and execution. Mao gave the number liquidated as 800,000 by 1959, but in the official Chinese Communist figure given by the mid-1950s, quoted by the East Asia Research Center at Harvard University, 2.8 million died, including the numerous suicides of those and some Christians who were objects of accusation, harassment and persecution.[361]

There were seven classes of undesirables known as the seven black kinds, which were the capitalists, landowners, rich farmers, rightists, anti-revolutionaries, "capitalist-roaders in positions of power," and those termed as "no goods." People identified within these categories could not hold citizenship or enjoy the privileges of citizenry, and their children were referred to as "the children of the seven non-desirables".[362] Even though many died, there were those who admitted to being of the class that exploited, begged for mercy and gave everything to the village peasants. These had to bear the label: "an enlightened son of a landlord family," or something similar.[363] The benefactors were those peasants who gained land, and in return supported the Communist Party.[364]

Mao was not only concerned about the support of the people for the newly formed Chinese Communist Party, but also of an international alliance. Specifically, the established relationship with the Soviet Union was comforting in the case of imperialist invasion. The example that the Soviet Union afforded, as a more established socialist government, gave the Chinese government a goal to work towards. Mao also concerned himself with the enemy from within, or those of the Party who disagreed with his methods and those who were counter-revolutionaries within society.[365]

---

[361] Leslie T. Lyall 'Church, 1949-1966,' David Aikman (ed.), *Love China Today* (Wheaton: Tyndale House Publishers, Inc., 1977), pp. 49-50. ??
[362] Jonathan Chao (interview), Richard Van Houghton (ed.), *Wise as Serpents Harmless as Doves* (Pasadena: William Cary Library, 1988), p. 67.
[363] Li Maoxiu, son of a landlord, interviewed, Williams, *China Revolution*.
[364] Yang Ge, Communist Party member, interviewed, ibid.
[365] Mao Zedong, Chairman, speech after first visit to Russia, ibid.

Aid-Korea, Campaigns and Reforms

Even before the unification of China was completed, war was declared in Korea, and the USA military was involved in Taiwan and the straits between China and Taiwan.[366] With Hong Kong returned by Britain to China on June 30, 1997, and Macao returned by Portugal on December 20, 1999[367], Taiwan remained the only contention concerning Chinese national integrity.

General Douglas MacArthur of the USA military had his own agenda. Beyond repelling North Korea from the borders of South Korea, he wanted to remove Communism from China, and he enticed China into the war.[368] The Chinese people were given reports on how the Chinese soldiers were triumphant over the Americans in the icy cold of the North. Each family willingly sacrificed to give for the Korean War effort.[369] The retaliation and resilience of the Chinese toward encroachment employed the recognition of the world that Chinese Communism was a permanent international factor.[370]

Following their entrance into the Korean War in November 1950, the Chinese launched the campaign "Resist-America and Aid-Korea" along with a series of other campaigns within the next year. In February 1951, the "Suppression of Counter-revolutionaries" campaign began, and in September of that year among the cadres and government workers the "Three-Anti" campaign against corruption, waste and bureaucrats was instigated. Later that autumn another crusade to "Increase Production and Practice Economy" was proposed along with the "Five-Anti" campaign against bribery, tax evasion, fraud, theft of state assets, and exposure of state economic secrets.[371] With these campaigns in place to expunge the stains of traitors within China, Mao was ready to initiate his formula for building a socialist society.

The basis of Mao Zedong's thought on revolutionary change remained in rural organization, for he saw that there was poor utilization of the land. The indebtedness of the peasants to landlords and high interest rates were widespread. Small plots made it difficult

---

[366] Whitehead, *China Community,* p 20.
[367] *China Today,* Television News, December 1998.
[368] U. Alex Johnson, East Asian Affairs State Department, interviewed, Williams, *China Revolution.*
[369] Zang Ming and Li Hui, a couple supported the Korean War, interviewed,ibid.
[370] Johnson, State department, interviewed, ibid.
[371] Uhalley, *Mao Biography,* p. 110.

to utilize modern mechanisms and fertilizers for a higher rate of production, and labor was not utilized to its potential in the cold months of the Northern provinces.

The policy of land reform was reinforced on a nationwide basis. The farmland was divided into tracts among the peasants, and the property owners and the peasants eliminated creditors through struggles of grievances, when millions were executed preceding the pronouncement of land reform completion in 1952.[372]

The next step of agricultural development was to escalate production by placing all the private tracts of land previously divided into cooperatives of large plots, which the community of peasants operated together. The outcome was positive for the peasant farmers, who with the expansion of cooperative farming of larger plots of land and adequate labor could afford to raise a few animals to supplement their income with side marketing enterprises.[373] By 1955, over sixty percent of the farmers of China had joined in cooperative farming.

However, the transition into collectives of the entire village in 1956 rendered the peasants dissatisfied with not only another change, but also a sacrifice of properties and animals they had acquired under the cooperative system. Those who eventually conceded to this new arrangement were not always satisfied with the outcome of loss. The taxes collected by the central government from this arrangement were excessive, and the peasants complained that they were treated unfairly with barely enough to live. Their complaints went unheeded, even though officials from the province level verified their circumstances.[374]

Mao, nevertheless, sensed the tension building throughout the society in ramification to the modification in agricultural production and the burden levied on the peasant farmers. To relieve tension for the Communist Party, Mao gave a speech in May of 1956 that included the statement, "Let a hundred flowers bloom; let a hundred schools of thought contend." The latter part of this phrase was taken from an historical event of two thousand years earlier in China's past. At that time the philosophies of the Warring States were contending for supremacy. Again in February of 1957 Mao made a speech to further encourage freedom of

---

[372] Latourette, *China*, p. 9-10.
[373] Zhou Yuanjiu, peasant, interviewed, Williams, *China Revolution*.
[374] Geng Xiufeng and Zhang Chaoke, Village Party officials, interviewed, ibid.

speech.[375] Then on April 27, 1957, the new rectification campaign incorporated an important feature, which allowed for criticism from outside the Party. In Mao's words, this campaign would be carried out "as gently as a breeze or a mild rain" with only small discussion groups, but no large struggle sessions.[376]

The people thought that democracy was imminent, and soon the students placed big posters throughout the campus of Beijing University that voiced pent-up frustrations with criticisms of the government. Intellectuals were voicing their opinions and making requests of the Communist Party for changes.[377]

Mao decided to limit the criticism in his speech on June 18, 1957, to define legitimate criticism in six criteria. The justifiable criticisms would help to unite the people of China's various nationalities, be beneficial to Socialist construction, help consolidate democratic centralism, strengthen the leadership of the Communist Party, and be beneficial to the international Socialist solidarity.[378]

Then just as suddenly in late June of 1957 began the kill of the hundred flowers with an "Anti-Rightist" campaign. By the end of that year, over 300,000 people were identified as rightists,[379]and several million intellectuals were sent to labor camps to be re-educated by the peasants through labor reform.[380] Again Mao reverted to peasant support as the machine to carry out the vision for the socialization of China.

The Great Leap Forward

Mao's determination to build a socialist economy prior to the Soviet Union by acceleration of production and big industry was viewed as less of a task than fighting a war, which he had already accomplished. On a tour to see how production was progressing, he read a banner in one village that said, "People's Communes Are Good." A reporter beside him published the quote in the newspaper and that is how the People's Communes commenced throughout China during the Great Leap Forward.[381]

---

[375] Dreyer, *Political System,* p. 92.
[376] Uhalley, *Mao Biography,* p. 119.
[377] Yang Gi, Communist Party member, interviewed, Williams, *China Revolution.*
[378] Uhalley, *Mao Biography,* pp.120-121.
[379] Dreyer, *Political System,* p. 93.
[380] Leslie Lyall, *God Reigns in China* (London: Hodder and Stoughton, 1985), p. 140.
[381] Li Rui, Secretary to Mao Zedong, interviewed, Williams, *China Revolution.*

A commune was the unification of many villages consisting of thousands of families, and from April to September 1958 more than 98 percent of the peasant households were reorganized again into 26,578 communes with 123 million families in brigades and production teams.[382] This accomplishment was done by the Communist formula, "from each according to his ability, to each according to his need." Dining facilities were established for the people to eat together since the large quantities would save from waste and fewer people would be taken from the commune production. Homes for the aged were established and nurseries were provided for the children and, consequently, mothers could also be free for productive labor. All workers, married and single, were placed in dormitories segregated by sex.[383]

The quick production of steel was one of the plans for the communes to overtake England and catch up with the USA in production. "Backyard Furnaces", small steel furnaces, were constructed in all areas with neither the proper knowledge nor the proper equipment to make good steel, and they were kept in operation day and night by burning every available wood. Even tables, chairs, window frames and old coffins were opened and used.[384] The steel produced was inferior and people were unhappy with the results as they had melted down many useful tools and cooking pots making them useless, and shipping the valueless steel congested the transportation systems.[385]

Another endeavor was to increase agricultural production, which the people thought could be accomplished by simply adding more fertilizer and planting closer. Everyone became enthused and exaggerated production reports, and a photograph was produced of wheat in a field supporting the weight of children.[386] Fields with such high-yield production, were later found to be artificially produced by the peasants who moved grain from other places to one field just for show because of Mao's visit.

Mao finally recognized that there were problems with the Great Leap Forward when he visited his hometown of Shaoshan in the

---

[382] Lyall, *God in China,* p. 140.

[383] Dreyer, *Political System,* p. 97.

[384] Zang Ming and Li Hui, married couple who experienced the events related, interviewed, Williams, *China Revolution.*

[385] Alasdiar Clayre, *The Heart of the Dragon* (Boston: Houghton Mifflin Company, 1984), p. 27.

[386] Li Rui, Secretary to Mao Zedong, interviewed, Williams, *China Revolution.*

Hunan province and encouraged the people to speak freely.[387] Crops had died from neglect and animals were slaughtered to integrate them as communal property. Production quotas were unrealistically inflated; reports were exaggerated and at higher governmental levels they were still further distorted.[388] The national government exacted a produce requirement according to the figures given, which left little or nothing for the peasants to live on. Much of the grain was shipped to Russia or left to rot in storage.[389] The failure of the Great Leap Forward was obvious, and the burden on the peasants who most acutely suffered its consequences.

The Great Leap Forward coincided with three years of floods, drought and other natural disasters caused by campaigns that disturbed the balance of nature with uncontrolled insect pests over much of China, but the news was controlled so that the people only knew of their local area. To prevent the news from spreading, peasants were not allowed to leave their local village, even to beg for food.[390] It was at this point that Russia's Premier Khrushchev in July 1960 withdrew all 1,390 Soviet technical advisers and terminated the aid to China program that China was depending on for industrial development.[391]

People resorted to eating weeds and grass roots and finally ate what they called *Guanyin* earth, a clay which a legend said that Old Mother Guanyin provided for poor people. The people attempted to swallow it, but after a few days it destroyed their intestines and they died. At first when someone died they were buried, but later they did not have strength to take the body out. They watched the rats dig out the eyes and eat on the bodies. The people did not have enough strength to chase the rats away.[392] During these years of famine and failure of the extortionate amount of grain seized by the government an estimated 30,000,000 people starved to death.[393]

Mao finally, recognized failure in the Great Leap Forward campaign, and in a speech in July 1959 confessed his mistakes

[387] Dr. Li Zhisui, Physician of Mao Zedong with Mao on the inspection, Interviewed, ibid.
[388] Dreyer, *Political System*, p. 141.
[389] Li Rui, Secretary to Mao Zedong, interviewed, Williams, *China Revolution.*
[390] Wang Ruoshui, Communist Party member, interviewed, ibid.
[391] Uhalley, *Mao Biography*, p. 133.
[392] Ding Xueling, son of a peasant farmer, witness testimony, interviewed, ibid.
[393] Williams, documentation, ibid.

but defied his colleagues to overthrow him.[394] At one point he commented, "It's all right for you to oppose me. When I have no alternative, I'll just take the Liberation Army, go up to the mountains and carry out guerrilla warfare." No one thought himself equal to Mao Zedong, and nobody would oppose him. Therefore, there were no comments even if someone might have wanted to say something.[395]

FAILURE LED MAO TO INITIATE THE CULTURAL REVOLUTION

Mao's reaction on occasions like this often was that of withdrawal. He was offended; viewing himself as a mistreated and misunderstood leader whom was not appreciated for doing his best. Then he would become aggressive to defend his actions. He vacillated between a traditional Chinese attitude of being replaceable to acting out in a very non-Chinese characteristic of defiance. Typically of his leadership, Mao withdrew to observe the governmental process and, upon reflection, suddenly would intervene imposing his ideas in a dictatorial fashion. At one point he glorified conflict with clashes and confusion, and at the next instant he displayed delicate sensitivity.[396] Mao glorified in his physical prowess and readiness for military conflict, but used any physical disability to recapture attention. This type of vacillation in his disposition was noted in his irresponsible refusal to be a father to his own children, but his preoccupation with the socialization of China's youth.[397] The formation of Mao's thought and nature had a bearing on the fabrication of the new society of China in the twentieth century.

Mao and the Party decided to launch another campaign to restore the reputation of the Communist regime, for the people to remember the bitter past before the Communist Liberation of 1949 and think of the sweet present conditions of the Communist era. However, people forgot they were supposed to concentrate on the pre-communist era and not remember the deaths and misery of the famine of the last three years. They became very depressed and attributed all their misery on the Party and Chairman Mao.[398] It was at this point that

---

[394] Clayre, *Heart of a Dragon*, p. 27.
[395] Li Rui, Secretary to Mao Zedong, was in attendance at the meeting, interviewed, Williams, *China Revolution*.
[396] Pye, *Mao Tse-tung*, pp. 53, 55, 62.
[397] Ibid, pp. 134, 225.
[398] Ding Xueliang, son of a peasant and a university student during the Cultural Revolution, interviewed, Williams, *China in Revolution, The Mao Years: It's Right to Rebel! 1960-1979.*

Mao resigned as Head of State, and the People's Congress elected Liu Shaoqi to succeed him. During the parades to celebrate, even though Liu had authority and the respect of the people, they shouted for Chairman Mao to have a long life. However, through continual positive recognition by the power of positive news media Mao's reputation rose from that of not only a national hero but to a god-like figure.[399]

Instruction of Mao

The educational curriculum included indoctrination of love for the Party and Mao Zedong. Much of what Mao may have said was not understood by the students, but they were taught that as long as they did what he said, they would be acting correctly for he was the savior of China, the one who brought liberation from foreign powers and corruption.[400]

Throughout his life, Mao had expressed his thought in oratory and writings. Many of the writings attributed to Mao, his speeches and lectures including military strategy, philosophy, socialization and history were oral creations transcribed and edited by others. In his speeches, Mao would strive to aggravate emotions in relation to the problems of the masses without interjection of solution to disperse the anxiety sensed in the immediate situation.[401] Through controlled news reports, Mao manipulated the emotions of the people and swayed public opinion.

Mao became disgruntled with Liu Shaoqi because of his program of building the economy using capitalistic methods. Both Liu and Zhou Enlai wanted to restrain revolutionary incitement in administration, but Mao considered the suppression of radicalism to be wrong.[402]

It was at this point in the history of China that Mao, as a god-like figure, called upon students who were a part of society with no work or profession, to rebel against party officials opposing him. Mao's recognition of their potential towards this cause had a tremendous impact on students.[403] As identified members of the proletarian class,

---

[399] Wang Ruoshui, Deputy Editor of People's Daily newspaper, interviewed, ibid.
[400] Lin Chun and Ma Bo, young students in that era, interviewed, Williams, *China Revolution.*
[401] Pye, *Mao*, pp. 236-237.
[402] Wang Raochui, Deputy Editor of the People's Daily, Interviewed, Williams, *China Revolution.*
[403] Ding Xuilang, son of a peasant and student, interviewed, ibid.

the students were inspired by the vision of keeping the Chinese Communist Revolution alive. These youth were to become the new Chinese society, free from the exploiting class. According to Mao, this transformation in society would only transpire as the people experienced continual thought reform through manual labor. He set high ideals to which everyone was to agree in theory, although the slogans of the youth were remote from the actual daily life in China.[404] From December 1964 to January 1965 an important Central Committee work conference was called, and Mao decided that severe renovation of the Party was required to recapture the jeopardized Chinese revolution.[405]

Mao was overheard to have told a contingent of foreign guests of going to see God as if he sensed his active life was over. This speculation was dislodged on July 16, 1966, when he made a typical maneuver to exhibit his admirable state of health. At 73 years of age, Mao staged an allegedly one-hour ten-mile swim with the current in the Yangtze River. This incident conferred on Mao the title "Great Helmsman".[406]

Having regained the confidence of the people with this demonstration of heartiness, Mao was ready to return to the political arena. At a meeting for students from the University of Peking and other institutions, led by Liu Shaoqi accompanied by Deng Xiaoping and Zhou Enlai on the stage of the Great Hall of the People, Liu described the start of the Cultural Revolution. He said, "We veteran revolutionaries have encountered new problems, and we don't know how to deal with them." Mao and his private physician, Dr. Li, were backstage listening unknown to anyone in the auditorium. Mao interrupted with, "I hear you! What veteran revolutionaries? You're an old counter-revolutionary." It was clear that in Mao's estimation Lui Shaoqi was no longer the Head of State and was labeled as a counter-revolutionary. Deng Xiaoping was demoted to sixth in power, Liu to eighth, and Lin Bio replaced Liu as Head of State.[407]

The mobilization, organization and use of the Chinese students known as the Red Guards were fundamental to the fulfillment of

---

[404] Adeney, *Church's March,* p. 99.
[405] Uhalley, *Mao Biography,* p. 144.
[406] Ibid, p. 151.
[407] Dr. Li Shisui, Mao's physician eye witness, interviewed, Williams, *China Revolution.*

the Great Proletarian Cultural Revolution. The People's Liberation Army provided the logistics for student living accommodations, organization, and travel support while the Cultural Revolution Group contributed its political guidance. All educational classes were cancelled for the academic year, and approximately 10 million Red Guards converged on Beijing for a series of eight rallies, from August 18 until November 26 of 1966.[408]

At this pivotal point in China's history, many of Mao's works were published. In the year 1967 alone 76,400,000 copies of his *Selected Works*, 350,000,000 copies of the famous *Little Red Book*, and 47,500,000 copies of *Selected Readings of Mao Zedong*, besides 57,000,000 copies of his poetry, were placed in Chinese hands. Moreover, these works were translated into twenty-three languages for foreign distribution.[409]

Mao's specific aims for the revolution were to rebuild Party loyalty to himself and eliminate the four "olds" of China's bourgeois past: old ideas, old customs, old culture and old habits. Armed with Mao badges and the *Little Red Book*, the Red Guards were ordered to make revolution throughout China. Within that first year one of every ten persons in China sustained political harassment.

General Secretary Hu Yaobang estimated that 30,000,000 people were persecuted with nearly 1,000,000 deaths.[410] Writer Wang Ruowang related that after being struggled against – a local informal court of accusations with violent consequences were common – on the first visit from the Red Guards, his books and bookcases were confiscated. Later they returned and took his sewing machine, sofa and desk for no apparent reason other than to terrorize his family.[411] Landowners were humiliated and often paraded through the streets with dunce caps on their heads with a slanderous placard hung around their necks on a thin wire and tortured. Some family relationships were severed so persecution was not transferred to other members of the family.[412]

Red Guards

The Cultural Revolution soon became a reign of terror as intellectuals

---

[408] Uhalley, *Mao Biography*, pp. 152-153.
[409] Pye, *Mao*, pp. 248-249.
[410] Lyall, *God in China*, pp. 141-142.
[411] Wang Ruowang, writer, interviewed, Williams, *China Revolution*.
[412] Li Zhongxin, peasant who observed struggles against landowners, Li Maoxio, a rich landowner's son relates his experiences, ibid.

were displaced: surgeons sent to work in fields or clean latrines, artists and writers were silenced while their works were burned, ancient art and architecture were smashed. To be caught with Western literature could mean death. Many teachers of the Red Guards were murdered, and rape and sexual brutality were frequent occurrences.[413] The *Kwangming Daily*, as the voice of the intellectuals, reported that there were thousands of highly trained scientists and technicians underemployed, lab technicians worked as sales clerks, radar specialists raised pigs, and computer scientists employed as distillers.[414] Anyone with authority over another could be accused and tortured, and many were driven to suicide.

The Gang of Four

The Cultural Revolution Group, known as the "Gang of Four" of which Mao's wife, Jiang Qing, was a part, directed the Red Guards to overthrow Liu Shaoqi and Deng Xiaoping. Jiang Qing campaigned against Liu as a counter-revolutionary and claimed that he should die the death of a thousand cuts.[415] After being struggled against, Liu Shaoqi became ill and died alone and naked in prison, having been denied medical attention. The Red Guards forced the son of the Chinese Communist Party Secretary-general Deng Xiaoping to jump out of a window. That rendered him crippled for life, and Deng himself was tortured and discharged from his office.[416]

Other students and workers started organizations to join the revolution in defense of Chairman Mao. There was conflict between the Red Guards and these new rebels. The fractions began to fight among themselves for power and territorial control with weapons either stolen from military arsenals or from army units that supported one division or the other.[417] With ex-servicemen on both sides who had artillery experience, the Cultural Revolution became real civil war, and many died in battles.

At the universities those identified as the Dictatorship Team

---

[413] Clayre, *Heart of a Dragon,* p. 29.

[414] W. Stanley Mooneyham, *China: A New Day* (Plainfield, NJ: Logos International, 1979), p. 21.

[415] Zhang Langlang, a student with the experience of a Red Guard, interviewed and Jiang Qing, Mao's wife in a recorded announcement on the streets to the people, Williams, *China Revolution.*

[416] Dreyer, *Political System,* p. 104.

[417] Zhang Wen, female student of the rebel fraction, and Ma Bo, male student of Red Guards, interviewed, Williams, *China Revolution.*

would come into the classes and pull anyone declared a criminal out of his seat, handcuff him, and drag him away, and nobody knew who would be next.[418] One student reported that she was ostracized just for contradicting the statement of Lin Biao that every sentence of Mao was the truth. Another student was imprisoned for ten years for commenting that the chaos of the Cultural Revolution was due to Mao's wife, Jiang Qing, and that Mao should divorce her.[419]

Finally, schools were reopened, but eighteen million students, the former Red Guards, remained embittered after having been manipulated, betrayed and then sent to the countryside to work on the farms. The time of the Cultural Revolution was cited as the ten-year gap in real education, which included wholesale destruction of artifacts, waste of resources and energy and detriment to the development of China.[420] However, the Communist Party continued to hold power over the largest population of the world.

Lin Piao had been a loyal supporter of Mao, but his selection as Mao's successor was an unusual feature of the Ninth Party Congress, and this gesture was premature. A conspiracy against Mao included a plot to assassinate him. A Party cadre led by Lin Piao had tired of trying to persuade Mao to change his political views. Mao intended to secure relations with the USA against Russia. An assassination could be blamed on others who would be eliminated as Mao's enemies.

The plan failed when the People's Liberation Army, or PLA, officer, entrusted to plant a bomb on the train that Mao had boarded, purposely evaded the assignment. The officer's wife informed the authorities, who had Mao removed from the train before the second fateful scheme could succeed. Lin Piao tried to escape by using his son, the deputy director of operations for the Chinese Air Force, as his connection for a flight to Russia, but his flight went down in Mongolia with no survivors.[421] Lin's death was a shock to the people, for he was portrayed as the heir and second only to Mao Zedong, and the people considered him as an exemplary revolutionary. Suddenly he was a traitor.[422] Mao continued to maintain control as

---

[418] Ding Xueling, student, interviewed, ibid.
[419] Lin Chun, a female student experience and Zhang Langlang, imprisoned, interviewed, ibid.
[420] Lyall, *God in China*, p. 141.
[421] Uhalley, *Mao Biography*, pp. 174-175.
[422] Wang Raoshui, Deputy Editor of the People's Daily, interviewed, Williams, *China Revolution*.

Chairman of the Chinese Communist Party.

By late 1973 Mao demonstrated his authority and control in a dramatic gesture when he displaced top regional military commanders, who had accumulated power and avoided the authority of Beijing. At the end of 1973 and into 1974, a campaign illustrated Mao's concern to educate the people in an "anti-Confucius" movement, which included criticism of chauvinistic male dominance in China and was fused with an anti-Lin Piao campaign.

Mao's Death

It was evident by the persistent energy he put into it that the Chinese Revolution had been Mao's revolution.[423] Mao's health deteriorated, and he entrusted the succession to Hua Guofeng rather than any of the anticipated ideologues. Hua did not appear to be aligned with either the liberal reformer group or the hard-line Communist conservatives. He had been a party secretary in Hunan province, his home province as well as that of Mao.

On July 28, 1976, one of the most devastating earthquakes of history hit northeast China in the Tianjin-Beijing region, and nearly 500,000 Chinese lost their lives. Just a few weeks later, on September 9, Mao died after 27 years as Chairman of the People's Republic of China.[424] Mao Zedong's dominion shaped modern Chinese history more than any other individual or political power, and his influence was evident in the following decades as his portrait continued to dominate Tiananmen Square.

CHINA IN POST-MAO ERA: 1976 - 2000

Mao Zedong constructed the setting for the context of historical, social and spiritual developments in China into the next millennium by adopting historical techniques used by the dynastic powers to control their subordinates. Deng Xiaoping was very apt at this also after Mao's death. However, the very nature of the Chinese culture held the deeply rooted requirement for a ruling emperor.[425] Students were taught that Mao was the great liberating savior of China, raising him to the level of divinity. This concept was impressed on their minds through the state

---

[423] Uhalley, *Mao Biography*, pp. 191-192.
[424] Dreyer, *China's Political System*, p. 108.
[425] W. J. F. Jenner, *The Tyranny of History* (London: Penquin Press, 1992), p. 44.

school system.[426]

Mao's physician, Dr. Li Zhisui, confirmed that Mao often referred to himself as the emperor and described his time in service for Mao as "life in the imperial court." Dr. Li also revealed that Jiang Qing, Mao's wife, who had planned to seize power after Mao's death, assumed herself to be a modern day Wu Zetian, the only female empress of China, to the magnitude that she had copies of Wu's gowns made for herself.[427]

For the demise of an emperor the usual character for death is not used in classical Chinese, but the proper ideograph depicts the fall of a mountain or that of a cataclysm or earthquake. On July 28, 1976, a few months before Mao's death on September 9, the most disastrous earthquake in China's history became an evil symbolic mark to many Chinese people, indicating not only his status, but also his character. An honorable symbol of noble quality would have been rain.[428]

SHIFT OF POWER WITHIN THE COMMUNIST PARTY

Hua Guofeng claimed the succession of rule from Mao Zedong under the pledged understanding that he would support whatever decisions Chairman Mao had made and persist in following whatever directives as Mao had outlined. This arrangement, alluded to as the "two whatevers," later placed Hua in an awkward position with others of the Communist Party.[429] It was noted that the request to fulfill the "two whatevers" negated a fundamental Maoist dictate that "practice is the parameter for evaluating truth," it demonstrated the characteristic of idealist empiricism.[430] The verification of this dichotomy was evident in the record of events that China had suffered in the past decade during the Cultural Revolution.

Those who came to power in China, along with most of the citizenry, remembered the Cultural Revolution of 1966-1976 with a

---

[426] Liu Qiao, Chinese business woman in Madrid, Interview, 26 July 1998, and Ma Bo, Williams (dir.), *China In Revolution,* An AMBRICA Production (Interview 1989).
[427] Li Zhisui, *The Private Life of Chairman Mao* (New York: Random House, 1994), pp. 480, 637.
[428] Chin Ying, [pseud.], Chinese Student in Costa Rica (Interview, October 1979).
[429] June Teufel Dreyer, *China's Political System* (Boston: Allyn and Bacon, 1996), p. 111.
[430] Lin Liangqi and Dai Xiaohua, 'Persistently Emancipating the Mind,' *Beijing Review,* June 15-21 (1998) 9.

particular aversion. These ten years were ascribed as the years of chaos, or the lost years. The Communist ideology that had founded the People's republic in 1949 was to continue into the 1980s after the lamentable aberration of the Cultural Revolution.[431] Most of the Standing Committee had personally suffered through the ten dark years as did each Chinese citizen, or at least had witnessed others, close to them, sustain loss or humiliation. The memories of the anti-rightist campaign in the late 1950s made China's advancement plummet into regression, and the devastating results of the Great Leap Forward left a sense of disillusionment and abhorrence toward Maoism. The rightist contingent preferred economic incentives as motivation, which was endorsed by Deng Xiaoping as a reformer, while they rejected the political incitement of mass movements, as supported by the ideologues or hard-liners.[432] With this new shift in control of the government and power over the official press, changes in China were certain.

The declamation of the news media against formerly demoted Deng Xiaoping soon ceased as they turned their venom against the Gang of Four. Jiang Qing, who as Mao Zedong's wife, had maneuvered to cling to the power, was declared to be selfish and decadent. She was pronounced responsible for virtually everything that had a negative effect on society throughout the lost decade of chaos. Within a month after Mao's death, Hua arrested the Gang of Four. Then after Ye Jinying, Wei Guoqing and Xushiyou insisted on Deng Xaioping's restoration, Hua rehabilitated him. However, Deng was coerced into writing a letter vowing his allegiance to Hua as Mao's rightful successor and another as a confession of his errors.

Soon, though, Deng's supporters accused Hua of initiating a personality cult, and they ridiculed his inability to lead by incorporating the policies of the "two whatevers," slavishly duplicating Mao. As early as 1977, it appeared that Deng Xaioping was regaining power, and by 1978 he had become Party Vice-Chairman and Deputy Prime Minister. It was apparent that he was edging out Hua Guofeng as Mao's successor.[433] Because of the

---

[431] Jonathan Chao (interviews), Richard VanHouten (ed.), *Wise as Serpents, Harmless as Doves* (Pasadena: William Cary Library, 1988), p. 23.

[432] Dreyer, *Political System*, p. 112.

[433] David Aikman (ed.), *Love China Today* (Wheaton: Tyndale House Publishers, Inc, 1977), pp. vii-viii; Dreyer, *Political System*, pp. 113-114.

uncertainties at the level of the Standing Committee, 1976 to 1978 was a time of increased freedom, even though local cadres would demonstrate their authority according to their personal aspirations.[434] It was not until December 11 through 22, 1978, during the Third Plenum that active steps were made toward reform.

The Third Plenum, a full meeting of 200-member Party Central Committee as appointed at the Eleventh Party Congress, met to achieve modernization. As Deng Xiaoping emphasized the characteristic of more work and less empty talk, the Plenum stressed individual initiative and responsibility. Workers should receive wages according to their production or contribution to the nation's advancement.

This plan for economic revitalization was based on anti-Maoist principles and was supported by Hua Guofeng as Party Premier and Chairman, although as Mao's heir he remained interested in preserving Mao's stature, as his heir. However, criticism of Mao began to surface, and the *People's Daily* criticized those who held Marxism as an object of faith. By late 1978, the *Little Red Book* of Mao's quotations disappeared from newsstands, and the Red Guards were formally disbanded. Deng remained consistent with Communist Marxism, although he may have de-emphasized its ideology in his vocalization of the principles of the new order on truth, in which he defined as its practice to be the criterion and to be sought from facts.[435]

The Gang of Four was put on trail in November 1980 for the implementation of policies favored by Mao. Carefully edited television broadcasts of these proceedings were publicized. Jiang Qing was defiant in describing herself as Mao's dog, fulfilling his demands.[436] Although Deng gave the appearances that indicated a severance from Mao influence, when he gained ascendancy over Hua Guofeng in late 1980, he introduced the Four Basic Principles in the December 1980 Party work conference. These included the insistence on socialism, the people's democratic dictatorship, leadership of the Communist Party, and Marxism-Leninism and Mao Zedong Thought.[437] There was an exchange from a Maoist form of Communism to Deng's continued leftist ideology into

---

[434] Chao (interviews), VanHouten (ed.), *Serpents Doves*, p. 56.
[435] Ibid, pp. 78-79.
[436] Dreyer, *Political System*, p. 118.
[437] Chao, (interviews), Vanhouten (ed.), *Serpents Doves*, pp. 138-139.

modernization.

The democratic misconception fostered by the Chinese Communist Party, CCP, was that the country ran on the coordinated efforts of its members, while in reality, the various Party committees dictated the policy, not so much from the point of ideology as from the power of authority. Party membership continued to be the channel of advancement, but the lack of interest in membership indicated a decline in Party authority.[438] Some who had been Party Youth Leaders declined the opportunity to solicit for CCP membership from the disappointment in what they had seen and experienced.[439]

It has been a great challenge for China to simultaneously restructure political institutions and modernize its economy. The gradual strengthening of the legislature, the National People's Congress, NPC, realized growth from 20 members in 1978 to over 2000 by 1990. This expansion enhanced the availability of written legislation, which could have a vast impact on the division of power in China. The influence had been noted as the NPC passed 175 laws between 1978 and 1994 and local people's congresses passed 3000, the number of lawyers rose from 31,000 in 1988 to 90,000 in 1995, and more citizens were depending on the legal system for rights protection.[440] China became a series of quasi-feudal pyramids of power, work units, and social values promoted and developed over the past forty years, all more influential than the Communist Party.[441]

Deng Xiaoping's announcement of the open door policy encouraged foreign trade, welcomed the technology of advanced countries, and sent Chinese students to Western and Japanese universities. The advice of intellectual experts would be solicited rather than ridiculed. In 1982 the Constitution reverted to the language of the 1954 state Constitution as it defined China as a people's democratic dictatorship rather than the 1978 definition as a dictatorship of the proletariat.[442]

The CCP continued to develop as China faced the new century and millennium, as it fought Party corruption and enforced

---

[438] Jennier, *Tyranny*, pp. 61-62.
[439] Liu Yun [pseud.],Former Communist Youth Leader in Madrid, Spain (Interview 25 July 1998).
[440] Myron Ivey (ed.),'Inching Toward Democracy?' *China News and Church Report*, 2624 February 16, (1998) 1-2.
[441] Jennier, *Tyranny*, p. 63.
[442] Dreyer, *Political System*, p. 116.

Party discipline. The ability of the Party to maintain the people's confidence depended on its competence to control the Party's nature, purity, cohesiveness and fighting capacity.[443] In February 1980, the landmark document titled, 'Some Principles on the Party's Internal Policies,' outlined basic rights for members of the CCP. It modified the power struggles, which resulted in massive purges. A mandatory retirement age for government officials was established to provide for leadership by middle-aged educated technocrats, rather than allow the poorly-educated aging revolutionaries to continue to dominate. In 1978, when Deng came to power, none of the essentials for political reform were in place. These essentials consisted of establishing norms to govern elite politics, restructuring of institutions to govern the state and strengthening of institutions of political participation.[444]

Deng instituted an atmosphere of more freedom of expression, which the constitution had promised, through his instigation of the Big Poster Campaign on a wall, known as the Democracy Wall, outside the Forbidden City near Tainanmen Square in Beijing. These walls were copied in many other cities and served until many adverse criticisms were stated against the Party elite, including Deng. His progressive economic policies and liberating open contact with the West were perceived as the cause of a rise in crime. To counter crime and appease his critics Deng instituted the Anti-Crime Campaign with an estimated 100,000 arrests and 10,000 executions. This was followed by the Anti-Spiritual Pollution Campaign focused on religious groups and unregistered churches in particular. The series of campaigns ended with the Party Rectification Campaign for the purge of leftists from the Party so Deng could successfully promote pragmatic policies.[445]

For the 12th Congress on September 1, 1982, Deng Xiaoping outlined the priority goals of the 1980s: to intensify modernization of socialist construction, pursue the unification of Taiwan with the motherland, oppose hegemony, and preserve world peace. The priority for the 1990s was decisively to develop Chinese society from the fulfillment of these goals. The central essential was economic construction that would constitute the fundamental

---

[443] Jiang Zemin, '15th congress,' *BR*, October 6-12 (1997) 30-33.
[444] Ivey, 'Inching,' *CNCR* (1998)1.
[445] Arthur Wallis, *China Miracle* (Columbia, MO: Cityhill Publishing, 1986), pp. 32-33 and Dreyer, *Political System*, p. 114.

solution of national and international problems.[446] Deng firmly refuted the deep-rooted definition of planned economy as socialism and commodity economy as capitalism.[447] His ability to unify the concept of international relations to economic growth reformed the conservative concept of capitalism.

Deng remained concerned with maintaining the Communist Party. This was noted in his proposal of a balance of power among the different branches of administration to prevent Party stagnation and stem corruption through an institutional change. At the age of 90, Deng followed Mao's method during the Cultural Revolution in protecting the direction of China in his final directives that the domestic politics of economic construction and open door policy were never to be altered. He exhorted the leadership of the CCP to be unshakable and never to allow the rise of a multi-party system to challenge its power. He advised Jiang Zemin to hold the People's Liberation Army, PLA, tightly and keep a handle on the military through frequent visits. Deng rallied 20 of the senior generals to support comrade Jiang for a trouble-free succession and to foster stability in central authority by avoiding growth of regionalism. Later Deng, however, expressed doubts in Jiang's ability to maintain functional balance.[448]

The theme that Jiang proposed for the 15th National Congress of the CCP on September 12, 1998, was to uphold the political theory advocated by Deng Xiaoping for national independence, the people's liberation, and to bolster the economy for common prosperity for the people. The progression of change in the history of China was recounted in the fact that Dr. Sun Yatsen executed change by the Revolution of 1911, Mao founded the People's Republic of China in 1949, and Deng initiated reform through opening China to international relations for modernization.

To build on the foundation of Deng Theory of Marxism in China was to uphold principles of emancipating the mind and seeking truth from facts, uphold achievements of scientific socialism, observe the world in perspective of Marxism and building socialism with Chinese characteristics. It was recognized that Socialism was the primary

[446] Yin Chingyo, *Politica Exterior de China Comunista en la Etapa Presente* [Communist Chinese External Politics in the Present Stage] (Republica de China: La Liga Mundial Anti-Comnuista, 1985), p. 3.
[447] Lin and Dai, 'Persistently Emancipating,' *BR*, (1998)11.
[448] Willy Wolap Lam, *China after Deng Xiaoping* (Hong Kong: PA Professional Consultants, 1995), pp. 385-386, 393, 425.

stage of Communism and that China was merely in this necessary primary stage, which in part was the period of New Democracy for industrialization and modernization of the economy. Reforming the political structure and strengthening democracy and the legal system were advocated for unity through constitutional safeguards and integration of Party members, law and public opinion. The renewing of the campaign, "letting a hundred flowers bloom and a hundred schools of thought contend," was advocated for diversity to create art works of ideological content, though it seemed necessary to place controls on the press to optimize its structure in society and improve its publication quality.[449] The government policies in turn affected the realities of life from lifestyles, freedoms and economic security to even family relationships for the Chinese people.

CHINA WAS EFFECTED BY GOVERNMENT POLICY

The effects of policy were realized in 1979 when many destitute people entered Beijing to demand food, clothing and an end to oppression. With each additional political movement, peasant life became more intolerable. The *People's Daily* reported in 1980 that 100 million peasants had not benefited from collectivization but remained as deficient as in 1949 and subsisted only from governmental assistance.[450] In 1980 some 50 beggars demonstrated in Datong in Shanxi province for free train rides to Beijing to petition for their needs. The government leaders recognized that these faults from the lack of science and technological development due to the persecution of the intellectuals during the Cultural Revolution, when Mao labeled them as the "stinking ninth class".[451]

Later in 1983 the commune system was abolished and township government was established which annulled the fixed-state agricultural produce purchase policy.[452] The land was divided into small plots to be privately farmed in family units, and each peasant paid a small rent and an agriculture tax. Excess production could then be retained or marketed which created profit, raised morale, and increased initiative. Even small industry and business were

---

[449] Jiang Zemin, 'Hold High the Great Banner of Deng Xiaoping Theory for an All-Round Advancement of the Cause of Building Socialism with Chinese Characteristics into the 21st Century,' *BR*, October 6-12, (1997) 10-27.

[450] *Far Eastern Economic Review,* 7 March (1980).

[451] David H. Adeney, *China: The Church's Long March* (Ventura, CA: Regal Books, 1985), pp.82-83, 89.

[452] Lin and Dai, 'Persistently Emancipating,' *BR*, (1998) 10.

encouraged as the government removed the negative tainted image of being a rich farmer, and replaced it with praise for rich farmers as model workers.

There were problems with this fresh view of decollectivization, for it caused the peasants to become more independent. Motivated by economic self-interest rather than ideology, they were less controllable to the point that throughout 1983 and 1984 reports in newspapers reported a rise in economic crime and corruption.[453]

Government leaders refuted the charges that capitalist policy had betrayed the Marxist principles. An article in December 7, 1984, issue of the *People's Daily* stated, "We cannot expect the works of Marx and Lenin in their day to solve our modern problems."[454] A drawback in the new system was the danger of inflation. Premier Zhao Ziyang gave an impressive report in May 1984 that the average income per capita among peasants rose 14.7 percent while urban income was up 15.5 percent. Another side effect was that even with the sufficient funds for peasants to build better homes, land development planning precluded building on land assigned for food crops that held priority.[455] Furthermore, China's greatest claim to human rights achievement was providing food and clothing for 1.2 billion people and helping 50 million to rise above poverty level.[456]

In the cities where work units were established, schools were provided along with housing and medical facilities, which caused dependency of employees on the State from birth to death. The strongest work unit was among the military, with civilian counterparts to form checks and balances to ensure control and security from an officer becoming over-zealous for power.[457] The basic value in China was to serve the people, and individual fulfillment was found in community effort. With 14 million new births each year added to the present generation, people instead of machinery planted, cultivated and harvested crops from the valuable soil with nothing wasted. A weakness in the system was that some cadres had limited understanding of the Party's policies and were unable to match individual aptitude and talents to the

---

[453] *China Daily,* 23 March (1984).
[454] Adeney, *Church's March,* p. 84.
[455] Ibid., pp. 80-81, 83, 86.
[456] 'US Human Rights Criticism Refuted,' *BR,* March 5-9 (1998) 5-6.
[457] Jennier, *Tyranny,* pp. 56-57.

community task. Therefore, the strength of China's massive human element was also her weakness. Natural individual capabilities and gifts were not allowed to develop, but work was dictated as a community. This, in actuality, minimized production needed to support the population.

Nationally, the greatest political concern of China remained as that of geographic unity and international independence.[458] However, the greatest practical concern encompassed absorption of technology through international means. The literacy level of the country remained low even among the CCP membership. The plan proposed by Huang Hsiang, a counselor of the Institute of Social Sciences, was for China, by the end of the 20th century, to reach the technical level that advanced nations were in 1970.[459] The freedom to retrieve information from other countries was limited through bureau censorship, although normal citizen did not perceive the censoring for they became accustomed to the lack of information.[460] Both social and political limitations to the technological advancements of China had to be overcome before modernization could be realized.

NATURAL DISASTER EFFECTED CHINA'S ADVANCEMENT

The devastation of flood and drought had also taken a toll on China's advancement. The disastrous 60-day flooding of the Yangze, Songhua and Nenjiang rivers during the summer of 1998 affected 29 of China's provinces and over 240 million people, causing an estimated 36 billion U.S. dollars in damage. These floods involved the greatest peacetime mobilization of 250,000 PLA troops to help civilians reinforce dikes. An estimate of 33,000 people died; however, the central government declared as policy that nobody would die of hunger and took the responsibility to provide grain for the surviving victims on a loan basis. Then these loans were to be repaid, as the people were able.[461] The real concern of China was not as much flooding as that of lack of water, according to Daniel Gunaratnam, a water expert from World Bank. Floods cost China an average of 10 billion U.S. dollars a year through the 1990s while water shortages

[458] Raymond L. Whitehead and Rhea M., *China: Search for Community* (New York. Friendship Press, 1978), pp. 7, 11-13, 27-29, 36, 39.
[459] Yin, *Politica* [Political], p. 47.
[460] Huang Wenyan [pseud.], Chinese art student in Madrid, Spain (Interview, 25 July 1998).
[461] Gail V. Coulson, (ed.), 'China's 1998 Flood,' *China Talk*, November (1998) 1-2, 12-13

cost 35 billion.[462] The unplanned natural phenomenon can help a nation come together with human compassion on projects to aid victims and minimize damage. Construction on the Yantze River Dam of the Three Gorges as the Xiaolangli Water Conservancy Project was started, and the Wanjiazhai Water Conservancy Project on the Yellow River began operation October 1, 1998. Construction commenced at Huaihe River also in October, and the Taizhou Water conservancy Project was under construction the same year. These projects indicated the progress China attempted.[463]

POLITICAL DECISION EFFECTS CHINA

Political limitations to China's advancement were evident on June 4, 1989, from the incident in Beijing. Tiananmen Square was the stage of rallies as Red Guards faced the reviewing stands on Tiananmen Gate with Mao Zedong and Lin Biao to preside over the ceremonies in late 1966. Since then, demonstrations have faced inward to the Monument to the People's Heroes in the center of the Square as in 1976 when Zhou Enlai staged a demonstration against the Gang of Four and in 1979 when the democracy wall movement had a pro-democracy rally. It seemed no different for the funeral of Hu Yaobang to make use of the same venue in 1989. The historical memory of demonstrations against the Treaty of Versaille on May 4, 1919, and date for the Deng and Gorbachev summit with a massive presence of international media provided a pretext for a small demonstration.

The Chinese government had intended as a symbolic ceremony of significant Sino-Soviet history for Gorbachev to lay a wreath at the Monument of the People's Heroes, to affirm the solidarity of the two Communist Parties on equal terms. The students took the stage of Tiananmen Square and appropriated the planned media for their purposes. A Styrofoam statue of the Goddess of Democracy, similar to the Statue of Liberty, was a potent symbol of desired democracy.[464] Newspaper reporters brandished banners asking to be free to print the truth, some demonstrators denounced inflation

---

[462] Myron Ivey (ed.), 'China Is Running Dry,' *CNCR*, 2654, October 12 (1998) 3-4.
[463] Li Rongxia, 'China Enhances Water Conservancy Construction,' *BR*, December 7-13 (1998) 9-11.
[464] Mckenzie Wark, 'Vectors of Memory…Seeds of Fire,' *New Formations China Tiananmen Square 4th June Globalization* (The Western Media and the Beijing Demonstrations, mwark@laurel.ocs.mq.edu.au, 1999), pp. 3-5.

and official corruption while others sought freedom and democracy, and even criticisms of Party leaders and their monopoly on power were paraded.[465] Short-wave radios relayed information to other parts of China where demonstrations in support broke out. Foreign journalists wired for updates, and Beijing was the global focal point as never in history.

On June 3, 1989, martial law was declared, satellite links were cut, troops were brought in from border provinces, and the Hong Kong stock market plummeted. Even though many workers were not favorable toward reform, nevertheless, workers and other citizens of Beijing were not willing to allow troops to harm Chinese students and blockaded the streets and railway station. Perhaps a million people held back 150,000 soldiers, but the troops were finally moved into position through the subway system and a network of underground tunnels Mao had built as fallout shelters. It turned into a battle over control of the city. The CCP leaders observed this student demonstration with alarm because many of them had suffered under students as Red Guards.[466] Seven military personnel drafted a letter to oppose the use of armed PLA troops against the demonstrators in Tainanmen Square in 1989, and the members of all field armies signed it.[467]

Suddenly the students were no longer referred to as patriots but counter-revolutionaries as Deng Xaioping and Li Peng held firm control. They held the power and support of all except the Beijing military district and a few of the liberals, like Zhao Ziyang who tried to tell the students to disband. He clearly feared the repercussions of the hard-line leaders against his more liberal faction and for his own life.[468] Early on the Sunday morning of June 4, tanks smashed barricades and soldiers fired into the crowd of demonstrators in full view of foreign news cameras. Live bullets flew and many were killed, both students and soldiers.[469] Chinese television stations used American news media interviews of Chinese citizens to identify participants. They broadcast a telephone number for anyone who recognized any interviewees to report them as counter-

---

[465] Dreyer, *Political System*, p. 129.
[466] Wark, 'Vectors of Memory,' *NFCTSJG*, pp. 5-6. Meng Xiangzhi [pseud.], Confirmed by Chinese professor in the USA (Interview, 21 October 1998).
[467] Dreyer, *Political System*, p. 16.
[468] Wark, 'Vectors of Memory', *NFCTSJG*, p. 7.
[469] Dreyer, *Political System*, p. 130, and Wang Li [pseud.], Chinese eyewitness now living in Madrid, Spain (Interview, 16 July 1998).

revolutionaries. The CCP had turned the western media feedback into a tool for discouraging resistance, to prompt compliance with the state, and as a surveillance system. Chinese embassies in the West taped newsreels and took clippings of newspapers to be used as evidence for the roundup. News photos were also used to identify overseas Chinese who had demonstrated in their host countries.[470] The relative political openness that had indicated an inclination toward democracy was put to rest with what became referred to in the West as the 1989 Tiananmen Square massacre.

The Chinese youth became cynical distrusting a system that depended on absolute power of the ruling Party and no absolutes in moral standards. They had no voice against official wrongs and gave up any idea of a political solution. Their interest turned to endeavors to improve their personal living conditions. Then again, even this avenue of personal comforts had been stifled with the memory of the 1983 Anti-Spiritual Pollution Movement that fought against efforts for personal gain as stipulated in the Constitution.[471] The ideals of Communism had subsided for the Chinese youth, and a moral standard of Confucianism resurfaced with the desire to learn the ancient Chinese language and quote Confucian phrases. The young generation turned its attention and priority to hard work for the sole purpose of earning money.[472]

There has been an effort to migrate from China, not only for prospects of financial opportunities, but also for freedom from political oppression. At times, the employment found outside China was more menial with less financial benefits than what was left in China. Nevertheless, there was a willingness to leave, as reported in the *Asiaweek*, 17 May 1992 edition, even through illegal routes by paying 18,000 U.S. dollars for fraudulent visas or passports. According to the publication *Cheng Ming* April 1992, international gangs gained 11,000,000 U.S. dollars through selling counterfeit Venezuelan legalization documents in 1990. The *Bai Shing*, 1 March 1992 issue, documents that there were approximately 49,600,000 overseas Chinese, or an amount equal to the population of France.[473]

---

[470] Wark, 'Vectors of Memory,' *NFCTSJG*, p. 8; Zheng Xianyu [pseud.], Chinese personal experience, Madrid, Spain (Interview, 27 July 1998).
[471] Aleney, *Church's March*, pp. 102-103, 106-107.
[472] Dreyer, *Political System*, p. 123; Huang Wenyan [pseud.], Chinese Art Student in Madrid, Spain (Interview, 25 July 1998).
[473] Chao, *CNCR*, 2018, September 4, 1992, and Interviews by the author from Chinese living in Europe confirm information.

Political History: China in Context

CHINA'S ATTEMPT TO RECOVER AND TO UNITE

Over the intervening years, with a noted openness to the world in trade and an attractive business future, China drew many of her citizens back and made the prospects of migrating less attractive. The start in this direction began on February 6, 1985, with the Japanese Shimizu Construction Company and Iwai Company that signed contracts with the Chinese International Trust & Investment Corporation and the Beijing Institute of Architectural Design. This became the first Chinese-Japanese company.[474] In 1997 the gross domestic product reached 7,477.2 billion yuan, for an increase of 8.8 percent over 1996, and grain production reach the highest at 492.5 million tons. China increased communication of public transportation by rail, expressways and road systems along with improved telecommunications. The successful launches of the satellites Dongfunghong-III and Fengyun-II and the operation of the supercomputer Galaxy-III were real Chinese accomplishments for 1997.[475] The 1997 world trade list by World Trade Organization put China before Belgium & Luxembourg in the position of one of the top ten in world trade.[476] Chinese international relations continually progressed even through human rights disputes, international marketing boycotts, political differences, domestic incidents and natural catastrophes.

To bolster the credibility and support from the people the CCP utilized the May 1999 incident of the alleged military intelligence error of the NATO bombing of the Chinese Embassy in Belgrade, Serbia. This drew attention away from the 10th anniversary of the Tiananmen Square incident of 1989. The government bussed in students from universities and encouraged a nationalistic demonstration against the USA Embassy in Beijing.[477]

Hong Kong

A real concern China harbored was the return of landmasses

[474] Yin, *Politica* [Political], p. 45.
[475] Chen Jinhua, 'Report on the Implementation of the 1997 Plan For National Economic and Social Development And on the draft 1998 Plan,' *BR*, April 13-19 (1998) 19-20.
[476] Li Ning, 'China Enters Top Ten In World Trade,' *BR*, March 30-April 5 (1998) 10.
[477] Fang Bay, 'China at 50, on a Long March to Modernity,' *U.S. News & World Report*, 4 October (1999) 2.

considered part of China. Hong Kong was returned from the British lease on July 1, 1997, under a policy of one country with two systems. A Hong Kong Special Administrative Region entrusted to the Hong Kong banker, Tung Chee Hwa, as its director was established. A survey showed that 61 percent of Hong Kong residents expressed full confidence in the future of Hong Kong and that large numbers of former Hong Kong residents, who left in apprehension of what the unification may implicate, were returning. The probability of the 50-year arrangement of two systems was doubted by some that lacked confidence in the Communist system's willingness to uphold the stipulations of the arrangement.[478]

The proposed reunification of Taiwan with the China motherland had a totally different status of circumstances. While Hong Kong was reunified after the termination of a lease, Taiwan was separated under a civil war act of possession. The People's Republic of China regarded Taiwan as a renegade province to be brought back under its authority. In the viewpoint of the Republic of China in Taiwan, the island was regarded as a sovereign nation.

Taiwan

The Nationalists or Kumintang had the greatest influence over Taiwan with manipulation of the news media and a record of success in leading the society into stability and prosperity with freedom. The alternative of the Democratic Progressive Party in its struggle with the People's Republic for independence had the possibility of producing an angry response from the Mainland. The atmosphere important to maintain was the tendency toward peace with minimum danger of violent interaction between Taiwan and China. Unification may take place under appropriate circumstances with development of the Taiwan model for China's modernization. The conditions Taiwan proposed for reunification specified a vast ideological, institutional, and economic transformation of the Mainland with the prerequisite that unification be the desire of the people of Taiwan.[479]

---

[478] Dai Xiaohua, 'Good Beginning for the One Country, Two Systems,' *BR*, July 6-12 (1998) 8; Song Shaozhou [pseud.] Overseas Chinese, Madrid, Spain (Interview, 20 July 1998).

[479] Thomas A. Metzger, *The Unification of China and the Problem of Public*

On October 14, 1998, in Shanghai's Peace Hotel, the president of the Association for Relations Across the Taiwan Straits, Wang Daohan, met with Straits Exchange Foundation chairman Koo Chenfoo as his Taiwan counterpart. Chairman Koo's visit was to create stable relations across the straits conducive to peaceful reunification under the one China principle, and end hostility between the two entities. Reunification concerned territorial and sovereign integrity of the nation, rather than discussion over the best political system. The People's Republic opposed the concept of "two Chinas" or "one China and one Taiwan," and the cession of Taiwan would not be tolerated. Sentiments within the Republic of China were mixed, as some desired to return to the Mainland as their motherland; however, others see the character of the two governments and lifestyles each to be completely different and in favor of independence.[480]

Macao

Beijing had refused Portugal's offer to return Macao twice before. The first time was during the riots fused by the Cultural Revolution in 1967 and the other in 1974, after the fall of Portugal's dictatorship, which incited the freedom of all her colonies.[481] Finally, the important documents were ratified for the future of the reunification of Macao in the second plenary session, held in Beijing, of the Preparatory Committee for the Macao Special Administrative Region. These sessions terminated on July 12, 1998, and the committee passed the proposal for public holidays to be declared between December 20, 1999, the date of Macao's reunification with the People's Republic of China, to December 31,1999.[482] After 442 years Macao became unified with China at midnight starting Monday December 20,

---

Opinion in the republic of China in Taiwan (Board of Trustees of the Leland Stanford Junior University, 1992), pp. 1, 5-7; Liu Yun [pseud.] Representative of Chinese Firm in Madrid, Spain (Interview, 25 July 1998).

[480] Huang Wei, 'A Firm Handshake Makes History' and ' Qian: Taiwan Should Face Up to The Int'l Situation,' *BR*, November 23-29 (1998) 11, 13, 15; Chang Naian, from Taiwan in Madrid, Spain (Interview, 18 July 1998); Ip Chiming, from Taiwan in Madrid, Spain (Interview, 19 July 1998);
Liu Yun [pseud.],Representative of Chinese Firm in Madrid, Spain (Interview, 25 July 1998).

[481] Dirk Beveridge, 'Chinese celebrate the return of Macau,' *USA Today*, Monday, 20 December (1999) 13A.

[482] 'Session Passes Documents on Macao,' *BR*, July 27-August 2 (1998) 5.

1999. Macao remained a special administrative region of China with autonomy for 50 years.[483] This historical victory of the People's Republic of China and the Communist Party of China was another step in the unification of China as a nation without international intervention.

In China, 1999 was a year of significance not only for the reunification of Macao, but also for historical anniversary events. It marked the 80th year since the May 4th Movement, 20th year of economic reform, 10th year of the June 4th Tiananmen Square Democratic demonstrations. On October 1, 1999, Tiananmen Square was the site of the celebration of the 50th Anniversary of the founding of the People's Republic of China.

---

[483] Beveridge, 'Chinese return of Maco,' *USA today,* Monday, 20 December (1999) 13A.

3
CHINESE CHURCH HISTORY

The historical context of China was the setting in which the seed of the Church was planted. It was in this contextual understanding of the physical and spiritual world that the first introduction of Christianity penetrated Chinese society. China's cosmology included neither the biblical creation nor a supernatural being who ordered life. The beginning was not even contemplated in a theory similar to the Big Bang.

Before the Xia Dynasty in 2205 BC, two rulers of the Legendary Period, Yao and Shun who lived in the post-flood period, were thought to have been the leaders of the Chinese migration from the Tower of Babel in the Middle East to China.[1]

One indication of biblical influence in China was noted in the Chinese written character for boat as *chuang*. This character depicts a vessel with eight mouths, which symbolizes people. In the story of Noah and the ark as found in the book of Genesis of the Bible, God had Noah build a large seaworthy craft and the only people saved from the flood waters were the eight within the ark: Noah and his wife, their three sons and their wives.[2]

---

[1] Samuel Wang and Ethel R. Nelson, *God and the Ancient Chinese* (Dunlap, TN: Read Books Publisher, 1998), p. 16.
[2] Ibid., p. 18; and the book of Genesis 11: 5-8 of the Bible.

Alopen, a missionary of the Nestorian Christians, came from Persia to Changan in 635 AD and introduced Christianity to China.[3] Then until the 1800s, Christianity had very little lasting impact on Chinese society, even though all levels of the nation had been touched at different times and by distinct methods. As did Islam, Christianity required the belief in a personal God who created all things, which was a more difficult concept for Chinese to grasp than the continual family relationships.[4] The identification of Christianity with foreign powers was a concept firmly established from the very beginning through Papal intervention. The disagreement of methods and doctrines of different orders left doubts and lack of understanding as to the basis of Christianity. These barriers continued to form a misconception of the feasibility for its adaptation into Chinese society.

THE MODERN MISSIONARY ERA

Although China went into isolation and rejected the Christian religion, there were still foreigners looking at the potential for marketing and missionary endeavor. The Catholics had been thrust out by decree because of Papal refusal to compromise authority over the Church in China, and the Chinese Emperor's rebuff of that refusal. The Protestants had not attempted to enter to establish a presence until the 1800s. However, the Russian Orthodox had begun to proclaim its doctrines in Beijing and Heilongjiang by the mid-seventeenth century. The Czar sent a Russian Orthodox mission to Beijing in 1715, and a permanent mission station was established by 1727 through the Treaty of Kiakhta.[5]

Christianity was much more difficult to propagate than Buddhism or Confucianism. Buddhism was full of superstitions and was easily accepted by people who, according to Princeton Hsu in his article 'China's Indigenous Christian Movements,' were naturally superstitious. Confucianism describes mankind as naturally good and kind, and evil acts were due to the lack of education, wrong choice of friendships, or perhaps the result of

---

[3] Luo Zhuteng (ed.), *Religion under Socialism in China*, trans. Donald E. MacInnis and Zhang Xian (London: M. F. Sharpe, 1991), p. 22.

[4] Clayre, *Heart of Dragon*, p. 51.

[5] Luo Zhufeng, (ed.), *Religion under Socialism in China*, trans. Donald E. MacInnis and Zheng Xian (London: M. E. Sharpe, Inc, 1991), p. 23.

poor circumstances. Christian doctrine propagated that all are guilty of sin, and salvation from a hell of eternal torment could only be accepted through the belief in Jesus Christ.[6] Nevertheless, as Bishop K. H. Ting had written: "The gospel convicts man of sin and that makes it something foreign to human nature as it is. But... [it is] intrinsic to the Christian message which we simply cannot do away with without changing the gospel to something else."[7] Nonetheless, Confucians criticized Christianity as superstitious and heterodox since the days of Yang Kunghsien, the leading opponent to Christianity in the seventeenth century. It was inconceivable to Confucianists that an omnipotent and merciful God had permitted original sin that permeated further generations. Those who had claimed to be Christians were the Taiping rebels, who had terrorized China and lived inconsistent doctrines, and barbarian invaders from the West with opium as their introduction, which did not give Christianity a positive reputation.[8] The fact that Christian missionaries were reformers brought them into conflict with the gentry-elite, for both were involved with reform within the Chinese society and were immune to the magistrate's authority. Also, the two taught their own version of a cosmic doctrine.[9]

PROTESTANT MISSIONARY ENTRANCE INTO CHINA

It was the arrival of Robert Morrison at Guangzhou, the only city open to foreigners, in 1807 as a passenger on an American ship from New York that the first Protestant missionary historically entered China. Even though Morrison was a Scottish Presbyterian, the British East Indian Company merchant ships would not grant him passage for fear that such an idealist would hinder their activities in the immoral trade of opium.[10] Morrison could not

---

[6] Princeton Hsu, 'China's Indigenous Christian Movements,' David Aikman (ed.), *Love China Today* (Wheaton: Tyndale House Publishers, Inc., 1977), p. 31.
[7] Philip L. Wickeri, *Seeking the Common Ground* (Maryknoll, NY: Orbis Books, 1990), p. 34.
[8] John K. Fairbank,; Edwin O. Reischaver and Albert M. Craig, *East Asia* (Boston: Houghton Mifflin Company, 1989), p. 572.
[9] John King Fairbank, *China, A New History* (Cambridge MA: The Belknap Press of Harvard University Press, 1992), p. 222.
[10] Stanley W. Moonyham, *China: A New Day* (Plainfield, NJ: Logos International, 1979), pp. 134-135; and David H. Adeney, *China: The Church's Long March* (Ventura, CA: Regal Books, 1985), p. 36.

seem to establish a foundation for starting a mission station or church. He spent twelve years in Macao studying the language and during that time translated the entire Bible into Chinese. After seven years proclaiming the message of Christianity while translating, he finally baptized the first convert.[11] Other Protestant missionaries from Portugal, Holland, France, United Kingdom and lastly the USA arrived even though their work was confined to Macao, and still there were others who prepared Chinese literature in Singapore while waiting to enter.[12]

The priority for missionaries became any means to gain entrance into China. While Morrison worked on translating the Bible, he accepted a position as a translator for the East India Company to gain entrance into China. He promoted the idea of Consular Jurisdiction, and he became a deputy consul for Britain within China. His son later joined the invasion army during the Opium War in 1839 and participated in the signing of the Treaty of Nanjing in 1842, which ensured foreign presence in China. Karl Gutzlaff with the Netherlands Missionary Society came into China on an opium ship. He distributed Christian literature from the ship and claimed that he had evangelized more than all the other missionaries put together. Other missionaries took part in the signing of different unequal treaties within the first hundred years of Protestantism in China. Some of these treaties even had suggested the extermination of China as a nation.

Missionaries were instrumental in promoting colonialism and supported armed force to serve that purpose. Article 17 of the Treaty of Wangxia granted missionaries the right to own land in the five port cities gained through the First Opium War. In 1856 a local government within Guangxi Province killed French Catholic missionary Chapdeline after he entered this interior region without authorization. Under the pretext of the "Father Chapdelaine Incident," the French started the Second Opium War in 1858, and through the Treaty of Tianjin and the Treaty of Beijing opened the interior of China to missionary endeavor. These incidents forever linked the concept of Christian missionaries to

---

[11] Arnold Lea, 'Christian Churches in China, 1807-1949,' David Aikman, (ed.), *Love China Today*, pp. 12-13. Morrison was in Guangzhou, or Canton. Therefore, his translation was in Cantonese.

[12] Adeney, *Church's March*, p. 37; and Kenneth Scott Latourette, *The Chinese, Their History and Culture*, 3rd edn. Rev. (New York: The MacMillan Company, 1959, p. 333.

imperialism and the iniquitous trade of opium carried on by the East Indian Company in the memory of the Chinese.[13]

Different attitudes were reflected from the missionary community that entered China under the protection of gunboats and in the wake of opium trade. Missionary Peter Parker, who inaugurated medical missions with an eye hospital in Guangzhou, expressed that he was "constrained to look upon the present not so much as an opium affair, or an English concern, but as a great design of Province to make the wickedness of man subserve his purpose of mercy towards China."[14] Huc, a French Lazarist Catholic, took a different position than that of most Protestants. He recognized the opium situation as "a mind brutalized, a body enfeebled, the premature death of the smoker followed by the sale of all his and his wife's and children's worldly possessions and their descent into a life of misery and crime – these are the normal consequences of this fatal passion."[15] Baldus observed that most Europeans cared very little, "and particularly the English, in whom love of humanity never prevails over the love of gain."[16] In many cases greed seemed to motivate missionaries who were attracted by the additional income that the supplementary position as an official translator for the invading nations afforded them, because their pay through the missionary societies was usually meager and invariably late in its arrival.[17]

Catholic missionaries rarely had economic or technical connections for penetration into China. They secured the right under the treaties of 1858-1860 to reoccupy the land they had lost during the decree that proscribed Roman Catholicism. The majority of the Catholic ministry was in the small towns and villages of the interior.[18] The Catholic priests dressed and lived as the Chinese, and they refrained from teaching European languages in the schools they established. They also abstained

---

[13] Luo, *Religion in China,* pp. 41-42; Adeney, *Church's March,* p. 37; and Wallis, Arthur, *China Miracle* (Columbia, MO: Cityhill Publishing, 1986), p. 35.

[14] Parker to Anderson, 24 June 1840, South China 1833-1844, ABCFM.

[15] Peter Ward Fay, *The Opium War 1840-1842* (Chapel Hill, NC: The University of North Carolina Press, 1975), pp. 242, 332-333.

[16] Baldus to Etienne, 3 Aug 1835, *Annales,* 10: 70-71; and Fairbank and others, *East Asia,* p. 464.

[17] Fay, *Opium War,* p. 87.

[18] Jean Cheneux, Marianne Bastid and Marie-Claire Bergere, *China, from the Opium Wars to the 1911 Revolution* (New York: Pantheon Books, 1976), p. 184.

from direct attacks on Buddhist and Daoist idols and Chinese social customs.[19]

MISSIONS AND MISSIONARIES PRESENTED MIXED IMPRESSIONS

Many Chinese who became Christians depended upon the mission compounds, schools and hospitals and were considered denationalized. Observing this, Chinese had composed the saying, "The addition of a Christian to the church means a loss of a citizen to China."[20] They used privileges secured through their connection with the missionaries under the unequal treaties, and Chinese officials dared not to oppose them. If there was a lawsuit between a church member and another non-Christian Chinese citizen, the local government always favored the former. Many of the Manchu officials conspired with church members to seize land from peasants.[21]

The American missionaries with their proclamation of moral law were accepted because of their opposition to the opium trade. The first Protestant missionaries lived in business settlements and carried on a very Western life-style, which magnified the foreignness of Christianity. Conversely, James Hudson Taylor arrived in China in 1853 but soon became sick, consequently he went back home to the United States and finished his studies in medicine. He returned to China in 1854 and was anxious to identify with the Chinese people in his manner of dress and living conditions. He suffered criticism, but he noticed an attitude change of the Chinese along with an acceptance of the Christian message.[22] Taylor was under the Chinese Evangelization Society, but later founded the China Inland Mission in 1865 and gave a new impetus to Protestant missions in China. He initiated a call for almost 1,000 missionaries on an interdenominational perspective, which was realized by the time of his death in 1905.[23]

Under the teachings of the missionary Issachar J. Roberts, Hong Xiuguan became the founder of the *Taiping Tianguo,* or

---

[19] Fairbank and others, *East Asia,* pp. 464-465.
[20] Jiang, 'Foreign Christianity,' Ting K. H., *Chinese Christians Speak Out* (Beijing: New World Press, 1984), p. 21.
[21] Tung Cheming, *An Outline History of China* (Hong Kong: Joint Publishing Company, 1982), pp. 168-169.
[22] Adeney, *Church's March,* pp. 38-39; and Patterson, George N., *Christianity in Communist China* (Waco, TX: Word Books, 1969), p. 29.
[23] Mooneyham, *China: New Day,* pp. 135-136.

the Heavenly Kingdom of Great Peace. Hong was born to poor peasants of Hakka stock and of Confucian ideology. From having failed the Confucian examinations twice mixed with the perceptions of Roberts's fundamental teachings, Hong became embittered and neurotic. He sensed a confirmation from the Bible for visionary hallucinations that he contributed to his concept of a divine and liberating mission.[24] He and his followers ruled much of Southern China from Nanjing from 1853 to 1864 and preached an Old Testament Protestant Christianity. Hong was a militant, moralist, monotheistic evangelist, who outraged the missionary community for his embellishment on God's Word. He proclaimed himself to be the brother of Jesus, and injected the Chinese family system into the concept of heaven with wives for God and Jesus.[25] The Christianity Hong declared was distorted to unite people in rebellion. In the beginning the missionaries supported him and his endeavors, until they discovered what heretical doctrines he represented in Nanjing.[26] However, Hong, in the minds of the Chinese people, was connected to the missionary movement.

The Chinese intellectuals found it difficult to accept Christianity because of the inconsistency between imperialistic attitude displayed by the Western countries in their political aims against China and what the Bible taught against this type of oppression. Then they noted that these governments were using religion for their bureaucratic benefit.

The missionaries caused conflict by deviously acquiring more access to different areas of China and demanding indemnities for minor incidents against them. Even though the missionaries protested the inhumane punishments exacted by the Chinese, many complained that the discipline rendered against their opponents was too lenient. The situation worsened when the Protestant missionaries arrived in the interior for they quarreled with the Catholics, who established work there years earlier. Their aggressive manners with a lack of the Chinese language and customs exasperated the diplomats.[27]

---

[24] Cheneaux and others, *China - 1911*, p. 89.
[25] Fairbank, *China*, pp. 107, 211.
[26] Wu Qiwei [pseud.], Professor at Nanjing Union Theological Seminary (Interview, 6-9 December 1998).
[27] Cheneaux and others, *China-1911*, p. 275.

Events Influenced Attitudes towards Missionaries

The weak Qing Dynasty could not resist the growing Western encroachment on China. The unequal Beijing Treaty of 1861 permitted both Catholic and Protestant missionaries into the interior where soon institutions were established in every province. Then more missionaries arrived to work in the hospitals, schools and colleges, introducing Western science and technology and leading in campaigns against opium smoking, prostitution, and the long-time social custom of foot-binding of baby girls. The education and suggested changes may have been of great value; nonetheless, strong spiritual Chinese leaders were not being produced.[28]

Unequal treaties augmented the animosity against the Western missionaries throughout the 1860s, and the Confucian scholars distributed printed leaflets and placards containing anti-Christian propaganda. Usually property damage was the only repercussion experienced; however, at times violence ensued and people were slain. In 1868 at Yangzhou an estimated ten thousand people attacked the China Inland Mission compound. By 1869 the incensed Chinese had killed three Catholic priests and 130 Chinese Christians.[29]

In Tianjin, during the summer of 1870, unchecked violence erupted after rumors that Christians were maiming Chinese people and that all types of illicit sex acts were being performed. In actuality, the zeal for saving souls had led Catholic mission orphanages to accept, and even seek out, those who were fatally ill and those abandoned, to baptize them before they died. When hostile Chinese exhumed these infants, it invariably led to a highly emotional response.[30] The Catholic Sisters of Charity came under scrutiny and suspicion for accepting all orphans and even offering pay to those who delivered them to their care. In some cases kidnappers may have exploited the orphanages for the small fee involved. Priests were portrayed as extracting a dying person's eyeballs for scientific purposes while administering extreme unction. The accusations of sexual perversions were portrayed in pamphlets as outright pornography, which attracted readers

---

[28] Adeney, *Church's March*, p. 40.
[29] Ibid, pp. 187-189.
[30] Jonathan D. Spence, *The Search for Modern China* (New York: W. W. Norton, 1990), p. 204-206.

and helped to discredit Christianity.[31]

The Xinjie Church, the first Protestant church built in China, was constructed in 1848 in Xiamen of Fujian Province, declared a treaty port city at the end of the First Opium War.[32]   Brochures pointed out that church structures were built adversely to the *feng shui*, or the geomantic spirits of the wind and water.   The display of this literature aroused the public to take action.   The interruption of traditional order through the misunderstanding of the Christian meaning of salvation stirred hostility and incited thousands of incidents, and some 240 riots or attacks on missionaries within the years 1860 to 1899.[33]

In May 1895, rumors of a plan for foreigners to invade Sichuan provoked violence in Chengdu and surrounding communities where seven churches were burned.   That August a White Lotus Society group, the Vegetarian Sect, murdered nine foreign missionaries and two children, and each incident caused the foreign powers to demand heavy compensations reinforced by the gunboat policy.[34]   The next step was accusations that missionaries were foreign spies, and arrests were made.   Even groups of missionaries were arrested – some without being formally charged – and sent to prison for a few years, then expelled from the country.   Chinese Christian clergy and believers were also tormented.[35]

During the great famine of 1877 through 1879, the Christian outreach touched many not only with the message of personal salvation but also with relief to basic human needs.   Mission hospitals sought to minister to the plight of the blind and deaf, and the orphanages cared for homeless children.[36]   Dr. Timothy Richard, a convert during the Welsh revival who came to China under the English Baptist Missionary Society, wrote the following in his diary about the famine:

> Heard stories at the inn that night of parents exchanging their children as they could not eat their own, that one dared not go to the pits for coal as mules, donkeys, and

---

[31] Fairbank and others, *East Asia*, p. 573.

[32] ' "Oldest Protestant Church in China" Prepares for 150th Anniversary,' *Amity News Service*, Vol. 7, January-February (1998) 26.

[33] Fairbank and others, *East Asia*, p. 573.

[34] Cheneaux and others, *China-1911*, p. 324.

[35] Ladany, 'Religious Policy,' David Aikman (ed.), *Love China Today* (Wheaton: Tyndale House Publishers, Inc., 1977), pp. 75-76.

[36] Mooneyham, *China: New Day*, pp. 136-137.

their owners were liable to be killed and eaten... I heard from other eyewitnesses that they had seen 270 dead on the roadside in three days.

Richard saw that China needed the technology of the West especially during the famine. Religiously, he was one of the very few missionaries who made an attempt to bridge the differences between the Roman Catholics and the Protestants.[37]

Although many positive contributions of compassion complimented the Christian message of Christ, the Chinese always remembered those who came in the name of Jesus were on missionary gunboats. This memory fueled the Boxer Rebellion, encouraged by Empress Cixi.[38] Boxers entered Pingyuan in October 1899 and, because of the advantage taken by Christians through unequal treaties, they ravaged the homes of the Christians. At that time the Chinese authorities executed most of the dangerous Boxer leadership. Then on June 13, 1900, groups of Boxers entered Beijing to unite with other bands in the city. American soldiers provoked them that evening, and they started to burn churches and massacre Christians.

The officials whom Empress Cixi had assigned to negotiate with the Boxers persuaded her to place her trust in them to clear out the foreigners. She then gave the foreign ministers twenty-four hours to evacuate Beijing, and ensured them safe passage to Tientsin. However, after the Boxers murdered a German official, Von Ketteler on his way to the *Tsungli Yamen* government offices the morning of June 20, 1900, Cixi declared war on the foreign powers on June 21, 1900.[39]

The foreigners and Chinese Christians were placed under siege in Beijing within the Catholic cathedral and the legation quarter.[40] There, 76 foreign combat soldiers, 6 foreign children, and several hundred Chinese Christians lost their lives, though the Boxers suffered even more casualties. All aliens in China were in danger, but missionaries and Chinese Christians were in more danger because most of them were beyond the security of ready exit that the port cities provided. In the outlying provinces to

---

[37] Patterson, *Christianity*, p. 29.
[38] Mooneyham, *China: New Day*, p. 138.
[39] Cheneaux, *China-1911*, pp. 331-332.
[40] Latourette, *The Chinese*, p. 391.

the Northeast over 32,000 Chinese Christians were slaughtered.[41] During the summer of 1900 the Boxers murdered 188 missionaries and missionary children.[42]

The victims of the Boxers suffered some terrible atrocities. Many missionaries and families were burnt alive in their homes. Women were soaked in gasoline and then set afire, and some European wives had their breasts severed and then were placed on the city wall until death. The Boxers hacked off the heads of many missionaries, their wives and children and Chinese Christians.[43]

Many of the foreigners did not want to retaliate; however, a number of American missionaries, to the criticism of fellow countrymen, were blood thirsty for revenge and demanded restitution.[44] It was Fredrick Brown, an American Methodist missionary, who led the eight allied foreign powers from Tianjin to Beijing to suppress the Boxers.[45] Upon the arrival of the alien troops, thousands of Boxers fled Beijing, and the allied soldiers pillaged the city. Some of the international military units were sent to the countryside after the Boxers to ostensibly track them down, but en route looted, raped and murdered innocent Chinese citizens indiscriminately.

Estimates of the number of Boxers killed reach into many thousands. The tally of innocent Chinese victims at the hands of both the Boxers and the International Relief Forces also was calculated into the thousands. During the rebellion, a grudge against a neighbor was opportunity to identify that neighbor to the Boxers as a Christian, and in the suppression the regiments failed to identify Boxers in hiding from the village peasants. An American general estimated, "it is safe to say that where one real Boxer has been killed since the capture of Peking, fifteen harmless coolies and labourers on the farms, including not a few women and children, have been slain."[46]

Although they had suffered and witnessed many of the

---

[41] Cheneaux, *China-1911*, p. 333.
[42] James and Marti Hefley, *China! Christian Martyrs of the 20th Century* (Milford MI: Mott Media, 1978), p. 13.
[43] Dennis Bloodworth, *The Chinese Looking Glass* (New York: Farrar, Straus and Giroux, 1966), p. 179.
[44] Nat Brandt, *Massacre in Shansi* (Syracuse, NY: Syracuse University Press, 1994), pp. 278-279.
[45] Jiang, 'Foreign Christianity,' *Chinese Christians Speak*, p. 25.
[46] Brandt, *Massacre*, pp. 269-270; Fleming, *Siege at Peking*, p. 253.

harrowing experiences, over 2,500 missionaries survived the Boxer Rebellion.[47] However, many China watchers thought that Protestant Christianity had been terminated in China. They claimed that the only converts were Christians just for the benefits they sought in association with the foreign missionary. The poor, who had nothing to lose by associating with foreigners, often responded to the Christian message for the wrong motives. They were known as "rice Christians," and it was thought that because of them the national church would die.

On the contrary, soul-searching revival resulted in confessions from missionaries that they had been ministering with arrogance and pride, and they beseeched forgiveness. Chinese pastors and church leaders admitted failing to provide adequate spiritual guidance for their churches. Family relations were united and prodigals plead for pardon. Within six years following the massacres the Protestant Church more than doubled.[48]

There was a definite lack of evidence of any indigenous work initiated by the Chinese Church from the time of the Opium Wars through 1900. A Western style of worship was maintained, and Christ was not portrayed as someone for the Chinese.[49] Throughout the 1890s about 200 Protestant missionaries arrived in China per year. By 1893 there were 1,500 Protestant missionaries with 40,000 converts, whereas the Catholics had 550 missionaries and 530,000 believers.[50] The 41 different Protestant mission boards represented a variety of denominational distinctions and varied patterns of church government. National church leadership was lacking because the focus of ministry was compassion for the poor, ill and suffering rather than leadership training, but where identification and integration with the populace was evident, there was acceptance and a following.[51] The missionary endeavor often was centered around denominational lines, adding confusion to defining Christianity, and Western forms of worship and community church structure that were culturally foreign to the Chinese.[52]

---

[47] Ibid., p. 270.
[48] Hefley, *Martyrs*, pp. 40-41.
[49] Hsu, 'Indigenous,' *Love China Today*, pp. 32-33.
[50] Cheneaux and others, *China-1911*, p. 273.
[51] Lea, 'Christian Churches, 1807-1949,' *Love China Today*, pp. 15-16.
[52] Wallis, *China Miracle*, p. 36.

MISUNDERSTANDINGS

Missionaries went to China with misunderstar
mores and were received with misconceptions
that which was observable and led to rumor. 1
very apt at concealing their true feelings, and e
were polite and intensely curious, it was known that they hated
foreigners. The Chinese found the alien to be grotesque, and since
they obviously lived on ships, they came to China to acquire land.
The opium market was then a scheme to deplete the strength
of national forces, and the Christian message was to gain the
confidence of natives to entice them to become traitors and spies
for these foreign powers. Then through these methods the final
plot was to bring soldiers upon China in her weakened condition,
and this foreign kingdom would take possession. Jesus the King,
according to the doctrine preached, was from a poverty-stricken
state and had come to take the beautiful and wealthy land of
China, and this is why his people had left their country. The two
Opium Wars were inadequate to secure China by force; therefore,
emissaries were sent as missionaries to convert Chinese citizens
to become traitors.[53]

There were many reasons why the Chinese were unreceptive
to Christianity. The failure of the missionary to observe the
importance of *feng shui*, for buildings to harmonize with the
natural setting in accordance with defined rules, was the cause
of much conflict.[54] The missionaries lacked grace in exacting
biblical law, and if a man had a wife and a concubine, the union
with the latter had to be dissolved to receive salvation. If a man
were even betrothed to a non-Christian girl, the relationship
would be terminated at the instigation of the missionary. When
the girl's family brought charges of promise breach, for which
Chinese law allowed heavy damages, the missionary would
appeal through his consul.[55] The Christian cliches that were
repugnant to the scholar as, "washing one's heart in the blood,"
and the label of *sinner*, for someone whose life obviously was
very moral without committing any blame-worthy act, was

---

[53] John Ross, *Mission Methods In Manchuria* (Edinburgh: Fleming H. Revell
Company, 1903), pp. 33, 60, 146-147.
[54] Chesneaux, *China-1911*, pp. 4-5.
[55] Victor Purcell, *The Boxer Uprising* (Cambridge: The University Press, 1963),
p. 135.

ted.[56] Of course much depended upon faith in what the Bible said to be truth and in a concept of the Holy Spirit to give illumination to the scripture and conviction of wrong.

The term *spiritual* was misleading in the Chinese concept if it was used in the Christian view of the spirit. There are two Chinese expressions for spirit: *jing shen*, or the humanistic term to describe mental attitudes and motivation, and *ling hun*, the eternal human spirit. Both were used but not in the Biblical sense, and *ling hun* did not describe a deity in spirit.[57] Therefore, the translation of the Bible was of utmost importance, and literacy to be able to comprehend its concepts was another concern.

There were many different versions of the Bible being produced in abundance. The problem of illiteracy hindered the expansion of the Christian message by the printed page. To facilitate literacy, some Bible societies decided to put the Chinese dialect in Roman letter form, which possessed the advantage of being quickly learned but lacked means of fully representing the sounds of the Chinese language.[58] Many methods were used to enhance the propagation of Christian ideology, and the most successful was to identify with the Chinese and their culture in acceptance and genuine respect.

DEVELOPMENT OF RELATIONSHIPS

Some of the missionaries who went to China became catalysts of influencing the West with Eastern civilization. Many changed the attitudes of their constituencies as internationalists and intermediaries between the two civilizations. In their quest to Christianize China, these missionaries were changed into broader persons, embracing both Western and Eastern cultures.[59] The Roman Catholic missionaries translated many of the Chinese classics and wrote extensively on China. During the 18th century, items from the Far East became a fad and Chinese plants were introduced. Chinese porcelain and designs were

---

[56] Wu, 'Confucianism and its Significance to Christianity in China,' *Ching Feng*, vol. XII, No. 1 (1969) 12-13.
[57] Adeney, *Church's March*, pp. 97-98.
[58] Herbert Hoilap Ho, *Protestant Missionary Publications in Modern China 1912-1949* (Hong Kong: Chinese Church Research Center, 1988), pp. 109-110.
[59] Steven W. Mosher, *China Misperceived* (Montclair: A New Republic Book, 1990), p. 45.

produced for the first time in Europe. Although there was foreign input into China all throughout the 19th and 20th centuries, very little of the Chinese basic lifestyle had altered with the exception of the introduction of Buddhism, which entered China through peaceful foreign contact.[60]

Many Chinese had misconceptions of Christianity as black magic, and they were convinced that missionaries used orphaned Chinese children for human sacrifice rituals.[61] However, they had not been a people limited by preconceived ideas but relied on *li*, or abstract reason. More than most races, the Chinese would give up their presuppositions when research proved this not to align with reason.[62] Chinese scholars expected a ready answer, and if a missionary was unable to give an answer, neglected to answer, or considered discussion of the issue as a waste of time, the scholar would scornfully walk away. Ignorance was considered unpardonable, and the teacher was determined to be unqualified. For a teacher to win respect of students, he or she should entertain the interruption of a question, and if it was suspected to be for foolishness, they must be able to disarm the opponent in good humor and maintain the esteem of the audience. Self-control was especially demanded of religion teachers as evidence that what they professed as truth was guiding in their own lives. Therefore, how an interruption was handled would be influential, for self-control was the most essential element of politeness in China.[63] The attitudes of compassion and desire to improve and be more productive demonstrated other virtues of character.

Chinese also responded to kindness demonstrated by institutions established by the Protestants for the Chinese society. They introduced the Red Cross, utilization of public play areas, social-service organizations, labor-saving machines, and improved methods of processing quality silkworm eggs.[64] It was also the missionaries who stood against the opium distribution and helped effect change in value of women in the Chinese society. While Hudson Taylor started from the bottom with personal salvation evangelism, Richard Timothy,

---

[60] Latourette, *The Chinese*, pp. 334, 341-342.
[61] Edwin E. Moise, *Modern China*, 2nd edn. (London: Longman, 1994), p. 36.
[62] Ross, *Manchuria*, p. 233.
[63] Ibid, pp. 138-139.
[64] Patterson, *Christianity*, p. 31.

from the top, in the late 1870s established the first hospitals, schools, a newspaper and a university, and worked down to evangelistic effort. Likewise, John Leighton Stuart was a missionary and an ambassador who founded the University of Peking in Beijing. He also taught Greek and New Testament and was dean of Nanjing Union Theological Seminary. These approaches contributed to the establishment of Christianity in China. By the early 1900s, ten to twelve percent of all college students, the future leadership of China, were Christians.[65]

Mission schools throughout China offered basic educational opportunities to both boys and girls of meager means. However, these schools were often viewed with suspicion, and missionary teachers often had to attract students with free food, housing, medical care, clothing and even a monetary allowance. These missionaries through schools and hospitals offered options and alternative worldviews, which influenced Chinese thought and practice in ways impossible to calculate.[66]

EXPANSION OF CHRISTIANITY

Revival movements characterized the Protestant Church in China throughout the early 1900s. Wang Mingdao's church drew thousands in Beijing. Canadian missionary Jonathan Goforth took part in this movement, and John Sung, the first to go into Manchuria in 1908, was recognized as China's greatest evangelist.[67] This era, referred to as the Chinese quickening, began through the prayer movement between 1900 and 1905. As a result of prayer, there was a noted widespread awakening during the years 1906 and 1907 with real revival throughout 1908, which continued until the 1911 revolution. This revivification even spread among Chinese university students in Japan.[68]

The number of missionaries began to double every eight years, and by 1905 there were 3,445 of which over 90 percent came from the USA or Britain. Their major Christian ministries were education and medicine.[69] The mission stations ministered

[65] Wu [pseud.] , Nanjing Seminary Professor (Interview).
[66] Spence, *The Search*, pp. 207-208.
[67] Wallis, *China Miracle*, pp. 37-40.
[68] Mooneyham, *China:New Day*, pp. 139-140.
[69] Mosher, *Misperceived*, p. 43.

to the sick, which proved a point of contact with the people. As the medical personnel helped with the ailments of their bodies, it was easier to speak to them about their spiritual lives.[70] Although signs of revival were obvious, at the 1907 Protestant centennial there was not a single Chinese present. This was evidence that the Christian missionaries, after one hundred years of ministering together with the Chinese, had not identified themselves with their Chinese coworkers sufficiently to recognize, respect, approve and accept them with equality as a vital part of the Church in China.[71] This attitude, whether intentionally or unintentionally, caused mistrust, but Christianity in China continued to grow and be vital.

With medical missions primary, missionary doctors were especially vulnerable to diseases during epidemics of smallpox, cholera, typhus, dysentery and malaria due to their proximity to patients during these plagues. More missionaries died of these dreaded diseases than from violence, yet the greatest loss of life was during the famine of 1906.[72] Through these times of pestilence, the Protestant Church continued to grow. By 1914 there were 5,462 Protestant missionaries in China, according to the 1915 edition of the *China Mission Yearbook*. In 1915 the number of all communicants, baptized or under instruction, forming the Protestant community totaled 526,108.[73]

During and after the revolution of Sun Yatsen in 1911, Christianity became a popular religion because the revolution was not anti-foreign; therefore it was also not anti-Christian. Christianity flourished and the fact that Sun, as father of the new republic, was a Christian helped tremendously. His successor, Chiang Kaishek, later became a Christian along with his brothers-in-law, T. V. Soong and H. H. Kung.[74]

Protestant groups used varied methods of evangelization to meet obvious needs to improve life and living conditions. In the realm of education, girls did industrial projects such as braiding

---

[70] L. C. Osborn & Mrs., Pearl Denbo and Catherine Schmidt, Data for 'Fresh Facts' received November 8, 1920, from the Chao Chend Mission Station (Archive 262-61 Missionary Headquarters of the Church of the Nazarene).

[71] Jiang, 'Foreign Christianity,' *Chinese Christians Speak*, p. 25.

[72] Hefley, *Martyrs*, pp. 59-60.

[73] Patterson, *Christianity*, pp. 30-31.

[74] Ibid, p. 37.

straw to supplement their studies while the boys learned to use industrial machines.[75] The Roman Catholics did not promote such diverse activities; their concentration was on building Christian communities by bringing thousands into echelon schools and often paying the tuition. Much of their time and energy was expended on baptizing infants in endangered health and maintaining orphanages to care for destitute children, to indoctrinate them into the Catholic Christian faith. Although the methods of the Catholics resulted in more converts, the Protestants formed more of a permanent impression upon the life of the country at large.[76]

The Bible, as a tool of evangelism, was the most widely circulated literature in 1910, but sales decreased by 1916 because the old Beijing version was depleted until the new translation came out in 1919. With the new editions of scripture available, commerce of Bibles increased significantly accompanied by the sales of portions to over 4,000,000 a year. This did not reflect the demand, as much of the distribution was gratis, but merely indicated the extent to which these portions could be supplied.[77]

EVENTS TOWARDS THE INDIGENIZATION OF THE PROTESTANT CHURCH

The missionaries' enthusiasm to enter China and propagate the Christian message was usually met with suspicion since they were the first to take advantage of the treaty terms. They were regarded as the cultural vanguards of imperialism. No denial of the accusation that missionaries were paid agents of their governments was ever accepted. The Communist Party utilized this theme in the 1920s to vilify the Christian movement.[78] Russian Communism, with its atheistic convictions, was especially influential through the anti-religious movement organized in 1922. The radical Communists elements in the Kuomingtang United Front were zealous in their activities, especially in 1926 and 1927 during its culmination of power, directed particularly against Christianity.[79]

---

[75] Proceedings of the First Four Annual Assemblies of the China District Church of the Nazarene, 1917-1920, (Archive 1091-29), p. 20.
[76] Latourette, *The Chinese*, pp. 470-471.
[77] Ho, *Literature*, pp. 182-183.
[78] Leslie Lyall, *God Reigns in China* (London: Hodder and Stoughton, 1985), p. 126.
[79] Latourette, *The Chinese*, pp. 466-467.

In the shadow of these sentiments, on May 1922 the National Assembly of the Chinese Church published the *Declaration of the Church*. Nine of the articles described the indigenous Church, which promoted the three selves of ecclesiastical church structure and the cultural concern of Christianity to be united with Chinese thought and traditions, to enhance the acceptance of Christianity by the Chinese people.[80] The first indigenous church to gain prominence in China was the True Jesus Church of Beijing, founded by Paul Wei in 1917. There were the Evangelical Church in Shanxi led by Xi Shengmo; the China Independent Mission founded by Yu Guozhen; the Church Assembly led by Tuosheng, and the Christian Chapel led by Wang Mingdao.[81] The final indigenous movement, before Communist governing of China in 1949, was the Jesus Family conceived from the Shangdong renewal in the early 1930s.

Although most missionaries did not become involved in politics, there were some who assisted their governments in drawing up treaties and legal documents, and these unequal treaties remained in effect until 1943.[82] Most mission boards stated their intentions not to meddle in government matters and described their activities of evangelism, establishing churches and schools, medical, literacy and industrial works.[83] This was intended to disarm any misunderstandings, or propaganda and be forthright with motives and plans for being in China.

With confidence that education was offered to promote literacy and vocational training, the Chinese took the opportunity. Many of the children who attended these mission schools remembered the Bible stories and songs and the fact that at Christmas time they received candy and gifts.[84] A desire for a Western education was evident, and the Protestants opened many schools, secondary, higher education, and for the handicapped. Some of the leading

---

[80] Eric S. Y. So, 'Timothy Tingfeng, Lew and the Indigenization Movement of the Church in China,' *Cheng Feng*, 39/3 September (1996) 240-241.
[81] Ibid., 241.
[82] Adeney, *Church's March*, p. 41.
[83] Policy of the General Missionary Board of the Pentecostal Church of the Nazarene to Govern the Work in China [see Minutes 1922], (Archive 305-14), p. 4.
[84] Chen Yenling, elderly Chinese, Madrid (Interview, July 18, 1998); and Zheng Xianyu [pseud.], elderly Chinese, Madrid (Interview, July 27, 1998).

Chinese educators were Protestant Christians or had studied in Protestant schools. Also they were instrumental in organizing Young Men's and Young Women's Christian Associations, as YMCA and YWCA, and leper asylums. Certain national leaders and heads of ministry of the Nanjing government were baptized Protestant Christians.[85] The Protestant YMCA and YWCA introduced modern sport activities and various social service reform programs. These events made a lasting impression on a great portion of the students even if it may not have been evident until later in their lives.[86]

On a national basis, the Protestants had made an impact; however, their organizational fractions created confusion and conflict. The First National Christian Conference organized by Dr. John R. Mott in Shanghai in 1922, virtually a clearing house of 130 mission organizations with a total of 6,250 missionaries, submitted all decisions to London and New York for approval. Only English was spoken in all the meetings for reports and minutes. In addition, the mission boards divided China into denominational spheres of influence. A survey in 1922 was entitled in Chinese, *China for Christ*, but the English, *The Christian Occupation of China*, seemed to disregard the feelings of the Chinese. Then with the May 30, 1925 massacre of Chinese laborers and students at the British Settlement in Shanghai, the students of the mission schools were not permitted to join students of the government schools in a demonstration in protest. These obvious acts of insubordination were incentives to attack Christianity as imperialist oppression and cultural invasion and for Chinese Christians to seek separation from foreign missions.[87]

Leaders of the anti-Christian movement of 1925 and 1926 were students who had returned from their studies in America, many of whom had been professing Christians. The most prevalent and influential cause for the animosity of these students toward Christianity was the character of reports on China delivered by missionaries on furlough and heard by these students.[88] The violence of the movement became characteristic, from kidnappings with a slice of an ear sent as warnings to killings if demands were not met. Finally, in 1926 the British Navy sailed up the Yangtze

---

[85] Latourette, *The Chinese*, p. 470.
[86] Luo, *Religion in China*, p. 28.
[87] Jiang, 'Foreign Christianity' *Chinese Christians Speak*, pp. 25-27.
[88] Wu, 'Confucianism,' *CF* (1969) 13.

Gorges and bombarded the city of Wanxian, and hundreds of Chinese were killed. Retaliation inflamed hundreds of Chinese churches to sever relations with foreign mission boards.[89] At that time there were more than 600 independent churches in China. When the Japanese invaded Jinan in May 1928 and slaughtered Chinese citizens, students from the Catholic school broke through the locked campus gates to join in the encounter against the aggressors.[90]

During the persecution that escalated in 1927, the missionaries migrated toward the coasts of China, and they discussed the three-self alternative of self-support, self-government and self-propagation. Even in recognition of the high rate of missionaries returning to their homelands, numerous missionaries and Chinese leaders still found it difficult to accept this proposal.[91] From 1927 on, an increased number of articles were written on politics and Christianity in direct response to the anti-Christian charges. Wesley Shen, in his article 'Christian Proclamation on Current Affairs,' contended that "Christians should not avoid politics should instead actively participate in it," that "imperialism and capitalism should be overthrown," and that, "missionaries who came with foreign gunboats should be opposed."[92]

Chiang Kaishek unified much of China under the Nationalist Party by 1928, and in the eyes of the missionary movement he won prestige because of his marriage to Wellesley graduate Song Meiling and his conversion to Methodism. With China's new Nationalist government headed by this Christian couple and a number of graduates of mission schools and American universities in official positions, the Protestants seemed to have become established in a way that the Jesuits nearly did over 300 years prior.[93] This was a time of enthusiastic growth among Protestants, of which Americans formed three-fifths of the total personnel within Protestant mission organizations throughout China in 1929.[94] Then November 7, 1931, Article 13 of the Chinese Soviet Constitution stipulated the aim was that all people have

---

[89] Hefley, *Martyrs*, p. 51.
[90] Luo, *Religion in China*, pp. 48-49.
[91] Lea, 'Christian Churches, 1807-1949,' *Love China Today*, p. 18.
[92] Ho, *Literature*, p. 216.
[93] Mosher, *Misperceived*, p. 45.
[94] Latourette, *The Chinese*, pp. 467-468.

real freedom of religious belief, and that the policy of separation of state and religion was to be carried out.[95]

Many of the Chinese Christians played an active role in the National Salvation Anti-Japanese Movement, and on July 6, 1936, Liu Liangmo, YMCA secretary, led some 5,000 youth in expression to defend their country. Christian churches organized shelters for refugees, rescued those who were wounded, gave condolences, and collected money for needs. Numerous progressive believers cooperated with the Chinese Communist Party.[96]

From 1930 through 1937 marked another period of Christian revival in China. Dr. Sung Sangtie preached about sin and personal conviction of sin. Through his work thousands of laymen were impressed to propagate the Christian message. Watchman Nee challenged people to a more profound commitment to the Christian faith, and Yung Chaotang taught the biblical pattern for the local church. Dr. Jao Yuming had a conference ministry and was founder of a particular series of spiritual training centers. Wang Mingdao took a courageous stand in his teaching Christian principles during the Japanese War.[97] The Protestant community numbered over 700,000 in 1936. In 1941 the Catholics reported more than 3,250,000 baptized believers in China.[98] Foreign missionaries had brought the Christian message of Jesus Christ, as savior to the Chinese people, a fact that must never be forgotten.[99]

The Sino-Japanese War in 1937-1945 was a time of testing for Christians. Many refugees from coastal areas fled Japanese tyranny to live in the northwest, which was very different from the comfortable life in the east. It was a radical break with the past including the unhealthy foreign mission control. The spiritual maturity through Biblical instruction and practical Christian disciplines received in the East came as a challenge to the rather immature Christians of Western China.[100] This war period resulted in a growing demand for Christian literature in the interior West and Southwest of China. The Christian Literature Society sent 18 tons of books to Kunming by way of Haiphong in 1939 to alleviate

[95] Luo, *Religion in China*, p, 135.
[96] Ibid., p. 49.
[97] Lea, 'Christian Churches, 1807-1949,' *Love China Today* , pp. 21-24.
[98] Latourette, *The Chinese*, p. 469.
[99] Wickeri, *Seeking*, pp. 33.
[100] Lea, 'Christian Churches, 1807-1949,' *Love China Today*, pp. 24-26.

the scant supply. Myron E. Terry's description of the situation:

Stocks of Bibles were parceled out with utmost care. If someone wanted to buy one, he must come personally. He must be introduced and must bring credentials from a pastor or a known Christian worker. When he had established his identity, he was then asked why he wanted a Bible. When he had established the sincerity of his purpose, the fact that he really wanted one for his own study, then he was allowed to purchase one copy, never two.

The effectiveness of Christian literature for influencing converts was not accurately calculated in that the intellectuals rejected it and most peasants were illiterate. Except for the Bible, which held best-seller position, most pamphlets and periodicals had low circulation. Chinese literati criticized the early Chinese Protestant periodicals written in easy literary form as grammatically wrong with poor literary style. Nevertheless, Protestant publications made a contribution to Chinese society. The *Woman's Messenger* was credited as the first women's magazine, and *Happy Childhood* was well received by both Christians and non-Christians as one of the three top children's magazines. The most important contribution to rural communities was the *Christian Farmer*, for it had a simple format of information. The Bible translated into the vernacular and different dialects made the greatest contribution during the Republican period. In 1946 the Christian Literature Society accomplished the biggest endeavor of the year in reprinting 5,000 copies of the hymnal.[101] The amount of literature that was printed and accepted, under the apprehension of the intellects and the illiterates indicated the openness to Christianity.

By the 1940s, the Chinese were more responsive to Christianity than in previous history although missions were suffering depletion in personnel. As the missionaries left, the missions distributed their properties to the churches, or Chinese Christian workers or the military confiscated it.[102] A growing nationalistic fervor was evident in anti-foreign Christian sentiments. Bandits struck missionaries because they were supposedly rich and valuable to hold for ransom. Therefore, scores were captured and numerous

[101] Ho, *Literature*, pp. 177, 187, 202, 248-250.
[102] Letter to the Swiss Counsel General in Charge of American Interests in China, Tamingfu (Archive Church of the Nazarene International Headquarters), June 25, 1942.

missionaries lost their lives.[103]   Again missionaries were being scandalized with rumors and charged with torturing hospital patients, refusing to feed the children in their orphanages, and murdering Chinese to eat their hearts. During the trial period they suffered cruelty. Confession brought release and exile from the area; otherwise, they were often imprisoned, beaten or put to death. On August 17, 1947, twelve Cistercian monks were brutally tortured before being buried alive. Authorities estimate that nearly a hundred foreign and Chinese priests were executed during that year.[104] This persecution gave rise to independent churches with no foreign connections.

Each indigenous church group had different doctrinal emphases, but in general they all maintained stress on basic Biblical principles. Their various weekly meetings consisted of prayer, Bible study, serving the sacraments of the Lord's Supper and social interaction. The most influential groups were the True Jesus Church, Christian Assemblies, of which there were more than 700 local churches by 1949 with excess of 70,000 members, and the Jesus Family started by a converted Buddhist. The leaders were men recognized as evangelists and teachers. In addition to the recognized organized churches there were many home gatherings, small groups of family members, friends and neighbors to have intimate Christian instruction and worship in the setting of a family dwelling. These communities of churches and groups were in opposition to the Communists' ideals, which could not be tolerated.[105] Still, the church had been prepared for the 1945 to 1949 period of atheistic antagonism.

In 1945 the Christian work among the students had gathered such momentum that a gathering of 200 students from all parts of China formed the first inter-university conference under the leadership of Pastor Tao Chungyin. This congress of youth was characterized with prayer and spiritual introspection, and marked by commitment of their lives to Christian principles and lifestyle.[106] This was a strong point of the Protestant Church for its encounter with the Communist Revolution of China in 1949.

[103] Latourette, *The Chinese,* pp. 472-473
[104] Richard C. Bush, Jr., *Religion in Communist China* (New York: Abingdon Press, 1970), p. 50.
[105] Patterson, *Christianity,* pp. 78-80.
[106] Lea, 'Christian Churches, 1807-1949,' *Love China Today,* p. 27.

On the eve of the formation of the People's Republic of China, the religious world of China revealed about 40,000 Buddhist temples and monasteries with 500,000 monks, nuns and uncounted followers, among the Han Chinese. An additional 4,600,000 Buddhists were counted among minority groups. The Daoists did not submit any statistics, but from ten Islam ethic minority groups there were 8,000,000 Muslims. Orthodox Christians were predominantly Russians residing in China. The Christian Catholics reported from 140 dioceses a total of 15,000 churches and 3,000,000 believers. Protestant Christians numbered 700,000 converts from 70 denominations and 121 mission societies that established 20,000 churches.[107]

The characteristic of the Protestant Church in 1949 was that of a short history of 115 years with nearly 1,000,000 adherents and a mixed but liberal dominance in theology. It was growing spiritually as it had experienced a revival movement each decade of the 1900s. It had accomplished independence from Western control as an autonomous body accompanied by well-trained mature leadership in all sectors of the Church.

The Church was, however, ill prepared for confrontation with Marxist ideology, which regarded Christianity as unscientific superstition to be opposed by progressive thought. Christianity has always been questioned as a tool of imperialism. These factors, along with Christian support of the Nationalist regime and their reluctance to participate in radical social reforms, placed them in a difficult position with the Communist Party.[108]

Thus had the Protestant Christian religion developed as it entered the era of Chinese Communism that formed the People's Republic in 1949 under Mao Zedong. All foreign missionaries were unable to contribute any support even from the outside, and the Chinese Church was forced to survive independently and autonomously as the Christian world from outside looked on, especially from Hong Kong and Taiwan.

THE CHINESE CHURCH UNDER COMMUNISM : 1949 – 1975

After a struggle for power with the Nationalists and Japanese, the People's Republic of China, PRC, under Mao Zedong as

---

[107] Luo, *Religion in China*, pp. 35-36.
[108] Leslie Lyall, 'The Chinese Christian Church under Communism 1949-1966,' *Love China Today*, pp. 41-42.

Communist Party Chairman was recognized as the government in control of Mainland China. The Nationalists had established their government on the island of Taiwan claiming to be the rightful government of China, which was recognized as such throughout the Western democratic world for some decades. The Christian Church in China found itself in this atheistic political context, which affected the status of foreign missionaries and the attitude of the Chinese Church in establishing its identity as an independent religious entity.

THE POLITICAL PERSPECTIVE OF THE CHINESE PROTESTANT CHURCH

A patriotic tradition developed within the recognized religions of China because there had neither been a national religion nor integration of religion and politics. The Catholic and Protestant Christians had gained their substantiation through Western powers. The attempt of Nationalists to use Protestant Christianity as a stage for foreign endorsement through regulations for the control and restriction of temples and monasteries led to the Haigu Muslim revolt in the late 1940s. After this Muslim rebellion assisted in establishing the People's Republic, in 1950, the Communist government enjoined the local governments to grant the customary holiday for marking the end of the fasting month of Ramadan to all Muslims. They were also given preferential treatment on their special foods and a tax exemption on slaughtering the beef and mutton used in their three Islamic festivals.[109] Otherwise, religion had very little interaction in the political strata of Chinese society and even less in the atheistic Communist regime.

According to Communist theory, religion originated from the incapability of primitive mankind to control nature with his simple mechanisms or explain the phenomena of their surroundings. Thus, they resorted to the help of spirits and the supernatural in the form of religious belief and ritual. The fundamental nature of idealism and religious theology derived from the imaginations of believers that developed apart from the material nature of the world. It was the result of the spiritual action of God or another divine force. The four authorities recognized by the Chinese

---

[109] Luo Zhufeng (ed.), *Religion under Socialism in China*, trans. Donald MacInnis and Zheng Xian (London: M. E. Sharpe, Inc., 1991), pp. 45-47, 71.

were political, religious, clan, and husband. They all became unstable when the Nationalist political authority was defeated. Communism expelled the Nationalists to become a new order, focused on eradicating the superstition of religious authority.[110]

At the heart of Marxist Communism was the aspiration to abolish the idea of God, yet provide hope of salvation for the human race.[111] Writer Chang Chihi developed the classic Communist thesis in an article, 'A Correct Understanding and Implementation of Party Policy Concerning Freedom of Religious Belief.' According to Chang, religion was a result of fear regarding forces in nature, which was eventually replaced by systematic religion when the exploiting classes used religion as a tool of oppression over the lower classes. While focusing on the spiritual world, the exploited were distracted from their misery, and their desire to revolt against their oppressors was weakened. They then bore their distress in the hope of a future utopia. Chang held that only when class exploitation had been eliminated from society and man's influence over nature had been developed would man's consciousness and scientific progressiveness been sufficiently nurtured that religion might gradually vanish.[112]

The assumption that human beings were the product of their environment and that dishonesty and cruelty of selfishness and corruption would disappear in a socialist society was proven false in that these characteristics were found in both capitalistic and socialistic societies alike. The proposed progressive scientific ideology of Communist atheism had not produced the positive qualities desired to establish the new society.[113]

Mao Zedong had certain intellectual and moral needs that required answers for personal salvation and hope for the human race. He refused the concept of a personal God, but his own statements denied some basic Marxist principles. In referring

[110] Stuart R. Schram, *The Political Thought of Mao Tse-tung* (NewYork: Frederick A. Praeger Publishers, 1969), pp. 184, 188, 257-258.
[111] David Aikman, 'Marxism, Leninism, The Thoughts of Mao Tse-Tung and Christianity,' David Aikman (ed.), *Love China Today* (Wheaton: Tyndale House Publishers, Inc., 1977), p. 103.
[112] Richard C. Bush, Jr., *Religion in Communist China* (New York: Abingdon Press, 1970), pp. 17 18, 24.
[113] David H. Adeney, *China: The Church's Long March* (Ventura, CA: Regal Books, 1985), 100-101.

to his own death, Mao expressed, "When I go to meet God."[114] Edgar Snow related from his interviews with Mao, who seemed to anticipate death, "going to see God," and "getting ready to see God very soon." Mao also had observed that "some people who claim to be well informed said there was a God. There seemed to be many gods and sometimes the same god [when called forth for self-serving political purposes] could take all sides."[115]

Chairman Mao recognized the attitude that the Party must maintain concerning religion in his 1957 essay 'On Correct Handling of Contradictions Among the People':

> We cannot abolish religion by administrative decree or force people not to believe in it. We cannot compel people to give up idealism any more than we can force them to believe in Marxism. The only way to settle questions of an ideological nature or controversial issues among the people is by the democratic method, the method of discussion, of criticism, of persuasion and education and not by the method of coercion or repression.

Nonetheless, the realities of persecution have been beyond doubt.[116] Mao's paradox was in denouncing the need of religion with a coherent set of ideas peculiar to Confucian moral and ethical behavior. He then linked these values to Daoist principles of achievements beyond human reasoning. Chinese people traditionally had been curious in respect to the relation between religion and communal concerns, and Communism provided them with a new set of ethics and an understanding of non-rational phenomenon. Consequently, Mao made his political thought into an ideology encompassing reasoning and faith.[117]

In the interest of promoting Communism among the religious sector of Chinese, writer Ya Hanchang made an astute observation: he recognized that administrative orders to abolish theism

---

[114] Aikman, 'Marxism & Christianity,' *Love China Today,* pp. 104-105, 117.
[115] Robert Jay Lifton, *RevolutionaryImmortality, Mao Tse-tung and the Chinese Cultural Revolution* (New York: Vintage Books, 1968), pp. 12-13.
[116] Lesie Lyall, 'The Chinese Christian Church under Communism – 1949-1966,' in David Aikman (ed.), *Love China Today* (Wheaton: Tyndale House Publishers, 1977), pp. 51-52; Bush, *Religion,* pp. 32-33.
[117] Lucian W. Pye, *Mao Tse-tung* (New York: Basic Books, Inc. Publishers, 1976), p. 254.

would only serve to drive religion underground and turn an open activity into something clandestine. It also would promote and strengthen the faith of the theists who would become more fanatical and promotional of their beliefs, and less possible to dissuade from their religion to become advocates of the ideals of Communism.[118]

Communism thrived on class aversion and anger at exploitation, for these were the life of revolution and struggle. Christianity revealed an opposite view with the attributions of the Holy Spirit, the third person of the Christian Trinitarian Godhead, as love and joy.[119] Yet, the missionaries and church leaders noted a certain level of moral discipline from the advancing Communist soldiers who never resorted to plunder, rape, or abuse, nor were any immediate demands placed on the churches. At that point the Communists did not want to antagonize the Christians before establishing their regime, for they also had realized that the missionaries afforded them certain needed expertise.

Nevertheless, by mid-1950s the Chinese Communist Party had implemented a plan to dislodge the influence of Christianity throughout China.[120] A fundamental Party policy and condition was to respect and protect the freedom of religious belief. The aim to establish the socialist system was to unite the religious believers and the nonbelievers for the endeavor to attain Communism. To exclude religious believers from participation due to their differences of world-view would hinder the objectives of the Party and commit the error of the closed-door policy of the political conservative Marxists.[121]

Communists are historically materialists who realize the existence of religion as a fact. Convinced that religion would disappear from society as it develops, there would be no need for coercive measures to eliminate a creed. To realize socialist construction within a united front effort, all people were needed to participate, including the religious citizens. To encourage such cooperation, the policy of religious freedom,[122]was ensured in

[118] Bush, *Religion*, p. 33.
[119] Aikman, 'Marxism & Christianity,' *Love China Today,* p. 120.
[120] Arthur Wallis, *China Miracle* (Clumbia, MO: Cityhill Publishing, 1986), p. 43.
[121] Luo, *Religion in China*, pp. 132-133, 137.
[122] Philip L.Wickeri, *Seeking the Common Ground* (Maryknoll, NY: Orbis Books, 1990), p. 93.

Document 19 of the Constitution of the People's Government. In China's first constitution adopted in 1954 at the People's Congress, Article 8 declared that "Citizens of the PRC enjoy freedom of religious belief."[123]

Article 147 of the Criminal Code admonished cadres who might illegally deny citizens to practice their legitimate right to freedom of religious belief or impinge the customs of the minorities with legal measures of up to two years imprisonment. The clergy of the different religious organizations were assured the freedom to fulfill their religious function, but they were to be politically educated to become united in support of socialism. Each religion was to have its own national and local organization. Specific places of worship were to be arranged for *normal* religious activity. Each religion had the right to edit, publish and distribute its literature. The various religions were free to open religious schools and colleges to train a new generation of patriotic clergy. The citizens of China had the constitutional right to believe in a religion and propagate theism, or conclude the validity of and propagate atheism. To ensure this freedom, in 1951 the government instituted offices of the Religious Affairs Bureau, RAB, at every level. The Chinese Communist Party, CCP, had the task of educating the people about dialectical historical materialism and a scientific worldview without compromising relations with religious followers.[124]

Religious believers had the same responsibility as ethnic nationalities to support the leadership of the Communist Party, and the socialist system, be patriotic, maintain national unity, pursue the four modernizations, and be active for socialism. A method was to be devised to distinguish *normal* religious activities from those considered illegal, criminal and counter-revolutionary in religious disguise as superstitions and concepts of spirits.[125] Responsibility meant the freedom to make decisions about religion. For this reason freedom of religious belief was to be reserved for adults. To indoctrinate a child would deprive that child of this freedom, but the children were placed in national boarding schools where atheism would be taught daily.[126]

The Central Committee of the CCP had ordered a former RAB

---

[123] Luo, *Religion in China*, p. 143.
[124] Ibid, pp. 139-140. Italics added by author for emphasis.
[125] Ibid, pp. 141-142. Italics added by author for emphasis.
[126] Hank Paulson, *Beyond the Wall* (Ventura, CA: Regal Books, 1982), p. 38.

official, according to his report, to promote the constitutional provision for people who had religious belief and to maintain that freedom, and to ensure the non-believer to have freedom, including the freedom to counter religion. People also had the right to change religious belief, which would enable them to be affiliated with several religions groups at once as well as introduce different religious ideas and openly oppose doctrines and practices within each religious association.[127] A creed was to be an internal private concern, not to affect relations with others or the state, as true freedom. When doctrine was expressed in a sermon, inspiring action or association, it might be considered as counter-revolutionary on ambiguous grounds determined by the state. Religion was only to be taught within the confines of the church or temple structure. Public places were not religiously orientated and might be used for atheistic teachings. The strict separation of church and state severely restricted the range of religious activity. To conduct atheistic education in the school and university systems was not considered contradictory to the religious policy of the CCP. [128]

The provision to restrict religious counter-revolutionary activity was accounted for under Article 99 of the PRC Criminal Code to guard against those who organize feudal superstitions and sects involved in these activities with a prison sentence, or public surveillance and deprivation of political rights.[129] These documents of order for the new Communist Party were put in place to protect and augment its plan to maintain control. The implementation of religious policy meant the involvement of each individual with their neighbors in dialectic encounter. This was to encourage disclosure of thoughts that were considered wrong and to accuse the neighbors of such thinking. Polite engagement of accusation was considered bourgeois. Each person was involved in three peer groups: immediate residence, those with whom he or she worked, and associates. Everyone had an active involvement in at least one of these groups. At all levels of society and at regular intervals throughout the years, intensive programs of ideological education were instituted to counteract religion with

---

[127] Bush, *Religion*, p. 18.
[128] Ibid, pp. 18-21.
[129] Luo, *Religion in China*, p. 142.

atheistic training.[130]

From the beginning of the new regime, Catholic missionaries were in a vulnerable position since the Vatican was known for its emphatic position against Communism. Those missions involved in education opposed the educational policy of the Communist Party; religious freedom was permitted but religious classes could only be authorized after regular class time and on the freewill of students without coercion.

The new requirements for all students from the level of normal school to university in all departments included courses in historic and dialectic materialism and the doctrines of the New Democracy. An additional prerequisite for Arts and Law Schools was a three-hour a week course in approved political economics. The faculty and students of all educational institutes were to listen to interminable lectures and participate in intensive discussion groups so they could place their confidence in the Party objectives. Communist students soon secured control within these groups over Christians as well as other non-Communist entities. The Young Communist League attained power as a prominent organization on every university and college campus, and chances for honorable employment depended upon the student's adjustment to the re-educational process.[131]

Methods Used by Communist Government to Discredit Religion

Rural Chinese Christian leaders who maintained their sectarianism and anti-Communist stand with the Nationalists against the Party were another source of conflict. The Communist cadres viewed religious activities as superstitious or foreign.[132] Marxism taught that religion was unscientific and a superstitious opiate to calm the distressed into an indifference and prevented social change. Consequently, Marxists portrayed Christianity as an evil allied with imperialism, as an implement of oppression for the political subjugation of China.[133] It was commonly known that Karl Marx borrowed the choice phrase "opiate of the people," in reference

---

[130] Bush, *Religion,* p. 34.
[131] Ibid, pp. 62, 72-76.
[132] Wickeri, *Seeking,* p. 119.
[133] Leslie Lyall, *God Reigns in China* (London: Hodder and Stoughton, 1985), p. 127.

to religion, from Charles Kingsley.[134] Another well-known phrase by Friedrick Engles described religion as "the fantastic reflection in men's minds of those external forces which control their daily life."[135] The Communist statements about religion were adopted to portray of its eventual decline and disappearance from society and to promote methods to expedite its degeneration.

In conjunction with the effort to effect Party policy, the RAB was to investigate the religious organizations and the activities of their personnel. They were to control all religious activity and direct the different religions into the appropriate organization with Protestant Christians in the Three-Self Patriotic Movement, or TSPM. The purpose of the RAB was to fulfill the religious policy determined by the central government and to teach these policies to religious leaders and their disciples for the construction of socialism. Their position also was to confront counterrevolutionaries of all religions with regular visits to any suspect, promoting labor reform for resisters and prison or even death for those who did not cooperate or who openly rebelled against the Communist system. They were also required to entertain any foreign religious guests.[136]

The Communists had a plan to deal with those who resisted their systematic strategy of constructing a socialized state. Accusations were arranged with evidence enough for an arrest and imprisonment, interrogations and different forms of mistreatment followed a showcase trial until the accused signed a confession. Then the person, in a damaged emotional state of despair, was released to the authorities in Hong Kong.[137]

The Chinese Communist Party had published a Spanish publication, *The Catholic Church and Cuba: Program for Action*, for Cuban leaders, which described a method for subjugating the Catholic Church. The aim was to isolate any anti-patriotic elements and put them under such pressure that they would compromise their position through protest and become martyrs for their cause in criminal acts. Yet, Communists claim that no religious persecution occurred in China. To the contrary, they claimed to

---

[134] Bush, *Religion*, p. 22
[135] Ibid, p. 23.
[136] Ibid, pp. 29, 31-32.
[137] Heflay, *Martyrs*, p. 69.

promote liberation from the feudal, unpatriotic and reactionary forces of religious oppression to help release all Chinese people to unite in socialist construction.[138]

To motivate the peasants to oppose the religious temples and churches, Mao Zedong asserted that these shrines should have their idols removed, and the peasants should demolish them with their virgins and sacred arches. He said: "The gods and goddesses are indeed pitiful; worshipped for hundreds of years, they have not knocked down for you a single local bully or a single one of the bad gentry. Believe in the gods or believe in the peasant association."[139]

In many areas of China the peasant association made its offices from temples of the gods. They advocated appropriation of temple properties of superstition to defray the expenses of school maintenance for the association.[140] With the People's Republic Land Reform Movement issued by the Communist Party in June 1950, the property of temples, churches, schools, collective units and public land were confiscated except those buildings reserved according to law. Thereupon, the religious workers of each religion received the same tract shares as the peasants.[141]

The tactics advocated by the Communists for dismantling the Christian Church were to have it investigated and use agents to isolate and divide local churches from associating with each other and the outside world. Then individual Christians were to be segregated and this condition was to be used as proof that they were out of touch with the progressive world. Pastors or leaders were to be detached from the youth. These clergy were then to be discredited through rumors, but those who discredit themselves were to be promoted. Intimidation was to be utilized on the Christians with demands of endless reports, licenses, and regulations against allowing parents to bring their children to church or afford them Christian instruction. The constitutional law confined evangelism within the local church structure. The Party was to impose instrumental hierarchical structures to

---

[138] Bush, *Religion*, pp. 36-37.
[139] Mao Tse-tung, *Selected Works, Vol. 1, 1926-1936*, (New York: International Publishers, 1954), p. 48
[140] Ibid, p. 46.
[141] Luo, *Religion in China*, p. 65.

create competition and demise spiritual vitality. The discredit of Christian ideals was to begin at seminary level with state approval and regulation. They would attempt to seduce Christians to compromise Biblical principles, and those who resisted were to be encouraged to emigrate to the West. For Communism to maintain a positive image for world opinion, the dissenter would be allowed to leave.[142]

In 1950 the Communists implemented even more control over the Chinese Protestants when Zhou Enlai persuaded some of the Christian leaders to draw up the "Christian Manifesto." The contents affirmed Protestant loyalty to the Communist government and opposition to foreign imperialistic powers, feudalism and bureaucratic capitalism. Eventually three hundred thousand Chinese Protestants signed the Manifesto.[143] This meeting was the highest level of governmental attention given to the Christian Church, and the delegates considered it as an honor. However, it was an expression of the end of the missionary era. The Manifesto signified that missionaries would soon withdraw from China.[144] To refrain from agitating world opinion, missionaries were not executed, but their ties of financial support from constituents were suddenly severed between China and the West, and all properties owned by Western organizations were confiscated.[145]

A conference was called in April 1951 at Beijing for Chinese Christian leaders to consult with the Administrative Council of the national government on how connections with American Imperialism could be severed. The method proposed was the use of accusation meetings with those who had links with the USA. Although the rally for charges took place on April 18th, those accused were not imprisoned. Conversely, it was decided that those Christian organizations that had accepted American subsidies and were dealing with financial difficulties as the result of the American freeze on Chinese assets were to receive a tax exemption on their properties.[146]

---

[142] Paulson, *Wall*, pp 84-92.
[143] Hefley, *Martyrs*, pp. 73-74.
[144] Lyall, *God Reigns*, p. 125.
[145] James and Marti Hefley, *China! Christian Martyrs of the 20th Century* (Milford, MI: Mott Media, 1978), p. 69.
[146] Bush, *Religion*, pp. 44-45; Luo, *Religion in China*, p. 73.

The Implementation of Religious Patriot Organizations

Five religions were approved as the religions with legal authorization to be organized, hold properties and be practiced by Chinese citizens in China. Those recognized were Daoism, Buddhism, Islam, Catholicism and Protestantism.

May of 1953 marked the establishment of the Chinese Buddhist Association in Beijing, but it was not until April 1957 that the Patriotic Chinese Buddhist Association was activated. Buddhist reactionaries, supported by imperialist countries, instigated a militant rebellion in an attempt to attain Tibet's independence from China in March 1959. For the first time in history the national Daoist representative conference was held in Beijing for the formation of the Chinese Daoist Association during April of 1957.[147]

On December 16, 1950, a month after China entered the Korean War; the United States government froze all Chinese assets in the USA. China's reaction came on December 29 as an anti-American response addressed to Christian institutions demanding that "Chinese Christian churches and other organizations should immediately sever all relations with American mission boards."[148] After the Three-Self Patriotic Movement, TSPM, Protestant association, originally the Resist America, Aid Korea, Three-Self Movement, had been instituted in 1951; church services were only permitted in authorized buildings at prearranged hours with a government representative present. By 1958 the number of open churches had diminished in Shanghai from two hundred to twelve admissible churches, and in Beijing only four of sixty-five were still in operation.[149]

In conjunction, denominational ties were attacked, and the RAB ordered churches to unite in integration, which resulted in many church buildings closing. During the Chinese New Year of 1958, a conference of all pastors was called for political training, and a strong attack was made against supernatural miraculous effects.[150] A reformation program for intellectuals was initiated with special studies to align their thinking, world-view and habits with Marxist concepts and categories of expression. Particularly,

---

[147] Luo, *Religion in China*, pp. 68-69.
[148] Ibid, p. 77.
[149] Hefley, *Martyrs*, p. 74.
[150] Lyall, 'Church 1949-1966,' *Love China Today*, p. 46.

missionary influence from foreign schooling was to be restricted if not eliminated.[151]

Communist Party Campaigns that Effected Chinese Christians

Mao Zedong released many political prisoners in 1957 marking a deceitful calm in a promotion of the state policy, "Let all flowers bloom and all schools of thought contend." Church leaders accepted this invitation to voice grievances and charged the Three-Self Movement with placing limitations on their political rights. Then the Anti-Rightist Campaign of that summer attacked those who had spoken out. Through these open complaints, the Communist Party knew who the resisters were and arrested them for crimes against the state. Those pastors were forbidden to preach or visit members of their congregations, and the majority were labeled as "rightists" and arrested in April 1958.[152]

Religion also became a major target during the Proletarian Cultural Revolution, 1966 to 1976, that aimed at eliminating the four olds of customs, thoughts, habits and cultures. The Red Guards, devised by Mao Zedong, abolished organized Christianity and may have been the peasants Mao had cited to for pulling down the idols. Maoists would agree that when Mao referred to the peasants pulling down idols it signified that any idols would serve when the peasants finally decided to act. During this time of chaos, Mao was attempting to produce what the Christian Church had claimed to accomplish: a new nation of people who were selfless and devoted to service toward their fellow citizens.[153]

During the Cultural Revolution, the Chinese Communist Party's prominent theoretician, Liu Shaochi, fell from favor. He experienced the prophesy he had written in September 1954 that "circumstances... in accordance with the law, to deprive feudal landlords and bureaucrat-capitalist for a given period of their right to vote and stand for election." Accordingly, counterrevolutionaries were excluded from their rights as citizens, a

---

[151] Steven Uhalley, Jr., *Mao Tse-tung a Critical Biography* (New York: New Viewpoints, 1975), p. 111.

[152] Hefley, *Martyrs,* p. 75; and Chao, Jonathan (Interviews), Richard Van Houten (ed.), *Wise as Serpents Harmless as Doves* (Pasadena: William Cary Library, 1988), pp. 18-19.

[153] Lyall, 'Church 1949-1966,' pp. 557-58; Bush, *Religion,* p. 31.

category in which religious believers have on occasion been classified. By this provision, the constitutional freedom of religious belief was withdrawn on the premise that the citizen had committed an unlawful act.[154]

During these Cultural Revolution years it was unlawful to read the Bible, and the people were not taught to live out normal human relationships. Communism said that one's desires were not important, and father, mother or brother may be close but not as close as Mao Zedong.[155] Mao was placed at a level of divinity during that time, and his little *Red Book* was considered the light of instruction for all.

THE CHRISTIAN CHURCH PERSPECTIVE OF ITS EXISTENCE IN CHINA

Christianity was isolated as it failed to gain the confidence of the Chinese people. At the threshold of a new political change for China in 1949, the Chinese Church was required to find its own identity within its people and culture.[156]

During the civil war between the Nationalists and the Communists, the Communists as policy would convert churches into horse stables for the People's Liberation Army. After the new regime was in place, such abuses against religious sites were investigated and denounced as erroneous. Prime Minister Zhou Enlai declared religious freedom in a document published in 1950; though, he confided to Christian leaders, " Don't put your faith in this paper to change things. The only way that your religion can be vindicated before the people is through your own exemplary conduct. Now that the foreigners are gone, this burden rests on your shoulders."[157]

Three situations characterized Protestant Christianity in the commencement of new China. First, there were degrading rumors towards the Communist Party, and others clamored for the restoration of the Nationalists. Second, some Protestant Christians sought ways in which the churches could maintain their dependence on foreign missions, and third, there were those

[154] Bush, *Religion*, p. 16.
[155] Yuan Aiguang, Medical Doctor, Madrid (Interview), 17 July 1998.
[156] Denton Lotz (ed.), *Spring Has Returned* (McLean, VA: Baptist World Alliance, 1986), p. 33.
[157] Timothy Wu, *Sheltered Through the Storms: A Chinese Pastor Preserved by God* (Palo Cedro, CA: Wayside Impressions, 1996), ch. 10.

who sought independence and self-sufficiency.[158]

The Termination of the Role of Foreign Missions

The missionaries concluded that their presence was either a source of embarrassment to Chinese Christians who had already been labeled as running dogs for the imperialists, or that their imperiled situation was cause of concern for the Chinese Christians who already were under stress. It must be remembered that a foundation had already been established toward church indigenization and diminution of the missionary role in China.[159]

As expressed by Steven Neill in his book *Call to Mission,* "Christian missionary work is the most difficult thing in the world. It is suprising that it should ever have been attempted. It is suprising that it should have been attended by a measure of success. And it is not at all suprising that an immense number of mistakes have been made."[160]By the early 1950s a post-mortem of foreign missions had begun. Professor Arthur Glasser of Fuller Theological Seminary, who had been a missionary in China during this epoch, identified mistakes made by missionaries: they displayed an abysmal ignorance regarding Chinese history and culture and an indifference to local customs; aggressive teaching of Western values became prevalent with public denunciation of idolatry, local religions, and ancestor adoration; and missionaries failed to contextualize the scripture for practical application in the Chinese setting. They also were insensitive in establishing extensive mission compounds and asserting certain rights for foreigners gained through the foreign military victories of Opium Wars; these were used even to legally protect their converts and provide for their social needs while neglecting those of non-Christians.[161] The semi-colonial status created unemployment and an atmosphere where many were forced into thievery, begging, prostitution, and superstitious practices.[162]

The American governmental economic sanction against Chinese

---

[158] Lou, *Religion in China,* pp. 55-56.
[159] Bush, *Religion,* pp. 48-49.
[160] Stephen Neill, *Call to Mission* (Philadelphia: Fortress Press, 1970), p. 24.
[161] W. Stanley Mooneyham, *China: A New Day* (Plainfield, NJ: Logos International, 1979), pp. 153-156. Arthur Glasser, retired professor at Fuller Theological Seminary (Interview, 15 December 2000) Confirmed, although he could not give exact reference since the disruption of his files since retirement.
[162] Mao Tse-dung, *Selected Works,* p. 95.

assets on December 16, 1950, not only cut financial support from all Christian organizations throughout China but also caused a reactionary response from the Communist government. An edict, just weeks later on December 29, stipulated registration within three months of all societies that had received foreign funds and subsequent reports every six months.[163]

It was also in 1950 when the great exit of missionaries from China began. Before they could receive permission to leave, the missionaries were to transfer the deeds to all properties and the control of educational, medical and charitable institutions to the government. Furthermore, the prerequisite for an exit visa was to place a notice in the local newspaper that invited anyone who might have a complaint against the missionary to file it. Then a local citizen had to sign as a sponsor for each missionary leaving for assurance of positive future conduct. Some missionaries were detained for public trial and sentencing.[164]

It was seldom that the Communist government would simply deport a missionary as other countries have done in the history of Christianity. Strategically essential for the Communists was the priority to charge these missionaries with some crime against the people to justify their expulsion to the outside world, the people, or to the government. Thus, an old radio receiver found in a missionary's possession could be interpreted as ownership of a transmitter for espionage. Even if a search group found a typewriter, it might have been concluded to be a telegraphic instrument. Many missionaries who suffered accusations from the press and accusation meetings, in which many of their Chinese Christian colleagues and friends participated as accuser, were able to accept the fact that these actions were due to social and political pressure. Chou Enlai and other officials had clearly communicated that all ties were to be severed with imperialistic nations if the Church was to survive in Chinese Communist society.[165]

In deciding what was best for the Chinese Church, the Protestant mission boards determined that their presence would only serve to hamper the Chinese Christians. To conform, it was agreed to evacuate, and by early 1952 all missionaries except for the

---

[163] Bush, *Religion*, p. 186.
[164] George N. Patterson, *Christianity in Communist China* (Waco, TX: Word Book, 1969), p. 48.
[165] Bush, *Religion*, pp. 61-63.

Roman Catholics had left China.[166] It was recognized by many that this sudden evacuation was the end of an era in Chinese Church history. The majority of the missionaries were hopeful, and when all foreign funds were terminated some like the pastor of the Tamingfu Church of the Nazarene initiated a business of a watch-repair shop to support himself and his ministry. The Chaochung Church of the Nazarene agreed to donate a tenth part of its grain for their pastor. On the other hand, it was also assumed that missionaries were needed for many more years, and many expected that the Chinese Church would dissolve.[167] The Western world was convinced that when the missionaries left it was as if God had been evicted from China, which was referred to as the "Closed Door." China was far from being closed, but the missionaries left the Chinese Christians with two different prominent situations. Some Christians were isolated, and others were in areas where they enjoyed Christian camaraderie and growth.[168]

The Beginning of the Chinese National Church Leadership

With all the missionary personnel expelled, the national church needed leadership with adequate Biblical training. The leaders of the new Communist order were avowed atheists but had a commitment to retain and protect the freedom of religious belief. In the beginning of the new regime, 1949 to 1950, this attitude was evident, and a document introduced to ensure that freedom. Those pastors trained by missionaries before the evacuation helped train others to pastor congregations. Timothy Wu was allowed to open a Bible school to train new pastors in Guiyang. After graduation these newly trained ministers would return to their home villages to pastor existing churches or start new ones. These short-term Bible schools offered a six-month course covering the entire Bible. Even the church leaders from minority groups of Miao, Yi and Buyi were trained through this course. The Church throughout China was finding a new identity, because the people had rediscovered faith in God for themselves. Christmas celebrations were allowed, and Christian literature was published. Church

---

[166] Wallis, *China Miracle*, p. 44.
[167] Peter Kiehn, 'The Past, Present and Future of the Church of the Nazarene,' Church of the Nazarene International Headquarters (Archive 604–15).
[168] Mooneyham, *China*, pp. 157-158.

169

leader Timothy Wu published a second edition of *New Life in the Wilderness* with some hymns attached, of which he was required to submit quadruplicate copies to the government for review. It was not only approved for publication, but reduced postal rates were granted for its distribution across China.[169]

Wu Yaozong, the YMCA secretary, drafted the instrument to ensure freedom of religious belief as the way for Chinese Christianity to give itself to the construction of new China, known as the "Three-Self Manifesto." This manifesto was sponsored by forty Chinese Christians and initially signed by 1,527 church leaders. It formed a pledge of allegiance by the Chinese Church to the People's government and obedience to the Communist Party. The Manifesto was given enthusiastic support through a special editorial in the *Rinmin Ribo, People's Daily,* that published it along with the list of signatures in the September 23, 1950, issue. Only the Anglicans refused to sign the document and were instrumental in generating a separate agreement. A number of the top clergy at the China Christian Council's fourteenth annual meeting that convened in October 1950 attempted to counter the Three-Self Manifesto with another declaration.[170] The distribution of the Manifesto, indoctrination groups within the church, the accusation movement, the Five Anti- and Three Anti- campaigns, Land Reform, and supporting the Korean War had placed the Church in a state of confusion.[171]

In 1952 a transition of power placed the conservative Communist Marxists in control of the PRC. This led to a more militant stance against foreign influences including Christianity. If the Church was to survive with governmental approval it would only be under a patriotic format. Foreign mission operations were forcibly closed, and the Chinese Christians reorganized into the Three-Self Patriotic Movement with the principles of self-government, self-support, and self-propagation.[172]

The Chinese Church still was comparatively young and had not had to concern itself with political relationships; it was unprepared to encounter State demands. Church buildings could only be used for worship on Sundays for one service a week, and the portraits of Mao

---

[169] Wu, *Sheltered,* ch. 8.
[170] Luo, *Religion in China,* p. 57; Lyall, 'Church 1949-1966,' pp. 42-43.
[171] Bush, *Religion,* pp. 199-200.
[172] Wu, *Sheltered,* ch. 9.

and Stalin were to be in place. In rural areas the church building was frequently used as a granary, which meant when it was full of grain no worship service could be held.[173]

The TSPM reported 18 percent growth in Chekiang Province, 22 in Shandong, 30 in Yangtse or Chiangnan. Anhwei Province increased in church membership by 2000 and Hunan by 3000 between the years 1953-1956. A conference held by students in 1954 reported 600 baptisms. The years from 1949 to 1955 was a period of missions, conversions, baptisms, and miracles. The different provinces reported sizable increases in church membership as the result of revival meetings after a period of religious persecution. In 1955 to 1960 even Tibetans were becoming Christian, and in 1960 there were 146 male and female students attending theological colleges in Beijing and Nanjing.[174]

The Opposition Faced by the Chinese Church

To support governmental policy meant that those charged as counter-revolutionaries or reactionary suspects were required to write out a detailed autobiography from age seven to the present and nothing could be left out, including thoughts. To encourage the process and ensure that no omissions occurred, receptacles were placed in every city, town and village into which the people were encouraged to inform on any suspicious elements by inserting an accusation slip.[175] A truck driver who had defected to Hong Kong gave the following description of his gruesome duties:

> I was conscripted by the Communists to drive one of their death trucks...at night... The victims were tied up hands and feet and loaded into trucks like logs – 120 of them to a truck. All night long I drove back and forth from the prisons to the river banks... They were simply dumped into the river and drowned.[176]

Missionary Helen Willis narrated her account of happenings during this era:

> It was a terrible time [the summer of 1951]. The victim, nicknamed the "Tiger," would be placed at a table round

---

[173] Bush, *Religion*, p. 186.
[174] Lyall, 'Church 1949-1966', *Love China Today*, pp. 54-55.
[175] Patterson, *Christianity*, p. 51.
[176] Harold H. Martinson, *Red Dragon over China* (Minneapolis: Augsburg Publishing House, 1956), p. 153.

which all his fellow workers were seated. All would point at him and shout "Confess." ...It was a wonderful opportunity for anyone who had a grudge, and many false accusations were brought...many businesses failed. There were endless suicides; ...I think it was forty suicides a day were taken to one hospital alone, and there were dozens of hospitals in Shanghai; and many more were taken straight to the morgue.[177]

The author lodged with a Chinese family in Shanghai that related the tragedy of family members who under the stress of being struggled against and fear had taken their own lives. The father had hanged himself in the very room where the family hosted the author, and the father's sister had jumped headlong from their home to her death in the alleyway below.

During this time many of the founders of indigenous Protestant Christian movements and their members were arrested. The son of the founder of the Jesus Movement was arrested in 1951, and in 1952 both Jing Tianying of the Jesus Family and Ni Tuoshen, known as Watchman Nee, were arrested. Wang Mingdao was arrested and given a fifteen-year prison sentence on August 8, 1955, without a trial. After thirteen months of torture, he broke down and signed a confession of being a counter-revolutionary offender and was released. Soon after his release he publicly retracted his confession with anguish over his weakness in denying his convictions and was imprisoned again. Wang was finally released in 1980 at the age of eighty.[178] These men had not compromised their conviction to not join the TSPM, but after the Cultural Revolution the Little Flock later known as the Local Assemblies and the Jesus Family, which dispersed into independent churches, registered and cooperated with the TSPM but remained independent to the point of being denominational.

In January 1956 the Shanghai Public Security Bureau arrested the followers of Watchman Nee in *Juhuichu*, the Shanghai Christian Assembly halls, as counter-revolutionaries. They were charged with colluding with American and Chiang Kaishek spies, plotting against the Communist Party by offering plans to bomb power

---

[177] Patterson, *Christianity*, p. 52; Willis, Hellen, *Through Encouragement of Scriptures*, pp. 125-126.
[178] Wallis, *China Miracle*, pp. 45-46.

plants, and raping numerous women.[179]

The pressure on the Catholic Church was evident as its leaders were brought to a final massive demonstration in Chongqing. Father John Tung appeared at the microphone and unannounced to offer himself as a sacrifice to bring understanding between the government and the church. Among the 4,000 Catholics gathered to witness this fraudulent trial of the Bishop of Shanghai, not one spoke to accuse him.[180]

Before 1952 about 100 clergy had died in jail, and in that one year more than 200 perished. By 1954 an estimated 500 additional priests had become martyrs, and after the Pope denounced the Patriotic Movement established in 1958, those who opposed the new church were imprisoned.[181]

The first representative conference of Catholic clergy in Beijing in 1957 adopted the decision to sever relations from Vatican control and realize the independence and self-reliance as the Chinese Catholic Church. During this time the National Chinese Patriotic Association was formally established. In March 1958 the priests of Wuchang and Hankou elected two bishops. The Vatican responded by declaring the elections invalid and threatened the participants with excommunication.[182] This marked the break with Rome, and within the next five years 45 priests were ordained as bishops by governmental direction. Many churches were then closed except those with priests who signed as part of the patriotic church. All of those did not necessarily deny their faith or compromise, but they had decided to preserve what could be rescued of Christianity in the atheistic setting. The priests who refused to sign went to jail and into forced labor.[183]

In 1957 Bishop Kaung claimed that Christianity in China was becoming more illuminated on the role of Christianity and the world, the church and state, belief and unbelief, faith and works. According to him there was a trend away from a world-denial theology to world-affirmation tendencies. This could be viewed from the opposition towards Mrs. Charles Cowman's devotional

---

[179] Luo, *Religion in China*, p. 59.
[180] Mooneyham, *China*, pp. 145-146.
[181] Hefley, *Martyrs*, p. 73.
[182] Luo, *Religion in China*, p. 64.
[183] Ladany (Father), 'Religious Policy,' David Aikman (ed.), *Love China Today* (Tyndale House Publishers, 1977), p 79.

book *Streams in the Desert,* which was condemned because of its view of acceptance of pain, suffering and sorrow as part of God's will. The fact that this was a favorite devotional of Chiang Kaishek contributed to its denunciation in Communist China.[184]

The campaigns promoted by the government did not accommodate religious beliefs or practices. The Great Leap Forward movement in 1958 called for complete collectivization into communal living. These communes were not devised to be anti-religious, but they did drive for increased production. The church laymen did not have the time or strength for worship and church activities. Many former church pastors worked full time in communes and tried to fulfill the ministry of a church in the little spare time they could muster.[185] The RAB started a struggle movement in all churches in the latter months of 1958, and innumerable church lay leaders were arrested. Some had no family in Shanghai, where they were taken, and had nothing to take with them to prison. With the food shortage in China from 1959 to 1962, an incalculable number of prisoners died of starvation. Some from outside the country tried to mail food to them, which aided survival of a few.[186] The isolation of prison was a time of purification through self- examination for many prisoners, who often propagated their faith to the prison guards.

During the years of severe oppression, whether a part of the official church or from independent congregations, while in public the Christians avoided even brief contact with each other if possible to circumvent any incidents of prolonged interrogation. The re-education labor program allowed no time for solitude and introspection.[187] It was an advantage for the growth of Christianity to have intervals of freedom for further evangelization to be followed by persecution to separate those who were not ready to commit themselves to the Christian life.[188] Many of the Chinese leaders experienced abuse and even loss of family members and demonstrated their commitment through the display of remarkable restraint and forgiveness.[189] Even though contact with other Christians was avoided, it could often

---

[184] Bush, *Religion,* pp. 234-235.
[185] Ibid, pp. 229-230.
[186] Chao, *Serpents Doves,* p. 13.
[187] Adeney, *Church's March,* pp. 193-195.
[188] Paulson, *Wall,* p. 98.
[189] Hefley, *Martyrs,* p. 42.

be sensed that another in the work place was a believer. It was a universal phenomenon, but it would put both parties in jeopardy to inquire.[190]

The situation in China can be very misleading: while the representative of the Party was present a tour guide claimed that religion was perfectly free. However, when alone he whispered in French to the priest who understood, not to believe a word he was being told.[191] In the family situation a Christian father related how he and his wife prayed together in bed, but feared telling their kindergarten daughter lest she might say something at school to bring distress upon them.[192] The author had two different Chinese reports on how they had learned English by secretly listening to Voice of America under the quilt in bed and reading Western books by flashlight. They knew it was forbidden because the Communist government feared the loss of control.

The most severe testing of the Christian faith was to see children suffer for the cause of their parent's religious conviction. Some families faced affliction from the children's school indoctrination that anything suspicious or reactionary about their parents must be reported. It must be noted that many children witnessed their parents' steadfast faith and accepted Christianity on their own as their parents risked the loss of employment opportunities for the Christian faith.[193]

A Christian teacher had to relinquish the coveted position of a high school teacher for the lesser wage as a factory laborer.[194] Party members who had power and influence often helped secure a position, benefits or privileges for a timely gift, and Christians also were frequently tempted to gain advantages in this manner. By falsifying reports a work unit could gain extra benefits, which would then be divided among the unit members. If Christians in the unit refused to collaborate because of their conviction for honesty, they could be in serious difficulty with their peers. Even the political attitude of a Christian was often evaluated for counterrevolutionary thoughts. Those who maintained distance from political discussion and avoided Party contact were frequently

---

[190] Ladany, 'Religious Policy,' *Love China Today* pp. 82-83.
[191] Ibid, pp. 77-78.
[192] Hefley, *Martyrs*, p. 77.
[193] Adeney, *Church's March*, pp. 195-197
[194] Paulson, *Wall*, p. 37.

suspect of subversive intellectualization.[195]

During the Second National Christian Conference of TSPM officials in 1961, the rural churches were criticized for permitting religious practices such as faith healing and exorcism, said to interfere with commune production. The impoverished conditions of church members were blamed on their excessive contribution for the church construction project. The time church members could have spent on digging irrigation ditches was perceived as wasted on meeting for prayer, and when the needed rains came the time of expeditious planting appeared to be squandered on a gathering for thanksgiving. These commentaries of Christian priority verify the vigor of life in the churches.[196]

However, in 1957 Bishop Ting Kuanghsun, an official of the TSPM and president of the Nanjing Union Theological Seminary, had declared that a theology of vague Christian moralism, liberalism, rationalism or the social gospel could not give spiritual satisfaction for China. Therefore, Chinese Christians have come to have a fuller faith in Jesus Christ as Prophet, Priest and King being Lord over all, and that his resurrection from the dead was victory over transgression, death and the spiritual enemy, Satan. Bishop Ting commented that Christians rejected the conclusion that materialists were progressive and idealists unenlightened, and he confirmed that Christians in reality are neither. Although it pertains to history, in essence Christianity was never a dogma and it had no economic base. The substance of Christianity was revelation and incarnation of deity, which transcended human, social and philosophical standards. He denounced the concept that Christianity was an opiate while the atheistic society blamed all evil on a corrupt social system. He argued that a transgression as sin was real in human life even in a positive social environment that might only limit the effectiveness of the transgressions of God's law. Forgiveness, salvation and grace, not social progress, could heal the sin dilemma.[197]

In a Communist society, where policy continuously changed and thought control was conspicuous, truth became relative: people endeavored to say the right thing regardless of its validity. For a Christian, integrity could result in dangerous consequences.[198] An

[195] Adeney, *Church's March*, pp. 200-202
[196] Bush, *Religion*, p. 243.
[197] Ibid, pp. 236-238.
[198] Adeney, *Church's March*, p. 199.

act of compassion could be interpreted as political subversive. In 1963, during a famine, one church learned that the neighboring commune was near starvation and initiated a project of sharing food. They were accused of sabotaging the distribution system and stealing, so two members pleaded guilty on behalf of the group. The commune reduced the ration for all church members, and they were required to replenish by installment that which had been given away.[199]

The Christian social norms taught by the Church were difficult to maintain. Christians, especially young women, were limited in finding a life partner with the same religious beliefs. Since there were fewer Christian men than women and some men chose non-Christian brides, it was difficult for Christian women to find a Christian mate. Beyond this, the Communist government opposed teaching that encouraged discrimination for marriage only within a certain religious faith.[200] The author observed this in Europe, where this dilemma remained or intensified for those Chinese who migrated overseas, especially if they wanted to remain within their ethnic community.

A compromised position often afforded a rationalized way of coping with social-cultural pressures in China. According to Hsu from his personal observation, for Catholics, an important part of their belief was to hire a religious leader to perform rites to improve the situation for relatives in purgatory. Especially in the villages, Christianity had been intermeshed with the traditional Chinese adoration of ancestors, and these rites would encourage the spirits of the deceased to help the living descendents. Because the fundamental way of life was polytheistic, a monotheistic religion was transformed into a polytheistic monotheism found in the saints, rituals and priestly hierarchy of the Catholic faith.[201] A great percentage of Chinese Christians were Catholic due to this paradoxical phenomenon.

The situation for both the Catholic and Protestant Church in 1964 was a naturally-formed contextual union in cooperative relationship with the Communist Party. They adopted a shrewd,

[199] Raymond Fung (compiled and translated), *Households of God on China's Soil* (Maryknoll, NY: Orbis Books, 1982), pp. 14-15.
[200] Adeney, *Church's March*, pp. 202-203.
[201] Hsu, Francis L. K., *Americans and Chinese*, 3rd edn. (Honolulu: University of Hawaii, 1981), pp. 250-251, 274-275.

realistic and positive approach toward the regime, perceiving the situation in China as an opportunity for additional growth of influential expansion in society.[202] Nevertheless, the most severe test of Christianity under Communism was during the Cultural Revolution's intensive Red Guard control from 1966 through 1969. It actually lasted over a decade with the Gang of Four in political power, when even the TSPM offices were closed.[203] Christianity was clearly indicated among the four old qualities to be eliminated, along with the demons and monsters allegedly opposed to Mao Zedong. The Red Guards closed churches throughout China and put them to an alternative use as schools, factories or warehouses, and they defaced or removed all religious symbols. Christian literature along with Bibles and hymnals were confiscated and usually burned.[204] In Beijing on August 22, 1966, at the YMCA building a poster was placed with the following inscription:

> There is no God…Spirit…Jesus…Mary…Joseph. How can adults believe in such things?…Priests live in luxury and suck the blood of the workers…is a reactionary feudal ideology, the opium of the people, with foreign origins and contacts…We are atheists; we believe only in Mao Tse-tung. We call on all people to burn Bibles, destroy images, and disperse religious associations.

It was reported in the August 24, 1966, in Shanghai's *South China Morning Post* about the devastation the Red Guards ravaged on churches, sacred scriptures, religious edifices and archives. They placed placards on churches charging to "Discard the old!" or "This is forbidden!", and in the foreign cemetery of Beijing they removed crosses and other religious symbols from tombstones.[205]

Not only the church buildings and religious symbols suffered damage, but the believers as well were subject to Red Guard fury. Many Christians were tortured or driven to suicide. Two Christian doctors at a former mission hospital killed themselves. Red Guards confiscated and destroyed the American clothes, shoes, books, and university diploma of an American-educated Chinese young lady. One group of Red Guards, estimated ages between

---

[202] Bush, *Religion*, pp. 251-252.
[203] Wallis, *China Miracle*, pp. 46-47.
[204] Lyall, *God in China*, pp. 147-148.
[205] Bush, *Religion*, p. 257.

eight and twenty years old, forced an evangelist and his wife to kneel beside a stack of burning Bibles, hymnals and religious materials all night, and poured hot tea on the wife's head.[206]

After knowing of cruel beatings, rapes and torture at the hands of Red Guards, some Christians, weakened under the fearful pressure of threats and demands, denounced their faith. Those who endured were strengthened in their faith.[207] Very few Christians took part in the chaos, preferring to suffer torture rather than transgress the Bible's commandments.[208] Christian students, called into the campus Red Guard office to be harassed about their religious practices in contrast to Marxist-Leninism and Mao Zedong Thought, were advised not to become defensive for that would have been fruitless. Consequently, they accepted their disgrace in silence.[209] There were fellow-Christians who betrayed other Christians and their faith during the revolution, but it was not that their belief was not genuine; in fact many regretted grievously what they had done under pressure.[210]

Letters to Far East Broadcasting Company in Manila from refugees and overseas Chinese who had returned from visiting relatives in China reported that home gatherings were thriving during the Cultural Revolution. The attempt to destroy all Bibles gave significance to one report of a charred page from a Bible burned by the Red Guards. The verse that was still readable on that page was Matthew 16:18, "Upon this rock I will build my church; and the gates of hell shall not prevail against it."[211] Not every copy of the Bible was destroyed, but generally the Church was without Scriptures, church buildings and leadership. Most church clergy had been imprisoned or silenced or sent to the countryside for re-education labor. By Easter of 1967, the annihilation of the visible Church was complete, and devotees were forced underground into home gatherings. Any Bibles preserved by a group were shared, and each Christian would keep one for a week or two and pass it on to another. In some cases it was unbound and divided among those of the group to be

[206] Ibid, p. 258.
[207] Lyall, *God in China*, pp. 157-158.
[208] Luo, *Religion in China*, p. 123.
[209] Fung, *Households*, p. 25.
[210] Adeney, *Church's March*, p. 197.
[211] Hefley, *Martyrs*, pp. 77-78.

copied. Radio stations from outside China would read scripture at dictation speed and believers would take the risk to listen and write out passages.[212]

Japanese professor Maseo Takenaka traveled in China in 1967 and observed that all churches had been closed. Only the one next to the Rumanian Embassy still bore crosses on the steeples.[213] In 1972 a delegation of Indonesian and African diplomats went to the governmental authorities and asked if there was freedom to worship in China. Assured that the constitution guaranteed freedom of religion, they petitioned for a place to be opened for them to worship as Christian believers in accordance with the constitution. Through their appeal, the Roman Catholic South Cathedral and the Protestant Rice Market Street Church were reopened for the first official services since 1967.[214]

THE HOME GATHERINGS PERSPECTIVE OF THE CHINESE CHURCH

Materialization of the Communist expectancy that the Christian Church would collapse was not realized, evidenced by the various policy shifts used for organizational control over the churches. The Plenary conference of church leaders in 1949 at Beijing claimed to have established an organization representative of the Protestant Church in China, which was misleading. The Communist government could seize control of an organization, but the Church was not a structured order, but it is a growing, living organism. The weakness of Protestantism by its individuality and local autonomy became its very strength, which an insurgent power cannot disable.[215] The CCP faced the dilemma of how to deal with the Christian churches, for if they were restricted severely or outlawed the believers had the capability of going underground, out of reach of governmental control. China must superficially abide by the Helsinki agreement on Human Rights to advance its cause, which depended on world opinion. That transaction prevented the Communists from pursuing eradication of the Church.[216]

---

[212] Lyall, *God in China*, pp. 148-149, 155.
[213] Bush, *Religion*, p. 258.
[214] Thompson Brown, *Christianity in the People's Republic of China* (Atlanta: John Knox Press, 1983), p. 126.
[215] D. Vaughan Rees, *The 'Jesus Family' in Communist China* (Montreal: Christian Literature Crusade, 1973), p. 116.
[216] Paulson, *Wall*, pp. 82-83.

The Formation of the House Church Movement

The historical concept of Christian home gatherings was not new. At the inception of Christianity, during Pentecost after the resurrection of Jesus Christ and the arrival of the Holy Spirit on the believers, regular gatherings in homes became prevalent. Paul, one of Jesus' followers, was known to teach Christian doctrines in public and from house to house.[217] Even before foreign missionaries left China the home gathering concept was prevalent.

As mentioned, some well-known movements followed the home-gathering concept: Yu Kuochen instituted the China Jesus Independent Church in Shanghai during 1906, and the China Christian Independent Church was chartered at Shantung in 1912. Paul Wei began The True Jesus Church in 1917, Ching Tienying established the Jesus Family in the year 1921, and Watchman Nee founded The Little Flock in 1926. Timothy Dzao inaugurated the *Ling Liang*, or Spiritual Food Church, which was followed by the Spiritual Work Church and offspring groups.[218] These indigenous Church movements, representing different backgrounds were unconnected to any other similar grouping throughout the world. They were the only simile of a church in China during the Cultural Revolution.[219]

The two largest indigenous church movements in China owe their origin to two foreign ladies. Miss Dillenbeck of the American Methodists influenced Mr. Ching, the founder of *Yesu Chiating*, or Jesus Family. This group was extraordinarily indigenous in communities by using the chapels as workshops during the week, and converts would utilize a room of their house for worship services. They tithed, or contributed from their monetary gain, at first 10 percent, and then 90 percent and finally 100 percent. Except for food they ate, any profit was given for helping the needy. The leadership saw it as a privilege to do the most menial and lowly labor as exemplary servitude. Watchman Nee had Miss Barbour, an English worker with the Church Missionary Society, as the force behind establishing the Little Flock movement.[220] Nee was critical of the missionary movement and the Chinese

---

[217] Adeney, *Church's March*, p. 143; *The Holy Bible*, Acts 20:20.
[218] Patterson, *Christianity*, pp. 38-39.
[219] Adeney, *Church's March*, p. 144.
[220] Rees, *Jesus Family*, p. 113.

Church's dependency on the West. Even some missionaries and the churches they founded had joined the Little Flock, and within twenty years it grew to some 700 churches with more than 70,000 members.

During the Five-Anti campaign in April 1952, Watchman Nee was arrested on the charges of being a capitalist and without trial was sentenced to fifteen years imprisonment. His colleague, Witness Li, who had been based in Taiwan, became the leader, and his followers became known as The Shouters and labeled as counter-revolutionaries in China. It was reported in the February 1953 issue of the *Tien Feng* that Ching Tienying, the patron of the Jesus Family was denounced. His nephew had accused Ching of tyranny and sexual irregularities.[221]

The truly indigenous churches had no roots in the denominational Western mission influence but were spontaneous products of Christian witness derived from the Bible. The Biblical principle of church structure and discipline offered self-governing and the prescript of voluntary contribution taught self-support, while the New Testament standard of self-propagation eliminated the necessity of clergy and ordination: each individual devotee was responsible to communicate the message of Christian doctrines. These home gatherings were to be free from governmental control, power politics, and institutional or traditional bondage, with neither committee meetings nor buildings with specified worship hours. Chinese social structure was evident: they were rooted in family units and emphasized the lordship of Jesus Christ, with confidence in the sovereignty of God for timely protection. They demonstrated a dependency on the Bible by even hand copying portions and prayer for healing, endurance of suffering, exorcism, and confession. Their caring attitude was a force of spontaneous evangelism that was zealously characterized by lifestyle and friendship, and many of those imprisoned even evangelized fellow prisoners.

Because they lacked clergy, they depended on lay leadership – often women because the ministers were in prison. From the scarcity of Bibles, they also lacked biblical teaching, which gave entrance to heresies from an instructor, who might claim a special or superior truth. However, with suffering as the purifying

---

[221] Wallis, *China Miracle*, pp. 38-39; Patterson, *Christianity*, p. 81; Rees, *Jesus Family*, pp. 14-46.

force, there were no nominal or rice Christians. Nevertheless, there were some who denied Jesus as Lord and betrayed fellow Christians.[222]

Outside the control of the Chinese Communist government, these churches claimed their only allegiance to Jesus Christ, and there was little the government could do. After all, with organizational control there would be hardly anything outside the control of state. A subversive cannot be placed in every gathering location.[223] Yet, in 1974 home groups came under persecution, and their leaders were arrested on the charge of being lazy, unproductive, and wasting time not working.[224]

The Attempt of Governmental Control over Home Gatherings

The Three-Self Movement had made it clear that the home gatherings must register or dissolve, but this led only to fortified faith and counter-measures on the part of the home gatherings. These groups began to inspect membership identity to prevent infiltration of TSPM representatives. They started breaking into smaller units with different and varying locations and times. Avoiding contact with clergy from abroad would help to elude the Chinese Communists' attention.[225]

Many Protestants were unhappy attending the post-denominational church registered under the TSPM and preferred the intimacy of the informal home gatherings. In some there would be evidence of miracles and healing practiced, approaching what the state would define as superstition.[226] Since meetings were not at a fixed time or place and all participants could not arrive at the same time, a home gathering was not easy to manage. Hymn-singing, prayer, a Bible passage exposition, and a personal testimony of an event or sharing a concern or answer to prayer were items of a regular meeting in a room with approximately five by two and a half meters floor space where 30 to 40 persons gathered. Many times a gathering would take place in the mountains or

---

[222] Adeney, *Church's March*, pp. 146-165.
[223] Rees, *Jesus Family*, p. 117.
[224] Chen Xiaoya, Manufacturer, Madrid (Interview) trans. He Yanli and Chu Lijung, 17 July 1998.
[225] Peter Humphrey, *Religious Suppression in Mainland China* (Republic of China: World Anti-Communist League, 1983), p. 18.
[226] Mickey Spiegel, 'Freedom of Religion in China,' *Asia Watch* (New York: Human Rights Watch, 1992), p. 4.

in the countryside or perhaps as a picnic in a park, with two hours for a time of worship.[227] During the Cultural Revolution, especially in the 1966 to 1968 period, it was common to break up into groups of three or four under a tree, in a field or in a park to pray with eyes open and mouth smiling as if sharing a joke. The hymns or scripture were placed on portions of palm-sized photographic paper to be handled like a snapshot.

When a home gathering became too large it would divide into two cells, but there was no organizational association to link the groups together. Some did join together in an isolated area for special retreats lasting several days for instruction, preaching, singing and socializing with other Christians. The inner courtyard of a unit for several families was convenient especially if all of the block were Christians. Party officials or village cadres could not condone meetings, but they were often sympathetic and did not interfere, especially since they recognized that the Christians were the hardest working and frequently the best qualified members of the commune. It was evident that Christianity was alive in the community, for the youth were often the most responsive.[228]

Without structure the Church grew with neither outside support nor inside control by Church or governmental political factors. In the latter quarter of the twentieth century, the Church continued to be flexible in its adaptation to the context of the Chinese political and social situation with little international intervention.

THE CHINESE CHURCH AFTER THE DEATHOF MAO ZEDONG 1976 – 2000

The years of the Cultural Revolution from 1966 until 1976 were considered the epoch of chaos when a generation in China missed an opportunity for education to being Red Guards and causing havoc throughout the country. It was a time of total religious suppression by extreme Marxists known as the Gang of Four, led by Mao Zedong's wife, Jiang Qing. She stated that religion was dead, and with all established church buildings, temples and mosques closed it appeared that religion in China had ceased to

---

[227] Theodore Marr, 'Research Information Training,' David Aikman (ed.), *Love China Today* (Wheaton: Tyndale House Publishers, 1977), pp. 66-68.
[228] Brown, *Christianity*, pp. 127-128; The author heard in a conversation with a Chinese Christian in Spain about the method of placing scripture and hymns on photographic paper.

exist.
Mao Zedong died on September 9, 1976, and October of that year marked the subsequent subjugation of the Gang of Four. With this abrupt suppression of the leftist faction of the Communist Party, the pressures on religions were alleviated somewhat. After Deng Xiaoping gained firm control in 1978 and a dramatically new policy was inaugurated in favor of modernization with openness to the West, the governmental policy on religion was seriously reconsidered.[229] A much more tolerant religious procedure was announced with the permission to reopen temples and churches to resume services for worship and ritual. The government offered to rebuild any church, mosque or temple that had been destroyed during the Cultural Revolution.[230]

PRESERVATION OF THE CHURCH IN CHINA

Throughout those years of political and social upheaval, Chinese Christians in isolated groups did not know that there were similar groups of believers meeting in nearly every province of China. It was to their amazement, and the awe of the world that such widespread religious practice existed. The only explanation theChinese Christians offered was the enterprise of the Holy Spirit, the third person of the Christian Triune Godhead.[231]

The population of China had increased tremendously with an acute shortage of housing, especially in metropolitan areas. A noted 20 percent decrease in living area per person from 1949 to 1978 with a mere 3.6 square meters created the situation of several families living in a single room. Home gatherings were difficult to manage with such limited space. Still, the older housing, with courtyards covered by mat roofing that were prevalent both in the cities and throughout the countryside, could accommodate hundreds.[232]

The Rice Market Street Church that reopened on Easter 1972 provided a place to worship mainly for diplomatic personnel. After the expulsion of the Gang of Four, the first church to reopen

[229] David H. Adeney, *China: The Church's Long March* (Ventura, CA: Regal Books, 1985), pp. 116, 123.
[230] June Teufel Dreyer, *China's Political System* (Boston: Allyn and Bacon, 1996), p. 117.
[231] Thompson Brown, *Christianity in the People's Republic of China* (Atlanta: John Knox Press, 1983), p. 159; Jones, Tracy K., Occasional Bulletin of Missionary Research, July 1979. p. 90.
[232] Adeney, *Church's March*, p. 85.

for worship services was the Bainian Tang at Ningbo during April 1979 to an overflow congregation. Then in February 1980, for the first time in nearly fifteen years, the enlarged TSPM Standing Committee met and especially emphasized the pastoral needs of the newly-opened churches.[233] Many of the pastors had been imprisoned, so their wives continued the ministry. It was common for young women to be participants in evangelistic teams sent to different areas by groups from home gatherings. Women actively took part in the pastoral committees of TSPM registered churches, and a number became ordained ministers.[234] Suddenly the openness led to a thrust for evangelism, which consequently led to tremendous Church growth and required a greater amount of the church leaders' time and energy to concentrate on administrative responsibilities to support the growing congregations.[235]

Potential Leaders of China Exposed to Christianity

Since 1978 thousands of Chinese youth have gone overseas to study. For many of these future leaders in China, this opportunity was coupled with a first-time contact with a clear presentation of the Christian faith. It was especially difficult for those whom the government sponsored to publicly profess Christianity and many opted for their faith to remain secret.[236]

When the Nanjing Union Theological Seminary opened in March 1981, 51 students, 29 men and 22 women, came from the twenty-two provinces, municipalities and autonomous regions of China. The traditional curriculum included Christian doctrines, Church history, pastoral studies, and a major emphasis on Bible. As in every institute of learning in China, several required hours each week were dedicated to political education. An invitation was extended to the seminary faculty to present five lectures on Christianity at the University of Nanjing. Surprisingly, 1,000 students responded to the opportunity, and as a result, Dean Chen Zemin offered Christian Doctrine as an elective at the University. Originally the course was programmed for 40 students, but when 180 students enrolled, a larger lecture room was required. This

---

[233] Philip L. Wickeri, *Seeking the Common Ground* (Maryknoll, NY: Orbis Books, 1990), p. 188.
[234] Adeney, *Church's March*, p. 95.
[235] 'Does The Church Have Anything To Say To Modern China?' *Amity News Service*, Vol. 7, ¾, 4.1 (1998) 17.
[236] Adeney, *Church's March*, p. 90.

indicated the interest of Chinese students in a subject that so long had been prohibited by the government. Accordingly, the faculty prepared a correspondence course for laypersons and leaders of home congregations, and 10,000 copies of the first edition were promptly in demand.[237] This irrevocable interest and acceptance of Christianity and its doctrine gave evidence of a change in basic values of Chinese society.

Legal Reinstatement of Religious Beliefs

The new Article 36 of Document 19 reinstated the freedom of religious belief in China; however, the policy was not consistently enforced throughout the country in that some officials continued the anti-religious bias of the Cultural Revolution. In some areas Christian literature was being confiscated in the mail, and youth under the age of eighteen were being denied their rights to attend church. The policy was stated in a way that could be interpreted in distinct manners, as the state protects *legitimate* religious activities, and no person was permitted to conduct *counterrevolutionary activities* or activities of *disrupting* social order, *harming* peoples health or *obstructing* the educational system of the nation.[238] The wording of *freedom of religious belief* did not ensure the liberty to practice or proclaim that conviction. Finally, in May 1982 the Chinese Communist government utilized the TSPM to suppress unregistered or underground church groups, to gain organizational control over the Christian community of China.[239]

The Church in China continued to thrive in every part of the country. Home gatherings were known to exist in nearly all twenty-two provinces with a total of 2,007 counties. An estimated 30,000 to 50,000 such groups represented the bulk of Christianity in China in 1985. Approximately 27,000 Chinese people a day, in the three years following 1980, became Christians. This growth was not even imagined by missionaries before 1949, has been attributed to worldwide intercessory prayer or petition to the

---

[237] Brown, *Christianity in China*, pp. 175-177.
[238] Ibid, p. 164; Luo Zhufeng (ed.), *Religion under Socialism in China*, trans. Donald E. MacInnis and Zheng Xian (London: M. E. Sharpe, Inc., 1991), p. 146. Italics for emphasis by author.
[239] Peter Humphery, *Religious Suppression in Mainland China* (Republic of China: World Anticommunist League, 1983), p. 15. Italics for emphasis by author.

Christian God on behalf of China and her people.[240]

GOVERNMENTAL RESTRICTION IMPOSED TO CONTROL THE CHURCH

Chinese Communism, on the other hand, perceived Christianity as a tool of imperialistic aggression and these unregistered home gatherings or underground churches as espionage organizations to be abolished.[241] Religion was tolerated on the basis of its contribution to China's unity, modernization, socialization, and production, with the belief that eventually religion would fade into non-existence. Until the inevitable disappearance of these idealistic creeds, they were to be harnessed to serve China's national interests. Restriction on the number of recognized religions was limited to the five; Daoism, Buddhism, Islam, and Christianity with Catholicism and Protestantism enumerated as two different religions. The Party could then exercise strict control over their organizations and leadership through their appropriate associations.[242]

Definition of Religious Policy

Still, these creeds were observed as negative influences on the modernization of a socialist state by retaining certain beliefs that were obstacles to the socialist-accepted scientific concepts: the existence of God, immortality of the soul, heaven as eternal paradise, and hell for everlasting damnation. The Party and the People's government were burdened with fashioning the constructive role of religion for their aspired objectives. Those involved in social sciences, cultural studies, and the media were directed to study the facts of religion and Marxist views about religion along with the current religious policies.[243] The constitutional regulations were the apparatus used to regulate, confine and defuse any conflicting interest religion might present in interference to the projected modernization.

The primary requirement was for religious organizations

---

[240] Lesllie Lyall, *God Reigns in China* (London: Hodder and Stoughton, 1985), p. 178.
[241] Humphery, *Suppression in China*, p. 18.
[242] Mickey Spiegel, *China: State Control of Religion* (New York: Human Rights Watch, 1997), pp. 2-3.
[243] Gong Xuezeng, 'Reflections of Religion and Modernization,' trans. by Michael Sloboda, *Tripod*, No. 103,Vol. XVII, January-February (1998) 19-21.

and individuals to observe all the laws and regulations of the Constitutions. They must be committed to unity, social order, and ethnic harmony. No organizational or individual use of religion for interference in either civil or judicial administration or *education* would be tolerated, through the law continually protected the legal rights of religious organizations: their locations, leaders, and believers, and their *normal* activities.[244]   Only an imprudent Christian would publish an article of dissident nature or commit any other fracture of confidence that would cause the government to risk world opinion to arrest or imprison some churchman or defy a constitutional guaranteed church activity.[245] Many Chinese, however, believed in discretion of communication for the embarrassment it might cause for their position as Party member, official or professor.[246] Those under the public educational system, especially as Party members, had accepted the notion of religion as an opiate and only for the uneducated without culture and understanding of progressive society.[247]   Nonetheless, the theories taught in school to children of Christian background were filtered through the biblical indoctrination from their church and the parents.[248]

It must be emphasized that as late as the 1990s the leftist influence was manifested in some cadres who had little understanding of the party policy regarding religion. They tried to restrict, interfere or control internal religious affairs; thus, they abused the legal rights of religionists, which discouraged their patriotic cooperation.[249]

A political change or event of political repercussion could also be accompanied with tense relations between officials and churches. The reunification of Hong Kong initiated reactionary control from the suspicion that the church would have a motive to take advantage of the circumstance to do something unlawful. Even a slight deviation from a prescribed religious activity was often

---

[244] 'Regulations for Guangshou No. 118 of religious Affairs Bureau,' *Tripod*, No. 103, Vol. XVIII, Jan. – Feb. (1998) 36; Chapter 1 Article 5. Italics for emphasis by author.
[245] Wang Zhikang, Representative of Chinese Firm, Madrid (Interview, 25 July 1998).
[246] Yuan Aiguang, Medical Doctor, Madrid (Interview, 17 July 1998).
[247] Zhou Xingli, Student, Madrid (Interview, 20 July 1998).
[248] Ye Jianwei, Business Man, Madrid (Interview, 17 July 1998).
[249] Luo, *Religion in China*, p. 147.

suppressed even as late as 1997, such as if a church, constructed under the permission of the government, started a Sunday school program. Those responsible for this approach of instruction and the ones who prepared the materials would be imprisoned, because their initiative went outside the prescribed governmental program. Certain incidents created a political strain, such as when a church that had desired to become registered with the TSPM aborted the process upon learning that the membership role would have to be submitted. A church's contact with foreigners could suggest a liability for drug traffic activities.[250] Even the hymns that a church chose to sing from hymnals of Taiwan origin could motivate official constraint and confiscation,[251] according to certain regulations. All religious organizations were subject to government supervision and must operate under their respective statutes.[252]

Further Governmental Regulations on Religious Activities

Party control over religious activity was through regulations, from one viewpoint a means of restrictive domination and from another a filter for the elimination of negative elements. Only recognized leaders positioned by their respective organizations could conduct religious activity in locations specified for that purpose. Those leaders invited to another area, or visitors asked to participate from outside the region, must be authorized by a religious body higher than the municipality and must register with the RAB at a level higher than the city. No propagation of religion other than that designated for a particular place would be permitted. Fortune telling, divination, palm reading, casting of lots, exorcism, and healing practices were prohibited inside any location of a religious movement. Only legitimate religious participation might be practiced in those localities designation by the local RAB, but citizens would be permitted to employ their chosen religion within their own homes.[253]

In practice, these regulations took freedom from a speaker or teacher of religion at the discretion of an official, who usually was placed in the audience to police the content of the message. If there

---

[250] Xiao C. P., Woman, Madrid (Interview, trans. Chu Lijung, 26 July 1998).
[251] Zhou E. W., Female Youth, Madrid (Interview, trans. Chu Lijung, 26 July 1998).
[252] 'Regulations,' p. 37; Chapter 2, Article 10.
[253] Ibid, pp. 38-39; Chapter 4, Articles 26 and 27; Chapter 5, Article 30; Chapter 13, Articles 16 and 18.

were a desire to teach from the Bible book of Revelation, a private meeting would need to be convened. A normal layman would not recognize these intricate political adjustments in the church, but an overseas Chinese, who returned for a visit, discerned these subtle criterion by comparison to the Biblical teachings learned in another country.[254]

Internal control was demonstrated in the manner in which printed matter was supervised, for all religious articles had to be printed on government-approved presses. Publishing, printing or reprinting needed to be issued in accordance to predetermined number and limits for distribution. No person or organization could transport, import, sell or reprint religious publications without government approval. Foreigners would be allowed to bring religious literature into China only for their own personal use.[255] A foreigner or overseas Chinese who returned for a visit would have to solicit governmental approval to be able to address a congregation. Any attempt to evangelize, as a foreigner, could be assumed to be without restriction; nevertheless, a leading correspondent from Beijing explained that those with whom the non-native converses might be required to explain the contact with an alien.[256] A Chinese evangelist or Bible teacher could instruct to love a neighbor or not to hurt or rob another, but anything eschatological would be prohibited. Because of this type of firm domination many churches meet illegally and in fear of official reproach.[257]

Suppression

The official system continued to pursue two goals to socialist modernization through Marxism, Leninism and Mao Zedong Thought. The first was to construct a highly developed socialist material world, and the second was to develop the socialist spiritual world. In this context, the spiritual side alludes to politics. The people were to be educated about the advantages of the four facets of modernization, which would create the spiritual realization of strength through production of wealth.[258]

The basic attitude of CCP had not changed toward religion

---

[254] Chen Y. P., Evangelist, Valencia (Interview, 21 July 1998).
[255] 'Regulations,' pp. 41-42; Chapter 7, Articles 43, 44, 46; Chapter 8, Article 54.
[256] Wallis, *China Miracle*, p. 11.
[257] Chen Y. P. (Interview, 21 Jul. 98).
[258] Clayre, *Heart of Dragon*, pp. 58-59.

in pursuit of these goals. Their post-1989 actions verified the prevailing attitude stated in senior-statesman Chen Yun's letter of warning to the Party head, Jiang Zemin, that religion would be in competition against Communism. Tightened surveillance over religious festivals, notably that of the Christian Christmas celebration, resulted. The CCP policy towards the Catholic Church remained: divide, attack, and divide again. The open Church, registered with the TSPM, was the object of its United Front Policy, while the unregistered illegal home gatherings or house churches as the underground Church remained the target of direct offensive. Their goal was to maintain control by containing church activities within their locations.[259] The official attitude towards Christianity differed from that for Daoists or Buddhists, because the Christian churches led to the fall of Communism in Eastern Europe in 1991. When Communist leaders sensed insecurity they became defensive, which affected all church groups and actually became an opportunity for the Church.[260]

The open churches were encouraged to develop as non-denominational in China's post-denominational era. Thus, the Body of Christ consisted of the Church in China without denominations, which had forever passed from Chinese church history.[261] For the attack by the CCP against the underground segment, long-term imprisonment and violent physical abuse continued, though less frequently. By 1997, isolated cases were reported, but there was no evidence of widespread systematic purges.[262] From Wenzhou in 1997 a report declared incidents of churches and Christian cemeteries desecrated by explosive devices placed by the government.[263] Sympathy and calls for Democratic reform by officials had been factors in minimizing religious persecution.

---

[259] Bao Sidong, 'Today's Church in Mainland China,' trans. Norman Walling *Tripod*, No. 103, Vol. XVIII, Jan.-Feb. (1998) 23-24.
[260] 'China Church and News Update,' *Tripod*, Vol. XVIII, No. 103, Jan.-Feb. (1998).
[261] Denton Lotz (ed.), *Spring Has Returned* (McLean, VA: Baptist World Alliance, 1986), p. 33.
[262] Spiegel, *China: Control*, p. 1.
[263] Xu Shulian (Interview).

Movement towards Democracy

A former vice director of the Planning Commission of Fuzhou revealed that the younger officials advocated democratic reform within Chinese politics and government, a historical first for internal leaders of the Communist Party. Therefore, it would no longer be possible for the Party to ignore supporters of a democratic government inside its own structure. The issues included freedom of expression and religious tolerance as well as electoral autonomy for both Taiwan and Tibet.[264]

In other countries, overseas Chinese had established organizations to promote democracy in China. Some linked Christianity with their emphasis in that they recognized that democracy usually was instituted under cultures where Christianity dominated. They discerned that China had suffered under Communism and only God could fulfill the role in the Chinese people that the Communist Party had tried to emulate.[265]

MODERNIZATION INFLUENCE ON THE CHURCH

According to Gong Xuezeng's article in the *Tripod*, religious believers were recognized as the front line force of production and promotion of China's modernization and those who advocated patriotism. Religions advanced moral values of benevolence and avoided depravity, and believers were taught positive discipline of citizenship. Therefore, religion was perceived as a definite force in the modernization program for construction of a socialist society.[266] The Standing Committee of the Politburo was the highest organ of the CCP for all key policy decisions. Then the United Front acted as the Party organ to implement that administrative decision, and the Religious Affairs Bureau was organized on provincial, municipal, district and county levels to execute policy.[267]

The attitude of the officials included in the Protestant Church in China had been that of cooperation with the Communist Party's

---

[264] Myron Ivey (ed.), *China News and Church Report*, 2 February 1998, 2620; Fang Jue (pseud.), a former vise director of the planning commission of Fuzhou, insists that he represents many other mid and high-level officials in their forty and fifties.

[265] Wang Li [psued.], former President of the Chinese Christian Democratic Union, Madrid (Interview, 16 July 1998).

[266] Gong, 'Reflections,' *Tripod*, pp. 18-19.

[267] Spiegel, *China: Control*, p. 13.

proposal for a United Front, which included all patriots of the motherland. The objective of modernization would be to cooperate for the benefit of Chinese society as a whole.[268]The trends of China's social and economic development in 1998 demonstrated a secular materialism imbalance that began to replace religious values. However, the relaxed application of policy had theists thinking of it as an era of religious growth. The new sense of patriotism toward modernization encouraged a new probe of theology to include cultural refinement with an opening to the international community and their religious organizations. An intermingling of religions had created other social disorders, especially in minority regions where separatism had been adhered and advocated. All of society was in transition toward a new system of democracy ruled by law, but internal contradiction occurred wherever religion and society interacted.[269] Governmental change of control methods allowed citizens to express their faith within the confines of the law, but the real problem was the laws themselves.[270] In February 1994 the author attended the International Church in Shanghai where the dean of Shanghai Seminary addressed the lack of specific laws in China to promote the Christian ethics of honesty, fairness, justice and service.

Effects of Modernization on Chinese Society

Deng Xiaoping had coined a political slogan, "to get rich is glorious," to promote economic growth on an international level. David Lutz noted that this mentality caused serious moral problems in China. Communistic ideology had not provided China's utopia; therefore, the people expected financial gain rather than politics or even ethics to lead to the perfection of society.[271] Russian novelist Alexander Solzhenitsyn summarized China's status perfectly: "Where the state is sovereign, there can be no place for any other religion," but the post-Mao situation in China forced the people to question Communistic values in search of

---

[268] Ting K. H., *Chinese Christians Speak Out* (Beijing: New World Press. 1984), p. 5.
[269] Gong, 'Reflections,'pp. 15-17.
[270] Spiegel, *China: Control,* pp. 9-10.
[271] David W. Lutz, 'Ethics and Morality in China Today,' John Tong (ed.), *Tripod* (Aberdeen, Hong Kong: Holy Spirit Study Center), Vol. XVIII, No. 107, Sept.-Oct. (1998) 12.

a cause worthy of their devotion.[272] Many turned to religion for purpose, and a great portion converted to Christianity.

Since the early 1990s, the youth of China were no longer open to Communistic ideals for fulfillment of their social needs. To be a Party member would not help these young people much in career advancement and was no longer a deterrent for them to become Christians.[273] The trend away from Communism was the result of many different influences of the past few decades of the 1900s. International communication through e-mail, Internet, cellular telephones, satellite news networks, and intercontinental travel had inspired investigation into other avenues for life's fulfillment. This included religious instruction through outside resources.

Modernization Indorsed Opening to the West

The TSPM perceived that foreign anti-Chinese Christian organizations were financing, from solicited funds, underground resources for evangelism and literature distribution in a wanton manner for a hidden agenda. They professed to have established illegal or *underground* churches in China and this type of activity would often be comprehended as a breach of national security.[274] An overseas church developed plans to establish a seminary in a remote area of China without consideration of the TSPM policy. The publication of the church claimed "our seminary in China" in reference to this project over which their requisite control dominated for the design of buildings, appointment of board of directors, hiring the teaching staff, and curriculum content.

In some parts of China even the church workers have become dependent upon foreign groups for their salaries and expenses. When a foreigner was in the region the church would invite him or her to establish contacts without inquiry about motive or affiliations. Missionaries, sent into China from abroad under pretense as teachers, business personnel or students, have advocated that members of churches linked with the TSPM could not be real Christians. They also provoked debate between believers and non-believers. Some groups had illegally imported

---

[272] Arthur Wallis, *China Miracle* (Columbia, MO: Cityhill Publishing, 1986), pp. 54-55.
[273] Liu Yun [pseud.], former Communist Youth Member, Madrid (Interview, 25 July 1998).
[274] Ting, *Chinese Speak*, p. 13. Italics for emphasis by author.

Bibles into China, and many of these taught that Communism in China might be defeated in the same manner as it was in Russia and Eastern Europe.[275] The author heard personal testimony from individuals and groups that admitted that they were involved in the types of Christian activities described. While visiting church in China he was approached by church leaders on how to contribute financially to the church on a periodic basis.

Many overseas Chinese have returned to China after becoming Christians and have been instrumental in evangelizing their region.[276] The government charged Christianity for hindrance from the radical change that China was to experience in her society through Communistic ideals. However, according to Chinese Christians from Adeney's record, when change would finally be realized, it would only be the Christian lifestyle that could sustain it under the self-seeking, dishonest corruption prevalent in modern society.[277] This phenomenon was evident in the comment of a law-enforcement officer to a church leader from Zhejiang Provincial Christian Council that the crime rate was much lower in their district than other areas because the church had produced so many good citizens in the region.[278] In the vicinity of Wenzhou this sentiment was prevalent. The author attended a church in a village near Jingtian of Jiangxi Province, and upon entering; a police officer was mingling with members of the congregation. The pastor assured the author that the officer was a Christian as well as a church member and enjoyed the order the church had brought to the community.

Churches that Modernization Produced

Many churches practice a form of utilitarianism with Christianity as a means to receive blessings and avoid misfortunes. These remained suspicious of systems of ethics and morals, mixed with academic scholarship, modernization and cynicism.[279] However, it

[275] 'Does the Chinese Church Need to Protect Its Independence Today?' *Amity News Service*, Vol. 7, March-April, (1998) 2-3.
[276] Chen Xiaoya, Manufacturer, Madrid (Interview, trans. He Yanli and Chu Lijung, 17 July 1998).
[277] Adeney, *Church's March*, p. 101.
[278] Chen Xida, 'The Life and Witness of the Church in China,' Gail V. Coulson (ed.), *China Talk*, October (1997) 37. Address at LWF Assembly Hong Kong, July 1997, Chen Xida of Nanjing Theological Seminary.
[279] Chen Zemin, 'Relations Between Christianity and Intellectuals since

was found in the beginning of 1999 that the believers and pastoral workers of most churches registered with TSPM were fundamental or evangelical in their conservative theologically orthodox beliefs of being saved by a spiritual rebirth through the transformation experience of accepting Jesus Christ and His claims.

This was the case with the orthodox Protestant church that started in the Xu family who opened their home in 1980 to Protestants of all backgrounds to worship together. From this home gathering within Dachang, a city of 300,000 residents, a new church of over 900 baptized members was built and dedicated in October 1998. The interior furnishings were purchased through overseas donations, and the government had conferred upon it a tax-free exemption for operational costs.[280]

YOUTH IN THE CHINESE CHURCH

The youth of China was another facet of society responding to the claims of Christian instruction. As of 1997, a church of Nanjing with over 1500 in the congregation had more than 300 young people meeting each Saturday evening. After an hour of Christian worship, ten different groups were available for participation in prayer, theological discussion, family counseling, and even a group for migrant workers. The church had become the place to learn and heal emotional and spiritual needs, for love to be shared, trust built, and confidence gained.[281] In the year 1996, the youth group from the church at Jingtian solicited permission from the local Department of Religion and organized an evangelistic expedition to another village. They had meetings throughout the entire day with singing, exposition on Bible passages, theater plays and personal testimonies of the Christian life that communicated the gospel or Christian message of Jesus Christ.[282]

The author was with a group of about 50 youth in a village near Jingtian in 1994 that had just returned from remote villages in the mountains after a week of evangelistic gatherings of preaching, song and skits. In Wenzhou there were regular weekly meetings

Liberation (1949),' Gail V. Coulson (ed.) *China Talk,* Vol. XXIV, April (1999) 21. Extract from a speech by Dr. Chen Zemin, Vice-Principle of Nanjing Union Theological Seminary and Vice-President of the China Christian Council.
[280] Gail V. Coulson (ed.), 'Church Grows from a Three Generation Family's Home Worship,' *China Talk,* Vol. XXIV, April (1999)16-17.
[281] Chen, 'The Life,' *China Talk,* p. 37.
[282] Liu Qiao, Businesswoman, Madrid (Interview, 26 July 1998).

scheduled for the youth in the church. Wednesday and Saturday evenings were designated for Bible study and singing Christian choruses, then on Sunday afternoon and evening they assembled for more singing, prayer and preaching.[283] It was interesting that a number of the youth wanted to identify with the West and would wear a cross on a chain around their neck.[284]

It must be emphasized that the religious regulations were not enforced exactly the same over all of China. The variation depended on the local cadre and how the ordinance was interpreted. The sympathy or apathy the officials had toward religious activities or perhaps the experiences and observations encountered with the members of a certain Christian group or church could influence their perspective.

THEOLOGY PROMOTED BY THE CHURCH IN CHINA

Generally the Church in China held to the Reformation Principle of *sola Scriptura*, the view that the Bible is the ultimate authority, and only that which had been established on the revelation of God is acceptable.[285] The first translations of the Bible by missionaries were somewhat inaccurate and irrelevant because there was minimal Chinese collaboration. Both Western and Chinese scholars cooperatively translated the 1911 version, the most popular translation. A new *simplified* version had been printed, but the more conservative facet of the Chinese Church did not accept its interpretation.[286]

Context of Theological Formation in China

The greatest contribution of foreign Protestant missionaries was the translation of the entire Bible into the Chinese language, but it was not until 80 years later that T. C. Chao, Jia Yuming, Xie Fuy and Y. T. Wu were writing Chinese theology. These theologians had been nurtured in traditional Chinese culture and mindset, evident in their theological formation.[287] This was revealed in Bishop Ting's observation in disagreement with the Liberation

---

[283] Xu Shilian, Businesswoman, Madrid (Interview, 24 July 1998).
[284] Zheng Xianyu [pseud.], English Professor, Madrid (Interview, 27 July 1998).
[285] 'Chinese Theology,' *CTR: 12*, p. 12. Italics by author for foreign phrase.
[286] Wu Qiwei [pseud.], Professor, New Haven, CN (Interview, 8 December 1998); and Hu Wei, Professor, Houghton, NY (Interview, 31 May 1999). Italics for emphasis by author.
[287] 'Chinese theology,' *CTR: 12*, p. 13.

Theologians of South America that political liberation would not be a solution between human beings and ultimate foundation of the universe. He sensed that they had not adequately dealt with life in Jesus Christ.[288]

Even though the Chinese Church does experience some persecution, Christianity in China has proven to be somewhat like a basketball, for the harder it is hit the higher it bounces. The more the Church had been persecuted the stronger it has become. Doctrines taught in preserved copies of the Bible, *Streams in the Desert*, and *Pilgrim's Progress* helped to sustain faith during time served in labor reform during the Cultural Revolution. Only since the 1990s was it possible to purchase a Bible without registering its procurement.[289] In the late 1990s toward the interior of Zhejiang province with permission from the local RAB or an invitation by the government, a foreigner would be allowed to participate in a church worship. Usually if a foreigner was a tourist and not introduced as a missionary evangelist, even without permission, could speak without much repercussion.[290] However, in the same area and timeframe, it was found that fellow employees would ridicule a Christian while the church leader was hurt physically. Government officials confiscated the tables and chairs of the church because it initiated the addition of its own program, and youth under 16 years of age were prohibited to attend.[291]

Doctrines Approved by TSPM

The theology of the majority of Chinese Christians was conservative and rooted in the fundamentals of the Bible. They do not accept Biblical criticism, for the Bible itself was seen as the absolute standard of authority and power for truth. All human beings were sinners, both with original sin, inherited from man's first disobedience to God and overt sins of personal acts contrary to God's will. Human beings were made in God's image to be honored, but humanism was rejected as man being substituted for God. The most accepted form of evangelism was through friendship; some areas of China held a more politically conservative enforcement on governmental policy, which prohibits evangelism

---

[288] Brown, *Christianity in China*, pp. 181-182.
[289] Wu [pseud.] (Interview).
[290] Chen Xiaoya (Interview).
[291] Xiao (Interview).

outside the church and of those under the age of 18 years of age.[292] To be an example of Christ's love when in contact with people would be the key to evangelizing in China, for it was his love for mankind that Christ died, and the world needs love.[293]

Chinese theology for salvation defined an inner life change or rebirth from selfish motivation to godly pure actions, which can be instantaneous or gradual growth. Jesus Christ was God incarnate as the Son of man and became Savior when he died as a sacrifice for man's reconciliation to God. Jesus became the mediator between God and man, and he is to be worshiped as the Son of God. The Trinity includes God as Father, Jesus as Son, and the Holy Spirit who works at his will to complete the work of Jesus in man. An example was his work for the Church to grow in China during the era when pastors were imprisoned and there was no one to nurture the Church. Mankind would have a choice to make in receiving salvation for it could not be the fate of predestination. One who deliberately sins could lose his or her salvation, but if that person was determined to live a godly life, he or she might receive forgiveness to continue in the Christian life.

The theology for sacraments within the Protestant Church promoted the celebration of the Lord's Supper in communion of the Body of Christ as all Christian believers. They share grape or berry juice to represent the blood of Jesus Christ and *bing* or Chinese bread to symbolize his body. The accepted means of baptism for being identified as a Christian was by the New Testament concept of being buried with Christ by immersion or the Old Testament version of sanctification by sprinkling. A baby may be baptized in dedication, but upon making a decision for salvation must be baptized again as an adult.

Traditional Western hymns were considered to be most sacred while the more familiar Chinese tune would be perceived as secular. In the hymnal that had been published in 1997, just 100 of the 400 entries were Chinese indigenous hymns. Some Protestant churches use the traditional Apostles Creed, but most do not use a formal creed. The church, with a minuscule **c**, would be that which was visible in organization and structure, and the

---

[292] Wu [pseud.] (Interview).
[293] Chen Yenling, an elder Chinese who was a soldier under Chiang Kaishek, Madrid (Interview, trans. Chu Lijung, 18 July 1998).

Church, with a capital C, enveloped the Body of Christ to be the believers as followers of Christ of the Open Church registered with the TSPM, home gatherings and the Catholic Church. The students of Nanjing Seminary are urged to remain close to God, maintain a vital relationship with Jesus Christ, honor the Church and respect the government.[294]

THE PROMINENCE OF THE HOUSE CHURCH MOVEMENT

Unregistered home gatherings, popularly known as the underground Church or house church movement, were known to be throughout China although not recognized by the Communist Party for they would not submit to their authority by registering with the TSPM. It was not a federation of churches or an organization that established home gatherings even though some had systematically made cell groups as the original assembly grew to proportions that could not be adequately nurtured in the faith. These meeting places were more prevalent in some areas as in Guangzhou there were several hundred, and the coastal regions of Wenzhou and Ningbo in Zhejiang Province were known for the density of home gatherings, even with numerous Communist cadres as participants. Those who attend underground churches in Shanghai number in the millions. Some cities, as Shenzhen of Guangdong Province, were considered void of religious faith, but Shenzhen was used as a haven for illegal importation of Bibles. Other areas, such as Yantai in Shandong Province lacked Bibles.[295]

Pastors were not able to bring spiritual nourishment without Bibles, or a deficiency in good study habits resulted in the lack of a proper theological base, which caused their congregations to misunderstand different doctrines. This combination conceived a legalistic emphasis on outward appearance and rules formed by the group leaders to take precedence over Biblical doctrinal principle.[296] The author met a Christian young lady working in Wenzhou who was from a nearby village, and she incidentally had her devotions from a hymnal because no Bible was available. She complained of the legalism of her home church that would forbid women to use cosmetic make-up and wear dresses or skirts,

---

[294] Wu [pseud.] (Interview). Bold letters used as identification by author.
[295] Humphrey, *Suppression in China*, pp. 20-24.
[296] Chen Y. P. (Interview)

but they were obligated to dress in slacks.

The TSPM was more vigilant of the church groups in the countryside with people of less education, theological instruction and leadership preparation; thus, a tendency toward heretical teachings. For an older experienced pastor who traveled to different neighborhood locations within a city to teach classes for pastoral training might be the only instruction in these areas.[297]

On his visit to the Wenzhou area in 1994, the author intended to schedule a visit for worship with a home gathering; however, another American had visited with a group the week before and later the home resident was imprisoned. Therefore, that part of the trip was canceled, and the acquaintance who was to afford this experience reported that this still was an obstacle as late as 1998. However, she related that some years earlier, as a Communist government teacher, she had surprised some of her students at a house church. They asked how a Marxist could be part of a Christian home gathering, and she answered that "the end of man was just the beginning of God."[298]

Independence of Each Congregation

Each church or home gathering had its autonomous operation due to different needs, circumstances and pressures. With no building construction costs and the pastors employed outside of their church ministry, finances were minimal and no offerings from the congregation were required.[299] Another church gave its Christian worker, who also was salaried, enough for bus fare to evangelize in other areas. The members financially supported him to that extent as well as gave moral endorsement in the early 1990s when the government intended to make a spectacle of him by parading through the streets wearing a dunce hat.[300] In a wealthier area, the government questioned an unregistered assembly how they could afford to build their large and beautiful church, even though permission had been granted for its construction. This group had also used offerings as a means to help establish another congregation and share with another group where there was less

---

[297] Zhou E. W. (Interview).
[298] Lin Yurong [pseud.], Businesswoman and former Communist Government teacher, Madrid (Interview, trans. Chu Lijung, 24 July 1998).
[299] Chen Y. P. (Interview).
[300] Ye Jianwei (Interview).

prosperity.[301] It was usual that offerings were taken to defer expenses of electricity and water of the location of the meeting and for relief funds to aid those in other sections of China who suffered from flood or famine.[302]

It had been estimated in 1998 that three new church buildings were completed in construction somewhere in China every two days.[303] In the city of Wenzhou nearly every section has a church or two plus meetings of home gatherings. Therefore, with a population of 6,000,000 there were many churches, some with 1,500 in attendance and numerous youth. Very little doctrinal variation existed, though in some churches the custom of women wearing a head covering as a symbol of submission to the husband or some legalistic practice marked a difference.[304]

The Attraction of the Home Gathering

Curiosity as to what Christianity had to offer or disillusionment and cynicism with Communist ideology drew Chinese to attend churches. Some sought truth, while the warmth and companionship of the Christian community and character of Christian associates attracted others. It certainly had not been perceived as a movement alien to Chinese life.[305] In some areas it was considered quite in mode to be a Christian.[306]

Even though doctrinal creeds were uniform, the worship practice varied some in distinct sections and political historical contexts of China. After the Communist revolution the sacraments of baptism and celebrating the Lord's Supper with bread and wine communion nearly ceased, but after the Cultural Revolution these practices became more prominent. Often baptisms were conducted in the country at a barn with a water tank or in a mountain stream, seaside or riverside and normally by immersion. Some home gatherings would meet every evening with different people for varied purposes. The prayer meeting was a free meeting spent in prayer, and everyone was expected to participate in a Bible study

---

[301] Zhou E. W. (Interview).
[302] Jonathan Chao (Interviews former Red Guard), Richard Van Houten (ed.), *Wise as Serpents Harmless as Doves* (Pasadena: William Cary Library, 1988), p. 69.
[303] 'Everyone's Building!' *Amity News Service*, Vol. 7, ¾,, 3.2, (1998) 3.
[304] Chen Xiaoya (Interview).
[305] Brown, *Christianity in China*, p. 179.
[306] Liu Yun [pseud.] (Interview).

gathering. Christians gathered to encourage each other in witness meetings with testimonies of what their Lord Jesus was doing among them. Each person had some training in Christian service and speaking, men and women alike. Worship was the service of Bible reading, hymns sung from the *Putian Songzan*, Hymns of Universal Praise, and a preacher, usually itinerant, expounded the Scripture portion. Non-Christians were not invited to most home gatherings for security against official intervention.

To practice the gifts given by the Holy Spirit; speaking in an unlearned language, praying for a person to be released from evil spirits and healing, were characterized as a part of worship in certain assemblages. Healing led many non-Christians and even Communist Party members to become believers in Jesus Christ as their Savior.[307] It was this phenomenon that the government through the TSPM had intended to eliminate from practice within the Protestant religious community. Therefore, the government targeted to suppress those itinerant evangelists who ministered through these gifts.

THE WORK OF THE ITINERANT EVANGELISTS

Itinerant evangelists on the home gathering or house church system numbered over 8,000 in the beginning of 1999. They started in their ministry at the age of 15-17 with vitality and vision. After three months of training in the basics of evangelism, they would be sent in pairs with a one-way ticket to wherever they sensed God had led them. After gaining a few converts through their ministry, they would live with a family of the community who provided for them as a form of Biblical Christian hospitality.[308]

Older and more established evangelists would often travel alone to contacts formed while speaking in different locations or by way of reputation. A weekend with one of these evangelists, called Jonah, from Shanghai, at the non-typical age of 73 revealed the life of these determined and vigorous Chinese disciples of Jesus Christ. This weekend in 1990, Jonah, accompanied by the one who reported the incidents, rode bicycles for 9 hours, traveled 40 hours on hard-seat class by train and 8 hours by a typical bus on rural roads. They went to a village of a convert who had attended a

---

[307] Chao, *Serpents Doves*, pp. 57-58, 61, 68-70, 74-75

[308] Jonathan Chao, Pasadena,CA: China Ministries International, Letter, 22 March 1999.

meeting where Jonah had spoken in another location. Of the 200 villagers who gathered to hear his message over 50 responded to become new Christian converts, and later he spent several hours training three of the new believers whom he had sensed would make exemplary leadership for this newly founded congregation. He had given an all-night seminar to 10 eager young people on the train, and in another city he reconciled the leadership of a church movement with over 5,000 members that he had helped establish years before. A Communist cadre of high rank sought him out to pray for the healing of his afflicted son, and both the official and his son became Christians due to this pastoral care. At one point the Public Security Bureau pursued him for arrest. Then upon arrival back at his home in Shanghai he had received mail requesting his ministry in another village, to which he responded by boarding another train that evening.[309]

The author met some of these evangelists while traveling in China in February of 1994. One was a 63 year-old man who traveled among 125 established churches and some 40 home gatherings in Jingtian County of Jiangxi Province to train church leaders. Another young man in Hangzhou had just returned from the far northern region where over 3,000 gathered in a wooded area to hear the Christian message, and the crowd was forced to continually stomp their feet to prevent their freezing.

Beyond the pastoral duties of preaching, leading worship in different locations over a large area, counseling individual believers, praying with the sick, and visiting the housebound and elderly, these Christian servants did tasks of maintenance and repairs on the church buildings. Often, duties at all hours made it prohibitive to adequately study the Bible, and their own spiritual life and family relationships suffered. The quality of their work deteriorated and at times sermons were ill prepared and delivered without enthusiasm, or inspiration, and worship became meaningless.[310] Married evangelists, especially after the birth of a child, could no longer stay with a host and must return to their home village to farm their own land or find employment.

---

[309] Ron MacMillan, 'A Weekend in the Life of a Chinese Itinerant Evangelist,' A News Network International Special Report, 11 December 1990; recorded in *Message of the Cross*, Jul.-Aug.-Sept. (1991).
[310] Gail V. Coulson (ed.), 'Believers Called Upon to Help Lighten Evangelist's Load,' *China Talk*, Vol.XXXIV April (1999) 14.

Some neglected to further their education and were not prepared for any profession, but evangelization continued to be their greatest passion.[311]

INTELLECTUAL CULTURE CHRISTIANS

The openness and reform demonstrated in the 1980s gave rise to the interest in learning from the West. This trend included the translation of over 300 Christian works into Chinese. This method was an alteration from Christianity being imported by foreigners to that being initiated by Chinese intellectuals searching for truth through the writings and translations from the West. These Chinese students, who were referred to as "Culture Christians," re-introduced Christianity and its theology from the West.[312]

A phenomenon in the last decade of the 20th century in China was intelligentsia who came to the knowledge about Jesus Christ and formed another part of the Chinese Church. Under the situation of general reform, academic circles had opened to religious research and separate departments or research centers were established.[313] Due to the disillusionment with Communism resulting from the 1989 Tiananmen Square incident, many of these intellectuals found an interest in Christianity. They had been taught that religion was for the uneducated peasants. Some through their international exposure had met Christians who shared their faith and for the first time in their lives heard the name of Jesus. To hear the singing of Christian songs was an attraction to Christianity for those who had only sung to Mao Zedong as the sun, moon and navigator.[314]

Preference for Christianity

An overseas Chinese art student related that, as an atheist, if he were to choose a religion it would be Christianity. He thought Buddhism to be for elderly women and Daoism to be suited for those who cared to live in seclusion with no knowledge of the world, but Communism, in comparison to any religion, was vacant. Christianity seemed to be a religion able to attract youth;

---

[311] Chao, Letter, 22 March 1999.
[312] 'Chinese Theology and Its Cultural Sources,' *Amity News Service,* Vol. 7, ¾,3.7 (1998) 14.
[313] Chen Zemin, 'Relations,' *China Talk,* p. 20.
[314] Yuan Aiguang (Interview); Hu Wei (Interview).

however, nearly 80 percent of Chinese have no religion but follow Confucian teachings.[315] The new Confucianism accepted among the Chinese intellectual circles in the current of reform and openness to Western scholarly trends had more influence than did Confucian thought of ancient China.

Expression of Christian Influence

The emergence of Culture Christians within China's society was due to profound understanding of Christianity through scholarship and research. A number had identified with Christianity in their thinking to convert and receive baptism. They had no tendency toward involvement in church activities, but they were interested in spreading the influence of Christendom among intellects of Chinese society.[316] The expression of their faith was revealed through their philosophy and art. Systematic translation of 20th Century Western philosophical, literary and religious classics was an integral part of China's cultural modernization and the source of the Culture Christian phenomenon.[317]

Within the last few years of the 20th Century, Chinese intellectuals were open to Christianity and were curious about the significance of the church in the large atheistic, modernizing socialist society of China.[318] A number of Christians among the intellectuals were not willing to confide their faith to colleagues and acquaintances, but maintained Christian devotion in the confines of their own home. Of course those who practiced a more open evangelistic role encountered more opposition.[319] Even though Christianity had been labeled as an "opiate," various Chinese literati have come to the conclusion it was what they needed in their lives, along with the wisdom of biblical instruction.[320]

THE CHURCH IN CHINA

A survey by the Central Committee of the Chinese Communist Youth League and the All-China Federation of Trade Unions in 1992 substantiated that 18 percent of China's citizens believe in

---

[315] Huang Wenyan [pseud.], art student, Madrid (Interview, 25 July 1998).
[316] Chen Zemin, 'Relations,' p. 21-22.
[317] Liu Xiaofeng, 'The Phenomenon of "Culture Christians",' Chinese Around the World, January 1999, pp. 20-21.
[318] Chen, 'The Life,' p. 36.
[319] Adeney, Church's March, p. 203.
[320] Yuan (Interview).

religion. The State Statistic Bureau completed another two-year survey project in May 1992 and found that the Chinese Protestant Church numbers 63,000,000, and 12,000,000 was the size of the Catholic Church of China.[321]

Christianity in China developed, due to the sociopolitical context, from foreign mission denominationalism to the post-denomination church of varied expression including Catholicism. The TSPM registered Church in its variations was determined to minister to the Chinese people and maintain legal status with the Communist government. The legal home gathering as a fellowship related to the registered churches, cared for intimate relationships in worship and a natural setting for influence. Those movements of house churches, considered clandestine, found their convictions to preserve Biblical principle with evangelical fervor rather than submit to governmental policy and register under the TSPM. Culture Christians were the latest 20th Century phenomenon without a church group identity except being within the scholarly literati, and their influence comes from foreign sources reaching out to peers. All of these facets of the Church in China were included in the identity of the Body of Christ with each part functioning as a whole in China.

---

[321] Thomas Lawrence, 'New Straightjacket for China's Expanding Church,' Jonathan Chao (ed.), *China Prayer Letter,* Hong Kong: No. 123, Oct.-Dec. (1992) 1.

4
HISTORY AND PHILOSOPHY OF THE THREE-SELF PATRIOTIC MOVEMENT 1950-1966

China was in a radical change at the inception of the Three-Self Patriotic Movement, known as the TSPM, conceived to represent Protestantism in China. In the political realm, the Chinese Communist Party had liberated the nation from the threat of Japanese occupation and from the Nationalist government that withdrew to Taiwan. All foreign agencies had withdrawn because of the anti-imperialistic sentiment that prevailed, including the mission boards with thousands of missionaries and the social services they initiated. The People's Government was in place to dominate China as a sovereign nation.

Traditionally, China had a pyramid power structure to wield state control over every facet of influence, according to Jonathan Chao's study as diagramed in *Wise as Serpents Harmless as Doves*. He showed that Confucianism was the recognized official orthodoxy of philosophical thought. Other recognized religions, which had been a part of the Chinese society, were tolerated through this structure. Any sectarian beliefs outside these endorsed associations were suppressed.[1] This contextual system remained in place under the People's Government of China in 1949. Christianity

---

[1] Jonathan Chao (interviews), Richard Van Houten (ed.), *Wise as Serpents Harmless as Doves* (Pasadena: William Cary Library, 1988), p. xi. Chao is a renowned researcher from Taiwan on China's Church and politics.

was considered an imperialistic implant not to be tolerated because of its alliance with Western powers and with Christian missionaries as implements of these alien nations. Richard Bush, the author of *Religion in Communist China,* quotes Wu Yaodong, the principle promoter of the implementation of the TSPM. Wu cited Leighton Stuart, Presbyterian missionary and President of Yenching University and his position as the American ambassador to the Nationalist government, as a case of imperialistic utilization of missionaries.[2]

With the knowledge of Christianity's historical framework as a foreign religion, Bishop Ting declared in an interview for the *China Avanza* that the TSPM might be able to improve the image of Christianity and open communication with the Chinese people.[3] A Chinese professor verified that the TSPM, organizationally, was not considered a church, but it mediated between the atheistic Communist government and the Chinese Christian Protestant churches. At times the TSPM heavily favored the governmental position[4] and used the Chinese traditional role of state control over religions. The Communist Party dominated the pinnacle of power while Marxism, Leninism and Mao Zedong Thought offered the official orthodoxy of ideology, and the churches registered with the TSPM or the Chinese Patriotic Catholic Association were tolerated as heterodoxy under state authority. Any Christian religious enterprise outside these patriotic organizations was considered illegal and to be repressed.[5]

The name, as a patriotic movement, identified the TSPM as an organization to encourage Christians to develop national self-respect and dedication to community progress and prosperity. Bishop Ting defined TSPM in his book *Chinese Christians Speak Out* and stated that these patriotic Christians influence society with the positive reputation of Christianity as a religion with Chinese

[2] Richard C. Bush, Jr., *Religion In Communist China* (New York: Abingdon Press, 1970), pp. 63-64.
[3] 'Situacion del Protestantismo,' *China Avanza* (Beijing: Beijing Informa, 1986), p. 4. An interview of Bishop K. H. Ting. *China Avanza* is a Spanish periodical printed to politically inform foreigners.
[4] Wu Qiwei [pseud.], Professor, New Haven, CN, Interview, 6 December 1998. Name withheld by request. Family spent years in labor camps.
[5] Chao (interviews), VanHouten (ed.), *Serpents Doves,* p. xxv.

characteristics.[6] Philip Wickeri in *Seeking Common Ground* reported that some discussion before 1949 formed a dichotomy between Communism and Christianity, but the TSPM provided an identity for the Chinese people and encouraged cooperation with the CCP on political and social issues. He declared that it also promoted the preservation of the Christian stance for believers.[7]

Mickey Spiegel stated in his book *Freedom in China* that the patriotic associations were a key part of the bureaucracy and directed by general secretaries who reported to the *Zong Jiao Ju* or Religious Affairs Bureau.[8] The TSPM provided locations for the Chinese Protestants to worship legally in open churches, where inquirers about the Christian religion may attend, and venues of contact for churches on the international level. Further, TSPM seminaries contributed theological training in a legalized locale, and their literature production served to help fulfill the Chinese Church's needs.[9]

The change of the TSPM title reflected willingness to identify and minister in the Chinese context. Leslie Lyall relates in 'The Chinese Church under Communism' a speech in 1954 by Wei Chingwu, the TSPM president. Wei reviewed the first four years at the national conference held in Beijing and reported notable growth in spiritual unity with the Little Flock and the True Jesus Church as the largest independent church movements formally represented. He stated that formerly the TSPM organizational title included the word "Reform" which some assemblies feared implied theological connotations. Therefore, the conference changed the designation to become known as the Chinese Christian Three-Self Patriotic Movement, now abbreviated as TSPM.[10]

Even with the TSPM as its representative, the Protestant

---

[6] Ting K. H., *Chinese Christians Speak Out* (Beijing: New World Press, 1984), pp. 7-9.
[7] Philip L. Wickeri, *Seeking the Common Ground* (Mary Knoll, NY: Orbis Books, 1990), pp. 19-20. Is known for his close relationship with the TSPM and Amity Foundation.
[8] Mickey Speigel, *Freedom in China* (New York: Human Rights Watch, 1997), p. 3. An advocate of human rights, focused on China.
[9] Jonathan Chao, *A History of Christianity in socialist China,* 1998, e-mailed material from the introduction and conclusion of his new book. Conclusion, p. 8.
[10] Leslie Lyall, 'The Chinese Christian Church under Communism 1949-1966,' in David Aikman (ed.), *Love China Today* (Wheaton: Tyndale Publishers, Inc., 1977), p. 45.

Chinese Church was weak in tradition, and the activities of the Church were circumscribed by defined limitations. Yet, without a historical heritage to perpetuate, there remained the capacity of freedom to venture toward other objectives. Though the Chinese Christians represent a small percentage of the Chinese population and had insignificant involvement in the Communist revolution, they increasingly sought to identify with the people's movement under the direction of the Communist Party. Wickeri agreed with Bishop Ting's view from the fourteen-point article he wrote that patriotism of the Chinese Christian community affirmed its association with the achievements of the Communist Party and identification with it, as well as a love for the New China.[11]

It must be recognized, on a theological basis, that the TSPM was established by the grace of God under the power of the Holy Spirit and the Lordship of Jesus Christ and not under the influence of another external force. The TSPM called the Church to accountability for responsible self-reliance and to assure its survival. The difficulty was that some RAB cadres lacked understanding of religions and their practices and tended to regard religious adherents with cynicism. Beyond that, some had inadequate comprehension of the united front approach, which the TSPM fulfilled as advocated under Marxist-Leninist and Mao Zedong Thought.[12]

On the other hand, the understanding of the role of the united front was questionable in a case Lyall related that demonstrated the lack of prudence under an atheistic Communist government brought consequences. Rev. Marcus Chang, vice-president of the TSPM, who attained one of the five Christian positions on the People's Political Consultative Council, experienced humiliation when faced with an opportunity for perhaps a justifiable criticism. In 1957, during the Hundred Flowers Campaign, Rev. Chang denounced the government for its insensitivity towards Christians and exhorted the constitutional rights for religion.[13] In 1984 *The South China Morning Post* stated that Bishop Ting related to reporters in Hong Kong that the Church had suffered persecution only during the Cultural Revolution period from 1966 to 1976. David Adeney, however, confirmed that hundreds

[11] Wickeri, *Seeking*, pp. 20-21, 24.
[12] Ibid, pp. 39-40, 71.
[13] Lyall, *Church 1949-1966*, p. 45.

of Christian pastors were arrested in the 1950s and spent years imprisoned before the revolution. Many were held until the subsequent moderation of the government in 1979 when they were released.[14] Furthermore, Timothy Wu, in his personal account *Sheltered Through the Storms: A Chinese Pastor Preserved by God,* said that by 1959, when the Leftists persecuted many Christians, some in the TSPM not only denied Christ but betrayed other Christians to the secret police. Unwarranted charges were often pressed to gain favor for the prosecutors and satisfaction for the persecutors.[15]

However, the Communist Party wished to encourage Christian involvement in the society for it believed that the political and material interests of all Chinese should be the same, under socialism. To separate from society because of a religious difference could not be tolerated, and any attempt to do so would indicate a religious authority to be repressed for the establishment of harmony, patriotism and national unity.[16]

The TSPM committee managed all administrative church affairs. Hymns were edited and Bible commentaries were examined, while preaching was restrained that dealt with eschatology, vanity and the prohibition of marriage between a believer and non-believer. All religious activity was restricted to church buildings, and the clergy had to register with the TSPM, even those who had ministered in home gatherings. Pastors and evangelists were not permitted to leave their designated area to perform ministry.[17]

After the Cultural Revolution and the subjugation of the Gang of Four, reconstruction of the government took place. In 1979 the TSPM initiated an effort to recover the confidence of Chinese Christians for participation in a united front. The second clause of Article 36 of the 1982 Constitution stated: "No state organ, public organization or individual may compel citizens to believe in, or

---

[14] David Adeney, *China: The Church's Long March* (Ventura, CA: Regal Books, 1985), p. 120. Information of *South China Morning Post,* April 11, 1984.
[15] Timothy Wu, *Sheltered Through the Storms: A Chinese Pastor Preserved by God* (Palo Cedro, CA: Wayside Impressions, 1996), ch. 10. Personally experienced persecution.
[16] Wickeri, *Seeking,* pp. 100.
[17] Adeney, *Church's March,* pp. 120-121, 174. Information of *Tian Feng,* 561, September 22 (1958) 20. A periodical of the TSPM.

not to believe in, any religion; nor may they discriminate against citizens who believe in, or do not believe in any religion." Article 147 of the new Penal Code held an even more explicit proviso: "Any government official who attempts to restrict religious belief of any citizen is subject to up to two years imprisonment...." This condition likewise referred to public organizations and individuals that may coerce persons to believe in a religion. This provision was particularly explicit for areas monopolized by Muslims.[18]

Thus, the TSPM had a role that provided the capacity for the Chinese Christian Protestant Church to legally exist in the Communist context of China. Different views gave varied responses to its role, and each could justify their prejudices due to their particular experiences and circumstances. However, the TSPM has been historically established for the Chinese Church, and it had affected all Protestants of China.

TSPM: HISTORICAL ROOTS

History Before 1949

The Chinese Communist Party in an effort to create the utopia society rooted in dialectical materialism conflicted with the ideological Christian Church. Historical experience shaped an inseparable relationship between Christianity and Western imperialism and capitalism. During the Qing Dynasty, Chinese Christian believers divided their loyalty between the state and the Pope subsequent to the rites controversy. The foreign aggression of the Opium Wars permanently connected Christianity with the unequal treaties that ensued, which required the official gentry to protect the detested foreign missionary. Consequently, anti-foreignness became synonymous with anti-Christian.[19] For the Christian Church to survive as a part of Chinese society a provision needed consideration and to maintain positive world opinion the government required an organizational structure to ensure ascendancy. The Three-Self Patriotic Movement was not a spontaneous conception of the Chinese Christian Church, but its origin by the government linked the Church with the

---

[18] Wickeri, *Seeking,* p. 104.
[19] Jonathan Chao, *A History of Christianity in Socialist China,* 1998, e-mailed material from the Introduction and Conclusion of his new book, Conclusion, p. 2.

secular state.[20]

Some of the imperialistic reputation earned by the missionary movement was justified and wrong. On the other hand, misunderstandings were generated by missionaries' ignorance of the Chinese mindset or from the lack of consideration for their cultural and national sensitivity, which accounted for anti-Christian sentiments. Nonetheless, Y. T. Wu, the initiative factor in the TSPM, related that the slogan of one missionary enterprise, "Evangelize the World in this Generation" was interpreted as that of imperialistic occupation of China.[21] George Patterson listed evidence of Western aggression: church architecture, religious rites and liturgy were adopted straight from the West, prayer books were poorly translated, and hymnals contained only 62 Chinese hymns from the total of 512. Missionaries maintained their Western lifestyle, and Chinese Christian workers attempted to imitate them. It was sensed that the missionaries rated the value of Chinese believers for the work of the Church in China according to their grasp of English, rather than their knowledge of Chinese literature and language skills.[22]

The main concern of the Church was to produce the Protestant Church in China with Chinese characteristics. In his article 'The Origins and Evolution of the Three-Selves in Relation to China,' published in the *International Bulletin of Missionary Research,* Wilbert Shenk relates that this concept was not new, for in 1793 William Carey arrived in India with the philosophy that emphasized training an indigenous ministry with native preachers. He also wrote the account of a leading Congregationalist pastor, J. A. James, who exhorted a congregation in 1826, "Let it be a great object with us, to render our missions self-supporting and self-propagating. The only work to be done by foreigners is to introduce the gospel into a country and then send it forward by the hands of native converts."[23] His thought modeled missions after the Church of the first century.

---

[20] Leslie Lyall, 'The Chinese Christian Church under Communism 1949-1966,' in David Aikman (ed.), *Love China Today* (Wheaton: Tyndale Publishers, Inc., 1977), p. 47.

[21] Wu, Y. T., 'Y. T. Wu on the New Missionary Strategy,' February 1962, Merwin, *Documents of TSPM,* 1963, p. 202.

[22] George N. Patterson, *Christianity in Communist China* (Waco, TX: Word Books, 1969), p. 47. Cary-Elwes, *China and the Cross,* pp. 212-215.

[23] Wilbert R. Shenk, 'The Origins and Evolution of the Three-Selves in relation to China,' *International Bulletin of Missionary Research,* Vol. 14, January (1990) 28.

The *Asia Journal of Theology* published Yeo Khiokkhng's article 'The Rise of the Three-Self Patriotic Movement (TSPM): Chinese Christianity in the Light of Communist Ideology in New China.' It told that as early as the 1800s, Missionaries S. L. Baldwin and V. Talmage had initiated the three-self concept in China.[24] In 1850, Henry Venn, the chief executive of the Church Missionary Society of England, reiterated the three-self theory in a paper entitled *Native Church Organization*, which captured the concept with the phrase "euthanasia of mission," as missionaries were to consider themselves dispensable.

Chen Mingnan, a Baptist scholar credited by Richard Zhang in 'The Origin of the "Three Self"' as the first Chinese Protestant to establish a *zili hui*, an independent church, in Guanzhou of Eastern Guangdong in the year 1872. By 1924, just two years after the National Christian Conference, there were over 330 independent local churches. After the tragic massacre of students by British soldiers on May 30, 1925, the May 30th Movement provided the incentive for the Church to consider indigenization within the Three-Self principles.[25] The book *Religion under Socialism in China* by Luo Zhufeng recorded that a Shanghai pastor, Yu Guozeng, led an active opposition to the mission protection by unequal treaties and stimulated churches and Chinese Christians to become independent, self-managing and self-propagating.[26] Philip Wickeri reported from an unpublished paper written by Shen Yifan and Cao Shengjie that in 1906 Yu founded the Chinese Jesus Independent Church in Shanghai and continually called all Chinese Christians to refuse the jurisdiction of Western church organizations.[27]

There was some encouragement for indigenization of the Chinese Protestant Church from the English Presbyterian Mission, which began ministry in the Swatow area during 1858. Twenty-three years later, in 1881, it summoned a meeting of all Chinese national leaders and missionaries of the chartered congregations

[24] Yeo Khiok Khng, 'The Rise of the Three-Self Patriotic Movement (TSPM): Chinese Christianity in the Light of Communist Ideology in New China,' *Asia Journal of Theology*, Vol. 6, No. 1, April (1992) 3.
[25] Richard X. Y. Zhang, 'The Origin of the "Three-Self",' *Jian Dao*, Vol. 5, 1996, pp. 178, 187-188.
[26] Luo Zhufeng (ed.), *Religion under Socialism in China*, trans. Donald E. MacInnis and Sheng Xian (London: M. E. Sharpe, Inc., 1991), p. 47.
[27] Philip L. Wickeri, *Seeking the Common Ground* (Mary Knoll, NY: Orbis Books, 1990), p. 41.

to propose the organization of a Presbytery under the principle that "the native church ought to be self-governing, self-supporting and self-propagating."[28] However, Princeton Hsu's article 'China's Indigenous Christian Movements' substantiated that the official call for autonomy came in 1924 for three actions: self-dependence, self-support and self-propagation, but the May 30, 1925, incident provided impetus for Church indigenization. In 1926, the Presbyterian, Anglican and Baptist mission boards conferred all church properties to the Chinese, an important step in Chinese Church history. Then 1929 marked the initiation of the Indigenous Movement, and Chinese Protestants took active measures in that direction.[29] Many Chinese had the desire, persuasion, and vision for autonomy, but they lacked unity of churches and mission boards for it to become a national movement.

THE MANIFESTO

The Chinese Communist Revolution of 1949 sealed a turning point in Chinese Church history. The Communist Party incorporated all dimensions of social endeavor under its disposition, which included the Protestant Church in China. Christians called for a compromise for Church survival in an evolutionary phase of self-renovation, self-reform and self-reliance, which developed into the three-self concept. Church leaders requested governmental protection with their affirmation of religious rights, but the Party demanded church members to confess and declare their loyalty.[30] Chinese Christians concluded that to remain in their country as citizens of China they could manage within the environment of a socialist state. At this time there were approximately 1,000,000 Protestant Christians, related to twenty-three major denominational groups, represented by both indigenous and foreign mission organizations.[31] The YMCA and YWCA were two of the organizations independent of foreign connections with Chinese support and staff, the first Christians to overtly support the cause of Chinese Communism. Y. T. Wu, Liu Liangmo, and Tu

---

[28] Shenk, 'The Origins,' *IBMR*, p. 32.
[29] Princeton Hsu, 'China's Indigenous Christian Movements,' in David Aikman (ed.), *Love China Today* (Wheaton: Tyndale House Publishers, Inc., 1977), pp. 33-34; and Zhang, 'The Origin,' p. 193.
[30] Zhang, 'The Origin,' *Jian Dao*, pp. 195-196.
[31] Wickeri, *Seeking*, pp. 116-118.

Yuching as the YMCA leaders along with Miss Cora Ting or Ting Yuchih of the YWCA encouraged Protestant leaders to support the Three-Self Movement.[32] Before the Communist Revolution the Three-Self could not fully realize its potential as a nationwide movement.[33]

Many of the Church leaders chose the attitude, regarding entrance under Communism or advocated by Bishop Ting, to perhaps err of the side of naivete rather than that of cynicism. They chose to persist in their Christian ministry and allow the consequences to prove reality, which would afford redeeming possibilities rather than frustration.[34] Bishop K. H. Ting in *Chinese Christians Speak Out* determined that the possibility for the Christian Church in China to legally thrive was by God's providence; God provided the policy of freedom of religious belief in the People's Republic of China, through the CCP, and the formation of the TSPM through the Chinese Christians themselves.[35]

On the dates of May 2, 6 and 13, 1950, Premier Zhou Enlai met with Y. T. Wu of the YMCA and Cora Ting of the YWCA. Zui who represented the Church of Christ in China, Ai Niensan the Lutherans of Shanghai, Bishop Z. T. Kaung the Methodists, T. C. Chao the Anglicans along with fifteen other delegates in Beijing, joined them. This assembly convened to discuss how the Protestants might pledge their loyalty to the new Communist regime. It resulted in the Christian Manifesto drafted by Y. T. Wu and approved by the Premier.[36] The Manifesto was placed on the back of pews throughout the independent churches. Individuals were encouraged to sign it as their patriotic duty and to avoid public censure.[37] Patterson reported that in September 23, 1950, the Christian Manifesto was published in all daily newspapers with the signatures of 1,527 Christian leaders.[38] Then according to Wickeri the indigenous Jesus Family of Shandong provided

---

[32] Richard C. Bush, Jr., *Religion In Communist China* (New York: Abingdon Press, 1970), p. 96.
[33] Wickeri, *Seeking*, p. 41.
[34] Ibid, p. 127.
[35] Ting, K. H., *Chinese Christians Speak Out* (Beijing: New World Press, 1984), p. 4. Bishop Ting's Retrospect and Prospect, Opening Address at the Third National Christian Conference.
[36] Bush, *Religion*, p. 177.
[37] Paul R. Spicard, 'The Church in the Crucible: Chinese Protestants Since liberation,' *Fides et Historia*, Vol. 22, Fall 1990, p. 35.
[38] Patterson, *Christianity*, pp. 46-47.

381 endorsements as the largest number of any denomination or movement. Within six months 180,000 Christians had signed, and finally the Manifesto bore 417,389 names of Chinese Protestants.[39]

A copy of the Christian Manifesto revealed that its fundamental aims were to help Chinese Christians to recognize the evils of imperialism and its use of Christianity. It fostered measures "to cultivate a patriotic and democratic spirit with a psychology of self-respect, self-reliance and self-criticism." The methods to achieve these aims were secure in "self-rejuvenation through deeper understanding of the nature of Christianity, closer fellowship and unity among various denominations, the cultivation of better leadership personnel, and reform in the systems of church organization." It emphasized "anti-imperialistic, anti-feudalistic and anti-bureaucratic-capitalistic education."[40]

ORGANIZATIONAL STRUCTURAL FUNCTION OF THE RELIGIOUS PATRIOTIC MOVEMENT

David Adeney charted the organizational structure in *China: The Church's Long March*. It proceeded from the Chinese Communist Party, CCP, to the United Front Work Department, UFWD, utilized for unity and cooperation to achieve Party goals. Under the UFWD the Religious Affairs Bureau, RAB, regulated all religious patriotic organizations of China, of which the Three-Self Patriotic Movement, TSPM, was the Protestant Christian association.[41]

Chinese Communist Party, CCP

The New China News Agency recorded Lu Tingyi's 1951 speech on culture and education, which affirmed that dialectical materialism provided the ideological worldview of Marxist-Leninist and Mao ZeDong Thought, and this rationale along with historical substance built the conventional platform for Communism. The expectations of the CCP were for Christianity to align against imperialism and collaborate with the People's Government on the common

---

[39] Wickeri, *Seeking*, p. 131.
[40] Patterson, 'Appendix I, Manifesto: May 1950,' *Christianity*, p. 168.
[41] David H. Adeney, *China: The Church's Long March* (Ventura, CA: Regal Books, 1985), p. 116.

foundation to form the New China.[42] Premier Zhou Enlai in his 'Peking Edict of December 29, 1950,' given at the 65th Session of State Administration Conference, declared that registration gave evidence of allegiance. The recording consisted of the name of the organization; name of the leader with his age, nationality, history; his capital listed along with his subsidies, their amount and source. The nature of work and conditions for using of funds was accompanied by a detailed strategy. Only organizations that had registered to signify detachment from foreign nations as "reported ... to the Special Committee under the Local, Municipal or Provincial Committee shall be released from the regulations governing the Special registration."[43]

Compliance to regulations assured non-interference with authorities when churches engaged in normal religious activities. C. T. Chao, whose holy orders were revoked during the Three-Anti Campaign in 1952, declared the intention of the government and rights of the people, in his address of 1956:

> If the Government should do something wrong, morally wrong, such as oppressing or injuring anyone, the people themselves would criticize it. The people have the liberty to do it, and we in the church as a part of the people have the right, the responsibility and the freedom to do this. The reason we have not opposed or condemned the government is because it is a good government.[44]

However, political conditions with the government of China brought periods of restriction on religious policy and periods of relaxation. Whenever the situation for the Christians was agreeable, it was also acceptable for the Buddhists and Muslims. An example: in April 1971, when China's relations with the United States became favorable; the Chinese Muslims' contingent for the

---

[42] Lu Tingyi, 'Speech on Culture and Education,' New China News Agency for April 25, 1951, Merwin, *Documents TSPM* (New York: New China Committee, 1963), pp. 30,32.

[43] Chou Enlai (Chairman), Peking Edict of December 29, 1950, 65th Session of State Administrative Council, Merwin, *Documents TSPM,* NY: NCC, 1963, p. 23.

[44] Chao, T. C., 'Address by "Brother" T. C. Chao,' April 16, 1956, Merwin, *TSPM Documents,* 1963, p. 130. Dr. T. C. Chao underwent severe criticism in the Three-Anti Campaign of 1952, and his holy orders were revoked. Accordingly he is here called "Brother," that is, layman.

annual pilgrimage to Mecca was the second largest of all foreign countries. This was not a phenomenon that the Chinese Muslims had specifically planned. Thus, the situation usually was not a special approach that focused just on Christians.[45]

United Front Work Department, UFWD

The United Front was shaped through alliances formed of associates, enemies, and those in the intermediaries. Friends supported the objectives of the Communist Party, and enemies were aligned with imperialists, anti-revolutionaries and anti-Communists. The United Front sought a link of cooperation that would center on those holding the median position to be persuaded to embrace the Communist cause.[46] The UFWD, an arm of the People's Government, was to supervise various non-Communist sectors of the new socialist society. Its policies, shaped through the conflicts with the Nationalist government and the Japanese, which involved the cultivation of support for its policies by the majority of society "while reducing to an ineffective minority, then isolating, neutralizing and ultimately destroying die-hard opposition."[47] The United Front approach was criticized for its tactic of deceit through an oblique focus on cooperation with the Communists, who then would manipulate it for its advantage. The use of initiatives for mutual esteem, peace and cooperation might signal a united front approach.[48]

The presence of the United Front was evident whenever the Communists sought support from non-Communists. Principled participation coupled with infiltration, solidarity and assistance, organization and control on both national and international scope were implicit or explicit expressions of the united front. Under the auspice of patriotism in the 1950s, the CCP sought to develop enthusiasm for socialist reconstruction.[49] Peter Humphrey recorded in *Religious Suppression in China* that the Buddhist Association, Islamic Association, Taoist Association, Catholic Patriotic Association, and the Three-Self Patriotic Movement are

---

[45] David H. Aikman, 'Religious Policy,' in David Aikman (ed.), *Love China Today* (Wheaton: Tyndale House Publishers, Inc., 1977), p. 95.
[46] Wickeri, *Seeking*, p. 56.
[47] Adeney, *Church's March*, p. 117.
[48] Wickeri, *Seeking*, p. 64.
[49] Ibid, pp. 45, 47.

all results of the Chinese Communist united front through the Religious Affairs Bureau.[50]

Religious Affairs Bureau, RAB

The RAB was formed as a state organization concerned with religious policy for religious adherents throughout China. Especially at the local level its purpose coincided with the function as a united front organization.[51] The RAB was formed in Beijing in 1950 to sever overseas connections from any religious order and to promote autonomous religious movements including the expulsion of foreign religious workers.[52] The RAB had become the intermediary between the Buddhists, Muslims, the Catholics and Protestants as Christians and diverse government establishments. These religious groups might appeal to the RAB when their religious freedom had been violated. The RAB was also concerned with the "non-antagonistic contradictions" of religious superstition, discrimination as well as "antagonistic contradictions" of religious policy and foreign influential penetration.[53]

The RAB functioned to investigate religious orders and the activities of their personnel, to control any religious activity and to influence Protestants to join the TSPM. Through the enforcement of governmental policy the RAB enhanced political consciousness of the patriotic religious organizations. The RAB aimed to cultivate a closer relationship between church leaders and the state to produce a positive alliance for socialist construction. It protected the Church by suppressing reactionary and counter-revolutionary elements that infringed on normal religious activity. Any foreign religious visitor to China came under the responsibility of the RAB to host and entertain for the duration of the stay.[54]

Some RAB officials interpreted the policy as a function of control and required organizational historical reports, an account of membership roles with a record of daily congregations, and financial and property assets. Meeting proceedings were submitted

---

[50] Peter Humphrey, *Religious Suppression in Mainland China* (Republic of China: World Anti-Communist League, 1983), p 28.
[51] Wickeri, *Seeking,* p. 66.
[52] Yeo, 'The Rise of TSPM,' *AJT,* p. 2.
[53] Wickeri, *Seeking,* p. 70.
[54] Patterson, *Christianity,* pp. 3-4.

to the RAB, and every clergy was obligated to present each sermon for censorship of any materials contrary to the interests of the Communist Party. These officials found some parts of the Bible reasonable, those which were philanthropic and advocated peace. The ideology of the RAB countered the supernatural, eschatology, resurrection and immortality. The RAB approved "propaganda in promotion of world peace, patriotism, love of the people and support of the realistic world."[55]

Three-Self Patriotic Movement, TSPM

The primary initiator of the TSPM, Wu Yao Tsung of the YMCA, by Patterson's account, had received a directive from the executive officer of the Department of Propaganda of the Central Committee of the CCP, Lu Tingyi. Wu was charged with approaching the Christian leaders of Beijing, Tientsin, Shanghai and Kwangzhou for signatures on the Christian Manifesto that instituted the TSPM.[56] Yeo recorded that in April of 1951 the RAB invited 151 Protestant leaders to a conference in Beijing. In this meeting they voted for the Chinese Church to become self-governed, self-supported, and self-propagated. To accomplish this all relations with imperialistic foreign mission must be severed.[57]

Arthur Wallis, executive secretary of the Foreign Mission National Council of Churches, documented that the formation of the TSPM circumvented the earlier established National Christian Council of China, NCC. The NCC had the stigma of imperialism conceived by the International Missionary Council, which also identified with the liberal facet of Protestantism. Many conservative churches had refused to join the NCC, and the intention of the TSPM was to attempt to unify the churches.[58]

TSPM Involvement with "Oppose-America Aid-Korea"

The outset of the Korean War set the stage for the TSPM as an organization promoted by the united front concept, Patterson noted. The Communist leadership feared the possibility of Chinese Christians conforming to Western thought as an accessory for imperialistic aggression. A campaign to "Resist

[55] Ibid, pp. 4-5, 12.
[56] Ibid, p. 7
[57] Yeo, 'The Rise of TSPM,' *AJT*, pp. 3-4.
[58] Arthur Wallis (Ex. Sec.), Jones (ed.), Merwin, *Documents of TSPM* (New York: FEODFMNCC, 1963), p. iii.

American Aggression and Aid Korea" was begun by the CCP to apply pressure on religious groups to publicly renounce foreign associations and embrace an anti-Western disposition. The person who refused was labeled as a counter-revolutionary or as an agent of imperialism and met with severe consequences.[59] Therefore, as Britt Towery explains in his book *The Churches of China*, the exodus of missionaries and the cessation of their funds were not implemented by the TSPM, but were triggered by American involvement in the war in Korea.[60]

Lyall found in his research that by the end of 1951 the Chinese Christian Church was totally isolated from any foreign relationships; church leaders had disposed of mission properties and had promoted full Church indiginization. Most Christian ministers immediately were required to become state or self-employed. Sermons were censored; baptisms restricted and Christian schools, hospitals, and charitable institutions were appropriated from the jurisdiction of the Church. The People's Government financed the anti-imperialism and socialism construction re-education for Christian clergy.[61] Lu Tingyi spoke of three widely-advocated, large movements: the "Oppose-America Assist-Korea Movement," agrarian reform, and suppression of counter-revolution. All Chinese Christians were expected to actively approve and participate in these movements.[62]

Accusation, Denunciation and Thought Reform

Within a week of the April 1950 inaugural conference with Lu Tingyi as the Cultural, Educational and Religious Bureau chair of the Government Administrative Council, there were 16,000 arrests in Shanghai alone. An unknown number, according to Leslie Lyall, succumbed to the extreme pressure and committed suicide. Lyall records the accusation meeting later on June 10, 1950, organized by the TSPM, at that time referred to as the Three-Self Reform Movement. Representatives of all Christian organizations and churches were ordered to attend. Church laity sat in shaded stands while the employees of Christian organizations stood in

---

[59] Patterson, *Christianity*, p. 8.
[60] Britt Towery, *The Churches of China* (Hong Kong: Long Dragon Books, 1987), p. 214. From an address by K. H. Ting, Protestant Christian Bishop.
[61] Lyall, *Church 1949-1966*, pp. 44-45.
[62] Lu, 'Speech,' *Documents TSPM*, p. 33.

the open on concrete exposed to the sun. Medics helped those who fainted while long speeches of fabricated statements against missionaries, made with facial expression of indignation droned on, in the effort to inflict loss of face to America, the missionary movement, and the Christian Church.[63]

Nearly a year later on April 19, 1951 the denunciation movement began at an assembly in Beijing called by the State Affairs Council. Its purpose was for the Chinese Christians to intensify their criticisms against American imperialism in the method of a broader patriotic movement. Former colleagues and associates mentioned missionaries and Chinese church leaders in discourses of reproach. Denunciation was primarily a negative dynamic of vulnerability while renunciation remolded ideology for socialist construction.[64]

The Party concentrated on the formation of thought through socialist education in every area concerning society. Bush detailed in *Religion in Communist China* that, on August 25 through 29 of 1952, the major event of unification of eleven seminaries of East China was achieved under the sponsorship of the TSPM at a conference in Shanghai. The formation of Jingling Union Theological Seminary resulted with the aims of studying the Bible, raising the comprehension level of national loyalty, preparing the New Church leaders to serve the people, and encouraging the principles of the Three-Self Reform Movement.[65] From *Documents of the Three-Self Patriotic Movement*, Wu Y. T. proposed in accordance with the three-self principles that the TSPM encourage Christians to endorse the Constitution of the Chinese People's Republic by working to achieve a socialist society. The TSPM was to summon all Christians to maintain anti-imperialistic views for world peace and have church members in continued studies on patriotism to terminate any imperialistic influence. The purpose was to consolidate churches into the character of self-direction, and to study the difficulties of self-reliance to encounter solutions.[66]

---

[63] Leslie T. Lyall, *Come Wind Come Weather,* pp. 30-32; Reiterated by Patterson, *Christianity,* pp. 62-63.
[64] Wickeri, *Seeking,* p. 134, 140.
[65] Bush, *Religion,* pp. 86-87.
[66] Wu Y., '54 Conference,' *Documents TSPM,* 1963, pp. 92-94.

Promotion of the Three-Self Principle

As reported in the January 15, 1953, edition of *Tien Feng* periodical, the Three-Self Reform Movement was considered a success by the end of 1952. Imperialistic influences had been minimized, and Christians had proven loyal to the government and the Oppose-America-Aid-Korea Movement. Church leaders had been united because of their purging experiences, and many churches had registered as members of the TSPM.[67] Even a message of respect was written by the TSPM to Chairman Mao ZeDong as found in an article in the *Asia Journal of Theology* by Yeo KhiokKhun.[68] It assured the promotion of unity of Christian churches through the Three-Self policies. It supported the Draft Constitution of the People's Republic of China and agreed to strive to help construct a socialist society. The letter assured continued opposition to imperialist aggression, for world peace, and encouraged Christians seriously to learn patriotism. The promotion of mutual respect for all citizens was considered in a study on self-propagation, which rejected any imperialistic contamination and facilitated the proclamation of Christianity. Finally, the goal of the TSPM was to cultivate the spirit of love-country and love-church, and patriotism for a law-abiding Church of purity. Bush stated that September 23 was declared as a special "Chinese Christian Church Three-Self Movement Day." This served as a testimony to encourage the Chinese Protestant Church to join the TSPM, participate in socialist construction, and support world peace.[69]

In his book *Religion under Socialism in China,* Luo Zhufeng related the concept of religion suggested by Zhou Enlai in the conference of national construction. Zhou proposed that the five natures possessed by religion were the "mass nature, long-lasting nature, international nature, complex nature and [minority] nationalities nature."[70] The TSPM was concerned with "indigenization and ecclesiastical renewal". These two contentions between political and religious concerns were considered inclusive and united in purpose. The First National Christian Conference held in Beijing from July 22 to August 6, 1954, had 232 representatives from 62

---

[67] *Tien Feng*, January 15, 1953, quoted in Lyall, *Come Wind*, p. 22.
[68] Yeo, 'The Rise of TSPM,' *AJT,* p. 4.
[69] Bush, *Religion*, p. 245.
[70] Luo, *Religion under Socialism*, p. 10.

churches and Christian organizations. This conference produced a "Letter to Christians throughout China" as to the purpose of the TSPM. Its goal was to unite Protestant Christians nation-wide to foster self-government, self-support and self-propagation in the Chinese churches and to actively oppose imperialism, assist in the affirmation of patriotism, and protect world peace. This letter was a contribution to the united front principle, and it helped in the implementation of the religious freedom policy.[71] Yeo confirmed this view from the Communist perspective on religious freedom in his article in the *Asian Journal of Theology*. He cites Article 88 of the 1954 Constitution, which states: "Citizens of the People's Republic of China enjoy freedom of religious belief." Article 88 was aligned with Marxist dogma and understanding as to the establishment of the TSPM.[72]

Wu asserted during the July 1954 conference that church members who had not registered to aid in the TSPM movement really had not come to an understanding of its function. In that era as the Three-Self Reform Movement, the TSPM had a sectarian view of non-participants and labeled them as being backward and non-progressive. He advocated empathizing with their situation and giving understanding by listening to their questions. Thus, with patience an avenue of cooperation might be found. Wu in this conference recounts the accomplishments by TSPM in its first four years as the liberation from foreign "imperialistic influence," the rise of "patriotic consciousness," and a new spirit to "love country and love church."[73]

The National Committee of the TSPM asserted on March 3, 1958, that the missionary movement had been a tool of imperialism for subversion. The committee quoted an editorial of September 28, 1955, from *The Christian Century*, which admits:

Accusations of espionage cannot be so confidently dismissed... It is known that strong pressures have been brought on individual missionaries and mission boards to place information at the disposal of our intelligence services. Some missionaries and some mission boards have responded to such appeals.

---

[71] Wickeri, *Seeking*, p. 114, 150-151, 153.
[72] Yeo, 'The Rise of TSM,' *AJT*, p. 1.
[73] Wu Y., '1954 Conference,' *Documents of TSPM*, pp. 87-91.

However, as a committee they continued to uphold international contact for the Chinese Christians with vigilance to demonstrate the impossibility for imperialists to utilize these Christian international relations and activities.[74]

Along with the vigilance against imperialistic encounters, the Shanghai Municipal Congress noted on August 20, 1958, that due to the misunderstanding of national religious policy on part of cadres, prejudice was demonstrated against some religious adherents.[75] This action caused depression among Christians who doubted if love for country and love for the Church could be united and diminished their enthusiasm for their work. They recognized this condition existed, and that when the government penalized a Christian who had proven to be a counter-revolutionary, some comrades retained the attitude that proper religious activity and all Christians were also counter-revolutionary.

The Congress acknowledged complaints from Christians who claimed that their efforts had never procured meritorious mention or promotion, a hindrance to positive Christian participation in the national endeavor. Christians had been labeled as non-progressives because of their religious beliefs and for declining to join the atheistic Communist Party. It was determined that the people were considered to be progressive when they portrayed a patriotic attitude and made efforts to promote socialism. Recognition was given for governmental assistance with the reconstruction of seventeen churches destroyed by the autumn typhoon. Employers gave their Christian employees time off for the celebration of Christmas, and the Shanghai daily newspapers gave a fair account of the Christmas religious activities. One thousand Christians of Shanghai received recognition from the government with Model Worker awards.

The government provided positive assistance for churches and the TSPM as referenced by Wickeri. The termination of foreign funds placed the properties of mission schools and hospitals in the administration of the state; in conformity to Article 5 of the Constitution, which demonstrated the extent of care for the people to include Chinese Christians, taxes on buildings used for religious, YMCA or YWCA, services were remitted. Then Article

[74] National Committee of the Three-Self Movement, 'Imperialism: Exploiter of Religion,' March 3, 1958, Merwin, Documents TSPM, 1963, p. 178.
[75] Shanghai Municipal Congress, 'Shanghai Manifesto,' August 20, 1958, Merwin, *Documents TSPM*, 1963, pp. 147-149.

6 approved Chinese Christian organizations to collect rent for supportive income on buildings they no longer occupied.[76]

The Post-Denominational Protestant Church in China

The unification of churches started in August 1958. In Beijing alone the sixty-five locations of worship were reduced to four, one for each quarter of the city, and the remaining structures were relinquished to the government. In the late 1950s the Chinese Church entered into the post-denominational era, identified merely as Chinese Protestant Christian Churches or Chinese Catholic Christian Churches.[77] In the TSPM document on Church Reorganization and Practice, the unification of churches in China was verified. The original committee of each church terminated its ministration and the administration united under the TSPM committee. Ceremonies and rites were condensed to unified worship, and hymns were varied with teaching on unity and in favor of socialism. To preach on eschatological topics or any stress on distinction between marrying a non-believer to a believer was prohibited, but believers were encouraged to love labor.[78]

The TSPM campaign for the unification of churches was to end the denominational structure perpetuated by foreign missionaries. In 1960 the churches no longer had any delusion about the Party's promise for religious freedom. The TSPM Committee had essentially ceased to defend the Church under suppression.[79] During the Second General Conference of the Three-Self Movement held January 9 through the 14th, 1961, Wu Yitang defended the situation, stressing the great changes in political thinking the Church had experienced. The Protestant Church of China had by that time accepted the Party leadership in following the direction of socialism and redirected "the exploiter class by way of increased political study and by participation in labor."[80]

---

[76] Wickeri, *Seeking*, pp. 98-99.

[77] Ibid, p. 219.

[18] Adeney, *Church's March*, p. 225.

[79] Leslie Lyall, *God Reigns in China* (London: Hodder and Stoughton, 1985), p. 147.

[80] Wu Yitang, 'The Second General conference of the Three-Self Movement,' January 9-14, 1961, Merwin, *Documents TSPM*, 1963, p. 198.

History Reflected in the TSPM Title

Richard Zhang claimed that the Three-Self Reform Movement was the original title for TSPM. In April of 1951, due to the Korean conflict involving the USA, political interests renamed it the Chinese Christian Resist-America-and-Help-Korea Three-Self Reform Movement. Then finally in 1954 upon the suggestion of Y. T. Wu the movement was renamed as the China Christian Three-Self Patriotic Movement.[81] The word "Reform", which held negative connotations of the 16th Century Reformation, was discussed in the August 5, 1954 letter to the churches drafted in the China Christian Conference. These implications had discouraged organizational participation; therefore, to dispel suspicion, they agreed deleting "Reform" from the title.[82] James Myers stated that the Chinese title adopted for the movement was *San Zi Yun Dong*, literally translated into Three-Self Movement.[83]

The TSPM Closure During the Cultural Revolution

The Red Guards in 1966 sealed all churches and confiscated properties, furnishings and equipment. Church leaders suffered humiliation and physical assault as did with leaders of the government-sanctioned TSPM, and 1966 was the first year that Christmas had not been celebrated in China since 1842, and the church lost its institutionalized status by the Gang of Four, as ruling hierarchy of the Communist Party, who claimed that: "Religion no longer exists in China."[84] The TSPM ceased to function as the legal organization of the Chinese Protestant Church until after the years of the Cultural Revolution.

PHILOSOPHICAL INTENT OF THE TSPM POLICY

The Communist Party used the patriotic religious movements to mediate between the governmental standard of China's political formation and the religious organization's respective religious disciples. Thus, a series of organizations and departments

---

[81] Zhang, 'The Origin,' *Jian Dao,* p. 197.
[82] China Christian Conference, 'Letter to the Churches,' August 5, 1954, Merwin, *Documents TSPM,* 1963, p. 98.
[83] James T. Myers, *Enemies Without Guns* (New York: Paragon House, 1991), p. 68.
[84] Leslie T. Lyall, *New Spring in China* (London: Hodder and Stoughton, Ltd., 1979), pp. 177-178.

were established for policy configuration, interpretation, and enforcement.

Dr. Jonathan Chao produced an outline of the organizational strategy determined by the CCP to fulfill the requirements agreed upon by the government agencies involved. The religious policies originated from the UFWD office, which was a department of the Central Committee of the CCP. In turn, the provincial, municipal and prefecture offices in agreement with the RAB implemented these policies. He asserted that the objective was to assimilate religious devotees into the national program and innovate means to restrain the influence of religion. The RAB was responsible to direct the patriotic organizations, including the TSPM, the representative organization for the legalization of the Protestant Christians of China. The charge of the TSPM was to educate those who adhered to the doctrines of the Protestant churches to become patriotic citizens and vigilant against foreign domination.[85]

The guidelines were assigned to the church leaders with certain expectations to be fulfilled, according to Pastor Timothy Wu. These directives always aligned with the three-self principles as chartered in the Christian Manifesto. The governing body of the church could only be native Chinese with a patriotic perspective. Its object was to enhance the reputation of the Chinese Communist government, and preaching was to advocate adherence to governmental rule and policy. No sponsorship or direction could be received from foreign sources. Pastor Wu affirmed that preaching was restricted to registered church structures, and no coercion could be practiced to proselytize converts, especially youth. Wu did not voice opposition, but he was committed to submit only to God no matter what was instructed by the RAB. This was a conviction for which he spent twenty-one years in prison.[86]

ORGANIZATIONAL PHILOSOPHY

The UFWD, RAB and TSPM were interlocked functionally. The Public Security Bureau re-enforced these organizations as a policy system that ministered closely with the procurator and

---

[85] Jonathan Chao, *A History of Christianity in Socialist China* e-mailed material from the Introduction and Conclusion of his new book, 1998, Introduction, pp. 9-10.

[86] Timothy Wu, *Sheltered Through the Storms: A Chinese Pastor Preserved by God* (Palo Cedro, CA: Wayside Impressions, 1996), ch. 14.

the judicial court system. All reports went through the TSPM to the RAB for consultation with the UFWD.[87] The State Council Information Office declared that the agreement and authority of these organizations were recognized to enforce the Manifesto of July 1950 published by Wu Y. T. as the "Three-Self Declaration," titled "The Way in which the Chinese Christianity Works for New China's Construction." The signatures of over 400,000 Chinese Christians indicated a democratic agreement to compliance.[88]

The proposals adopted by the TSPM for the Chinese Christians were to Oppose America and Aid Korea as an important entity of the church's duties along with the cleansing and destruction of all imperialistic influence. The Chinese Christians had to participate in the search and segregation of those with benevolent relations towards imperialists. They were also to "support the Land Reform program and increased production" and "increase their knowledge of politics" as an exemplary "leading force for all these movements."[89]

The TSPM could not exist as an organization within the People's Republic of China directed by the CCP without the government's knowledge. It would have been senseless to even discuss the possibility that the TSPM was a spontaneous movement.[90] Aikman asserted that it was an encouragement for the Christians to realize that they were not specified as a religion for the focus of discriminatory oppression. However, Chinese Christians suffered persecution because of the government's efforts to achieve specific ends of control. The channels of organizational, vertical, political power structure originated from the CCP, the central committees, provincial cabinets, district congresses and local councils; the institutions on the horizontal structure were established according to profession, class origin, economic group, and special interests.[91]

[87] J. Chao, *A History,* Introduction, p. 11.
[88] State Council Information Office, 'Freedom of Religious Belief in China,' October 1997, *Beijing Review,* November 3-9 (1997) 20.
[89] Richard, C. Bush, Jr., *Religion in Communist China* (New York: Abingdon Press, 1970), pp. 190-191.
[90] Leslie Lyall, 'The Chinese Christian Church under Communism 1949-1966,' in David Aikman (ed.), *Love China Today* (Wheaton: Tyndale House Publishers, Inc., 1977), pp. 48-49.
[91] Aikman David, 'Religious Policy,' in David Aikman (ed.), *Love China Today* (Wheaton: TH Pub. , 1977), p. 94.

The Peking Edict of December 29, 1950, regulated all educational and medical institutions, religious bodies, and social services as well as literature, communications, and cultural and studies groups subsidized with foreign funds. Each organization was obligated to register under its respective bureau and committee at the provincial, city, and local levels of the People's Government. A report had to be submitted every six months to verify funds received and the way they were used. Violators were subject to reorganization or closure, and those not registered were liable to investigation and penalty by the People's Government. The regulations were enforced by the Committee on Cultural and Educational Affairs of the State Administrative Council as provided by the Premier's Administrative Council, of the People's Government.[92]

REGULATIONS TO EXPOSE CHRISTIANS

Governmental regulations determined theological doctrines to be taught in China. During the 1950s the Christian Church in China did not emphasize the improvement of society by removal of sin from the world, but it was secured through the creative function of labor. Physical work was regarded as an important principle of spirituality in humanity. Production, thus, was emphasized as a Christian conviction for the good of society and gave purpose to creation. The abundant life as proposed in the Bible was to be achieved through participation in the world.[93]

Those Christians who were not in agreement with the policy of the new China society, claiming that they were above politics, were exposed for using the church to criticize China and deceive Chinese believers. Documents submitted by Liu Liangmo on May 15, 1951, presented explicit instructions on how to conduct an accusation meeting. The first procedure eliminated the concept that many Christians maintained, to conceal evil and focus only on the good in their lives. The second process was to organize an accusation committee to determine which persons should be accused and who was to be invited to devise the accusations. Those selected to meditate charges were invited for motivation and instruction in the procedures of allegation. In the preliminary

---

[92] George N. Patterson, *Christianity in Communist China* (Waco, TX: Word Books, 1969), Appendix II, Peking Edict of December 29, 1950), p. 170.
[93] Philip L. Wickeri, *Seeking the Common Ground* (Mary Knoll, NY: Orbis Books, 1990), pp. 262-263.

accusation meeting each one to vocalize an arraignment was to express their opinions enthusiastically in brief, clear speeches.

Liu continued that the content of an accusation revealed facts without regard for sentiments and was to be uninhibitedly expressed in a sincere, outspoken and thorough method to define the position of the Chinese people. The gatherings were to be conducted in an atmosphere of dignity fostering high tension followed by moderate, then another of high tension. The object was to emotionally stir the people and encourage their applause as a form of agreement. The representatives of the RAB were invited along with those of the People's Government. Each accusation was recorded and submitted to the local newspapers for publication and sent on to the TSPM for its archives. Any evidence of imperialist crimes including photographs, correspondence, radios, and weapons were to be reported to the local police.

All Christians were to improve their knowledge of current affairs, continually promote the TSPM for suppression of counter-revolutionary sentiment, and help clear the nation of imperialist elements. Participation in the "Oppose-America Assist-Korea" movement was an important role in the expectation of the Christian Church. Every church was counted upon to accept its function as an organ to help abolish imperialistic influences with knowledge on how to convene a successful accusation confrontation.[94] Bush verified the role of accusation meetings and cited cases of churches that were intent on registration with the TSPM for tax remission and to qualify for balances: as a prerequisite for registration they were required to have had a successful accusation meeting against at least four of their members.[95] The intention of the TSPM was to maintain the Chinese Christians and churches within the policies instituted by the designated agencies under the CCP.

POLITICAL ATTEMPT TO MANAGE RELIGION TOWARDS SOCIALIST ENDS

Before the date of the formation of the People's Republic of China, the CCP under the leadership of Mao Zedong, utilized situations for the benefit of the Party. As already discussed, the principle

---

[94] Patterson, *Christianity*, appendix III How to Hold a Successful Accusation Meeting and Accusation Meeting by Liu Liangmo, May 15, 1951, pp. 171-173.
[95] Bush, *Religion*, p. 192.

of a united front was a formula devised to bring others into the plan to accomplish their purpose. The hidden strength of the CCP was its ability to employ available sources. Church members who had committed crimes punishable by imprisonment were used as a resource. These offenders would receive special consideration for their willingness to gather information in the church, to be used at an appropriate time. In the political realm, members of the Nationalist Party or other reactionary associations were forced to become informants for the Public Security Department with official promises that their efforts would "achieve merits to redeem crimes."[96]

THE MANIFESTO AS AN INSTRUMENT OF COOPERATION

The CCP formed an avenue for the cooperation of religious groups to cooperate in the cause of socialist construction without interference in the cause of Communism. The purpose of the Patriotic Associations was to encourage the participation of religious believers. For the Protestant Christians, the Three-Self Patriotic Movement, or TSPM, fulfilled that function as characterized in the description outlined by Jonathan Chao. During the primary stage, in the years 1949 and 1950, the State sought to establish direction for the Protestants through sanctioning the establishment of the TSPM. The TSPM under the direction of Y. T. Wu encouraged churches to declare their support for the New China.[97] The Christian Manifesto was used as a pledge of Chinese Christians to declare their support. Bush also listed other instruments that were promoted as patriotic pacts. The citizen's pact began with pledges to champion Chairman Mao, the Communist Party, the People's Central Government, and the People's Liberation Army. Christians sustained a special pact, especially due to the Roman Catholic connection with the Vatican, with a pledge to uphold the Common Platform of patriotism. The resolution to support the principles promoted by the Second World Peace Congress was also included.[98] The Christians who

---

[96] George N, Patterson, *Christianity in Communist China* (Waco, TX: Word Books, 1969), p. 17.
[97] Jonathan Chao (interviews), Richard Van Houten (ed.), *Wise as Serpents Harmless as Doves* (Pasadena: William Cary Library, 1988), p. xv.
[98] Richard C. Bush, Jr., *Religion in Communist China* (New York: Abingdon Press, 1970), p. 183.

did not conform to the declarations of the pledge as outlined in the Manifesto were denounced under the biblical rationalization of Christ's charge against the Pharisees.

The launch of the Accusation Campaign occurred in April 1950 by the Beijing Conference of the TSPM. The national setting was that of fear as government cadres organized criticisms and demanded self-reproach as well as the usual charges of association with foreigners. Imprisonment or labor camps were the punishment for crimes of disloyalty to the state; "reform, rebirth and reinstatement" was the claimed intent of such treatment. Hundreds of pastors were relieved of their ministries, especially those who had studied abroad, and were assigned to menial and degrading tasks. Others committed suicide, while some lost their reasoning. After these purges the churches were accepted into the community as "reformed" congregations.[99] The accusation gatherings ruined the atmosphere of love and obedience to truth within the church, Adeney pointed out. Christians attacked each other in criticism; therefore, the institutional church was avoided, and the house church movement began.[100]

Segments of the Catholic Church were suffering direct persecution during this time. In 1950 there were approximately 5,300 Catholic missionaries in China. By 1952 only roughly 1,500 remained, and many of these were in prison. The Communists singled out the Legion of Mary for special attention, and 70 of their order died by the end of 1953. Kitter was quoted from *The Mary Knoll Fathers* to have found that "Others had been beheaded, burned alive, had their heads crushed between stones, had been dragged and beaten by mobs until they died."[101] This modeled an example of how the CCP was determined to limit the effect of Christianity in socialist China.

The TSPM attempted to conform to the direction of the CCP by unifying all churches to confine the effectiveness of the Chinese Christian Church, Patterson asserted. All church properties and financial assets were surrendered to the local TSPM committee.

[99] Leslie Lyall, 'The Chinese Christian Church under Communism 1949-1966,' David Aikman (ed.), *Love China Today* (Wheaton: Tyndale House Publishers, Inc., 1977), pp. 52-53. Referred to the Bible book of Matthew 23:1-3.
[100] David H. Adeney, *China: The Church's Long March* (Ventura, CA: Regal Books, 1985), p. 120.
[101] Patterson, *Christianity,* p. 112.

Those religious establishments involved agreed upon the articles of union.[102]

METHODS OF INFLUENCE USED FOR THE SUPPORT OF SOCIALISM

Jonathan Chao concurred that to establish the Chinese People's Government the CCP continually adjusted its approach to impel its citizenry to cooperate in a socialist construction. The State sought to control the churches during the period from 1951 to 1954 as it rallied them behind the formation of the Chinese Protestant Anti-America and Aid- Korea Three-Self Reform Movement. The Party gave directives through the TSPM to maintain ascendancy over the Protestant Christian churches.[103]

To promote an awareness of the history of imperialism in the Protestant Church of China, Y. T. Wu reported on an investigation that took place by 1954, within the first four years of the formation of the TSPM. It cited the activities of missionaries who had been involved in imperialistic aggression against China, and reported that some of the unequal treaties were even planned by the missionaries themselves: Gutzlaff took part in drafting the Nanking Treaty, Bridgmand and Parker were both involved in the Wang-hsia Treaty, S. W. Williams and W. A. P. Martin in the Tientsin Treaty. Martin, along with Charles Denby and Timothy Richard, was also implicated in the Boxer Treaty.

Wu named the founder of China Inland Mission, Hudson Taylor, as one who breached the confidence of the people in 1888 at the London Centennial Missionary Conference where he was understood to refer to the natural mineral assets of China, and was quoted: "These resources can make western nations rich." It was perceived that Hudson's motive was to utilize the privileges granted to missionaries by the unequal treaties to deceive the Chinese and aggressively extend imperialism against China. He was quoted as saying, "Now under protection of these treaties we can take our passports in hand and go comfortably by road or riverboat to every province in China."[104]

The CCP was preoccupied with Christians and especially church leaders in their devotion of loyalty to the central government

---

[102] Ibid, p. 126.
[103] Chao, *Sepertents Doves*, p. xxii.
[104] Wu Y. T., 'Y. T. Wu's Report to the July 1954 Conference in Peking', Merwin, *Documents of TSPM* (New York: NCC, 1963), p. 86.

and its purposes.   According to Patterson, in September 1954, the TSPM requested delegates from all churches in Beijing for an accusation meeting against Wang Mingdao, a recognized leader who declined association with the TSPM. The charges were for his lack of sympathy with the government and his refusal to participate with the TSPM. Furthermore, his preaching was said to be individualistic and unclear in purpose. Within several days after these accusations the student organization in Beijing initiated a campaign to oppose the persecution of Wang.[105] In June of 1955 Wang Mingdao published an article in Beijing which read:

> All is gone! The virgin birth of Jesus is an "allegory!" Jesus' redemptive sacrifice – there is no such thing, only a "demonstration of the power of God's love!" Belief in the physical Resurrection has "no vital importance for Christian faith!" Genesis is not credible, the prophets are not to be believed, nor the Gospels, nor the Epistles, nor the witness of the apostles, nor even the words of Jesus Himself! Thus the essential doctrines of the Bible are denied by these modernists; they are completely overturned. What, I ask, is left? What is left?[106]

Political education became the mechanism from 1954 to 1958 for the state to reform the churches. The CCP continued to require all churches to unite under the TSPM, and the TSPM encountered those churches that refused to join with an educational approach.[107] Hsi Zhungxun, the vice-director of the Central Propaganda Department, declared that Catholicism and Protestantism, from the political perspective, are both opposed to Communism. The materialistic worldview of Marxism-Leninism determined that the material world, which verified thought, was of the first order and the spirit was definitely secondary. The attitudes of these two orders of Christianity as perceived by the Patriotic Movements were that Catholics opposed the movement while the Protestants participated superficially, undermined it in secret. Concentration was placed on Catholicism to disarm their

---

[105] Patterson, *Christianity,* pp. 114-115.
[106] Wang Mingdou, 'We, Because of Faith,' June 1955, Beijing, Merwin, *Documents of TSPM,* 1963, p. 103. Wang was arrested on August 8, 1955 and imprisoned.
[107] Chao, J., *Serpents Doves,* p. xvii.

reactionary approach, and the TSPM was to remain aware of the Protestant activities.[108]

In March 1957, Marcus Cheng delivered a speech arguing that because some cadres mistakenly interpreted the religious policy was no reason to assume that religious freedom did not exist in China.[109] Patterson quoted Chairman Mao Zedong who had proclaimed to Tibet in a speech on November 22, 1952: "The Communist Party protects religion. Believers and unbelievers, believers in this or that religion, all are protected and respected." Nonetheless, just five years later in November 1957 the period of grace ended as leaders of the TSPM denounced "rightist" church leaders.[110] Also, within this year Mao initiated the campaign to Let a Hundred Flowers Blossom, a Hundred Schools of Thought Contend. Bush detailed that by mid 1957 Reverend Marcus Cheng was one of the Protestants to respond. He stated that there was lack of respect shown to religious believers, and they sustained discrimination. In late 1957 the Standing Committee of the TSPM denounced Cheng through accusations of attacking the CCP as an anti-socialist and for inferring that a problem existed between believers and non-believers. He was implicated for comparing the CCP and the People's Government to Imperialists.[111]

According to Patterson very few defied the authorities, for the RAB compiled a dossier on each clergyman and administrator of every religious institution, filed photographs, samples of handwriting, biographies, and accounts of political activities. Any evidence of anti-Communist expressions were filed, and when the person would commit a misdemeanor, this information was used as evidence to accessory crimes.[112]

FULL COOPERATION OF TSPM FOR SOCIALIST ENDS

Jonathan Chao reported that from 1958 to 1966 an alliance was formed between the Church and the state to develop official Three-Self churches. There remained a nominal institutional separation, the union of the state government and the TSPM openly maintained the official church. All churches or gatherings

---

[108] Patterson, *Christianity*, pp. 14-15.
[109] Marcus Cheng, 'Marcus Cheng's Speech,' March 19, 1957, Merwin, *Documents of TSPM*, 1963, p. 153.
[110] Patterson, *Christianity*, pp. 124-125.
[111] Bush, *Religion*, pp. 224-226.
[112] Patterson, *Christianity*, p. 12.

outside their jurisdiction were considered illegal.[113] Patterson confirmed that by 1958 the TSPM no longer emphasized the Three-Self principles, which were considered political issues settled by the government. Its main ministry was to organize political and current affairs training for all clergy and to ensure that each church activity satisfied the law.[114]

The TSPM celebrated its tenth anniversary in 1959 with parades in major cities displaying claims of organizational maturity. In the Fourth National Conference, held in Shanghai in 1960, the master of ceremonies announced that since the revolutionaries Watchman Nee and Wang Mingdao had been brought to justice, the churches were free of reactionaries. The TSPM Committee was now collaborating more in political activities to illustrate camaraderie with the Chinese people. One of the Ten Prohibitions listed by provincial TSPM administrators: "Keep religion to yourself and do not travel from commune to commune to spread religion!" According to Lyall, this prohibition reduced the TSPM principle of "self-proclamation" to "no proclamation."[115]

A discussion published in the *Kwangming Daily* declared that the single danger to socialism was religion; therefore, Communists were atheists. Socialist revolution was designed to replace oppression and exploitation along with the destruction of classes. Communism reasoned that religious superstitious thought presented a threat in that it might diminish revolutionary ardor into a hope of happiness in an after-life through prayer. [116] Engles, a renowned Communist writer, categorized ancestor worship along with considering natural objects to be divine as a "spontaneous religion." Superstition held exorcism, supernatural healing, fortune telling and physiognomy outside the realm of religion. Christianity, Buddhism, Taoism and Islam were considered "artificial religions." The objection to "artificial religions" was "because of their next life theory."[117]

In his article 'Religious Policy' Aikman interpreted that the religious policy of China derived from the principle defining conditions for international and domestic Communism. Social and economic policies were to promote socialism for introduction of Communism

---

[113] Chao, *Serpents Doves*, xix-xx.
[114] Patterson, *Christianity*, p. 16.
[115] Lyall, 'Church 1949-1966,' *Love China Today*, p. 46.
[116] Patterson, *Christianity*, pp. 135. Information was released from the April 2, 1964 edition of the *Kwangming Daily.*
[117] Ibid, p. 136.

into China. The significance of domestic political control was that the power had been placed with those who maintained Communism as their paramount objective. The first aim in Chinese foreign policy was the extension of diplomatic relations; second the supporters of the USA and Russia were to be isolated; third to donate active assistance to revolutionary movements in other nations by means of propaganda or materials.[118] Y. T. Wu's report of March 1956 verified their method:

> Today the people of Taiwan lead miserable lives, and earnestly desire to return to the embrace of their mother country. We believe that the desire of the Chinese people to liberate Taiwan by peaceful means will certainly be warmly supported by all peace-loving peoples of the world. In order to promote world peace, we Chinese Christians are at one with the Chinese people in the struggle to liberate Taiwan peacefully. We will lovingly receive all Christians and church workers who return to their mother country on the mainland, we will gladly join our forces with theirs...[119]

Religious policy was subordinate to the principle of social and political evolvements within any era of time. The overriding political attitudes as they come down through the levels of departments determined the national and local approach of policy enforcement towards religious devotees in China. The political struggle experienced in China concluded the level of religious activity permitted throughout the nation, and the international developments were as much a deciding factor as the events in Beijing.[120] All religious policies were directed to further the construction of socialism in China. The method as a means to that purpose was justifiable by law under the People's Government.

THE CHINESE CHURCH'S MOTIVE TOWARD THE SPIRITUAL ENDS

Chinese Christians declined the classification of all thought as either materialistic or idealistic. Bishop Ting K. H. insisted in his commentary on Christian Theism of June 12, 1957, these two

[118] David Aikman, 'Religious Policy,' in David Aikman (ed.), *Love China Today* (Wheaton: TH Pub., 1977), pp. 91-92.
[119] Wu, Y. T., 'Report on the China Christian Three-Self Patriotic Movement, July 1954 to March 1956,' Merwin, *Documents of TSPM*, 1963, p. 130.
[120] Aikman, 'Religious Policy,' p. 93.

ideologies not only "stand opposed" as "mutually exclusive" in "disagreement," but they also "interpenetrate each other" jointly and influentially in "agreement."[121]   Timothy Wu, a pastor who suffered imprisonment as an experienced church leader during the late 1950s in China, agreed with Ting. He claimed that Chinese Christians under the confines of the new Communist government policy spontaneously organized the Three-Self Movement. Wu's conviction was that the Church's independence came through the TSPM as a manifestation of maturity in God's providence. It allowed the Church in China to find its own identity in Jesus Christ as its leader rather than foreign patronization.[122]

Chinese socialism in an advanced stage of historical development must consider accepting the challenge of Christianity that had failed to come to a natural termination according to the Communist theory. Christianity had undergone a transformation under socialism and enabled Christians to share their vision for the future as a factor belonging to all Chinese.[123] As a Church in the realm of a Communist state, Wu Y. T. indicated in his report that the Chinese Church governed by the Chinese did not insinuate that all international relations were to be terminated. He proposed that Chinese Christians would oppose colonialism and its aggression, not the Christians of other nations. Christ was regarded as head and Lord of all followers of the Christian faith.[124]

On the national level, the Church encountered strong Christian principles as propagated by the TSPM Committee. The 1956 Bishops' Pastoral Letter reminded Chinese Christians of their responsibilities to maintain a positive family life and exhorted parents to provide "general and religious education" for their children. They promoted the attention to children's literacy, moral standards, and cultural activities for piety and exemplary conduct.[125] The spiritual realm of society was an evident part of the TSPM ministry to the churches of China under and through the People's Republic of China and the CCP.

[121] Ting K. H., 'Christian Theism,' June 12, 1957, Merwin, *Documents TSPM,* 1963, p. 157.
[122] Timothy Wu, *Sheltered Pastor* (Palo Cedro: WI. 1996), ch. 9.
[123] Phillip L. Wickeri, *Seeking the Common Ground* (Maryknoll, NY: Orbis Books), pp. 290-291.
[124] Wu Y. T., 'Report,' p. 127.
[125] Bishops of the Chung Hua Sheng Kung Hui, 'Bishops' Pastoral Letter of May 1956,' Merwin, *Documents TSPM,* 1963, p. 145.

China, a vast area with a massive population of which the majority resided in the rural areas, remained perplexing to govern even as a homogeneous people. The Communist government had exerted great effort to unify all Chinese through their written language of simplified characters. Rather than reading up and down, from right to left and turning pages from left to right, they changed to reading from right to left down the page and turning the page from right to left. They declared the official national language as Mandarin, which further united the Chinese people for a unified government, education and relations of people between areas and provinces, especially as the people of China had become more mobile. Yet, each area cadre and religious organizational official had distinct manners and ideas of how to superintend his or her specific region. Therefore, consistency of enforcement for even a centralized established policy remained improbable. This was particularly true with policy that governed religion, because of distinct belief or non-belief and interpretation of policy. The improbability intensified with an administrator who emphatically desired to cooperate with the central government.

For this reason, in many areas of China the Christians suffered severe persecution, but through persecution the Chinese Church continued to persevere even as many were martyred for their faith. The October 1952 issue of the *China Missionary Bulletin* claimed that "the blood of martyrs is the seed of the Church," which was understood by faithful youth who dedicated their lives and blood to count toward the cause of Christianity. Their consecration was not with a narrow nationalistic attitude, but they claimed their right to suffer for Christ as head of the Church. To these youth it became clear that "the Church in China has reached maturity and achieved her birthright."[126]

THEORIES PENETRATING TO SPIRITUAL ENDS

Y. T. Wu, who revealed in his writing that he sought to minister within the governmental policy and promote national unity, felt that the solution was doing the will of God as a Christian or atheist or of another religion. Goodness, then, was acceptable to God as doing His will, for all good comes from God. Wu cited from the Christian Bible that salvation was only through Jesus. Yet,

---

[126] George N. Patterson, *Christianity in Communist China* (Waco, TX: Word Books, 1969), p. 113.

The Church in China 1950 – 2000

he argued that those who call Jesus "Lord" are not saved, but it was those who do the will of the Heavenly Father, God.[127]

Bishop Ting, who was not only very involved in the ministry of the Chinese Church but became the president of the TSPM, claimed that although Christianity had been influenced by history it was not the fruit of history. It never was an ideology to be placed in opposition to Communism as another ideology, but it came as the free revelation of God in Jesus Christ through whom all was created. God's lack of material form presented reason for faith, which Bishop Ting declared to be "higher than scientific demonstration." Faith motivated men to great achievement and sacrifice. He illustrated faith in God's creation as to taking a walk in the desert and finding a wristwatch. The conclusion could only be that someone had been there before and left it. In no manner could the sands produce an instrument so complicated. The world, much more complex than a wristwatch, must have had a creator: God.[128]

THE ATTITUDE OF THE CHINESE CHURCH TOWARDS THE GOVERNMENT

The Communists were atheistic, Kiang Wenhan observed in his article on 'Church and State,' but the constitution reflected their commitment to protect the Christian faith throughout its duration in China. Communists and Christians of China differ in conviction, but all were Chinese with the desire to cooperate for increased prosperity and dignity for the nation.[129] In agreement, Bishop Ting assured Christians that the Church could coexist with atheism and agnosticism, and it should profit through their criticism. Theism and atheism were expressions of faith and worldview, but they were not subjects of legislation. He warned against the seduction of their reasoning, and he encouraged learning on how to present

---

[127] Wu, Y. T., 'Freedom Through Truth,' *Tien Feng*, Jan. 11, Feb. 1 & 22, 1954, in Merwin, Wallace C. (Ex. Sec.), Francis P. Jones (ed.), *Documents of the Three-Self Movement*, New York: Far Eastern Office, Division of Foreign Mission National Council of the Churches of Christ in the U. S. A. (1963) 84. Wu cited the Bible in the book of John 14:6 and The Acts of the Apostles 4:12.
[128] Ting, K. H., 'Christian Theism,' June 12, 1957, Merwin, *Documents of TSPM*, pp. 158, 160-161. *China Missionary Bulletin*, Vol. IV, October (1952) 648.
[129] Kiang Wenhan, 'Church and State,' August 1957, Merwin, *Documents of TSPM*, p. 172.

effectively the Christian message to those influenced by these theories. These differences, Ting suggests, did not prevent political unity. Although Christians disagreed with atheistic Communism they could welcome their political leadership and frank attitude regarding religion.[130]

Kiang quoted the Apostle Paul, who recommended obedience to the government: "Let every soul be in subjection to the higher powers, for there is no power but God, and the powers that be ordained of God." [131] Allegorically he explained that indeed there were things that belonged to Caesar's jurisdiction, still Caesar was not God. Governments were formed as instruments to serve the people and should be obeyed, but were to be resisted if they did not. Kiang claimed that in either case the action taken would be a witness for God. China formed the freedom of individual and public worship as well as evangelism and internal administration. With improved standard of living and public morals, the opportunities for proclaiming the Christian belief were enhanced, of which one area of attesting Christianity was through participation in the government.

Richard X. Y. Zhang in his article, 'The Origin of the "Three-Self"' published in a 1996 issue of the *Jian Duo*, recounted that the October 28 to December 4, 1957, meeting of the Anti-Rightist Movement declared free individualistic ministry as an anti-socialist activity. This convocation requested an injunction from the government against reactionary religious activity. The Church's autonomy with the Three-Self principle declared its dependence upon God and did not deny his activity by the Holy Spirit. The projection of "self" as a principle referred to the local indigenous Christian community, which neither inferred independence nor dependence in the irrational sense. Zhang emphasized the decision to define "self" not as "absolute self-sufficiency, self-satisfaction, or self-contained," and certainly not "self-isolation." The assembly concluded that Apostle Paul's teaching, "Bear ye one another's burdens, and so fulfill the law of Christ," did not relieve the personal responsibility to "let every man prove his own work," for each person must participate in the labor. This demonstrated

---

[130] Ting, 'Christian Theism,' *Documents of TSPM*, pp. 166-167.
[131] Kiang, 'Church and State,' pp. 172, 174. He referred to the Bible in the book of Romans 13:1.

in the contemporary context the concept of interdependence.[132]

The Chinese Church remained dependent on the truth of its message. Y. T. Wu connected his personal testimony as a Christian believer for forty years in his June 30, 1958, discourse 'My Recognition of the Communist Party.' His sentiments were that if Christianity is not truth might it perish quickly. From his experience Christ became truly "the way, the truth and the life"; consequently, he discharged any anxiety about the future of Christianity. Wu insisted that the Communist Party as atheistic taught atheism, but it constituted absolutely no threat to the Christian faith.[133]

CHRISTIANITY ADJUSTED TO GOVERNMENTAL POLICY

Even the unification of churches had a positive effect, Lu Wen reported in an article 'Unification of Worship' on August 25, 1958. There were billboard arguments and small group discussions about the reduction of the number of churches in Beijing to just four congregations. Apparently this contraction would release many locations for the reconstruction of Beijing as the capital city. The increased unification of Christian fellowship would prevail, and there would be a reduction of the extra expense of building maintenance. According to Lu there were other advantages: the discharged clergy along with YMCA secretaries encountered an opportunity of enduring the discipline of labor.

Lu disclosed certain adjustments for unification, inevitable for groups like the Little Flock: the women's group was abolished along with the personal interviews in connection with the Lord's Supper. Women were allowed to speak in worship gatherings, a practice restricted by that group. The Salvation Army discontinued all reference to military regulations. The Seventh Day Adventists terminated morning prayers, observance of the Saturday Sabbath, programs of good works and economic production, and their tithe system. The content of the worship message emphasized unity of faith and practice, the dignity of labor, control over nature and its resources, the recognition of enemies, and difference between right

---

[132] Richard X. Y. Zhang, 'The Origin of the "Three-Self",' *Jian Dao*, Vol. 5 (1996) 176-177. The *Jian Dao* is a Chinese journal of Bible and Theology. Zhang referred to the Bible book Galations 6:2, 4-5.

[133] Wu, Y. T., 'My Recognition of the Communist Party,' June 30, 1958, Merwin, *Documents of TSPM*, p. 191.

and wrong. Lu revealed that negative and pessimistic instruction concerning vanity and the end of time had been restricted.[134]

Bishop Ting validated the ministry of the Chinese Church through the biblical passage from Isaiah, "All we like sheep have gone astray; we have turned everyone to his own way," in his description of man in the presence of God. The change of a governmental social system might limit the effectiveness of sin, as a transgression against God's will and towards others, yet sin could only be amended through forgiveness, grace and salvation given by God in Jesus Christ. It was not in the quest for social progress.[135] Theodore Marr in his discussion on 'Religious policy' agreed with the people who realized through the apparent failure of the Great Leap forward that governmental policy was not their salvation, for religion resurfaced as a trusted force. Nevertheless, the continued ambivalent attitude of the government towards religion indicated the Marxist axiom of the termination of religion upon social progress.[136]

Bishop Ting refuted the Marxist teaching that religion, as an opiate, would disappear with development through a positive affirmation that religion was at times a sedative. It must be considered that history had shown scores of people who had used atheism as a pacifier to avoid responsibility for their sin and "stifle the reproaches of their consciences." Ting illustrated the existence of God in granting the discovery that religion had a narcotic effect on some individuals. One, nonetheless, cannot conclude from a man who might draw calmness from looking at the sky through a telescope that the moon and planets, which he saw, did not really exist.[137]

EXAMPLES OF CHRISTIAN WITNESS IN CHINA

In his book, *The 'Jesus Family' in Communist China*, Vanghan Rees chronicles how Christian testimony had a spiritual effect on those working within the Communist political system. A pastor who had been harboring Nationalist soldiers was labeled a "rightist"

---

[134] Lu Wen, 'Unification of Worship,' August 25, 1958, Merwin, *Documents of TSPM*, pp. 181, 184.
[135] Ting, 'Christian Theism,' *Documents of TSPM*, pp. 163-164. Bishop Ting referred to the Bible book Isaiah 53:6.
[136] Theodore Marr, 'Religious Policy,' Aikman (ed.), *Love China Today* (Wheaton: TH Pub., 1977), p. 87.
[137] Ting, 'Christian Theism,' *Documents of TSPM*, pp. 158, 164-165.

and awaited trial, which assuredly meant a sentence of burial alive. His wife gathered a group in the church to pray when a chicken came in and disturbed the gathering by laying an egg. The pastor's wife unthinkingly tied money and a note to the leg of the chicken in payment for the egg. Soon a woman came with the Communist judge and told him they were the Christians. After the judge asked about the money and note, stated, "Such honesty I have not seen before, how did you become like this?" They told him about Jesus, and he dismissed the trial.

Rees told of a man who was standing trial for his faith, and when the Communist official asked him what Christianity had done for him, he answered, "Made me a better man." The crowd affirmed his answer when they were asked if his testimony was accurate, and they reported that his farm had been the dirtiest but now it was the best of their village. When asked how this happened, the man testified, "I was a drunkard and an opium smoker... But I accepted Jesus as my Savior and He changed me." The Communists could not refute that type of confirmation of faith.

Another testimony related by Rees was from a Christian soldier who applied for a pension, and during his interview the official reproached him for having "eaten" a foreign religion. The soldier replied, "But isn't what you have eaten a foreign religion, belonging to Marx and Lenin?" Nonplussed by the response, the officer remarked, "You can't beat these Christians in an argument."[138]

The reality of Christianity in China was substantiated by TSPM leaders against the Communist governmental policy, regulations and persecution, which was, in some cases, perpetrated by TSPM officials. However, the perspective of what constituted a reactionary religious activity continued to hinder the unity of Christianity, as Wu Yifang explained in the Second General Conference of the TSPM in January 1961. According to Wu, those groups that had not registered with the TSPM were considered damaging to socialist construction. Even though they had been dealt a severe setback during the call for accusation meetings, it was recognized that they had not been removed. Wu determined that the autonomous home gatherings must be eliminated. He lamented that these elements continued to practice

---

[138] D. Vaughan Rees, *The 'Jesus Family' in Communist China* (Mobile Christian Literature Crusade, 1973), pp. 71-73, 89-90.

illegal dynamics, which in turn impaired health and poisoned the thinking of Christian believers.[139] This dichotomy remained from the effort to cooperate with an atheistic system to govern the policy of religious activities within China.

RESULTS FROM THE ADMINISTRATION OF THE TSPM

In the title Three-Self Patriotic Movement states the purpose of the organization. As a Chinese Christian Protestant institution cooperating with a government, determined to eliminate foreign elements from the nation, a declaration of independence was inevitable for the Church also. The "Three-Self" principle was the fulfillment of that manifesto, and it included a guard against future international involvement by asserting instruction against imperialistic Western influences. This was especially emphasized during the conflict in Korea in 1951 when a clear demarcation divided the East from the West as acknowledged within the title "Resist-America Aid-Korea." As an association with a "patriotic" accentuation, it was imperative that the TSPM assuredly pledged allegiance for the intent of its policy to maintain a nationalistic sentiment. The "movement" ensured its perpetuated action to coordinate the patriotic standard.

Zhou Enlai, as premier, designated the details of cooperation required of the religious patriotic associations. In his book, *The Fish of the Dragon,* George Young – a missionary in China for twenty-seven years – provided the background of Zhou, whose name Enlai signified "grace comes." Zhou was born to a Mandarin family and educated in a Christian school in Moukden, then studied in Paris and travelled in England, Germany and Russia. After this exposure to the West, he returned to China dedicated to revolution. Even though he was a Communist party leader, he knew the language and thought patterns of Christians and foreigners; therefore he recognized the validity of an established organized movement to encourage cooperation in socialist construction. The question Young presented was "Why did these Communist leaders educated in our western countries not become Christians?" He received the same answer from many Chinese students who had studied abroad: "In your country we did not

[139] Wu Yifang, 'The Second General Conference of the Three-Self Movement, January 9-14,' 1961, Merwin, *Documents of TSPM,* p. 198

see people living like Jesus, whom we admire."[140]   It was from this personal history that Zhou tried to weave Christianity into the socialist structure of China through establishing the patriotic organizations.

After the TSPM helped shape the Protestant Church in China for participation in the New China through different adjustments to national policy, it came under the scrutiny of political criticism. Lyall recorded that in 1964 the national press initiated an inclusive assault on all religions.   By 1966 the TSPM collapsed under the offensive of the Red Guards, which proved to be the most concentrated effort against the Chinese Christian Church.   Easter of 1967 marked the complete liquidation of the visible Church and its order, for its leaders had been humiliated and maltreated. They suffered in correction camps, and for many their plight ended in suicide.[141]

ENFORCEMENT REVEALED THE REALITY AND INTENT OF RELIGIOUS POLICY

The policies filtered down from the Central Government by the CCP through the united front's enterprise of consolidating all activities toward the fulfillment of socialist construction.   The RAB then enforced these policies that constituted affect from the different recognized religious groups.   In turn, the appropriate religious group required the compliance of those within the spectrum of believers under its agreed jurisdiction. The TSPM, as the recognized association for management of Protestant church activities, held the responsibility to urge full collaboration of each church leader and member in policy.

Bush reviewed the People's Republic of China's constitutional Article 88, which declared that citizens of China enjoy the freedom of religious belief. According to the previous article, number 87, freedoms of assembly and association along with procession and demonstration would apply to religions as well. However, for the sake of freedom of religious belief a provision was made for

---

[140] George A. Young, *The Fish and the Dragon* (Kippen, Sirling: Arndarroch, 1985), p. 21. Young had been a missionary in China for twenty-seven years and returned to China for a survey visit in 1975.
[141] Leslie Lyall, 'The Chinese Church under Communism 1949-1966,' in David Aikman (ed.), *Love China Today* (Wheaton: Tyndale House Publishers, Inc., 1977), p. 54.

freedom not to believe. Therefore, religious activity was restricted to the designated churches, temples or mosques of each particular religion.[142] Even in the early years of adjustment to rule as a Party, pressures were placed on Chinese Christians for conformation to their Communist ideology. Young witnessed a zealous Communist declare to a group of Christians, "If you don't obey us we will beat you to your knees." That was precisely what happened in the local churches Young knew in Sian where each started prayer and Bible-study meetings.[143]

The policies appeared legitimate and those who objected or rebelled against them were considered an anti-socialist. In his article 'China's Official Church – A Cry from Within,' Paul Davenport quoted a Chinese senior seminary staff member:

At the end of the fifties, all the Christian denominations and churches were forced to amalgamate and close down to participate in the so-called socialist education movement. The leaders of every denomination, without exception, were attacked as 'imperialist elements', 'rightists' and 'counter-revolutionaries', and imprisoned or sent to labor camps. In my province alone, the number...sent to labor camp under pretext by the (TSPM) were about 80 Christians. [144]

Church denominations were eliminated to minimize Western influence and maximize the management effectiveness of the TSPM. From Bush's description the unification policy was acclaimed by the TSPM as evidence of Christian unity and an economic desire to utilize properties and personnel, but there were those who suspected an ulterior motive of procuring ascendancy over the religious affairs of churches. He produced the articles of union for the churches of Taiyuan capital of Shansi province, claiming that the established "governing boards and committees of individual churches were abolished in favor of the Three-Self Committee, which would be in complete control." Church clergy and Bible women, who proclaimed the Christian message,

---

[142] Richard C. Bush, Jr., *Religion in Communist China* (New York: Abingdon Press, 1970), p. 15.

[143] Young, *Fish and Dragon*, p. 41.

[144] Paul Davenport, 'China's Official Church – A Cry From Within,' September 23 (1998), e-mail version of *Campus Direct*, in Myron Ivey (ed.), *China News and Church Report*, September 28 (1998) 2.

were released to participate in productive labor, and the vacated buildings were made available for other uses.[145] During a visit to China in 1994, the author worshiped in a reclaimed church in Jingtian City of Anhui province once used as a factory during the unification campaign. Others had been used as granaries or even as public latrines.

During the Cultural Revolution all visible signs of Christianity were obliterated, churches closed, and clergy quieted by leftist governmental leaders who claimed that religion did not exist in China. Nevertheless, believers held their faith, some in private and some in secret groups as home gatherings. Jonathan Chao reported on a Christian from central China who offered her experiences with house meetings during the early 1970s. The first years of the revolution the house congregation was held in secret, she recalled, but after 1972 it became overt in its activities when the group grew from thirty to over eighty. A great cloth covering was extended from the house to protect those on the outside. Later in 1974 more than 150 worshippers expanded down the lane. The local officials were known to be polite and rational in their contacts with these Christians, but at times they received orders to terminate this type of religious gathering. It always seemed like a believing relative of an officer would notify the churches to take precautions.[146] When the Chinese Christian Church had no means to legally congregate for worship, it resorted to underground groups that kept their faith alive and the Church in China growing.

BENEFITS AND ADVERSE EFFECTS TO THE CHINESE CHURCH

It was not that over 400,000 Chinese Christians had diluted their faith to sign the Christian Manifesto, which put the Church under the realm of the People's Republic and involved with the patriotic movement through the TSPM. These Christians, Young agreed, were patriots who loved their country and were grateful for the positive changes in society promoted by the Communist Party and initiated by Chairman Mao Zedong.

These Christians sensed a transformation with security and a

---

[145] Bush, *Religion*, p. 231.
[146] Jonathan Chao (director), *China News and Church Report*, No. 1904, 17 January (1992).

hope for the future of China. They sought to live in identification with their fellow-countrymen as fruitful citizens of the country where God had placed them.[147]

According to Bush's account, the fundamental aims of the Chinese Christian Church then were to recognize and be vigilant against imperialistic influence through self-criticism. They agreed to stand in opposition to war and promote peace, and maintain the governmental policy of agrarian reform. The church's ministry advocated patriotism with democratic, self-reliant and self-respectful spirit represented through the TSPM, and this could be accomplished through deliberate independence from foreign financial sustenance. Chinese Christians fixed their priority on unity in the nature of Christianity, with enhanced fellowship and reform produced by efficient leadership and church organization. This attitude sought anti-feudalistic, anti-imperialistic and anti-bureaucratic capitalistic education through forms of social service.[148]

Some Christian church leaders disagreed with the aims promoted by the TSPM with such certainty that they could not be coerced into conforming to its structured goals. Young described the strong conviction of Wang Mingdao, the founder of the Christian Tabernacle in Beijing. He was arrested before the Cultural Revolution in 1955 and spent twenty-four years in confinement; four years after the revolution ended in 1979 he was released at the age of seventy-eight. From prison he was sent to a Labor Reform Camp factory in Shansi province to work as a male nurse. His sense of victory for maintaining his certitude was reflected in a letter sent to his sister-in-law in Hong Kong. "I am very well and happy. Please be of good cheer. My feelings are just the same as yours. All things work together for good. Be of good cheer, I am much more precious than sparrows."[149] Although the Cultural Revolution was not specifically an anti-religious movement, for some Christians the strain was overwhelming; many were tortured to death, murdered, or driven to suicide.

---

[147] Young, *Fish and Dragon*, p. 90.
[148] Bush, *Religion*, p 178.
[149] Young, *Fish or Dragon*, pp. 91-92. Wang's quoted statement refers to Bible passages. The one was from Apostle Paul to the citizens of Rome in the book Romans 8:28, and the other was from the noted Sermon on the Mount by Jesus in encouragement of people's worth in the book of Matthew 6:26.

Philip Wickeri reported that the Nanjing Theological Seminary closed in June of 1966. The TSPM was exposed when many of the leaders tried to help the Christian community to secure Bibles, helped minimize church property damage, and impartially volunteered imprisonment to divert abuse from other believers. There were those, though, who denied their Christian faith and joined the assault against their former friends and fellow believers. Wickeri credited the Zhou Enlai with having done the most to protect the acknowledged religions and intellectuals by sending telegrams ordering the preservation of certain religious buildings or individuals.[150]

Determination within the Church during the anti-foreign and anti-religion sentiment displayed in 1968, as told by Young, was commendable. The Chinese Christian's Bibles had been confiscated and destroyed, they were persecuted, indoctrinated, and had no church buildings or institutions. Their leadership had been eliminated, no missionaries, no money, no literature for spiritual nourishment; notwithstanding, the Chinese Christian Church not only survived but grew both spiritually and quantitatively. With no churches and with open-air meetings forbidden, these Christians simply told the Christian message to others in natural conversation, and they gathered in homes for Bible study and prayer. They adapted to the circumstance in a biblical principle of accommodation.[151]

The Church was functioning only through underground house churches, and Christians who had purified their faith through the suffering that they endured were the heart of such groups. Kauffman recounted a surgeon in Shanghai who reported, "Every Sunday for almost 15 years I rose at dawn and stood in the street outside this closed church and prayed that the doors would open again." The Church in China had not weakened because of nominal Christians, for they had not survived the pressure produced on the Christian community during Cultural Revolution. Chinese Christians have taken account of the price for their faith and decided that the way of Jesus Christ was worth more than their own lives. There were no Christians who cared to be a part of a church for

[150] Philip Wickeri, *Seeking the Common Ground* (Mary Knoll, NY: Orbis Books, 1990), pp. 181-183.
[151] Young, *Fish or Dragon*, pp. 92-93. The biblical principle Young referred to was from the Bible in the first book of Corinthians and the ninth chapter.

the physical or monetary gain it may bring, and Christianity was not for social prestige. Motives for being a Christian had become clear as a pure Church with faith in Jesus Christ.[152]

Young recalled his experience in 1975 as he was with a secular group surveying China. He had let it be known of his desire to visit Christians in China. When they reached Beijing his guide informed him that his instructions were to take Young to a church on Sunday at 9:30 AM. He remembered:

Next day we were welcomed by the Chinese pastor and led to an upper room where 25 people were assembled for worship – 10 Chinese men and women, 4 Africans, 3 British girls teaching in schools and colleges, and some members of the diplomatic corps. The pastor sounded the Call to worship and Confession of Faith, "Come let us sing unto the Lord, for He is a great God and a great King above all gods. He is our God and we are his people." Then we sang, "O God, our help in ages past", prayed together the Lord's prayer and joined the responsive reading of Psalms 104. The pastor's prayer made us aware of God's Presence with His people and his readings from the Bible were most illuminating – Luke 11:27-36 and I Peter 13:25 [sic]. The two hymns were sung fervently "Take time to be holy" and "I need Thee every hour."

A communion service of the Lord's Supper was followed by the hymn "Rock of ages cleft for me." It was not allowed by law to preach a sermon.[153]

In the time immediately after the Cultural Revolution, even the displacement of the TSPM was evident by its absence with closed churches that had registered as patriotic participants. Young cited the confirmation of tourists who had witnessed and reported, "There is no Church left in China. We saw closed church buildings, burned Bibles and no Christians." If they had gone to Shanghai, they would have seen the Catholic Cathedral closed along with the other churches, and its Roman Catholic Bishop would have been in prison. Yet, later they would have seen

---

[152] Paul E. Kauffnman, *China, the Emerging Challenge: A Christian Perspective* (Grand Rapids, MI: Baker Book House, 1982), pp. 175, 191, 198.
[153] Young, *Fish or Dragon*, p. 89. The Bible reference I Peter 13: 25, which does not exist, was again referred to on page 93 as I Peter 1: 13-25.

the bishop in the sports arena dressed in shorts and his hands secured behind him. The People's Court tried him, and after he listened to the accusations, he was brought in his weakened state to the microphone where he was expected to confess to counter-revolutionary activities. Instead, he exclaimed in a loud voice, "Long live Christ the King."[154] The effects of the TSPM as an organization to ensure patriotism at the cost of limitations of Church activity to the total abolition of all visible and legal religious practice caused Christians suffering. Moreover, in its distress, purification took place that enabled it to proliferate without any supports except the faith in the claims of Jesus Christ.

[154] Young, *Fish or Dragon*, pp. 88-89.

5
THE REINSTATEMENT OF THE TSPM

After the death of Mao Zedong and the arrest of the Gang of Four, the years of chaos during the Cultural Revolution ended and the political climate in China changed. This made adjustments in every area of life possible, and China embarked on a new chapter of history with optimism overshadowed by cynicism. Religion had been a focal point for the devastation raged upon the "four olds" of ideology, thought, habits and customs throughout the Cultural Revolution, and Christianity emerged with mixed sentiments towards the validity of the constitutional freedom for religious belief.

As Dreyer pointed out, it was unpredicted that the 1975 Constitution would uphold the assurance of freedom to believe, though, the rights to not believe and to propagate atheism were added as well as the right to strike, and the four big freedoms. These freedoms become known as the "four bigs": to "speak out freely, air views fully, hold debates, and write big-character posters."[1]

In his book *The Resurrection of the Chinese Church*, Tony Lambert confirmed that by the summer of 1979 the TSPM committees,

---

[1] June Teufel Dreyer, *China's Political System* (Boston: Allyn and Bacon, 1996), p. 169.

which consisted of the trusted pastors and church workers from prior to the Cultural Revolution, reactivated work in Shanghai, Guangzhou, Beijing and other major cities.[2] The period from 1979 to 1982 marked a governmental restoration of the soft-line religious policy to re-establish the patriotic organizations, according to Jonathan Chao.[3] The TSPM was activated as the Protestant patriotic organ, which eventually formed the China Christian Council, CCC, as an ecclesiastical body. Then the TSPM and the CCC jointly administered the Protestant Christian churches. Still, any Protestant group outside of their administrative management was considered illegal. Thompson Brown asserted in *Christianity in the People's Republic of China* that it was inevitable that many Chinese believers remembered the unjust actions of the TSPM leaders from before the Cultural Revolution, which made them distrustful. However, every Christian, whether he or she opposed or supported the TSPM, suffered during the revolution. But it was a time for a new start with unity of purpose and understanding.

On March 1, 1980, the first national Christian meeting in over ten years convened with the Standing Committee of the TSPM who cited past achievements in bringing Chinese Christians closer to the people of China. They outlined future priorities of Bible and literature publication, ministerial training, and correcting governmental policy.[4]

It had been twenty years since the Three-Self Movement held a congress when the third National Christian Congress convened on October 6 to 13, 1980, with 176 delegates, which also included minority peoples of China. This body approved the new association of the China Christian Council as a sister organization to the TSPM, designed to undertake the pastoral ministries, while the TSPM continued its liaison role between the churches and the government. The two were to interact as arms of the same body.[5] It called for allegiance in support for the national modernization

---

[2] Tony Lambert, *The Resurrection of the Chinese Church* (Wheaton, IL: Harold Shaw Publishers, 1994), p. 40.
[3] Jonathan Chao (interviews), Richard Van Houten (ed.), *Wise as Serpents Harmless as Doves* (Pasadena: William Cary Library, 1988), pp. xxi-xxii.
[4] Thompson Brown, *Christianity in the People's Republic of China* (Atlanta: John Knox Press, 1983), pp. 165-166.
[5] Leslie Lyall, *God Reigns in China* (London: Hodder and Stoughton, 1985), P. 191.

program, efforts at cooperation in the unification of Taiwan to the motherland, support of world peace, and "opposition to hegemony and aggression." There was, on behalf of the Chinese Church, a pledge "to make all efforts in defending religious freedom of the public" and to "help the government to fully implement its policy of religious freedom." Chinese authorities demanded, "Religion must then be organized and controlled so that its strengths may be channeled in the desired direction."[6] Bishop Ting, as the new TSPM chair, gave affirmation to the government for its efforts in raising China out of poverty, and elevating the level of morality and respectability. In support of patriotism, he advocated approval of the governmental policy of religious freedom. Also through his proposal, an amendment to Article 46 of the Constitution deleted the clause, "right to promote atheism."[7]

In his speech recorded by *Christianity Today* as reported in the September 9, 1980, issue of the *People's Daily*, Bishop Ting said:

> The mission of our Three-Self Patriotic Committee is to unite all Christians in the country. We cannot consider the house church Christians as a separate party. As one of the leaders of the Three-Self Committee, I cannot comfortably say that house churches are illegal.[8]

Bishop K. H. Ting was also elected as the new president of the newly formed CCC. He welcomed those who worshiped in homes, which alleviated the fears of restriction to officially-sanctioned church buildings. The council extended a proposal for international church relationships under defined conditions.[9] There were those who had maintained that there were two Protestant Churches in China, the registered churches that had joined the TSPM and the unregistered house church movement. This distortion of the complexity of a changing situation had been an insult to both the TSPM and CCC leaders, in that while there had been differences of views among Chinese Christians in these two factions, the Church of Jesus Christ was presented as one Body.[10]

---

[6] 'China's Three-Self Congress Makes Rehabilitation of Religion Official,' *Christianity Today*, Vol, 25, January 2 (1981) 46.
[7] Lyall, *God in China*, p. 192.
[8] 'China's Three-Self,' *CT*, Vol. 25, January 2 (1981) 47.
[9] Brown, *Christianity in China*, p. 167.
[10] Philip L. Wickeri, 'A Three-Self Movement Perspective', http://lausanne. org/0697wick.html, 11/9/98, 3:29 PM, p. 1.*

In October of 1980 Pastor Timothy Wu attended a National Christian Representatives Meeting in Nanjing to discuss the future of Christianity in China. This assembly recognized the abuses of the Cultural Revolution as the activities of extreme leftists, who betrayed the constitutional declaration of religious freedom. The representatives agreed that the government accepted the important contribution that religion had made to the development of society, and that it should not be opposed by force. They recognized that the Communist Party realized that even though they are atheistic that the whole Chinese society could use the stabilizing factor of religious influences.[11]

The TSPM claimed the establishment of confidence by representing the sincerely patriotic Christians and that they had removed the foreign stigma from Christianity for the Church of China. They re-opened buildings as well as provided a legal channel for access to Bibles by supplying paper and permission to print Christian literature. The problems the TSPM leaders encountered included the renovation of churches and finding accommodations for the occupants of the buildings that were recovered for the churches. Then the provision for pastors presented a challenge, for the pastors of the 1950s were nearing or in their eighties. The liberal theology proclaimed before the Cultural Revolution had drained the confidence of the people. To recover the people's trust, an auxiliary organization to the TSPM, the CCC, was established. The CCC provided the urgently needed theological training of new pastoral staff through short-term Bible schools, and it had the Nanjing Theological Seminary reopened in March of 1981.[12] The TSPM and CCC became complimentary sister organizations.

Neither the TSPM nor the CCC were bureaucratic associations but coordinating agencies with few staff members. Both of these organs defended the rights of Christians before the People's Republic government.[13] However, Lambert found that they were organizationally self-perpetual through the Standing Committees of both bodies. According to their constitutions, the Standing

---

[11] Wu, Timothy, *Sheltered Through the Storms: A Chinese Pastor Preserved by God* (Palo Cedro, CA: Wayside Impressions, 1996), ch. 14.

[12] David H. Adeney, *China: The Church's Long March* (Ventura, CA: Regal Books, 1985), pp. 168-172.

[13] Wickeri, 'A Perspective,' http://lausanne.org/0697wick.html, p. 1.

Committee may nominate members to the National Committee, and the method of elections for the Chinese National Christian Conference was determined jointly through the Standing Committee.[14] The National Chinese Christian Conference, according to Article 5 of the CCC Constitution, was the largest body of the Council convened by both the CCC and TSPM Committees. It made any drafts or revisions to the Constitution and elected the Committee.[15]

The governmental bureau connected to religious affairs of all legally recognized religions was the State Council's Religious Affairs Bureau, RAB, whose main duties were listed in the article 'The Ministry of the Public Security and the Religious Affairs Bureaus' by Anthony Lam.[16] This agency formed the policy for governing religious activities and established regulations for them. They ensured religious freedoms by authorizing religious officials to maintain normal control over religious activities, support patriotism and socialism, cooperate in the educational system, and encourage national harmony through strengthened efforts with the United Front Foundation to mobilize believers for assistance toward reform. The RAB assisted each religion to develop according to its particular characteristic and within the law. The national organization directed the ministry of the provincial and local chapters through courses for cadres at these levels and assisted the government to monitor religious events that threatened social stability. The RAB was to organize religious education for its theory and practice, teach the legal system and government policy, and promote atheism. The Public Security Bureau included a special branch to supervise religious matters and deal with religious activities not recognized by the government and outside the RAB's jurisdiction, such as counter-revolutionaries, spies, special agents and criminal activity that might pose a threat to national security.

Between 1982 and 1988 the government, through the RAB, consolidated its control over religion and in particular Protestant

---

[14] Lambert, *The Resurrection*, p. 48. Taken from the Document of the Third Christian Conference, pp. 25-28.

[15] 'Constitution of the China Christian Council,' Article V, [Passed ? January 1997], Janice Wickeri (ed.), *Chinese Theological Review: 12* (Holland, MI: Foundation for Theological Education in Southeast Asia, 1998, p. 52.

[16] Anthony Lam, 'The Ministry of the Public security and the Religious Affairs Bureaus,' *Tripod*, No. 104, Vol. XVIII, March and April (1998) 48, 50-51.

churches through requiring house gatherings to join the TSPM. Those that refused to join were considered illegal and not recognized as legitimate religious groups.[17]

Document 19, as a supplementary religious policy of the constitution, was ratified in March 1982. It confirmed religious policy under the Chinese Communist Party, CCP, which continually regarded religion as a relic with no place in the new socialist society. From the Party's perspective, the landowner class had been basically eliminated, and it had been this class that exploited the peasants, who gave emergence to religion as a future hope. Nevertheless, the CCP reasoned that the reality of the people's ideology developed slower than social actuality; therefore, religious sentiments remained that had not yet been eliminated. Although CCP assumed that there was no purpose for religion in an authentic socialist society, the Party recognized that suppression of religion would be counter-productive and not practical in effecting the cooperation of religious believers.[18]

Section III of Document 19 stated that opposition to the conservative Marxist error, demonstrated during the Cultural Revolution, was necessary to implement the CCP's religious policies, though attention was needed to guard against the tendency to relinquish control. Events of Chinese religious history must be reviewed, while promoting the understanding of the theory of religion to emerge, develop and terminate by maintaining the scientific direction as determined by Marxism-Leninism and Mao Zedong Thought. As defined in Section IV, Communists were atheists but recognized the fruitless harm of dealing with religious issues by coercion. The concentrated objective was to minimize the differences between believers and non-believers and eliminate any aggravation towards religious fanaticism. However, as outlined in Section V, the goal was to involve patriotic believers in the formation of a United Front toward socialist modernization.[19]

Patriotic religious organizations, as delineated in Section VII in Document 19, were to implement the policy of freedom of

[17] Chao, *Serpents Doves*, pp. xxiii-xxiv.
[18] Lambert, *The Resurrection*, pp. 53-55.
[19] Document 19: The Basic Viewpoint and Policy on the Religious Question During Our Country's Socialist Period by the Central Committee of the Communist Party of China, 31 March 1982, Sections III-V.

religious belief and raise the consciousness of each religious adherent to patriotism and socialism. The patriotic religious movements were to represent religious lawful rights and manage normal religious activities and affairs. Section VIII stated that the seminaries were to create young religious personnel who were patriotic and support the Communist Party's leadership. These students were to possess religious knowledge and help sustain the socialist system.[20]

Document 19, Section IX, declared that Communist Party members were not permitted to be religious believers, for the freedom to believe as guaranteed in the constitution did not apply to them. The Party members belonged to a Marxist political party, which was a declaration of atheism. To strengthen the potential of the Party's leadership, Section XII declared that the Party committees at every level must direct all the relevant departments of state within China's society, which included the RAB for religions, to unify ideology, policy and knowledge.[21]

On December 4, 1982, the National People's Congress adopted a new Constitution that contained Article 36. The English translation published in Adeney's book stated that Chinese citizenry enjoy the freedom of religious belief, and that:

> No state organ, public organization or individual may compel citizens to believe in, or not to believe in any religion; nor may they discriminate against citizens who believe in, or do not believe in any religion.
> The State protects legitimate religious activities. No one may make use of religion to engage in activities that disrupt public order, impair the health of citizens or interfere with the educational system of the state.
> Religious bodies and religious affairs are not subject to any foreign domination.

The interpretation that Adeney had identified for the two phrases "freedom of religious belief" and "legitimate religious activities" was instituted in their implementation on December 5, 1982, when the TSPM closed down the largest home gathering in Guangzhou. The report submitted to justify the action revealed

---

[20] Ibid., Sections VII-VIII.
[21] Ibid., Sections IX, XII.

that books had been printed privately and tapes of the pastor's sermons had been illegally recorded and sold. Prayer for healing of the sick without medical help was an infraction of the set phrase "impair the health of citizens," while "interference with the educational system" referred to the exposure of minors to religious teachings.[22]

However, according to Wickeri, the conservative perspective on China considered Communism as the ideology of the enemy. This view left no possibility of dialogue, and any Christian who cooperated with the Communists was considered a betrayer. These conservatives formed their understanding of Christianity in societies different from the context found in the People's Republic of China. The liberal perspective on China was biased against Communism and unable to understand any Christian's affirmation of the Chinese Communist Revolution with integrity, and it was unconcerned about a sense of patriotism. The challenge was to institute an ecclesiology, theology and church structure that reflected both Christianity and the Chinese sociopolitical system.[23] This concept prompted Bishop Ting's denial of governmental interference with religious affairs, as quoted in *Protestantism in Contemporary China* by Alan Hunter and Chan Kimkwong:

> There are some people overseas who, consciously or not, have created confusion by saying that the RAB of the State Council supervises us and that Chinese Christian churches and organizations are parts of the RAB. This would be totally at odds with our social and political system. The bulk of the work of the RAB is to represent the state and government in implementing the policy of religious freedom... The RAB only handles the religious affairs of the state. As to the development of the Chinese Christian TSPM and the administration of the Chinese church, these are our own concerns.[24]

The author interviewed Xu Rulei, who served as a Standing Committee member of the CCC and as chairman of the Jiangsu

[22] Adeney, *Church's March*, pp. 136-138.
[23] Philip L. Wickeri, *Seeking the Common Ground* (Maryknoll, NY: Orbis Books, 1990), pp. 6, 9-10.
[24] Alan Hunter and Chan Kim-kwong, *Protestantism in Contemporary China* (Cambridge: Cambridge University Press, 1993), p. 55.

Provincial and Nanjing Three-Self Committees. Professor Xu stated, "The TSPM and CCC do not report to the RAB, but the RAB is invited to come to their meetings. The RAB gives directives, and we consider the suggestions, but we are independent."[25] The CCC general secretary Shen Chen-en stated that the TSPM and CCC related very closely, *Liang Hui*, as the two societies. He said that the TSPM related to the RAB along with the CCC, and that the RAB was part of the government while the United Front Work Department, UFWD, was part of the Communist Party.[26]

Also, the author sent copies of the organizational charts outlined in David Adeney's book *China: The Church's Long March* and *The Resurrection of the Chinese Church* by Tony Lambert to Shen Chen-en in Shanghai, China. These two accounts connected the TSPM organizationally to the CCP through the RAB, which was joined by way of the UFWD. Shen returned the charts, which had been marked, along with a letter of November 23, 1999, with his response:

I think they have made the same mistake, to organizationally relate the church with the government, because how can the church become a part of the government? I draw two red lines to cut off the relations (I mean organizational relations) between church and government. For your reference.[27]

The Document 6 and Section III that was ratified on February 5, 1991, placed all of the religious organizations including the TSPM under the responsibility "to accept the leadership of the Party and government." In accordance with the law they were to "educate their religious staff in patriotism, socialism, the policy on current developments" and enhance the "interests of the state and the nation and upholding the principle of independence and managing their religious undertakings themselves."[28]

---

[25] Xu Rulei, Standing Committee Member of CCC, Vice Chairman of Jiangso Province Three-Self Committee, Chairman of Nanjing Three-Self Committee and Deputy Director of the Center for Religious Studies at Nanjing University (Interview, 11 September 1999).

[26] Shen Chen-en, Associate General Secretary of CCC, Chief Editor of *Tian Feng* or 'Heavenly Wind Monthly' and Pastor of the Shanghai Community Church (Interview, 10 September 1999).

[27] Ibid. (Letter, Shanghai, China, 23 November 1999).

[28] Documant No. 6, Circular Issued by the Central Committee of the Chinese Communist Party and the State Council On Some Problems Concerning Further Improving Work of Religion (5 February 1991), Section III.

Moreover, during the 1990s the government assiduously promoted atheism. Chen Junsheng of the 13th Party Central Committee addressed the leaders of the RAB:

...religious departments must cooperate and join with the relevant departments in promoting dialectical materialism, including atheism, among the masses, especially among the young; and also promote scientific education to establish a humanistic world view... [This] emphasis must be placed on religious work in rural areas, and materialism [must continue to be] propagated in urban areas. [29]

In 1993, Jiang Zemin, president of the People's Republic of China, encouraged cadres to intensify the propagation of atheism. Then in 1995, according to Lam's account, the RAB underwent a major organizational change when a number of new research departments and publications were added. Their quarterly *Religions in China* was presented to the general public, reducing politics to become more intellectual for "a positive religious dialogue" between the RAB and the patriotic religious organizations.[30]

The TSPM and CCC in 1997 wrote into their Constitution, as reported by the Human Rights Watch, that the TSPM's objective was to "foster patriotism" among Protestant Christian believers, promote unity among them and guard independence. Also, because of its dedication to the CCP and People's Republic, the TSPM was entrusted to protect the "unity and stability" of China and construct a "spiritual and material civilization."[31] The *Chinese Theological Review* substantiated the account cited in the TSPM Constitution Articles II, III and V, endorsed on January 2, 1997. The aims of the TSPM were "to love the nation and the church" along with cooperation with the CCC.[32]

Samuel Wang, author of *God and the Ancient Chinese*, confirmed that the TSPM was organizationally on the same level as the

[29] Lam, 'The Ministry of PSB & RAB,' *Tripod*, p. 52.
[30] Ibid., p. 53.
[31] Human Rights / Asia, *China: State Control* (New York: Human Rights Watch, 1997), pp. 13-14. Reference to the 'TSP/CC Constitutions.'
[32] 'Constitution of the National committee of the Three-Self Patriotic Movement of the Protestant Churches in China,' passed January 2, 1997, Janice Wickeri (ed.), *Chinese Theological Review* (Holland, MI: Foundation for Theological Education in Southeast Asia, 1998), pp. 46-47.

CCC, but the CCC was more practical in church ministries while the TSPM was administrative. He referred to Bishop Ting's exclamation that the TSPM had finished its purpose and task for self-reliance, which led to the separation of personnel for each organization's leadership; before, the same people held the same positions within both the TSPM and the CCC. The CCC headquarters in Nanjing consisted of an academic setting while the TSPM headquarters in Shanghai was more political. When the CCC ordained ministers, for example, it had to seek permission from the TSPM, and at times the two did not agree.[33]

The accounts in the *Chinese Theological Review* and in Lambert's book agreed that the aim of the CCC according to Article II of the CCC Constitution was to unite all Chinese Christians who believe in God as the Heavenly Father and acknowledge Jesus Christ as Lord. The CCC agreed to manage the Church in China well under the guidance of the Holy Spirit with unity of purpose and obedience to the Bible. It was to uphold the principles of patriotic self-dependence, church order, and the laws and policies of the people's constitution.[34] Article III claimed that the CCC exalted Jesus Christ and his cross, and with him as the Head of the Church was to unite the churches of China to build up the Body of Christ to be an excellent witness to the Gospel of Christ. The CCC advocated mutual respect in matters of doctrinal faith and the form of worship with the spirit of "bearing with one another in love, making every effort to maintain the unity of the Spirit in the bond of peace" in member relationships.[35] The character of the CCC differed from that of the TSPM, for its ministry was to spiritually nurture the Chinese Protestant churches in the Christian sense of spirituality and faith.

THE EVENTS LEADING TO RELIGIOUS POLICY REVISION

To regain the confidence of the people the CCP, purposely reviewed the events of the Cultural Revolution for damages inflicted on the reputation of the Chinese Communist government, the People's

---

[33] Samuel Wang, Scholar of the *Four Books* collection of Confucius and Mencius teachings and coauthor of *God and the Ancient Chinese* (Interview: 21 December 1999).
[34] 'Constitution of CCC,' Article II, p. 51; Lambert, *The Resurrection*, p. 48.
[35] 'Constitution of CCC,' Article III, p. 51. Ephesians 4:2b-3 of the Bible is quoted within the text of Article III in the Constitution.

Republic of China, as a socialist society. Having wrestled control from the conservative Marxist political faction, the moderates proceeded to recover sociopolitical stability. Chinese sociologist Drew Liu stated in his article in *China Strategic Review* that by the late 1970s the CCP concluded to abandon the harsh religious policy held throughout the past decade, and a new policy governing religious activities took shape.[36] According to Adeney, it had been undeniable that Christianity had multiplied in both numbers and strength. The CCP was faced with the problems of providing an explanation for the growth of Christianity, a turnaround in religious policy, and a method to enforce a new policy.[37]

IMMEDIATE CHURCH ACTIVITIES AFTER THE CULTURAL REVOLUTION

Radical changes took place in the implementation of renovated religious procedures. In his book, *!China Today!*, Paul Kauffman cited that as early as 1978 Christian churches were being restored, and even retroactive rent was being paid by the CCP for the use of these church buildings for the past twenty years.[38] Bishop Ting confirmed that since 1979 at least one church a day was reopened or newly built somewhere in China. However, he also reported that the clergy spent the first few years after the Cultural Revolution in political rehabilitation to restore their status as Chinese citizens and to recuperate financial and material losses before they returned to their positions of ministry.[39] The TSPM was restored to its function as a patriotic organization to help in this process.

Though the TSPM had been organized over thirty years earlier, it was inoperative throughout the Cultural Revolution and had to be reinstated. Wu Gaozi, in his article in the *Chinese Theological Review,* credited the TSPM with enabling the Chinese Church to become independent of foreign influence. The TSPM had helped

---

[36] Drew Liu, 'State Policy and Christianity in China,' *China Strategic Review,* Vol. 1, 1996, China Strategic Institute, p. 2.

[37] David H. Adeney, *China: The Church's Long March* (Ventura, CA: Regal Books, 1985), p. 124.

[38] Paul E. Kauffman, *!China Today! Through China's Open Door* (Hong Kong: Asian Outreach, Ltd., Rev. edn. 1980), p. 119.

[39] Ting K. H., 'The Church of Jesus Christ is There in China:' [Address to the Lutheran World Federation Executive Committee, July 12, 1987], *Currents in Theology and Mission,* Vol. 17, October 1990, p. 377.

to increase the self-respect of Christianity in China and interact on an international basis with a sense of equality. The determination of the TSPM to become post-denominational proved that Chinese Christians with different theological doctrines were able to unite on major doctrinal positions yet retain their minor religious perceptive differences.[40] Kauffman stated that the reasons for the reactivation of the TSPM were to enable negotiations with the government about resuming control over church properties, reactivate the Three-Self principles, and develop relations with international Christians.[41] The CCC was then formed to minister to the Chinese Christian churches.

ACTIVITIES OF THE TSPM AND CCC

The documents of the Third National Christian Conference in 1980 verified that Bishops Ting and Jianye planned the course for the CCC. It was not to be a national organization church but to serve Chinese Christians and the Protestant churches with Bible translation and publication. The CCC was to nurture Christians through Christian literature publications and promote the training of church leadership by opening seminaries.[42] While the role of the TSPM remained administratively consistent with the *Ching Feng's* account of Article 2 of the TSPM Committee Constitution, its main objective was to maintain patriotism among the Chinese Protestant Christians. It was to assist the government in implementing religious freedom and contribute to the cooperation of Christians for the modernization of socialist China. The TSPM's assistance with the return of Taiwan to the motherland for national unity and preservation of world peace was also a priority aim.[43]

During the third national conference of 1980, Bishop Ting clarified the intention of the TSPM not only to be content with relating to the Christians of churches joined to the TSPM; he insisted that those who worshiped in homes were also an

---

[40] Wu Gaozi, 'On the Revision of the Constitutions', Janice Wickeri (ed.) [Documents from the Fourth National Christian Conference, Shanghai, August 1986], *Chinese Theological Review,* Vol. 3 (1987) 6-7.

[41] Kauffman, *!China Today!,* p. 184.

[42] Tony Lambert, *The Resurrection of the Chinese Church* (Wheaton, IL, Harold Shaw Publishers, 1994), p. 47. From the documents of the Third National Christian Conference, p. 46.

[43] 'Committee of the Chinese Christian Three-Self Patriotic Movement,' *Ching Feng,* Vol. 23, No. 3-4, (1980) 170.

intrinsic part of the Chinese Church. In May of 1982 the People's Government of Guandu, according to Thomas Lawrence's article 'New Straightjacket for China's Expanding Church,' released a document sounding alarm over the increase in itinerant evangelism and flourishing Christian gathering points in homes and work places. All meeting points were to be closed down by the end of July 1982. The object was to eliminate house churches and abolish any church built without governmental permission.[44]

Later in 1982 the CCP stated that in principle the house churches should be prohibited. Late in 1983 many house church leaders were arrested,[45] even though the CCP had published Amendment 19 the previous year. Pastor Timothy Wu commented that this document had reinstated religious freedom in recognition that religion was a stabilizing force within society and must not be opposed by force, which seemingly strengthened the nation while it was weakened. Pastor Wu said that his parishioners experienced an answer to prayer when the secretary of the local city council, Liu Chao, announced to their local church congregation that they were granted 270,000 yuan in recompense for the seizure and occupation of their church building many years before.[46] However, to maintain balance the second section of Document 19 stated that because of the historical background of Christianity in China, each level of the Party ought to adopt the attitude of precaution as proposed by Lenin who said, "Be especially alert," "Be very strict," "Think things through thoroughly." Therefore, to panic or to allow matters to continue unheeded were regarded equally erroneous.[47]

THE CHURCH ADJUSTED TO THE POLITICAL CONTEXT

According to Bishop Ting, patriotism was the key bridge between the Church and government with trust and cooperation. He praised patriotism no matter its form: whether it may have been

---

[44] Thomas Lawrence, 'New Straightjacket for China's Expanding Church,' Jonathan Chao (ed.), *China Prayer Letter,* Hong Kong: No. 123, October-December (1992).
[45] Adeney, *Church's March,* p. 173.
[46] Timothy Wu, *Sheltered Through the Storms: A Chinese Pastor Preserved by God* (Palo Cedro, CA: Wayside Impressions, 1996), ch. 15.
[47] Document 19: The Basic Viewpoint and Policy on the Religious Question During Our Country's Socialist Period, by the Central Committee of the Communist Party of China, 31 March 1982, Section II.

induced by "grief and indignation over danger to the motherland, or from exaltation of her progress, arises from a sense of right and wrong, a sense of justice, and a sense of national belonging."[48] Patriotism motivated people to perform heroic deeds and endure sacrifice for the welfare of their country. Ting called for patriotic support of Chinese Christians for the new socialistic system by defending it and eliminating the negative aspects that might remain while promoting improvements. The CCP in its August 1985 report on research of minority nationals and religious groups encouraged an educational approach for teaching of government policy among cadres and to strengthen patriotism through the United Front theory. With insufficient publicity and lack of education after the long-standing influence of conservative Marxist ideology, there remained mistaken views of the theory and policy of the United Front.[49]

Since 1979, along with the United Front principle and in connection with its ministry to Chinese Christians, the TSPM transformed the Three-Self Principle from pursuing independence to the development of well-managed churches. Philip Wickeri found that from 1980 to 1986 the TSPM and CCC had concentrated on reconstruction and restoration of the Church, and since then their emphasis had changed to edifying the Church as the Body of Christ.[50]

However, in February 1988 there was discussion as to whether TSPM had outlived its purpose. Bishop Ting, a liberal with an open moderate stance from the Nanjing office, favored disbanding the TSPM organization in sharp disagreement with the conservative TSPM leaders from the Shanghai headquarters, who were determined to preserve it. Lambert referred to a March 1989 letter from a former TSPM pastor who stated that the campaign to abolish the TSPM was an effort to dissociate the names of some TSPM leaders from the dark reputation the TSPM gained during the Cultural Revolution. During that time the TSPM had held accusation meetings that led to many pastors being imprisoned

---

[48] Bishop Ding Guangxun, 'Another Look at 3-Self,' *Ching Feng*, Vol. 25, No. 4, December (1982) 256.
[49] Lambert, *The Resurrection*, p. 97.
[50] Philip L. Wickeri, *Seeking the Common Ground* (Maryknoll, NY: Orbis Books, 1990), p. 234.

for up to 20 years. He found from the April 1989 report on the TSPM's December conference that the TSPM reduced its political role, and the CCC at different levels was to take a more active function in coordinating church work in conjunction with the church congregations. However, Lambert pointed out that the Tiananmen Square incident in June 1989 ended the reform of the religious policy; under the control of the conservative Marxist facet of the CCP, reform deteriorated towards harshness in its implementation.[51]

The 'Notice of Problems on further and better Administrating Religious Works' issued in 1991 by the Chinese People's Republic viewed all religious effort as the "struggle between infiltration and anti-infiltration, subversion and anti-subversion, peaceful evolution and anti-evolution." A 1994 regulation regarding temples and churches placed the authority to control and arrange religious activities in the hands of county-level government agencies rather than the local religious community.[52]

From the March 14, 1995, on the theory page of the *People's Daily*, Ye Xiaowen, director of the Bureau of Religious Affairs of the China State Council, explained that the central idea was to administer religious affairs according to law, to protect legal activities and curb the illegal by prosecuting violators according to the process for handling religious affairs. Ye recalled that Jiang Zemin, president of the People's Republic, emphasized that three phrases were imperative regarding religion. First, Party policy toward religion was to be implemented in the correct manner. Second, the administration of religious affairs was to be strengthened according to law. Finally, religions were to be actively guided in order to adapt to the socialist society.[53] Policies were to be constructed to comply with the aims that the CCP had for the constitutional religious freedom and to unite all religions to the sociopolitical ideology of the people's government.

---

[51] Lambert, *The Resurrection*, pp. 100, 208-209, 242.
[52] Liu, 'State Policy,' *China Strategic Review*, p. 5.
[53] Ye Xiaowen, Director, Bureau of Religious Affairs, the State Council, 'Appendix X: China's Current Religious Questions of Religion: Once again an Inquiry into the Five Characteristics of Religion,' in Human Rights / Asia, *China: State Control of Religion* (New York: Human Rights Watch, 1997) pp. 143-144; From 'Selection of Reports of the Party School of the Central Committee of the Chinese Communist Party'.

THE CHANGES MADE IN POLICY AND POLITICAL STRUCTURE

To fit the new ideals into the political structure and objectives of the People's Republic of China toward the desired direction designated by the Chinese Communist Party, the appropriate changes were to be made in religious policy. The direction desired was away from the harsh conservative Marxist dogma to eradicate religion. Modernization without compromise on the Marxist ideology was the new ideal goal, which required the cooperation of religious citizenry.

GOVERNMENTAL ADJUSTMENT OF POLICY

Dr. Theodore Marr expressed in a symposium on religious policy in China that the Marxian theory considered religion a superstition; it would eventually disappear from society as human control over the world was accomplished. This position was reflected in the religious policies adopted in China. The 1940 Communist United Front Policy, Article 5 of the Common Program in 1949, Article 88 of the 1954 Constitution, and the 1975 Constitution all reflected this presupposition.[54] The Third Plenary Meeting of the 1978 Eleventh Central Committee witnessed a change toward a more moderate religious policy. In place of a ban on religious activity, the emphasis was to contain religious practices to enhance China's international image. The CCP came to recognize that administrative pressure neither controlled religious activities nor prevented its growth. Chairman Deng Xiaoping recognized the political advantage of abandoning religious repression and submitting a more moderate stance on religious policy for modernization.[55]

Tony Lambert emphasized that even though the Communist Party promised freedoms of religious belief, it maintained strict limitations. The parameters were mediated through the TSPM and enforced through the hierarchy from the CCP to the UFWD and the RAB. Religious freedom was a calculated policy toward modernization, which the Party was willing to risk.[56] The CCP

---

[54] Theodore Marr, 'Symposium: The Religious Policy of the People's Republic of China: A Protestant View,' in David Aikman (ed.), *Love China Today* (Wheaton, IL: Tyndale House Publishers, 1977), p. 86.
[55] Drew Liu, 'State Policy and Christianity in China,' *China Strategic Review,* China Strategic Institute, Vol. 1, (1996) 1.
[56] Tony Lambert, *The Resurrection of the Chinese Church* (Wheaton, IL: Harold Shaw Publishers, 1994), p. 49.

Central Committee directive published in 1982, 'Fundamental Viewpoints and Policy on Religious Issues in Our Socialist Period,' was the foundation for religious affairs during the reform era. The freedom of religious belief was to be protected and respected to ensure individual choice of what to believe, but Party members retained certain rights to promote atheism. All religious activities were brought under the control and management of the State through a legal structure, and finally religion would serve religious policy, economic development, and international relations. Representatives of the respective religious organizations would bridge the relation between the CCP and the religious communities.[57] Philip Wickeri found that the point of the deletion of the phrase "freedom not to believe in religion and to propagate atheism" had been the striking similarity between the 1954 and 1982 People's Constitutions, which had been included in religious policy of the constitutions ratified in 1975 and 1978.[58]

The important of documents that regulated the religious policy of China included Document 19, the basic policy on religion released by the Central Government on March 31, 1982 and Document No. 6 that compelled the observance of the established policy issued on February 5, 1991 by the State Council. Decrees No. 144, which regulated religious activities among foreigners within China, and 145, which governed the registration of Chinese religious groups, were both released by the State Council on January 31, 1994.[59] However, it was reported in the June 8, 1998, issue of the *China News and Church Report* that the cadres at the enforcement level were unfamiliar with the basic policies other than orders 144 and 145 and the public had no knowledge of them.[60]

The CCP had certain objectives for Document 19, 'Concerning Our Country's Basic Standpoint and Policy on Religious Questions During the Socialist Period.' It confirmed that Marxist ideology regarded religion as a stage in human social development. The

---

[57] Liu, 'State Policy,' *China Strategic Review,* pp. 2-3.
[58] Philip L. Wickeri, *Seeking the Common Ground* (Maryknoll, NY: Orbis Books, 1990), p. 102.
[59] Jonathan Chao, 'The Church in China Today – Officially Registered Churches and House Churches,' *Challenger,* Vol. XXXVI, No. 4, August-September (1997) 6.
[60] Myron Ivey (ed.), 'TSPM Leaders Call for a National Religious Law,' *China News and Church Report,* June 8 (1998) 1.

CCP used Document 19 as a control, developed in terms of the United Front principles in connection with the eight patriotic religious organizations. Training the leaders of the patriotic societies was fundamental to establishing policy. International congenial relations depended on the religious policy, but it also controlled religious growth and unregistered religious assemblies.[61] Document 19 outlined the duties of the TSPM as the Central Committee deemed necessary to assist the People's Government and Party to implement the religious policy of freedom of belief, raise patriotic consciousness for socialism, represent religious rights, and organize as well as implement religious activities efficiently.[62]

Lambert found that the CCP regulated religion in accordance with Section IV of Document 19 for the private sector of society, and forbade it in governing in terms of education and the legal system. Section VI then presided over aspects of religion in relation to social, production and work orders.[63] According to the CCP:

The essence of the policy of religious freedom is to make religious faith a matter of private free choice for the citizen, a private and individual matter... We emphasize mutual respect in order to broaden the scope of our unity; we should unite with all patriotic believers, their special liturgical practices should be respected. This is a progressive, not a regressive attitude.[64]

Section IV gave all Chinese citizens the freedom to believe in any approved religious sect, to be a believer or forego religious belief "to become a non-believer."[65]

To augment Document 19 another circular, known as Document

---

[61] David H. Adeney, *China: The Church's Long March* (Ventura CA: Regal Books, 1985), pp. 125-134.
[62] A. P. B. Lambert, 'Supervision of Christianity in the People's Republic of China,' *Religion in Communist Lands,* Vol. 18, Autumn (1990) 216.
[63] Lambert, *The Resurrection,* pp. 55 56.
[64] Shen Xilin, 'Seeking the Common Ground and Unity,' Janice K. Wickeri (ed. & trans.) [Documents form the Fourth National Christian Conference, Shanghai, August 1986], *Chinese Theological Review,* Vol. 3, (1987) 37-38.
[65] Document 19: The Basic Viewpoint and Policy on the Religious Question During Our Country's Socialist Period, by the Central committee of the Communist Party of China, 31 March 1982, Section IV.

No. 6 was published in February 1991 to further improve religious work. Section I involved the protection of national unity from any religious ambition that may oppose the leadership, social stability, interests of society, or rights of the Chinese citizenry. The role of the patriotic religious organizations outlined in Section III "served as a bridge by which the Party and government unite with and educate religious personages." It was a "guarantee for the successful implementation of the Party's policy towards religion and the normalization of religious activities." Section V attached further attention to training cadres for improved competence while dealing with religious matters. A new emphasis stressed their responsibility and the significance of their duties in religious education, with further studies on Marxist philosophy and the Party religious policy along with the laws governing those policies.[66]

The duties of Party leadership concerning religious activities were delineated in Document No. 6, Section VI, that defined a new level of religious awareness required for officials to influence religions to cooperate in the socialist society. This section stressed the importance of education at all social and age levels in dialectical and historical materialism for high ideals, moral standards and discipline. It limited the belief and participation of Party members in religion and its activities with a warning of disciplinary action of reform to acquire the desired world-view or be expelled from the Party. The only acceptable exception was for members working directly among religious minority groups; even then, the Central Committee stipulated certain guidelines.[67]

At a national meeting on January 14, 1996, convened in Beijing, an agenda was compiled for regulating religious factions by the turn of the century. The Ministry of Public Security had issued a document in November 1995, 'On Further Reinforcement of the Leadership and Supervision Towards Religious Groups.' This contained parts of Party Secretary and President Jiang Zemin's speech that portrayed the policy concerning Christianity

---

[66] Document No. 6, Circular Issued by the Central Committee of the Chinese Communist Party and the State Council On Some Problems Concerning Further Improving Work of Religion, February 5, 1991, Sections I, III, V.
[67] Document No. 6., Section VI.

as "a war to be conducted quietly."[68] Conversely, a speech by the director of the State Council's Religious Affairs Bureau, Ye Xiaowen, on June 9, 1997, pointed out that Article 36 of the Chinese Constitution ensured the freedom of religion as the basic right of all China's citizens. He stated that no religious endeavor might be used to disrupt public order, endanger health of citizens, or interfere with the State's educational system, but the State committed itself to protect normal religious activity.[69] According to Article 7 the RAB, as the principle administrative body of religious affairs of the People's government was to supervise the implementation of regulations from national to local levels.[70]

Guidelines for religious regulation implementation were stipulated in Article 251 of Criminal Law, which specified up to a two-year imprisonment for any personnel of the State who would deprive any Chinese of freedom of religious belief.[71] But even though religion was legally protected, Ye Xiaowen declared that the government focused on the long-term character of religious existence during the socialist period of political evolution to Communism. The Party plan was to dissuade Chinese people from religious belief and to deteriorate religious influence through political, cultural, social and educational development, and social reform. The CCP utilized the mass character of China's population for cooperation to enhance the political and economic interests of the nation, though individuals might have different beliefs. The policies to protect freedom of belief encouraged the unification of the masses for national construction. The CCP conceded that the employment of the "mass character" of China must not influence them to accommodate primitive ideas or inflict damage on society from a minority faction, but the interests of the majority must be safeguarded. Chairman Deng Xiaoping promoted "patriotism and love of the Church and unity for progress." He recognized the fallacy of administrative measures to deal with religion, which

[68] Liu, 'State Policy,' *China Strategic Review*, p. 5.
[69] 'RAB Chief Says China Respects and Protects Religious Freedom,' *Amity News Service*, Vol. 6, July-August, (1997) 4.
[70] Mickey Spiegel, 'Appendix IV: RAB Regulations,' *China: State control of Religion* (New York: Human Rights Watch, 1997), p. 91; Chapter 1, Article 7.
[71] State Council Information Office, 'Freedom of Religious Belief in China,' October 1997, *Beijing Review*, November 3-9 (1997) 17.

led to fanaticism, but he also believed that to allow it to function without direction would lead to the same outcome.[72]

ADJUSTMENTS WITHIN THE TSPM THROUGH INTEGRATING THE CCC

Samuel Wang, a Chinese scholar who worked with both the TSPM and the CCC in translation work, confirmed that neither the TSPM nor the CCC had organizational relations to the CCP through the UFWD or RAB. He related that from the beginning of the People's Republic in 1949, because of the hatred generated toward Christianity in connection with the unequal treaties, Zhou Enlai, as a Christian, lectured for six sessions to show Christianity to be Chinese. Then at the start of the Korean War in 1951 the patriotic organizations were established and the government could reasonably accept religions on this basis. He cited that the TSPM did not follow directions from the Central Government in 1982 when Bishop Ting stated that the Chinese Communist leaders had souls "and we need to lead them to Christ."[73]

The Three-Self principles of the TSPM had primarily been established for the purpose of independence of the Church in China. Han Wenzao, president of the CCC, stated that these principles were inseparable from accomplishing the work of the Church. He stressed that the principle of self-propagation not only should increase the number of Christian believers, but believers must find growth in understanding biblical truth.[74] The TSPM leadership influenced the quality of how

---

[72] Ye Xiaowen, Director of Bureau of Religious Affairs of the State Council, 'Appendix X: China's Current Religious Question: Once again an Inquiry into the five Characteristics of Religion,' from a Selection of Reports of the Party School of the Central Committee of the Chinese Communist Party, 1998, No. 5 in Human Rights / Asia, *China: State Control of Religion* (New York: Human Rights Watch, 1997), pp. 18-19, 125-128.

[73] Samuel Wang, Scholar of the *Four Books* collection of Confucius and Mencius teachings, Co-author of *God and the Ancient Chinese,* Director of the Chinese Department of Laymen Ministry News Ministries, had done translation work for TSPM and CCC and in the U.S. worked closely with Human Rights Watch (Interview: 21 December 1999).

[74] Han Wenzao, 'Build Up the Body of Christ with One Heart and United Effort: Running the Church Even Better According to the Three-Self Principle,' Janice Wickeri (ed.), *Chinese Theological Review: 12* (Foundation for Theological Education in Southeast Asia, 1998) pp. 30, 33.

the Church was nurtured.

Adeney identified the three types of leaders: the first, from the 1950s, had been involved in the persecution of Christians. Then there were those who participated in the betrayal of fellow Christians, but in turn suffered during the Cultural Revolution and were restored. Finally, there was a group that had contact with house churches during the Cultural Revolution and later joined the TSPM to more easily minister as an evangelical witness to the general Chinese public plus be in a position to promote change in religious policy.[75]

Influence in policy usually came from adjustment to CCP directives. As chairman of the TSPM, Luo Guanzong reviewed the changes for the TSPM Constitution revision of Article II indicating its aims and duties. The first was from "deeply love their homeland" to "deeply love their socialist homeland." The second change of wording was from "to observe the national constitution," to "to observe the national constitution and the laws, regulations and policies of the land." An addition included "safeguarding the legitimate rights of the church."[76]

Therefore, the TSPM daughter organization, established in 1980 as the CCC, had identified itself to minister not only to the churches registered and joined to the TSPM but also to Protestant Christians who had chosen to worship in homes. The aims outlined in Article II of the CCC constitution stated, "to unite all Chinese Christians who believe in the heavenly Father and who acknowledge Jesus Christ as Lord and Savior." Article III stated that the CCC "advocated mutual respect in matters of faith and worship."[77] As vice chair of the TSPM, Ms. Wang Juzhen pointed out a further change made for the July 7, 1997 revision in Article II of the CCC Constitution. From merely, "...to uphold the national constitution and laws, regulations and policies of the land..." there was an addition to include leading the Chinese Christian Church under the guiding influence of the Holy Spirit. This premise

---

[75] David Adeney, 'Division time in China: To join the TSPM or not,' *Evangelical Missions Quarterly*, Vol. 19, No 3, July (1983) 201.

[76] Luo Guanzong, 'The Revised Constitutions' [Three-Self Movement], trans. Janice Wickeri, *Chinese Theological Review* (1991) 38-39. Luo was President of CCC.

[77] 'About the China Christian Council,' *Amity News Service*, www.hk.super.net/-amityhk/ccprot.htm, 11/9/98, 3:26 PM.

pledged obedience to the truth of the Bible, the patriotic principles set forth by the TSPM, order of the Chinese Church and the laws, policies and regulations of the national constitution.[78] The TSPM formulated policy based on political and ecclesiastical context.

Kan Baoping, lecturer at Nanjing Union Theological Seminary, identified the organization of the CCC, in connection with the TSPM, not as the decision-making body, although it was consultative to provincial Christian councils.[79] Article IV of the CCC Constitution stated the duties of the CCC:

> The CCC promotes theological education and the publication of the Bible, hymnbooks and other literature for the Chinese church, the exchange of information among local churches in evangelism, pastoral work and administration, and promotes the formulation of church orders for local churches and the development of friendly relations with churches overseas.[80]

To relate on an international basis the CCC had become a member of the World Council of Churches, although publication of Bibles held priority. Under the direction of the CCC twenty different versions of the Bible had been published, to produce different styles for the varied educational levels and backgrounds of the people along with several translations for different minority groups within China. *Today's Chinese Version* was the version with the broadest circulation. The United Bible Societies published this version in 1979, and about 70 different translations since the 1950s were referenced. The 1995 edition used the original Bible languages in translation.[81]

By accommodating persons with Bibles for adequate worship

---

[78] Wang Juzhen, 'On The Revisions to the Constitutions,' Janice Wickeri (ed.), *Chinese Theological Review* (Holland, MI: Foundation of Theological Education in Southeast Asia, 1998), p. 57. Ms. Wang was Vice-Chairperson of the TSPM, a scientist and inventor.

[79] Kan Baoping, 'Theology In The Contemporary Chinese Context,' *Amity News Service*, Vol. 7, January – February 1998, reprinted from *World And World*, Luther Seminary, St. Paul, MN, Vol XVII, No. 2, Spring (1997) 15. Kan Boaping was a lecturer in systematic theology and historical theology at Nanjing Union Theological Seminary and a member of the Chinese Religion Association.

[80] 'About the China Christian Council,' *Amity News Service*, www.hk.super.net/-amithk/cccprot.htm, 11/9/98, 3:26 PM.

[81] 'Different Chinese Translations of the Bible,' *Amity News Service*, Vol. 7, January-February, 98.1.3, (1998) 5.

and churches to congregate in, the TSPM and CCC pursued a policy to bring all Chinese Protestant believers under their leadership. There were nearly 4000 churches either newly built or reclaimed and renovated by 1995, to be used by those who had met in homes before.[82] The two organizations became known as the *Lianghui*, or Two Joint, Committees, because they worked so interdependently. The October 1997 issue of their periodical, *Tian Feng*, announced eight special committees to oversee their ministry throughout China and be represented internationally.[83]

Until 1996 the TSPM and the CCC shared the same leadership. During the Sixth National Christian Conference on December 29, 1996, Bishop K. H. Ting announced his retirement as chairman of the TSPM and president of the CCC. He had held these offices for fifteen years, and then two different individuals filled these positions.[84] Although the TSPM and the CCC then had separate leadership there was no indication of a division in ideals or purpose.

THE AMITY FOUNDATION AS AN ADDITION TO THE CCC

While president of the CCC, Bishop Ting helped organize the Amity Foundation in 1985 and became president of it as well. It was established to promote education, welfare and cultural exchange for the Chinese people.[85] Amity was founded as an independent Chinese organization on the initiative of Chinese Christians. It provided an avenue for Christian participation in China's social development and an opportunity for international contact. It involved Chinese Christians in rural development, social welfare, relief and rehabilitation, health care and various forms of education.[86] In the onset, Amity's workforce consisted of three people, but by 1995 there were 24 in staff positions. Their

---

[82] Jonathan Chao (interviews), Richard Van Houten (ed.), *Wise as Serpents Harmless as Doves* (Pasadena: William Carey Library, 1988, p. 140.

[83] 'Lianghui Announces Formation of Eight Special Committees,' Myron Ivey (ed.), *China News and Church Report*, 2054, 1997.

[84] Ting K. H., 'Greetings to the Sixth National Chinese Christian Conference,' Janice Wickeri (ed.), *Chinese Theological Review* (Holland, MI: Foundation for Theological Education in Southeast Asia, 1998), pp. 2 3.

[85] 'Christian Work – China,' *Global Prayer Digest*, www.calebproject.org/nance/n1632.htm, 3/12/98, p.6.

[86] Philip Wickeri (overseas coordinator), *The Amity Foundation*, Kowloon, Hong Kong: brochure.

qualifications were compassion, dedication and proficiency, and every effort was to be made to repress any idea that Amity was a charity organization.[87]

The Amity Foundation, as described by Han Wenzao, was instrumental in changing the reputation of Christianity with the Chinese people, for it demonstrated that Christians were patriotic and not nationalistic with an ambition to facilitate the establishment of Christianity in China. The programs of Amity were not restricted to only Christian participation, which provided the realization that "all human efforts, all ethical concerns and all humanitarian work stand within God's mercy and under God's judgement." Its work was within the teachings of Jesus in the Bible about Christians as salt and light of the world as found in Matthew 5. It provided the opportunity to demonstrate the Christian faith without a hidden agenda as a part of the pre-evangelistic task of Christians.

The Amity Foundation also promoted the sense that the church was never established as God's representative in the world, but was to "act in the world and for the world, not simply in the church and for the church." The Bible taught, "For God so loved the world...," which they asserted did not exclusively segregate the church for His love. In that realm, the definition of evangelism, through restricted to the church building, was recognized as: "to make systematic efforts to persuade others to believe in Jesus Christ." This did not exclude telling others that you were a Christian, or encourage a friend to read the Bible, nor did it prevent a teacher from answering a student's questions about Christianity for discussion of the faith in a natural and appropriate way.[88]

In the concept of missions, Amity expanded into new areas of opportunity to be effective in ministry. The sphere of Christian art and its research was used to generate intellectual, scientific and financial international exchange projects as an ecumenical partnership. Therefore, in cooperation with the CCC, TSPM,

[87] Han Wenzao, 'In the Course of Ten Years,' *Compassion and Development*, On the Tenth Anniversary of the Amity Foundation, 1985-1995.
[88] Philip L. Wickeri, 'Development Service and China's Modernization: The Amity Foundation in Theological Perspective,' *The Ecumenical Review*, Vol. 41, January (1998) 83-84, 86-87. Reference to the Bible, Mathew 5:13-15 and John 3:16a.

Nanjing Union Theological Seminary and the Amity Printing Company, an organization entitled The Amity Center for Cultural, Technological and Economic Exchange, ACCTEE, was founded.[89]

ADJUSTMENT FOR THE CHURCH

Religious policy mandated churches or religious organizations to register their sites with the RAB in accordance with the law. The State Council Information Office stated that there were six requirements stipulated as a prerequisite for registration. The congregation must have "a permanent site and name; regular attendance; a management organization composed of adherents to the relevant religion; clerical personnel for officiating religious activities...; management regulations and lawful income."[90]

Many religious buildings had been confiscated during the Cultural Revolution; consequently, a congregation without a site could not register. Pan Fubao, a lawyer and Christian, explained Document 188, 'Report on the Handling of Religious Property Questions,' issued in July 1980 by the State Council. If a religious organization could clearly provide evidence that they had previously owned the property occupied by a work unit or business enterprise, it must be returned. If the property had been altered to such an extent that rendered it impossible to be returned, compensation must be paid.[91]

The January 1997 Chinese Church Order approved at the Sixth National Christian Conference determined that after a meeting point satisfied the registration requirement it could become an approved church only when the municipal or county RAB recorded its decision to grant the church status. Then a roster of membership must be established for historical records of that particular church or meeting point. The church property would be collectively owned, and the church as a registered organization would assume responsibility for its function. Therefore, a designated person or committee would assume accountability for the property and institute a system of management to implement

---

[89] Han, 'In Ten Years,' Wickeri, *Amity*, brochure.
[90] State Council Information Office, 'Freedom of Belief,' *Beijing Review*, November 3-9 (1997) 17.
[91] 'Section III: Protestant Church,' *China Study Journal*, Vol. 13, No. 1, August (1998) 56.

the Three-Self principles. The object of this precaution was to preempt individuals or institutions that might intend to disrupt these principles. Democratic methods were to be employed in church organizations for a mutual representation of the members for unity in making decisions. A trained church worker of the group was then required to perform the teaching and preaching to dissuade any heretical instruction.[92]

According to documents from Shaanxi province in central China, pastors were to maintain loyalties to the Communist Party and support the four principles of the Party. These principles state allegiance to the "supremacy of the party, the supremacy of the Socialist system, the dictatorship of the people, and the supremacy of Marx, Lenin and Mao Zedong thought." It was forbidden to proclaim religious dogma to a minor less than eighteen years of age or to a Communist Party member. For adults to become members of a congregation through baptism, they were to be observed and investigated to ensure that they conformed to certain doctrines and maintained a reputation and political position for unity toward Socialist construction. Sermon content was to be patriotic without pronouncements on marriage, education or the law.

This publication prohibited the infiltration of Bibles or Christian literature from abroad along with listening to outside religious radio broadcasts. Also forbidden were any activities including healing the diseased, demon exorcism, charismatic demonstration, or anything that might be defined as cheating people or damaging to their health.[93]

POLICY FOR THE HOUSE CHURCH MOVEMENT

Document 19, Section VI, stipulated that gatherings in homes should be prohibited in principle, although they might be tolerated. It was the responsibility of the patriotic organizations to persuade these groups to register with the RAB and join the TSPM or unite with a congregation that had already done so.[94] Leslie Lyall recorded that in January 1979 a visiting group from Hong Kong

---

[92] 'ANS Documentation,' *Amity News Service*, Vol. 6, November – December (1997) 14.
[93] Megan Gabriel Lanham, *Snatched from the Dragon* (Nashville: Thomas Nelson Publishers, 1990), pp. 153-154.
[94] Document 19, Section VI.

discovered that house gatherings were very suspicious of the TSPM and reluctant to become legalized for fear of jeopardizing their independence.[95]

In September 1980 Bishop Ting of the Chinese People's Political Consultative Conference, CPPCC, reiterated that the obligation of the TSPM was to unite all Chinese Protestant Christians. Those who met in homes, which made up a majority of Chinese Christians, were not to be labeled separately nor in his opinion were they illegal. Ting pointed out that the constitution ensured freedom of belief in homes as well as in church buildings. However, house church Christians reported a significant change in this policy in late 1983 when the CCP reinstated the Anti-spiritual Pollution Campaign for a brief time, and then arrests were made for infractions of unclear areas in policy.[96] Anti-spiritual was not a term used in the sense of religious spirituality, but it indicated the spirit of cooperation toward socialist construction in the Communist governed society.

EFFECTS OF CHANGES UPON THE PRACTICES OF THE CHINESE CHURCH

Many factors converged to produce the changes for Chinese Church indigenization. Historically, when the Church came under the Communist government, it was left without foreign mission board direction and leadership. With the governmental change, the political regulations to govern all aspects of the society were transformed. Therefore, not only religious polity was modified but also secular variations in economics, international relationships, educational priorities, living arrangements and land distribution were affected. These adjustments then became uncertain and arbitrary, which stimulated insecurities and a wane of confidence in the system. The accumulation of factors affecting the attitudes of citizens produced reactions, and in the sphere of religion different methods to cope became apparent.

THE REFLECTED ATTITUDES

An article published in September 20, 1979, issue of the *Workers Daily*, cited by Tony Lambert, revealed an attitude in Chinese youth of resentment and disillusionment toward the government. For them

---

[95] Leslie Lyall, *God Reigns in China* (London: Hodder and Stoughton, 1985), pp. 190-191.
[96] Lambert, *The Resurrection*, p 71.

the constitutional provisions of freedoms of thought, speech, press and association adopted in the Second Session and Fifth National People's Conference had become merely pieces of scrap paper. The Constitution's words and the actions of the CCP were far apart, and arrests of ideological criminals, who vented expression of beliefs, exhausted their trust in the Communist Party. Lambert claimed that in the spiritual vacuum created from disillusionment with political resolution many Chinese turned to Christianity, evidenced by the tens of thousands of letters received since 1979 by foreign Christian radio stations.[97] Amid the understanding that Marxist ideals were unfulfilled, Christianity, Buddhism and even fatalism expressed in palm reading and fortune telling became fashionable.[98]

After the confirmation that Christianity had survived and grown through the bitter persecution of the Cultural Revolution, Bishop Ting convened the elders of the Chinese Protestant Christian churches in March 1980 for a seven-day session. They were encouraged to air their suffering of this past decade, but the response revealed the attitudes of these Christian leaders. Not a single grievance was made publicly, but all conversation centered on plans for the future and how to recuperate the lost decade.[99] A new TSPM constitution was published, the CCC was founded, and new policies were declared concerning freedoms and moderation.

The Anti-spiritual Pollution Campaign in 1983 did not discourage itinerant evangelists, who were objects of police search. Over 100 evangelists became fugitives and never returned to their homes but travelled constantly.[100] The attitude of commitment enabled them to travel into the remote mountainous regions where no Christian had gone with the message of Christ, and they established new congregations.[101] There was a commitment to take the Church of China forward without dwelling on past injustices.

---

[97] Tony Lambert, *The Resurrection of the Chinese Church* (Wheaton, IL: Harold Shaw Publishers, 1994), pp. 104, 109.

[98] Peter Humphrey, *Religious Suppression in Mainland China* (Republic of China: World Anti-Communist League, 1983), pp. 8-9.

[99] Han Wenzao, 'Work Together with One Heart to Build Up the Body of Christ,' Janice Wickeri (ed.), *Chinese Theological Review: 12* (Holland, MI: Foundation for Theological Education in Southeast Asia, 1998), p. 118.

[100] Jonathan Chao (interviews), Richard Van Houten (ed.), *Wise as Serpents Harmless as Doves* (Pasadena: William Cary Library, 1988, p. 140.

[101] 'Christian Work-China,' *Global Prayer Digest*, www.calebproject.org/nance/n1632.htm, 3/12/98, pp. 1-9.

THE POLITICAL EFFECT ON THE CHURCH

It was advantageous politically for the CCP to assure freedom of religion, as affirmed in Section IV of Document 19, for it was a "means of strengthening the Party's effort to disseminate scientific education as well as to strengthen its propaganda against superstition." For young ministers graduating from the seminaries, the Party had plans to ensure their loyalty to promote the religious policy as outlined in Section VIII. This directive held these young, impressionable, and perhaps eager church workers to imitate respectfully the older patriotic religious leaders of the older generation for their integration into the system.[102]

The implementation of policy was the responsibility of the RAB. According to Han Wenzao, even though the People's Republic or the CCP had no organizational connection with the TSPM, their channel of communication went through the RAB. The function of the RAB in cooperation with regional and local authorities was to accomplish the religious policy arranged in the Constitution. "With the vastness of China there is a dependence of officials on the local level of education and understanding."[103] Especially in the remote Guizhou province, many RAB cadres had a conservative Marxist orientation and little acquaintance with the progress of religious policy, and they maintained that religion was counter-revolutionary as their discriminated practices proved throughout their jurisdiction.[104] Dr. Han reported the religious-freedom violation complaints were to be "channeled through the RAB under the State Council." An advisory board unique to China, the Standing Committee of the Chinese People's Political Consultative Conference, CPPCC, was made up of 37 representative groups; less than 40 percent of them were Communist Party members. Then the National People's Conference, NPC, acted as a parliament and requested investigation and restitution on the part of the violator. The CCC represented the church for securing rights. Dr. Han continued:

---

[102] Document 19: The Basic Viewpoint and Policy on the Religious Question During Our Country's Socialist Period, by the Central Committee of the Communist Party, March 31, 1982, Sections IV, VIII.
[103] Han Wensao, Dr, President of China Christian Council, Nanjing (Interview 14 September 1999)
[104] 'Section III: Protestant Church,' *China Study Journal,* Vol. 3, No.1, April (1998) 92.

Procedures are different here in China, for example in Bible printing is to get a printing permit, but we can get things done for we are called by God to work on this piece of land and in the local context. The gospel message is unchanging and we must consider the context.[105]

It was the responsibility of Party Committees, as provided for by Document 19, "to clearly delineate the line dividing normal religious activities from criminal ones." The procedure then was not to attack the criminal conduct but to protect the normal religious activities by securing the confidence of religious believers and through education produce normalization.[106] The Human Rights Watch of Asia found from the Regulations of the Shanghai Religious Affairs Bureau ratified on November 30, 1995, that the officials at province, county and local levels of jurisdictions, in accordance with their Bureau, "have the authority to be even more restrictive when they issue implementing regulations." A registered church may not be free to practice what it considered normal, according to the religious regulations of the central government.[107]

The fact that churches that registered with the RAB and joined with the TSPM experienced discrimination was evidence that the implementation of government policy lacked consistency. The deficiency of remedial action against discriminative practices on the part of governmental agencies inferred approval to cadres with conservative Marxist ideals to act with biases.[108]

As of September 1999, over 25,000 meeting points were known, and some, because of their refusal to collaborate with an atheistic regime, had no contact with the RAB, TSPM or CCC. Dr. Han reasoned that:

> It is important in that it is the people's government and that we support the Party politically because most Chinese are willing to build a prosperous nation. The CCP could play the leading role. Old China could not be changed to New China without the CCP. The CCP freed the Chinese

---

[105] Han (Interview, 14 September 1999).
[106] Document 19, Section X.
[107] Human Rights/ Asia, *China: State Control of Religion* (New York: Human Rights Watch, 1997), p. 20.
[108] Gail Law, 'Ding,' Jonathan Chao (ed.), *China Prayer Letter*, No. 126, p. 3.

people and challenged people to work very hard. They have made it possible to have a religious choice. Zhou Enlai seeks common ground to help build China.

Since Communist Party members only embody 5 percent of China's population, Han concluded that the united effort of the people was imperative. Therefore, it was vital that the CCP maintain respect for religious believers to obtain their support. An example was that of Samuel Lamb of Wenzhou to whom the local CCC supplied Bibles even though he accused them of being collaborators with the atheistic regime. As president of the CCC, Dr. Han reiterated that, "We can accomplish Church work by the Bibles we print and seminaries provided."[109]

At times the TSPM leadership was obliged to cooperate with the desires of the CCP as demonstrated in a statement Lambert found recorded in the September-October 1989 issue of the *Bridge*. This article cited a regional Religious Affairs Bureau Director who on December 31, 1988, said that "the number of Christians in our region has doubled in the past five years, and in some districts this increase has been fivefold. This has created confusion in the church and harmful effects on society." Within a few days of this statement the local TSPM office issued a decision to forbid laymen from persuading converts to Christianity.

Lambert cited the April 1990 *Zhenming* that reported an alarming statistic in Beijing declaring that Communist Party applicants declined while growth in church membership increased. In fact there was a 45 percent decline in Party membership while the registered churches experienced a 170 percent increase. He also found that a September 1990 issue of the *Workers Daily* gave an account that a student survey conducted in Zhejiang province revealed that 10 percent of the students attend a Christian church regularly.[110] This demonstrated the confidence in Communistic ideals had diminished, and the Chinese people were turning to other credos.

EFFECTS ON INTERNATIONAL RELATIONS

Missionary societies and the Vatican were considered reactionary

---

[109] Han (Interview, 14 September 1999).
[110] Lambert, *The Resurrection*, pp. 236-237, 244.

groups with intentions to reenter China as stated in Section XI of Document 19. This section encouraged friendly exchange with international religious organizations, but warned against any infiltration by antagonistic religious institutes.[111] No religious association or representative individual was authorized to establish offices, promote publications, or disturb China's religious affairs as delineated in Section II of Document 6. This section specified norms for non-religious firms to notify the RAB of any influential foreign religious personnel they may invite into China.[112]

THEOLOGICAL IMPLICATIONS

The Bible was the main curriculum of the seminaries, Bible schools, and lay training programs promoted by the CCC all over China. The Bible was considered a most prized possession to Chinese Christians due to incidents in their lives during the Cultural Revolution. Chen Xida of Nanjing Theological Seminary confirmed this from his own experience.[113] The National TSPM Committee reported that eighteen seminaries and Bible schools had been established since 1981 to meet the demand for theological training and production of church leadership, yielding 3,100 graduates by July 1998.[114] Document 6, Section II, prohibited any unauthorized Bible college, seminary or convent and their products of self-appointed clergy.[115] The curriculum of the approved institutions no longer offered separate courses for conservative and liberal students as during the 1950s, but professors from each discipline exposed the students to the different perspectives.[116]

Section VI of Document 19 forbid entry into a place of worship to propagate atheistic teaching and prevented any religious believer from promoting his or her religion outside the designated religious sites.[117] Samuel Wang acknowledged that by policy a preacher was not

[111] Document 19, Section XI.
[112] Document No. 6: By Central Committee of the CCP and the State Council February 5, 1991, Section II.
[113] Chen Xida, 'The Life and Witness of the Church in China,' *China Talk*, October (1997) 35. Address at LWF Assembly in Hong Kong in July 1997 from Chen Xida of the Nanjing Theological Seminary.
[114] National Three-Self Movement Committee China Christian Council, *Protestant Christianity in China*, Shanghai, Nanjing, 1999.
[115] Document No. 6, Section II.
[116] Philip L. Wickeri, 'Theological Reorientation in Chinese Protestantism 1949-1984, Part II,' *Ching Feng*, Vol. 28, No. 2-3, August (1985) 125.
[117] Document 19, Section VI.

to speak unless in an assigned church building, but the government would not enforce this on home gatherings, except when the crowd became large.[118] The Three-Self principle of self-propagation included confinement to the local religious location for evangelization.

The Self-Propagation Symposium in Shanghai from November 18 to 20, 1997, intertwined self-propagation with the Three-Self principle of self-support. The representatives concluded that when a church met the spiritual needs of the people through teaching the doctrines of the Christian faith, the support of the people would be offered willingly. It was decided in the symposium that evangelists should only be those who maintained a close relationship with God plus a strong sense of moral integrity and had personally applied their own instruction. The level of education for an evangelist must be adequate, especially in theological training, to relate with a broad spectrum of society and accurately and plainly share Biblical knowledge. It was agreed in the symposium that the basic Gospel message never changed, but its application might vary with time and ages. It was imperative to teach the doctrines of creation, original sin, and the atonement in an understandable and acceptable method for the traditional society of China. The message should promote Christian ethics and speak to the current problems of Chinese society as to "how believers should deal with new wealth in the midst of a developing economy, how believers should face the threat of unemployment or early retirement, marriage breakdowns and divorce."[119]

THE EFFECTS OF THE TSPM AND CCC

Samuel Wang declared that "the greatest defining factor of the Church of China was the Three-Self principles, which have shaped the Church and caused Christians to grow. There has been less human leadership and more dependence on the Holy Spirit."[120] Since 1979 the TSPM had reopened churches at the rate of one a day.[121] The government funded most of the cost for church building renovation to reimburse for the rent during their

---

[118] Samuel Wang, Scholar and Co-author, St. Maries, ID (Interview, 27 December 1999).
[119] 'Self-Propagation Symposium,' *Amity News Service*, Vol. 7, 1 / 2 (1998) 20. 47 Representatives from provincial Christian Councils and theological institutes throughout the country met in Shanghai between 18-20 November 1997.
[120] Wang (Interview, 27 December 1999).
[121] 'Christian Work,' *GPD*, 2.

confiscation of the Cultural Revolution epoch.[122] The National TSPM Committee claimed in 1999 that 70 percent of the 13,000 churches had been newly built.[123] This was a factor that could induce trust in the TSPM and its concern for Church growth.

Philip Wickeri gave perspective to the TSPM and the CCC organizations, for they had expected church groups to register with them, though they proposed that registration would be a civil matter.[124] Membership of the churches that joined the TSPM was estimated at 13 million by 1999.[125] There was no means to estimate of the number of Chinese Protestant Christians because it was represented in four groups. One group included the churches registered with the RAB and joined to the TSPM; another held those who may have reservations about a relationship with the TSPM and CCC but sustain the officially recognized churches. Another grouping, the majority of Christians in China, included those who held the conviction not to join with any organization that would collaborate with an atheistic system, so they gather into private homes for worship. Still another group of mostly intellectuals known as "culture Christians" remained alone without association to the official churches or the house church movement.[126]

As the official representative organization for all Protestants of China, the first notable accomplishment of the TSPM was the recovery of churches; the second, acquiring governmental authorization to print Bibles and New Testaments, was just as noteworthy.[127] In 1985 a 3 million U.S. dollar project for Bible printing was underway with permission for funds to be procured through the American Bible Society and other Bible societies. November 1986 marked the beginning: the foundation stone for the Amity Press was placed on an eight-and-a-half acre site just at the edge of Nanjing donated by Jiangning Industrial Corporation. The United Bible Societies financed the presses, personnel training, and the expenditure for starting production.[128]

---

[122] Leslie Lyall, *God Reigns in China* (London: Hodder and Stoughton, 1985), p. 196.
[123] National TSPM Committee, *Protestant Christianity.*
[124] Philip L. Wickeri, 'A Three-Self Movement Perspective,' http://lausanne.org/0697wickhtml, 11/9/98, p. 1.
[125] National TSPM Committee, *Protestant Christianity.*
[126] Lyall, *God in China,* pp. 198-199.
[127] Ibid, pp. 193-194.
[128] 'Christian Work,' *GPD,*5.

The Nanjing Amity Printing Press was established as a functioning concern in 1987. By the beginning of 2000 over 23 million Bibles and more than 10 million copies of the hymnal with 400 hymns, 100 indigenous to China, had been published and distributed from the sixty-five CCC distribution points throughout China.[129] Anyone was eligible to buy a Bible from churches and bookstores supplied by the distribution centers. In September 1999 it was claimed by Wang Jian Guo of the East China Theological Seminary in connection with the TSPM office in Shanghai that the supply of Bibles was sufficient for demand without foreign organizations bringing them in from abroad.[130] A house church elder in Beijing, however, within that same month claimed that the need for Bibles from outside China remained evident in the countryside.[131] China's size prohibited complete understanding of needs, reasons for shortages, attitudes, restrictions and just implementation of policy and distribution. The different strata of political power and events along with the differing realms of Protestant Christian facets contributed to the complex nature of how the TSPM and the CCC related to the Chinese Protestant Church.

---

[129] National TSPM Committee, *Protestant Christianity.*
[130] Wang Jian Guo, Acting Dean of East China Theological Seminary, Shanghai (10 September 1999).
[131] Steven Liu [pseud.], elder in *An Ti Ya*, Antioch Church, Beijing (16 September 1999).

6
CHURCHES ESTABLISHED
AFTER THE 1979 REVISION

After 1979 the change of government to a moderate stance and the move toward modernization of China was swift. However, in a country so large it was apparent that change was not completed consistently in every area of government or in all provinces simultaneously. It was also apparent that a complete change of government had not occurred but merely a change in political position for the purposes of modernization. This change toward modernization was to encourage international collaboration, which included a moderate religious policy.

In an interview with the *China Avanza,* Bishop Ting said that the most profound obstacle for the advancement of the Chinese Church was "ultra-leftist" attitudes that demonstrate a lack of respect for religion to allow the nation to progress under the United Front principle. The Church found that it could work with Marxists revolutionaries who recognized the value of unity to include those of religious persuasion for progress.[1]

An intellectual declared in 1998 that ever since reform 20 years earlier, Christians in China still experienced persecution depending on the area in which they lived. The interior provinces usually held a more conservative Marxist stance and religious discrimination

---

[1] 'Protestantismo,' interview with Bishop Ting, *China Avanza II* (Beijing: Beijing Informa, 1986), p. 9.

was often stronger than that advocated by the central government. The qualifications of church workers depended on the biblical training available, and heretical doctrinal interpretation gave rise to unlawful sects in some areas. However, on the coastal areas of Wenzhou, Shanghai and Hangzhou, openness toward religion was experienced. The government had returned church buildings, taken to facilitate other enterprises during the Cultural Revolution, to congregations for worship.[2]

Since the Cultural Revolution the CCP was concerned about the phenomenal growth of the Chinese Christian Church, and it was referred to as *Jidu jiao re*, Christianity fever.[3] Especially since 1991, when Christianity was credited for the collapse of Communism in Eastern Europe, the rapid expansion of Christianity in China caused alarm among Chinese governmental officials. According to Jonathan Chao the State Council had issued a directive to the RAB that year to restrict the development of Christianity.[4] However, the council's goals continued under the United Front effort towards modernization.

To allow churches to reopen was a step in the direction of national unity. The first church to be reopened in China was the *Bai Nian Tang* in Ningbo on April 18, 1979. On August 26, 1979, the *Xinjie Tang*, or Church in Xiamen, Fujian Province, was the second to be restored and reopened. In 1998 there was a celebration for the 150th anniversary of this church, for Xiamen was one of the original treaty ports after the Opium Wars, and this church was the first built in China.[5] According to Rev. Ms. Zhu Minghui in 1998:

> The church has three evangelists, six elders and twenty-six stewards. Activities include a choir, children's group, youth fellowship, Bible study, prayer fellowships, fellowship for the elderly, and a network for providing home visits to

[2] Wang Li [pseud.], Former President of the Chinese Christian Democratic Union, Madrid (Interview, 16 July 1998).
[3] Tony Lambert, *The Resurrection of the Chinese Church* (Wheaton, IL: Harold Shaw Publishers, 1994), p. 139.
[4] Jonathan Chao, 'The Church in China: Needs and Opportunities for Ministry,' Myron Ivey (ed.), *China News and Church Report*, Pasadena: China Ministries International, May 11 (1998) 1-2.
[5] 'China Connection News Exchange,' *China Chronicles*, Vol. VIII, No. 2, Spring (1998) 2.

those in need. Since 1979 there have been 15 baptismal services, admitting 949 new believers. By December 1997 the total membership was 2,200.[6]

Eva Stimson reported the reopening of the third church in China. It was the magnificent *Mu En Tang*, known in English as the Moore Memorial Church, a gothic cathedral prominently constructed on the riverfront and a busy street corner in Shanghai. Pastor Shi Qigui approached the church at 2:00 AM on September 2, 1979, the morning of its reopening. At 3:00 he heard people congregating outside to attend the church after a decade of it being a government-administered school. Two hours before the planned opening at 6:00 AM, those waiting to worship commenced to sing the chorus and hymn, *Jesus Loves Me* and *Rock of Ages*, in Chinese. In 1997 this church had a 5000-member congregation and on a yearly basis was baptizing approximately 350 new believers into its fellowship.[7]

By July 1982 in excess of 500 Christian assemblies had been recovered throughout China, which had taken considerable time and effort on the part of the TSPM and RAB in negotiation with former occupants of the church properties. Those buildings damaged by the Red Guards or tenants were renovated by funds the government had collected for rent through the RAB.[8]

A letter from Shanghai in 1980, reported by Jonathan Chou, revealed that an open-air gathering in Shanghai People's Park in front of the Moore Memorial Church had become the largest Christian public assembly of Shanghai. With no overall leadership, Christian songs of worship and praise were taught and testimonies of God's intervention were aired, expository teaching of the Bible was shared, and there were prayers for healing or exorcism.[9] This was significant in that the change in government and reactivation of the TSPM brought about a real sense of freedom of religion.

Chao found that before 1985 about 3000 Protestant Christian meeting points had registered, and an estimated 100,000 or

[6] 'Xin Jie Church Celebrates 150 years,' *China Talk,* October (1998) 27.
[7] Eva Stimson, 'The Church in China,' *Presbyterians Today,* November (1997) 1-2.
[8] Thompson Brown, *Christianity in the People's Republic of China* (Atlanta: John Knox Press, 1983), p. 168.
[9] Jonathan Chao (interviews), Richard Van Houten (ed.), *Wise as Serpents Harm-*

more groups without affiliation with the TSPM were meeting with only a network of itinerate evangelists to give them a fraternal relationship.[10] A writer for the *China Chronicles*, Kathy Call, ascertained that in 1998 there were above 12,000 registered churches and 25,000 legal home gatherings, or more than 37,000 open meeting points of Protestant worship in China. These comprised of 43 percent of the venues for worship open, at that time, to Chinese of all religions.[11]

The churches in China were non-denominational since the unification of all Protestants. Consequently, an informal consensus for nomination of a pastor was submitted to the RAB for approval, to omit any political dissidents or latent agitators. The pastoral team of a church might include of representatives of different doctrinal backgrounds; the Rice Market Church in Beijing had three pastoral staff: one had been Presbyterian, one Anglican and one Methodist.[12] The *San Yi Tang*, Trinity Church, in Xiamen, with a congregation of 1,700, had four ministerial workers, two pastors and two evangelists, and the church incorporated four different denominational traditions using the same facility at different times. The Church of Christ of China met for Sunday morning worship, the Little Flock gathered for a service in the afternoon, the Seventh Day Adventists assembled on Saturdays, and the True Jesus Church held its worship ceremony whenever convenient.[13]

Adequate pastoral leadership was a main concern for many congregations of newly opened churches. During the Cultural Revolution leaders from the TSPM had been sent to re-education camps even though they tried to cooperate with the government, and their offices were closed while the RAB terminated their operation. The churches had been locked and left vacant or used as factories, schools or warehouses.[14]

An open letter was sent on March 1, 1980, from 24 members of TSPM Standing Committees in 16 provinces to the Protestant Christians throughout China. It stated that although there was

---

[10] Ibid, p. 141.
[11] Kathy Call, 'For Precious Bibles, We Give Thee Thanks!' *China Chronicles*, Vol. VIII, No. 2, Spring (1998) 2.
[12] Brown, *Christianity*, p. 170
[13] 'San Yi Tang (Trinity Church) Xiamen,' *China Talk*, October (1998) 28.
[14] Brown, *Christianity*, p. 125.

persecution during Cultural Revolution countless Christians had remained steadfast in their faith, and they had held the conviction that the governmental stance against religion would change. It rallied the people to support the TSPM, which in turn would be able to relate to Christian communities and respond to their needs.[15]

Several reasons were outlined by David Adney as to why a meeting point would consent to join the TSPM. Since the government considered a religious movement outside its control to be an illegal entity, many church groups joined the TSPM for fear of being regarded counter-revolutionary. The freedom experienced with the TSPM allowed people to come to the open churches, and it was reasonable for those who cared to evangelize to remain where they could legally minister. In addition, it was a way for some assemblies to recover their buildings with the TSPM's help with the authorities, and this relationship could develop into a means to receive government funds. Moreover, the TSPM, in collaboration with the "security forces," could help suppress the undesirable heretical religious groups and maintain freedom of religion as specified in the constitution.[16] The president of the CCC, Dr. Han, in an interview with the author encouraged registration for the purpose of government protection. For those who resisted because of fear of control, he assured that the required annual report provided confidence that the group had nothing to hide. The purpose of this report was merely to record the estimated number of baptized and worshipers, the type of center with location, committee, leader, constitution and source of income. Also, if for some reason a local official would refuse the registration of an assemblage that intended to register with the RAB, the CCC would be available to assist the group to register legally.[17]

The registered, open churches attracted a variety of worshipers, and Lou Zhufeng listed several different types. The singing or the use of colloquial language in preaching attracted some to the services, and many non-believers appreciated each church's strong sense of community.[18] The elderly rejoiced at the opportunity to

[15] Lambert, *The Resurrection,* p. 42.
[16] David Adney 'Division time in China: To join the TSPM or not,' *Evangelical Missions Quarterly,* Vol. 19, July (1983) 202.
[17] Han Wenzao, Dr., President of CCC, Nanjing (Interview, 14 September 1999).
[18] Lou Zhufeng (ed.), *Religion under Socialism in China,* trans. Donald E. MacInnis and Zheng Xian (London: M. E. Sharpe, Inc., 1991), p. 88, 107.

have corporate worship again, and new Christians had been invited by friends to join them for services. There were the curious who went to observe or had been attracted by the music, and then informers came to report anything that might be interpreted as subversive.[19]

A diversity of clergy also was evident within each church, as Adeney described in an article for *Evangelical Missions Quarterly*. Political appointees lacked spirituality but retained influence over church policy. Also, some maintained their denominational distinctions, while others set priorities on the Gospel's core doctrines.[20] However, the TSPM attempted to maintain a standard for the Chinese Protestant Churches.

The Church Order, described in the *Chinese Theological Review*, provided the churches a perspective for ministry in China:

> The Christian Church is called by God to be a community of believers to serve Christ as Lord. Christ is the head of the Church, the Church is the Body of Christ, the Household of God, the Temple of the Holy Spirit. The faith of the Church is founded upon the Bible and the Apostles Creed.[21]

> Sun Xipei expounded that the Church, as the home of God, the Body of the Son and the temple of the Holy Spirit, demonstrated its relation to the Christian Triune God.[22] The Church consisted of the believers within the Christian faith.

Each believer was to be recognized to have a different spiritual experience and needs; therefore, mutual respect as to liturgy and style was to be accepted with unity under the leading of the Holy Spirit.[23] The form of simple and functional worship had not changed since the missionary era with hymns, prayers, scripture readings and a usually lengthy sermon.[24] Only seekers, who

---

[19] David H. Adeney, *China: The Church's Long March* (Ventura, CA: Regal Books, 1985), pp. 176-177.
[20] David Adeney, 'Division,' *EMQ*, p. 201.
[21] 'Chinese Christian Church Order,' Janice Wickeri (ed.), *Chinese Theological Review* (Holland, MI: Foundation for Theological Education in Southeast Asia, 1998), p. 64.
[22] Sun Xipei, 'Family, Body and Spiritual Home,' Wickeri (ed.), *CTR: 12*, pp. 106, 108.
[23] 'Chinese Church Order,' *CTR: 12*, p. 65.
[24] Brown, *Christianity*, p. 169.

had participated in church activities for a length of time, usually a year, with evidence of repentance of wrong to receive Christ as their Savior, were to be allowed to apply for classes of catechism. Upon the approved achievement on examinations the person could receive membership by baptism and be eligible to take Holy Communion as a sacrament for the Church community.[25]

Zhao Fusan said that the major obstruction to construction of community in churches was the issue of church polity, which in 1986 had been a type of congregationalism.[26] To establish a self-governed National Church structure in China, Shen Mingcui declared that human faults must be eliminated and aligned with God's will for the goal of church unity.[27] Sun Xipei stated that self-propagation was the Three-Self principle needing development because of the lack of leadership training. For such a large membership, the Chinese Christian Church lacked sufficient trained ministers. The wide use of volunteer workers with little biblical knowledge for preaching and teaching, especially in remote rural area meeting points, had resulted in perhaps enthusiastic though fragmented and at times ambiguous Bible teaching.[28] In 1998 Dr. Han Wenzao recognized that in every province of China there was an acute deficiency of pastors, and he acknowledged that:

> There are many pastors in our church who work very hard with very few holidays. They have to preach two, three, or even more times every Sunday. This has become commonplace: there are over ten million Christians in China, but only slightly more than a thousand pastors.[29]

Shen held seminaries responsible for the lack of research in the area of self-propagation, training future pastors, encouraging church life, and promoting literature. He admitted, however, that the hindrance also was inherent in the people who favored

---

[25] 'Chinese Church Order,' *CTR: 12*, p. 66.

[26] Zhao Fusan, 'Prospects of Christianity in China,' Janice Wickeri (ed.,) [Documents from the Fourth National Christian Conference, Shanghai, August 1986], *Chinese Theological Review*, Vol. 3, (1987) 14.

[27] Shen Mingcui, 'Three-Self Continues to Move Forward,' J. Wickeri (ed.) [Documents of 4th Conference, Shanghai, Aug 1986], *CTR*, Vol. 3 (1987) 31.

[28] Sun, 'Family Home,' *CTR*, Vol 3 (1987) p. 55.

[29] Han Wenzao, 'Work Together with One Heart to Build Up the Body of Christ,' J. Wickeri (ed.), *CTR: 12*, p. 121.

methods of religious activity that bordered on fallacy and who continue to prefer Western hymns rather than those in the new hymnal composed by Chinese.[30]

Gao Ying focused on another area of self-propagation that needed particular attention. He recognized the need to minister to women, for they accounted for more than 70 percent of Chinese adherents to the Christian faith. For that reason the development and prayer for this ministry within the church was a priority.[31]

From 1980 through 1998 a total of 2,700 students graduated from China's seminaries to fulfill the urgent needs of the Church, Dr. Han reported. Nearly 1,000 enrolled for the year 1998 and of these 50 percent were women. Within China there were 17 seminaries, of which 12 were either newly constructed, had completed new additions, or for which new construction was being prepared. He stated that the Nanjing Union Theological Seminary had also established a three-year correspondence course that enrolled 1,000 new students a year.[32]

Another aspect for fulfilling the needs of the church was economic. Luo Yingzhong, a pastor in Anshun City of Guiyang Province, interconnected the principles of self-government and self-propagation with the wealth of parishioners. The prosperity of the believers would provide for further development of the Church, for church programs could then be enhanced.[33] For the proper management of church property, Shen Mingcui agreed that attention must be placed on stewardship of church assets with economic preparation and "financial planning instituted and self-support enterprises developed." He summarized the "leftist" position on free-will offerings from believers "as a form of oppression."[34] At the Fourth National Chinese Christian Conference in Shanghai during August 1986, Sun explained that some churches started factories and small businesses as enterprises for self-support and fulfilled their part in promoting

---

[30] Shen, 'Three Self,' *CTR*, (1987) 32-33.
[31] Gao Ying, ' Sharing Women's Work,' J. Wickeri (ed.), *CTR: 12*, p. 95.
[32] Han Wennao, 'Build Up the Body of Christ with One Heart and United Effort: Running the Church Even Better According to the Three-Self Principle,' J. Wickeri (ed.), *CTR: 12*, pp. 9, 12.
[33] Luo Yingshong, 'Self-Support Difficulties in Mountain Churches,' J. Wickeri (ed.), *CTR: 12*, pp. 101, 105.
[34] Shen, 'Three Self,' *CTR*, (1987) 34.

the modernization of the socialist society. He also advocated that a church provide such services as facilities for medical treatment, education, or housing the elderly, which would have a practical promotional impact on the community for Christianity.[35]

Chinese churches were to have two different concerns in their ministry. The first was the spiritual ministry to Christians with the effort to build up the Body of Christ. The other facet was to function as social organizations complying with the policies of the government and the constitution in support of the socialist government and promoting international peace.[36] The latter was to be accomplished through Christians being encouraged to participate in "socialist construction" and their demonstration of hospitality to foreign visitors. In turn their support for governmental policy confirmed confidence in the Party leadership. According to Shen, under this pretext the Christian community might be enabled to have a voice when the People's Republic or CCP prove to be ineffective in certain areas. Moreover, it was the duty of the TSPM and CCC to guard the rights of Protestant Christians as religious believers, manage the Church under the Three-Self principles, and elevate patriotic awareness in Chinese Christians.[37] An important priority for the TSPM and the CCC in ministry was to nurture the Protestant Church within the political system of China.

Therefore, the ministry changed with the political climate within China. Thompson Brown reported in 1983 that there were no Sunday Schools and churches were not involved in social work in the secular community of Beijing. Any Christian work with those under 18 years of age was discreet, and church weddings were in the minority. People were apprehensive to be identified as a Christian on a church membership roster.[38] However, Philip Wickeri found evidence by 1990 that the government protected those religious activities considered normal and was concerned about those that "disrupt public order, impair the health of citizens, or interfere with the educational system of the state." Chinese families routinely gave Christian religious instruction

[35] Sun Xipei, 'From Three Self to Three Well,' trans. Jean Woo, Janice K. Wickeri (ed.), [Documents of 4th Conference, Shanghai, Aug 1986], Vol. 3 (1987) 56.
[36] 'Chinese Church Order,' *CTR: 12*, p. 65.
[37] Shen, 'Three Self,' *CTR*, (1987) 34-35.
[38] Brown, *Christianity*, pp. 170-171.

to their children, and it was common to see children attending church worship services as witnessed by the author both in the rural areas and in city churches in 1994 and again in 1999. There were also religious schools to enroll Chinese minors for religious work.[39]

Also in 1983, David Adeney, in his article on division among Chinese Christians as whether or not to join the TSPM, pointed out that those in opposition reasoned that the church was being used as a platform for political instruction. Informers within the churches would report a newcomer, who would then be admonished by his work unit.[40] The vice-chairman and general secretary of the TSPM, Deng Fucun, in a 1999 interview, argued that "The CCP is atheistic and does not want to use religious organizations to promote a political policy."[41]

The Communist government had prohibited many topics including eschatology and the resurrection of Christ from being mentioned in churches, and at one time these prohibitions might have been enforced. Yet, there was an account of a woman from an unregistered home gathering who had thought that she would never go to a registered church for that reason, but as she walked by the *San Yi Tung*, Trinity Church, she heard pastor Chen speaking on the resurrection. Finally, after she had attended there for some time, she became a member and the church's youth leader of several hundred youth.[42] Kathy Call recalled from her experience that the closing hymn of a service in a Chinese church she attended was *When Jesus Comes, Will He Find Us Watching?*, and in spite of reports, she noted that they were singing a definite message of the second coming of Christ.[43] The author had experienced the same in some officially registered churches throughout China where both songs and messages indicated a full range of biblical teaching.

Biblical standards and acceptance of Jesus Christ as Lord defined Christianity. The Catholics and the Protestants are both

---

[39] Philip L. Wickeri, *Seeking the Common Ground* (Maryknoll, NY: Orbis Books, 1990), pp. 104-105.

[40] Adeney, 'Division,' *EMQ*, (1983) 203-204.

[41] Deng Fu-cun, Vice Chairman and General Secretary of Three-Self Patriotic Movement, Shanghai (Interview, trans. Wang Jian Guo, 10 September 1999)

[42] 'San Yi Tang,' *CT*, (1998) 28.

[43] Call, 'For Bibles,' *CC*, (1998) 2.

Christian, but in China they were considered as two different religions because of historical factors. According to Samuel Wang the political relations with the Vatican created the difference. He stated that Chinese churches registered with the RAB as Catholics considered the Pope to be the Anti-Christ referred to in the Bible. He recognized that many Christians regard all believers in Jesus Christ to be of one body.[44] Catholic Bishop Fu Tieshan of Beijing described the Catholic Church, on an international level, as being a colony of the Vatican. He asserted that the Vatican maintained a hostile political relationship with China without respect for the independence of the Chinese Catholic Church. This was especially true since it gave diplomatic recognition to Taiwan, which was considered by the People's Republic of China as a province, and considered this recognition as the diplomatic relationship to all Chinese people. The Vatican disregarded China's sovereignty and maintained intentions to intervene in the affairs of the Catholic churches in China.[45] Chairman Jiang Zimin, quoted by Ye Xiaowen in his speech in 1998, said, "Our system of reform has been eradicating the manipulation and control of imperialism within the Catholic and Protestant Churches."[46]

The Catholics in China continued to advocate patriotism and remained independent, autonomous and self-administered with the selection and consecration of their own bishops. These declarations of self-reliance were centered on the provisions of Constitutional Article 36. Otherwise, there was no significant divergence between the practices, doctrines and faith within Catholic Church of China and those of other nations.[47] The only exception had been that in 1979 when the Catholic Association of China started ordaining women priests in Shanghai.[48] As of 1997 the estimate of the number of Chinese Catholic Christians

[44] Samuel Wang, Scholar of the *Four Books,* Co-author, Director of Chinese LMN Ministries (Interview, 21 December 1999) He referrenced the Bible book of John 2:22.
[45] 'Communidad Chistiana en China, *China Avanza II,* (Beijing: Beijing Informa, 1986), p. 16.
[46] Ye, 'Speech,' *Tripod* (1998) 52.
[47] Ye Xiaowen, 'Speech of Ye Xiaowen, Head of the Religious Affairs Bureau of the State Council, at the Sixth National Congress of Catholic Representatives, January 17, 1998,' *Tripod,* Vol. XVIII, No. 107, September-October (1998) 52-53.
[48] 'Protestants en Shanghai,' *CA,* Beijing: BI, 1986, p. 23.

was 10 million, to make the total Christian population of China estimated at near 30 million with three new churches being established every two days. "Less conservative estimates of the Christian population range as high as 80 million."[49]

The unregistered churches of China rendered the Christian population impossible to accurately estimate. All open churches had been closed during the Cultural Revolution, and the house church movement became increasingly more important as worshipers gathered in intimate home gatherings. In some cases these groups were known and permitted by the government if they remained self-sufficient.[50] Even after the Cultural Revolution and the reformation of the TSPM, many of these gatherings remained independent and unregistered.

The reasons for church groups to not join under the TSPM stemmed from reflections on the past reputation of open churches, which had been in alliance with the TSPM leadership of the 1950s. These open churches had disseminated a liberal theology and Communist political indoctrination, and the Christian faith was effectively being limited in growth and power. Their emphasis in ministry was solely to Protestant Christian believers without an outreach in evangelism. Adeney expressed that those who chose to remain unregistered considered the TSPM regulations, such as prohibiting preachers to preach outside of their assigned location or to teach the gospel to youth, to be unbiblical. The Christians of independent gatherings reasoned that they must follow the biblical example "We must obey God rather than men!" Adeney added that the needed Bibles, literature and instruction received through radio programs broadcast into China by foreign means were denounced by the TSPM. These materials and radio broadcasts provided a method to reduce heretical teachings from sectarian factions.[51]

Lambert confirmed the value of radio broadcasting by citing a letter received in Hong Kong from the northern part of Anhui Province early in 1988. The letter stated that there had been no Christians in that area prior to 1982. "People had turned to

---

[49] Stimson, 'The Church,' *PT,* (1997) 3.

[50] Richard C. Bush, Jr., *Religion In Communist China* (New York: Abingdon Press, 1970), pp. 254-255.

[51] Adeney, 'Division', *EMQ,* (1983) 203. From the *Bible* in the book of *Acts of the Apostles* 5:29 where Peter spoke for the apostles of Jesus the Christ.

Christ through listening to gospel radio programs beamed from overseas, and then through miracles and healings." It verified that in the area of the city of Fuzhou even children were welcome to attend meetings in the open churches, and Bibles were plentiful in the city. Conversely, within thirty miles of the city in the mountainous countryside, Bibles were unobtainable or the number was insufficient for the many meeting points with over a hundred members each.[52] Moreover, in some areas the house church groups became quite large and some had built regular church buildings. The author attended some of these rural churches in 1994, although the majority met in private houses.[53]

The house churches remained independent because they were apprehensive about the possibility of failing to maintain their prophetic role if they collaborated with the government and relinquished control over their own political reasoning. Even if they did not sustain an "anti-Communist" outlook "in terms of a socio-economic system," they resisted the mandate to "uphold the four basic principles" of Chinese Communism.[54] Most members and leaders of house churches loved China and the Church in general as the Body of Christ, but their experiences and interpretation of the Bible Scriptures would constrain them to live according to their convictions of not collaborating with an atheistic government nor with any organization that did so.

Pressures and Methods for Religious Restriction

In the endeavor to maintain Communist doctrines and support the constitutional guarantee of freedom of religious belief, the CCP and the People's Government of China presented religious restrictions through laws and regulations. By these legal methods there was an attempt to form a socialist society and limit the effects of religion while securing the participation of religious believers in national construction.

Communist Restriction of Religion

As a research assistant of Social Sciences at the Chinese Academy, Liu Peng stated:

[52] Lambert, *The Resurrection,* pp. 89, 121.
[53] Authur Wallis, *China Miracle,* Columbia, MO: Cityhill Publishing, 1986, p. 63.
[54] Adeney, 'Division', *EMQ,* (1983) 204.

Religion is accepted by the state on the premise that it admits the state's political authority, accepts its leadership in all social sectors, and carries out its policies. The state administration manages religious organizations... (whose) role in society is strictly limited. [55]

Deng Zhaoming in his article for the *Tripod* agreed in his response to Liu that the freedom of religious belief policy was not an admission of theism. However, it was a pragmatic solution for religion to serve the purposes of the CCP, and it was used as a means to govern China. The reports from the Chinese press and a delegation of USA religious leaders to the People's Republic of China in February 1998 revealed that religion was at its highest point of agenda throughout China.[56] The CCP insisted that "religion must serve the state and adapt – or be adapted – to socialist society."[57] In analysis, the objective of the CCP was to restrain religious extremism and to interpret all doctrines of religious theology to benefit the socialist governing of China.

Dr. Brent Fulton, managing director of the Institute of Chinese Studies at Wheaton College, cited in Document 19 that the Chinese Communists claimed that religion would cyclically expire on its own. For the CCP, religion was a secondary condition to its desire for the cooperation of religious believers in building a socialistic political structure.[58] The atheistic Communist Party counteracted religious organizations; conversely, Shen Chen-en the associate general secretary of the CCC, observed that the RAB was organized to ensure the protection of religious belief. The CCP had learned through the experience of the Cultural Revolution that when faith came under adversity people held to it.[59] Scholar Samuel Wang affirmed that the CCP was committed to diminishing of religion

---

[55] Deng Zhaoming, 'Church and State Regulations in China: Characteristics and Trends: A Response', trans. Michael Sloboda, *Tripod*, (July-August 1995) 19.

[56] Donald Argue, Theodore E. McCarrick and Arthur Schnwer, 'Religious Freedom', *Tripod*, Vol. XVIII, No. 105, (May- June 1998) 54.

[57] Human Rights/Asia, *China: State Control of Religion*, (New York: Human Rights Watch, 1997), p 8

[58] Brent Fulton, Ph.D., Executive Director of Chinasource, Managing Director of the Institute of Chinese Studies at Wheaton College, Served 8 years with China Ministries International in Pasadena, Served 2 years with Chinese Church Research Center in Hong Kong, Wheaton, IL (Interview, 19 November 1999).

[59] Shen Chen-en, Associate General Secretary of China Christian Council, Chief Editor of *Tian Feng* or Heavenly Wind Monthly and Pastor of Shanghai Community Church, Shanghai (Interview, 10 September 1999).

until after 1978, and by 1981 it had aided in reopening churches. He denied claims that churches were used as political platforms or showcases for foreigners, and he advocated for believers to give allegiance to the People's Republic.[60]

The strictness by which TSPM adhered to the desires of the Central Government Dr. Fulton confirmed; on the national level communication was held fairly rigid while the local level usually afforded more flexibility. This depended on current events and their national impact such as the Tiananmen Square incident that rendered a TSPM action to approach the National People's Congress to minimize restrictions.[61] The goal of harmonizing religion in a socialist society depended on the cooperation of religious believers working together with the non-religious for the prosperity of the nation. Beliefs and ethics ought to correspond with the demands of the social order, and specialties should be used effectively for national construction and international relations with the Party guarding the rights and freedoms as specified in the constitution.[62]

The concern of the CCP was political unity and social progress, encompassing the entire population of China, whereas freedom of religious belief included a relatively small portion of the citizens.[63] In 1993 President Jiang Zemin outlined the methods of controls on religion:

> (1) Implement the Religious policy of the state as stated in Document 19 of the Party Central Committee issued in 1982.
> (2) Control and manage religious activities through legal means, and (3) make religious persons and organizations suit the development of Chinese socialist modernization.[64]

---

[60] Samuel Wang, Scholar of the *Four Books,* Co-author of *God and the Ancient Chinese,* Director of the Chinese Department of LMN Ministries, Had done translation work for TSPM and CCC, Worked closely with Human Rights Watch, St. Maries, ID (Interview, 27 December 1999).

[61] Fulton, Wheaton, IL (Interview, 19 Nov 99).

[62] Luo Zhufeng (ed.), *Religion under Socialism in China,* trans. Donald E. MacInnis and Zheng Xian (London: M. E. Sharpe, Inc., 1991), pp. 115-116.

[63] Philip L. Wickeri, *Seeking the Common Ground* (Maryknoll, NY: Orbis Books, 1990), p. 101.

[64] Jonathan Chao, 'The Church in China: Needs and Opportunities for Ministry,' Myron Ivey (ed.), *China News and Church Report,* Pasadena: China Ministry International, May 11 (1998) 2.

The open door policy of China had a counter-balance effect on the conservative Marxists within the Party, and for this reason ambiguity of policy implementation resulted at national and local levels. Tony Lambert quoted a reporter, from the March 1979 issue of *People's Daily*, who had visited officials for governing religious affairs, and stated:

The policy of religious freedom ensures the normal religious activities carried on by religious workers and their congregations. However, they must observe the government's relevant policies and decrees... We must not permit the class enemy to engage in counter-revolutionary and other illegal activities by using religion. For this reason, the government must strengthen the control of religious bodies. [65]

By 1980 church buildings outside of TSPM patronage were being opened, which was objectionable by the CCP. Consequently, the first order of business of the Christian Conference was to establish organs to control and unite the Christians all through China. The Communist Party had assigned personnel to those churches not registered to report activities that might be interpreted as illegal and also to agitate discord among the members of the meeting point, or to hire instigators to raise dissension. The most frequent charge that could be brought against this type of group was illegal assembly.[66]

The *People's Daily* reported a discussion on religious policy that Party general-secretary Jian Zemin initiated in a speech on January 31, 1991, with the leaders of the Patriotic Associations of the five recognized religions in China. He asked for the Party to "prevent and curb illegal elements from using religion or religious activities to stir up disorder," and to incapacitate any type of foreign infiltration and resist any ramification of the political change in Eastern Europe from Communism. The Party faced a predicament: many within their own membership, who according to Document 19 must be atheist, had become religious believers.

[65] Tony Lambert, *The Resurrection of the Chinese Church* (Wheaton, IL: Harold Shaw Publishers, 1994), pp. 32, 34, 44.
[66] Peter Humphrey, *Religious Suppression in Mainland China* (Republic of China: World Anti-Communist League, 1983), p. 20.

These comrades had encouraged religious devotion and countered the Party's Four Basic Principles.[67]

By 1997 the Party was in the second year of implementing of a campaign *Yan da,* to reinforce against crime. Security forces were under orders to arrest for any form of crime, and many Christians became targets with the charge of illegal assembly.[68] Richard Zhang in his article in *Jian Dao* claimed that China's combination of government and Communist Party had caused dilemmas in public life, especially in religious affairs. The government's opposition to religion was labelled as discriminatory while any support or help rendered to religious groups was suspected. Thus, there was an assertion that the open churches were government-sponsored churches. Those churches so recognized by the government should stress that their object for following the Three-Self principles was to discard the external relationship with foreign mission boards and not then become dependent upon the internal interference from Chinese governmental sources.[69]

Ye Xiaowen, head of the RAB of the State Council, related in a 1998 speech that President Jiang had stressed the implementation of Party policy for management of religious affairs with the importance of mutual adaptation, or that religion must adhere to the national laws, regulations and directives.[70] The legal means of restriction required governmental intervention, but also provided protection against heresies and liberty for citizens who had religious interests to walk into an open church.

LAWS AND REGULATIONS

On February 5, 1991, the Central Committee of the Chinese Communist Party issued the noticeably hard-line Document No. 6 with the stated concern for foreign powers that endorse "peaceful revolution." Another apprehension was the "separatists

---

[67] Lambert, *The Resurrection,* pp. 110, 227.
[68] Samuel Ling, 'Approaching China in 1997,' *Chinese Around the World,* May (1997) 3.
[69] Richard X. Y. Zhang, 'The Origin of the "Three Self",' *Jian Dao,* Vol. 5, (1996) 199-200. The *Jian Dao* is a journal of Bible and Theology.
[70] Ye Xiaowen, 'Speech of Ye Xiaowen, Head of the Religious Affairs Bureau of the State Council, at the Sixth National Congress of Catholic Representatives, January 17, 1998,' trans. Norman Walling, S. J., *Tripod,* Vol. XVIII, No. 107, September-October (1998) 53.

among national minorities who have been using religion to stir up trouble."[71] Each region had its own interpretation and clarification of the law as it was to be implemented in its district. The Shandog Provincial Regulations Governing Venues For Religious Activities, issued on November 18, 1993, stipulated that no government organization could discriminate against citizenry who held religious beliefs or remained atheistic. They could neither coerce citizens to believe in a religion nor to renounce their religious faith.[72]

According to Lambert the "regulation, which is most restrictive of pastoral ministry and growth of the church" was RAB Document No.16 stipulating that clergy were to be chosen from local citizens with resident permits who were accepted with TSPM approval through the church regulations. Then they must have been registered at the county or district branch of the RAB.[73]

Premier Li Peng signed Decrees 141 and 145 of the State Council on January 31, 1994, to manage foreign religious activities and place all national religious activities under the control of the five recognized patriotic religious groups. The second constitutional article regulated religious sites by requiring registration with the government through the RAB, which put unregistered house churches at risk under the law unless they sought registration. However, for the legal venues under the TSPM, State protection was strengthened.[74] The RAB then issued a regulation in April of the same year, 'Methods for the Registration of Places of Religious Activities.' Later in September it published 'Seriously Do the Work of Registration of Places of Religious Activities' as a summary.[75] Article 2 of the RAB regulations outlined the prerequisites for church registration as having a specific place of worship, regular participants as religious believers, a management staff, trained clergy, a constitution, and

[71] Lambert, *The Resurrection*, pp. 227-228.
[72] Deng Zhaoming, '[Chinese Regulations Affecting Religious Activities, English translation of documents with editorial introduction]', *Bridge*, Vol. 66, August (1994) 4. Shandog Provincial Regulations Governing Venues For Religious Activities published November 4, 1993.
[73] Lambert, *The Resurrection*, p. 229.
[74] Ibid., p. 259. The February 18, 1994 Chinese News and Church Report included a full English translation of these decrees signed by Premier Li Peng.
[75] Chao, 'The Church,' *CNCR*, May 11 (1998) 2.

source of legal income.[76]

Another decree from the RAB in July 1996 was 'Methods of Annual Inspection of Place of Religious Activities.'[77] Criteria from Article 4 stipulated the inspection of cites for religious devotion to assure obedience to policy by laws and regulations and implementation of management regulations. The principle religious and foreign activities were scrutinized as were changes regarding conditions of registration, financial matters for income, and expenditure and management of any enterprise for self-reliance.[78]

Articles 21 of chapter four and 37 of chapter six from the Regulations of the Shanghai RAB contributed to the policies for the management of religious sites, and both of these articles specified that each locality must "accept administrative supervision from the pertinent government departments." Article 21 dealt with committees, programs, and systems of management for places of religious devotion, while Article 37 treated the maintenance of control over the internal management systems of each point of gathering.[79] Laws and regulations to govern devotional sites had their restrictive quality, but there was also an inclusive feature of protection.

TSPM REGULATIONS

At the 1981 Christian Conference in Shanghai a statement was presented that stated, "To be anti-TSPM is to be anti-government, for religion must be organized and under control."[80] CCC associate general secretary Shen claimed that the relationship between the atheistic CCP and the Christian organizations TSPM and CCC was that of mutual respect and communication. He stated that

---

[76] Mickey Speigel, 'Appendix VIII: Registration Procedures for Venues for Religious Activities,' *China: State Control of Religion* (New York: Human Rights Watch, 1997), p. 109.

[77] Chao, 'The Church,' *CNCR,* May 11 (1998) 2.

[78] Speigel, 'Appendix IX: Method for the Annual Inspection of Places of Religious Activity,' *China: State Control,* p. 112.

[79] Speigel, 'Appendix IV: Regulations From the Shanghai Religious Affairs Bureau,' *China: State Control,* pp. 93, 95. Approved on November 30, 1995 by the Standing Committee of the Shanghai 10th People's Congress at its 23rd Meeting. According to Chapter 10 Article 63 these regulations were effected from March 1, 1996.

[80] 'SBC works with Liberal China Christian Council,' http://www.whidbey.net/-dcloud/fbns/sbcworks.htm, 11/9/98, 3:17 PM.

for any changes, which may affect the other, the two entities confided in each other as required.[81] At first, as Zhang pointed out, the TSPM's original commission was to preserve the Protestant Christian Church in the Communist political setting. Though in its effort to cooperate with the government, "the major critique in this regard is its overdone compromise with...the government, for whom it provides a framework for communication and united action in church."[82]

By the mid-1980s the TSPM was the main mediator for the RAB in its effort to subdue and control the house church movement. Bishop Ting, as head of the TSPM in 1980, had emphasized the lack of distinction between those churches joined to the TSPM and the house churches. Many home gatherings were registered, after which "their leaders must attend the Three-Self movement indoctrination classes to learn about Party politics."[83] Nonetheless, during this time those gatherings that refused to register were systematically closed, and the itinerant evangelists became fugitives or were arrested for non-compliance to register. Then the CCC implemented the Ten Don'ts such as: it was forbidden for youth under eighteen years of age to attend religious services, to arrange church night activities, to receive foreign Christians, or to preach from the Bible book of Revelations.[84]

In 1999, TSPM vice-chairman and general secretary Deng Fucun recalled from an experience that a group of visitors asked him if his message must be approved by the RAB. He had responded that in seminary he was taught that for a sermon to touch the lives of others it must first touch the speaker. Therefore, it would have been useless for officials to see his outline, and it was usually so sketchy that they would not have been able to make sense of it. Moreover, he declared that it was not necessary to have a message checked, and that the preaching was about the Bible, their faith and creed.[85]

Also in the 1980s, according to Wallis, the TSPM of the

---

[81] Shen Chen-en, Associate General Secretary of CCC. Shanghai (Interview, 10 Sept 99).

[82] Zhang, 'The Origin,' *JD*, (1996) 199-200.

[83] Arthur Wallis, *China Miracle* (Columbia, MO: Cityhill Publishing, 1986), p. 59.

[84] 'SBC works with CCC,' http://www.whidbey.net, 11/9/98, 3:17 PM.

[85] Deng Fu-cun, Vice-Chairman and General Secretary of the Three-Self Patriotic Movement, Shanghai (Interview, trans. Wang Jian Guo, 10 September 1999).

Henan Province submitted a Ten Commandments declaration for registered meeting points. These said that the organization of a church could only be by governmental approval, and only government appointed clergy could baptize. Contacts with foreign religious organizations and their books were forbidden at the risk of prosecution, and the printing of Bibles and religious books without permits was forbidden. Travel between communes for evangelism was prohibited, religion should be kept to the individual, and prayer was to be restricted to only Sundays. To even talk about religion or sing religious songs with youths less than eighteen was banned. It was unlawful to solicit funds for religious purposes, placing an additional financial burden on religious advocates.[86]

The Yunnan Province Christian Council's decision that those who form the church management group must have the qualities of integrity, to be law-abiding, ethical, responsible, and sustain the Three-Self principles. Clergy were obliged to conduct religious activities only within their church buildings, to not obstruct public order and cause confusion, and they could not use public properties or distribute wealth. Any program of the church was required not to interfere with education, government, birth control, marriage, and culture. Ministers were expected to preach the Bible message, be patriotic, and oppose those who contribute to heresies such as praying for the sick and preventing medical treatment, exorcism, or coercing money from citizens. It was the responsibility of the Chinese Church to evangelize without foreign influence and intervention.[87] Wickeri maintained that it had become problematic for Chinese Christians when well-financed foreign entities sponsored the infiltration of foreign printed Bibles and other clandestine procedures, which are unlawful by the constitution of Chinese People's government and contrary to what the TSPM had striven to accomplish.[88]

The Yunnan Provincial TSPM regulations required Christians to endorse the Four Basic Principles and the Four Modernizations. They were to honor the laws and policies of the state and live in

[86] Wallis, *China Miracle*, pp. 59-60.
[87] Lambert, A. P. B. (ed.), 'Supervision of Christianity in the People's Republic of China,' *Religion in Communist Lands*, Vol. 15, Summer (1987) 214-215.
[88] Wickeri, *Seeking*, p. 236.

mutual respect and harmony with non-Christian compatriots.[89] In 1999, Xu Rulei as a standing committee member of the CCC, said that the Christians in China accepted the Four Basic Principles to love their country and recognize the leadership of the Communist Party. The Christians, he added, were adopting two principles: unity and cooperation in beliefs, and to maintain religious mutual respect. CCP president Jiang Zemin announced the aphorism: "love country, love church," which encapsulated the united front theory. Xu continued that the value of Bishop Ting as chairman of the Chinese People Political Consultative Conference, CPPCC, on the national level and he as a CPPCC member of the Jiangsu provincial branch was that they had the opportunity to provide a contribution on political affairs at these different levels.[90]

Before the unification of Hong Kong with China in November of 1992, a delegation of sixteen representative Protestant leaders of the TSPM and the CCC from China went to Hong Kong for the purpose of constructing a united front. Their object was to form links with the all the Christian organizations of Hong Kong that would cooperate with the *Lianghui* associations while segregating those that were not supportive.[91] The main object of the TSPM was for dialogue with the government in an effort to bring the Chinese Protestant Church under law in cooperation with the People's Government, yet promote church activities for the fulfillment of the Christian faith.

REGISTRATION POLICY

The most important means of CCP supervision through the religious associations within China had been the policy of registration since 1991 under Document No. 6, a circular to improve religious affairs.[92] Lin I Shuan, a retired pastor of the Mo Chou Road Church in Nanjing, stated in 1999 that the purpose of church registration not only provided constitutional protection but protected the Protestant Chinese Church from cults that "look like

---

[89] Lambert (ed.), 'Supervision,' *RICL*, Summer (1987) 215.
[90] Xu Rulei, Standing Committee Member of the China Christian Council, Vice-Chairman of Jiangsu Providence Three-Self Committee, Chairman of Nanjing Three-Self Committee, Deputy Director of Center for Religious Studies at Nanjing University (Interview, 11 September 1999).
[91] Pao H. K., 'China's Church Leaders Pay a Visit to Hong Kong,' Jonathan Chao (ed.), *Chinese Prayer Letter,* Hong Kong: Vol. 124, (January-February 1993) 5
[92] Human Rights, *China: State Control,* p 17.

sheep but really they are wolves. We agree that the government counsel cults...The way to counsel is to arrest the leaders and educate the others."[93]

A Christian engineer in Beijing related that the importance of church registration depended upon the objective of the group. For instance if its goal was to establish church groups, the TSPM church could be used as a base from which small groups could be formed for teaching Christian doctrines and values, and then allow them to multiply themselves. These newly formed groups in turn would help in the ministry of the parent church.[94] According to Mickey Spiegel, from the government's point of view it was the refusal to register that rendered a group illegal. The constitution justified personal individual freedom for religious belief, but the form of corporate worship was what the officials spent effort to monitor.[95]

Dr. Han, the national president of CCC, declared that the Protestant religious organizations grappled with a long-standing problem in the process of registration of churches and meeting points. He pointed out that "We must continue in our efforts to persuade meeting points which are temporarily unwilling to register." The CCC had arranged for those who had not qualified for registration to acquire a temporary registration and helped them to attain the criteria for qualification.[96] According to a Chinese Science professor who was a Christian, a typical unregistered church needed a seminary-trained pastor to grasp the larger scope of what God is doing in China. Especially in remote rural areas, the only contact with Christianity for these Christian believers was their circle of relatives and members from their particular congregation.[97]

In his letter of December 1992, Jonathan Chao revealed

---

[93] Lin I Shuan, Retired Minister of Mo Chou Road Church, Nanjing (Interview, trans. He Yanli, 13 September 1999).

[94] Tok Kai Hua, Engineer in Project Management from South East Asia, Beijing (Interview, 6 September 1999).

[95] Mickey Spiegel, *China: State Control of Religion* (New York: Human Rights Watch, 1997), p. 2.

[96] Han Wenzao, 'Build Up the Body of Christ with One Heart and United Effort: Running the Church Even Better According to the Three-Self Principle,' Janice Wickeri (ed.), *Chinese Theological Review: 12* (Foundation for Theological Education in Southeast Asia, 1998), p. 43.

[97] Meng Xiangzhi [pseud.], Science Professor, New York (Interview, 21 October 1998).

the pressure for independent house churches to register with the government through the RAB and join the TSPM. This coercion moved many groups who refused to register, for fear of consequences, to terminate their meetings while others continued to meet secretly.[98] In July 1992, Bishop Ting spoke out in the National People's Congress, NPC, against suppression in China, targeted at unregistered meeting points. According to Chao this speech confirmed that the government had renewed determination to terminate any suspicion of "peaceful revolution" through registration requirements.[99]

The Registration Procedures for Venues for Religious Activities in Article 3 of the RAB regulations provided the requirement for registration application. The following documents must be submitted in order: first, the application forms; second, all documentation and credentials of the venue; and third, the written opinion of the village, township government, or the city zones committee. Upon completion of registration an annual management report must be submitted to the RAB "during the first quarter of each year." According to Article 14, the "interpretation of these procedures is the provenance of the Religious Affairs Bureau of the State Council."[100]

For the protection of normal religious activity, each registered church group was required to change its name into a uniform title, and it was understood that the Three-Self Principles must be endorsed as well as the restrictions of activities within the specified location for religious functions. The qualifications for ministers were specific as to training required, patriotism, and limitations regarding religious teaching of youth. Any clergy who had been sentenced or relinquished political rights for contravention of the law also lost their position with the church. For restoration to their previous station, they must submit to investigation, and then the TSPM and CCC committees decide whether or not to receive them.[101] Registration was a method of monitoring, a form of standardization with certain qualifications for religious sites, and for procuring modifications to agree with the socialist setting

---

[98] Jonathan Chao, Letter from China Ministries International, December 1992.
[99] Jonathan Chao (dir.) 'Bishop Ding Speaks Out Against Wind of Suppression sweeping China,' *China News and Church Report,* December 31, 1992.
[100] Deng, 'Chinese Regulations,' *Bridge,* (1994) 3-4.
[101] David H. Adeney, 'Appendix 4: Decisions Regarding the Safeguarding of Normal Religious Activity,' *China: The Church's Long March* (Ventura, CA: Regal Books, 1985), pp. 230-232.

in which it found itself.

EDUCATIONAL ELEMENTS OF SOCIETY ON RELIGIOUS MATTERS

To direct the input of information into a society of people, the governing body could manage, to some degree, the attitudes and actions of that people. Chinese mathematics professor Hu Wei revealed that this was the concept maintained by the administration toward radio programming in China. He also related the notion, "if we did not hear about it we cannot know about it," to the church where it was acceptable to preach about Jesus but not about His Second Coming. It was intimidating to the CCP that the Second Coming would be more powerful than the first; therefore to mention it was discouraged. Professor Hu told of his school experience that "we were taught from the beginning of the class that there was no God. Chairman Mao tried to make people believe that he was god, savior of the Chinese people."[102]

Another method of management was to ascertain the attitude and experiences of the people. As recently as 1984, Adeney found that school children, even at the elementary level, were expected to write self-criticisms. With the rewrites, which were required, it was important to remember what was written before as to not contradict previous accounts. With religious issues, the difficulty resided in the question as to what constituted the denial of Christ in these essays.[103]

Ye promoted the concept that understanding the political system would help in religious matters. If there were more education among the seminarians to publicize China's history and the humiliations suffered, they would better understand the formation of Chinese socialism.[104] The curriculum taught, according to Deng Fucun, included Bible, evangelism, homiletics, and also law. He stressed President Jiang Zemin's words, "religious matters should be administered according to the law." Deng claimed that Protestant Chinese Christians carried out activities contrary to the law because of not knowing the laws, especially those pertaining to religious

---

[102] Hu Wei, College Mathematics Professor, New York (Interview, 31 May 1999).
[103] David H. Adeney, *China: The Church's Long March* (Ventura, CA: Regal Books, 1985), p. 191-192.
[104] Ye, 'Speech,' *Tripod,* (1998) 56.

matters.[105] They must know the legislation of China's Communist government to perform religious affairs legally.

POLITICS AND RELIGION DURING THE TIANANMEN SQUARE EVENT

Anthony Lambert relayed the events of the Tiananmen Square incident: On May 18, 1989, Bishop Ting supported the student's patriotic activities in a statement to the leaders of the State Council for promoting dialogue. Then on the 19th Zhao Ziyang went to the square to communicate with the students there. After Martial Law, on the 25th Ting along with fifteen leaders of the *Liang Hui* organizations remitted a letter to Wan Li, head of the Standing Committee of the NPC. The correspondence favored the students and their activities as well as that of the masses and asked for an emergency session of the NPC to discuss this national quandary. At the June 1, 1989, convening of the NPC, Bishop Ting emphasized the necessity for the People's Government to eliminate corruption within the CCP and evaded the events that were taking place at Tiananmen Square.

Lambert reported that the Christian students, from both Catholic and Protestant seminaries, were in the square with banners in declaration of their faith. They sang Christian hymns, which attracted bystanders as the first public Christian evangelistic proclamation within the People's Republic of China in forty years. Nevertheless, the Beijing Massacre of June 3 and 4, 1989, seriously affected the Chinese Church, for the conservative Marxist faction of the Communist Party extracted power from the reformists whose leader, Zhao Ziyang, was expelled and dishonored. Those in positions of influence to discard Maoist ideology were arrested or released from office.[106] The TSPM's open support of reform placed Bishop Ting and the *Liang Hui* in jeopardy. Consequently, as anticipated, shortly after the confrontation the TSPM and the CCC leaders conveyed an expression of support to the Communists hard-liners. On June 6, 1989, Bishop Ting corresponded his regrets with associates abroad for what had happened in Beijing, but he affirmed confidence that God's justice and the People's Democracy would triumph. He continued in his letter that many Christians

---

[105] 'An Interview with Deng Fucun Shanghai, 15 March 1997,' *Amity News Service*, Vol. 6, 5 / 6 (1997) 17.

[106] Anthony P. B. Lambert, 'The Church in China: Pre and Post Tiananmen Square,' *Religion in Communist Lands*, Vol. 18, August (1990) 244-247.

attended worship services as usual on that Sunday of June 4, 1989, and "as the news of the massacre spread they fell to their knees in the pews, weeping and imploring God's mercy for China."[107]

All of the patriotic religious organizations expressed their support to the government for suppressing the apparent counter-revolutionary demonstrations in the capital. The *Liang Hui* Committees on June 27, 1989, requested all Christians to study President Deng Xiaoping's speech to the soldiers enforcing martial law in Beijing, and they affirmed endorsement of the policies presented in the speech.[108] However, their delay in response revealed evidence of resistance in the carefully-worded statement by the Protestant leaders toward the governing party's direction and a struggle within the *Liang Hui* organizations.[109] Then the absence of the TSPM at the official tea party held for representatives of all the religious patriotic organizations over the Chinese New Year in 1990 was conspicuously noted as a form of protest. Finally, Bishop Ting submitted a self-criticism effected under political duress.[110]

Zhao Fusan, a leader in the TSPM and vice-president of the Chinese Academy of Social Sciences, after delivering a speech to the United Nations Educational Scientific and Cultural Organization, UNESCO, on June 9, 1989, disappeared in Paris. The news of his decision to defect was publicized on June 28. For the reformists faction of the *Linag Hui* this was at a very inopportune time, for he had been an influential Protestant leader. Later he voiced his disagreement with the action taken against the democratic movement in Beijing. In March 1990 the TSPM officially released Zhao from his local position, and in August 1990 the national *Liang Hui* organizations relieved him of his permanent membership and vice-presidency of the CCC; Zhao was denounced for "disgracing and attacking the CCP and People's Government."[111]

Sociologist Drew Liu expressed that the Tiananmen incident was a turning point in governmental religious policy. Since Christians

---

[107] Lambert, *The Resurrection*, pp. 217-218. The letter of Bishop Ting was taken from an article in the *Bridge*, (September-October 1989) 3.
[108] Lambert, 'The Church,' *Religion in Lands* (1990) 246.
[109] Kenneth H. Sidney, 'The Church Seeks a New Place in China,' *Christianity Today*, Vol. 33, (September 8 1989) 55.
[110] Lambert, 'The Church,' *Religion in Lands* (1990) 247.
[111] Lambert, *The Resurrection*, p. 219. *South China Morning Post*, (June 30, 1989) and *Tian Feng*, (November 1990) 24.

had supported the student movement, the CCP viewed Christianity as a political influence of opposition, which had been instrumental in the disintegration of Communism in Eastern Europe. However, the people's attitude toward Christianity changed. Many of the pro-democratic students turned to Christianity for solace and purpose. A revealing survey, conducted in late 1989 by the Central Institute of Educational Research in Shanghai, discovered that a mere 2.96 percent of 500 students claimed to believe in Communism and 41.8 percent declared belief in God. This was in contrast with a survey of seven years prior, which gathered data that 60 percent believed in Communism while 6 percent professed belief in God. Then "in 1993 the University of Beijing offered a series of lectures on religion which attracted thousands of students."[112] Different events both national and international affected the political climate of China, which in turn produced changes in the relationship between the religious sector and the government. In this incident it was especially true from the direct implication Christianity bore with similar events in Eastern Europe.

CHURCH AFFAIRS

Since 1979 the Chinese Protestant Church had grown at an exceptional rate, but was not free of difficulty from those who misused authority. Cases of embezzlement of church funds and illicit relationships were reported as becoming prevalent.[113] With an increase of wealth on the national level and stress on materialistic values, the temptation existed for Christians to secure assets through illegal means.[114] For this reason Pastor Lin I Shuan emphasized submitting reports to the RAB on suspected cultic practices. He affirmed that government policy prohibited the interruption of religious affairs.[115]

From this interrelated context of Christians and the Communist government came a provision for Christians in the Preliminary Session of 1984-1985. Said Deng Fucan:

---

[112] Drew Liu, 'State Policy and Christianity in China,' *China Strategic Review,* Vol. 1 (1996) 4.

[113] 'Call For Church To Bring In Its Own "Anti Corruption" Mechanism,' *Amity News Service,* Vol. 7, 3 / 4 (1998) 19.

[114] Adeney, *Church's March,* pp. 84-85.

[115] Lin I Shun (Interview 13 September 1999).

At that time the CCP stated that religious believers are not required to accept Marxist teaching, but the other three basic principles such as Mao's Thoughts were okay, for the Christian worldview is considered. In China it is a reality that the political system is Communism. This is the reality in which we live, and these principles are as a pledge of allegiance.[116]

Independent house churches in China experienced their pastors being imprisoned because of their deliberate rejection of governmental authority and policies, which the CCC never considered as persecution especially to an international forum.[117] House church pastor Lin affirmed that he and his congregation had experienced very little maltreatment in Beijing as compared to remote areas. He attributed it to the understanding that the Beijing police had of the religious laws; in the countryside they did not have sufficient knowledge and often overreact in some situations. Nonetheless, Lin affirmed that freedom of religion was not supported for unregistered meeting points.[118]

A Chinese science professor who was a Christian from the interior of China related a typical example of the divergence of government intervention in the affairs of religious groups in different areas of China. He told that his mother, who was involved in evangelism, had no conflict with authorities for the policy there in the countryside was fairly liberal, particularly with registered meeting points.

She had started evangelizing from 1995, and it became more open since, even to meet as a house church as long as they do not criticize the government, they have the freedom to believe in the one and true God. The church had certain independence from the government even though they are registered. They are not allowed to preach openly outside the church. My mother does not organize meetings, but goes door to door to individual families and individuals.[119]

Another Chinese Christian professor of mathematics recounted

---

[116] Deng Fu-cun (Interview 10 September 1999).
[117] 'SBC Works with CCC,' http://www.whidbey.net, 11/9/98, 3:17 PM.
[118] Lin, Pastor of the An Ti Ya Church, Beijing (Interview, trans. He Yanli, 17 September 1999).
[119] Meng Xiangzhi (pseudo), (Interview, 21 October 1998).

that the best form of evangelization in China was to do what you are supposed to do and do it very well no matter what the profession. In this way the people notice by example, "for to be well recognized with credibility in an institution is important to establish acknowledgment."[120]

In other parts of China, it may be quite the opposite from what the professors had claimed in their regions. Mickey Spiegal reported on areas where the proselytizing of minors was prohibited, as were sermons addressing the biblical themes of the Second Coming, judgment day and creation. The RAB could examine message content, and the membership rolls were to be made available to them. Those who desired baptism were required to apply with forms in triplicate and photos attached for the RAB, TSPM, and their work unit. These three agencies must agree or the request for baptism would be denied.[121] However, Xu Li, a missionary of the Mo Chao Road Church in Nanjing, confirmed that in his district there was no limitation on what he could teach if it was "what the Bible says."[122] Some restriction of sermon content, according to a Chinese graduate student, was due to the depth of the subject, such as that of eschatology. She also clarified that "there are no age restrictions for church attendance, but to take communion one must have been baptized and those under 18 are not baptized."[123] There also had been some exceptions by the TSPM to the prohibition of Sunday school for youth in the open churches.[124]

Another factor distinct to China was the registration of one's name upon the purchase of a Bible, for the science professor clarified that "this information may be used in evidence if that person speaks out against the government. There is religious freedom, but when you get in trouble all that is gathered as evidence. The bookstore must submit records." He also elucidated as to why certain people may experience suppressive action:

---

[120] Hu Wei, (Interview, 31 May 1999).

[121] Spiegal, *China Control,* p. 18.

[122] Xu Li, Missionary of Mo Chou Road Church, Nanjing (Interview, trans. He Yanli, 13 September 1999).

[123] Yilin Gu [pseud.], Assistant to Headmaster at Beijing BISS International School, Parents are involved with the House Church Movement and she had been in a TSPM church a year, Beijing (Interview, 5 September 1999).

[124] Lambert, *The Resurrection,* p. 108.

It depends a lot on what you have done before you were a believer, such as if you have a history of dissidence against the government, or if you have political agenda for becoming a Christian. However, Christians do continue to be persecuted...they may fire you or cut your benefits, send you to remote areas with no facilities, or put you in prison. It is happening.[125]

Even though Christianity in China may differ from area to area in how it may be received or restricted, the atheistic government has provided limited liberties, and Christianity continued to thrive in varied forms. The professor acknowledged that:

The body of Christ is everywhere in China, not just in the house church. God is doing things in China by using the system there. The style is diverse in China from the situation, but those that seem to struggle are the most sincere. They may not know much about theology but they are richly blessed. This is the time for Christianity to grow in China with the growth of economy. In the future it will impact the world.[126]

The population of China alone gave it an international impact. As China might become more influenced by Christianity, this influence could also become international.

FOREIGN ACCESS

The United Nations denied intolerance of religious beliefs within the limitations of the law for the protection of public security, order or the fundamental rights of other citizenry. In a speech, Ye emphasized that no nation would tolerate the use of religion to impair the state, bring harm to the people or denigrate the religion.[127] The State Council Information Office confirmed China's amiable attitude toward religious associations that reciprocated their friendship by respecting the sovereignty of China and the self-reliance principle maintained by the religions of the nation. This was evidenced in 1991 upon the enlistment of the China

---

[125] Meng Xiangzhi [pseud.], (Interview, 21 October 1998).
[126] Ibid.
[127] Ye, 'Speech,' *Tripod*, (1998) 54.

Christian Council with the World Council of Churches.[128]

The concept of respect for national sovereignty eliminated religious broadcasting into China as being lawful. A Chinese graduate student argued that the vast population of China merits this religious contact with remote areas of the nation. For them it would be an opportunity to receive the instruction offered on the broadcast. She also reasoned that the broadcasts were invaluable to the Christian community and social construction for Christian seekers, new Christians, and especially youth because social life was not sufficient in many parts of China.[129] Moreover, according to Lambert, young Chinese Christians revealed in private conversations that the more political faction of the TSPM had reported their relationships with foreign Christians living in China to the Public Security Bureau.[130]

In 1997, the regulations had been reported by the Human Rights agency for any foreign Christians coming into China as a guest or to tour:

A guest must report to the entry and departure desk at the local Public Security Bureau (PSB), apply for temporary residence and provide a copy of the application to the local Religious Affairs Bureau. After his departure the hosting unit must submit a written report about the visitor's activities to both bureaus. As a precaution against unplanned events, an outsider who comes to visit friends or relatives or as a tourist must notify the PSB and RAB of his or her planned activities.[131]

Allen Hunter along with Chan Kimkwong in 1993 informed religious personnel, journalists or academic visitors that since 1989 the Chinese government had monitored their movements within the country more closely.[132]

The author traveled into China in September 1999 to interview for research on the Church in China. Appointments were made with both TSPM and CCC officials in Shanghai and Nanjing,

[128] State Council Information Office, 'Freedom of Religious Belief in China,' October 1997, *Beijing Review,* (November 3-9 1997) 20.
[129] Yilin Gu [pseud.], (Interview, 5 Sept 99).
[130] Lambert, *The Resurrection,* p. 108.
[131] Human Rights, *China: State Control,* p. 21.
[132] Alan Hunter and Chan Kim-kwong, *Protestantism in Contemporary China* (Cambridge: Cambridge University Press, 1993), p. 102.

but there was no reporting to the PSB or notification of planned activities to the PSB and RAB. However, on the day before this author arrived in Beijing and also the day after departure, officials had called the Chinese native that was the translator and companion during the research tour. He had been told that all the travels and engagements within China had been observed. Furthermore, this was a date close to a national event that the government took precaution against any possible anti-Communist activity, for it was on the eve of the 50th anniversary celebration of the Communist revolution and establishment of the People's Republic of China. In fact, notices had been posted in public to inform all non-residence of Beijing to be out of the Capital City by a certain date before the celebration scheduled on October 1, 1999.

NEW FOUND RELIGIOUS FREEDOMS AND CONSEQUENCES

The regulations and policies were implemented in different ways at various stages of socialistic development and leadership inclination. Regional diversity placed Christianity in a distinctive perspective, and the consequences of its activities fluctuated accordingly. Therefore, any generalization would be a false statement in another district of China. When speaking of a situation, the location and circumstance would consequently need to be specific.

GOVERNMENTAL ACTION

In September 1979, Xiao Xianfa, as director of the RAB, pointed out the CCP religious policy in an interview with the New China News Agency. His statement underscored the futility of administrative measures opposed to religion, which would continue as part of Chinese society in the role of an individual matter for some time to come. For a decade later the leftists resisted this new policy, thus its disparity of application.[133] The CCP had discovered that forcible manipulation of Christianity only intensified its growth and potential. Consequently, they admitted error in their treatment of Christians during the Cultural Revolution, but with no intention of special treatment in the future. However, Christianity would

---

[133] Tony Lambert, *The Resurrection of the Chinese Church* (Wheaton, IL: Harold Shaw Publishers, 1994), pp. 36, 38.

not be subjected to ridicule or discrimination as a superstition, but considered acceptable as a religion for China.[134] For this reason, Chinese citizens of each religious belief benefited from equal opportunities for education and employment, and it became unlawful to use discriminatory content against religious or ethnic factions on trademarks or in advertisements.[135]

The November 30, 1980, issue of the *Guang Ming Daily* published an article titled 'Freedom of Belief is a Basic Policy of the Party towards Religions.' It reiterated the theory that the existence of religion depends on "ideological causes," which the "democratic method" of education and direction would solve. It declared that the Party's detailed religious policy must be consistent with its primary duty and subordinate to its objective. The CCP confused aspiration for morality with technical ability by promoting slogans such as "Four Emphasis" and "Five Beautifuls" or devised a campaign as "Be Courteous Month" that lacked the influence to produce moral people.[136]

Archbishop Robert Runcie of England questioned China's President as to the aim of the "Spiritual Pollution Campaign" in regards to religion, and he was assured that there was definitely no reference to religion. Yet, suppression of groups that refrained from TSPM contact notably increased during the initial months of the campaign. Religious literature along with pornographic materials was barred from entrance into China, and a Bible was displayed along with contraband items.

If a Bible was printed in China it was considered legal, but from the CCP's perspective the Christian message was a spiritual pollutant because its worldview challenged Marxist philosophy. Accordingly, the government permitted religious belief but intended to prevent the influence of Christianity, especially on Chinese youth.

The *China Youth News* magazine declared: "The Party should provide the solution [to any of life's problems] through warmth and understanding – only then shall youth no longer turn to

---

[134] Britt Towery, *The Churches of China* (Hong Kong: Dragon Books, 1987), p. 182.
[135] State Council Information Office, 'Freedom of Religious Belief in China,' October 1997, *Beijing Review*, (November 3-9 1997) 15.
[136] David H. Adeney, *China: The Church's Long March* (Ventura CA: Regal Books, 1985), p. 101 and Appendix 2: Chinese Communist Party Policy towards Religions,

other worldly beings for assistance." The December 1983 issue called for atheistic instruction at the elementary school level for protection "from the harm of superstition and the bad influence of religion."[137]

On the other hand, laws were developed to protect religious beliefs and their regulations. Article 17 of Decree No. 145, signed by the Chinese Premier Li Peng on January 31, 1994, stated that the RAB would report any infringement of the basic religious rights of a religious venue to the People's Government at the proper level. It, in turn, would be responsible to halt the infraction and enforce restitution for any economic loss.[138] Article 30 in Chapter 5 of the RAB Regulations listed the approved religious activities:

> Worshiping Buddha, recitation of prayers, reconciliation services, following a vegetarian diet, fasting, prayer, Sunday services, Bible sharing, preaching, baptism, celebrating mass, anointing the sick, requiem services, observing feast days, etc. One can also practice religion at home.[139]

The People's Government circulated the 'Regulations on the Administration of Sites for Religious Activities' for the protection of those locations that lawfully supported these procedures. It also permitted foreigners to participate in Chinese religious services in recognized sites, and even preach upon invitation. They might also arrange religious activities for aliens as approved at or above the county level.[140]

Regulations were promoted in China for the benefit of her religious believing citizens, and a statement by Bishop Ding demonstrated independence. He said, "Our Chinese churches

---

[137] Ibid., pp. 107, 108, 135. Richard Van Houten, 'Party Politics-The Great Spiritual Polution Hunt,' *China and the Church Today,* (January-Febuary 1984) 12-16.

[138] State Council of the PRC, 'Decree No. 145: Regulation Governing Venues for Religious Activities,' signed by Premier Li Peng, 31 January 1994, China Religious Law, *Amity News Service,* pp. 1-3.

[139] Mickey Speigel, 'Appendix IV: Regulations from the Shanghai Religious Affairs Bureau,' Approved on November 30, 1995 by the Standing Committee of the Shanghai 10th People's Congress at its 23rd Meeting. According to Chapter 10 Article 63: These regulations are effective from March 1, 1996, *China: State Control of Religion* (New York: Human Rights Watch, 1997), p. 94.

[140] State Office, 'Freedom in China', *BR* (1997) 15; and Speigel, 'Appendix IV: RAB Regs., Chapter 8 Article 49' and 'Appendix VI: Regulations on the Supervision of the Religious Activities of Foreigners in China,' *China: Control,* pp. 97, 104.

are independent not only of foreign churches, but also of the National People's Congress, the Political Consultative conference, the government and the Party." Li Weihan, director of the UFWD, negated this apparent concept for the furtherance of Christian ministry. He stated: "In the final analysis, to implement correctly and properly the policy of freedom of religious belief in our country's situation is more helpful for accelerating the decline of religious belief than for promoting its development."[141] While officials claimed that no citizen was imprisoned on the basis of his or her faith, the implementation of law had been irregular with their expression of concern for the destabilizing aspects of uncontrolled religious groups.[142] Government agencies had labeled such groups as cults rather than branches of a recognized religion, a device to eliminate some religious organizations.[143]

The RAB held the authority to terminate the operation and confiscate the equipment or funds of any religious assembly for different violations, include the distribution of religious literature outside the designated area or literature considered illegal within the region. To obtain money under duress or organize gatherings to view or listen to foreign-produced religious videos or radio broadcasts, or to promote any religious activity disruptive to society, was liable for discipline.[144] Training pastors in an unregistered church group would be considered illegal and   could be reported by the TSPM to the RAB. Officials would be sent to investigate and deliver a warning, and if the warning was disregarded the UFWD would confer with the Public Security Bureau to procure arrests. PSB cadres would effect interrogations where coercion might be used to extort confessions and fines,   or those accused were referred to the procurator's office for   further investigation and prosecution, sentencing and imprisonment.[145]

However, Shi Zesheng in a forum on China's religious conditions

[141] Deng Zhaoming, 'Church and State Regulations in China: Characteristics and Trends: A Response,' [to Liu Peng, pp. 5-18], trans. Michael Sloboda, *Tripod*, (July-August 1995) 20.
[142] Donald Argue, Theodore E. McCarrick and Arthur Schnwer, 'Religious Freedom,' *Tripod*, Vol. XVIII, No. 105, May-June (1998) 56-57.
[143] Human Rights/Asia, *China: State control of Religion* (New York: Human Rights Watch, 1997), p. 30.
[144] Jonathan Chao, *China News and Church Report*, No. 1934, 13 March (1992).
[145] Jonathan Chao, e-mailed material from the Introduction and Conclusion of his

declared that church registration ensured legal protection, but it was not for the purpose of governmental control. He refuted the accusation that the Chinese government had closed "family churches" when in fact, he claimed, the "family churches" do not exist in China. The government authorities respected family gatherings of Christian devotees that consist mainly of family members who read Bible and prayed, and such groups were not required to register.[146] "Church" indicated an approved organized gathering of religious believers.

From March 1 to 7, 1998, Shanghai hosted a campaign to publicize China's religious laws to improve awareness of regulations governing religious practices. Religious buildings posted banners exhibiting this information for citizens, to establish that the freedoms of religious belief were basic Chinese policy.[147] Effort was made to bring religious activities within the law for protection and secure a level of management.

TSPM ACTION

Deng Xiaoping introduced the "Four Modernizations" program for religions to consider and incorporate into their support for social construction. The UFWD directed and staffed the RAB, which in turn corroborated the TSPM and the CCC. Article 29 of the TSPM constitution clarified the interdependence of the political and religious endeavors of the TSPM. Reports confirmed cases of TSPM collaboration with the PSB in the arrest of independent preachers. The concluding section of the Yunnan TSPM polity document substantiated this: "All who transgress the above decisions should undergo re-education, and if they have not changed after re-education, the relevant department of the government can be requested to deal with them."[148]

However, according to Dr. Brent Fulton, the TSPM possessed no political authority, but it might intervene if a pastor was unjustly treated by over zealous cadres. Then again, he added, in most

---

new unpublished book, *A History of Christianity in Socialist China*, 1998, Introduction, p. 11.

[146] Shi Zesheng, 'Forum on China's Religious Conditions,' *Beijing Review*, September 1-7 (1997) 18.

[147] 'Section III: Protestant Church,' *China Study Journal*, Vol. 13, No. 1, (August 1998) 57.

[148] Adeney, *Church's March*, pp. 118, 175.

cases those arrested would have been labeled as cult leaders or criminals.[149] Normally, those arrested were house church leaders or itinerant evangelists with the house church movement. By 1984 pressure to conform was endured by house churches, but a shortage of facilities for the number of new Christians required the TSPM to grant recognition to house meeting points that accepted its authority, to which over 10,000 house groups consented.[150] Many of these groups were persuaded after the TSPM published the "Ten Don'ts," assigned meeting points, and distributed Bibles, and then invited many of the leaders to a meeting where they were entertained and led to join the TSPM.[151] Jonathan Chao, who worked with the house church leadership, claimed that the "Ten Don'ts" were released collectively by the TSPM, UFWD, and PSB as an instrument to encourage church groups to comply under the authority of the TSPM. Often when a home meeting began, security officers would attend to observe and allow their presence to apply pressure for compliance without any warnings or arrests.[152]

A Chinese educator in Beijing whose parents participated in a house church claimed that the key to house church survival was neighborhood relations. She held that if there were no illegal activity the group would not be interrupted; otherwise, interrogations were certain. These home gatherings were not required to register unless the crowd became too large, "so small would be safe."[153] Britt Towery, who had studied and worked in China for decades, asked Professor Chang as a teacher of sociology and head of the English Department of Anhui Normal University in Wuhu, Anhui Province, if he knew of the TSPM to have imprisoned anyone. Professor Chang emphatically exclaimed,

---

[149] Brent Fulton, Ph. D., Executive Director of Chinasource, Managing Director of the Institute of Chinese Studies at Wheaton College, Served 8 years with China Ministries International in Pasadena, Served 2 years with Chinese Church Research Center in Hong Kong, Wheaton, IL (Interview, 17 November 1999).
[150] Leslie Lyall, *God Reigns in China* (London: Hodder and Stoughton, 1985), pp. 200-201.
[151] Jonathan Chao (interviews), Richard Van Houten (ed.), *Wise as Serpents Harmless as Doves* (Pasadena: Willaim Cary Library, 1988), p. 142.
[152] Ibid., p. 143.
[153] Yilin Gu [pseud.], Assistant Headmaster at Beijing BISS International School, parents are involved in the house church movement and she had been in a TSPM registered church a year, Beijing (Interview, 5 September 1999).

"Three-Self putting Christians in jail! Three-Self is doing all it can to get people out of jail!"[154]

Nevertheless, Bishop Ting, president of TSPM and CCC, reported to president Jiang Zemin that on the local level cadres cursed, physically abused, and fined Christians. These cadres not only had confiscated Christian literature and Bibles, but also bicycles, watches, and other items. Then Ting defended church leader Wan Weifan who had asked why his Christian center had not yet been approved but was designated as "unlawful, illegal, and an underground power," for which he had been subsequently punished.[155] In a 1988 letter Bishop Ting also complained, "We have seen Communist Party members taken out of the Religious Affairs Bureau and put into the churches as atheistic church leaders."[156] Then since 1988 Ting reported:

> ...cadres make it their personal responsibility to struggle against religion. Religion to them is like a splinter in the eye. Disregarding the experience of the past fourteen years, they try hard to counteract religion with administrative decrees. They exploit religion and deprive believers of their legal rights. The government does not allow many sites for religious activities. Furthermore, it uses every kind of excuse to disallow normal religious activities to take place. It uses unwritten methods to downgrade numerous religious venues to illegal status, leaving believers no choice but to resort to underground places of worship.

Bishop Ting again addressed this problem with a statement:

> ...quite a few cadres exceed their functions and meddle in other's affairs under the pretext of fitting religion into socialism. As a result, relations between the Party and the masses are strained. What they are doing is making religion fit their own intention and interests. Some Christians who are pained by this leave the so-called "official" church and join a privately-run church. This does not broaden unity, but weakens the prestige of the Party and government and

---

[154] Towery, *Churches*, pp. 203-204.
[155] Deng, 'Church and State,' *Tripod*, (1995) 21
[156] Lambert, *The Resurrection*, p. 206.

the unifying force of the Three-Self...[157]

The TSPM attempted to balance governmental policy and constitutional rights with the actual practice and implementation of those regulations. In that effort they were forced to recognize the extent of the law in compliance and stand firm against poor enforcement.

CADRE ACTION

During the "Anti-Spiritual Pollution Campaign" in 1983 and the "Anti-Bourgeois Liberalization Campaign" in 1987, the implementation of the religious policy demonstrated a repressive trend. Then the cadres at the local level who may have had conservative Marxist tendencies executed the policy with even more severity than the regulation may have intended.[158] This was an issue to which Bishop Ting drew attention while commending the Party for its implementation of the liberties of religious belief. In the process, though too many of the cadres took the attitude that "supervision of religion must be strengthened" or that "religious activities must be conducted underground."[159] Deng Zhaoming pointed out known cases where governmental cadres had selected as leaders for churches those who may have had problems with finances, personnel, or property rights. Their selection for leadership might have had no religious training, or perhaps were not even a member of the congregation.[160]

The governmental policy in China was to restrict illegal churches or religious activities. Eighty percent of the population resided in the rural areas, where the local officials had no understanding of illegality or had a predisposition against religious orders.[161] Churches had been arbitrarily closed, fined, denied permission for registration and had their leaders imprisoned because of cadres who misunderstood the religious policies. The CCC availed itself to intervene in these cases with

---

[157] Deng, 'Church and State,' *Tripod*, (1995) 21-22.

[158] Lambert, *The Ressurection*, p. 58.

[159] Ding Guangxun, Bp., 'Bishop K. H. Ting's View of the Present Situation of Christianity in China,' Interview by C. Kwok, *Bridge*, No. 33, January February (1989) 7.

[160] Deng, 'Church and State,' *Tripod* (1995) 20.

[161] Myrrl Byler, 'Debate over religious persecution in China is often simplistic,' *News Service*, Akron, PA: Mennonite Central Committee, June 27 (1997) 1.

appropriate government agencies.[162] As China's economy grew, officials became acquisitive and used their authority to attain money. The village police in remote areas arrested Christians merely to extract a fine from them.[163] One government official who was sympathetic to Christianity verified that the parts of China most visitors see on the eastern coast and the capital with religious freedom were atypical from the majority of the nation.[164] Deng Fucan recognized these inconsistencies as reason for teaching religious law in seminaries, and then church leaders could point out discrepancies to cadres who do not comply. Another advantage was that the church workers would be assured of conducting religious activities legally.[165] With the vastness of China and the great rural population, cadres sensed the separation from their supervising officials, and officiated by their own integrity or lack thereof.

ACTION REGARDING CHRISTIANS

Not only during the Cultural Revolution but at any time in Chinese history, the greatest hurts of any persecution was that of betrayal and accusations by those considered Christian brothers and sisters who had failed to remain faithful to God and loyal to their fellow Christians.[166] Yet, the varied examples dealt with here included only direct encounters and treatment from government related officials over various areas of the country and at assorted times in the final quarter of the twentieth century. The most prime to attract official attention were itinerant pastors and evangelists who travelled outside the designated assigned areas and constantly faced the prospect of arrest.[167]

Another obvious group that the government found delinquent was the unregistered house churches. The PSB's recent method of treatment for these gatherings was implemented in May 1991

---

[162] Eva Stimson, 'The Church in China,' *Presbyterians Today,* (November 1997) 4.
[163] Hummer, Earnie, 'Thoughts from the President, China Puzzle Part Two,' *Panda Bearer,* (September-December 1998) 4. Interview of Daniel Su who was the special assistant to the COM President.
[164] Lambert, *The Resurrection,* p. 72.
[165] 'An Interview With Deng Fucan, Shanghsi 15 March 1997,' *Amity News Service,* Vol. 6, (May-June 1997) 17.
[166] Arthur Wallis, *China Miracle* (Columbia, MO: Cityhill Publishing, 1986), p. 108.
[167] Chao, *Serpents Doves,* p. 144.

when ten believers in central China were arrested and then released upon payment of a 300 *yuan*, 35 U.S. dollars, fine. Some of those arrested borrowed the money from relatives, friends or their church to pay the charge. Foreign visitors in an unregistered house meeting caused even more concern for a group of 120 local believers in a training session in September 1992. The three foreign Christians were released after 3 weeks, but at least 108 of the Chinese believers remained in custody at the time of the report in November 1992.[168]

A superintendent of over 80 unregistered churches was arrested, had his head shaved, and was beaten until he lost consciousness. He was later released, but placed under 24-hour surveillance.[169] A Christian worker, Brother Steven, was beaten and tortured in interrogation for as many as 70 times. Reports claimed his condition as being ill and coughing up blood yet treatment at a hospital was withheld. Another Chinese Christian, Chan Nien, in November 1992 suffered injury from being beaten by the butt of a rifle.[170]

Different provinces represented a variety of action taken against Christian gatherings in a spectrum of situations. Police sealed off a house church in Shanxi Province where more than 100 Christian worshippers assembled, and then they broke in upon those inside and beat them with electric police batons. The police took twelve of these Christians into detention where they were interrogated and beaten repeatedly. In the areas of Anhui Province affected by floods in Huoqiu, Hao and Taihe counties, the police refused to grant the Christians relief. Also in this vicinity Christians had to pay authorities a fee just to be allowed to meet. In Su County each Christian was required to register, pay a charge, and submit two photos before being allowed to attend a church.[171]

The source of Bibles in China had been a point of strict regulation by Chinese authorities. In 1992 the border patrol checked more closely for foreigners entering with Bibles. They

---

[168] Chao, *CNCR*, 12 July (1991), 6 November (1992).
[169] 'China: The Untold Story', *The Voice of the Martyrs*, Los Angeles (1993) 13. Servants of the Persecuted Church.
[170] 'Bibles in China: A Great Deception!' *VOM*, LA, (May 1993) 7.
[171] Thomas Lawrence, 'New Straightjacket for China's Expanding Church,' Jonathan Chao (ed.), *China Prayer Letter,* Hong Kong: No. 123, (October-November 1992) 6.

would permit them to pass through in order to apprehend those who received the Bibles for distribution.[172] The Bibles published in China by Amity Press in Nanjing were considered legal, so the house church leaders from Sichuan Province went to Nanjing and ordered 400 Bibles to be delivered to a registered church in Chongqing of Sichuan Province. Still, in April 1992 when they went to collect these Bibles these house church leaders were asked about their involvement with unregistered churches. Eventually the TSPM church relinquished the Bibles, but within a month the PSB invaded the house gathering to arrest and fine the people there. Others who desired to purchase a couple of Bibles were required to submit forms with their name, address and identification number, which resulted in a visit from the UFWD or PSB. For these reasons the house church leaders prefer to use foreign sources for acquiring Bibles rather than through the means of official TSPM and Amity Press resources.[173]

By April 1997 the Amity Press, the only printer with governmental authorization to print the Bible in China, had printed 15 million Bibles.   Even though secular bookstores were not permitted to sell Bibles, the Bible was the second most published book in China after the *Selected Works of Mao Zedong*.[174] Then again, authorities confiscated Bibles and books mimeographed by house church leaders as evidence of the production and distribution of counter-revolutionary materials.[175] This method was used to control religious activities and publications.

Varied manners of stifling religious activities were employed. Christians who attended church may be disregarded for a career promotion, and members of the Communist Party were not permitted to join a religious organization. Therefore, when a family became Christian, a husband might allow his family to attend church without him until after his retirement.[176] In Beijing as a part of a campaign to raise work standards, a move was made against the pastor of Gangwashi Protestant Church in December

[172] Ibid., p. 7.
[173] 'Bibles,' *VOM,* (May 1993) 7.
[174] Stimson, 'The Church,' *PT* (1997) 4.
[175] 'SBC Works with Liberal China Christian Council,' http://www.whidbey.net/-dcloud/fbns/sb cworks.htm, 11/9/98, 3:17 PM.
[176] Alan Hunter and Chan Kim-kwong, *Protestantism in Contemporary China* (Cambridge: Cambridge University Press, 1993), pp. 174-175.

1994. The press reported that 200 agents took Yang Yudong, the 73-year-old pastor, from his pulpit with the charge that he was over the mandatory age of 70 for retirement.[177] Nationwide societal security in June 1996 intensified with the "Strike Hard Campaign" against crime. One house church leader reported that his home was searched and all Christian books, cassettes, videos and photos were pronounced illegal and confiscated.[178]

Unregistered house gatherings have been considered cults since early 1996, and the leaders who experienced arrests were placed in labor-education camps for three years or were allocated exorbitant fines. In a female labor camp in Zhengzhou, Hennan Province, nearly a third of the inmates were Christian evangelists, and in the male labor camp of Pingdingshan, twice the population of the women's camp, a sixth were evangelists or pastors. Their two meals a day consisted of a piece of *mantou*, steamed bread, and a bowl of soup. These circumstances placed many Christian families in serious poverty.[179]

The government became concerned about the growth of house churches. In April 1997 a report confirmed that eight Protestant leaders of the house church movement had been arrested from the Puebla Program on Religious Freedom. Puebla, a New York-based human rights organization, was a division of Freedom House. Peter Xiu, who had the largest known church movement in China of 4 million members called the "Wilderness," was one of those arrested.[180]

With certainty, the Human Rights Watch reported the determination with which officials attempted to reduce the mobility of growth within the unregistered groups through campaigns, incursions, and impositions of charges aimed at bankruptcy of these movements. Any accusations were difficult to refute; as an informant explained, "If they meet in the dark, they are accused

[177] Communists vs. Christians,' *Wall Street Journal*, Eastern Edition, New York: (December 12 1994) A14.
[178] Myron Ivey, 'The Ransacking of a House Church during the Strike Hard Campaign: A Testimony of God's Blessing,' *CNCR*, 2639, (May 25 1998) 1-2. Transcribed and translated from a cassette recording by Ronald Yu, 1998.
[179] Jonathan Chao, 'The Material Needs of the Church in China,' *CNCR*, 2655, (October 26 1998) 2; and Chao, 'The Church in China: Needs and Opportunities for Ministry,' *CNCR*, (May 11 1998) 2-3.
[180] 'China Continues Assault of Non-official Churches,' *The Christian Century*, Vol. 114, Is. 15, (May 7 1997) 446.

of rape." Another said, "When we try to collect tithe, we are accused of trying to cheat people or amass wealth. When we preach that 'there is hope in the world so we believe in God,' the government says that it means that it (the government) is hopeless and we want to overthrow it."[181] Arrests and treatment were directed at renowned leaders of the movement like Peter Xiu and Ms. Cheng Meiying. On October 26, 1998, Cheng was arrested on her way to a national meeting for house church leaders. She had been instrumental in the conversion to Christianity of hundreds of thousands of Chinese and had established thousands of house churches. This was just one of several times she had been arrested, but this time she was beaten with a water-soaked hemp whip and a police baton until she lost consciousness. At her release on November 21, 1998, she had suffered complete memory loss and exhibited insanity.[182]

According to David Zhang, spokesman for China's house churches, in different parts of China, even in the latter years of the twentieth century and under various circumstances, the Christians faced the consequences for their choice to gather for worship. On October 26, 1998, the PSB assaulted a group of 40 at a house gathering, in Liuwan Village of Wugong County near Wugang City in Henan Province. The next day, 11 prominent leaders were imprisoned at Fancheng where they were tortured. In Nanyang of Henan Province on November 5, 1998, at 8:00 PM, the PSB detained 100 devotees including the two prominent house church leaders, Lu Lianquan and Zhang Fushan, and these believers suffered beatings.[183] A description of some of the maltreatment received: beatings during the first week of interrogations with deprivation of sleep around the clock for several days. One report told of a man who had been forced to drink his own urine and a woman who had boiling water poured onto her lap during interrogation. Another

---

[181] Human, *China: State Control*, pp. 23, 31.

[182] Human Rights In China Press Release, (November 24 1998) 1.

[183] David Zhang, Spokesperson for China's house churches, Urgent Letter of Appeal: The Chinese Government has begun a new round of Religious Persecution, November 9, 1998. To: U.N. Secretary – General Kofi Annan, U.S. President Clinton, U.S. State Department, Amnesty International, Human Rights Watch/Asia and Human Rights in China.

woman was requested to enter an official's bedroom for her interrogation.[184]

In August 1999 the PSB invaded various house meetings in Henan Province, and 39 Christian leaders were arrested. First, eight men were arrested for an illegal Bible class in the city of Wu Gang on August 18th. The afternoon of August 23rd in Tanghe County during a Bible study at a farmer's home, 31 house church leaders were arrested.[185]

It could be noted that these recorded arrests involved the house church movement and their leaders. Pastor Lin informed that many of these groups do not register because they do not want the government to know their location. Even if they might have acquired the six specified qualifications they might be rejected for registration, because the officials have their own idea of the requirements. There are house churches that care to register but are afraid of rejection. "So if they do not go for registration they may continue in the underground stage, and they do not have to worry about the government's rejection then being shut down." He mentioned that in Beijing the restrictions against unregistered groups were very strict. However, in some areas away from the capital there would be more leniency, and there would be districts where the TSPM even had a working relationship with house churches.[186]

Timothy Wu observed that the Christian life portrayed benefits for everyone. He recounted an account of a Christian laborer in the Guiyang Electric Factory, who had worked more diligently then his peers, but his foreman was prejudiced against Christians and would not promote him. One night the water main burst and the laborer came and worked all night to make the necessary repairs. His fellow workers noted his loyalty and sense of duty to the citizens of the city even though the foreman had not regarded his rights.[187] Han Wensao also conveyed that just within

[184] Chao, 'The Material,' *CNCR,* (1998) 3.
[185] Steven L. Snyder, 'Chinese Police Arrest Thirty-nine (39) In Raids on Prayer Meetings,' *International Christian Concern,* www.persecution.org, September 7, (1999) 1.
[186] Lin [pseud.], Pastor of the *An Ti Ya Tang*, Antioch Church, Beijing (Interview, trans. He Yanli. 17 September 1999).
[187] Timothy Wu, *Sheltered Through the Storms: A Chinese Pastor Preserved by God* (Palo Cedro,CA: Wayside Impressions, 1996), ch. 16.

the years from 1992 to 1994 there were about 20,000 Christians selected as model workers and advanced producers. He stated, "The political and social status of Christians is constantly rising, and there are Christian representatives and members at every level of the National People's Congress (NPC) and the Chinese People's Consultative Conference (CPPCC) now."[188] Donald Argue commented that the Chinese Christians participated in a positive role in China's modernization, and if given the freedom to do so could accomplish much more.[189] The dilemma between the Chinese Church and the State was that both required the total commitment of the believer whether to Communism or Christ, and some groups could not support the contention of interests. Therefore, they chose to become completely independent of any organization in cooperation with the Communist regime. Implementation of policy presented a diverse reaction in interpretation and sympathies according to the orientation of the local officials.

RATIONALE FOR ACTION

Article 36 of the 1982 People's Constitution guaranteed the freedom of religious belief to the citizens of China. However, Article 34 stated that the legal age to vote or stand for election was 18, which resulted in uncertainty as to the other freedoms for minors under the age of 18 assured under the constitution. The ambiguity of interpretation of Article 36 in the conditions of 34 was an ultraconservative Marxist manifestation.[190] The misinterpretation of policy and the uncertainty of directives accounted for the differentiation of treatment as with Samuel Lamb, a known leader in the house church movement. His arrest and treatment was because of who he was and the approach of the officials rather than the objective policy.[191] Another factor in the case of Samuel Lamb, in which the international exposure and

---

[188] Han Wensao, 'Build Up the Body of Christ with One Heart and United Effort: Running the Church Even Better According to the Three-Self Principle,' Janice Wickeri (ed.), *Chinese Theological Review: 12* (Foundation for Theological Education in Southeast Asia, 1998), pp. 7-8.

[189] Argue, 'Religious Freedom,' *Tripod* (1998) 55-56.

[190] Philip L. Wickeri, *Seeking the Common Ground* (Maryknoll, NY: Orbis Books, 1990), pp. 103-104.

[191] Karen Young, [pseud.], Chinese writer of financial economic and political news in *Zong Guo Zeng Juang,* Children's English teacher, Beijing (Interview, 5 September 1999).

world opinion did not protect him, was that he had become an embarrassment to the government and they would not lose face.[192] Wang recognized that Lamb was arrested because of a violation of the law, for he had contacted foreigners without permission then flaunted it against the constitution.[193]

Hunter stated that personal relationships were respected when TSPM regulations on the local level were implemented with flexibility. With strong interpersonal relationships the possibilities are expanded, even to the extent of "co-ministering in China with overseas Christians," especially during the formation of the open-door policy and economic development in South China. The RAB had even encouraged churches to welcome overseas visitors for potential foreign investment.[194] However, what might be tolerated or even encouraged in Guangzhou or rural Zhejiang Province as normal religious activity would not be permitted in Beijing and the rural areas of Henan Province.[195] Conversely, a personal conflict with an official might cause trouble for an individual Christian, which may cause complexity. As Au Yeung Chekwong affirmed: "An official may not like a Christian and cause him trouble for his own benefit." Even for that Christian "to write an article is cause for serious problems, for something can always be picked out to be interpreted as against the government."[196]

Heresies presented situations that the government could not endure for the security and protection of the nation. The group called The Shouters propagated 23 rules for shouting and weeping in their form of veneration. In one case an elderly woman who could not shout had died from the exertion of trying.[197] A woman, Li Congmei, of Henan Province in Chenghuan who resided in the Tani Brigade wrote a Letter of Repentance, for she had supplied

---

[192] Carl Franklin Kelly [pseud.], Professor at a University in Beijing over fifteen years, Involved in International Christian fellowship, Beijing (Interview, 6-7 September 1999).

[193] Samuel Wang, Scholar of the *Four Books*, Co-author of *God and the Ancient Chinese*, Director of the Chinese Department of Laymen Ministry News Ministries, had translated for TSPM and CCC and in U.S. worked with Human Rights Watch, St. Maries, Idaho (Interview, 21 December 1999).

[194] Hunter, *Protestantism*, p. 183.

[195] Lambert, *The Resurrection*, p. 73.

[196] Au Yeung Chikwong (Andrew), Chinese Student, New York (Interview, 25 May 1999).

[197] Wang, (Interview, 27 December 1999).

food and lodging to a group of The Shouters sect.[198] Therefore, most arrests were focused on the following infractions: first, the involvement with The Shouters, who by 1982 had been indited as counter-revolutionaries. Second, the prominent growth through active evangelism of itinerant evangelists drew official attention. International associations interconnected with the fourth, illegal distribution of Christian literature from abroad or copied clandestinely in China. Fifth, any opposition to the TSPM brought condemnation.[199]

Any religious body that did not submit to the leadership of the government and cooperate was treated as a hostile force. The Chinese Communist socialist government utilized all possible influence including the TSPM to bring the unregistered churches in compliance.[200] The PSB agreed that the China Evangelical Fellowship maintained proper conduct, but the fact that they had "evangelistic commandos," a term borrowed from the book *Missionary Sending China*, caused suspicion. Also, they had been charged as a cult, because they were an unregistered group comprised of more than twenty members.[201] Often the government's interconnected authority produced occasions when it had affronted its own policy, as with the "Three-anti Campaign: anti-peaceful revolution, anti-subversion, and anti-infiltration."[202]

Rationale for action must be understood against hearsay as in the issue of registration. As TSPM vice-chairman and general secretary Deng Fucun denounced the rumor that Protestant church members were required to register with the TSPM:

Registration has nothing to do with TSPM. Neither congregation nor member needs to register with the TSPM. The requirement with the RAB is that religious sites must be registered with the RAB. Every Chinese has a registration book, which covers all about them *except* religious belief. My daughter was in Public Concern and nothing was on religious faith. Why? Her boss said China is free in religious

[198] Adeney, *Church's March*, Appendix 5.
[199] Lambert, *The Resurrection*, p. 95.
[200] Deng, 'Church and State', *Tripod*, (1995) 21.
[201] 'Section III,' *CSJ*, (1998) 61.
[202] Deng, 'Church and State,' *Tripod*, (1995) 21.

belief. Today one may believe, tomorrow not.[203]

Tok Kai Hua clarified that if the congregation presented a plan of operation, registration would not be obligatory. The government sensed a threat if it did not understand the motive or interest of a congregation. Consequently, the more undercover a church activity remained the more conflict the group would experience.[204]

Understanding of rationale for policy implementation would reduce conflict. According to Han Wenzao, president of the CCC, there is no limit to biblical teaching in the Chinese churches as had been reported:

> Eschatology and the Second Coming are okay to teach as long as it is biblical. However, some groups promoted stopping work and just praying, because August 28, 1999, was to be the end of the world. Three years ago a Korean said August 28 of that year would be the end. Another group was asked to go to the river and pray and Jesus would come, and finally they went into the river and drowned. This is why training is so important.[205]

The logic behind treatment of religious policy complicated by motive, political views, relationships and understanding brought perspective as to how management was implemented. Christians who use prudence in their church activities without blatantly disregarding governmental aims in socialism could reduce discord.

---

[203] Deng Fu-cun, Vice-Chairman and General Secretary of TSPM, Shanghai view, trans. Wang Jian Guo, 10 September 1999). Italics for his emphasis.
[204] Tok Kai Hua, From Southeast Asia, Engineer in Project Management. Serves in a registered church, Beijing (Interview, 6 September 1999). We Shen, General Manager of Don Shen Enterprise, Parents are Christian Shanghai (Interview, trans. He Yanli, 12 September 1999).
[205] Han Wensao, Dr., President of CCC, Vice-Chairman of Amity Fo Vice-Chairman and General Secretary of China Committee on Rel Peace, Representative to the World conference on Religion and P York, Nanjing (Interview, 14 September 1999).

7
THE HOUSE CHURCHES AND THE TSPM

The phenomenon in China with religion was the interaction of the Chinese Communist government and the TSPM as the Christian Patriotic organization incorporated by Chinese Christians to integrate the Church as a Chinese Protestant religious group into the Chinese socialistic society. As the TSPM represented ˈll Protestant Christians of China, a further dilemma presented ˈˈ in the conviction of some Chinese Christians against any ˈn collaboration with atheists. It was exacerbated by ˈt many independent Christian religious groups had formed before the establishment of the TSPM. ˈplications arose from the interruption of the Revolution when all organized religious ˈn along with the patriotic associations. ˈ of the Chinese Christian Church ˈ Church Movement," which in

ˈre was an era of political ˈastors who wanted to ˈ, there were the leaders ˈfluence. Christians, who ˈ TSPM leadership insisted ˈsts, became distrustful about joining the TSPM.[1] Bishop Ting understood the negative image of the TSPM because it was believed to be a department of the government, empowered to rule over the Protestant Church. As in Guangdong, various governmental levels had considered the TSPM and CCC to be subordinate departments in working together to suppress religious freedom.[2]

Because of the loss of confidence, pastors and believers alike demonstrated a half-hearted acquiescence.[3] However, the fact that the Nanjing Union Theological Seminary and its Beijing corresponding institution had trained over 300 religious leaders during the years just before the Cultural Revolution encouraged the Christian community. These middle-aged leaders formed a bridge for the age-gap of church workers in China until confidence could be built for younger leaders to join the ministry and lead the newly formed churches.[4]

Just because a church had registered as a religious site with the RAB, Britt Towery argued, it did not warrant the reference as a Three-Self church, which was a misnomer. The churches in China were independent entities of cooperative federations with an expression of their faith as a witness to the reality of God in their communities. These churches adapted their activities and message to their contextual experience.[5] Four variations of churches can be identified according to the socio-political context in which they were founded. The first is the *libai tang*, or the "open churches" that identified with the TSPM. Second, the *juhui dian*, or the "meeting points" called "home gatherings" that predate churches and were registered. The third type is the *jiating juhui*, or the groups that were formed where there were no prior churches, and they had registered but had little contact with the

---

[1] Tony Lambert, *The Resurrection of the Chinese Church* (Wheaton, IL: Harold Shaw Publishers, 1994), p. 99.
[2] Bp. Guangxun Ding, 'Bishop K. H. Ting's View of the Present Situation a Christianity in China,' interview by Kwok, *Bridge*, No. 33, (January-February 1989) 6.
[3] Anthony P. B. Lambert, 'The Church in China: Pre and Post Tiananmen Square,' *Religion in Communist Lands*, Vol. 18, Autumn (1990) 242.
[4] Zimin, 'Theological Education in China,' Denton T otz (ed.), *Spring Has Returned* (McLean, VA: Baptist World Alliance, 1986), p. 42.
[5] Britt Towery, *The Churches of China* (Hong Kong: Long Dragon Books, 1987), p. 196.

TSPM. Then there are the *ziyou jiating juhui,* or the "unregistered meetings" that normally met in homes of believers.[6]

As with any organization in China, it was essential for the TSPM to accept the leadership of the CCP and display a patriotic respect for the nation and its socialistic government. In the balance between the Church and the People's Republic there was a precedence of the country over Church. The Church was to re-educate and adapt to the governmental priorities.[7] A Chinese professor clarified that the object of the TSPM was to maintain the Church within the parameters of the government; however, he stated, "Sometimes they lean toward the government too much."[8]

It had been noted that, higher the position in the TSPM, the closer the links were with the CCP and the more political were their activities. A great portion, though, were committed to Christ and to the Church and to ministering to those who attended the open churches. The typical worshipper was simple in biblical faith and in his/her quest for Bible teaching, baptism, the sacraments and Christian companionship. The government's relationship to the TSPM and church was not his or her concern.[9] David Adeney found that there were believers who searched out the speakers who were preaching in the different churches of the city on a particular Sunday to hear the best biblical sermons. Those pastors who had purified their faith through suffering were known for their evangelical fervor, or they may have been involved in the independent home gatherings but had joined the open church that they might effect a positive impact on these congregations.[10]

Towery explained that it had been understood by some that the government paid the pastors of the open church connected with the TSPM. On the contrary, he told of one pastor who confided that the pastors drew their salaries from church offerings and rent from buildings owned by churches that business enterprises in

---

[6] David Adeney, *China: The Church's Long March* (Ventura, CA: Regal Books, 1985), pp. 175-176.

[7] Qingguang, 'Three Self or Not Three Self,' *Bridge,* Vol. 59, No. 1, (May- June 1993), 13.

[8] Wu Qiwei [pseud.], Seminary Professor, New Haven, CT (Interview, 6-9 December 1998).

[9] Authur Wallis, *China Miracle* (Columbia, MO: Cityhill Publishing, 1986) 57-58.

[10] Adeney, *Church's March,* pp. 178-179.

the area continued to use. This pastor declared, "The government and the political party allow and tolerate religion, but they do not subsidize it."[11] The main governmental requirement was for church registration.

The primary reason for registration of a site with the RAB and joining the TSPM was for legality. All social groups had to submit to the Chinese government supervision. To publicly promote Christianity as legal registration was required, and in this way inquirers could be invited to meetings without restriction. New believers may be taught the Bible and Christian literature can be acquired legally.[12] Wang Jian Gao, acting Dean of East China Theological Seminary, clarified that registration enabled the church with its estimated 30,000 meeting points to be more open as a public witness, which was to its great advantage.[13]

The regulations for registration of a group specified that leadership was a necessary qualification. As Director of Chinese Studies at Wheaton College, Dr. Fulton clarified that, depending on the local situation, a group would appoint a leader or be encouraged to join another registered congregation of Christian believers.[14] In areas such as the villages of Fujian and Eastern China, where some of the churches had no leadership, as in one village in May of 1993, the local TSPM committee provided leadership for two of the meeting points.[15] Registration was not to divert or pressure groups to change the substance of their faith, according to Bishop Ting. He sensed that registration according to the regulations would be acceptable to any Christian conscience, but refusal, in his opinion, neither glorified God nor supported the church.[16]

---

[11] Towery, *Churches*, p. 190.
[12] Adeney, *Church's March*, pp. 180-181.
[13] Wang Jian Gao, Acting Dean of Faculty at East China Theological Seminary, Shanghai (Interview, 10 September 1999).
[14] Brent Fulton, Executive Director of Chinasource, Managing Director of the Institute of Chinese Studies at Wheaton College, served 8 years with China Ministries International, served 2 years with Chinese Church Research Center in Hong Kong, Wheaton IL (Interview, 19 November 1999).
[15] 'China: The Untold Story,' *The Voice of the Martyrs*, Servants of the Persecuted Church (1993) 13.
[16] Deng Zhaoming, 'Chinese Regulations Affecting Religious Activities, English translation of documents with editorial introduction,' *Bridge*, Vol. 66, (August 1994) 2. This was from the Editor's Desk as an interview of Bishop K. H. Ting by the *Tian Feng*.

The church order as produced by the TSPM and the CCC on December 30, 1991, demonstrated the plausibility of registration. First, it verified God's call on the church to serve Christ as a community of his followers. The Bible and the Apostles Creed were the foundations of the Church. The Chinese Christian Church as equals, rather than patronized by foreign missions, shared as friends in the universal Church, and endeavored to edify the Body of Christ as well as observe the constitution and governmental policy for social progress. Churches were formed to assist the TSPM in uniting Chinese Christians and sensitizing them to the people's various experiences and needs.

Those inquirers who repented of wrongs in their lives, accepted Christ as Lord, verified by righteous behavior, and passed the exams of catechism classes for Bible and Duties as Christians, formed the church community. After baptism these believers could partake of the Sacrament of Holy Communion.

All who ministered in the church were required to possess a purity of faith and character with a willing heart to serve Christ, and they were to be held in high regard by the parishioners. Church leaders must maintain a superior reputation and uphold the patriotic Three-Self principle. The Bishop, with a broad area of responsibility, had to have been a Pastor more than 10 years with a firm theological understanding. The pastor, as manager of the church, should be seminary educated with three years experience. Teachers were required to have attained a formal theological education and two years experience while Deacons and Elders were to advocate orthodox Christianity and should have had extended experience in serving the church. For the exclusion of heresy and disorder, all gatherings should have endorsed appropriate liturgies with preaching by trained clergy, and a plan of biblical discipline was to be devised for those who committed criminal acts or challenged church instruction.[17]

In January 1992, the Fifth National Christian Conference attempted to change the focus of the Three-Self, which had virtually been accomplished, to the Three-Well movement. The bishop emphasized that the TSPM as an organization was dedicated to

---

[17] 'Church Order for Trial Use in Chinese Churches,' *Bridge*, No. 52, (March-April 1992) 6-9. Passed by the Standing Committee of the TSPM and CCC on 30 December 1991.

the development of the Church, not its destruction. Therefore, he advocated that the people select a pastoral staff that they respected and to whose authority they could trustfully submit.[18] The diversion from pastoral duties for a building program was one example of poor leadership that could not maintain the respect of the church's membership. According to one article, even though the new building was needed and the members had sold eggs, forewent medical treatment, and sacrificed with self-denial of food to donate for the project, there was an over-extravagance in decoration. Then there were groups who had their adequate buildings demolished to build anew because a neighboring congregation had built a large spectacular church. Many members were lost through these types of non-essential activities, which were allowed to dominate the ministry.[19]

The growth of the Church was still evident after the reformation of the TSPM, for in 1980 there were but 13 churches open, and by 1986 there were 4000. Bible printing escalated to the point that they were printed in Fuzhou and Nanjing as well as in Shanghai. The effort broadened from the popular 1919 Union Version to an edition to accommodate the youth with scriptures printed in the new Chinese simplified script that was learned in the revised educational system. The Bible was also printed in Korean and minority languages, and with the continued demand for Bibles throughout China, the Amity foundation and Jiangsu Teachers University initiated the Amity Press for operation in Nanjing.[20] Even though Bibles were becoming more available, the crisis of leadership remained evident with growth from 4,000 churches in 1986 to 7,000 in 1993, plus over 20,000 registered meeting points. In the ten years prior, only seventy-five graduates from the thirteen seminaries of China were ordained for ministry.[21]

Church growth had been phenomenal, but not because of open evangelism. Each Christian was encouraged to be an evangelist through conduct in the market place, at employment and to neighbors. The demonstration of love for people, country

[18] Qingguang, 'Three Self,' *Bridge* (1993) 14.
[19] 'Everybody's Talking About Church Building,' *Amity News Service*, Vol. 7, (March April 1998) 3-4.
[20] Zheng, 'The Place of the Bible in the Life of Chinese Christians,' Denton Lots (ed.), *Spring Has Returned* (McLean, VA: Baptist World Alliance, 1986), p. 50.
[21] 'China Story,' *VOM* (1993) 13.

and church was the key method of evangelism.[22] Due to their evangelism restrictions, the TSPM had endured much criticism from both international and domestic sources. A Chinese Christian professor in New York stated that most TSPM leaders were true to the Christian faith and had worked uncompromisingly in the context of China. He affirmed that authority comes only from God, and God places people in different circumstances to live out their faith.[23] A Chinese news writer, a Christian, confirmed that there were pastors who ministered according to policy; although they had been accused as of being like Judas, they served God within the governmental limitations. She acknowledged that the masses knew about the open churches, and if they had a desire to learn of Christianity that was where they would go.[24] Within its context the TSPM ministered for church growth and accommodated the Chinese Protestants with Bibles and biblical literature, but admittedly had recognized mistakes and deficiencies especially in the number of pastors compared to the Church growth in China.

The phenomenal church growth was mainly due to the house church movement. Home gatherings started in the 1950s, according to a Chinese seminary professor. These were meetings in homes or small buildings of the immediate family or perhaps up to over a hundred people. He acknowledged that some areas of China did not implement the freedom of belief but had criticized religion, which required clandestine activity for some of these assemblies.[25] Bishop Ting described his own experience during the Cultural Revolution when he gathered with a group in homes to have tea, study scripture, and comment on its meaning. When their Bibles had been confiscated, they relied on the memory of Christians who would recite various passages and each would write it in a notebook. They also celebrated the Sacrament of Holy Communion, referred to merely as thanksgiving or breaking bread. As late as the 1987 Ting recognized that even with thousands

---

[22] Shen Chen-en, Associate General Secretary of CCC, Chief Editor of *Tian Feng,* Pastor of Shanghai Community Church, Shanghai (Interview, 10 September 1999).

[23] Meng Xiangzhi [pseud.], Science Professor, New York (Interview, 21 October 1998).

[24] Karen Young [pseud.], Chinese Writer of financial and political news in *Zong Guo Zeng Juang*, a Chinese financial magazine, English Teacher for Children, Beijing (Interview, 5 September 1999).

[25] Wu Qiwei [pseud.], (Interview, 6-9 December 1998).

of churches reclaimed and built there were literally tens of thousands of home gatherings.[26] For those who had converted to Christianity during the Cultural Revolution, this was the only mode of worship they had known and would not be comfortable in a church setting.[27]

Thompson Brown said that the open churches were a small minority of Christian meeting points in China, for the majority of Chinese Christians gathered in homes as did Christians in the first century. Principally in the rural areas, this was the only form of Christian community, for in most villages there were no churches.[28] Wallis claimed that since there usually was no one main pastor in these gatherings, the use of lay-workers had initiated new ministries; one night a week was devoted to learning ministry skills.[29]

Various rationales explained the existence of home gatherings over joining the registered open churches. Some Chinese Christians expressed discontentment with the TSPM, and others cited actual TSPM disregard for their form of worship. The memories of some retained feelings of resentment toward the TSPM personnel for their politically-correct activities against Christians during the 1950s.[30] Some groups with leadership that lacked formal theological training could not register, and there was an unnumbered amount that had no permanent location for meeting as required. Registration was rendered unlawful for those who had not defined their sphere of ministry. Other groups had formed a network of international contacts that rendered them illegal.[31] The CCC associate general secretary Shen claimed that a large portion of these gatherings deemed the Church as a spiritual body that should have no interaction with the government as a human institution.[32] For many, Bishop Ting

---

[26] Ting K. H., 'The Church of Jesus Christ is there in China,' *Currents in Theology and Mission,* Vol. 17, October (1990) 376-377. Address to Lutheran World Federation Executive Committee, July 12, 1987.
[27] 'Communidad Cristiana en China,' *China Avanza* (Beijing: Beijing Informa, 1986), p. 7.
[28] Thompson Brown, *Christianity in the People's Republic of China* (Atlanta: John Knox Press, 1983), pp. 171-172.
[29] Wallis, *China Miracle,* p. 120.
[30] Ding, 'Bishop Ting's View,' *Bridge* (1989) 5.
[31] Fulton, (Interview, 19 November 1999).
[32] Shen, (Interview, 10 September 1999).

concurred, the content of sermons from the open churches had a theological perspective contrary to their view of scripture, or the liturgy did not match their tradition, or even that there were not enough meeting times throughout the week became a point of contention. He argued that they were patriotic citizens who wanted a satisfactory worship experience and should be free to meet without interference. Cadres would prohibit them from meeting because their activities were unknown, but Bishop Ting continued in their defense that personal correspondence also remained private in China.[33]

Qingquang identified the freedom experienced by the home gatherings known as house churches. They assumed the actuality of separation of Church and state and had gone forward on that basis. There was no burden of power or benefit, and they had put the Three-Self principle into action without it being an issue as a goal. Being in isolation, as most were in remote areas, influence and monetary gain from foreign sources were of minimal concern. They also took prayer to heal the sick and hospitality to strangers as part of basic Christian life of the Church. Their greatest fault was the lack of theological training of leadership to distinguish heresies that had emerged in various areas of China.[34]

Systematic pastoral training and biblical teaching for the members in both volume and depth was a factor of need for home gatherings due to their rapid expansion, Jonathan Chao observed. There was a shortage of Christian literature to inform on heretical factions and for intellectuals in the area of science and culture.[35] Methods for the needed training were implemented when the availability of the expertise, a facility, and the means to apply them were in place. Older leaders trained the younger in an experiential format. Where technology was available, videos and cassette tapes were used, but in the primitive countryside these young Christians gathered for night classes and slept in farmhouses or caves.[36] Underground seminaries had been established in secluded areas in caves or up in the mountains where students came for a few months of classes, and each day

[33] Ding, 'Bishop Ting's View,' *Bridge* (1989) 4.
[34] Qingguang, 'Three Self,' *Bridge* (1993) 14, 17, 19.
[35] Jonathan Chao, 'The Church in China: Needs and Opportunities for Ministry,' Myron Ivey (ed.), *China News and Church Report*, 11 May (1998) 4.
[36] 'China: Story,' *VOM* (1993) 13.

was started in prayer at 5:00 AM before a full day of classes.[37] A Chinese professor with a Ph.D. and others with master of divinity degrees established a yearly seminary program of biblical and theological studies for leaders of home gatherings. The curriculum included Bible survey, studies of separate Bible books, systematic theology, hermeneutics, apologetics, and spirituality as well as courses for marriage and family counselling.[38] There were also courses offered by Jonathan Chao, Korean pastors and Americans like T. L. Os and Oral Roberts who sent missionaries to China to train pastors.[39] Many clergy, who had formerly been pastors of traditional churches, became involved with the home gatherings.

The reception of the instruction offered in home gatherings was exceptional. The Chinese were a family and community-oriented people, characterized by mass decisions to become Christian. In the districts where Christians predominated and the churches were large, itinerant preachers visited at the risk of being arrested. Evangelism was done at night or during the times of less work, for since 1982 the government had returned the land to the private farmer and as long as production progressed, there was freedom to be involved in other things. These home meetings were known to exist in all twenty-nine provinces and their 2000 counties.[40]

The itinerant evangelists contributed to the massive growth of the house church movement in China, for they would go with a one-way ticket wherever they sensed God's leading and stay for several weeks. When they left, (using a ticket they bought perhaps by selling their blood,) they would leave conceivably a half dozen established home gatherings. Many in their enthusiasm neglected their health and suffered from bronchitis, tuberculosis, malnutrition, nervous breakdowns, and depressions. In 1995 a group selected 50, from 8,000 of their evangelists, and trained them as paramedics to care for

---

[37] 'Christian Work – China,' *Global Prayer Digest*, www.calebproject.org/nance/n1632.htm, 3/12/98, p. 4.
[38] Ivey, Myron (ed.), 'Profile of a New House-Church Training Program,' *CNCR*, 2 March (1998) 3.
[39] Lin [pseud.], Pastor of *An Ji Ya Tang*, Beijing (Interview, trans. He Yanli, 17 September 1999).
[40] Wallis, *Church Miracle*, pp. 65, 67, 69, 71.

their fellow evangelists and use their skills with the people as a means to evangelize.[41]

Wallis recognized that there was opposition from the TSPM because of evangelism, which encouraged house church leaders to draft a resolution to spread the Christian message clearly with a willingness to suffer. They resolved to meet at night in smaller groups and teach the reality of the Body of Christ. Christian fellowship was increasingly encouraged for the strengthening of the church and spiritual growth with new converts. With a missionary zeal, these evangelists went into remote regions where the message of faith in Jesus Christ had not reached, and they promoted the essential teaching programs for the spiritual growth of new believers.[42] In agreement and defense of the home churches and their ministry, Bishop Ting reasoned that the only way to govern home gatherings was to do nothing but allow them to supervise themselves for any illegal content in their activities. He insisted that there could be a form of intercommunication through contact with the clergy of the TSPM and CCC, without assumption that the house church movement was amiss in management.[43]

In actuality, Alan Hunter and Chan Kimkwong proposed a change in the terminology with reference to the house church movement that would be more acceptable. The term "movement" was misleading with connotation of a clandestine anti-Communist union, and "church" affords the concept of structure with defined leadership and ideology. Their submission for designation of those groups since 1980s was "Autonomous Christian Communities," which was definitive and inoffensive. These communities demonstrated a vibrant faith, conservative theology, evangelistic fervor, informality, spontaneity and flexibility. Their leadership, although usually without much formal training, often proved to be strong charismatic personalities.[44]

On August 22, 1998, an appeal was made to the government in a united effort from the leadership of the autonomous Christian

---

[41] Jonathan Chao, 'The Material Needs of the Church in China,' *CNCR*, 26 October (1998) 3.

[42] Wallis, *China Miracle*, pp. 93-94.

[43] Ding, 'Bishop Ting's View,' *Bridge* (1989) 4.

[44] Alan Hunter and Chan Kimkwong, *Protestantism in Contemporary China* (Cambridge: Cambridge University Press, 1993, pp. 81, 178.

communities from the Henan Province. The logic rested on the imbalance of the 10 million members of the TSPM's open churches to the over 80 million who met in homes, to represent the Chinese Christian Church. This they paralleled with the feasibility of Taiwan's 22 million people to represent China when the mainland population was 1.2 billion. They requested there definition of a cult according International Standard. Their petition included an appeal to terminate official legal action against home gatherings for they had only brought harm to China, and countered the blessing the Chinese people could receive through the message proclaimed by these groups.[45] Effort was made to form an understanding among the TSPM, the government, and these autonomous Christian communities for their mutual satisfaction and benefit.

The government continued to intervene. The use of the Bible as an exceptional work of literature was reinstated, and in 1980 a lecture on the Bible at Nanjing University drew an overwhelming response. However, in the Chinese Academy of Social Sciences the Chinese government founded the Institute of World Religions for studies from the Marxist position. Then in 1982 this institute invited Hans Kung, a German theologian, to lecture on God's existence. Yet, in the year 1983, Deng Xiaoping, in his determination to purge China of the ultraconservative facet of the government, crime and Western influence, assigned an apportionment of arrests and executions for each city. By November of that year more than of 5,000 executions were reported, and unfortunately these included many Christians.[46]

Further, restrictions were implemented in 1992 with a revised policy of registration with the RAB and new religious laws, which the provincial administrative systems augmented.[47] Dr. Fulton substantiated, "The legal status of registration was important, for no social group within the Chinese society could be unconnected with the government."[48] Bishop Ting verified that the problems at the providence level were the cause of negative impact on religious activities. He outlined the quandary with the Guangzhou

---

[45] Glen Braden, 'Faith in Action #8,' *The Discussion Network*, gbraden@visi.net, 29 October (1998) 2.

[46] Leslie Lyall, *God Reigns in China* (London: Hodder and Stoughton, 1985), pp. 195, 203.

[47] Jonathan Chao, 'Projecting,' Chao (ed.), *China Prayer Letter*, No. 125, March (1993) 5.

[48] Fulton, (Interview, 19 November 1999).

Municipal Religious Affairs Bureau, which stipulated that a gathering point might register if the group did not surpass 30 persons. Through this regulation many home gatherings would be eliminated, or forced to go underground, which would enhance religious fanaticism, proselytizing, and antagonism against the government. Ting argued that it administratively deprived people of their constitutional freedom of belief.[49]

Bishop Ting recounted that registered churches also had experienced discrimination in Shanxi, Hebei and Yunnan provinces throughout 1991 and 1992. An incident in Shanxi province involved the No. 9 Coal Mine Church that had been built with the governmen's permission and had properly registered. It was demolished in September 1991 by the PSB on the charge that "it was too prominent." On the other hand, he gave an illustration of how persecution had perpetuated the growth of the Church in Wenzhou of Zhejinag Province. Wenzhou had been declared as "a city without Christians," but then through the tribulations of the Great Leap Forward by the 1950s it had the highest percentage of Christians in China. All maltreatment did was harm the Communist Party's image both nationally and internationally.[50]

The government realized the existence of the autonomous Christian communities, but according to the Chinese scholar Samuel Wang it did not recognize their legality as an approved religious entity. A petition presented in 1997 for the legalization of these communities, was rejected.[51] Progress was made when Bishop Ting presented a RAB clarification that a small group of family or friends might gather for prayer or devotional activities as a part of a church meeting point and would not need to register.[52]

One official, sent to observe if a church had complied with the government policy, told the pastor that at the rate Christianity was spreading, all of China would soon be Christianized. He then joked that the police would be out of

---

[49] Ding, 'Bishop Ting's Views,' *Bridge*, (1998) 4-5.
[50] Kit Law, 'Bishop Ding Speaks Out Against "Wind of Suppression",' Chao (ed.), *China Prayer Letter*, No. 126, (April 1993) 1-3.
[51] Samuel Wang, (Interview, 21 December 1999).
[52] *Amity News Service*, Vol. 7, (January-February 1998) 12.

work if that happened.[53] The admission that Christianity made an impact on China for positive social construction still was met by a socio-political structure that must maintain jurisdiction over any social activity. This was especially true with Christianity with its disputable historical past in China and the element posed by the autonomous groups.

The open churches congregated in buildings built before 1949 or in new structures, while house churches were meeting in private homes. Many of the unregistered meeting points in Wenshou area outgrew their houses and built regular church buildings.[54] Other than differing in theological convictions and tradition, the TSPM continually intended to bring these independent gatherings under its auspices. The People's Government suspected that secret assemblies might produce subversive action; therefore, the TSPM to abide within the Communist system had prevailed in the task to gain the trust of the unregistered assemblies.[55] A professor at a university in Beijing clarified the definition between the groups designated as house churches and those as home gatherings. He explained that there was no intended distinction, but a non-registered gathering cannot be a church unless it is organized. The home gathering, however, was an informal portion of a registered church.[56]

Nevertheless, the integration of religion with politics was characteristic of the registered congregations. Their structure included institutional hierarchy with a cosmic Christology that included social involvement. In contrast, autonomy and a charismatic Christology that emphasized the forgiving, teaching, healing and ethical Jesus Christ, characterized the house assembly, which stressed the life with the personal practical values of the Christian faith.[57] A Southeast Asian Christian engineer who lived and was employed in Beijing discovered the unregistered meeting points to be based on a denominational structure from foreign influence, or dependent on the leader. The registered churches,

[53] Myron Ivey (ed.), 'Getting Acquainted With Relatives In China, Glimpses of Life in the Mainland,' *CNCR*, 2646, 3 August (1998) 5.
[54] Chao, 'The Needs of the Church,' *CNCR* (1998) 1.
[55] Lyall, *God in China*, p. 199.
[56] Carl Franklin Kelly [pseud.], (Interview, 6-7 September 1999).
[57] Paul Varo Martinson, 'The Protestant church in post-Mao China: Two Paradigms,' *Ching Feng*, Vol. 31, No. 1, (March 1988), 20.

nonetheless, maintained a basic liturgy with no programs.[58] When asked why he left the registered church, Pastor Lin said:

> When they preach, they give much on the humanity of Jesus and not enough on the spiritual. The pastors just do their jobs, not because they are called by God, it is just their position... The difference between the TSPM church and the house church is with the Great Commission. The TSPM churches carry it out, but the house churches have a real burden.[59]

The TSPM relied upon social action to complete the Great Commission. Social involvement surfaced in the TSPM-registered churches during the Tiananmen Square incident in 1989. The students from the authorized seminaries and TSPM leaders supported the democracy movement, while the house assembly Christians remained detached from these demonstrations. The Christians of the unregistered meeting points considered participation in political events as worldly or unspiritual and those from remote areas were oblivious to the events of Tiananmen.[60] The differences between the TSPM and the autonomous house assemblies range in world-view, definition of spirituality, emphasis in ministry, understanding, political involvement, biblical interpretation and personal preference.

It had been noted how vocal Bishop Ting had been to include the autonomous Christian communities as legal entities. As early as 1983, there were TSPM leaders in areas of China who had supported and encouraged house congregations and noted their needs for training, Bibles and Christian literature. Bibles had been in so short supply that portions were hand-copied and circulated. As a result, printing of scripture became priority.[61]

No matter what differences may set them apart, the open churches and the unregistered house assemblies had growth as a common factor since 1989 with an especially rapid rate noted in 1997 and 1998. Some whole villages had been referred to as 'Christian villages' with 50 to 80 percent of their population

[58] Tok Kai Hua, (Interview, 6 September 1999).
[59] Lin [pseud.], (Interview, 17 September 1999).
[60] Lambert, 'The Church,' *RCL*, (1990) 143-145.
[61] Brown, *Christianity*, pp. 172-173.

becoming Christian.[62]

In the city of Wenzhou, Jonathan Chao found the relationship between the house congregations and the open churches to have been unique in that the house assemblies controlled the relationship. A select group of leaders managed to maintain contact with TSPM to foster relationship. The dissimilarity between the two groups was indistinguishable, and the house assemblies might even refer to themselves as Three-Self to augment the acquisition of land or permits from the government. Some of the open churches and house assemblies even used the same church facility for worship.[63] Within a five county area around Nanjing there were about 300 meeting points of which several were unregistered. Xu Rulei, a standing committee member of the CCC, said that leaders from the CCC regularly attended these house assemblies and even provided preaching.[64]

Raymond Fung observed forty-two communities throughout eleven provinces, and declared, "nowhere have we discovered the kinds of division that lend support to the theory that there are two Protestant churches in China, the 'Three-Self church' and the 'house churches.'"[65] Bishop Ting affirmed that in China there were not considered to be two Protestant churches as the "official" and the "unofficial." There was no official church for all Christians who honor Christ as Lord embody the Church. In that, religion was a private matter in China; the CCC did not consider itself to be the representative of an official church.[66] In stating their views on the TSPM, five house church leaders concurred with Bishop Ting: "...we hope that foreign Christians do not divide us into house churches and Three-Self churches. There is only one Church with Christ

[62] Chao, 'The Needs of the Church,' *CNCR*, (1998) 1.
[63] Jonathan Chao, 2015, *CNCR*, 27 August (1992).
[64] Xu Rulei, Standing Committee Member of the CCC, Vice-Chairman of Jiangsu Province TSPM, Chairman of Nanjing TSPM Committee, Deputy Director of Center of Religious Studies at Nanjing University, Nanjing (Interview, 11 September 1999).
[65] Philip L. Wickeri, *Seeking the Common Ground* (Maryknoll, NY: Orbis Books, 1990), p. 187.
[66] Ting K. H., 'The Chinese Church Since 1949,' Denton Lots (ed.), *Spring Has Returned* (McLean, VA: Baptist World Alliance, 1986), pp. 24-25.

as its head."[67]   The focal point of both registered-unregistered, official-unofficial, open-underground, TSPM and autonomous Christian communities was Jesus Christ, honored as Lord.

Both the registered open church and the house assemblies were reluctant to accept the young Chinese intellectuals who responded to Christianity. The TSPM saw former Party members as being disloyal, and the leaders of the house groups accused them of attempting to serve two masters, God and Communism.[68] After the Tiananmen Square democracy demonstration when the conservative Marxist Party members seized domination, the disillusioned intellectuals turned to Christianity. According to Lesley Francis, director of the China Program with Overseas Missionary Fellowship, "the house churches and the ...Three-Self churches are having huge problems coping with a terrific influx of converts from the intelligentsia." Conversely, these intellectual converts sensed a shallow teaching in the open churches, as for an "inquirer's class." In the home assemblies, the usually older pastors had rich content to their sermons, but they seemed unable to communicate with the scholarly.

An anti-intellectual atmosphere also prevailed in the house assemblies, where free thought and questioning were regarded as derisive. As a physics graduate from Beijing University told, "I was nearly put out of my house church when I asked, 'Is Genesis literal?'... The leader rebuked me for lack of faith, but I was only asking!" Of the social problems that were brought to these assemblies, Francis said, "Premarital sex is very common among the intellectuals, and divorce may be as high as 50 percent...it is hard for house-church leaders to show the learning sympathy required to deal with them." However, the greatest barrier for the activist academic in a traditional house assembly setting was the apathy for political matters. A philosophy professor in Shanghai related, "We got fed up with being lectured on Romans 13...that the state should only be obeyed if it is a terror to evil... Our government is a terror to good! Why shouldn't we work

---

[67] Jonathan Chao (Interviews), Richard Van Houten (ed.), *Wise as Serpents Harmless as Doves* (Pasadena: William Cary Library, 1988), p. 193. The view of 5 house church leaders on the TSPM.
[68] Lyn Cryderman, 'For God and Deng,' *Christianity Today,* Vol. 34, 10 (September 1990) 18.

to change the government of China? We are not advocating rebellion, just involvement." Both church groups had been found unsatisfactory for the intellectual, and a new facet of home-based gatherings may be established.[69] Many have become involved with international Christian fellowships.

There were new converts who remained Communist Party Members particularly in the Wenzhou area. With determination they retained their membership for the position to exert political influence for change. The traditional home assembly again rebuked such action as hypocritical.[70] The intellectual sector had introduced a practical aspect of life-on-the-edge in China that must be recognized and included in ministry of the Chinese Christian Church.

INTERRELATIONSHIPS OF THE CHINESE CHRISTIANS

The interrelationships of the Chinese Christians involved many facets of the society of China, and the variations of areas within China entailed differences in those relationships. The political atmosphere, the different levels of trust built by the TSPM and the autonomous Christian community's acceptability or international contact determined the rapport. As a Chinese seminary professor claimed:

> Some pastors of the open churches help in some home gatherings, and some people will attend both the open church and the home gatherings. Some of the gatherings are forced underground by the local situation on the religious policy being badly implemented. Some groups want to register but the local government will not allow them to register, but then treat them as illegal. They want to limit development or growth of the Church.[71]

The complexity of the situation in China rendered the Church with flexibility to adapt and grow no matter what the local condition.

---

[69] Ron MacMillan, 'House Church Struggles with New Converts,' *CT*, Vol. 34, 20 August (1990) 39-40.
[70] Ibid, p. 40.
[71] Wu Qiwei [pseud.], Seminary Professor, New Haven, CT (Interview, 6-9 December 1998).

Governmental Relationship with Chinese Christians

Harmony was maintained where the religious groups cooperated with the Chinese government for mutual benefit. One autonomous Christian community, the Jesus Family, gathered in chapels, which were mostly enlarged rooms on a private house, and the *Ye-Su jiao tang*, Jesus chapel, was the only building in the countryside large enough for the propaganda meetings for the local Communists. Therefore, even in the early 1970s because the Communists used the chapels, they implied permission for the Christians to use them also.[72] Bishop Ting admitted that he did not expect over 4,000 churches to be returned for Christian congregations to use after the Cultural Revolution. Since 1980 there was a revival of Christian faith, and those who had met in homes wanted to return to churches for worship. Reports from various provinces verified how the government had restored the possession of these churches to the local Christian believers.[73]

According to Britt Towery, there was an incident in 1984 in Jiangxi Province with RAB officials who decided to wield their authority before the Christian leaders, and they arrested a pastor. The parishioners decided to report the incident to the Residential Area Committee with legal action, and the pastor was released. The RAB admitted that it had acted in ignorance of the constitutional laws of freedom of religious belief.[74] Then in 1996, Mr. Wang of the local RAB told of a case in Jiangsu Province where the local government compelled a church to maintain the road leading to its site. Without the financial resources for the project the tensions rose between the congregation and the officials who finally tried to close the road. However, the local RAB and UFWD mediated and came to an agreement that the County Finance Department and the Christian believers would share the cost.[75]

Rev. Sun Xipei, president of the Zhejinag CCC, emphasized that the positive relationship with the local RAB helps the church

---

[72] D. Vanghan Rees, *The 'Jesus Family' in communist China* (Montreal: Christian Literature Crusade, 1973), p. 55.
[73] Denton Lotz (ed.), *Spring Has Returned* (McLean, VA: Baptist World Alliance, 1986), p. 28.
[74] Britt Towery, *The Churches of China* (Hong Kong: Long Dragon Books, 1987), pp. 202-203.
[75] 'Section III: Protestant Church,' *China Study Journal*, Vol. 13, No. 1, (August 1998) 64.

to function smoothly without internal interference for it bridges the church with society. He admitted that the cadres were better educated, studied religion to better discharge their duties, and did not act so much out of ignorance as in earlier years.[76] Evangelical pastors with positive relationships with the RAB officials promoted more liberty to exercise pastoral duties as desired.[77]

In Longzhan in 1988, no open churches existed but house gatherings were numerous; the government knew of the activities but because of constructive interaction it had never disturbed them from assembling.[78] To fulfill the constitutional policy of freedom of belief was the resolve of the CCP and the People's Republic, and the concern of Christian believers for the practicalities of life was their incentive to support socialism. For the most part, Luo Zhufeng advocated for Christians to adjust their religious concepts voluntarily for the sake of contentment in life that "love of country and love of church" might unite for socialistic construction and "a better paradise on earth."[79]

The balance of ideal implementation of policy varied with RAB cadre ambition to escalate Communist ideology. Some cadres who instigated tension between the government and the Church by imprisoning, or placing fines on Christians and even imposing their approval for the custodial staff used by churches. Under these circumstances, some Christians preferred imprisonment to church registration with the municipal RAB.[80] In Cixi County in 1984 the RAB released an edict with governmental and UWFD approval, but without conference with the TSPM. It authorized eleven Christians to form a church committee to arrange appropriate church activities under leadership of the CCP, but eliminated all home gatherings in that jurisdiction.[81]

---

[76] 'Success Must Not Lead To Complancency: How the Church in Zhejiang Seeks to Grow Further,' *Amity News Service*, Vol. 6, November-December (1997) 21.

[77] Tim Yates, 'US Baptist Conflicts in Cooperating with the TSPM, Part II,' *China News and Church Report*, 2650, 14 (September 1998) 5.

[78] Jonathan Chao (interviews), Richard Van Houten (ed.), *Wise as Serpents Harmless as Doves* (Pasadena: William Cary Library, 1988), p. 115.

[79] Luo Zhufeng, (ed.), *Religion under Socialism in China*, trans. Donald E. MacInnis and Zheng Xian (London: M. D. Sharpe, Inc., 1991), pp. 117-118, 121.

[80] Deng Zhaoming, 'Chinese Regulations Affecting Religious Activities,' *Bridge*, Vol. 66, August (1994) 3. From the editor's desk. English translation of documents with editorial introduction.

[81] Tony Lambert, *The Resurrection of the Chinese Church* (Wheaton, IL: Harold Shaw Publishers, 1994), p. 75.

The government's arbitrary formation of policy according to events in Chinese society affected the Church in China. Rev. Jimmy Lin related that the 1996 implementation of the Strike Hard Policy against crime set up an atmosphere for the misuse of power against independent home gatherings.[82] The apprehension of religion's influence on political strength long reigned over China's leadership. Deng Zhoaming, a renowned Chinese church observer, said, "No emperor would tolerate an organized group that he did not control. In China, Ceasar is above Christ, no question; Christ can never be head of the Church. It's the State that's the head of the church."[83]

The need for CCP domination extended out especially in the area of informative communication, which made the broadcast of a special news bulletin that announced the local Christian activities on Fengjie County TV in 1996 a first for Chinese mass media.[84] Wen Xuandao's report confirmed that governmental approval was also imperative for printing and publishing of religious books. In cooperation with the TSPM or by compliance with prescribed regulations, a printer might be used under the approval of the RAB. Literature published through the TSPM would be without registration numbers for distribution only through registered churches under a long authorization process. An example was the TSPM publication of Mrs. Cowman's book *Streams in the Desert*, which took two years for RAB approval.[85]

In respect for governmental direction, in 1998 four Chinese house church leaders released a statement of their attitude toward the government. They declared their love for Christ, the Chinese people, and the state, and their support of national unity and the harmony of the peoples of China. They supported the constitution, and affirmed that they contemplated no reactionary attitude or action. They vowed never to betray the interests of the Chinese people, but only would do that which would

[82] Jimmy Lin, Rev., 'Nurturing Chinese Christians,' Internet report (1997) 2.
[83] B. Palmer, 'Caesar vs. Christ,' *U.S. News & World Report,* Vol. 123, 4 August (1997) 41-42.
[84] 'Church's Acts of Faith find Wide Publicity,' *Amity News Service,* 97.2.3, Vol. 6, January-February, (1997) 10.
[85] Wen Xuandao, 'Literature Work in Mainland China,' *China Around the World,* March (1998) 16-17.

benefit the nation.[86] This statement reflected an effort to form a relationship with the government without the commitment to the registration process for whatever varied sets of reasons. The Local Assemblies churches of Zhejiang debated the issue of registration, and they sensed that the church belonged to heaven and no earthly registration was viable. Then they reasoned that they were residents of a particular country with obligations as its citizens. They concluded that they were registering a place, the church building, not the Church as part of the Body of Christ.[87]

Often reality toward the government would develop a more positive workable attitude. Just as the question of governmental censuring of sermons in China continued to be forwarded, Dr. Han Wenzao related that a delegation from Hong Kong came to the mainland with this notion. They were asked to preach, and they spoke freely without manuscripts and some without notes but only set of ideas that they wanted to relate.[88] The author verified that the preaching he heard translated from mainland pastors was also very Biblical and not political.

The change in the political climate and relations toward religious leaders and Christian believers was a part of China's norm with shifts of political influence. At the August 1999 annual Beidaihe top level CCP meeting, a conservative Marxist trend of the government followed some decisions made in light of the economic conditions in China at that time. Premier Zhu Rongji announced, "even the economy has to look up to politics." It was on September 7 and 8, 1999, that Christians reported of mass arrests in Lixin County of Anhui Province.[89]

The relationship of Protestant Christians with the state

---

[86] Myron Ivey (ed.), 'Chinese House Church Leaders Issue Confession of Faith and Declare their Attitude Toward the Government,' *CNCR*, 21 December (1998) 7. Shen Yiping represented China Evangelistic Fellowship, Zhang Ronliang represented the mother church in Fangcheng, Cheng Xianqi represented the church in Fuyang, and Wang Chunlu (pseudo) represented another church in China.

[87] Ian Groves, 'In the World But not of the World: Portrait Of An Indigenous Chinese Church Community In Zhejiang,' *ANS*, Vol. 6, November-December (1997) 23.

[88] Ian Groves, 'Interview with Dr. Wenzao Han, President of the China Christian Council,' *ANS*, Vol. 6, July-August (1997) 9.

[89] 'Top Chinese House Church Leaders Face Persecution After Publicity Declaring Their Faith Last Year,' *China Prayer Letter*, March-September (1999) 1.

depends on many factors, some of which were identifiable. Other dynamics depended on location and attitudes of Christians and the authorities of governmental represented organizations there at that time.

TSPM RELATIONSHIP WITH CHINESE CHRISTIANS

Bishop Ting acknowledged that Chinese Christians in 1986, for the most part, had a respect for the TSPM with the Three-Self principle that would be important for Protestants of any nation. In that the Chinese Protestant Christians had a national identity the people assumed a friendly attitude toward the TSPM as an organization.[90] However, in their zeal to unite Chinese Christians with the objectives of the government, the TSPM had condemned former American missionaries and even intentionally forced the issue. This action had caused many Christians to collectively transfer away from the stance of the TSPM.[91] In some areas of China the TSPM had required pastors to proclaim patriotic covenants in their sermons, or issued the 'Ten Don'ts' or 'Eight Don'ts' or disallowed youth under 18 years of age to enter churches. These actions conflicted with any effort to rally Chinese Christians in favor of the TSPM.[92]

Bishop Ting, who had been president of both TSPM and CCC, outlined the relational task of the TSPM. He encouraged an educational approach to introduce new believers to the organization and promote Christian unity whether believers attended the open churches or gathered in homes to worship with the point to glorify God and benefit others. Ting endorsed the opposition of foreign organizations who sustained anti-China underground tactics of illegal evangelism and activities, and encouraged assistance in honoring the government with the accountability for maintaining the religious freedoms guaranteed by the constitution. This was the point of his attack on the conservative Marxist policy since the Tiananmen Square incident in June 1989:

> In some areas the authorities have closed down unregistered meeting-points, that is home-meetings. I think that our

---

[90] Ting (obisbo), 'Protestantismo,' *China Avanza* (Beijing: Beijing Informa, 1986), p. 5.
[91] Towery, *Churches*, p. 92.
[92] Anthony P. B. Lambert, 'The Church in China: Pre and Post Tiananmen Square,' *Religion in Communist Lands*, Vol. 18, Autumn (1990) 240.

TSPM/CCC organizations at every level should explain [to authorities] that this lack of making distinctions is harmful to stability and to the nation... These meeting-points have many good Christians in them, they are also part of the Body of Christ. We should protect them. [93]

Those within the TSPM upheld the right of some unregistered gatherings to continue meeting, because in some areas the authorities had withheld registration, to terminate Christian endeavors. Chinese sociologist Drew Liu exclaimed that it took real courage for Bishop Ting to address the interference of the local government with the Christian church affairs at the Eighth National Political Consultative Conference in 1993. He said it "was an act unheard of throughout communist rule."[94]

An attempt at consolidating all home gatherings under TSPM had been evident in areas of concentration of Christians as in Henan and Anhui provinces. A policy of only one meeting point in every rural district, the span of territory of a commune, was designed to force the issue on unregistered autonomous house churches to join the TSPM.[95] A Chinese seminary professor confided:

Often the TSPM cooperated with the government at the expense of the Church... The churches with weak leadership will be strangled out of ministry by regulations. Those with strong leadership will survive and go underground. There is still some persecution in China for Christians. Usually it depends on the area, local government and church leadership.[96]

Associate General Secretary and Executive Director of the CCC, Bao Jiayuan, explained:

The CCC serves all Christians. China is vast and some local policy is '*Tian guo huang di yuan*,' or 'The emperor is far and I am number one.' So we receive letters of complaint. The implementation of policy is getting better. Some have said, "Why do you want to build a church; why don't you

[93] Lambert, *The Resurrection,* pp. 46-47, 225, 276.
[94] Drew Liu, 'State Policy and Christianity in China,' *China Strategic Review,* Vol. 1, (1996) 3.
[95] Lambert, *The Resurrection,* p. 65.
[96] Wu [pseud.], (Interview, 6-9 December 1998).

go to the temple and worship and become Buddhist?" We refer all of these to the RAB. Most of what we refer to the party is well received and acted upon.[97]

Jonathan Chao, who had been an advocate for the independent house gatherings, agreed with the above evaluations of the TSPM's relationship with the Chinese Church:

> TSPM leaders who are loyal to the state often provide information leading to the arrest and imprisonment of the house church leaders... TSPM...majority...their hearts are one with the people of God who are engaged in evangelism...particularly true with house churches that chose to register with the government because of their size... there are more preachers in the TSPM who share common vision with the house churches than with cadres of the state.[98]

Wang Jian Gao described how the unregistered autonomous Christian communities and the open TSPM's churches relate with each other. He further identified the *ju hui dian* as the house meeting points that supplement the open churches with activities for believers who have irregular schedules, enabling them to meet on Sundays. Wang conceded that the house church movement was adverse to the TSPM, while the home gatherings were those Christians who gather for geographical convenience if a church is not close to their area.[99] A representative of a Chinese firm expressed indifference as to the type of Christian gathering or church he attended:

> The TSPM in China- I don't care about that, I just went to listen. I don't think it is very important if it is TSPM or not. We meet with some Christians and sometimes we worship at home. I never thought the TSPM was a barrier for me to reach God. Now more and more young people go to church. Every Sunday the church is full. If

[97] Bao Jiayuan, Associate General Secretary and Executive Director of CCC Office, Nanjing (Interview, 13 September 1999).
[98] Jonathan Chao, e-mailed material from the Conclusion of his book, *History of Christianity in Socialist China,* (1998) 9.
[99] Wang Jian Gao, Acting Dean of Faculty at East China Theological Seminary, Shanghai (Interview, 10 September 1999).

it is TSPM they don't care.[100]

With the greatest number of Chinese believers in the countryside the important factor for the TSPM according to Han Wenzao was for evangelists to work in the rural areas. In 1995 a rural work committee established a sub-committee to research the availability of lay training materials. This committee was responsible for the rural effort to raise the standard of Christian training in resisting heresy.[101] Throughout China seventeen theological training centers had been established at local, provincial and national levels by the TSPM since 1981 "to match the pace of Christian development" and to bridge "the age gap between the clergy and the church workers." Over 2,700 seminarians had completed training by July of 1995. Most of these institutions had also developed training classes for laity from municipal and rural areas.[102]

UNREGISTERED ASSEMBLY RELATIONS WITH CHINESE CHRISTIANS

The attitude of unregistered autonomous Christian communities usually determined their acceptability. Groups that were flourishing around Wenzhou maintained a working relationship with the TSPM. In nearby county, however, the government retained stringent dominance over Christians and would not allow house gatherings to exist. There were 50,000 Christians with only 140 open churches in the county, and the TSPM leaders did not hold the trust or respect of the Christian communities of their district.[103]

The TSPM and the CCC, as representatives of the Chinese Protestant Christians, must admit that most Chinese Christians were a part of the unregistered independent Christian communities. Some of the house churches criticized the theology and activities of the TSPM and regarded them as hypocrites and collaborators

[100] Liu Yun [pseud.], Former Communist Youth Member, Representative of Chinese Firm, Madrid (Interview, 25 July 1998).
[101] Han Wenzao, 'Build Up the Body of Christ with One Heart and United Effort: Running the Church Even Better According to the Three-Self Principle,' Janice Wickeri (ed.), *Chinese Theological Review: 12* (Foundation for Theological Education in Southeast Asia, 1998), pp. 12-13.
[102] Melissa Manhong Lin, 'A Modern Chinese Journey of Inculturation,' *International Review of Mission*, January (1998) 12.
[103] Thomas Lawrence, 'New Straightjacket for China's Expanding Church,' Jonathan Chao (ed.), *China Prayer Letter,* Hong Kong: No. 123, October-December (1992) 5.

with the anti-Christ. The self-righteousness of these groups blinded them to their own limitations and constructed barriers against others in referring to the open churches as 'Brother who kills Cain' or 'Judas.' Even though some of their accusation may hold truth, they fail to recognize what the TSPM had accomplished in maintaining religious freedoms in China's Communist context. This attitude had generated disharmony and created a barrier for non-believers to accept Christianity.[104]

A Christian Chinese writer substantiated that the relation between the TSPM and the house church demonstrated acceptance on the part of the TSPM while the house churches reserved their tolerance for the TSPM because of their cooperation with the government. She deemed the house churches as shortsighted, for many have grown inward and had become cultic.[105] Still, the house churches maintained the Three-Self principle, which they considered as a policy of the Church rather than a goal,[106] to more of an accurate degree than the open churches, which had many of their leaders educated in the West. Even so, the independent house churches, because they had refused registration, had to operate clandestinely and were considered political deviants.[107]

The leadership of the Little Flock, an independent Christian community of Fuzhou, coexisted with the TSPM without joining it. In this way they had benefited from the legality of the TSPM relationship and continued to act independently but with legal recognition.[108] A report from the Amity News Service, ANS, revealed that over 100 unregistered meeting points in area of Putian, not far south from Fuzhou, had not met the requirements of registration but the county CCC was assisting them to meet these stipulations.[109] Other independent groups had submitted reports just a year later to China Ministries International, CMI,

[104] Alan Hunter and Chan Kimkwong, *Protestantism in Contemporary China* (Cambridge: Cambridge University Press, 1993), pp. 87, 209.
[105] Karen Young [pseud.], Chinese Writer of financial economics and political news in *Zong Guo Seng Juang*, Children English Teacher, Beijing (Interview, 5 September 1999).
[106] Zhang, Richard X. Y., 'The Origin of the "Three Self",' *Jian Dao*, Vol. 5 (1996) 198.
[107] Hunter, *Protestantism*, p. 139.
[108] Lambert, *The Resurrection*, p. 122.
[109] 'Putian Church: Different Traditions, New Developments,' *Amity News Service*, Vol. 6, May-June (1997) 13.

and testified that they had sought to register only to be told that they did not qualify or were met with unaffordable fees.[110]

Even the relationship between some unregistered independent groups remained awkward due to the insistence on traditional denominational faith characteristics. Some groups tended to express a superiority attitude that they held the only truth. There were also those self-centered pastors who wanted to attract a following but overlooked people who may have needed their help but did not serve their purpose. The believers in these cases had to choose between groups or seek another place where their spiritual needs would be met.[111] Pastor Lin of an unregistered independent group in Beijing affirmed that fellowship was maintained between groups through their pastors and national missionaries who communicated. However, any interaction among the members of different congregations was not encouraged, for it might lead to difficulties and "they may become confused by the different points of view."[112]

Furthermore, twelve house church leaders from various provinces gathered in Henan Province to collaborate in drafting the appeal dated August 22, 1998, to the CCP to acknowledge God and the value of Christianity. They called for the release of Christians serving in labor reform camps and urged the CCP accept the fact that there are approximately eight times more to Christians from unregistered groups than in the open churches.[113] As the unregistered Christian communities related to the government, TSPM and each other with varied external and internal factors, the distinction between the areas within China revealed a spectrum of relationships.

PERSONALITIES IN RELATION TO CHINESE CHRISTIANS

Several Chinese Christian personalities known for their international sphere of influence became the focus of governmental

---

[110] TimYates, 'US Baptist Conflicts in Cooperating with the TSPM (Part I),' *CNCR*, 2649, 31 August (1998) 3.

[111] 'Why is Denominationalism Raising Its Head Again?' *ANS*, Vol. 6, November-December (1997) 5. Lou Liquang from Xinyu in Jiangxi Province probed into the reasons for the reappearance of denominationalism.

[112] Lin [pseud.], Pastor of the *An Ti Ya Tang*, Antioch Church, Beijing (Interview, trans. He Yanli, 17 September 1999).

[113] 'Section III,' *CSJ* (1998) 62-63.

attention because of their prominence. Some were known to exhibit their international renown and lacked the insight of consideration as to what the Chinese government might sense as a real or conjured threat to its ultimate authority in China. Others with particular theological distinctions were perceived as advocates of disunity within the Chinese Protestant Church.

Lin Xianguo, the leader of the Guangzhou house church and most popular group of Damazhan, had received letters from USA President Ronald Reagan, and American evangelist Billy Graham had spoken to his congregation in March of 1988. Authorities had arrested Lin on February 22, 1990, and other unregistered house gatherings in that area were closed that night.[114]

Those religious groups that operated outside the approved system of religious polity were often considered heretical, and action was taken against their leadership. The president of the CCC, Han Wenzao, had declared Xu Yongze, the founder of the All-Range Church as a break-off from the Shouters sect to be a heretic and leader of a *xie jiao*, or cultic religion. Xu's arrest and imprisonment in May 1997 became known internationally.[115]

Unregistered autonomus Christian community leader Daniel Kwan had a huge following that had drawn attention, and he was arrested on July 10, 1998. Also the prominence of the Guangzhou congregation of Li Dexian, also known as Samuel Lamb, concerned the Guanzhou PSB and the municipal UFWD enough for them to prepare sanctions for his arrest. Because Li had become an alarming influence in Huadu and had defied their education and warnings, "The Guangzou Public Security Bureau is prepared to send Li Dexian to labor re-education as prescribed under the law in order to hit hard on the fast proliferation of illegal religious activities in Huadu." In China the police were able to sentence a person to three years in a labor camp without a court trial.[116]

Zhen Xianqi was third of the four who had signed the issues of the Confession of Faith of the House Churches to be arrested. As the leader of the Anhui Huyang Church, Zhen was arrested on

---

[114] Lambert, *The Resurrection*, pp. 247-248.

[115] Myron Ivey (ed.), 'House Church Leader to be Sent to Labor Camp,' *CNCR*, 20 July (1998) 3. Interpretive notes on the Official Document of CCP in the city of Huadu.

[116] 'Section III,' *CSJ*, (1998) 59.

September 7, 1999, at the Bangpu train station. He was indicted for the breach of Criminal Law No. 61, which prohibited involvement with a religious cult organization.[117]

There would be a tendency to generalize cases, which were written from a different point of view from outside the system of China. At times the criticism would be too sharp and radical, and the writer could reflect an unjust evaluation.[118] These cases, representative of prominent Chinese personalities, are noted for their leadership in the unregistered congregations. They had not complied with the requirement to come under the management prescribed by the People's Republic of China.

INTERNATIONAL RELATIONSHIP WITH THE CHINESE CHRISTIANS

International involvement stemmed from the needs voiced by Chinese Christians. The need for Bible Scriptures to be printed for the Church immediately after the Cultural Revolution remained secondary for the Chinese Church in the process of actually becoming established again. Therefore, Bibles and Christian literature came from interested foreign Christians and overseas relatives.[119] The Mini-Library Project was sponsored by the China Research Center as a division of Christian Communications from Kowloon. A mini-library included parcels sent into China containing 15 volumes of Bible references and other literature, which was one answer to the need.[120]

The formation of Amity helped in the Christian ministry in China. In Chinese Amity translated as *Ai de,* or the two characters for 'love' and 'virtue,' expressed the means of the Christian message of social action. Relations for its establishment developed from Chinese Christians and internationals.[121] It was founded to promote health, education and social services as a non-government and non-church organization. Even though its president was also the president of both TSPM and the CCC there was not an organizational connection with either of these

---

[117] 'Top Chinese,' *CPL*, (1999) 1.
[118] Wu Qiwei [pseud.], (Interview, 6-9 December 1998). In the interview he mentioned specific names of such writers, which have not been mentioned.
[119] Luo, *Religion in China*, pp. 99-100.
[120] 'Christian Work-China,' *Global Prayer Digest*, www.calebproject.org/nance/n1632.htm, 12 March (1998) 5. The article was from 15 September 1982.
[121] Towery, *Churches*, p. 159.

associations.

The projects of Amity included procuring of international teachers to offer courses of higher education in China, and Amity supported a training program between Cooperative Services International and Nanjing Drum Tower Hospital on nutrition for dieticians in children's schools. They promoted a program of ecology and pollution control and financed equipment for social service agencies. The principle program concerning the Church in China was that of printing Bibles.[122] These projects started with an objective towards modernization of China, to promote the participation of Chinese Christians and to build international relationships. The Amity Printing Press started as a joint effort between the United Bible Societies and the Amity Foundation. Construction on the buildings near Nanjing began on November 8, 1986, and the equipment for the presses was imported from international sources duty free. [123]

The Amity Printing Press was established to uphold the Three-Self principle. As early as 1983 a sign was posted at the Amoy Customs House entry point prohibiting the import of Christian literature. Since then officials ordered university students of Beijing to voluntarily submit all Bibles and Christian materials received from foreign sources or risk expulsion.[124] The message interpreted by the Chinese government, from foreigners bringing in Bibles and Christian literature into China, was that Christianity continued to be a foreign religion with the attitude that it remained above Chinese law. Those who brought the Bible in illegally had caused it to be considered a political document, for foreign Christians claimed that it was the counter response to Communism.[125]

Bishop Ting addressed the ambition that allowed the good will of Christians from foreign nations to be used to smuggle Bibles into China under the merit of internationalism. According to him, this activity was perceived as a political act violating the sovereignty of China and was offensive to Chinese

---

[122] Lotz, *Spring,* pp. 53, 56-58.
[123] Towery, *Churches,* pp. 142, 159.
[124] Leslie Lyall, *God Reigns in China* (London: Hodder and Stoughton, 1985), p. 195.
[125] Towery, *Churches,* pp. 40, 143.

Christians.[126] Broadcasts from overseas were met with the same sentiment from Chinese Christian leaders, for the programming again posed the image of Christianity as a foreign religion to the Chinese government. Also the broadcasts often failed to relate to the Chinese context with its foreign flavor.[127] However, in the 1990s the TSPM and the CCC were intent on cultivating international evangelical relations with organizations that provided Christian literature and broadcasts to support the Church in China and maintained contact with autonomous Christian communities. In 1992 the CCC signed international agreements for assistance in printing Bibles for the unregistered independent Christian communities.[128]

An estimated 19.4 million Bibles were printed worldwide in 1996, and of these 3 million were produced in China.[129] In the first ten years of operation, the Amity Press printed more than 18 million Bibles in China, which had met the demand of the registered open churches. However, the growth and remoteness of the unregistered congregations had made their requests prohibitive to fulfill.[130] Pastor Lin verified that there remained a need among the independent congregations, and their main source continued to be from foreigners bringing Bibles into China from abroad. He related that in Beijing one person could not buy many Bibles from the distribution points of Amity Press to be circulated among the Christian communities in outlying areas. Yet, he had encouraged the members of his congregation to buy their Bibles at the TSPM bookstores.[131]

International cooperation had been built through perseverance, although certain districts were slow in response or perhaps resistant. The government continued to insist on legality via the sovereignty of the CCP and the People's Republic of China.

[126] Ibid., p. 212. An address by Bishop Ting K. H. in Nanjing on May 15, 1986.
[127] Ibid., p. 205.
[128] Lambert, *The Resurrection*, pp. 267-268.
[129] 'News in Brief', *China News Update*, September (1997) 9.
[130] Wen, 'Literature,' *CATW*, (1998) 16.
[131] Lin [pseud.], (Interview, 17 September 1999).

ORTHODOXY, BELIEFS AND LIMITATIONS OF THE CHINESE
CHURCH WITHIN ITS CONTEXT

Dr. Han Wensao, president of the CCC, reasoned that the context
in China, as in any political community, required all religious
groups and individual believers to be accountable to the national
constitution, laws and regulations.[132] An elder of the Little Flock,
Ji Jianhong, citing the authority of the Bible, pointed out that
God established the national boundaries and put each person in
a certain ethnic group. The individual had no choice as to race
or birth nationality; therefore, any Christian who would consider
patriotism to be ungodly might not be considered theologically
reliable.[133] In China, however, no matter how patriotic an
individual Christian, the major threat to a Communistic system
was the ultimate loyalty of the Christian faith.[134]

Chinese Christians proved that they were patriotic citizens and
not backward, remnants of the feudal system or bound to foreign
powers. The ethical practices and discipline of Christian values was
in harmony and supportive of socialist construction.[135] The proof
of the validity of Christianity was in its practice, for the Chinese
had endured the promises of theoretical principle. The action taken
on the ethical instruction of the Christian faith gave power to the
message of Christ. The youth of China had grasped the meaning
of the Christian message of forgiveness and reconciliation through
the death and resurrection of Jesus Christ. The joy and love
demonstrated by believers who practiced ethical relationships and
habits had drawn them to inquire about Christianity.[136] Spiritual
leader and pastor Jia Yuming proclaimed that Christianity was
the "most ethical and moral religion." He pointed out that Jesus

---

[132] 'Statement By China Christian Council President Dr. Wensao Han On China's
So-called "Religious Persecution" 20th June 1997,' *Amity News Service*, Vol. 6,
July-August (1997) 2.
[133] 'Can a Good Christian be a Good Patriot too?' *ANS*, Vol. 6, May-June (1997) 12.
Ji Jianhong, *Tian Feng*, May (1997). Ji was an elder of the Little Flock and Vice-
Chairman of the TSPM. He used Bible references: Psalms 74:17, Deuteronomy
32:8 and Acts 17:26.
[134] D. Knippers, 'How to Pressure China [Persecution of Christians and Most Favored
Nation Status]' *Christianity Today*, Vol. 41, 14 July (1997) 13
[135] Philip L. Wickeri, *Seeking the Common Ground* (Maryknoll, NY: Orbis Books,
1990), p. 90.
[136] David H. Adeney, *China: The Church's Long March* (Ventura, CA: Regal
Books, 1985), p. 111.

Christ had come to fulfill the law, which enabled citizens to act on virtues that transcended status and race with "the way, the truth and the life" into new relationships for the development of China.[137] Christianity adjusted to political demands and in the process made a positive influence on society through a legalized political organization that was intent on identifying with the government as a Chinese religion. In that adjustment there was concern with maintaining orthodoxy in theological doctrines.

BELIEF ENDORSED BY THE TSPM

To preserve focus, support and decisive input, the TSPM became a part of several organizations. Dr. Han Wenzao asserted that the TSPM was a part of the China Committee on Religion and Peace, CCRP and also a member of the religious sector of the Chinese People's Political Consultative Council, CPPCC. The TSPM was enabled to participate and contribute to the national constitution through its membership in the CPPCC. On an international level, as a part of the *Liang Hui* with the CCC, it became a member of the World Council of Churches, WCC.[138]

To the Three-Self principle of the TSPM, self-expression would be appropriate to include, for the product of Chinese Christianity was within the culture lived out in the Chinese experience. Historically the TSPM depicted a post-denominational ecumenical unity. From this perspective, resentment emerged for the concept of two Chinese Protestant Churches in China, the open registered churches and the unregistered autonomous Christian communities. The TSPM was not to be identified as a Communist Christianity but as a Chinese Christianity. The principles espoused by the TSPM were not to advocate China as a closed door, but indigenous and also transnational, intercultural and interdependent with every part of the Body of Christ.[139]   Dr. Han acknowledged that all

---

[137] Sun Jiaji, 'On Relationship: Community and Individuals,' *China News Update,* September (1997) 8. He used the Bible references Matthew 5:17 and John 14:6.

[138] Han Wenzao, President of CCC, Vice-Chairman of AF, Vice-Chairman and General Secretary of China Committee on Religion and Peace, Representative to the World Conference on Religion and Peace in New York, Nanjing (Interview, 14 September 1999).

[139] Yeo Khiok-Khng, 'The Rise of the Three-Self Patriotic Movement (TSPM): Chinese Christianity in the Light of Communist Ideology in New China,' *Asia Journal of Theology,* Vol. 6, No. 1, April (1992) 6.

followers of Christ made up the Church as the Body of Christ in China.[140]

Deng Fucun declared that theologically the Church of China could in all probability be categorized as the most conservative Church in the world. It maintained fundamentalism, not in the Western reference of legalism, in that members believed every word of the Bible was from God. Deng was grieved at the criticism from the West that the TSPM had started printing the simplified-script Bible as having simplified the message of the Bible. He explained:

> The traditional script is quite complicated. Students now use this simplified character so we have made a simplified version. In 1980 we started printing the Bible in traditional characters, and there were rumors that the CCP does not want youth to read the scripture because it was traditional character instead of the simplified. Still the traditional character is printed for the elderly. Rumor said Daniel is not printed in the simplified version. Visitors are invited to look at both to see. The doctrine is not simplified.[141]

A real dependency on the Bible came with the post-denominational era of China. Xin Jian, writer for the *Tian Feng*, clarified that the denominational distinctives were prevalent in many groups, such as observing the Sabbath on Saturday and the ordination of pastors. The goal was mutual respect, to allow religious experiences and approaches to co-exist.[142] The needs of the believers through consideration of their spiritual experiences of liturgy and traditions must be met with respect and mutual tolerance. Effort was promoted to maintain unity in accordance with the Holy Spirit without force.[143] Over the years, the basic tenets of the Apostles' Creed were generally accepted in principle, but there were minor differences in areas such as the celebration

---

[140] Han Wenzao (Interview, 14 September 1999).

[141] Deng Fu-cun, Vice-Chairman and General Secretary of the TSPM, Shanghai (Interview, trans. Wang Jian Guo, 10 September 1999).

[142] 'Section III: Protestant Church,' *China Study Journal,* Vol. 13, No. 1, August (1998) 70.

[143] 'ANS Documentation,' trans. Philip L. Wickeri, *Amity News Service,* Vol. 6, November-December (1997) 11. Chinese Christian Church Order adopted at the Sixth National Christian Conference in January 1997.

of Christmas on December 25. The incarnation of Christ was the common realization that became the point of unity.[144] The fundamental Christian Doctrines in accordance with the Bible were primary in the Chinese Protestant Church.

Christians in Communist China

In his address at the consecration of two Protestant bishops in 1986, Bishop Ting expressed the Chinese Christian's adjustment to socialism. After agreeing with the governmental policy, he added, "It is fine for the Church to be in tune with socialism. If we really abide by the teachings of the Bible, there are no questions that the Church is in tune with socialism..."[145] There was division among the Chinese Christians as to the basis of the government's authority. Some declared the State to be ordained by God while others maintained separation of government from spiritual life, and another view was that the state was the result of original sin in Adam, the first created being. The TSPM held that the State was under God's rule as the ultimate Ruler, and even though the Communist government may be atheistic, God continually worked through it. The Chinese TSPM Christians declared allegiance to their country, but the Three-Self principle also affirmed independence from both foreign missions and the CCP. The Chinese Church functioned through Chinese Christians, and the TSPM did not establish the "official" church. Again Bishop Ting commented that Christians were not to be seduced by Communist atheism, but live with them as a witness for Christ in a holistic approach of sharing the social and individual Christian message.[146]

The slogan for the Sixth National Chinese Christian Conference of 1997 said, "A good Christian should also be a good citizen." Dr. Han acknowledged, "As we understand it, being a good Christian is our identity, being a good citizen is our witness. Only by being a good citizen can we give a good witness."[147] However, the

---

[144] Shi Zesheng, 'Experiences of the Road to Church Unity,' Janice K. Wickeri (ed.), *Chinese Theological Review,* Vol. 3, (1987) 27-28. Documents from the Fourth National Christian Conference, Shanghai on August 1986 trans. William Dockery.
[145] Deng Zhaoming, 'Church and State Relations in China: Characteristics and Trends: A Response' [to Liu Peng pp. 1-18], trans. Michael Sloboba, *Tripod,* July-August (1995) 22.
[146] Yeo, 'The Rise of TSPM,' *AJT* (1992) 4-5.
[147] Ian Groves, 'Interview with Dr. Wenzao Han, President of the China Christian Council,' *ANS,* Vol. 6, July-August (1997) 8.

theology and political task of Bishop Ting through the UFWD agenda was to bring unity between Christians and non-Christians in support of the CCP and the governmental programs.[148] Even though the Church agreed that God ordained the government, it was accepted that Christians, as citizens, must adhere to the government.

Theology

According to Kan Baoping, theology professor at Nanjing Seminary, as far back in Chinese history as the mission era there was a sense that the expression of Western theology would not serve the Church in China. He referred to the theology criticized by T. C. Chao that was of the five characteristics known as TULIP of the Calvinist Synod of Dort, which included Total depravity, Unconditional election, Limited atonement, Irresistible grace, and the Perseverance of the saints. Kan agreed with Y. T. Wu who viewed the incarnation of Christ as God's love to be manifest in society with the Church assuming a role in socialist construction. In an attempt at dialogue between Christianity and Marxism, theologians Chao and Wu supported the program of social construction that the people's government initiated.[149]

The Dean of Nanjing Theological Seminary, Chen Zemin, stated the issue considered central in the theology of China to be that of independence with a critical view of the missionary endeavor. He endorsed identification with the Chinese people in socialist construction in affirmation of the revolution. Chen encouraged unity of denominational traditions in mutual respect, and he promoted evangelism in view of practical "materialism and the Christian faith" within the church setting.[150]

Chen described the theological training within China as a three-layered pyramid. First, for the grassroots lay church leaders serving the tens of thousands of Christian communities meeting in homes, a correspondence course had been designed. Second, the

---

[148] Jonathan Chao (ed. and trans.), 'Three Graduate Students Told to Leave Nanjing Theological College,' *China Prayer Letter*, March-September (1999) 11.

[149] Kan Baoping, 'Theology in The Contemporary Chinese Context,' *ANS*, Vol. 7, January-February (1998) 12-14. He was lecturer in systematic theology and historical theology and member of the Chinese Religious Association.

[150] Philip L. Wickeri, 'Theological Reorientation in Chinese Protestantism 1949-1984 (Part I),' *Ching Feng*, Vol. 28, No. 1, March (1985) 47-48. He outlined the issues of Chen Zemin.

short-term training course, which ranges from two weeks to four months, was intended for those selected from the correspondence courses. The final part consisted of the theological schools of China that offered a two to four-year program.[151] To shape the theology of China the Church's relationship to the government, the Chinese people, and contexts for training needed to be considered.

The Bible

The traditional respect for the classics was reflected in the Chinese Protestant fundamental view of Scripture, for the Bible was viewed as the source of highest authority. As to the relationship between the Bible and science, the youth of China who had been educated in a scientific and atheistic system found it important that Christians affirmed that the Bible and science were in agreement. The Chinese culture promoted a special affinity for the allegorical method of biblical interpretation, and its popularity was also due to the lack of hermeneutic terminology on the part of Chinese evangelists.[152]

The Nanjing theologians urged Christians to ingage with the biblical message as witnesses of the death and resurrection of Christ through the Chinese Revolution. Their concern was for humanization and salvation to be integrated without one superseding the other. The truth of the Bible, within the factors of interpretation to their expression in application towards Christian concern, depended on that theological orientation. The theological task was to place the intellectual understanding of the Christian faith within the context of human relationship in which one lived.[153] The Chinese theologian developed a concern for scripture in social application.

The Concept of God

Bishop Ting observed, "God loves and cares for all people irrespective of their religious traditions or disbelief." Chen Zemin added:

---

[151] Chen Zimin, 'Theological Education in China,' Denton Lotz (ed.), *Spring Has Returned*, McLean, VA: Baptist World Alliance, 1986, p. 43
[152] Ji Tai, 'Hermeneutics in the Chinese Church,' Janice Wickeri (ed.), *Chinese Theological Review: 12*, Holland, MI: Foundation for Theological Education in Southeast Asia, 1998, 139-140, 146.
[153] Wickeri, 'Theological Reorientation,' (Part I), *CF,* (1985) 55.

We are learning not to condemn but to appreciate and respect all the good works of people outside the Christian church and to regard them as coming from God and out of God's all-encompassing Love through the Holy Spirit... God's saving work is not coterminous with the boundary of the church. It has the whole cosmos as its limit.[154]

Ting declared that God's incarnation was a demonstration of his love in identification with human deprivation and the completion of salvation by his death on the cross. This indicated how Christians must regard physical things:

Bodily and material life, intellectual development, the sociopolitical sphere, ethics and morality are all included within the realm of God's love and concern. He wants us to escape from suffering, and enjoy peace and prosperity in a more reasonable social system.[155]

Y. T. Wu reoriented the Chinese theology through his own experience in leadership of the TSPM and the revolution, for in 1952 he wrote, "The one great cause for difficulties some Christians in China are facing is their inability to appreciate the true meaning of God's omnipresence. They are bewildered because they refuse to see God's light which comes through unexpected channels." He referred to the CCP and Communism as a vehicle God used for human development for all good works come from God.[156] God, in his encompassing love, had considered China at the point in history when he could use Communism in fulfilling his purpose for the Chinese people.

The Concept of the Cosmic Christ

Chen Zemin proposed the theological Trinitarian concept of the Cosmic Christ as the incarnation of God who dwelt among us, who in his humanity comprehended God's power to create and to deliver from sin and gave purpose in human history.[157] Melissa

---

[154] Melissa Manhong Lin, 'A Modern Chinese Journey of Inculturation,' *International Review of Mission*, January (1998) 10.
[155] Ding Guanggxun, (Bishop), 'Another Look at 3-Self,' *CF*, Vol. 25, No. 4, December (1982) 254.
[156] Wickeri, 'Theological Reorientation,' *CF*, (1985) 41-42. Wu referred to the Bible reference of James 1:17.
[157] Chen Zemin, 'Theological Reflections,' Ting K. H. *Chinese Christians Speak Out*, Beijing: New World Press, 1984, pp. 45-46.

Manhong Lin captured the Christology of Chinese theology as focused on Apostle Paul's writings to the Colossians and the Ephesians in the Bible. In these books Jesus Christ was depicted as in the image of God, and he was the creator and sustainer of all things, even dominions and powers. All was placed under his power for his Body, the Church.[158]

Chen summarized the concept of the Cosmic Christ as the revealer of God's love throughout the process of creation and His sanctification of it along with the plan of redemption. Chen then linked the Holy Spirit to have brought all creation together under the wisdom and capacity of the Triune Godhead. He maintained that people were created in the image of God with freedom of will, distinguished from other life forms by the ability to accumulate knowledge.[159] Christ as the essence of God's love in creation and incarnated redemption was posed as the sustainer of all for the Church, His Body of believers.

Concept of Sin

Culturally the Chinese people were attached to the physical world especially in the era of secularism. Therefore, they were less responsive to the transcendent aspects of Christianity. Also, their Confucian concept that man was inherently good inhibited their acceptance of the Christian concept of sin.[160] To the Chinese the concept of one being a sinner, as verified by Bishop Ting, was scorned, and the foreignness of it provoked resistance to the Christian message. Nevertheless, he exclaimed that this concept could not be eliminated to make it more palatable, for without it redemption became meaningless.[161] Socialism cannot alleviate the need for salvation, but as Bishop Ting affirmed, it could only limit the effectiveness of sin without bringing solution to it. He asserted that only forgiveness, salvation and grace, not social progress, could bring healing for the sin problem. Chen

---

[158] Lin, 'A Chinese Journey,' *IRM*, (1998) 9. She referenced the Bible Colossians 1:15-17 and Ephesians 1:22-23.

[159] Chen Zemin, 'Relations Between Christianity and Intellectuals Since Liberation (1949),' Gail V. Coulson (ed.), *China Talk*, Vol. XXIV April (1999) 22-23.

[160] Zhao Fusan, 'Prospects of Christianity in China,' Janice Wickeri (ed.), *Chinese Theological Review*, Vol. 3 (1987) 15. Documents from the Fourth National Christian Conference in Shanghai on August 1986.

[161] Ding, (Bishop), 'Another Look,' *CF* (1982) 258.

expressed full agreement with Bishop Ting, then introduced the concept of redemption beginning with the love of God rather than the depravity of the world.[162]

The Chinese could not comprehend the concept of sin as self-assertion against God, but Chen Zemin confirmed that they understood sin "as the concept of a failure to obey the two great commandments or violate God's will in human relationships." The theological task for China did not include liberation but reconciliation to God, from whom the whole of the human race had been alienated.[163] As a Chinese Christian, Shen Yefan defined freedom in the context of China to pertain to two aspects: freedom from sin by Christ and freedom to serve God to whom Christ brought us into harmony. He pointed out that freedom, as an end unto itself, would lead to licentiousness.[164]

Chen Zemin held that people were not complete in perfection but still working together with God in the whole of creation even with weaknesses and inadequacies. The redemption and sanctification of Christ was needed to expiate sin, the disobedience to God's will, to progressively acquire the stature and holiness of Christ. Consequently, "all who act in accordance with God's will putting into practice…righteousness… are looked upon with favor by God."[165] The definitions of sin, sinner and freedom became the focal point in the theology of redemption for the Chinese mindset toward Christianity.

Concept of Evangelism

Philip Wickeri described the Chinese concept of a living theology as that which developed out of a faith encounter with contemporary historical reality. It was an attempt to discover the meaning of the Christian faith in the circumstance of suffering. This theology presupposes the validity of involvement as well as a critical reflection on that participation. He wrote of Luo Zhenfang's opposition to the interpretation of Christian-non-Christian relationship, for his perspective included all of those who do

---

[162] Wickeri, 'Theology Reorientation,' *CF* (1985) 52-53.

[163] Chen, 'Theological,' Ting, *Chinese Speak*, p. 50.

[164] Shen Yifan, 'Freedom as Viewed by a Chinese Christian,' Ting K. H., *Chinese Speak*, p. 76. Shen referenced in the Bible Galatians 5:1, 13; I Peter 2:16 and Romans 6:16-22.

[165] Chen, 'Relations,' Colson (ed.), *CT*, (1999) 23.

justice, and maintained faith as what he referred to as, "reserved difference." However, Wickeri referred to Huang Xianglin who asserted that the Christian perspective must understand God's will as a new life in Christ to become heirs of God, which sets the Christian apart from the non-Christian.[166]

The Chinese argument was that God deemed creation to be good therefore Christians should be intent on its improvement through creative labor rather than its transcendence due to the removal of sin.[167] Consequently, Chen Zemin found that there was a shift from the traditional evangelism for Church growth to the improvement of the quality of the church relationship with the Chinese people through compassion and service.[168] Bishop Ting agreed with Chen that the arrogance of Jonah toward the Ninevites in pointing out their sin must be rejected, for "We should welcome any and every move Godward on the part of men and women no matter how slight."[169] C. T. Chao wrote in 1956, "Our duty to Christ is to love men in a practical way, in practice; and again in practice." In 1973 he again spoke, "Religion has no name in China today; it is not based on doctrine, dogmas or hypotheses, but practice."[170] The practical service to people in the improvement of society rather than individual salvation from sin encompassed the theological position of evangelism held by the TSPM in China.

View regarding Eschatology

As the Chinese Christians emphasized an appreciation of creation and society, world-affirmation in expectation of progress supplanted apocalyptic and eschatological issues. From what they regarded as impending themes of destiny, their attention was directed to a sense of future hope.[171] Chen questioned the

---

[166] Wickeri, 'Theological Reorientation,' *CF,* (1985) 43-44, 113-115.
[167] Ibid., p. 107.
[168] Chen, 'Theological,' Ting, *Chinese Speak,* p. 47.
[169] 'SBC Works with Liberal China Christian Council,' http://www.whidbey.net, 11 September (1998). From Bishop Ting's lecture of September 23, 1984 at Rikkyo (St. Paul's) University in Tokyo, Japan under the sponsorship of the Anglican-Episcopal Church of Japan. Written by Ting K. H. as an article 'Theological Mass Movements in China,' for *International Bulletin of Missionary Research,* July (1985) 98. Bishop Ting referred to the Bible reference of Jonah 3:4.
[170] Wickeri, 'Theological Reorientation,' *CF* (1985) 40-41.
[171] Ibid., p. 108.

validity of the traditional eschatology, but agreed with Jurgen L. Moltmann, a German theologian, in his "etymological analysis and criticism that the term *eschatology* (*eschatos* and *logia*) is wrong." Chen approved of his theme of hope, and asked, "Why speculate on the last things when history is just beginning?"[172] *Streams in the Desert* by Lettie Cowman came under attack for its exclusion of human effort for social change, but rendered the Christian message with pessimism and emphasis on suffering. According to Wickeri the important aspect was to find the origins of suffering in society for the discovery of the biblical hope that Jesus had overcome the world as the message of liberation.[173]

In 1999 CCC general secretary Shen Chenen declared that no restrictions were mandated on preaching on eschatological subjects. Nonetheless, these themes were not to be emphasized because some groups forewent going to school and work centers for Jesus Christ was coming. He cited articles in the August and September 1999 issues of *Tian Feng*, the TSPM magazine that he edited, which featured the themes of the Second Coming of Jesus and on the last days. He said, "We preach on the resurrection, Second Coming, and both the Apostles' and Nicene Creeds."[174] There remained sincerity to all biblical themes for Chinese Christians, though a positive outlook on efforts to change society towards progression and hope forthcoming.

Seminaries

In the Nanjing Union Theological Seminary the curriculum carried a strong emphasis on biblical studies. The unique feature of the seminary was the incorporation of both the conservative and liberal perspectives. In the 1950s there were separate courses for each of the viewpoints, but in the 1990s they changed so that the same course was taught by two different professors of the different positions for an overall exposure to the student-body.[175] Bishop Ting had introduced a pluralistic or even a relative theology for the support of the socialist construction program of the CCP, while

---

[172] Chen, 'Theological,' Ting, *Chinese Speak*, p. 48.
[173] Wickeri, *Seeking*, pp. 264-265.
[174] Shen Chen-en, Associate General Secretary of CCC, Chief Editor of *Tian Feng* and Pastor of Shanghai Community Church, Shanghai (Interview, 10 September 1999).
[175] Wickeri, *Seeking*, p. 277.

some of the younger faculty had a strongly committed evangelical theology based on the authority of the Bible as the standard for faith and life.[176] The author became acquainted with and interviewed faculty at the Nanjing Seminary of both perspectives.

Chen Zemin stated the development in theology advocated to teach in the seminaries was from *Selected Works of K. H. Ting*, which were printed by the end of 1999. These works were intent on adaptation to the Communist setting. A series, *Selected Papers of Nanjing Seminary* from conservatives, indicated that Bishop Ting was too liberal. The doctrine of dispensations with its seven stages of God's providence and the pre-millennial view of the rapture of the saints before the thousand year earthly reign of Jesus Christ promoted by the Little Flock were not part of the curriculum.

Personally, Chen did not believe in the infallibility of the Bible, but that God revealed His will over a period of time in a crude manner. God's revelation, Chen reasoned, then was continually exposed through all of history. Between creation and evolution, Chen held that the open mind would not accept the account in Genesis of the Bible and evolution was a theory with missing links. In the area of marriage he followed the reasoning of the State, in that with such a major gap between the number of Christians and non-believers, it should not be a church issue if the one married the other. However, in that seminaries were co-ed, he said that couples "later in their studies it is hoped they will couple up and become coworkers in the Church ministry."

Chen continued that theology in China had developed with cultural and contextual properties to accommodate the political context. He maintained that there was the urgency to be all things to all people but to remain true to the gospel. He observed:

Truth, good and beauty outside the Church all came from God. Inclusiveism is what I stand on for a socialized society, for those of these values are by the grace of God. Salvation is for those who will do God's will, anonymous Christianity. Christ is our Savior and revealer of God's will. I do not totally agree with substitutional redemption.[177]

---

[176] Chao, 'Three Students Leave,' *CPL*, (1999) 7.
[177] Chen Zemin, BD., DD., Professor of Theology at Nanjing Union Theological Seminary and Center of Religious Studies at Nanjing University, Nanjing (Interview, 13 September 1999).

The acting dean of faculty at East China Theological Seminary, Wang Jian Gao, affirmed that he taught theology and doctrine with no restrictions, "for we must be able to teach all biblical subjects such as the resurrection, miracles, the Holy Spirit, etc."[178] In China's seminaries a curriculum balance developed between the conservative and liberal interpretation of biblical doctrines to fit the sociopolitical context.

Aspects of Belief in the Rural Areas of China

Han Wenzao recognized that in order for the Church in China to progress there must be attention given to the rural churches. Most leaders in the countryside meeting points were lay workers with little systematic theological training, and they found it difficult to discern truth from heresy. A training program for these laymen took priority for several years.[179] Pastor Mei Chuan toured the rural suburbs and counties surrounding Wuhan, the capital city of Hubei Provience, in 1986 and again from April to August in 1996. On his first tour Pastor Mei observed:

> Churches would appoint special people to heal sick and cast out spirits, while some people shout and call out during meeting as if possessed, kicking their feet, rolling about the floor and trembling violently. Others would spread strange visions and dreams.

The second tour revealed the results of the municipal CCC training classes. There was evidence of understanding about normal religious activities of the Christian faith and superstition.[180] To be unable to read the Bible had inhibited the churches' ministry with the great numbers of converts in the remote rural areas, not that education would be equated with spirituality.[181] The problems

---

[178] Wang Jian Gao, Acting Dean of Faculty at East China Theological Seminary, Shanghai (Interview, 10 September 1999).
[179] Han Wenzao, 'Build Up the Body of Christ with One Heart and United Effort: Running the Church Even Better According to the Three-Self Principle,' Janice Wickeri (ed.), *Chinese Theological Review: 12*, Holland, Mi: Foundation for Theological Education in Southeast Asia, 1998, 37.
[180] 'From Chaos to Order: Churches Around Wuhan Revisited,' *ANS*, Vol. 6, July-August (1997) 11-12.
[181] Tony Lambert, *The Resurrection of the Chinese Church* (Wheaton, IL: Harold Shaw Publishers, 1994), p. 134.

of illiteracy and lack of formal training revealed the urgency of concentrated attention to lay leadership training within the rural churches.

UNREGISTERED AUTONOMOUS CHRISTIAN COMMUNITIES

Four leaders of the unregistered groups issued a document on their faith and attitude toward the government. In it they declared their belief in the Holy Spirit's infallible inspiration of the 66 books of the Bible as interpreted in its historical context. They accepted that Bible interpretation was through other biblical Scriptures, but not out of the context of the biblical passage. Their theological view of God was Trinitarian with each Person of the Trinity manifesting specific functional roles, and all in unity were to receive worship in spirit and truth. God the Father in His omniscience, omnipresence and omnipotence created the universe and all in it. Man was created, but Jesus as the eternally begotten Son was not created, and the Father and Son sent the Holy Spirit. Jesus as the Son identified with man in human form to endure temptation without succumbing to it. Jesus willingly was crucified to redeem from sin and death those who believe in him. He ascended into Heaven after his resurrection and sits on the right of the Father, and he will return to earth to judge the world.

Their confession of salvation relied on grace through faith with the evidence of salvation in the reception of the Holy Spirit by faith, for he led them to understand truth, and into an abundant life through obedience to Jesus Christ the Son. The Holy Spirit also gave power for miracles to the Church. The Church as the Body of Christ, with Christ as the head, was local and universal for all churches of orthodox faith and all believers throughout history.[182]

Jonathan Chao witnessed divisions among these autonomous groups over issues of traditional preference as to whether or not women should cover their heads while worshipping in the church, the Sabbath, and baptism. In one mountainous area where there were no preachers, they asked an elderly man to speak; however, his understanding of Christianity was mixed with Confucian

---

[182] Myron Ivey (ed.), Chinese House church Leaders Issue Confession of Faith and Declare their Attitude toward the Government,' *CNCR*, 21 December (1998) 2-5.

teachings and Buddhism. In some areas that had no Bibles and little understanding of salvation, the believers had remained at a stage of healing for their faith. Upon the healing of one who had been prayed for, the believers would build a meeting point to repay their vow.[183]

The unregistered meeting points had a warm simple faith and consuming zeal, but they needed Bible teachers with a mature faith. Leslie Lyall quoted an elderly pastor who in analogy said, "Before the Communists came, I remember that shepherds were searching for sheep. But now, all over China, it is the sheep who are searching for shepherds."[184] The problem with the unregistered gatherings was lack of theological training and the standardization of traditions of doctrine, which caused disunity and misunderstandings of Biblical truth. It was not for lack of faith and commitment, but they lacked the availability of trained Christian teachers.

THE MIRACULOUS

Alan Hunter found that a core feature in traditional Chinese spiritual life had been entreaty to spiritual beings for healing and exorcism. The Christians required a new orientation, but in reality the essence of custom remained.[185] According to Arthur Wallis the TSPM sought to discourage healing,[186] and the CCC asserted that Jesus's mission on earth, "was to preach the good news of the kingdom of heaven, rather than drive out demons and heal the sick."[187] Wang Sanyuan, a writer for *Tian Feng*, stressed that faith should be founded on the Bible and not in healing experiences alone. He cited the Bible warning that not only God but Satan could also do miracles, and many heretical groups used miraculous displays to deceive people to join them.[188]

---

[183] Jonathan Chao (Interviews), Richard Van Houten (ed.), *Wise as Serpents Harmless as Doves* (Pasadena: William Cary Library, 1988), 108-109, 146-147.

[184] Leslie Lyall, *God Reigns in China* (London: Hodder and Stoughton, 1985), p. 183.

[185] Alan Hunter and Chan Kim-kwong, *Protestantism in Contemporary China* (Cambridge: Cambridge university Press, 1993), p. 146.

[186] Arthur Wallis, *China Miracle* (Columbia, MO: Cityhill Publishing, 1986), p. 127.

[187] Corporate Author China Christian Council, 'One Hundred Questions and answers on the Christian Faith,' *The Chinese Theological Review*, Vol. 1 (1985) 220. They made reference to the Bible in Luke 4:40-44.

[188] 'How Should We Regard Miracles?' *ANS*, Vol. 7, May-June (1998) 4. Wang Sanyuan cited from the Bible in Mathew 24:24 and II Thessalonians 2:9.

Chen Liya recorded a case of malpractice in the Hunan Province when he exposed a group of believers that opposed medical assistance and medication with belief in prayer only, while deterioration of the condition was attributed to sin or lack of faith. He discerned that this afforded a reason to doubt God's existence or acquire the attitude to believe in Jesus only when they became ill.[189] Mr. Wang, a lay leader of a congregation, encouraged a woman to disregard the use of medicine and rely entirely on the Lord, and within four days she died.[190] In Eastern China Jonathan Chao recognized the theological problem of belief in Jesus Christ as the great doctor. After expanding their view that he was the great healer and the Lord of salvation, they recognized that their understanding had been inadequate.[191]

Official accounts from the *China Daily* dismissed the growth of rural Christianity as an atypical healing cult of peasants who lacked medical facilities and sought healing in Jesus. However, evidence revealed that those healed often experienced a more profound orthodox Christian faith later.[192] Liu, the elder of an unregistered gathering, established that his church believed in praying to heal the sick, but they also encouraged medical treatment to accompany the prayers.[193] TSPM vice-chairman Deng Fucan said that it was merely temptation for those who had medical facilities available to have thought that they could rely on the Lord to get well and even save money. He recognized Jesus as the final resource when medical sources had been consulted without results, much like the Bible account of the woman who had seen many doctors and finally touched Jesus' garment and was healed.[194] The illusion of free and quick medical help through healing consisted of the extent of widespread miracle expectations in China, although there had been verified cases of biblical prayers for healing that resulted in

[189] Cheng Liya, 'Section III: Protestant Church,' *China Study Journal*, Vol. 13, No. 1, April (1998) 96.
[190] Martinson, Paul Varo, 'The Protestant Church in Post-Mao China: Two Paradigms,' *Cheng Feng*, Vol. 31, No. 1, March (1988) 15.
[191] Chao, *Serpents Doves*, p. 104.
[192] Lambert, *The Resurrection*, pp. 112-113
[193] Liu [pseud.], Elder of the *An Ti Ya Tang*, Beijing (Interview, trans. He Yanli, 16 September 1999).
[194] 'ANS Documentation: An Interview with Luo Guanzong,' *ANS*, Vol. 6, May-June (1997) 19. Referred to the Bible book of Matthew 9:20-21.

healthy recoveries and growth in the Christian faith. The majority of Chinese Christians recognized that ultimately all healing came from God whether medical resources were used or not.

CHRISTIAN SECTS

Ye Xiaowen, director of the RAB, defined a sect of a religion to be multifaceted and incompatible with the orthodox and other sects of that religion. The sect took the scriptures and infused diverse and opposing interpretations.[195]

The Jesus Family was labeled as a sect from its communal lifestyle that fostered separation through compound type of living. It was formally disbanded in 1950, for the CCP viewed it as a feudalistic attempt at socialism and an obstacle to progression in the Shandong Province. The leader, Ching Tienying, was arrested in 1952. The communities were dissolved and the Jesus Family was reorganized into churches.[196]

The TSPM chairman, Lou Guanzong, gave an account of one sect that claimed knowledge as to the date of the establishment of the kingdom of heaven, and they stopped working and sold their possessions to wait for the Second Coming of Jesus. Finally, they were completely destitute, and the government intervened to prohibit their activities.[197]

Jonathan Chao described some of the sects prominent in China, such as The Way of Fasting, a group that advocated eating only one meal each day, but they did not attract many adherents. Another sect was The Seventh-Day Adventists who were known for their honor of the Sabbath on Saturday, but also prayed facing west toward the front gate of the Temple in Jerusalem. Their women believers wore veils, and they insisted on baptism by immersion. Still another group unique to Henan Province was called the Four-Gospel Sect, and they preached only from the four books of the Gospels in the New Testament and criticized the Apostle Paul.[198]

---

[195] Ye Xiaowen, 'Appendix X: China's Current Religious Question: Once Again an Inquiry into the Five Characteristics of Religion,' Human Rights/Asia, *China: State Control* (New York: Human Rights Watch, 1997), 134. Ye Xiaowen was Director of RAB and this article was from 'Selection of Reports of the Party School of the Central Committee of the Chinese Communist Party,' No. 5, 1996.
[196] Wickeri, *Seeking,* p. 161.
[197] 'ANS Documentation: An Interview with Luo Guanzong,' *ANS,* Vol. 6, May-June (1997) 7.
[198] Chao, *Serpents Doves,* p. 136.

Chao reported that the authorities of Henan Province in October of 1989 averted a mass suicide advocated by a woman preacher who had encouraged her congregation to drink poisoned liquor to accelerate the Second Coming of Jesus Christ. Another incident claiming Jesus' imminent return took place in the village of Fang Cheng, also in Henan Province. A stranger in the area promoted escape from the life of drudgery through the joy of seeing the Messiah who would meet them at the river nearby. After the people gave money, they gathered at the river to wait for Jesus, and their wait turned to disillusionment. Finally, in a step of conviction, the group entered the water where 20 drowned. Chao recounted the details of a church group in Zhejiang Province that prophesied of the Second Coming of Jesus on April 18, 1991. The people slaughtered and ate their animals, abandoned crops, and dressed in their best to be ready for His coming. April 18 came and went with the disenchanted believers left gazing into the heavens.

Chao also reported cases where some killed their sons in sacrifice to emulate Abraham of the Bible who had been called on by God to sacrifice his son Isaac, but God had intervened on Abraham's behalf. Others drowned in attempting to walk on water as Jesus had done.[199] Paul Martinson recounted the case of a charlatan who claimed power to convey the Holy Spirit to young women through a purification rite of fondling their nude bodies.[200] Over-zealous Christians whose ignorance was drawn by blind faith and perpetrated by untrained or dishonest leadership, led to disillusionment in sectarian beliefs.

The Wilderness Sect and the Disciple Society

The two sects known as the Wilderness Sect and the Disciple Society by 1992 had recruited more than 30,000 followers from Ankang district and over 10,000 from the Yunyang area. They had been known to batter security officials and work-group members as well as make verbal attacks on the local government and disrupt their meetings. They had caused casualties with firearms and had used religious façade to promote rape and defraud for money and properties.[201]

[199] Jonathan Chao, 2009, *CNCR*, 7 August (1992). Referred to the Bible book of Genesis 22:1-14.
[200] Martinson, 'The Protestant,' *CF* (1988) 13.
[201] Hunter, *Protestantism*, p. 264. Quoted in *Freedom of Religion in China*, Asia Watch, January (1992).

The All-Range Church or the Yellers

The Yellers sect, the most notable of the sect movements, apparently was an unorthodox form of a Pentecostal faction in Zhejiang, Fujian and Henan provinces.[202] In the early 1980s Xu Yongze split from the Yellers, also known as the Shouters, and in 1984 established a group called the All-Range, Holistic or Full-Scope church. He claimed that crying out was the only mark of the Spirit, and crying must be exercised in prayer and worship. He said, "You need to cry and sob out loud, for only then can you be reborn to salvation." He claimed that the end of the world was near with imminent disaster.[203] Many people abandoned their work to participate in orgies of weeping and lost their means of sustenance, and many had mental breakdowns. Some were reported to have gone blind, and another portion committed suicide. In 1988 at Beijing, Xu was sentenced to three years of labor reform, and after his release in April of 1991 he intensified his efforts in the movement. In June 1997 the Zhengzhou City Public Security Department in Henan Province arrested Xu, and he was sentenced to three-year imprisonment for social disorder.[204] According to CCC president Dr. Han, "The detaining of Xu is definitely not persecution of Christians by the Chinese government but a normal handling of a criminal prosecution."[205]

Through the course of cultivating fellowship with Christians, influenced by the Yellers in Sheng County and Xinchang in Zhejiang Province, those from the registered open churches shared spiritual truth. They eventually recognized that the open churches maintained a God-fearing faith, and the natural consequence was for them to join the TSPM as part of the recognized Church in China.[206]

Regardless of religious belief, all Chinese citizens shared in the

---

[202] Wickeri, *Seeking*, p. 237.

[203] 'Statement by Han,' *ANS*, (1997) 1-2.

[204] 'China Issues Commentary on US Human Rights Report,' *Beijing Review*, 23-29 March (1998) 12.

[205] Xinhua, 'President of Christian Council Defends Christianity in China,' Beijing: www.chinanews.org, (1997) 1.

[206] Shen Xilin, 'Seeking the Common Ground and Unity,' trans. Janice K. Wickeri (ed.), *Chinese Theological Review*, Vol. 3, (1987) 40. Documents from the Fourth National Christian Conference, Shanghai, August 1986.

constitutional rights and responsibilities. If one were to be found guilty of criminal action, he or she would be prosecuted according to law. However, a citizen would not be detained or arrested for religious beliefs or participation in normal religious activity.[207] The governmental authorities viewed sects as detrimental to social order, and the TSPM supported the CCP and People's government on both political and theological grounds against the sects with illegal and separatist tendencies.[208] The difficulty arose on defining a sect over the peculiarities of an unregistered group that followed orthodox theology.

CULTS

In 1998, the Far East Broadcasting Company received 13,800 letters from Chinese listeners, and 530 of those referred to harm caused by the different cults in China.[209] As defined by Ye Xiaowen a cult was "a mutation of religion" or heresies by rogue elements with secret societies that use "fragments from religious scriptures" and mix fallacy with doctrine, and they were to be eradicated by Chinese law.[210] A Taiwan researcher, Dr. Edwin Lee, believed the People's government wanted an adverse definition for cult, such as *xie jiao*, a cultic religion with closed content in its doctrine. The members had tendencies to look inward and did not live as normal citizens of society. He claimed that with this designation the government could assume legal action against the group.[211]

The characteristics of a cult included recognizing authorities other than the Bible and stressed behavioral evidence for salvation. It usually portrays a pride in possession of the truth with an emphasis on eschatology, and the founder may have acquired divinity status.[212] Wang Jiao Gao pointed out; "The government forbids other organizations besides the five recognized religions, so these cults try to attach themselves to one of the recognized

---

[207] A Responsible Member of the State Council's Bureau of Religious Affairs, 'Religious Affairs in China,' *BR*, 1-7 September (1997) 14.

[208] Wickeri, *Seeking*, p. 155.

[209] Bonnie Ho, 'Your Call has been Heard,' *Chinese Around the World*, September (1999) 25.

[210] Ye 'Appendix X,' *Human Rights, China: State Control*, p. 137.

[211] Ivey, Myron (ed.), 'House Church Leader to be Sent to Labor Camp,' *CNCR*, 20 July (1998) 4.

[212] Jonathan H. Y. Lee, trans. from *Pray For China*, 'The Prevalence of Cults,' *CATW*, July (1997) 14.

religions. In the countryside the untrained start some doctrines that lead to cults."[213]

Eastern Flash of Lightning

Dong Feng Shandian, or the Eastern Flash of Lightning that originated in Zhengzhou of Henan Province, believed that a female Jesus came to China.[214] This cult developed a theory and system of beliefs with paraphernalia for proliferation, which allowed it to expand rapidly. It obtained its name from the Bible reference of Matthew 24:27, "For the Son of Man will come like lightning which flashes across the whole sky from the east to the west." A writer for the *Tian Feng,* Wan Ge, found that the group had divided history into three stages. First, under Jehovah God came the law; secondly, Jesus as God in male human form came to provide grace; then finally, God came again to China in female form with the name of *Shandian,* or Lightning. The coming of the female Christ, for the group, rendered the previous beliefs about God as invalid, consequently the Bible was declared forbidden. They produced another scripture, a 600-page volume titled *Lightning From The East* without number, publisher or author. They denied the Trinitarian concept and opposed salvation by Jesus's death on the cross.[215]

Falung Gong

In 1999 the greatest cultic concern in China was the Buddhist cult Falung Gong. On October 31, 1999, an anti-cult law was established especially to punish the leaders and terminate the movement. Fulung Gong claimed to be related to *qigong,* an exercise of respiratory meditation from ancient Chinese culture. The exercises of Falun Gong were claimed to integrate with meditation to harness bodily energy through an inner wheel in the abdomen to attract good forces and expel the negative. Those in advance stages were to acquire supernatural capabilities.

The followers of Fulung Gong started coming into Beijing on October 25 to protest the governmental pressure on the group. Vans awaited at train stations and at Tiananmen Square to take

---

[213] Wang Jian Gao, (Interview, 10 September 1999).

[214] Jonathan Chao, ' The Church in China: Needs and Opportunities for Ministry,' Myron Ivey (ed.), *CNCR,* 11 May (1998) 3.

[215] 'The "Eastern Lightening" Sect: A Recent Threat To the Church in China,' *ANS,* Vol. 6, November-December (1997) 17. Reference to the Bible in Matthew 24:27.

them to detention centers in their own provinces. The leaders were charged with endangering national security and held liable for murder of followers who died after they refused medical treatment.

Li Hongzi, the founder of Falun Gong, created an atmosphere of panic in advocating a theory of fate. He taught that Sir Isaac Newton's law of gravity was in error, and there was a possibility that the earth could collide with the sun. Li claimed to be the oldest being in the universe and that he had created his own parents.

The director general of the State Administration of the RAB, Ye Xiaowen, described the Falun Gong as a dangerous cult, but he assured China's religious believers that the action taken against this cult would not become a threat to the religious activities of the authorized religions.[216]

Mormonism and Jehovah Witness

The Mormon and Jehovah Witness groups were in all parts of China, and they had even converted some known Christians. They were known to go to the unregistered meeting points to proselytize those who were vulnerable. The government authorities had not encouraged nor targeted these two cults to terminate their activities.[217]

According to Samuel Wang the Mormons invited a Chinese delegation to the United States to visit their temple in the state of Maryland in 1997 to promote Mormonism in China. By the year 2000 he claimed that approximately 20,000 Mormons were in China working subversively.[218]

The China Evangelical Fellowship Yu-E Mission

Shen Xianfeng, known as Pioneer Shen, developed the Yu-E Mission in an attempt to disregard the present society as the kingdom of Satan and to form another nation as the kingdom of God. The association attempted to challenge the constitutional religious policy and criticized the TSPM as, "The way of the

[216] 'Banned in China, Thriving in NewYork: The Controversy of Falun Gong,' *CATW,* January (2000) 25-27.
[217] Gu Yilin, Assistant to Headmaster, Beijing BISS International School, Beijing (Interview, 5 September 1999).
[218] Samuel Wang, Scholar of the *Four Books,* Co-author of *God and the Ancient Chinese,* Director of the Chinese Department of LMN Ministries, St Maries, ID (Interview, 27 December 1999).

whore." It disturbed social order by deceitfully arousing public anger against social laws and governmental policies.[219]

Fortune Tellers

Director of the Research Institute of Marxism-Leninism at the Chinese Academy of Social Sciences Fu Qingyuan sighed:

> It turns out that the majority of business-people in China believe in the god of fortune. And one-sixth of the people believe in the existence of gods or demons. One-twelfth believe they have seen ghosts or demons. Is it any wonder that 80% of Chinese visit fortune-tellers?"[220]

The problem with the government's attempts at maintaining control over cults in China was that it put pressure on legitimate religious communities. The unregistered Christian meeting points were grouped with illegal cults.[221] There was an attempt to preserve the religious rights guaranteed by the constitution, as addressed by RAB director Ye Xiaowen, in an effort to control cultic activity.

INDIGENIZATION MANIFESTED IN THE CHINESE CHURCH

Several factors were involved in the formation of the indigenous ministry of the Church in China depending on the area and the nature of each congregation in relation to the political context within which it ministered. The contribution of influences flavored each group with an aspect of uniqueness, but throughout China the whole of the indigenous Church had been fashioned. Christianity had adapted to whatever context into which it was introduced, and it made an impact on any part of society where it was proclaimed.

FOREIGN INPUT

Before 1978 China had been labeled as a closed nation to the Christian message from the standpoint that there were no foreign missionaries within her borders and the political regime of that era of the Cultural Revolution had declared that God was dead

---

[219] 'Section III,' *CS Journal,* August (1998) 60.
[220] Florcruz, Jaime A. and Joshua Cooper Ramo, 'Inside China's Search for its Soul,' *Time,* 4 October (1999) 73.
[221] Steven Liu [pseud.], Elder in *An Ti Ya Tang*, Beijing (Interview, 16 September 1999).

in China. The omnipresent characteristic of the Christian God in the triune person of the Holy Spirit sustained those Chinese believers open to the Christian faith and the teaching of the Bible as the Word of God even during this time. Small groups met in homes, and in remote areas larger assemblages gathered.[222] By 1987 Bishop Ting recognized that the tens of thousands of groups gathering in homes were financially self-sufficient, but the large churches and seminaries were dependent upon funds from the rent of unused church properties and the tax-exempt status the government had granted for religious organizations. He advocated that the acceptance of help offered through the unconditional love of international Christians would not be in violation of the self-support principle.[223] The formation of the Amity Foundation through the CCC created a channel of legal foreign involvement, with funds from abroad being used as the Chinese religious leaders considered appropriate. The United Bible Societies and the Southern Baptist Convention supported Amity as overseas organizations willing to work under the authority of the CCC.[224] The openness to international participation manifested an indication of maturity and oneness with the universal Church.

Clandestine Activities

According to the 1990 *Chinese Theological Review,* different foreign enterprises of religious infiltration had organized to publish literature in support of underground church activities under the auspices of Serve China International. Some used China's open policy to send missionaries under cultural or medical cooperation, as English teachers and tourists. Even seminaries had been established within the country as "wilderness seminaries" or outside of China to train personnel to be "dispatched to the interior." They attempted to attract Chinese students to go abroad for "theological training" to return to China as foreign-trained missionaries. Radio broadcasts were also used to propagate

---

[222] David H Adeney, *China: The Church's Long March* (Ventura, CA: Regal Books, 1985), pp. 142-143.
[223] Britt Towery, *The Churches of China* (Hong Kong: Long Dragon Books, 1987), p. 213.
[224] 'SBC Works with Liberal China Christian Council,' http://www.whidbey.net/-dcloud/fbns/sbcworks.htm, 9 November (1998)

in a way that circumvented the legal authority of the Chinese government. Those with an antagonistic attitude toward the People's government and the CCP used these means in a political "strategy of peaceful evolution" towards capitalistic democracy that formed division between Christians.[225]

In an indirect fashion literature and monetary support brought from abroad to Christian believers in China had caused churches to split. These items served the purpose of ministry of the church, but as this literature accumulated it became an indication of authority and power for the leader to command a following for the advantage that the information represented.[226] Also foreigners who visited China and overtly baptized converts provoked Communist authorities to link subversive acts to Christianity as counterrevolutionary. Even though the Chinese believers suffered the consequences of such thoughtless acts of either imprudent zeal or blatant self-indulgence, for converts could be legally baptized by their own clergy of registered churches or by leaders at independent meeting points,[227] it helped them form their identity as the Chinese Church.

The Two-Track Approach

Han Wenzao indicated disappointment in the International Mission Board, IMB, of the Southern Baptist Convention, for it had cultivated confidence with the CCC in a cooperative "open track" ministry in China. Then, at the same time without CCC consultation, the IMB directed foreigners to participate in "missionary work" on a "clandestine track" of ministry. The CCC informed the IMB representative that its partnership in ministry was dissolved in light of the "two-track approach."[228] The formal termination of cooperative relations on November 3, 1997, according to IMB personnel familiar with the immediate circumstances, resulted from the new IMB East Asia Director who favored collaboration with the independent unregistered Christian

---

[225] Janice Wickeri (ed.), *Chinese Theological Review, 1990* (Holland, MI: Foundation of Theological Education in Southeast Asia, 1991, pp. 10-11.

[226] Jonathan Chao, 2006, *China News and Church Report,* 31 July (1992).

[227] Tony Lambert, *The Resurrection of the Chinese Church* (Wheaton, IL: Harold Shaw Publishers, 1994), p. 130.

[228] Han Wenzao, 'CCC Statement On The IMB's Covert "Missionary Work",' *Amity News Service,* Vol. 6, November-December (1997) 2.

communities. The CCC presidency had also recently changed to Dr. Han, who was not as inclusive as Bishop Ting with the unregistered congregations. Again it was the Chinese national Christians who suffered and adjusted to any repercussions for the illegal activities of the Baptist missionaries.[229]

Alliances in Ministry

International relations had been strengthened when the CCC joined the World Council of Churches in 1991 as a full member. It had also become associated with the Lutheran World Federation, World Alliance of Reformed Churches, and the Baptist World Alliance.[230] In cooperation with the United Bible Society the CCC formed the Amity Press in Nanjing and printed 20 million copies of the Bible from 1986 to the year 2000. The CCC also sent Chinese nationals to Western countries to observe, participate and study at their seminaries.[231] Ten different publishers in China printed the beloved book *Streams in the Desert,* by American author Lettie Cowman, and many other overseas agencies supported China through Amity indicating world brotherhood in Christ as the TSPM does not promote self-isolation as a Three-Self principle.[232]

In September 1989, after the Tiananmen Square incident, Chen, who was a member of an unregistered church group, went to legally purchase a Bible at the bookstore of a registered open church. A few days after his purchase he was observed by a security official carrying his Bible and was accosted for possession of illegal and subversive literature. He then was allowed to go after he had shown that Amity Press had legally printed it in Nanjing, China.[233] According to an elder from an unregistered meeting point in Beijing, even though Bibles and reference books were available to buy, still there were not enough for the countryside. He said that his group received these materials from foreign sources

[229] Tim Yates, 'US Baptist Conflicts in Cooperating with TSPM (Part I),' *CNCR,* 31 August (1998) 2.
[230] Melissa Manhong Lin, 'A Modern Chinese Journey of Inculturation,' *International Review of Mission,* January (1998) 13.
[231] Bao Jiayuan, Associate General Secretary and Executive Director of CCC Office, Nanjing (Interview, 13 September 1999).
[232] Wang Jian Gao, Acting Dean at East China Theological Seminary, Shanghai (Interview, 10 September 1999).
[233] 'The Birth of a Historic Opportunity,' www.egmi.org/whatisehmi.htm, East Gates Ministries International, 9 November (1998) 1.

and had means of distribution to these remote areas.[234] Foreign cooperation existed on both the level of legal authority with the knowledge of the TSPM and the level with unregistered groups. The debate rose whether those acting in a clandestine manner were in violation of Christian teachings by not seeking the legal channel to give assistance with the Christian ministry in China.

Broadcasts from Overseas

From the viewpoint of the shortage of pastors, especially for the outlying districts of China, Tok Kai Hua, a Southeast Asian engineer, concluded that there was a need for foreign broadcasts, such as from the Far East Broadcasting Company for Christian instruction in these areas. For him, the fulfillment of reaching those people in remote villages and others who are illiterate legitimized the provision of the programs. The radio was an available tool, for the government had also used it for their means of communication with these areas.[235] Professor Wang of East China Theological Seminary agreed that the overseas broadcasts were the only means of getting the biblical message to those in the countryside in the past, but at the point of the late 1990s more preachers were available. His contention was that in the post-denominational stage of the Chinese Church the conflicting doctrines propagated over broadcasts caused division. He counted the Seventh Day Adventists broadcast, the Catholic Real Christian Voice, and other evangelical stations that promoted different dogmas. Knowledge of the context was important to be able to effectively minister to China; for example, a broadcast might preach that "divorce is bad" but nobody would be there to provide counsel, instruction, and support to those facing marital problems.[236]

Samuel Wang explained that the Chinese government no longer tried to block the foreign broadcasts into China. He said that it was the youth that listened mostly for the popular music that Christian stations broadcast to attract their attention.[237] In

---

[234] Steven Liu [pseud.], Elder at *An Ti Ya Tang* (Interview, 16 September 1999).

[235] Tok Kai Hua, Engineer in Project Management, From Southeast Asia, Beijing (Interview, 6 September 1999).

[236] Wang Jian Gao, (Interview, 10 September 1999).

[237] Samuel Wang, Scholar of the *Four Books,* Co-author of *God and the Ancient Chinese,* Director of the Chinese Department of LMN Ministries, St. Maries, ID (Interview, 27 December 1999).

the view of the People's government and the CCP, it remained illegal to broadcast into China and for Chinese to listen to these broadcasts. However, wherever the broadcasts were received, the instruction was integrated into the formation of the Chinese Church.

GOVERNMENTAL INFLUENCE

The News Network International reported in May 1992 that Party chairman Deng Xiaoping, since the Tiananmen Square incident in 1989, had intentions to secure political balance. He promoted economic reform by combating ultra-conservative suppression while still securely maintaining CCP control over the people. Therefore, the subjugation of Christian activities was on the increase.[238] The collapse of Communism in Eastern Europe caused the Chinese Communist government to watch the Chinese Church, for religious groups had contributed to that event. Nevertheless, Christian students formed prayer groups and remained optimistic in the continuance of growth in the Christian faith throughout China.[239]

Sociologist Drew Liu agreed with the evidence that the Chinese people had become disillusioned with Communistic ideology and turned to religion for the comfort and meaning to life. In the earlier stages of Communism, religion had been considered the result of ignorance, but by the mid-1990s it was realized that the demanding political and economic realities had become a factor in people turning to religion.[240] The Chinese people filled the officially recognized churches to capacity and concluded that even if this was the best they could find for corporate worship it was better than not being able to worship at all. Their devotion was as real as those who chose to become a part of an unregistered group, and the officials preferred to see the evidence of a progressive religious policy with people using authorized sites for their religious activities.[241]

As China entered 2000, the "market-based economy" was

---

[238] Jonathan Chao, 1979, *CNCR*, 4 June (1992).
[239] Jonathan Chao, 1940, *CNCR*, 27 March (1992).
[240] Drew Liu, 'State Policy and Christianity in China,' *China Strategic Review*, Vol. 1 (1996) 2.
[241] Human Rights/Asia, *China: State Control of Religion* (New York: Human Rights Watch, 1997) 64.

so foremost in the nation's ambition that atheistic ideals took a "distant second place." Leaders recognized that some religious faith had the capacity to help in national growth while moderating social unrest and the boredom referred to by the Chinese as *huise wenhua* or gray culture. The Shanghai Catholic leader, Bishop Jin Luxian, said, "The Communist Party realizes that religion has a good side and can contribute to the welfare of the people." The government had recently approved a humanistic program of *jinshen wenming*, or spiritual civilization, designed to ennoble life with the values of family and labor.[242] Even the government acknowledged the value of religion for the construction of society but attempted to minimize its effect through an appeal to the people's devotion. Christianity had been instrumental throughout China in the development of positive virtues.

The Influence of the TSPM

After the Cultural Revolution the TSPM had no anti-missionary intentions, but its concern included the independence of the Church of China to be organized, directed and financed by Chinese Christians. The TSPM intended to eradicate all suspicion from the bureaucrats in Beijing that the Church was dependent on foreigners again.[243] Li Duoma wrote for the *Tian Feng* January 1985 issue in disagreement of the objective of TSPM to bring "Chinese characteristics" to the Chinese Church. He argued that, "The Church ought to Christify," and to insist on "Chinese characteristics" could produce superficiality and lose its real Christian identity. However, as Paul Martinson pointed out, the TSPM had to concern itself as an organization with its function as a channel for two-way information flow between the government and the grass roots of the Chinese Protestant Church and to organize principles under which the Church was to function. On the local level, the churches maintained a strong sense of autonomy among the registered churches and those groups "beyond proper authorization."[244]

---

[242] Jaime A. Florcruz, and Joshua Cooper Ramo, 'Inside China's Search for its Soul,' *Time*, 4 (October 1999) 71, 72.
[243] Towery, *Churches*, p. 180.
[244] Paul Varo Martinson, 'The Protestant Church in Post-Mao China: Two Paradigms,' *Ching Feng*, Vol. 31, No. 1, (March 1988) 5, 7, 11.

Post-Denominational

In the effort to unite the Chinese Church, according to Shen Xilin, the TSPM declared, as a biblical principle of the post-denominational era, the premise that Christians shared basic beliefs and remained patriotic while reserving their minor differences.[245] Chen Zemin recognized that in pursuit of unity the seminaries must maintain a mutual respect for the different traditions and promote a willingness to learn and understand different spiritual practices in harmony.[246]

Running the Church Well

In the effort to be concordant Bishop Ting stressed that the TSPM must go beyond the Three-Self principles to running the Church well both politically and ecclesiastically. The Church should demonstrate "Chinese characteristics" and support socialism in a patriotic manner "opposing illegal activities." Then the ministry of the church must consistently express biblical truth to the people for their knowledge and spiritual growth.[247] TSPM general secretary Deng Fucun declared that the most urgent task for the church was to train lay workers, for he said, "Most of those who are preaching the Gospel to these new believers are actually lay workers. This is even more important than running seminaries"[248]

In the June 1998 issue of *Tian Feng* several church workers commented, "workers are only as good as their tools." Their primary tool was their own spiritual life and their biblical understanding of the Christian faith, which must continually be nurtured to effectively minister to others. Lin Zhien from Zhejiang wrote that an evangelist usually ministered in the churches within a large geographical area. The rigors of his ministry included pastoral duties, leading worship, and preaching in several locations, counseling believers in matters of the Christian faith,

[245] Shen Xilin, 'Seeking the Common Ground and Unity,' Janice K. Wickeri (trans. and ed.), *Chinese Theological Review,* Vol. 3 (1987) 38-39. Documents from the Fourth National Christian Conference at Shanghai in August 1986. Shen referred to the Bible in 1 Corinthians 1:10-17.
[246] Chen Zemin, 'On Nanjing Theological Seminary,' trans. Chaig Moran, J. Wickeri (ed.), *CTR*, Vol. 3 (1987) 47. Documents.
[247] Ting K. H., 'K. H. Ting Talks Again to Jiang Zemin, January 28, 1992,' *Bridge,* Vol. 53, (May-June 1992) 7.
[248] 'An Interview With Deng Fucun, Shanghai, 15 March 1997,' *ANS,* Vol. 6, (May-June 1997) 17.

praying for the sick and elderly and often the tasks in the church that others will not do.[249] To run the Church well the TSPM had concluded that preparation for the ministry and adjustment to the political context must be its focus.

Expanding Church Activities

It must be reiterated that the situation for religious activity throughout China was not uniform in availability or acceptance and under various degrees of restriction. There were areas where Sunday Schools and youth work were permitted and even unauthorized groups flourish unabated, while in other districts Christians worshipped under severe persecution. The Chinese Christians learned to adapt to the local political environment. In some areas children's work was possible under the guise of nursery in order not to antagonize the authorities. However, work with eighteen to thirty-year-olds, robed choirs, Christian books, and even Christmas cards published in China were becoming common in different areas.[250]

Publication of the Bible in different versions and in simplified forms had become a primary undertaking for the CCC. By the late 1990 the Bible printing committee had established 45 Bible distribution centers over China. The CCC had also published the Concordance of the Old and New Testaments, an Annotated Bible, the Chain Reference Bible, the Chinese Study Bible, an Order and Liturgy for Worship, and Notes on Composers and Hymns in the Hymnal. Also, by 1998 the CCC had printed thirty-five new titles of Christian literature along with many overseas Chinese publications and translated foreign publications.[251]

Although the CCC had printed the new hymnal with at least a quarter of the hymns being indigenous Chinese, the city church choir directors regarded the Chinese tunes with the Chinese instrumentation unsuitable for worship. They thought that for worship the Western music was superior. The rural areas found the Western diatonic scale difficult to sing but found that they

[249] 'Call for Believers to Help Lift the Burden on Evangelists,' *ANS*, Vol. 7, July-(August 1998) 3.
[250] Lambert, *The Resurrection*, pp. 254, 261.
[251] Han Wenzao, 'Build Up the Body of Christ with One Heart and United Effort: Running the Church Even Better According to the Three-Self Principle,' Janice Wickeri (ed.), *Chinese Theological Review:* 12 (Holland, MI: Foundation for Theological Education in Southeast Asia, 1998), pp. 13-14.

could express themselves in worship through the indigenous hymns accompanied by the *er-hu, pipa,* bamboo flutes and other Chinese musical instruments.[252] The TSPM had worked in every area to develop the Protestant Chinese Church to be manageable in the local political context and current national sociopolitical climate.

THE AUTONOMOUS CHRISTIAN COMMUNITY INFLUENCE

To define the Church as "our Lord Jesus Christ is there" covered a spectrum manifested in China from a person who had kept his faith a secret to a gathering of several hundred people. Between these two extremes was the immediate family who gathered for worship, the kinship worship with relatives and friends, and then a small group of those with a common commitment to Christ.[253] These differences accounted for the adaptability of Chinese Christians to the local circumstance in toleration of religious activity.

House Meeting Points

The Cultural Revolution created an atmosphere for a growth of house groups in China because of the closure of the authorized open churches during that decade. The desire for close Christian companionship and freedom from political control along with opportunities to evangelize, when the conservative Marxist religious policies were reversed, encouraged more Christians to congregate. Prayers to heal the sick manifested the power of the Holy Spirit of God, which had been attributed to revival of Christianity. Christian broadcasts from overseas convinced many to accept the Christian faith, and they began meeting with other Christians.[254]

Wang Mingdao, the popular pastor of a large unregistered congregation in Beijing, held the view, "where there were Christians, there was a Church." This defined the meeting points in homes as the legitimate Church, like the groups mentioned by Apostle Paul in the Bible. These meetings consisted of a simple program of prayer, hymn singing, personal accounts of spiritual

---

[252] 'Section III: Protestant Church,' *China Study Journal*, Vol 13, No. 1, (August 1998) 65.
[253] Ted Marr, 'The Church in China Today,' David Aikman (ed.), *Love China Today* (Wheaton, IL: Tyndale House Publishers, 1977) p. 65.
[254] Adeney, *Church's March*, pp. 145-146.

life from each member for the lack of pastors, more singing, and an offering taken to meet the financial expenses of the group.[255]

Itinerant Evangelists

The itinerant evangelists continued to be legendary figures throughout China for their exuberance of faith and disciplined ministry. Typically, they traveled mornings, rested in the afternoons and held meetings throughout the evenings and repeated the procedure the next day. Generally, they would stay in a village for one day with an average of two hours of sleep and go on to another the following day to visit as many villages as possible within a year or two. Any spare days were used as a time to go to a secluded spot for personal relaxation, meditation and prayer.[256]

In 1992, at Heilongjiang one unregistered autonomous church society had 1,500 full-time itinerant evangelists, who worked in pairs in every province of China doing pioneer evangelization. The greatest need was for follow-up personnel to conduct a series of meetings in a given location, known as Life Meetings, for 20 or 30 serious inquirers for several days of intensive teaching and saturation of basic biblical doctrines. Another need was for the new Christian families of a newly evangelized village to open their homes for hospitality to provide room and board for evangelists and also for meeting places. A serious problem regarding these evangelists was that of exhaustion from conducting pre-evangelism work, presiding the meetings, holding the Life and Truth sessions for training, and teaching laymen as well as field seminary training. Besides the strenuous schedule they usually forfeited eating food for three days and prayed before a series of sessions to condition themselves spiritually.[257]

Itinerant evangelists, who caused problems in the form of pride, had a tendency to patronize the lay workers condescendingly for having little systematic theological training. Often the older

[255] Jonathan Chao (Interviews), Richard Van Houten (ed.), *Wise as Serpents Harmless as Doves* (Pasadena: William Cary Library, 1988), pp. 63, 116. Interviews of evangelists on Hainan Island. Referenced the Bible books of I Corinthians 16:19 and Colossians 4:15.
[256] Ibid., pp. 105, 218. Interviews of evangelists from East China and a Woman evangelist.
[257] Jonathan Chao, Letter, Pasadena: China Ministries International, (December 1992).

church worker would criticize his or her younger counterpart and focus on weaknesses as being incapable for church ministry, which was a source of division.[258] The church leader, on the other hand, might not be adequately trained, and a new Christian might have taken a part in the life of the church. Then as he or she might have become mature in the faith and finally through an opportunity to study the Bible, possessed more biblical knowledge than the pastor. After a time, this type of person might separate from the church to his or her own private faith because he or she lacked a sense of benefit from being a part of the congregation.[259] An important ministry of the itinerant evangelist consisted of training the new converts and leaders, leaving them with adequate Christian literature and study guides for producing growth in the faith. Their passion was the source of growth for the Chinese Church.

Persecution and Suffering

Persecution took many forms. In the late 1980s a Christian teacher's son described an incident when there was a struggle against his father along with others who knelt on a platform. Heavy iron plates were hung about their necks with a thin wire that cut into their skin. Their crime as "Counter-revolutionary Christians" was written on the plates with their names shamefully crossed out. People grabbed their hair and pushed their heads down to face the ground.[260] Wang Weifan was an evangelical theologian of Nanjing Theological Seminary who kept his faith in both God and humanity during the 18 years he spent in the countryside. He stated, "One needs to see the suffering in history in the same way that one views the suffering of childbirth. In the end, a child is born." His experience deepened his sense of identification with the others who suffered.[261]

Still in the late 1990s, an eighty-four-year-old unregistered-church leader, Yuan, agreed that discrimination had not been a hindrance to the autonomous Christian communities. During

---

[258] 'Section III,' *CS Journal,* (August 1998) 70.
[259] Myron Ivey (ed.), 'Good Pastoral Care Needed In China,' *CNCR,* 2618, 19 (January 1998) 1.
[260] Chao, *Serpents Doves,* p. 133. An interview with a Teacher's son in Xinjiang Province.
[261] Philip L. Wickeri, *Seeking the Common Ground* (Maryknoll, NY: Orbis Books, 1990), p. 275.

USA President Clinton's visit to China in June 1998, the Public Security Bureau had closed Yuan's meetings with a warning that he was not to talk with any of the 2,000 reporters who had come to Beijing or have any of them to attend his worship services.[262]

It was through persecution that the Church in China was purified and the sense of urgency to spread the Christian message originated.

The Little Flock

In 1984 the Report of the Shanghai Academy of Social Sciences declared that the unregistered Little Flock indigenous group formed at least 95 percent of the 63,000 Christians in Xiaoshan County. It opposed the TSPM, but as an independent faction the Little Flock remained patriotic in every respect.[263] It was one of the major independent indigenous Christian communities in China founded in 1928 by Ni Duosheng, known in English as Watchman Nee. By the late 1990s Zhou Zaiqing of the Xiaoshan Christian Council reported that approximately 95,000 believers belonged to the Little Flock assemblies, with over 4,000 new believers being baptized into the group per year. They used their own hymnal containing hymns written by the Chinese Church before the 1949 Communist liberation and printed by Amity Printing and the Zhejiang Province Christian Council. The Little Flock did not believe in formal theological training, for it believed that the interpretation of biblical Scripture came from God and if a dispute arose the older and more experienced believers' interpretation would be accepted by the congregation.[264] Finally, in 1994 the Little Flock, as a Church community, decided to fulfill registration requirements by law, and chose Local Assemblies as their new name. They indicated that each individual congregation independently was "answerable only to God."[265]

[262] Jerry Sturdivant, 'Christian Persecution Part 5,' *The Discussion Network*, jerrys@pacifier.com, 29 (October 1998) 2.
[263] Lambert, *The Resurrection*, p. 86.
[264] Ian Groves, 'In the World But Not Of The World: Portrait Of An Indigenous Chinese Church Community In Zhejing,' *ANS*, Vol. 6, (November-December 1997) 22.
[265] Ibid., p. 23.

The Beginning of Renewal of Denominations

Along with the Local Assemblies, the most prominent indigenous Christian community in China, the True Jesus Church, had a certain relationship with the TSPM without losing independence as an indigenous group. These two movements, with the Seventh Day Adventists and the Korean Methodists, which are not Chinese indigenous church groups, had brought a revival of denominations back into the Protestant Chinese Church.[266] The TSPM had accepted these autonomous Christian communities for their patriotic intentions and cooperation in social construction and allowed them to maintain their particular distinctive denominational characteristics.

INDIGENOUS THEOLOGY

Chinese theologian Xie Yongqin contended that those who do the will of God were to be regarded as *dixiong*, or brothers. He proposed that evangelization was not to create a belief verses non-belief barrier to distinguish between Christian and non-Christian, but only between justice and injustice. His goal for Christians was to live at peace with all people. Xie challenged Chinese Christians to bring changes into Chinese society through truth, justice and righteousness in relation to the economy of salvation.[267] Beyond personal relations the Chinese Christian must find common communication with the People's Government. The principles of government relations as found in the Bible's Old Testament books of Ezra, Nehemiah, and Haggai were taught in the seminary classes.[268]

Concept of Theology

According to Jonathan Chao, because of the Confucian concept of human improvement through self-cultivation and education, the Chinese lacked an understanding of sin. They had dealt with moral issues through materialistic and socialistic solutions,

---

[266] Bao Jiayuan, (Interview, 13 September 1999), and Xu Rulei, Standing Committee Member of CCC, Vice-Chairman of Jiangsu Providence TSPM Committee, Chairman of Nanjing TSPM Committee and Deputy Director of Center of Religious Studies at Nanjing University, Nanjing (Interview, 11 September 1999).

[267] Philip L. Wickeri, 'Theological Reorientation in Chinese Protestantism 1949-1984 Part I,' *Ching Feng*, Vol. 28, No. 1, (March 1985) 58; Part II Vol. 28, No. 2-3, (August 1985) 112-113. Xie Yongqin referred to the Bible in Romans 12: 17-18.

[268] 'An Interview,' *ANS*, (1985) 18.

and from these misconceptions they lacked an awareness of redemption through Jesus Christ's atonement for the sin of all people. He affirmed that only the *su*, or forbearance, and *ren*, as tolerance, gave a Chinese concept of forgiveness, which left them to endure hate, mistrust and vengeance; Christianity taught them to forgive others as Christ forgave them. Chao explained that outside of festivals and family relations, community love was lacking among the Chinese people except in the Christian community as the Body of Christ. He reinforced that the Christian faith gave hope of eternal life after physical death to the Chinese understanding that lacked hope with the finalization of death in pain and despair.[269]

Events in Formulation of Theology

Theology professor Kan Baoping found that the theological themes acquired for the Chinese Church since 1979 surfaced after the Cultural Revolution and they united Christians of different denominational traditions on the standard of sharing as found in the Bible story of Jesus with the five loaves and two fish. The subject of reunification helped Chinese Christians to identify with other Chinese people. However, the change of focus to new church building construction and evangelization of new converts prevailed over these theological developments.[270]

Wang Jian Gao admitted that the development of the TSPM principle of self-propagation became theologically difficult in the Chinese society, for there was the isolation approach that recoiled from the evils of society. The reformer system idealized the view of Jesus for the transformation of society, and they theorized that the CCP had accomplished that task through the Theological Movement of the People. He defined the theology of incarnation as that which was formulated through culture and reality in Jesus Christ. Theology of what he termed as "The Great Consolation"

---

[269] Jonathan Chao, 'Christian Contributions to Chinese Culture: What Do Chinese People Lack that Christianity can Contribute,' *CNCR*, 22 (June 1998) 1-2.
[270] Kan Baoping, 'Theology In The Contemporary Chinese Context,' *ANS*, Vol. 7, (January-February 1998) 14. Kan Baoping was a lecturer in systematic theology and historical theology at Nanjing Union Theological Seminary and member of the Chinese Religious Association. Kan referenced the Bible in the New Testament books of the Gospels: Matthew 14: 15-21, Mark 6:35-44, Luke 9:12-17 and John 6:5-14.

had been fashioned by the Cultural Revolution when hatred was prevalent and love was considered "Western bourgeois." Samuel Wang agreed with Wang Jian Gao that after 1979 the theology of reconciliation had been dominant, with clergy being reconciled to each other for the Church to develop. This changed to a different portion of society from the late 1980s and 1990 with the government being reconciled to the Chinese people and the interrelationships of people being restored.[271]

A Chinese political writer verified that Chinese theologians who had lived through the Cultural Revolution wrote papers about the experiences and what they had learned about what God had done during this period. These papers, along with the input from students sent abroad to study by Chairman Deng Xiaoping, produced hope that China would change to a more democratic political policy. This hope, in turn, formed the events of June 1989 in Tiananmen Square that came to a dramatic end. It was through these events that Yuan Ziming became a Christian and developed theology for the context of China through the traditional Chinese philosophy of Taoism, which related to the early form of Christianity. The *Dao* referred to the Word, which he referenced to that of Jesus as found in the Bible New Testament book of John in chapter one.[272] Indigenous theology was formed from the context of these events and political changes in China. Biblical interpretation was viewed through the reality of the context.

CULTURE CHRISTIANS

According to Wang Jian Guo "Culture Christian" as a term could be quite ambiguous. It referred to Chinese intellectuals who had no interest in Christianity even though the Church had tried to evangelize them before the Cultural Revolution, but since had taken a keen curiosity toward Christianity. They then came to churches, researched, studied and translated many Western theological books into Chinese. They became interested in Christian values for the reconstruction of Chinese culture. These scholars challenged

---

[271] Wang Jian Gao (Interview, 19 September 1999) and Wang, Samuel (Interview, 27 December 1999). Samuel Wang added that Liberation Theology was not accepted in China.
[272] Karen Young [pseud.], Chinese writer of financial economics and political news in *Zong Guo Zeng Juang*, English teacher for Children, Beijing (Interview, 5 September 1999).

the Chinese Church, because many had come to churches and became bored from the lack of stimulation, and they realized that there was a gap between a personal faith and institutional Christianity. Wang defined the "Culture Christian" from different settings with those of the universities having developed theology with a scientific understanding. In the churches there was "no common ground to dialogue" for generally they did not claim baptism or participate in communion while those in the cultural setting feigned self-righteousness through self-justification.[273]

The fulfillment of these intellectuals came from the self-satisfied feeling of having compassion and being helpful, according to the evaluation from a foreign professor teaching in Beijing. He found that for the academic, Christian songs were clever with expression, and religion had become a gratifying manner to relate to foreigners. Christianity was certainly an alternative to cynicism and pleasure, but the Culture Christians were not impacted by the realities of Christ.[274]

Intellectual Christians

Dr. Brent Fulton, director of Chinese studies at Wheaton College, stated that many of the intelligentsia had truly become Christians even though they lacked connection with churches, but they may have formed their own small group for prayer.[275] Since 1989, in the post-Tiananmen Square period, the academics had turned from Marxism to Christianity in marked numbers.[276] In disillusionment with the political system there was an effort to find self-actualization through a personal relationship with Christ. One student stated, "Christianity is very realistic. Unlike our Chinese religions, it starts from the premise that what is wrong with the world is mankind, not circumstance – this attracts us!"[277]

[273] Wang Jian Gao, (Interview, 10 September 1999).
[274] Carl Franklin Kelly [pseud.], Professor at a university in Beijing, Attends a Christian group of intellectuals, the International Christian Fellowship, Beijing (Interview, 6-7 September 1999).
[275] Brent Fulton, Executive Director of Chinasource, Managing Director of the Institute of Chinese Studies at Wheaton College, Served 8 years with CMI and 2 years with CCRC.
[276] Lambert, *The Resurrection,* p. 216.
[277] 'China's Students Flocking to Christianity,' Beijing China, News Network International, www.nni-news.com, (1990) 1.

The CCC in Relation with Culture Christians

Whether they had accepted Christ personally or not, they were without links to the Church in China. Bao Jiayuan, executive director of the CCC office, acknowledged that the CCC had a goal to initiate dialogue with these intellectuals as a means of evangelism. An illustration he gave was Lu Shao Fung, who had translated many books about Christian thinking and theological books from a philosophical view of Christianity. Bao and his colleagues contend that "the translation was not properly done because of the lack of faith." He declared that the CCC lacked the resource at the academic level necessary to reach these scholars.[278] Steven Liu, an elder of an unregistered church group, asserted that Culture Christians approach Jesus like Nicodemus of the Bible, who thought of Jesus as a good man who sought truth, was educated, and already had a position in the established church. He said, "They think that through their own wisdom they can find truth, but because of Jesus' miracles it is hard for them to believe."[279]

MINORITIES

Some of the ethnic minority groups in China had their own religions, such as Islam, and were separated into their own communities. Their languages were distinct, and as a race they had different physical features from the Han Chinese.

The religious believers distinguished themselves as a minority within the overall population of China, and within this group there were the separate religions. Within Christianity, the Catholics were minority to the Protestants, as were the open registered churches to the unregistered autonomous Christian communities.

Women's Work

As a facet of the Chinese Protestant Church women formed a minority group for an emphasis of importance. The ordination of women did not become an issue through the liberation of women for equality. This area of ministry opened not from the need to

---

[278] Bao Jiayuan, (Interview, 13 September 1999).
[279] Steven Liu [pseud.], (Interview, 16 September 1999). Liu referred to the Bible New Testament book of John 3:1 21.

emphasize the abilities of women, but from the congregational needs for pastoral care. An illustration of their effectiveness was found in the Shenyang church where divorce had been on the rise within the community. The women's group wrote and performed small dramas on different issues of family life and the Christian faith and invited non-believing husbands of the ladies of the congregation to the performances. Within a few years after this group of women formed, Tian Yu reported in *Tian Feng* that 200 of the husbands had become Christians and applied for baptism.[280] Bishop Ting reported that an effective means of neighborhood evangelism was from an organization of women who served as mediators in domestic quarrels.[281]

Within the minority churches, the congregations consist of 70 percent women; therefore, they had a role of ministry in the church to affect the social needs of the community. Because the educational level of women was often lower, and since their character tended to be more open than that of men, they were inclined also to be more susceptible to heresies. Thus, to alleviate that risk there was an urgent need for thorough biblical training of women church leaders.[282] The author observed many Chinese women with pastoral duties in the churches in the capacities of speaking, leading hymns, and as elders.

National Minorities

Of the 55 national ethnic minority groups in China the Korean, Miao, Yi, Jingpo, Lisu, Wa, Hani, and Lahu were the eight with the greatest number of Christians.[283] As the smallest officially recognized minority group in China as of 1998, the Dulong had a census of only about 4,000 people. They were located close to the Burmese border in the northwestern corner of Yunnan Province, and they reveled in telling stories. Ye Xi of the *Tian Feng* said, "Anyone who is not able to tell stories about his own people cannot be considered a real Dulong." He discovered that the way to evangelize this minority group was to relate the Christian message to them with stories in the style that Dulongs use in their

---

[280] 'Section III,' *CS Journal,* (August 1998) 67, 72.
[281] Ting K. H., 'The Chinese Church Since 1949,' Denton Lotz (ed.), *Spring Has Returned* (McLean, VA: Baptist World Alliance, 1986), p. 24.
[282] 'Section III,' *CS Journal,* (April 1998) 87.
[283] Han, 'Build Up the Body,' *Review: 12,* p. 16.

narratives as Jesus did with parables.[284]   Each minority group presented a sociopolitical context to which the Church of China adjusted to become indigenous to the point of Bible translation into their minority language and the presentation of Christianity.

PRACTICAL INDIGENIZATION

To be an indigenous Christian Church the Chinese Protestants must manifest evidence of biblical cultural implications. In China this phenomenon revealed itself in the respectful relationship with parents, for instance. Second, evidence of a transformation experience as new people in Jesus Christ was essential for indigenous Christianity, which superseded Confucianism and other religions of China.[285]

The Church in China had identified with the values of labor, which the Chinese culture and ideal of Communism had advocated, with the clergy also being involved in secular employment. Bishop Ting declared that Protestant Christianity in China by 1978 had been "declergyized, deinstitutionalized," and without denominations.[286] Wallis confirmed Bishops Ting's declaration that even after nearly a decade the Chinese believers met in homes, warehouses, courtyards, open air and businesses: as their conviction that expenditure of finances for buildings impeded growth and was a misappropriation for their resources.[287] This was not only indigenously characteristic of Christianity in China, but also similar to the church of the New Testament as described by Apostle Paul.

Indigenous Concepts

For different strata of people throughout China there existed diverse concepts of indigenization. For some the Church's response to the sociopolitical atmosphere of the nation, and how it concerned itself with the four modernizations, became decisive. Others sought Chinese characteristics in the hymns, architecture, art,

---

[284] 'Section III,' *CS Journal*, (August 1998) 68.

[285] Princeton Hsu, 'China's indigenous Christian Movements,' David Aikman (ed.), *Love China Today* (Wheaton, IL: Tyndale House Publishers, 1977) 35-36. Hsu's concept referred to the Bible New Testament book of I Corinthians 5:17.

[286] Whitehead, Raymond L. and Rea M., *China: Search for Community* (New York: Friendship Press, 1978), p. 48.

[287] Wallis, Arthur, *China Miracle* (Columbia, MO: Cityhill Publishing, 1986), p. 148.

music, lanterns, and the version and translation of the Bible, even
the type of written character used. Still others were concerned
that the theology be shaped by a traditional Chinese culture
from the ancient relevant philosophers: Confucius, Laotzu and
Motzu. In general, however, the message of the Chinese churches
demonstrated almost a fundamentalist quality emphasizing sin,
grace, and moral standards to promote Christian conversion and
holiness of life.[288]

During the Cultural Revolution all Bible study commentaries
were destroyed along with Bibles, and the teachers of theology were
imprisoned or sent to rehabilitation labor camps. However, there
were those of the Christian faith that preserved the doctrines and
were dedicated to teaching them to others. In one home gathering
in Shanghai, the group produced a paper outlining doctrines, titled
Ten Main Points and Seven Points for Every Day.[289]   Each of the
seven points for every day were supported by a Bible scripture
references, and five referred directly to a personal relationship with
the person of Jesus Christ. The first to recognize of the assurance
of his care; second, an admonition to proclaim his salvation; third,
Praise him; fourth, seek his will; fifth, follow his example. The
other two were for general Christian behavior with the sixth an
exhortation to encourage others and the seventh to study the
Bible. The main ten points outlined devotional assurances of the
faith for living the Christian life until death.[290]

Revival sessions lasting several days, referred to as Life
Meetings, took place at a hospitality house where food and bedding
was supplied for the duration. The group understood the process
of confession in four stages. The first stage *shuo zui*, was for the
enumeration of sins in a list; second, *ren zui* or confession of these
sins before God. The third, *ao zui*, was the stage of contrition for
having been foolish enough to commit the sins, and the final stage
of *hen zui* was an attitude of hate toward sin engrained into the

---

[288] Martinson, 'The Protestant,' *CF,* March (1988) 6, 19.
[289] Leslie Lyall, *God Reigns in China* (London: Hodder and Stoughton, 1985), p. 156.
[290] Marr, 'Church Today,' Aikman (ed.), *Love China,* p. 69. The Scripture references for the Seven Points for Every Day were from the Bible in the Old Testament from Psalms 55:22; 68:19; 96:1-2; 145:1-2 and Isaiah 58:2, and from the New Testament from Luke 9:23, Acts 17:10-11, Hebrews 3:12-14 and I Peter 5:7.

character of the person.[291]

According to Chinese theologian Huang, "Christianity is the acceptance of a new life in Christ, and is not necessarily linked with any particular social system." A Christian should be able to endorse many of the socialist views. He gave the example, "the Bible teaches that all people are equal before God, and Christians should be able to support a social system which seeks to bring an end to class and racial oppression."[292]

Compensations for the lack of biblical teaching materials and theological relations with the sociopolitical system formed indigenous ideas and interpretations of Christianity.

Concentrations of Christians

Certain parts of China, especially along the southeastern coast, had higher concentrations of Christians. The churches in Wenzhou County of Zhejiang Province became models of Christian witness, for the area economic strength afforded confidence and enthusiasm for the development of the Christian community.[293] The Christians of Jiangzu Province were exemplary in relations with coworkers and family; they emphasized humility, respect, peace, justice and ethics according to principles of the Bible.[294]

The inland province of Hunan Province in south China was where Christians founded the Faith and Deeds Foundation in 1990. The foundation's ministry included leprosy prevention and aiding children with hearing impairments.[295] Some Christians had affected communities with humanitarian ministries, but the church in Putian County of Fujian Province was an example of the spiritual ministry crucial to the community throughout the week. Sundays were for congregational worship with the sanctuary filled to the 1,400 capacity three different times during the day as well as services on Wednesdays and Saturdays. Mondays were reserved for evangelistic meetings, and each member

[291] Joshua Hao, 'China's Revival Meetings and Tears,' Chao (ed.), *China Prayer Letter,* No. 125, (March 1993) 1-2.
[292] Wickeri, 'Theological Reorientation Part II,' *CF,* (August 1985) 117-118.
[293] Jonathan H. Y. Lee, 'The Chinese Jerusalem – A Report on Wen Zhou County,' *Chinese Around the World,* (May 1998) 17.
[294] Zhao Zhi-en, 'A Vast Field of Harvest,' *China News Update,* (September 1998) 6. Rev. Zhao Zhi-en was a Nanjing Seminary Teacher and Chairperson of the Commission on Rural Ministries, CCC.
[295] 'Section III,' *CS Journal,* (August 1998) 68-69.

was encouraged to bring non-believing friends, relatives and coworkers. Bible studies, youth activities, choir practices and prayer meetings were also scheduled each week.[296] This schedule was typical of different churches the author visited in Beijing, Shanghai, Wenzhou, Hangzhou, Nanjing and several town and rural churches in Zhejiang Province.

Sufferings

According to Raymond Fung, Christianity in China was no longer considered a foreign religion, through there was little evidence of its indiginization in expression. He declared that through suffering Christianity had established itself in China, but the Chinese Church had not reflected on its suffering or on its mission to the Chinese people in the midst of their affliction. They had learned to adjust to the political pressure placed on the Church at any point in time as a church of the Production Brigade in the early 1980s adapted to not having money, because they did not want to answer questions of suspicion from cadres. Therefore, whenever money was needed the members contributed for the presented cause.[297]

Jonathan Chao said in 1983:

> Christians in China interpret the last thirty-four years of prolonged suffering as a gift of God's profound grace to the Chinese Church to cleanse her from her impurities, to test the genuineness of their faith and loyalty, to train them for obedience and progress unto greater maturity, and to enable them to gain a deeper experience with Christ.

The question never arose as to why God had allowed the Chinese Church to suffer if He really loved it. The congregations were known locally for caring for one another as they shared with the needy and comforted the bereaved and sick. One Communist school teacher received care from Christians when

---

[296] 'Putian Church: Different Traditions, New Developments,' *ANS*, Vol. 6, (May-June 1997) 13.

[297] Raymond Fung, (compiled and trans.), *Household of God on China's Soil* (Maryknoll, NY: Orbis Books, 1982), pp. x-xii, 8. Stories of 14 Christian Communities from 42 on which information was gathered. This selection was to avoid stories of too similar experience. This selection spread over eleven provinces.

she was sick and finally became a Christian. While suffering ridicule in a confession session, she protested, "When I was ill, you did nothing to help me. It was the Christians who did everything!"[298]

One Chinese Christian from Hong Kong who had frequent contacts with Chinese Christians in the rural areas of China remarked, "In most parts of rural China poverty, disasters – both natural and man-made – and the lack of all kinds of resources drive the Christians to total dependence on God. He is not their last resort. He is the first and only resort."[299] It was not the unique Chinese fashion of worship or structure of church organization that gave an indigenous flavor to the Church in China, but it was its adjustment to circumstances that were unique to China.

Evangelization

A mass evangelistic campaign would be difficult in the Chinese setting, but each church or group had its own strategy for evangelization. Peifen recounts that some congregations took advantage of the New Year holidays to have special evangelistic services in their churches or dedicated one Sunday a month for evangelistic emphasis.[300] In agreement with Peifen, Samuel Wang gave the analogy of big Western-style evangelistic meetings, which are not used in China, to using a bomb in battle while personal evangelism was like the use of ground troops. The ground troops, in his analogy, were the ones who actually fought the war. It was laymen who really did most of the evangelization.[301]

Pastor Timothy Wu said that it was common to use the opportunity of a wedding or a funeral to preach the Christian message to those who would never come to the church for a regular service. A funeral also gave an opening into the community to minister to the relatives and friends who suffered loss.[302]

Electronic technology was used in evangelism in China. Many churches cannot adequately accommodate the large congregations,

[298] Lyall, *God in China*, p. 159.
[299] Lambert, *The Resurrection*, pp. 158-159.
[300] Peifen, 'Features of the Church in China,' Denton Lotz (ed.), *Spring Has Returned* (McLean, VA: Baptist World Alliance, 1986), p. 39.
[301] Samuel Wang, (Interview, 27 December 1999).
[302] Timothy Wu, *Sheltered Through the Storms: A Chinese Pastor Preserved by God* (Palo Cedro, CA: Wayside Impressions, 1996), ch. 16.

so many must participate in the activities of the service and benefit from the sermon by way of closed circuit television. Also Christian videos and cassette tapes of sermons are circulated for evangelistic purposes.[303] The author attended worship services in Nanjing in a facility away from the main sanctuary served by a closed-circuit television.

Music

The home gatherings during the Cultural Revolution and for years afterwards had been deprived of hymnals; as a result, these Christians sang portions of Bible scripture with Chinese tunes. Among the more popular scriptures to be set to music were the verses of the twenty-third Psalm and the Beatitudes as found in the Bible book of Matthew, fifth chapter.[304]

Rev. Wang Jisen, the vice-general secretary of the Zhejiang Christian Council, stated, "Christianity is a religion of music." In the province of Zhejiang music was certainly an important part of the Christian exposure. The churches of Hangzhou would combine the best singers of all their choirs to perform at festivals as well as Christmas and Easter, which never failed to draw crowds of those passing by on the street.[305]

In rural area of Shaanxi Province, a woman named Tao Bushen was known for singing a long Christian song titled The Life of Jesus. She sang in the Shaanxi folk style as a storyteller with simple and repetitive melodies. Different songs in this area were passed from person to person and written down by the singer but never printed for distribution. These rural Christians admitted that they do not like the hymnal produced by the CCC, but prefer Christian scripture set to folk music.[306] The rural areas where most of the Chinese Christians resided produced indigenous Christian music and preferred it to the Western translated hymns used mostly in the city churches.

---

[303] Gu Yilin (Pseudo), Assistant to Headmaster at Beijing BISS International School, Beijing (Interview, 5 September 1999).

[304] Lyall, *God in China,* p. 153.

[305] 'Success Must Not Lead To Complacency: How the Church in Zhejiang Seeks to Grow Further,' *ANS,* Vol. 6, (November-December 1997) 21.

[306] 'ANS Focus: Church Music: Sing Praises to the Lord: Inculturating the Gospel – Chinese Rural Church Music,' *ANS,* Vol. 6, (May-June 1997) 8.

Indigenous Christianity Manifested

Occurrences of supernatural healing through prayer for the sick were not unusual, a Christian leader in China testified. He said, "Our believers just simply trust the Lord like little children trusting their father. And our heavenly Father cares for and loves us so much that He often heals our sick and meets our needs."[307] Some Communist officials had Christians pray for a chronic disease they had suffered, experienced healing. Through the concern shown by these Christians and the healing experience, these Communists accepted Christianity even though the materialist Marxist system regarded these miracles as superstition.[308]

Another way in which Chinese Christians convinced authorities of the reality of the Christian faith and willingness to participate in the modernization of China was through their daily productive work, which exceeded their non-Christian counterparts.[309] This was obvious to the point that the non-Christians of a village complained to the officials that the Christians went to Church on Sunday and worked only six days. When the authorities noted that even in six days the Christians produced more and the crime rate among them was less, they concluded that working six days was better than working seven.[310] An incident in a hotel in South China was typical as a man noticed a cleaning lady with a manner of love and graciousness, and finally asked her if she was a Christian. She replied, "Yes. I cannot say much, but I seek through the life I'm living to reveal the Lord Jesus."[311] Pastor Wu confirmed that Communist government officials had come to favor law-abiding Christians for the welfare of society and maintaining stability and social order. He said, "It was our natural function before God to shine forth the virtues of His grace."[312]

Deng Fucun, the general secretary of the TSPM, affirmed, "One of the reasons for the rapid growth of the Church is that Christians

---

[307] Wallis, *China Miracle*, pp. 126-127.
[308] Lyall, *God in China*, pp. 153-154.
[309] Ibid., p. 181.
[310] Adeney, *Church March*, p. 142.
[311] David Adeney, 'Love China Vision,' David Aikman (ed.), *Love China Today* (Wheaton, IL: Tyndale House Publishers, 1977), pp. 164-165.
[312] Wu, *Sheltered Pastor*, ch. 15.

have borne a fruitful witness in their daily lives." Deci Su, the Secretary-general of the CCC, agreed that more people are attending churches because, "people are discovering that they have more than just material needs."[313]

At the Lunar New Year as the time for the Spring Festival it was customary for the Chinese people to paste couplets around their doorways. Those on either side of the door were to bear a message of hope for the coming year, and the horizontal four-character message above the door completed the greeting. Christians used Bible messages such as the following for the vertical aphorism: "God's Mighty Grace is as deep as the Ocean"; "Jesus's Great Love is as Strong as a Mountain"; "A family that possesses the Gospel is often joyful"; or "A Christian household enjoys peace in abundance." For the horizontal greeting they inscribed four-character sayings as "Emmanuel," "Hallelujah," "Praise the Lord," "Spread the Good News," "Be salt and light" or "Love your country Love the Church."[314] These methods of Christian expression formed the indigenous Church in China as it took the initiative and adjusted to the local context.

THE CHINESE CHURCH'S PROSPECTS FOR THE 21ST CENTURY

The renewed hope that accompanied the entrance into a new century superseded any problems facing the Chinese Protestant Church. Throughout its history the Church had adapted to the situation and continued to grow. There had always been adjustments to political change affecting the sociological elements of the Chinese society. International relations, internal events, and immediate dilemmas in search of solution allowed the Church in China to progress with expectation for future expansion and Christian impact throughout China.

CHRISTIAN EDUCATION AND TRAINING

Shen Chenen, associate general secretary of the CCC, identified the most pressing problem of the Protestant Church in China as the lack of pastoral staff for the number of churches throughout China. Most churches, according to his knowledge, had to rely

---

[313] Eva Stimson, 'the Church in China', *Presbyterians Today,* (November 1997) 3.
[314] 'Using Spring Festival Couplets To Announce The Good News,' *ANS,* Vol. 7, (January-February 1998) 24-25.

on untrained lay workers, who might unwittingly teach heresy. Every level of church leadership training, along with Christian literature for these congregations, was urgently needed as the Church entered into the 21st century.[315]   In agreement, Jonathan Chao reiterated the importance of training church workers due to the rapidly growing number of conversions among the Chinese people in recent years.   He stated that this predicament was compounded by the effort to consolidate groups that formed into churches at an inconceivable rate that lacked the required pastoral care and leadership. [316]

Proper evangelical Christian training had also become a mounting concern for Christian intellectuals of the cities in China and for those studying abroad.   Yu Jiang, a writer for *Tian Feng*, stated that the intelligentsia also must be encouraged to participate in the verve of the Church through theological debate. The church clergy had an obligation to elevate their training to enable dialogue and ministry through special fellowships for these scholars.[317]

In the throes of modernization the People's Government and the CCP had encouraged religious activities with unprecedented openness among the intelligentsia.   Given the opportunity to teach at Peking University in January 2000, Evyn Adams, as a global professor for the American organization OMS International, had twelve students in a class on 'The Influence of Christianity on Western Culture.'   He confirmed that just six years earlier there had only been courses on Marxism, Atheism and the Sciences. However, upon entering into the 21st century, Peking University inaugurated a master's degree program in Christianity into their new Department of Religious Studies.   For July 2000 Evyn and his wife, Neva, had been invited to teach the course 'Basic Issues in Christianity.'   While teaching at the university, Adams attended the Haidian Church of over 3000 members, which was within walking distance of the University.   This open registered church

---

[315] Shen Chen-en, Associate General Secretary of CCC, Chief Editor of *Tian Feng* and Pastor of Shanghai Community Church, Shanghai (Interview, 10 September 1999).

[316] Chao, Jonathan, Letter, Pasadena: CMI, 1 (February 2000)

[317] Yu Jiang, 'Meeting the Needs of Intellectual Believers,' Gail V. Coulson (ed.), *China Talk*, Vol. XXIII, 1st Quarter, (May 1998) 20.   There were 47 representatives from provincial Christian councils and theological institutes from throughout China that met in Shanghai between 19-20 November 1997.

had services at different times each Sunday to accommodate people in the limited sanctuary. The government had agreed to help in the construction of a new sanctuary and student center.[318] The author attended this church in September 1999, and the congregation was talking then of this new project.

PROSPECTIVE FOR EVANGELIZATION

A delegation of representatives from provincial Christian councils met in Shanghai for a conference and decided on the type of characteristics desired in Chinese evangelists to undertake the task of evangelism in China. These assets included: to maintain a close relationship with God, to sustain a sense of morality that was practiced in personal life, and to acquire the degree of education that would allow them to relate adequately to a wide spectrum of the Chinese society. The doctrines of creation, atonement, and original sin were to be rendered understandable and acceptable in their Christian message to the Chinese society. Traditionally and culturally these concepts were foreign to the Chinese mind.[319]

In an evangelistic role, Christian professionals were recognized in their manner of business and ethical practices as a benefit to Christianity in China in what was referred to as a tent-making ministry, or being a Christian witness in the daily workplace.[320] They could be open about their faith in a natural setting of everyday society and to a broader audience than of those who might be inclined to inquire about Christianity in a church. This would be true of international Christians who lived in China to pursue their profession as well as Chinese.

TECHNOLOGY

The director of the RAB in the State Council, Ye Xiaowen, was concerned with finding common communication between the Party and religious believers. He proposed the common desire for political unity, cooperation and stability to fulfill the rejuvenation of China by 2010. This goal was to enhance the material and

---

[318] Evyn Adams, Letter, Greenwood, IN: OMS International, February (2000).
[319] Gail Coulson (ed.), 'Who should undertake the task of Evangelism in China,' *CT*, (May 1998) 18.
[320] Fung Ho-Lau, 'Wanted! Professionals Where Are You? A Challenge Towards Global Evangelization,' *Chinese Around The World*, (February- March 1996) 1.

spiritual civilization of the people.[321] In the material sense the first factor to influence the course of China, according to Jonathan Chao, was the expansion of the world market, which influenced social change. Another factor was the expansion in mass communication and mass transit, to which the Chinese people adjusted rapidly in telecommunication, e-mail and Internet technology.[322] The author noted quite a contrast in the major cities of China from 1994 to 1999 in the number and size of automobiles, numbers of cell telephones, the amount and the higher quality of construction as well as improved facilities in airports and train stations. The expansion of air travel and general mobility was noticeable.

Ye voiced a concern of the government about the expansion of computer communications regarding the effects of intrusion from foreigners with religious evangelistic methods on palm-sized computers. There was a motion to have Chinese citizens who use computers with Internet capacity to register with governmental authorities. He said that effective administrative methods remained to be established with success and foresight in the interest of the Chinese society.[323] The extensive progress of computer systems and devices would render registration an expensive process and very difficult to monitor with precision.

THE CHINESE CHURCH'S MISSION EXCHANGE WITH THE WEST

In 1973 a Chinese pastor evangelist, Timothy Dzao, made a statement to the Western world that the time had come for Chinese to convey the Christian message to the West. He said that not only did China owe a debt to the West for its missionary effort to bring Christianity to China, but the Chinese as an accomplished people gained a perspective of biblical scriptures that had been written in an Eastern context to share with the

---

[321] Ye Xiaowen, Director of RAB, the State Council, 'Appendix X: China's Current Religious Question: Once again an Inquiry into the Five Characteristics of Religion,' Human Rights/Asia, *China: State Control* (New York: Human Rights Watch, 1997), pp. 141-142.
[322] Jonathan Chao, e-mailed material from the Conclusion of his book *A History of Christianity in Socialist China*, 1998, p. 20.
[323] Ye Xiaomen, 'Appendix X,' HR/A, *State Control*, p. 132.

Western world.[324] Peter Wagner, as an authority on international Christian movements, had projected, "The number of Chinese overseas missionaries may be the largest in the world in the year 2025."[325]

There were several different concepts of Christianity that the Chinese need to share with the West, according to Wang Jian Gao. He proposed that the post-denominational aspect of unity through focus on the basics in biblical Christian doctrines and respect for other traditions of worship was an important factor that would benefit the Church in the West. Moreover, the West could learn more from Christians in China about responsibilities to God rather than rights, and also the virtue of considering the community over individuality as the values Chinese Christians discovered during the Cultural Revolution.[326] The Chinese Christians had learned simple theology formulated through the pastor ordination prerequisite of reading the Bible through 30 to 40 times to be saturated with its teachings was what Samuel Wang, who had lived in the West for some years, sensed the Western world should imitate. He also observed that the Chinese Church's stress on prayer and evangelism as a personal witness were characteristics that could benefit the West.[327]

Those things that Wang Jian Guo noted that China could benefit from the Church in the West for prospective Church growth in China into the 21st century was the experience of administration. He said the Chinese needed training on managing a parish and for organizing programs and seminars. The pastors of churches in China made the decisions for the congregation while in Wang's estimation the Chinese Church would profit in adopting a Western democratic approach for church government. He suggested that the interchange of these advantages between the East and the West could take place with more professor exchange in seminaries.

[324] Authur Wallis, *China Miracle* (Columbia, MO: Cityhill Publishing, 1986), pp. 161-162.
[325] Maak Hay-chun, 'Partnership with China,' *Chinese Around the World,* (January 1998) 5.
[326] Wang Jian Gao, Acting Dean of Faculty at East China Theological Seminary, Shanghai (Interview, 10 September 1999).
[327] Samuel Wang, Scholar of the *Four Books,* Co-author of *God and the Ancient Chinese* and Director of the Chinese Department of LMN Ministries, St. Maries, ID (Interview, 27 December 1999).

For example, in 1999 Philip Wickeri taught a short-term class on eschatology in Nanjing Seminary and was invited for a future date to East China Seminary in Shanghai.[328]   For maximum benefit from the resources available, the exchange of formidable characteristics and materials on an international level would be to the advantage of all participants. Development for the Church in China would mature through the realization of the fact that it had a great deal to share with the world from the experiences and biblical principles discovered in its context.

---

[328] Wang Jian Gao (Interview, 10 September 1999).

8
CONCLUSIONS

The indigenous development of the Protestant Church in China depended on many factors of historical, sociopolitical, and contextual realities all influenced by international relations. The shape of the Church was affected by those who introduced Christianity to China. The contextual approach of service taken by the Italian missionary Matteo Ricci in 1582 was exemplary, for he learned about the culture and the language in an effort to identify with China as a guest. The Franciscans mission approach was by refuting the methods of Ricci and demanding papal authority over the Church. Then the 1800s were marked by forced entry through pressure of the opium trade and the unequal treaties. Finally, through the political and military weaknesses of China, the unchallenged missionary movement had access to the whole nation, often without any effort on the missionaries' part to learn the language and culture. Although many of the missionaries came to serve, a significant number maintained an attitude of superiority toward the Chinese people. This was the setting in which the Protestant Church entered the Chinese sociopolitical context of ruling dynasties.

The early 1900s marked a radical political change from dynastic rule to warlords and gentry rule to the Republic and Communist struggle along with international penetrations and unjust negotiations, and the Church on the most part remained dependent upon foreign missionaries and their agencies. It was not until 1949 that China, as a nation, regained its sovereignty and the missionaries were forced to relinquish their authority and influence on the formation of the Church in China. Even though the West referred to China as a nation closed to Christianity, the Church had not only survived but also flourished.

The Christian organization that formed to accommodate the new Communist government of the People's Republic of China was the Three-Self Patriotic Movement or TSPM. It allowed for the legalization of Protestant Christianity but was not organizationally connected to the Chinese Communist Party. Those Christian groups that had convictions against a link between Christianity and an atheistic government formed into independent church groups that the West referred to as the house church movement, but were more accurately defined as autonomous Christian communities.

CONTROVERSY BETWEEN THE TSPM AND THE AUTONOMOUS CHRISTIAN COMMUNITIES

The two parts of the Protestant Christian Church in China did meet in some very significant vortices, and even though they may seem to be at cross-purposes they proved to function toward the same objective. The situation was analogous to the Hong Kong rail system, where the Mass Transit Rail, MTR, runs underground as a subway system, and the Kowloon Canto Rail, KCR, traverses overland as a train system. However, the MTR surfaces in places, and where terrain demands, the KCR tunnels underground. The two intersect at strategic points for passenger transfers from the one system to the other. The TSPM as the legally registered Church organization with governmental recognition would be considered above ground while the independent Christian communities with the characteristics of unauthorized and unregistered were clandestine in nature. Yet both, for the most part, upheld Christianity in faith and the Bible as their scriptural authority.

The indigenous Chinese Church was recognized through four strata of contingents, which shaped its essence. These included the People's Republic government at national, provincial and local levels; the patriotic organizations of the Protestants as the TSPM and the Chinese Catholics as they function in society; the autonomous Christian communities both Protestant and the Roman Catholics with their effect; and those intellectuals known

431

as Culture Christians.

The Chinese government was Communistic, totalitarian and atheistic with rule over 1.3 billion citizens by the end of the 20th century. The form of justice in China, unlike the Western system, held the accused guilty until innocence was proven, and Chinese police may sentence a person to three years in a labor camp if deemed justified, without a case trial. This type of governmental system produced the religious policy that was based on the contribution that religion might provide toward socialistic construction.

China as a vast country with social diversity could not be expected to have governmental policy uniformly implemented. In many parts of the country the provincial or local cadres tried to anticipate any policy change by the CCP, whether it was an international political maneuver or a domestic incident that provoked the change. Usually the cadre would promote a more conservative Marxist implementation beyond that intended by the policy on the national level. The patriotic religious organizations took their place as agents of communication between the government officials and the religious believers.

The TSPM, in an attempt to remain within the legal boundaries prescribed by the government, found that certain adjustments had to be continually made. Then the change of leadership from Bishop Ting to Dr. Han Wenzao called for organizational adaptations. Ting would negotiate ecclesiastical situations with the government officials. For example, he tried to mediate with the government to eliminate church registration so that the autonomous Christian communities could be legally recognized. However, Dr. Han was not in sympathy with the independent unregistered groups, and he held a view that the Protestant Church should be more submissive to the governmental stipulations. Nevertheless, Dr. Han's theology proved to be more orthodox than that of Bishop Ting. Han maintained a traditional biblical interpretation, while Ting became more inclusive in humanitarian goodness as God's will for propitiatory purposes. The younger Christian theologians and seminary professors, many who had been educated in Western seminaries and universities, proposed a more democratic political stance and a conservative theological view for religious activities.

Because the legal institute of seminaries in which the TSPM provided Christian training for church workers used the Bible as their principal instrument for teaching, the theological doctrines followed the Apostles' Creed in its orthodox interpretation. The autonomous Christian communities also held to a conservative biblical theology and were fervently evangelistic in their faith. However, many of these independent house groups had few Bibles, and their Christian training was sporadic or non-existent in remote areas where illiteracy was prevalent, which allowed heresies to spawn without adequate checks.

Often, the very thing that attracted so many people to Christianity was identified by the government as a heresy. Faith healing and the miraculous helped to promote Christianity. However, the leadership of some groups became fanatical and avoided proper medical treatments to the detriment of the individual's health and the reputation of the independent groups in general. The fervency for evangelism of these unregistered assemblies and their ambition to send out itinerate evangelists was unauthorized and therefore placed in a category of criminal activity.

A VIEW OF CHINESE CHRISTIANS AND HELP OF THE OUTSIDE WORLD

The heretical teaching prevalent among the unauthorized Christian groups was obvious to the Chinese Christian community, and Bishop Ting strove to correct the inadequate supply of Christian materials for training church workers. He petitioned the government to allow these groups to legally obtain Bibles, commentaries, and other Christian literature through the Amity Press.

There were organizations from the West that held sympathies with the independent Christian community movement in critical conflict with the Communistic Chinese government. The problem became a concern to those who had an interest in the Church in China from abroad, and they had become involved in providing the unauthorized autonomous gatherings with Bibles, commentaries, and other Christian literature through a clandestine importation system. A method of providing unofficial training through unauthorized seminaries in some areas of China had also become common for these organizations.

However, other Western Christian organizations formed legal connections to help the Chinese Church through the Amity

Foundation in the provision of printing presses and funds. They also cooperated by means of negotiation for authorized Western teaching positions for courses on Christianity in the universities and seminaries, and this encouragement persuaded the opening of Christian Studies departments in several universities throughout China.

Whether foreign or domestic, personal or organizational, interpersonal relationships had proved to promote the corresponding results when encountering the Chinese. The relationship developed at the local level between the Christians and other Chinese citizens was critical for being accepted and receiving cooperation. Moreover, the interaction that the church leadership established with officials gained favor for further expansion in church activities within the community, or the lack of a positive rapport brought suspicion and discrimination against the group. Therefore, persecution was often due to the lack of positive relationships built within the local community.

Different forms of persecution were rationalized according to the mindset of an official or the interpretation of a policy. There was often a difference between situational truth and reality. The truth of constitutional freedoms of belief at times did not correlate with the reality of the implementation of the policy because of the sentiment, loyalties or prejudices of the enforcement agency. Even some TSPM leaders had tendencies to lean toward the gain of political influence and maintenance of controls on the church that might produce positive recognition from the government in its goals of socialist achievement. A cadre or TSPM leader who may not sympathize with the unregistered house groups and their illegal stance in society might effect judicial action against them. Imprudence on the part of a Christian writer who may word an article in a way that it could be interpreted as subversive might become the object of suppression.

TOWARD UNDERSTANDING THE CHINESE CHURCH IN CONSEQUENCE OF THIS RESEARCH

The dynamic growth of the Protestant Christian Church caused the government to recognize that the Marxist ideal of socialist progression that eventually would eliminate the tie to religion was only theoretical. As an advance in economic growth flourished in China, evidence had shown a shift in ideological priorities, especially in areas of China such as Wenzhao where a correlation between Christianity and affluence was evident. In these areas less attention as to whether a church group was registered or not became the norm. Many unregistered groups built a church building because the group had outgrown the capacity of private homes but still remained independent from the TSPM.

The organizational function of the TSPM provided the Chinese Protestants identification with Chinese culture, relations with the People's government, and maintained their position as the legal representative of the Protestant Christian Church in China. The Three-Self principle related to the separation from dependence on foreign missions and provided the identification for the Church with Chinese characteristics. The quality of post-denominationalism defined one of the marks of independence and uniqueness of the Church in China. However, the characteristics of worship remained very Western, even in the choice of translated Western music over Chinese indigenous Christian composition.

On the other hand, the autonomous Christian communities, the largest sector of the Chinese Protestant Church with estimates above 30 million adherents, conducted indigenous worship and favored Chinese music. However, prominent segments remained in contact with foreign entities. They even remained dependent on overseas sources for financial assistance, Christian literature, and training of clergy.

There was also an intellectual component of the Chinese Christian Church that basically rejected the open registered churches and the independent unauthorized groups for different reasons, but both lacked philosophical stimulation. The fascination that the intelligentsia developed for Christianity led to the translation of Western works on theology, and they acquired a sense of gratification through the caring lifestyle promoted by Christians. The incident at Tiananmen Square on June 4, 1989, initiated the search for reality that led many of these scholars to reject Marxism, Leninism, and Mao Zedong Thought for Christianity. Special groups for these Christian intellects, such as the International Christian Fellowship in Beijing, were formed to discuss theological issues.

These different strata of Chinese believers, including the entities of Catholicism, formed the Church in China. Some TSPM church leaders remain open to all Chinese Christians as a Christian community no matter what their legal status. They share the vision of evangelization, training church workers, and providing Bibles and other Christian materials for the purpose of Chinese Church growth. The goal of patriotism remains intact as all Christians must also be good citizens, but their primary priority is that of nurturing the Church within the Chinese society.

The indigenous feature of the Chinese Church remains in its adaptability to its sociopolitical context. No matter whether missionaries were present or not, political change, governmental prohibitions, persecutions, registration policies, organizations or domestic incidents of political or natural causes, the Church continued unabated to adjust and grow. Its growth did not depend on organizational skills, financial prosperity, constitutional amendments for freedoms, or charismatic personalities. It was upon the focus of biblical teaching and the Christian message of Jesus Christ that the Church has been built in China.

The consensus of Christians agreed that all Chinese who followed and believed in Jesus Christ and the Christian message of the Bible made up the Christian community of China. The TSPM leadership and churches, the pastors and members of unauthorized Christian groups, scholars on Chinese Christian Studies both in China and overseas concurred and did not dispute over Protestantism and Catholicism, the political implications of legality or policy at this point. All of these Chinese Christian believers came under the universal fatherhood of God to become a part of the universal brotherhood in Christ known as the Church or "the household of God" referred to in I Timothy 3:15.

THE STUDY OF THE CHURCH IN CHINA

In the introduction of this dissertation, the author stated questions to be researched extensively and resolved. Now the essence of each investigation is to be considered from the evidence available.

INDIGENIZATION OF THE CHURCH IN CHINA

The heart of this study is posed in the first questions: What constituted the indigenous aspects of the Chinese Christian Church? Were there particular elements that made it unique? Did indigenous indicate isolation? Could the indigenous Church be identified as one entity?

During the missionary era of China's Church history autonomous groups of Chinese Christians formed spontaneously with their own order, music, and self-reliance for indigenous

436

worship in homes that held to biblical doctrines. Upon the establishment of the People's Republic of China, the patriotic Christian religious organizations formed the Church independent of foreign missionaries and their sending agencies. The TSPM adapted to the Communist government with the Three-Self principles of self-government, self-support, and self-propagation, which verified indigenization. Also autonomous Christian communities continued to expand within their indigenous order and other groups formed because of Communism, known as the house church movement. After the Cultural Revolution, the TSPM changed through government moderation to running the Church well in adaptation to the political change, and encouraged the autonomous groups to join in registration.

The adaptability of Christianity as a body of believers not dependent on organization was the key factor of the indigenous Church in China as addressed in chapter 7. The historical sociopolitical context of China, especially in the latter half of the 20th century under totalitarian Communism was particularly unique to China. However, with the Protestant organization of the Chinese Christian Council as a member of the World Council of Churches, it has not been segregated from identifying with the international Church.

Several entities make up the Church in China as part of the Body of Christ. The open Church that has legally joined the authorized TSPM, the autonomous Christian communities that make up the majority of Christians in China, and their counterparts within the Catholic Church that the Chinese government actually considered a separate religion through historical events. Encompassed within these entities are the intellectual believers who have formed separately from a philosophical perspective.

THE CONTEXT OF THE CHURCH IN CHINA

The background for this research was in response to these questions: What formed the context into which the Chinese Church emerged? What historical events of China shaped the development of the Church? What political contributions affected the character of the Church?

Chapter 2 addresses the dynastic political history with the emperor elevated to a divine status, which collapsed under foreign dominance, and how Communism deflected alien subjugation and

437

ruled China for over a half century. The philosophy of Confucius with the concepts of *yin yang* or complimentary opposites, *feng shui* or social harmony, *li* or reasoning, and the principle that man was perfectible dominated. The social-cultural setting of family orientation with a hierarchy of submission formed the context of Chinese society.

Chapter 3 discusses the history of the Chinese Church and how it was shaped through the sociopolitical context. Christianity had been received through Catholic missionaries but was then purged from China. Finally, through foreign domination and the Opium Wars Christianity was established by missionaries who subsequently had gained entrance into China. With the missionary effort terminated after the People's Republic of China was instituted in 1949, the TSPM and the Catholic Patriotic Association gave the Christian Church legality. Autonomous Christian communities had started during the missionary era of the Church but escalated in 1949 under Communism and again in 1966 during the Cultural Revolution. Governing policies and management procedures of the Communist government placed limitations on the Church that had required contextual adaptation.

THE EXPRESSION OF THE CHURCH IN CHINA

Through the context of history the Chinese Church has become truly indigenous. Therefore, the adaptations taken were to be determined through answering the following:

How did the Chinese Church express itself within its context? Was the Church effective in the same manner throughout all of the Chinese provinces? Had power shifts and policy change affected religious activities of the Church in China?

Several different responses evolved from the context in which the Church found itself. Determination to remain within legal status, the enforcement of policy at different levels of government, and economic growth had effect on how the Church expressed itself. Christians who cared for legal recognition were loyal to the authorized churches, and took a post-denominational stance. The coastal provinces that grew economically proved to be less restrictive on religious issues.

The segment of the Church joined to the TSPM taught orthodox Christian doctrines and still cooperated with the policies produced by the CCP, which they recognized as being biblically ordained by

God for China at this point in its history. It maintained evangelism through having open churches that the masses knew could be utilized legally for worship, and provided seminaries that used the Bible as its ultimate authority in training national pastors. Although law prohibited overt evangelism, the TSPM encouraged Christians to be evangelistic in the work place through living the Christian life before fellow workers.

In provinces where religion was restricted, or believers held to the biblical interpretation that Christianity was not to have union with atheistic Communism, more autonomous Christian communities formed to provide worship and evangelization for Chinese citizens of these areas. The autonomous groups were more actively evangelistic by training and sending itinerant evangelists to villages and remote areas to take the Christian message where Christianity was unknown and establish other autonomous Christian communities.

When Deng Xiaoping succeeded Mao Zedong as chairman of the CCP a definite change in policy took place. The four modernizations promoted by Deng allowed China to open to foreign business and influence, and to accomplish this a moderate religious policy was adopted, which enhanced the ministries of registered churches and provided a more relaxed political atmosphere for the expansion of the autonomous Christian communities.

OTHER QUESTIONS

Three supplementary questions were considered, and response summaries of each appear below:

1.   What caused the changes in the philosophy of the TSPM after the Cultural Revolution? Did these changes affect the direction or ministry of the Church in China? Why were these changes introduced?
2.   Had the growth of the Church affected governmental policy change?
3.   How could those who viewed China from abroad better understand and best encourage Chinese Christians?

TSPM Philosophy Changes

The political change from within the Communist Party after

the Cultural Revolution in 1976 brought a change in focus from maintaining the quest for revolution to modernization. The TSPM was reinstated in 1979 and changed its policy from accommodating the Communist policy to ministering to the churches. To encourage the autonomous Christian communities to register, the TSPM formed a sister organization; the CCC to help build trust in the TSPM that was lost through suffering because of its zealous collaboration with the government in its campaigns to eliminate religion from Chinese society before the Cultural Revolution.

Growth of the Church

The expansion of the Church, both within the registered churches and in the autonomous Christian communities, caused the Chinese Communist government concern; therefore, it produced the policy known as Document 19 that outlined church management and stipulations for registration. The government also initiated the Anti-spiritual Pollution Campaign against criminal activity in 1983, and defined unregistered religious groups as subversive and their leaders as cultic or involved in counter-revolutionary activity.

The Tiananmen Square incident in 1989 and the collapse of Communism in Eastern Europe caused anxiety among the central government of the CCP. The policy of Document No. 6 was produced in 1991 to curb peaceful revolution. Document No. 16 stipulated clergy and Decrees 141 and 145 defined further regulations on religious site registration. Each of these policy changes was due to Church growth

Understanding and Encouraging Chinese Christians

From the author's observations and conversations with Chinese religious leaders, Chinese Christians are encouraged when Christians from the West attempt to identify with them as part of the universal Body of Christ by attempting to understand their sociopolitical context, their limitations because of their context, and that God placed them in that context with a plan for them to minister within it. If their ministry remains within the legal framework set by the government there is less conflict. However, if the boundaries restrict Christian believers from becoming the salt and light to penetrate society there is a point of departure from what might be considered legal. This should be accepted without judgmental criticism or condemnation, but with prayerful support.

The legal exchange of professors in seminaries and universities gives opportunity to the West to learn the positive attributes of prayer, evangelistic fervor, and Bible saturation that the Chinese Church practices. It would provide an opportunity to be a living testimony in the Chinese society as well as teach democratic church leadership that is lacking in the Chinese churches. It would be an encouragement for Western Christians to personally visit to see and witness how the Christian leaders are ministering in China rather than speculate from what writers, who may hold biases, say about China and the Chinese Church.

SOME GENERAL OBSERVATIONS

The author was overwhelmed at the Christian spiritual fervor he found in China under a totalitarian atheistic Communist government, which mandates its indigenization. The sacrifice for evangelistic thrust found in every province and every age group required consecration and dedication far beyond that found in the Western world. Church growth was phenomenal, and outreach is to the point that the missionary effort of the Chinese is estimated to surpass that of the West by 2025. At this writing it is estimated that there are more Christians in China than in the USA, which was considered a Christian nation just a few decades ago. This is astounding, even given that China's population is nearly five times larger.

In conclusion, the Church in China in all its entities adheres to orthodox Christianity with faith in the Lordship of Jesus Christ and claims the Bible to be the ultimate authority. The various entities of the Church are in agreement on these basics. The general masses of Chinese give little thought as to the legality of a group, for their main interest is to worship God. The post-denominational aspect of the Chinese Church has helped to perpetuate this attitude of indiscriminate worship. For some there is little preference between Protestant and Catholic churches. The author observed this phenomenon in the Chinese churches in Spain when worshipers would ask when mass began on Sunday, which indicated a desire to worship rather than to discern between the two faiths. Therefore, rather than the Western mentality of either-or the Chinese sustain the *yin yang* or both-and concept.

The official registered churches with a TSPM connection, the autonomous Christian communities, their Catholic counterparts, and the intellectual culture Christians all maintain some inherent

441

connection with the West. However, they are indigenous to China because they are governed, supported, propagated, controlled, and structured in China by Chinese citizenry. The indigenous aspect is how each entity adapted to the Chinese Communist context to achieve the aims of the group; nevertheless, they maintain the fundamental biblical Christian doctrines to form the Church in China.

BIBLIOGRAPHY

PRIMARY SOURCES

Interviews

Auyeung Chikwong, Middle-aged Chinese college student, Houghton, New York. Interview, 25 May 1999.

Bao Jiajuan, Associate General Secretary and Executive Director of China. Christian Council Office, Nanjing, China. Interview, 13 September 1999.

Chen Wei, Business woman and former Buddhist, Madrid, Spain. Interview, 26 July 1998.

Chen Xiaoya, Manufacturer, Madrid, Spain. Interview, trans. He Yanli and Chu Lijung, 17 July 1998.

Chen Zemin, Professor of Theology at Nanjing Union Theological Seminary and Center Of Religious Studies at Nanjing University, Nanjing, China. Interview, 13 September 1999.

Deng Fucun, Vice Chairman and General Secretary of Three-Self Patriotic Movement, Shanghai, China. Interview, trans. Wang Jian Gao, 10 September 1999.

Fulton, Brent, Executive Director of Chinasource, Managing Director of the Institute of Chinese Studies at Wheaton College, Served 8 years with China Ministries International – Pasadena, CA, Served 2 years with Chinese Church Research Center – Hong Kong, Wheaton, Illinois. Interview, 19 November 1999.

Glasser, Arthur, Retired Professor at Fuller Theological Seminary and former missionary to China, Seattle, WA. Interview, 15 December 2000.

Han Wenzao, President of China Christian Council, Vice-Chairman of Amity Foundation Vice-Chairman and General Secretary of China Committee on Religion and Peace Representative to the World Conference on Religion and Peace, Nanjing, China. Interview, 14 September 1999.

Hu Wei, College Mathematics and Computer Science Professor, Houghton, New York. Interview, 31 May 1999.

Ip Chiming, Seventh Generation Taiwanese, Student and Businessman,

Madrid, Spain. Interview, 19 July 1998.
Li Lanshen, Pastor of Mo Chou Raod Church, Nanjing, China. Interview, trans. He Yanli, 13 September 1999.
Lin I Shuan, Retired minister of Mo chou Raod Church, Nanjing, China. Interview, trans. He Yanli, 13 September 1999.
Shen Chenen, Associate General Secretary of China Christian Council, Chief Editor of *Tian Feng*, Pastor of Shanghai Community Church, Shanghai, China. Interview, 10 September 1999.
Tok Kai Hua, Engineer in Project Management, Southeast Asian, Tent-making ministries through a registered church, Bejing, China. Interview, 6 September 1999.
Wang Jian Gao, Acting Dean of Faculty at East China Theological Seminary, Shanghai, China. Interview, 10 September 1999.
Wang, Samuel, Scholar of the *Four Books* collection of Confucius and Mencius Teachings, Co-author of *God and the Ancient Chinese*, Director of Lamen Ministry News Ministries, Translated for TSPM and CCC and works closely with Human Righs Watch, St. Maries, Idaho. Interview, 21, 27 December 1999 and 12 January 2000.
Wen Shen, Businessman, General Manager of Don Shen Enterprise, Nanjing, China. Interview, trans. He Yanli, 12 September 1999.
Xu Li, Missionary of Mo Chou Road Church, Nanjing, China. Interview, trans. He Yanli, 13 September 1999.
Xu Rulei, Standing Committee Member of China Christian Council, Vice-Chairman of Jiangsu Province Three-Self Committee, Chairman of Nanjing Three-Self Committee, Deputy Director of Center of Religious Studies at Nanjing University, Nanjing, China. Interview, 11 September 1999.
Xu Shilian, Businesswoman, former Buddhist, Madrid, Spain. Interview, trans. Chu Lijung, 24 July 1998.
Ye Jianwei, Businessman, Madrid, Spain. Interview, 17 July 1998.
Yuang Aiguang, Medical Doctor, Madrid, Spain. Interview, trans. He Yanli, 17 July 1998.
Zhou Enwei, Student, Madrid, Spain. Interview, trans. Chu Lijung, 26 July 1998.

Interviews with Pseudonyms

Chen Y. L., Solder under Chiang Kaishek to Taiwan, Madrid, China. Interview, trans. Chu Lijung, 18 July 1998.
Chen Y. P., Christian Evangelist, Valencia, Spain. Interview, trans. Li, 21 July 1998.
Chin Ying, Spanish Language Student, San Francisco de Dos Rios, Costa

Rica. Interview, October 1979.

Gu Yilin, Assistant to Headmaster at Beijing BISS International School, Beijing, China. Interview, 5 September 1999.

Huang Wenyan, Art Student, Madrid, Spain. Interview, trans. He Yanli and Chu Lijung, 25 July 1998.

Kelly, Carl Franklin, Professor at a University in Beijing for over a 15 year period, and attends International Christian Fellowship, a group of intellectuals, Beijing, China. Interview, 6, 7 September 1999.

Lin, Pastor of the *An Ti Ya Tang*, Antioch Church, Beijing, China. Interview, trans. He Yanli, 17 September 1999.

Lin Yurong, Restaurant owner, former Chinese Communist Government Professor, Madrid, Spain. Interview, trans. Chu Lijung, 24 July 1998.

Liu, Steven, Elder in *An Ti Ya Tang*, Antioch Church, Beijing, China. Interview, trans. He Yanli, 16 September 1999.

Liu Yun, Representative of Chinese Firm, former Chinese Communist Youth Member, Madrid, Spain. Interview, 25 July 1998.

Meng Xiangzhi, Science Professor, Houghton, New York. Interview, 21 October 1998.

Song Shaozhou, Student, father is member of the Chinese Communist Party, Madrid, Spain. Interview, 20 July 1998.

Wang Li, former President of Chinese Christian Democratic Union, Madrid, Spain. Interview, 16 July 1999.

Wu Qiwei, Seminary Professor, New Haven, Connecticut. Interview, 6-9 December 1998.

Xiao C. P., A woman from Wenzhou area, Madrid, Spain. Interview, trans. Chu Lijung, 26 July 1999.

Young, Karen – Chinese, English teacher for children and writer of financial economics and political news in *Zong Guo Zeng Juang*, Beijing, China. Interview, 5 September 1999.

Zhang Ping, Businesswoman, Madrid, Spain. Interview, 26 July 1998.

Zheng Xianyu, former English Professor, has taken political asylum in Spain, Madrid, Spain. Interview, 27 July 1998.

Interviews of Documentary

Williams, Sue, *China in Revolution*, Parts 1 – 'Battle for Survival 1911-1936,' 2 – 'Fighting for the Future 1936-1949,' 3 – 'The Mao Years, Catch the Stars and the Moon 1949-1960,' 4 – The Mao Years, Its Right to Rebel!' co-director Katheryn Dietz, (ed.) Howard Sharp, associate producers: People's Republic of China, PRC – Carma Hinton, Taiwan – Shuhua Chang, additional interviews: PRC – Paul Pickowicz Film research: Raye

Farr, research: Jean Tsien, John Wentworth, Gong Xiaoxia, An AMBRECA production 1989.
- Bo Yi-ko, Communist Minister of Finance
- Chang Tieh-chun, Chinese student
- Chen Li-fu, Nationalist Official
- Chen Su-yi, Worked for Security Police
- Chiang Wen-kuo, Son of Chiang Kai-shek
- Chuan Shili-han, Chiang Kai-shek's Deputy
- Davies, John, Foreign Service Officier
- Ding Xueling, Student, Son of a Peasant Farmer
- Ge Yang, Communist Party Member
- Geng Xiu-feng, Village Party Official
- Guo Qui-min, Communist training
- Huang-wei, Nationalist General
- Johnson, U. Alexis, East Asian Affairs State Department
- Jiang Qing, Mao Zedong's wife
- Li Heng-xin, Rich Farmer, Party Member
- Li Mao-xiu, Son of Rich Landlord
- Li Rui, Secretary of Mao Zedong
- Li Xiu-ying, Peasant Woman
- Li Zhi-sui, Mao Zedong's Medical Doctor
- Li Zhong-xin, Young Peasant
- Liang Lian Heng, Communist Soldier
- Liang Xi Hua, Victim of Japanese
- Lin Chun, Student
- Liu Han-shao, Village Peasant, Communist Soldier
- Lu Di, Professor at People's University in Beijing
- Lu Chuan-cheng, Victim of Japanese
- Lu Zheng-cao, Communist Officer
- Ma Bo, Student
- Mao Chun-fen, Spokesman for Modernization
- Mao Zedong, Communist Party Chairman
- Mo Wen-hua, Red Army Officier
- Qui Hui-ying, Child Laborer and Communist Wife
- Rice, Edward, Foreign Service Officer
- Rong Yi-ren, Industrialist
- Shen-zui, Nationalist Security Police
- Soong His-lien, Nationalist Cadet, Officier
- Soong Mei-ling, Chiang Kai-shek's wife
- Sun Ming-jiu, Chuan Shili-han's Officer, Involved in kidnapping of Chiang Kai-shek

- Sun Yat-shen, Founder of Nationalist Movement, Speech
- Tsai Wen-tchih, Nationalist General
- Wan Xiang, Communist, sold at age 7 as a maid
- Wang Jin-mao, Son of Landlord
- Wang Ping, Communist Official, was on the Long March
- Wang Rou-shui, Deputy Editor of People's Daily
- Wang Ruo-wang, Writer
- Wang Tieh-han, Chuan Shilihan's Officer
- Wang Xin-lan, Communist Officer's wife, was on Long March
- Wu Fu-hai, Communist Worker
- Wu Xiu-quan, Communist Officer, Interpreter to Otto Braun
- Xie Pei-lan, Communist Soldier
- Xie Shao-han, Nationalist Soldier
- Xu De-liang, Communist Worker
- Yang Cheng-wu, Communist Soldier
- Zhang Jing-zhi, Peasant
- Zhang Lang-lang, Student
- Zhang Ming and Li Hui, Couple supported Chinese effort in Korean War
- Zhang Wen, Student, Red Guard
- Zhong Chao-ke, Village Party Official
  Zhou Yuan-jiu, Peasant

Manuscripts

Adams, Evyn and Neva. Letter, Greenwood, IN, OMS International, Februray 2000.

Bsldus. Letter to Etienne, 3 August 1835, *Annales*, 10: 70-71.

Chao, Jonathan. Letter, 22 March 1999, China Ministries International

_____, Letter, December 1992, China Ministries International

_____, Letter, 1 February 2000, China Ministries International

Church of the Nazarene Headquarters. Letter to the Swiss Council General in Charge of American Interests in China, Tamingfu, Archive Church of the Nazarene International Headquarters, 25 June 1942.

Kiehn, Peter, The Past, Present and Future of the Church of the Nazarene, The Church Of the Nazarene Archives 604-15, Kansas City, MO.

Osborn, L. C. and Mrs., Pearl Denbo and Cathrine Schmidt, Data for 'Fresh Facts,' 8 November 1920, from the Chao Chend Mission Station, Missionary Headquarters Of the Church of the Nazarene Archives 262-61, Kansas City, MO.

Parker. Letter to Anderson, 24 June 1840, South China 1833-1844, ABCFM.

Pentecostal Church of the Nazarene. Policy of the General Missionary Board to Govern The work in China [minutes 1922] of the Church of the Nazarene Archives 305-14.

Proceedings of the First Four Annual Assemblies of the China District Church of the Nazarene, 1917-1920, Church of the Nazarene Archives 1091-29.

Shen Chengen. Letter to author discussing the political organizational structure of the TSPM, 23 November 1999.

Wei Jingsheng. Testimony as Chairman Joint Conference of the Overseas Democracy Movement, House Committee on International Relations, Hearing of Nipping Democracy in the Bud: The New Crackdown on Dissidents in China, 8 January 1999.

Zhang, David. Spokesperson for China's house churches, Urgent Letter of Appeal: The Chinese Government has begun a new round of Religious Persecution. To: U.N. Secretary – General Kofi Annan, U.S. President Clinton, U.S. State Department, Amnesty International, Human Rights Watch/Asia and Human Rights in China, Human Rights Press Release, 9 November, 1998.

Documents

Adeney, David H., Appendix 4: Decisions Regarding the Safeguarding of Normal Religious Activities, *China: The Church's Long March,* Ventura, CA: Regal Books, 1985.

ANS Documentation, Chinese Christian Church Order adopted at the Sixth National Christian Conference, January 1997, trans. Philip L. Wickeri *Amity News Service,*Vol. 6, November-December (1997) 10-15.

ANS Documentation, An interview with Luo Guanzong, *ANS,* Vol. 6, May-June (1997) 6-8.

Central Committee of the Communist Party of China, Document 19: The Basic Viewpoint and Policy on the Religion Question During Our Country's Socialist Period, 31 March 1982.

Central Committee of the Communist Party of China and State Council, Document No. 6,

Circular on Some Problems Concerning Further Improving Work of Religion, 5 February 1991.

Chen, Marcus, Speech 19 March 1957, Wallis C. Merwin (ex. sec.), *Documents of Three-Self Patriotic Movement,* New York: Far Eastern Office, Division of Foreign Mission National Council of the Churches in the USA, 1963, p. 153.

Chen Zemin, 'On Nanjing Theological Seminary,' trans. Craig Moran,

[Documents from The Forth National Christian Conference, Shanghai August 1986], *Chinese Theological Review*, Vol. 3 (1987) 45-52.

China State Education Commission, Notice on Prevention of Some Places Using Religious Activities to Hinder School Education [China Document], *Tripod*, No. 67, (1992) 16-20.

Chinese Christian Church Order, trans. Philip L. Wickeri, Janice Wickeri (ed.) *Chinese Theological Review:12*, Holland, MI: Foundation for Theological Education in Southeast Asia, 1998. Pp. 63-78.

Constitution of the China Christian Council [Passed 2 January 1997] J. Wickeri (ed.) *CTR:12*, Holland: FTESA, 1998. Pp. 51-55.

Constitution of the National Committee of the Three-Self Patriotic Movement of Protestant Churches in China [Passed 2 January 1997] J. Wickeri (ed.) *CTR:12*, Holland: FTESA, 1998. Pp. 46-50.

Deng Fucan, An Interview, 15 March 1997, Shanghai, *Amity News Service*, Interview, Vol. 6, May-June (1997) 16-19.

Deng Zhaoming, Chinese Regulations Affecting Religious Activities, English translation Of documents with editorial introduction, *Bridge*, Vol. 66, August (1994) 2-8.

Han Wenzao, 'In the Course of Ten Years,' *Compassion and Development*, On the Tenth Anniversary of the Amity Foundation, 1985-1995.

Han Wenzao, 'Statement by China Christian Council President on China's so called "Religious Persecution," 20 June 1999,' *Amity News Service*, Vol. 6, July-August (1997) 1-2.

Human Rights In China Press Release, 24 November 1998, pp. 1-2.

Ivey, Myron, 'House Church Leader to be Sent to Labor Camp,' *China News and Church Report*, 20 July (1998) 1-4. Official Document of Chinese Communist Party Committee in the City of Huadu.

'Section III: Protestant Church,' *China Study Journal*, Vol. 13, No. 1, April 1998, pp. 81- 97.

'Section III: Protestant Church,' *CS Journal*, Vol. 13, No. 1, August 1998, pp. 56-74.

Shen Mingcui, 'Three-Self Continues to Move Forward,' trans. Janice K. Wickeri (ed.) [Documents form the Forth National Conference, Shanghai, August 1986] *Chinese Theological Review*, Vol. 3 (1987) 31-36.

Shen Xilin, 'Seeking the Common Ground and Unity,' trans. J. Wickeri (ed.) [Doc. 4th Nat. Ctn. Con., Shanghai, Aug. 1986], *CTR*, Vol. 3 (1987) 37-44.

Shi Zesheng, 'Experiences on the Road to Church Unity,' trans. William Dockery, J. Wickeri (ed.) [Doc. 4th Nat. Ctn. Con., Shanghai, Aug. 1986], *CTR*, Vol. 3 (1987)   26-30.

Spiegel, Mickey, *China: State Control of Religion*, Appendix IV: Regulations

From the Shanghai Religious Affairs Bureau, Approved 30 November 1995 by the Standing Committee of the Shanghai 10th People's Congress at its 23rd meeting [Translation from the *Tripod*, Vol. XVI, No. 92], New York: Human Rights Watch, 1997, pp. 90-99.

_____, Appendix VI: Regulations on the Suppression of the Religious Activities of Foreigners in China [Translated from *China News and Church Report*], NY: HRW, 1997, pp. 104-105. Came into force the day of issue, 31 January 1994, signed by Premier Li Ping, Order of the State Council of the People's Republic of China No. 144.

_____, Appendix VII: Regulations Regarding the Management of Places of Religious Activity [Translated from *CNCR*], NY: HRW, 1997, pp. 106-108. Came into force on the day of issue, 31 January 1994, signed by Premier Li Ping, Order of the State Council of the People's Republic of China, No. 145.

_____, Appendix VIII: Registration Procedures for Venues for Religious Activities [Translated from *CNCR*], NY: HRW, 1997, pp. 109-111. According to Article 15, these procedures take effect from the date of promulgation 1 May 1994.

_____, Appendix IX: Method for the Annual Inspection of Places of Religious Activity [Translated by UCA News], 13 January 1997, NY: HRW, 1997, pp. 112-115.
Religious Affairs Bureau State Council, 29 July 1996.

_____, Appendix X: China's Current Religious Question: Once again an inquiry into the Five Characteristics of Religion, by Ye Xiaowen, Director, Bureau of Religious Affairs, the State Council. NY: HRW, 1997, pp. 116-117. From 'Selection of the Central Committee of the Chinese Communist Party, 1996, No. 5.

Sun Xipei, 'From Three Self to Three Well,' Janice K. Wickeri (ed.) [Documents from The Fourth National Christian Conference, Shanghai, August 1986], *Chinese Theological Review*, trans. Jean Woo. Vol. 3 (1987) 53-56.

Ting, K. H., 'Christian Theism,' 12 June 1957, Merwin, *Documents of TSPM*, New York: National Council of Churches, 1963, pp. 158-167.

Wang Mingdao, 'We, Because of Faith,' Merwin, *Documents of TSPM*, NY: NCC, p. 103.

Wickeri, Philip, *The Amity Foundation*, Brochure, Kowloon, Hong Kong.

Wu Gaozi, 'On the Revision of the Constitutions,' Janice K. Wickeri (ed.) [Documents From the Fourth National Christian Conference, Shanghai, August 1986], *Chinese Theological Review*, Vol. 3, (1987) 5-8.

Wu Y. T., 'Freedom Through Truth,' Merwin, *Documents of TSPM*, NY: NCC, p. 84.

Wu Y. T., 'Report to the July 1954 Conference in Peking,' Merwin,

Documents of TSPM, NY: NCC, 1963.

Ye Xiaowen, Appendix X: China's Current Religious Question: Once again an Inquiry Into the Five Characteristics of Religion, Human Rights – Asia, *China: State Control,* New York: Human Rights Watch, 1997. Pp. 116-145.

Zhao Fusan, 'Prospects of Christianity in China,' Janice K. Wickeri (ed.), [Document From the Fourth National Christian Conference, Shanghai, August 1986], *Chinese Theological Review,* Vol. 3, (1987) 9-18.

Articles in Periodicals

Adeney, David, 'Division time in China: To join the TSPM or not,' *Evangelical Missions Quarterly,* Vol. 19, No. 3, July (1983) 200-204, 229.

Argue, Donald, Theodore E. McCarrick and Arthur Schnwer, 'Religious Freedom,' *Tripod,* vol. XVIII, No. 105, May-June (1998) 54-64.

Bao Sidong, 'Today's Church in mainland China,' trans. Norman Walling *Tripod,* Vol. XVIII, No. 103. January-February (1998) 23-24.

Beveridge, Dirk, 'Chinese celebrate the return of Macau,' USA Today, Monday, 20 December (1999) 13A.

Burchett, Wilfred, 'Lin Piao's Plot – The Full Story,' *Far Eastern Economic Review,* 20 August (1973) 22-24.

Byler, Myrrl, 'Debate over religious persecution in China is often simplistic,' *News Service,* Akron, PA: Mennonite Central Committee, 27 June (1997) 1-2.

Call, Kathy, 'For Precious Bibles, We Give Thee Thanks!' *China Chronicles,* Vol. VIII, No. 2, Spring (1998) 1-4.

Chao, Jonathan, 2009, *China News and Church Report,* 7 August (1992).

_____, 'Bishop Ding Speaks Out Against the Wind of Suppression Sweeping China,' *CNCR,* 31 December (1992).

_____, No. 134, *CNCR,* 13 March (1992).

_____, No. 1940, *CNCR,* 27 March (1992).

_____, No. 1979, *CNCR,* 4 June (1992).

_____, No. 2006, *CNCR,* 31 July (1992).

_____, No. 2015, *CNCR,* 27 August (1992).

_____, 'Projecting,' *CNCR,* No. 125, March (1993) 5.

_____, 'Christian Contributions to Chinese Culture: What do Chinese People Lack that Christianity can Contribute, *CNCR,* 22 June (1998) 1-2.

_____, 'The Church in China Today – Officially Registered Churches and House Churches,' *Challenger,* Vol. XXXVI, No. 4, August-September (1997) 5-7.

_____, 'The Material Needs of the Church in China,' *CNCR,* No. 2655, 26 October (1998) 1-5.

_____, 'The Church in China: Needs and Opportunities for Ministry,' *CNCR*, 11 May (1998) 1-6.

_____, 'Three Graduate Students Told to Leave Nanjing Theological College,' *China Prayer Letter*, March-September (1999) 2-7.

_____, 'Three *Undergraduate* Students Leave Nanjing Theological College in Protest over the *Graduate* Student Incident,' *China Prayer Letter*, March-September (1999) 8-11.

Chen Aemin, 'Post-denominational Unity of Chinese Protestant Church,' *Bridge*, No. 53, May-June (1992) 16-19.

Chen Jinhua, 'Report on the Implementation of the 1997 Plan for National Economic and Social Development and of the Draft 1998 Plan,' *Beijing Review*, 13-19 April (1998) 19-21.

Chen Xida, 'The Life and Witness of the Church in China,' *China Talk*, October (1997) 36-37. Address at LWF assembly Hong Kong July 1997, Chen Xida at Nanjing Theological Seminary.

Chen Zemin, 'Relations Between Christianity and Intellectuals Since Liberation (1949),' Gail V. Coulson (ed.), *China Talk*, Vol. XXIV, April (1999) 20-24.

Corporate Author China Christian Council, 'One Hundred Questions and Answers of the Christian Faith,' *The Chinese Theological Review*, Vol. 1 (1985) 211-243.

Coulson, Gail V., 'Who should undertake the task of evangelism in China,' *China Talk*, Vol. XXIII, 1ˢᵗ Quarter, May (1998) 18-19.

_____, 'China's 1998 Flood Disaster,' *CT*, November (1998) 1-13.

_____, 'Believers Called Upon to Help Lighten Evangelist's Load,' *CT*, Vol. XXIV, April (1999) 14-15.

_____, 'Church Grows from a Three Generation Family Home Worship,' *CT*, Vol. XXIV April (1999) 16-17.

_____, 'A Year of Sensitive Dates,' *CT*, Vol. XXIV, April (1999) 26-28.

Cryderman, Lyn, 'For God and Deng,' *Christianity Today*, Vol. 34, 10 May (1990) 18.

Dai Xiaohua, 'Good Beginning for the Country, Two Systems,' *Beijing Review*, 6-12 (1998) 8-11.

Deng Zhaoming, 'Church and State Regulations in China: Characteristics and Trends: A Response,' [to Liu Peng], trans. Michael Slobada, *Tripod*, July-August (1995) 19-25.

Ding Guangxun, Bp., 'Another Look at 3-Self,' *Ching Feng*, Vol. 25, No. 4, December (1982) 250-265.

_____, 'Bishop K. H. Ting's View of the Present Situation of Christianity in China,' [Interview by C. Kwok], *Bridge*, No. 33, January-February (1989) 3-8.

Fang Bay, 'China, at 50, on a Long March to Modernity,' *U.S. News & World Report*, 4 October (1999) 35-36.

Florcruz, Jaime A. and Joshua Cooper Ramo, 'Inside China's Search for its Soul,' *TIME*, 4 October (1999) 69-73.

Fung Ho-Lau, 'Wanted! "Professionals Where Are You?" A Challenge Towards Global Evangelization,' *Chinese Around The World*, February-March (1996) 1-4.

Gong Xuezeng, 'Reflections on Religion and Modernization,' trans. Michael Sloboda *Tripod*, Vol., No. 103, January-February (1998) 15-21.

Groves, Ian, 'In The World But Not Of The World: Portrait Of An Indigenous Chinese Church Community In Zhejiang,' *Amity News Service*, Vol. 6, November-December (1997) 22-23.

_____, 'Interview with Dr. Wenzao Han, President of the China Christian Council,' *Amity News Service*, Vol 6, July- August (1997) 8-9.

Guo Jincai, 'Chinese Clergy Who Have Returned from Study Abroad Hold Seminar in Xian,' *Tripod*, Vol. XVIII, No. 107, September-October (1998) 59-62.

Han Wenzao, 'CCC Statement On the IMB's Covert "Missionary Work",' *Amity News Service*, Vol. 6, November-December (1997) 1-2.

Hao, Joshua, 'China's Revival Meetings and Tears,' Jonathan Chao (ed.) *China Prayer Letter*, No. 125, March (1993) 1-2

Heller, Scott, 'Worldwide "diaspora" of Peoples Poses New Challenges for Scholars,' [Migration and Cultural Identity; Photos], *Chronicle of Higher Education*, 38:7-9, June (1992).

Ho, Bonnie, 'Your Call has been Heard,' *Chinese Around The World*, September (1999) 24-25.

Huang, Jennifer C., 'Chinese American Christianity and the Challenges of Diversity,' Part I, *CATW*, December (1995) 1-8.

_____, 'Chinese American Christianity and the Challenges of Diversity, Part II,' *CATW*, January (1996) 1-6.

Huang Wei, 'A Firm Handshake Makes History,' *Beijing Review*, 23- 29 November (1998) 11-14.

_____, Qian: 'Taiwan Should Face Up to The Int'l Situation,' *BR*, 23-29 November (1998) 15.

Hummer, Earnie, 'Thoughts from the President – Puzzled by China? Part 1,' *The Panda Bearer*, May-September (1998) 3-4.

_____, 'Thoughts from the President – China Puzzle, Part 2,' Interview of Daniel Su, Special Assistant to the COM President, September-December (1998) 3-4.

Ivey, Myron (ed.), 'Alan Yuan's Interrogation,' *China News and Church Report*, No. 2623, 27 April (1998) 1-2.

_____, 'Chinese House Church Leaders Issue Confession of Faith and Declare their Attitude Toward the Government,' *CNCR*, 21 December (1998) 1-10.

_____, 'Despite Floods, China is Running Dry,' *CNCR*, No. 2654, 12 October (1998) 3-4.

_____, 'Getting Acquainted with Relatives in China, Glimpses of Life in the Mainland,' *CNCR*, No. 2646, 3 August (1998) 1-5.

_____, 'Good Pastoral Care Needed in China,' *CNCR*, No. 2618, 19 January (1998) 1-3.

_____, 'Lianghui Announces Formation of Eight Special Committees,' *CNCR*, No. 2054 (1997). Lianghou – Two Joins, TSPM & CCC.

_____, 'Profile of a New House-Church Training Program, *CNCR*, 2 March (1998) 3-4.

_____, 'The Ransacking of a House Church during the Strike Hard Campaign: A Testimony of God's Blessing,' *CNCR*, No. 2639, 25 May (1998) 1-7.

_____, 'TSPM Leaders Call for a National Religious Law,' *CNCR*, No. 2640, 8 June (1998) 1-2.

_____, No. 2620-2622, *CNCR*, 2 February (1998).

Ji Tai, 'Is there a Chinese Theology?' *China News Update*, September, (1997) 4-6.

Jiang Zemin, 'Hold High the Great Banner of Deng Xiaoping Theory for an All-Round Advancement of the Cause of Building Socialism with Chinese Characteristics Into the 21st Century,' *Beijing Review*, 6-12 October (1997) 10-33.'Report Delivered at the 15th National Congress of Communist Party of China on 12 September 1997, *BR*, 6-12 October (1997).

Kippers, D. 'How to Pressure China,' [Persecution of Christians and the Most Favored Nation Status], *Christianity Today*, Vol. 41, 14 July (1997) 13.

Lam, Anthony, 'The Ministry of the Public Security and the Religious Affairs Bureaus,' *Tripod*, Vol. XVIII, No. 104, March-April (1998) 47-55.

Lam, Cyrus On-Kwok, 'Ten Mission Directions for the Chinese Church,' *Chinese Around The World*, October-November (1996) 1-6.

Lambert, Anthony P. B., 'The Church in China: Pre and Post Tiananmen Square,' *Religion in Communist Lands*, Vol. 18, Autumn (1990) 236-252.

_____, 'Supervision of Christianity in the People's Republic of China,' *RCL*, Vol. 15, Summer (1987) 213-217.

Law, Kit, 'Bishop Ding Speaks Out Against "Wind of Suppression",' Jonathan Chao (ed.) *China Prayer Letter*, No. 126, April (1993) 1-3.

Lawrence, Thomas, 'New Straightjacket for China's Expanding Church,'

Chao (ed.) *CPL*, No. 123, October-December (1992).

Lee, Jonathan, 'Oriental Expectations and Western Cultural Influence,' *Chinese Around The World*, January (1997) 14-16.

_____, 'The Chinese Jerusalem – A Report on Wen Zhou County,' *CATW*, May (1998) 15-17.

Lee, Peter K. H., 'The "Cultural Christians" Phenomenon in China,' *Ching Feng*, Vol. 39, No. 4, December (1996).

Li Ning, 'China Enters Top Ten In World Trade,' *Beijing Review*, 30 March-April (1998) 10-13.

Li Rougxia, 'China Enhances Water Conservancy Construction,' *Beijing Review*, 7-13 December (1998) 9-12.

Lin Liangqi and Dai Xiaohua, 'Persistently Emancipating the Mind,' *BR*, 15-21 June (1998) 9-12.

Lin, Melissa Manhong, 'A Modern Chinese Journey of Inculturation,' *International Review of Mission*, January (1998) 1-17.

Ling, Samuel, 'Approaching China in 1997,' *Chinese Around The World*, May (1997) 2-5.

Liu, Drew, 'State Policy and Christianity in China,' *China Strategic Review*, Vol. 1 (1996) 1-5.

Liu Xiaofeng, 'The Phenomenon of "Culture Christians",' *Chinese Around The World*, January (1999) 20-21.

Lo, Steven, 'Chinese Churches in Melbourne,' *CATW*, March (1997) 8-10.

Luo Guanzong, 'Interview,' *Amity News Service*, Vol. 6, May-June (1997) 6-7.

_____,'The Revised Constitutions,' [Three-Self Movement], trans. Janice Wickeri, *Chinese Theological Review*, (1991) 37-42.

Lutz, David W., 'Ethics and Morality in China Today,' *Tripod*, Vol. XVIII, No. 107, September-October (1998) 12.

Maak Hay-chun, 'Partnership with China,' *Chinese Around The World*, January (1998) 2-5.

MacMillan, Ron, 'House Church Struggles with New Converts,' *Christianity Today*, Vol. 34, 20 August (1990) 39-40.

Martinson, Paul Varo, 'The Protestant Church in Post-Mao China: Two Paradigms,' *Ching Feng*, Vol. 31, No. 1, March (1988) 3-23.

Palmer, B., 'Caesar vs. Christ,' *U.S. News & World Report*, Vol. 123, 4 August (1997) 41-42.

Pao H. K., 'China's Church Leaders Pay a Visit to Hong Kong,' Jonathan Chao (ed.), *Chinese Prayer Letter*, No. 124, January-February (1993).

Qingguang, 'Three-Self or Not Three-Self,' *Bridge*, Vol. 59, No. 1, May-June (1993) 13-19. The question for some Christian groups in Shanxi and Shanxi Provinces.

Ren Yanshi, 'Protecting Human Rights Calls for Punishing Crimes,' *Beijing Review,* Vol. 42, No 2, 11-17 January (1999) 12-13.

Responsible Member of the State Council's Bureau of Religious Affairs, 'Religious Affairs in China,' *BR,* 1-7 September (1997).

Shenk, Wilbert R., 'The Origins and Evolution of the Three-Selfs in Relation to China,' *International Bulletin of Missionary Research,* Vol. 14, January (1990) 28-35.

Servants of the Persecuted Church, 'Bibles in China: A Great Deception!' *The Voice of The Martyrs,* May (1993) 7.

_____, 'China: The Untold Story,' *The Voice of the Martyrs,* (1993) 13.

Shi Zesheng, 'Forum on China's Religious Conditions,' *Beijing Review,* 1-7 September (1997) 18.

Sidney, Kenneth H., 'The Church Seeks a New Place in China,' *Christianity Today,* Vol. 33, May-August (1989) 55-56.

So, Eric S. Y., 'Timothy Tingfing Lew and the Indigenization Movement of the Church In China,' *Ching Feng,* Vol. 39, No. 3, September (1996) 240-241.

Spickard, Paul R., 'The Church in the Crucible: Chinese Protestants Since Liberation,' *Fides et Historia,* Vol. 22, Fall (1990) 30-41.

State Council Information Office, 'Freedom of Religious Belief in China,' October 1997, *Beijing Review,* 3-9 November (1997) 13-22.

Stimson, Eva, 'The Church in China,' *Presbyterians Today,* November (1997) 1-6.

Sun Jiaji, 'On Relationship: Community and Individials,' *China News Update,* September (1997) 6-8.

Ting K. H., 'K. H. Ting Talks Again to Jiang Zemin, January 28, 1992,' *Bridge,* Vol. 53, May-June (1992) 6-7.

_____, 'The Church of Jesus Christ is there in China,' [Address to Lutheran World Federation Executive Committee, July 12, 1987], *Theology and Mission,* Vol 17, October (1990) 375-380.

Wen Xuandao, 'Literature Work in Mainland China,' *Chinese Around The World,* March (1998) 16-17.

Wickeri, Philip L., 'Development Service and China's Modernization, The Amity Foundation in Theological Perspective,' *The Ecumenical Review,* Vol. 41, January (1989) 78-87.

_____, 'Theological Reorientation in Chinese Protestantism 1949-1984, Part 1,' *Ching Feng,* Vol. 28, No. 1, March (1985) 36-62.

_____, 'Theological Reorientation in Chinese Protestantism 1949-1984, Part 2,' *CF,* Vol. 28, No. 2-3, August (1985) 105-129.

Wiseman, Paul, 'Taiwan wants China and World to Acknowledge Reality, Island's President seeks recognition as separate State,' *USA Today,* Monday, 19 July (1999) 14A.

Wong, Daniel L., 'OBC's –ABC's Toward Effective Relations and Partnerships in Ministry, *Chinese Around The World*, October-November (1995) 1-8.

Wong, Hoover, 'Toward Understanding and Reaching the Overseas-Born Chinese,' *CATW*, AUGUST (1996) 1-8.

Wu S. 'Confucianism and its Significance to Christianity in China,' *Ching Feng*, Vol. XII, No. 1, (1969) 12-13.

Yates, Tim, 'US Baptist Conflicts in Cooperating with the TSPM, Part I,' *China News And Church Report*, No. 2649, 31 August (1998) 1-4.

_____, 'US Baptist Conflicts in Cooperating with TSPM, Part II,' 14 September (1998) 1-6.

Ye Xiaowen, 'Speech of Ye Xiaowen, Head of the Religious Affairs Bureau of the State Council at the Sixth National Congress of Catholic Representatives,' January 17, 1998, trans. Norman Walling, *Tripod*, Vol. XVIII, No. 107, September-October (1998) 48-58.

Yeo Khiok-khng, 'The Rise of the Three-Self Patriotic Movement (TSPM): Chinese Christianity in the Light of Communist Ideology in New China,' *Asia Journal of Theology*, Vol. 6, No. 1, April (1992) 1-9.

Yu, Timothy and Iris Cheung, 'A Blessed Mission: Outreach of the Chinese People in U.K. and Europe,' *Chinese Around The World*, December (1995) 7-8.

Zhang, Richard X. Y., 'The Origin of the "Three Self",' *Jian Dao*, Vol. 5 (1996) 175-202.

Zho Zhi-en, 'A Vast Field of Harvest,' *China News Update*, September (1998) 4-7.

Articles in Periodicals without Authors

Amity News Service, Vol. 7, January-February (1998) 12.

ANS Focus: 'Church Music : "Sing Praises to the Lord": Inculturating the Gospel –   Chinese Rural Church Music,' *ANS*, Vol. 6, May-June (1997) 8-9.

'Banned in China, Thriving in New York: The Controversy of Falan Gong,' *Chinese Around The World*, January (2000) 25-27.

'Call for Believers to Help Lift the Burden on Evangelists,' *Amity News Service*, Vol. 7, July-August (1998) 3-4.

'Call for Church to Bring in its own "Anti Corruption" Mechanism,' *ANS*, Vol. 7, March-April (1998) 19 20.

'Can a Good Christian be a Good Patriot too?' *ANS*, Vol. 6, May-June (1997) 12-13.

'CCC Seeks to Assist in Rebuilding Collapsed Churches,' *China Talk*,

November (1998).
'China Church and News Update,' *Tripod,* Vol. XVIII, No. 103, February (1998).
'China Connection News Exchange,' *China Chronicles,* Vol. VIII, No. 2, Spring (1998) 4.
'China Continues Assault on Non-official Churches,' *The Christian Century,* Vol 114, Is. 15, 7 May (1997) 446-447.
China Daily, 23 March (1984).
'China Issues Commentary on US Human Rights Report,' *Beijing Review,* 23-29 (1998) 11-16.
'China's Three-Self Congress Makes Rehabilitation of Religion Official,' *Christianity Today,* Vol. 25, 2 January (1981) 46-47.
'Chinese Theology and Its Cultural Sources,' *Amity News Service,* Vol. 7, March-April (1998) 12-14.
'Church Order for Trial Use in Chinese Churches,' *Bridge,* No. 52, March-April (1992) 6-9.
'Church's Acts of Faith find Wide Publicity,' *Amity News Service,* Vol. 6, January- February (1997) 10.
'Committee of the Chinese Christian Three-Self Patriotic Movement,' *Ching Feng,* Vol. 23, No. 3-4 (1998) 170-171.
'Communists vs. Christians,' *Wall Street Journal,* Eastern Edition, New York, 12 December (1994) A14.
'Deng Xiaoping 1904-1997,' *China Talk,* March (1997).
'Different Chinese Translations of the Bible,' *Amity News Service,* Vol. 7, January- February (1998) 5-6.
'Does the Chinese Church Need to Protect Its Independence Today?' *ANS,* Vol. 7, March-April (1998) 2-3.
'Does The Church Have Anything To Say To Modern China?' *ANS,* Vol. 7, March- April (1998) 17.
'Everyone's Talking About Church Building!' *ANS,* Vol. 7, March-April (1998) 3-4. *Far Eastern Economic Review,* 7 March (1980).
'From Chaos to Order: Churches Around Wuhan Revisited,' *ANS,* July-August (1997) 11-13.
' "Homeward Bound" of Chinese in the Diaspora,' *Chinese Around The World,* August-September (1995) 12-13.
'How Should We Regard Miracles?' *Amity News Service,* Vol. 7, May-June (1998) 4.
'Nation Called to Study Deng's Thory,' *Beijing Review,* March (1998) 5-15.
'New Leaders Elected,' *BR,* 13-19 October (1997) 9-17.
'New TSPM and CCC Constitutions Approved,' *Amity News Service,* 28 December-January (1997) 6.

'News in Brief,' *China News Update,* September (1997) 9.

'News of Church Persecution in China Breaks,' *The Voice of the Martyrs,* September (1993).

' "Oldest Protestant Church in China", Prepares for 150ᵗʰ Anniversary,' *Amity News Service,* Vol. 7, (1998) 26-27.

'One China Principle To Be Firmly Upheld,' *Beijing Review,* Vol. 42, No. 7, February (1999) 5.

'Profiles of Newly Elected Chinese Leaders,' *BR,* 6-12 April (1998) 25-34.

Putian Church: Different Traditions, New Developments,' *Amity News Service,* Vol. 6, May-June (1997) 13.

'RAB Chief Says China Respects and Protects Religious Freedom,' *ANS,* Vol. 6, July-August (1997) 4-5.

'Registration Procedures for Venues for Religious Activities,' *ANS,* 1 May (1994) 1-2.

'Regulations for Guangshou No. 118 of Religious Affairs Bureau,' *Tripod,* Vol. XVIII

No. 103, January- February (1998) 36-39.

'Rev. Su Deci, General Secretary of the CCC,' *Amity News Service,* 28 December-3 January (1997) 9-10.

'San Yi Tang (Trinity Church) Xiamen,' *China Talk,* October (1998).

' "Self-Propagation" Symposium,' *Amity News Service,* Vol. 7, January-February (1998) 19-20.

'Session Passes Documents on Macao,' *Beijing Review,* 27 July-2 August (1998) 5.

South China Morning Post, 11 April (1984).

' "Success Must Not Lead To Complacency:" How the Church in Zhejing Seeks To Grow Further,' *Amity News Service,* Vol. 6, November-December (1997) 20-22.

Tian Feng, 22 September (1958) 20.

'Top Chinese House Church Leaders Face Persecution After Publicity Declaring Their Faith Last Year,' *China Prayer Letter,* March-September (1999) 1.

'US Human Rights Criticism Refuted,' *Beijing Review,* 5-9 March (1998) 5-6.

'US TMD Warned Not to Include Taiwan,' *Beijing Review,* Vol. 42, No. 4, 25-31 January (1999) 4.

'Using Spring Festivals Couplets To Announce The Good News,' *Amity News Service,* Vol. 7, January-February (1998) 24-25.

' Why is Denominationalism Raising Its Head Again?' *ANS,* Vol. 6, November-December (1997) 4-5.

'Xin Jie Church Celebrates 150 Years,' *China Talk,* October (1998).

'Yunnan Province: Many Christians, Few Church Workers,' *Amity News*

The Church in China 1950 – 2000

Service, Vol. 5, May-June (1996) 8.

Articles in Books

Adeney, David, 'Love China Vision,' David Aikman (ed.), *Love China Today*, Wheaton, IL: Tyndale House Publishers, 1977. Pp. 164-165.

Aikman, David, 'Marxism, Leninism, The Thoughts of Mao Tse-Tung and Christianity,' Aikman (ed.), *LCT*, Wheaton, IL: TP, 1977. Pp. 97-125.

Bautista, Lorenzo, Hidalgo B. Garcia, and Sze-Kar Wan, 'The Asian Way of Thinking in Theology,' Bong Rin Ro and Ruth Eshenaur (ed.) *The Bible & Theology In Asian Contexts*, TaichungL Tai Shin Color Printing, 1984. Pp. 167-183.

Bong Rin Ro, 'Contextualization: Asian Theology,' Bong Rin Ro and Ruth Eshenaur (ed.), *The Bible & Theology In Asian Contexts*, Taichung: Tai Shin Color Printing, 1984. Pp. 63-77.

Chen Zemin, 'Theological Education in China,' Denton Lotz (ed.), *Spring Has Returned*, McLean, VA: Baptist World Alliance, 1986. P. 42.

_____, 'Theological,' Ting K. H. (ed.), *Chinese Christians Speak Out*, Beijing: New World Press, 1984. Pp. 45-46.

Gao Ying, 'Sharing Women's Work,' Janice Wickeri (ed.), *Chinese Theological Review:12*, Holland,MI: Foundation for Theological Education in Southeast Asia, 1998. Pp. 91-95.

Han Wenzao, 'Build Up the Body of Christ with One Heart and United Effort: Running The Church Even Better According to the Three-Self Principle, J. Wickeri (ed.) *CTR:12*, Holland: FTESA, 1998. Pp. 6-45.

_____, 'Work Together with One Heart to Build Up the Body of Christ,' J. Wickeri (ed.) *CTR:12*, Holland: FTESA, 1998. Pp. 116-125.

Hsu, Princeton, 'China's Indigenous Christian Movements, David Aikman (ed.), *Love China Today*, Wheaton, IL: Tyndale House Publishers, 1977. Pp. 30-38.

Ji Tai, 'Hermeneutics in the Chinese Church,' Janice Wickeri (ed.), *Chinese Theological Review*, Holland, MI: Foundation for Theological Education in Southeast Asia, 1998. Pp. 137-147.

Jiang, 'Foreign Christianity,' Ting K. H. (ed.), *Chinese Christians Speak Out*, Beijing: New World Press, 1984.

Ladany, Ladislas, Theodore Marr and David Aikman, 'Symposium: The Religious Policy Of the Peoples Republic of China,' David Aikman (ed.), *Love China Today*, Wheaton, IL: Tyndale House Publishers, 1977. Pp. 73-96.

Lea, Aronald, 'Christian Churches in China, 1807-1949,' Aikman (ed.) *Love China Today*, Wheaton: THP, 1977. Pp. 11-29.

Luo Guanzong, 'Closing Address,' [To The Sixth National Chinese

460

Christian Conference] Janice Wickeri (ed.), *Chinese Theological Review: 12,*
Holland, MI: Foundation for Theological Education in Southeast Asia,
1998. Pp. 126-136.

Luo Yingzhong, 'Self-Support Difficulties in Mountain Churches,' *CTR: 12,*
Holland: FTESA, 1998. Pp. 101-105.

Lyall, Leslie, 'The Chinese Christian Church under Communism 1949-
1966,' David Aikman (ed.) *Love China Today,* Wheaton, IL: Tyndale
Publishers, 1977. Pp. 39-61.

Marr, Theodore, 'Research Information Training,' Aikman (ed.), *LCT,*
Wheaton: THP, 1977. Pp. 151-159.

_____, 'Symposium: The Religious Policy of the People's Republic of China:
A Protestant View,' Aikman (ed.), *LCT,* Wheaton: THP, 1977. Pp. 84-89.

_____, 'The Church in China Today,' Aikman (ed.), *LCT,* Wheaton: THP,
1977. Pp. 64-65.

Minus, Keith, 'Missions and Indigenization,' A Compendium of the Asia
Missions   Congress '90, *World Missions: The Asian Challenge,* 1992.
Pp. 260-265.

Nicholls, Bruce J., 'The Gospel in Indian Culture,' M. Ezra Sargunam (ed.),
Mission Mandate, Kilpauk, Madras: Mission India 2000, 1992. Pp. 377-388.

Peifen, 'Features of the Church in China Today,' Denton Lotz (ed.), *Spring
Has Returned,* McLean, VA: Baptist World Alliance, 1986. P. 39.

Schwartz, Benjamin I. 'The Philosopher,' Dick Wilson (ed.), *Mao Tse-tung in
the Scales Of History,* Cambridge: Cambridge University Press, 1977.

Shen Yefan, 'Freedom as Viewed by a Chinese Chrisrtian,' Ting K. H. (ed.),
Chinese Christians Speak Out, Beijing: New World Press, 1984. P. 76.

Spiegel, Mickey, 'Freedom of Religion in China,' *Asia Watch,* New York:
Human Rights Watch, 1992.

Sun Xipei, 'Family, Body and Spiritual Home,' Janice Wickeri (ed.), *Chinese
Theological Review: 12,* Holland, MI: Foundation for Theological Education
of Southeast Asia, 1998. Pp. 106-110.

Ting H. K., 'Greetings in the Sixth National Chinese Christian Conference,'
Janice Wickeri (ed.) *Chinese Theological Review: 12,* Holland, MI: Foundation
for Theological Education in Southeast Asia, 1998. Pp. 1-5.

_____, 'The Chinese Church Since 1949,' Denton Lotz (ed.), *Spring Has
Returned,* McLean, VA: Baptist World Alliance, 1986. Pp. 24-25.

_____, 'Protestantismo,' *China Avanza,* Beijing: Beijing Informa, 1986.

Wang Juzhen, 'On the Revisions to the Constitution,' Janice Wickeri (ed.),
Chinese Theological Review: 12, Holland, MI: Foundation of Theological
Education in Southeast Asia, 1998. Pp. 56-62.

Weerasingha, Tissa, 'A Critique of Theology from Buddhist Cultures,' Bong
Rin Ro and Ruth Eshenaur (ed.), *The Bible & Theology In Asian Contexts,*

Taichung: Tai Shin Color Printing, 1984. Pp. 290-314.

Wing-hung Lam, 'Patterns of Chinese Theology,' Bong Rin Ro and Ruth Eshenaur (ed.), *The Bible & Theology In Asian Contexts,* Taichung: Tai Shin Color Printing, 1984. Pp. 327-342.

Xu Xiaohong, 'Working Well at the Grassroots,' J. Wickeri (ed.), *CTR:12,* Holland: FTESA, 1998. Pp. 96-100.

Zheng, 'The Place of the Bible in the Life of Chinese Christians,' Denton Lotz (ed.), *Spring Has Returned,* McLean, VA: Baptist World Assiance, 1986. P. 50.

Articles from Books without Authors

'Protestantes en Shanghai,' *China Avanza,* Beijing: Beijing Informa, 1986.

'Communidad Cristiana en China,' Beijing: BI, 1986.

Articles from Internet

Braden, Glen, 'Faith in Action #8,' gbraden@visi.net, *The Discussion Network,* (29 October 1998), pp. 1-3.

Chao, Jonathan, Introduction and Conclusion of his unpublished book, *A History of Christianity in Socialist China,* 100261.2163@compuserve.com, (21 September 1998), Introduction, pp. 1-15, Conclusion, pp. 1-24.

Lin, Jimmy, 'Nurturing Chinese Christians,' *Internet Report,* 1997, pp. 1-3.

Snyder, Steven L., 'Chinese Police Arrest Thirty-Nine (39) In Raids on Prayer Meetings,' *International Christian Concern,* www.persecution.org, (7 September 1999), pp. 1-3.

Sturdivant, Jerry, 'Christian Persecution Part 5,' *The Discussion Network,* jerrys@pacifier.com, (29 October 1998), pp. 1-2.

Wark, McKenzie, 'Vectors of Memory...Seeds of Fire,' *New Formations China Tiananmen Square 4th June Globalization,* The Western Media and the Beijing Demonstrations, mwark@laurel.ocs.mg.edu.au, (1999).

Wickeri, Philip L. 'A Three-Self Movement Perspective,' http://lausanne.org/0697wick.html, (11 September 1998), pp 1-3.

Xinhua, 'President of Christian Council Defends Christianity in China,' Beijing: www.chinanews.org, (1997), pp. 1-2.

Articles from Internet without Authors

'About the China Christian Council,' *Amity News Service,* www.hk.super.net/-amityhk/cccprof.htm, (11 September 1998).

'China – Christian Persecution in China,' *International Christian Concern,* www.persecution.org, (27 August 1999), pp. 1-5.
'China's Relentless Persecution Continues,' *ICC,* www.persecution.org, (June 1999), pp. 1-2.
'China's Students Flocking to Christianity,' *News Network International,* www.nni-news.com, Beijing, China [NNI], (1990), p. 1.
'Christian Work – China,' *Global Prayer Digest,* www.calebproject.org/ nance/n1632.htm, (3 December 1998), pp. 1-9.
'SBC Works with Liberal China Christian Council,' http://www.whidbey.net/-dcloud/fhns/sbcworks.htm, (11 September 1998).
'The Birth of a Historic Opportunity,' *East Gates Ministries International,* www.egmi.org/whatisegmi.htm, (11 September 1998), p. 1-2.

SECONDARY SOURCES
Articles in Periodicals

Davenport, Paul, 'China's Official Church – A Cry From Within,' 23 September (1998).
E-mail version of *Compass Direct,* Myron Ivey (ed.) *China News and Church Report,* 28 September (1998), 1-3.
Kan Baoping, 'Theology In The Contemporary Chinese Context,' *Amity News Service,* Vol. 7, January-February (1998) 12-19. Reprinted from *World and World,* Vol. XVII, No. 2, Spring (1997).
Lee, Jonathan H. Y., 'The Mystification of Suicide,' *Chinese Around The World,* July (1997) 16-17. From, *South China Morning Post,* May (1997).
_____, 'The Prevalence of Cults,' *CATW,* July (1997) 14-16. From, *Pray For China,* May-June (1997).
MacMillan, Ron, 'A Weekend in the Life of a Chinese Itinerant Evangelist,' *Message of The Cross,* July-August-September (1991) 22-28. A News Network International Special Report, 11 December (1990).
Yu Jiang, 'Meeting the Needs of Intellectual Believers,' Gail V. Coulson (ed.), *China Talk,* Vol. XXII, 1st Quarter, May (1998) 14-20. From, *Tian Feng,* January (1998).

Articles from Periodicals without Authors

'Inching Towards Democracy,' *China News and Church Report,* 2624, 16 February (1998) 1-3. From, Minsxin Pei, *Foreign Affairs,* January-February 1998.
'The "Eastern Lightening" Sect: A Recent Threat To The Church In China,'

Amity News Service, Vol. 6, November-December (1997) 17-18. From, Wan Ge, *Tian Feng.*

Books

Adeney, David H., *China: The Church's Long March,* Ventra, CA: Regal Books, 1985.

Aikman, David (ed.), *Love China Today,* Wheaton,IL: Tyndale House Publishers, 1977.

Bloodworth, Dennis, *The Chinese Looking Glass,* New York: Farrar, Straus and Girour, 1966.

Bosch, David J., *Transforming Mission,* Maryknoll, NY: Orbic Books, 1991.

Bouc, Alain, *Mao Tse-tung: A Guide to His Thought,* trans. Paul Auster and Lydia Davis, New York: St. Martin's Press, 1977.

Brandt, Nat, *Massacre in Shansi,* Syracuse, NY: Syrcuse University Press, 1994.

Brock, Charles, *Indigenous Church Planting,* Nashville: Broadman Press, 1981.

Brown, Thompson, *Christianity in the People's Republic of China,* Atlanta: John Knox Press, 1983.

Bush, Richard C., Jr., *Religion In Communist China,* New York: Abingdon Press, 1970.

Chan Kim-kwong, *Towards a Contextual Ecclesiology,* Hong Kong: Phototech System, 1987.

Chao, Jonathan (interviews), Richard Van Houghton (ed.) *Wise as Serpents Harmless as Doves,* Pasadena: William Cary Library, 1988.

Cheneaux, Jean, Marianne Bastid and Marie-Claire Bergere, *China, from the Opium Wars to the 1911 Revolution,* New York: Pantheon Books, 1976.

_____, Francoise LeBarbier and Marie-Claire Bergere, *China from the 1911 Revolution to Liberation,* NY: PB, 1977.

Clayre, Alasdiar, *The Heart of the Dragon,* Boston: Houghton Mefflin, 1984.

Dreyer, June Teufel, *China's Political System,* Boston: Allyn and Bacon, 1996.

Fairbank, John King, *China, A New History,* Cambridge, MA: The Belknap Press of Harvard University Press, 1992.

_____, Edwin O. Reischaver and Albert M. Craig, *East Asia,* Boston: Houghton Mifflin, 1998.

Fay, Peter Ward, *The Opium War 1840-1842,* Chapel Hill, NC: The University of North Carolina Press, 1975.

Fremantle, Anne (ed.), *Mao Tse-tung An Anthology of His Writings,* New York: New American Library, 1972.

Fung, Raymond, trans. and compiled, *Households of God on China's Soil,*

Marynoll, NY: Orbis Books, 1982.

Gittings, John, *A Chinese View of China*, New York: Pantheon Books, 1973.

Glover, Carl A., *Victorious Suffering*, New York: Abingdon-Cokesbury Press, 1943.

Guillermaz, Jacques, *The Soldier*, Wilson (ed.), Cambridge: Cambridge University Press, 1977.

Hefley, James and Marti, *China! Christian Martyrs of the 20th Century*, Milford, MI: Mott Media, 1978.

Hiebert, Paul C., *Anthropological Insights for Missionaries*, Grand Rapids: Baker Book House, 1985.

Ho, Herbert Hoi-lap, *Protestant Missionary Publications in Modern China 1912-1949*, Hong Kong: Chinese Church Research Centre, 1988.

Hsu, Francis L. K., *Americans and Chinese*, 3rd edn., Honolulu: University Press of Hawaii, 1981.

Human Rights – Asia, *China: State Control of Religion*, New York: Human Rights Watch, 1997.

Humphrey, Peter, *Religious Suppression in Mainland China*, Republic of China: World Anti-Communist League, 1983.

Hunter, Alan and Chan Kim-kwong, *Protestantism in Contemporary China*, Cambridge: Cambridge University Press, 1993.

Hykes, *The Boxer Rising*, New York: Paragon Book Reprint, 1967.

Jenner, W. J. F., *The Tyranny of History*, London: Penguin Press, 1992.

Kauffman, Paul E., *China, The Emerging Challenge*, Grand Rapids, MI: Baker, 1982.

_____, *!China Today!*, Rev. edn., Hong Kong: Asian Outreach, 1980.

Lam, Willy Wo-lap, *China after Deng Xiaoping*, Hong Kong: DA Professional Consultants, 1995.

Lambert, Tony, *The Resurrection of the Chinese Church*, Wheaton, IL: Harold Shaw Publishers, 1994.

Lanham, Megan Gabriel, *Snatched from the Dragon*, Nashville: Thomas Nelson Publishers, 1990.

Latourette, Kenneth Scott, *China*, Englewood Cliffs, NJ: Prentice-Hall, 1965.

_____, *The Chinese, Their History and Culture*, 3rd Rev. edn., New York: The MacMillan, 1959.

Lifton, Robert Jay, *Revolutionary Immortality, Mao Tse-tung and the Chinese Cultural Revolution*, New York: Vintage Books, 1968.

Lotz, Denton (ed.), *Spring Has Returned*, McLean, VA: Baptist World Alliance, 1986.

Luo Zhufeng (ed.), *Religion under Socialism in China*, trans. Donald E. MacInnis and Zheng Xian, London: M. E. Sharpe, 1991.

Lyall, Leslie, *God Reigns in China*, London: Hodder and Stoughton, 1985.

_____, *New Spring in China,* London: H & S, 1979.

Mao Tse-tung, *Selected Works, Vol. 1 1926-1936,* New York: International Publishers, 1954.

Metzger, Thomas A., *The Unification of China and the Problem of Public Opinion in the Republic of China in Taiwan,* Leland Stanford Junior University, 1992.

Moise, Edwin E., *Modern China,* 2nd edn., London: Longman, 1994.

Moonyham, W. Stanley, *China: A New Day,* Plainfield: Logos International, 1979.

Mosher, Steven W., *China Misperceived,* Montclair: A New Republic Book, 1990.

Muirhead, William, *China and the Gospel,* London: James Nisbet, 1926.

Myers, James T., *Enemies Without Guns,* New York: Paragon House, 1991.

National Three-Self Movement Committee China Christian Council, *Protestant Christianity in China,* Shanghai: Nanjing, 1999.

Neill, Stephen, *Call to Mission,* Philadephia: Fortress Press, 1970.

Nicholls, Bruce J., *Contextualization: A Theology of Gospel and Culture,* Eseter: The Paternoster Press, 1979.

Patterson, George N., *Christianity in Communist China,* Waco, TX: Word Books, 1969.

Paulson, Hank and Don Richardson, *Beyond the Wall,* Ventura, CA: Regal Books, 1982.

Purcell, Victor, *The Boxer Uprising,* Cambridge: The University Press, 1963.

Pye, Lucian W., *China, An Introduction,* 4th edn., New York: Harper Collins Publishers, 1991.

_____, *Mao Tse-tung,* New York: Basic Books, 1976.

Rees, D. Vanghan, *The 'Jesus Family' in Communist China,* Montrial: Chrisitian Literature Crusade, 1973.

Ross, John, *Mission Methods In Manchuria,* Edinburgh: Fleming H. Revell, 1903.

Schram, Stuart R., *Mao ZeDong,* Hong Kong: The Chinese University Press, 1982.

_____, *The Political Thought of Mao Tse-tung,* New York: Fredrick A. Praeger, Publishers, 1969.

Schlossberg, Herbert, *A Fragrance of Oppression,* Wheaton, IL: Crosswan Books, 1991.

Schwartz, Benjamin I., *Chinese Communism and the Rise of Mao,* Cambridge, MA: Harvard University Press, 1979.

Snow, Edgar, *Red Star Over China,* New York: Grove Press, 1973.

Spence, Jonathan D., *The Search for Modern China,* New York: W. W. Norton, 1990.

Spiegel, Mickey, *China: State Control of Religion*, New York: Human Rights Watch, 1997.

Terrill, Ross, *Mao*, New York: Harper & Row Publishers, 1980.

Ting, K. H. (ed.), *Chinese Christians Speak Out*, Beijing: New World Press, 1984.

_____, *No Longer Strangers*, Maryknoll, NY: Orgis Books, 1989.

Towery, Britt, *The Churches of China*, Hong Kong: Long Dragon Books, 1987.

Tung Chi-ming, *An Outline History of China*, Hong Kong: Joint Publishing, 1982.

Uhalley, Stephen, Jr., *Mao Tse-tung, A Critical Biography*, New York: New Viewpoints, 1975.

Wallis, Arthur, *China Miracle*, Columbia, MO: Cityhill Publishing, 1986.

Wang Gunwu, Wilson (ed.), *The Chinese*, Cambridge: Cambridge University Press, 1977.

Wang, Mary, *The Chinese Church Will Not Die*, London: Hodder and Stoughton, 1971.

Wang, Samuel and Ethel R. Nelson, *God and the Ancient Chinese*, Dunlap, TN: Read Books Publisher, 1998.

Whitehead, Raymond L. and Rea M., *China, Search for Community*, New York: Friendship Press, 1978.

Wickeri, Janice (ed.), *Chinese Theological Review, 1990*, Holland, MI: Foundation of Theological Education in Southeast Asia, 1991.

_____, *Chinese Theological Review: 12*, Holland: FTESA, 1998.

Wickeri, Philip L., *Seeking the Common Ground*, Maryknoll, NY: Orbis Books, 1990.

Wu, Timothy, *Sheltered Through the Storms: A Chinese Pastor Preserved by God*, Palo Cedro, CA: Wayside Impressions, 1996.

Yin Ching-yao, *Politica Exterior de China Communista en la Etapa Presente*, Republica De China:La Liga Mundial Anti-communista, 1985.

Young, George A., *The Fish of the Dragon*, Kippen, Stirling: Arndarroch, 1985.

ABOUT THE AUTHOR

It was during the time Michael Suman served as a United States Airforce officer in East Asia from 1972 through 1975 that he developed an interest in China and her people.

After becoming a part of OMS International in 1979 he served in Spain where he became involved with overseas Chinese from 1986 through 1995. During that time he helped establish the Chinese Church in Madrid that has grown and spread to other cities throughout Spain and into Portugal.

In 2001 Michael received his Ph.D. in Intercultural Studies from South Asian Institute of Advanced Christian Studies (SAIACS). He completed his research through extensive interviews within China with officials of the Three-Self Patriotic Movement (TSPM), China Christian Council (CCC) as well as pastors of registered churches, the home church movement and other professionals connected with the religious activities in China. He also interviewed many overseas Chinese in both Spain and the USA. Most of his study research was completed at Harvard University and Yale University.

It was in 2002 that Michael moved with his wife, Nora, to Shenzhen, China in Guangdong Province to study Mandarin Chinese and teach English at Shenzhen University. In 2004 they moved to Urumqi, China in Xinjiang Province where he taught post-graduate students at Xinjiang Nong University.

Michael and Nora have two sons, Matthew and Andrew.